THE OFFICIAL®
PRICE GUIDE TO
ANTIQUES AND
COLLECTIBLES

THE OFFICIAL® PRICE GUIDE TO

ANTIQUES AND COLLECTIBLES

FOURTEENTH EDITION

ERIC ALBERTA AND ART MAIER

HOUSE OF COLLECTIBLES • NEW YORK

Important Notice. All of the information, including valuations, in this book has been compiled from the most reliable sources, and every effort has been made to eliminate errors and questionable data. Nevertheless, the possibility of error, in a work of such immense scope, always exists. The publisher will be held responsible for losses that may occur in the purchase, sale, or other transaction of items because of information contained herein. Readers who feel they have discovered errors are invited to *write* and inform us, so they may be corrected in subsequent editions. Those seeking further information on the topics covered in this book are advised to refer to the complete line of *Official Price Guides* published by the House of Collectibles.

 This is a registered trademark of Random House, Inc.

Published by: House of Collectibles
201 East 50th Street
New York, NY 10022

Distributed by Ballantine Books, a division of Random House, Inc., New York, and simultaneously in Canada by Random House of Canada Limited, Toronto.

http://www.randomhouse.com

Manufactured in the United States of America

ISSN: 1050-6144

ISBN: 0-876-37961-7

Cover design by Kristine Mills
Cover photo by George Kerrigan

Fourteenth Edition: March 1996

To Valerie Hoyt and Muriel Pearson

Contents

Introduction 1
Trends 1
Tips for Collecting 1
Tips for Buying at Auction 1
Selling 2
Tips for Selling at Auction 2
Prices 2
Fakes 2
Using This Guide 3
Collecting Related Publications 3

Americana 5
Canes 5
Chalkware 6
Coverlets 7
Fire Fighting Memorabilia 9
Folk Art 11
Hooked Rugs 13
Miniatures 14
Nautical Memorabilia 16
Needlework 17
Political Memorabilia 18
Political Buttons 19
Scrimshaw 20
Shaker Collectibles 22
Ship Models 26
Tools 27
Weathervanes 30

Autographs 32
Artists 32
Authors 33

Entertainers 34
Presidents 50

Books, Magazines, and Other Published Material 55
Bibles 55
Catalogs 58
Sears Roebuck 59
Classic Books 60
Comic Books 66
Little Golden Books 72
Magazines 77
Newspapers 89
Whitman TV Books 92

Coins 95
Half Cents 95
Large Cents 95
Small Cents 96
Two-Cent Pieces 97
Three-Cent Pieces 97
Five-Cent Pieces 97
Dimes 99
Twenty-Cent Pieces 102
Quarter Dollars 102
Half Dollars 104
Silver Dollars 107
Gold Pieces 109
Civil War Tokens 109

Furniture 110
Antique Furniture 110
Mission Furniture 122
Wallace Nutting Furniture 129
Wicker Furniture 130

Glass 133
Art Glass 133
Avon Bottles 147
Bottles 152
Cambridge Glass 155
Carnival Glass 156
Cut Glass 157

Depression Glass 159
Flasks 174
Fostoria 176
Fruit Jars 180
Heisey Glass 183
Insulators 186
Lalique 189
Pressed Glass 192
Steuben Glass 195
Waterford Crystal 198

Household Items 200
Advertising Memorabilia 200
Baskets 209
Beer Cans 212
Boxes 214
British Royalty Memorabilia 216
Cameras 218
Clocks 223
Coca-Cola Collectibles 233
Doorstops 237
Holiday Decorations 241
Ice Cream Molds 247
Motion Lamps 249
Radios 251
Wood 254

Jewelry and Clothing 256
Belt Buckles 256
Buttons 257
Clothing 259
Fans 260
Watches 262

Metal 271
Aluminum 271
Barbed Wire 273
Brass 274
Bronze 278
Chrome 279
Copper 280
Graniteware 282

Ironware 286
Pewter 289
Silver 292
Silver Flatware 297
Tin 305
Toleware 308

Military Memorabilia 310

Music 317
Records 317
Sheet Music 322

Orientalia 326
Assorted Orientalia 326
Chinese Export Porcelain 328
Cinnabar 334
Nippon Porcelain 336
Occupied Japan 338
Oriental Rugs 339
Satsuma 342
Snuff Bottles 343

Pottery and Porcelain 346
J.A. Bauer Pottery 346
Edwin Bennett Pottery 349
Bennington Pottery 350
Boehm Figures 353
Bookends 354
Camark Pottery 355
Cookie Jars 356
Cronin China 361
Crooksville China 362
Decanters 363
Earthenware Pottery 368
Fiesta Ware 374
Figurines 376
Frankoma Pottery 385
French-Saxon China 386
W.S. George Pottery 387
Gladding, Mcbean 389
Grueby Potteries 393

Hall China 394
Hall Teapots 402
Harker Pottery 403
Head Vases 406
A.E. Hull Pottery 408
Hummel Figurines 413
Iroquois China 420
James River Pottery 422
Josef Originals 423
Edwin M. Knowles China 426
Homer Laughlin China 428
Limoges China 433
Marblehead Pottery 435
Metlox Pottery 436
Morton Pottery 438
Newcomb Pottery 438
Niloak Pottery 439
George Ohr Pottery 440
Paden City Pottery 441
Pfaltzgraff Pottery 442
Planters 443
Collector's Plates 448
Purinton Pottery 465
Red Wing Pottery 466
Rookwood Pottery 468
Roseville Pottery 470
Royal China 471
Royal Doulton 472
Salem China 478
Sebring Pottery 480
Shakers 481
Shawnee Pottery 485
Staffordshire 486
Stangl Pottery 488
Stoneware Crocks 489
TV Lamps 491
Van Briggle Pottery 494

Prints, Photographs and Other Images 497
Audubon 497
Cigar Box Labels 510
Currier & Ives 512

Fruit Crate Labels 515
Louis Icart Prints 522
Maps 526
Maxfield Parrish Prints 535
Photographs 539
Wallace Nutting Photographs 542
Postcards 547
Vanity Fair Prints 550

Toys and Playthings 551
Baby Rattles 551
Barbie 553
Board Games 556
Character Toys 563
Children's Dishes 574
Comic Character Watches 577
Cracker Jack 581
Dolls 582
Dollhouses 590
G.I. Joe 592
Hot Wheels 594
Japanese Automotive Tinplate Toys 599
Lunch Boxes 603
Matchbox Toys 607
Mechanical Banks 609
Paper Dolls 614
Pez Dispensers 618
Premiums 622
Robots and Space Toys 625
Schoenhut Animals 632
Scouting Memorabilia 635
Star Trek Memorabilia 636
Star Wars Memorabilia 640
Still Banks 647
Tonka Toys 650
Toy and Miniature Soldiers 652
Lionel Trains 657
Trolls 661
Viewmaster 663

Transportation 665
Automobiles 665

Contents

xiii

Aviation 680
Bicycles 681
Railroad Memorabilia 682

Board of Collectors 684

Photography and other Contributions 685

Index 686

Introduction

TRENDS

The Great Art Market Crash of '89 (that's 1989) had a ripple effect throughout the antiques and collectibles market. Although no collectable that we know saw its value plummet like those of Chagall prints (some of which lost over 60% of their value), the overall market was dampened. At that time, the word around New York's Madison Avenue was, "Stay alive 'til '95."

Well 1995 has come and gone, and the various markets are waking up and showing signs of life. New markets are constantly emerging. On our trips to flea markets and auctions around the country we found an evolving landscape of nostalgia and history. Although glass insulators are still to be found, the buzz in the field is more concerned with post-war toys and fifties memorabilia.

Ten "hot spots" in the market are:

- Advertising Memorabilia
- Phonograph Records
- Barbie and GI Joe dolls
- Bakelite Jewelry
- TV Character Game Boards
- Maxfield Parrish Prints
- Radios
- Star Wars Memorabilia
- Premiums
- Cookie Jars

TIPS FOR COLLECTING

- In most areas, condition is everything. The difference between perfect and almost perfect can be the difference between $100 and $1000 or more! If an item needs restoration, know what that will cost before you buy. Also remember that a restored antique is generally worth much less than an unrestored piece in pristine condition.
- Just because something is rare, doesn't mean that it is valuable.
- Do your homework! The information age has created an explosion of material on all subjects and topics. Taking advantage of a public library's book search service is well worth the time. Books are often expensive, but a $50 book can often save you from many $100 mistakes.
- Pay attention to fakes and average pieces. Learning the ordinary teaches about the extraordinary.
- What goes up often comes down. Amazing prices are often reported, but a market that is slowly ebbing away will rarely be reported in the press.
- Always be sure whether or not the seller is providing a guarantee of authenticity. If he or she is, get it in writing; if not, know what you're buying!

TIPS FOR BUYING AT AUCTION

- Always thoroughly examine every piece before you bid on it. If you haven't examined it, DON'T BID.
- Always set your limit for yourself before you start bidding. Don't let auction frenzy drive your bidding.

• Make sure the auctioneer can see your bid. If you bid with just the nod of a head, the auctioneer may be selling to the woman in front of you.

• And yes, if your nose itches, you can scratch it without buying a fifteen-foot chandelier; just don't stare the auctioneer in the eye while you're doing it.

SELLING

A dealer must make his profit to stay in business and many businesses are expensive to run. The difference between a dealer's buying price and his selling price must cover the rent, the car, and everything else. Hence, the selling price of an item may be only a fraction of the price tagged in the window (or quoted in this guide!), especially for inexpensive items.

TIPS FOR SELLING AT AUCTION

• Choose your auction house by the service they offer, not the estimate they quote. You can't deposit an estimate in the bank.

• Don't be greedy. An item with a high estimate and reserve scares away many potential buyers. And once an item has failed to sell (or "bought in"), it is harder to sell the next time.

• Understand your contract:
  - What is the commission?
  - Who pays for photographs?
  - Who pays for insurance?
  - What is the reserve (or minimum price) set at?
  - Is there a "buy-in" fee for items that fail to sell?
  - When is payment made?

PRICES

Collecting is not the same as investing. If the value of your collection increases with time and rising markets, consider it a bonus. Most collections do not make money, they absorb it.

The prices in this book represent the average price that an informed buyer will pay a knowledgeable and specialized dealer for these items.

The antiques and collectibles market is not the stock market. Prices do not tick up and down on a daily basis.

FAKES

The ever increasing availability of cheap labor and expensive machines has resulted in the production of countless fakes in all fields. Most dealers are honest, but many honest dealers get fooled. We advise:

• Learn to recognize tool marks and which tools were used when.

• Learn to use a black light. (*The Black Light Book* is available from Antique & Collectors Reproduction News - see our list of publications)

• Visit museum gift shops and other places where high quality reproductions are sold.

• Learn the styles of the times. Many fakes give themselves away because they just don't "feel right."

• Subscribe to *Antique & Collectors Reproduction News* (see our list of publications). It's a great monthly report on fakes and reproductions that have appeared in the collectibles market.

• If it's too good to be true, it's probably not true.

USING THIS GUIDE

Sections are laid out by category.

Abbreviations are used throughout. Some that appear most often are:

Amer.-American	len.-length
attrib.-attributed	mah.-mahogany
c.-circa	mtd.-mounted
dec.-decoration	19th c.-ninetenth century
dia.-diameter	orig.-original
dr.-drawer	pr.-pair
ea.-each	ptd.-painted
Eng.-English	rect.-rectangular
'-feet (linear)	sq.-square
ft.-feet (standing)	varn.-varnish
ftd.-footed	uph.-upholstered
ht.-height or high	w.-width or wide
"-inches	w/ with

We have often abbreviated States of the Union by their two letter postal code (e.g. Maine-ME, Massachusetts-MA, etc.). The term "sight" preceeding a measurement refers to visible image.

COLLECTING RELATED PUBLICATIONS

Hundreds of periodicals on antiques and collectibles exist, some for very specialized areas. Here are some of our favorite general news publications:

A B Bookman's Weekly
70 Outwater Lane
Garfield, NJ 07026
(201) 772-4282

Antiques & The Arts Weekly
(" Newtown Bee")
Box 5503
Newtown, CT 06470
(203) 426-3141

Antique & Collectors
Reproduction News
Box 71174
Des Moines, IA 50325
(800) 227-5531.

Antique Toy World
Publisher and editor Dale Kelley
P.O. Box 34509
Chicago, IL 60364
(312) 725-0633

Comic Buyer's Guide
700 East State Street
Iola, WI 54990

Dolls The Collector's Magazine
P.O. Box 1972
Marion, OH 43305

Doll Reader
Hobby House Press
900 Frederick Street
Cumberland MD, 21502

Goldmine Magazine
700 East State Street
Iola, WI 54990

Inside Collector
PO Box 98
657 Meacham Ave.
Elmont, NY 11003
(516) 326-9393

Maine Antique Digest (MAD)
911 Main Street
Box 645
Waldoboro, ME 04572
(207) 832-7534

Today's Collector
700 East State Street
Iola, WI 54990

Toy Collector and Price Guide
700 East State Street
Iola, WI 54990

Toy Shop
Circulation Dept. AUE
700 East State Street
Iola, WI. 54990
(800) 258-0929

Unravel the Gavel
PO Box 171
Ctr. Barnstead, NH 03225
(newspaper covering New
England's country auctions)

Americana

Canes

Canes are either simple walking sticks or "gadget" canes that conceal a sword, pistol, musical instrument, or other device. The stylish canes of Europe came into vogue in the 17th and 18th centuries, while the 19th century saw gadget canes reaching their peak of popularity. When buying a cane or walking stick, examine it closely for indications of hidden compartments. Many devices go undiscovered for years.

Carved folk art canes are judged by their style and the skill of the carver. Many of the most desirable ones date from the mid-19th century. We've seen many of varying quality in the auctions of New England.

"Good" examples are undamaged with simple carving or simple forming. "Best" examples have superior carving or forming and (if wood or metal) a fine patina.

Left: Ivory headed canes with whimsical carving are among the most valuable.

Right: Simple canes sometimes contain hidden treasures. The arrow indicates a mircofilm view of the 1876 Centennial Exhibition.

	GOOD	BETTER	BEST
Amethyst, cut glass handle, c. 1880	$ 180	$ 245	$ 500
Bamboo, curved handle, c. 1920	17	25	45
Blown Glass, green	85	100	225
Bottle Cane, glass liner holds liquor, 36"	150	200	400
Clenched Hand, ivory, c. 1870	180	300	500
Dog's Head, painted and carved wood, c. 1880	200	250	500
Dog's Head, wood with brown eyes, c. 1900	40	65	125
Hound's Head, ivory, c. 1890	70	125	235
Monkey, hand-carved	95	132	275
Mother-of-Pearl, gold, c. 1900	65	100	200
Parade Cane, china clown head	40	55	115
Reproduction Oak Cane, Horse	7	18	30
Reproduction Oak Cane, Eagle	7	18	30
Reproduction Oak Cane, Duck	7	18	30
Umbrella Cane, wood case, 34"	90	135	265
Walking stick, gold head	110	145	300
Walking stick, sterling head	50	65	140

Chalkware

Figurines made from plaster of Paris and painted in bright colors are called chalkware. It was originally produced as a cheap imitation of Staffordshire and Bennington wares during the middle and late 1800s. Later examples were manufactured as carnival prizes during the first half of the 20th century. Of these, animals with nodding heads are especially rare. Few were produced and even fewer have survived through the years. They are sometimes found in the Midwest.

Because of their fragility, many pieces are restored. Check closely for condition. Measurements refer to largest dimension. Prices are for perfect (P), minor paint loss (M), and restored (R).

Early Chalkware is often patterned after Staffordshire designs.

	P	M	R
Bank, apple w/ red cheeks, c. 1900s	$ 40	$ 25	$ 17
Basket of Fruit, c. 1800s	425	275	200
Bird, nesting, c. 1800s	366	230	175
Black Child w/ Watermelon, c. 1900s, 4"	26	16	11
Bookends, pirates, c. 1900s, pair	57	37	25
Boy, reading books, c. 1900s, 10.5"	130	80	55
Cat, c. 1800s, 4.5"	218	142	110
Cat, c. 1800s, 10.5"	277	165	122
Charley McCarthy, c. 1900s, 15"	33	20	14
Dancing Lady, c. 1900s, 14"	38	16	13
Deer, c. 1800s, 9.5"	600	450	275
Dog, c. 1900s, 8.5"	180	120	85
Dove, c. 1900s, green w/ blue wings, 12"	275	185	130
Dove, c. 1800s, green w/ yellow wings, 6"	365	230	165
Duck, c. 1900s, 5"	77	36	25
Eagle, c. 1800s, spread, 9.5"	400	254	183
Gnome, German, c. 1930s, 11"	33	20	14
Horn of Plenty, c. 1900s, 14"	38	15	13
Indian, Cigar Store, reclining, 23"	275	187	130
Lamb, c. 1800s, gray body, 8.5"	365	230	165
Lamb, c. 1900, 6.5"	75	50	35
Owl, c. 1900, 12"	248	165	110
Parrot, c. 1800s, 10.5"	1800	1150	850
Pigeon, c. 1900, 10"	180	120	84
Poodles, c. 1800, 7.75"	277	165	122
Rabbit, c. 1900, 8"	125	89	60
Rooster, c. 1800s, 6"	450	300	214
Santa Claus, c. 1900, 24"	212	135	98
Sheep, mother w/ babies, c. 1900, 7"	130	75	50
Shepherd, German, c. 1900, 17.5"	124	75	50
Squirrel, c. 1800s, 10"	248	165	110
Stag, c. 1800s, rectangular base, 15"	366	231	168

Coverlets

Coverlets are bedspreads woven on a loom. They fall into two categories: geometrics and Jacquards. The geometrics are generally earlier and have small simple designs such as the star, diamond, or snowball. The Jacquards, produced using a loom device made by Frenchman Joseph Jacquard, have curving, ornate designs such as flowers, birds, and trees.

Coverlets were made from the 18th to the 20th century in the East, South, and Midwest. Some are made today in isolated areas. The early geometric coverlets were woven at home usually by women. The Jacquards were more often made by professional male weavers. The Jacquard device enabled the weaver to put his name on his work, the simple loom didn't. Two threads are used in weaving. The warp threads (vertical) are usually cotton, and the weft threads (horizontal) are usually wool. Red and blue dye was primarily used until the middle of the 19th century when synthetic dyes brought a greater color variety. The development of the power loom brought an end to most manual loom weaving.

Jacquards are more popular with collectors than the geometrics. Most coverlets are reasonably priced. Prices are higher for the rarer all-cotton or all-wool coverlets.

The listings are identified as geometric or Jacquard. Following the identification are color, description, and dates, when available.

For further information contact the Colonial Coverlet Guild of America, 7931 Birchdale Avenue, Elmwood Park, IL 60635.

	LOW	AVG.	HIGH
Geometric, blue and white, double weave	$ 280	$ 325	$ 370
Geometric, blue and white, c. 1840	430	535	640
Geometric, blue and white, design, c. 1830	560	620	680
Geometric, indigo and cream, double weave	480	580	680
Geometric, log cabin design	480	560	640
Geometric, red, white, blue, center seam	440	500	560
Jacquard, black and white, birds and flowers	600	675	750
Jacquard, blue and white, crossed rose sprays and stars center, with eagle corners, double weave, c. 1850	1200	1300	1400
Jacquard, blue and white, floral and geometric motifs, house, horse and tree border, double weave, center seam, c. 1835	800	900	1000
Jacquard, blue and white, floral medallions and Amer. eagles and star border, double weave, c. 1830	900	1200	1500
Jacquard, blue and white, garlands and flowers, spread-winged eagle, double weave, center seam, c. 1855	800	900	1000
Jacquard, blue and white, patriotic motif, signed, c. 1860	1600	2000	2400
Jacquard, blue and white, rosettes, leaves, snowflakes, double weave	800	890	980
Jacquard, red and white, floral motif	560	665	770
Jacquard, red and white, lilies and floral sprays, signed	600	660	720
Jacquard, red, blue, green, white, double house border, single weave, center seam	1200	1300	1400
Jacquard, red, eagle motif, unsigned	600	700	800
Jacquard, red, eagle motif, signed	650	750	850
Jacquard, red, green, white, oak leaf and flower design	600	700	800
Jacquard, red, gold, blue, stars and leaves with grapes on border, center seam, c. 1850	1000	1200	1400
Jacquard, red, tan, ivory, eagle motif, "Independence, Virtue, Liberty"	1350	1475	1600
Jacquard, red, white, blue, exotic birds	1200	1350	1500
Jacquard, red, white, blue, star and flower motif	560	665	770

	LOW	AVG.	HIGH
Jacquard, red, white, gold, bird medallions, double weave	$ 540	$ 630	$ 720
Jacquard, red, white, gold, green, central medallions and floral borders, double weave	560	665	770
Jacquard, red, white, green, flowers, stars, spread-winged eagle	640	745	850
Jacquard, Tree of Life, signed, c. 1848	830	880	930
Repro. "Old Colony," white & blue rosettes, double weave 48" x 68"	40	45	50
Repro. "Victorianna," white & blue w/ house border, double weave, 48" x 68"	40	45	50
Repro. 24-panel "Everlasting," 3 color, triple weave, 48" x 68"	60	65	70
Repro. 6-panel "Starburst," 3 color, triple weave, 48" x 68"	60	65	70
Repro. 24-panel "Bear Paw," 3 color, triple weave, 48" x 68"	60	65	70

Fire Fighting Memorabilia

Fire fighting collectibles run from the leather buckets people kept in their homes for fire emergencies, to full hook and ladder trucks. Much equipment used by firemen received heavy use, so today many early items are scarce. This accounts for price variations and the high price often placed on small items.

Top row, left to right: fire bucket, 1834, $650; fire helmet with eagle ornament, $200; Boston fire certificate, $500; fire helmet with lion ornament, $500; Fire bucket, 1817, $600. Bottom row, left to right, fire bucket, Eagle Engine Company, $1300; fire trumpet, 1889 $350; model of fire pumper, $500; fire trumpet, $350; fire bucket, Endicott, Beverly, $650. — Photo courtesy of Northeast Auctions.

	LOW	AVG.	HIGH
Axe, nickel-plated head, c. 1850	$ 500	$ 750	$ 1000
Banner, for parades, with lantern, axe and trumpet	330	365	400
Bell, brass, hand crank	700	900	1100
Belt, parade belt, leather	190	250	310
Belt, parade belt, leather with black, white and red trim, shield on buckle	100	125	150
Book, Our Fireman by A.E. Costello, history of New York fire departments, c. 1887	600	675	750
Bucket, leather, decorated with helmet and hatchet	530	645	760
Bucket, leather, painted	450	600	750
Bucket, leather with red design	850	1000	1150
Bucket, tin	80	100	120
Bucket, with owner's name inscribed, c. 1875	2000	6000	10,000
Bucket, wooden with iron banding and leather strap handle, ht. 13"	50	75	100
Buckle, "1811," brass with fire engine, engraved, c. 1970	180	225	270
Cap, fireman's dress cap with badge	200	250	300
Extinguisher, brass	90	110	130

	LOW	AVG.	HIGH
Extinguisher, bulb shape	$ 30	$ 45	$ 60
Extinguisher, glass	140	175	210
Extinguisher, tin	40	55	70
Fire Bell, nickel plated bronze, outside mechanism, mounted on board	400	600	800
Fire Engine, American LaFrance, 6 cyl., pumper, c. 1948	6000	8000	10,000
Fire Engine, American LaFrance, 6 cyl., type 40 pumper, c. 1917	40,000	50,000	60,000
Fire Engine, American LaFrance, 6 cyl., type 75 pumper, c. 1924	7000	9000	11,000
Fire Engine, American LaFrance, Auburn V.12 engine, ladders, siren, bell, c. 1944	5000	7500	10,000
Fire Engine, Chevrolet, 4 cyl., one ton, fully restored, c. 1927	11,000	13,000	15,000
Fire Engine, Ford, 8 cyl., restored, c. 1941	5000	6000	7000
Fire Engine, Ford, F-6, V-S, equipped. c. 1948	5000	6500	8000
Fire Engine, Ford, unrestored, c. 1947	3000	3600	4200
Fire Engine, Seagrave, Model "A," 4 cyl., restored. c. 1928	48,000	53,000	58,000
Fire Mark, cast iron, c. 1860	650	760	870
Fire Mark, hands clasped, Germantown National Fire, c. 1843	400	460	520
Fire Mark, hydrant, F.A., brass plaque, c. 1843	270	310	350
Fire Mark, hydrant, FA., brass plaque, c. 1817	570	660	750
Fire Mark, Insurance Co. of Florida, c. 1841	700	800	900
Fire Mark, Mutual Assurance Co., iron plaque	350	425	500
Fire Mark, Twentieth Century	100	135	170
Helmet, aluminum with eagle finial	150	190	230
Helmet, brass with eagle finial	600	700	800
Helmet, hand painted shield, c. 1880	1200	1500	1800
Helmet, leather, 6-seam, front shield	170	220	270
Helmet, leather, black embossed with brass eagle, c. 1889	260	315	370
Helmet, leather, ornamental parade helmet, 18th century	1700	2000	2300
Helmet, leather, white with eagle, c. 1890	280	355	430
Helmet, leather with trumpet finial	340	405	470
Helmet, spike top, used for parades	360	440	520
Helmet, three cornered, c. 1870	3550	4175	4800
Honor Roll, watercolor	800	900	1000
Horn, brass	600	800	1000
Hose Nozzle, brass, #12	180	215	250
Hose Nozzle, brass, #15	210	260	310
Hose Nozzle, copper, #25	240	290	340
Lantern, brass	300	450	600
Lantern, nickel plated	170	240	310
Lantern, wagon style with brass font	430	510	590
Spotlight, nickel plated brass	200	300	400
Tickets, fireman's benefit, c. 1860	20	25	30
Trumpet, brass, engraved	800	1000	1200
Trumpet, nickel plated	410	475	540
Trumpet, silver plated with red tassel	830	890	950
Trumpet, sterling silver	1200	1400	1600
Watch Fob, copper	60	90	120
Watercolor Drawing, pumpers, crowd, c. 1875	1000	1200	1300

Folk Art

American folk art of the 19th and early 20th centuries has become a sophisticated field. Carvers such as Wilhelm Schimmel and John Bellamy have seen extremely high prices. But beware! Only pieces of the highest quality command the prices listed below. We have included listings for damaged pieces to show how steeply the values can fall. Many pieces are restored. Check closely for condition.

Measurements refer to largest dimension. Prices are for auction (A), damaged (D), and retail (R).

Above: Bellamy eagle, $5500 at auction. Left: Schimmel eagle, $14,000 at auction. Below left: whirligig, $14,000 at auction. Below right: fire bucket; $2000 at auction. — Photos courtesy of Northeast Auctions.

Left to right: Dapper Dan whirligig, $1500; Indian Chief carving, $2250; sign painter's portrait of Washington, $4000; Washington figure $1100; Lincoln figure, $800. — Photo courtesy of Northeast Auctions.

	A	D	R
Birdcage, fret-carved, ptd. & elaborately decorated w/ cartoon characters, marked "KOM," John O. Komon, Detroit, MI, 1932–33, h. 28," len. 32"	$ 15,000	$ 1500	$ 40,000
Chalkware Deer	350	100	600
Eagle, Amer., carved & ptd., John Bellamy, Portsmouth, NH, w. 23"	800	300	2250
Eagle, Wilhelm Schimmel, PA, c.1880, carved & ptd., spread wing, h. 11," w. 16"	14,000	2000	37,000
Figure of Seated Youth, carved & ptd., w/ sunbonnet & fishing pole, MN, c. 1920, h. 18"	350	100	1000
Figurehead of Woman, half-length, carved & ptd. w/ feathered headdress, h. 50"	3600	900	9000
Folk Art Blue Heron, carved & ptd., driftwood stand, h. 30"	200	75	500
Folk Art Mallard, carved & ptd., w/ tin wings, mtd., len. 13"	350	50	1000
Grotesque Jug, Lanier Meaders, glazed redware, w/ inset eyes & teeth, Cleveland, GA, inscribed, h. 10"	650	300	1700
Horsehead, gilt-copper hollow-molded, h. 23"	750	412	2000
Man Wearing Beaver Hat, carved & ptd., h. 16"	300	165	800
Nantucket Basket	150	82	400
Pastel Portraits, pr., 18th-century man & woman, h. 18"	1200	660	3200
Powderhorn, w/ amorous scenes & eagle, marked "HB," c. 1810	850	400	2200
Rocking Horse, Amer., carved & ptd., leather saddle & horsehair tail, 37"	400	220	1000
Shaker Hooded Cloak in blue-gray	125	60	300
Silhouette, Amer., black ptd. tin depicting couple w/ dove, c. 1860, w. 15"	700	385	2000
Soldier, painted sheet-iron, w/ sword on horse, h. 13"	350	192	945
Watercolor, by New England Schoolgirl, allegorical figures at riverside, eglomisé mat, h. 16"	500	275	1350
Watercolor, Strawberries in Tea Bowl, dated 1820, h. 6"	1500	825	4000

Hooked Rugs

American homes of the 19th century were filled with American ingenuity. Oriental rugs and the fine European carpets were too expensive and too easily damaged in ocean transit (by saltwater in leaky sailing ships) to cover many floors of America. The hooked rugs made from discarded rags or scraps from the cutting room show a wealth Early American imagination.

Watch out for rotted and unraveled examples. They may look good from the back of the auction hall, but restoring them can cost more than the value of the rug itself.

Floral rugs are rarely as valuable as figural rugs.

	AUCTION	RETAIL	
		Low	High
Baltimore Steps, Before and After, by B. Merry, 34" x 40"	$ 850	$ 1600	$ 2800
Barbara House, Rainbow, w/ farm animals, signed, 40" x 50" ...	1000	1900	3300
Christmas Tree and Stars, New England, 40" x 25"	450	800	1500
Floral, 58" x 107"	450	800	1500
Four Six-Point Stars, brown, black, red, and white, 30" x 36" ..	300	600	1000
Hearts & Geometric Motifs, 84" x 96"	500	900	1600
Leaf Spandrels centering medallion w/ horse, 15" x 35"	650	1200	2100
Rooster, circular, w/ braided border, dia. 29"	625	1200	2000
Sleigh Ride in Town, 31" x 41"	350	700	1100
White House, 24" x 37"	225	400	700

Miniatures

Before the days of the wallet photo or the Polaroid, miniature paintings filled the need of a quick keepsake. Although some of these likenesses bear no more resemblance to the sitter than a cartoon character, they often capture a style and a mood of a bygone era. Most of the artists did not sign their work and many names have been lost to history. However, some artists (e.g., Rufus Porter) have a positive effect on the value of a piece.

Left to right: pen and ink sketch, $1500 at auction. Ivory portrait 1835, $875 at auction, Newburyport watercolor of child, $1600 at auction.
— Photos courtesy of Northeast Auctions.

	AUCTION	RETAIL Low	High
Boston Gentleman, on ivory, 3.5" x 2.5"	$ 550	$ 1000	$1500
Boy Holding Book, watercolor, attrib. to Thomas Skynner, c. 1860 ..	1400	2500	3500
Child in Blue Shirt: Thomas C. Bell, 1810, half-length watercolor eglomisé mat, ht. 2.5"	450	750	1250
Child in Cobalt-Blue Outfit, on ivory, attrib. to Joseph Whiting Stock, c. 1843, ht. 2.5"	7500	12,000	20,000
Child in Red Outfit, full-length watercolor, attrib. to R. Porter, ht. 4" ...	8750	14,000	22,000
Gentleman, bust-length profile, watercolor, attrib. to Michel Corne, c. 1800, ht. 3.5"	400	700	1000
Gentleman, on ivory, ht. 2"	800	1400	2000
Gentleman in Blue Coat w/ Brass Buttons, watercolor on ivory, c. 1830, ht. 3"	1300	2200	3000
Gentleman on Red Seat, watercolor, James S. Ellsworth, ht. 3.5" ..	1800	3000	5000
Girl, "age 12 yrs., ink profile, Apr. 23, 1827," ht. 4"	1300	2000	3500
Girl in Polka-Dot Dress, pen and ink, full-length, inscribed "Merit," c. 1830, ht. 5.5"	950	1500	2500
Lady in Bertha-Collar and Watch-Fob, watercolor half-length, attrib. to Justus Dalee, c. 1835, ht. 3", sight	1000	1700	2600
Lady in Black Balloon Sleeve Dress, half-length watercolor, attrib. to John S. Blunt, c. 1830, Found in Portsmouth, NH, ht. 4", sight ..	700	1200	1800
Lady in Red Dress, watercolor and pencil, c. 1830, ht. 3.5"	1800	3000	5000
Lady with Tortoiseshell Comb, profile, watercolor, signed and dated			

	AUCTION	RETAIL	
		Low	High
"Jarvis, Sept. 1807"	$ 600	$ 1000	$ 1500
Man in Striped Coat, bust-length profile, watercolor, attrib. to Rufus Porter, c. 1815, ht. 4.5"	2700	5000	7000
Military officer, on ivory, ht. 1.75"	300	500	750
Newburyport Child, watercolor, ht. 4"	1600	2500	4000
Phebe A. Gurney, 1835, attrib. to Field, on ivory, ht. 2.5"	875	1400	2200
Phoebe Phelps Edwards and Child, on ivory, c. 1830, ht. 2.5"	700	1200	1800
Portraits, pr., Joseph & Sally Adams, attrib. to R. Porter, ht. (frame) 5.5"	7500	12,000	20,000
Portraits, pr., Man and Woman in Cap, watercolor, attrib. to Justus Dalee, c. 1830, ht. (frame) 5"	1400	2500	3500
Portraits, pr., oval, watercolor, attrib. to J. Gillespie, c. 1835, ht. 4.5" .	900	1500	2500
Red-Headed Gentleman, on ivory, ht. 1.5"	275	500	750
Rev. Stephen Westbrook, ht. 2.5"	625	1000	1500
Sea Captain, on ivory, ht. 2"	400	680	1000
Sea Captain, on ivory, ht. 2.5"	600	1000	1500
Two-Sided Oval Portrait Miniatures, each of young child w/ plaid outfit, c. 1840, attrib. to John Carlin, ht. 5"	2100	3000	5000
Woman, bright-cut engraved frame, on ivory, ht. 2"	1300	2000	3500
Woman with Blue Neck-Ribbon, watercolor and applied gilt details, c. 1835 ht. 3"	1000	1600	2400
Woman in Elaborate Collared Dress, pencil, attrib. to J.M. Crowley, ht. 3"	650	1200	1600
Woman in Empire style Dress, on ivory, ht. 4"	600	1000	1500
Young Man, watercolor, with applied gold-leaf spectacles, attrib. to J.H. Gillespie, within oval format and case, ht. 3", sight	400	700	1000

Nautical Memorabilia

Items from the 18th- and 19th-centuries Age of Sail are highly prized. Fine specimens command high prices. Finds can still be made in small New England auctions and estate sales.

Signal cannon on oak casson (see below)

	AUCTION	RETAIL Low	High
Back Staff, C. Elliott, New London, CT, 1765, w. 23"	$ 7500	$ 15,000	$ 22,000
Billet Head, foliate scroll-carved and gilt, w. 23"	1700	3400	5100
Captain's Mah. Liquor Chest, c. 1825 w/ glasses, w. 17"	5000	10,000	15,000
Captain's Oak Liquor Chest, c. 1845, w/ glasses, w. 20"	1200	2400	3600
Captain's Speaking Trumpet, brass, c. 1860, 8"	700	1400	2100
Chronometer, Eng., John Arnold, c. 1770, mah. case, w. 3.5"	4500	9000	13,500
Chronometer, in mah. case, Bliss & Creighton, NY, w. 7"	3250	6500	9750
Compass and Thermometer, Eng., Somalvice & Co., dia. 3"	300	600	900
Compass, Boston, Thaxter & Son, c. 1860, w/ hood, ht. 36" ...	3500	7000	10,000
Compass, in brass case, Kehew, New Bedford, MA	400	800	1200
Dead-Eye, lignum vitae, w/ rope fitting, dia. 5.5"	125	250	380
Globes, pr., celestial and terrestrial, London, ht. 10", dia. 7" ...	6500	13,000	19,500
Pulley, hardwood & brass, Agnall & Loud, Boston, w. 10"	450	900	1350
Quadrant, by Spencer, Browning & Co., case w/ U.S. flag	1500	3000	4500
Quadrant, Eng., ebony and ivory inlaid, signed, c. 1850, 14"	450	900	1350
Sailor-Form Umbrella Stand, ptd. cast-iron, h. 27"	2000	4000	6000
Salute Cannon, on iron carriage, w. 18"	1000	2000	3000
Sea Captain's Iron Strongbox, w/ bail handles, w. 18"	600	1200	1800
Sea Chest w/ ship and house flag, "H" on blue ground, w. 37" ...	1000	2000	3000
Ship's Hanging Clock, Eng., w/ barometer, ht. 10"	1750	3500	5250
Ship's Lanterns, pr., copper, h. 26"	700	1400	2100
Signal Cannon, on oak casson, by Wm. Hawkes, w. 26"	3000	6500	9000
Sundial Cannon, French, marble and brass, inscribed, w. 11"	1700	3400	5100
Water Bucket, sailor's brass-bound, w/ rope-work handle	450	900	1350
Whale Oil Lamps, pr., turned-brass, h. 9"	375	750	1120

Needlework

Embroidery or decorative needlework uses diverse threads such as silk, gold, wool, or cotton stitched into any type of fabric including cloth or leather. The most valuable and rarest embroidery work is from the 1700s. Embroidery pieces from the 1800s and 1900s are more readily available. The condition, workmanship, materials, design, and age of a piece are equally important in determining value. Many hobbyists collect all types of embroidery while others collect by motif, stitch, or country.

Left: Hoffmaster 1823 sampler, 9" x 6", $300 at auction. Below left: 1803 Weston sampler, 18" x 12", $2000 at auction. Below right: memorial picture, $400 at auction. — Photos courtesy of Northeast Auctions

	AUCTION	RETAIL	
		Low	High
Bell-Pull, Victorian, w/ brass tip, len. 66"	$ 125	$ 200	$ 300
Bellows w/ floral needlework panel	55	100	150
Bonnet, colonial period	650	1000	1500
Book Cover, William and Mary, ht. 12"	750	1200	2000
Courting Couple & Landscape, w/ animals and brick mansion, Eng Queen Anne, 25" x 20"	7250	12,000	18,000
Floor-Cloth from Ship *Nancy Louise*, Deer Isle, ME, dated 1939, 46" x 22"	600	1000	1500
Memorial for William Weston by Caroline Weston, 1837, 16" x 13"	1200	2000	3000
Pictorial by Eliza Greenawalt, 1822, depicting shepherd and sheep, 15" x 17"	900	1500	2500
Pocketbook, "John Clark, 1757," flame stitch	450	750	1250
Portsmouth Sampler, "wrought by Mary Elizabeth Coffin," 20" x 17"	650	1000	1500
Sampler, by Elizabeth Lilly, 1797 w/ verse on education, ht. 18"	1000	1750	2500
Sampler, by Maria Atkinson, 1800, of "Hope Beside an Anchor, and Adam & Eve," 18" x 14"	1400	2500	3500

Political Memorabilia

Every political campaign from dog catcher to president produces memorabilia. In addition to the familiar campaign buttons, there is literature of all types, including posters, pictures, brochures and newspaper ads. Such variety and the number of candidates over the years creates a rich and broad collecting field. Political memorabilia offers a history lesson, a chance to discover the movers and shakers of other eras. Most collectors concentrate on national elections and well known politicians. There are others that focus on third party and more obscure candidates.

Buttons are a favorite area of specialization for many collectors. There are several types of buttons. Celluloid buttons are produced by placing a thin piece of paper over a metal disc and then sealing it with a coating of celluloid. Tin lithograph buttons are produced by printing directly on to the tin. A curious term to novices is "jugates," which are buttons picturing both presidential and vice presidential candidates.

Although some items are worth thousands of dollars, this collecting field offers items for every budget. Our consultant for this area is long time collector Karen Gagliardi (she is listed in the back of this book).

Nixon Record,
$8-$10.

VALUE

"America's Pride," colored and embossed cigar box label, pictures George Washington, 7" x 9"	$ 10-25
"Bottom Is Out Of The Full Dinner Pail," Postcard, 1908	10-20
"First Banner," cigar box label picturing Washington, an eagle and a shield, 7" x 10"	10-25
Bryan, "Back To The Farm-Three Strikes And Out," Anti-Bryan cartoon postcard	14-20
Bryan, "Next Occupant Of The White House," campaign postcard for William J. Bryan	8-14
Carter, The Interview," Carter Talks in Playboy," Playboy Magazine folder with 2 1/2" button, 1976 campaign	8-12
"I Like Ike," sticker, 1952 or 1956, 3" x 3 1/2"	6-9
"Lincoln Bouquet," colored and embossed cigar box label, c. 1910, 6" x 10"	10-25
Nixon, "Let's Back Nixon," paper sticker showing Nixon pointing his finger at Khrushchev, 1960 campaign, 4" x 6"	15-20
Roosevelt, "Dee Lighted," a postcard picturing Teddy Roosevelt, 1905	12-20
Roosevelt, Teddy, "Puck" Magazine, issue contains two large political cartoons, one of Teddy Roosevelt, 1906	15-25
Taft, "Nation's Choice," embossed postcard picturing Taft and Sherman	10-15
Taft , "Our Next President William H. Taft: Glory And Prosperity For Our Country," colored postcard picturing Taft	8-12
Taft , "Our Next President And Vice President," postcard picturing Taft and Sherman	8-12
"Vote Democratic," paper window sticker, c. 1948, 4" x 4"	7-12
Wilson, "I Think We've Got Another Washington And Wilson Is His Name," song sheet, 1915	15-20
Wilson, "Never Swap Horses When You're Crossing A Stream," song sheet with portrait of Woodrow Wilson, 1916	15-20

Political Buttons

VALUE

Carter, "The Grin Will Win Jimmy in '76, Carter for President" .... $ 6-10

Chafin, "Eugene Chafin for President," 1908 Prohibition Party candidate, black and white, 7/8" 36-40

Coolidge, lithographed tin, blue and white 14-18

Coolidge/Davis, Jugate, celluloid, black and white, 7/8" 35-45

Eisenhower, "I Like Ike," lithographed tin, red lettering on white background, no illustration, used in 1952 2-3

Hoover, black and white, 1 1/4" 45-50

Hoover, lithographed red, white and blue, 7/8" 4-8

Johnson/ Humphrey, Jugate, photos in outline of the U. S., "Vote Democratic," red, white and blue, 3 1/2" 10-15

Kennedy, "For President John F. Kennedy," red, white, blue and black ....: 10-14

Mckinley/Hobart, Jugate, mechanical gold bug, 1896 200-250

McKinley/Theodore Roosevelt ,Jugate, "Employment for Labor, A Full Dinner Bucket," sepia, 1 1/4" 100-145

Nixon/Lodge, Jugate, lithographed tin, from campaign of 1960 which Richard Nixon lost to John Kennedy 2-3

Reagan, "Ronald Reagan for Governor," lithographed tin, white border 2-3

Roosevelt, "Carry On," lithographed tin, 1" 4-8

Roosevelt, "Rally Round Roosevelt, The People's Choice for President, RRR," red, white and blue 25-35

Roosevelt, FDR/Wallace Jugate, sepia with red, white and blue border 42-52

Smith/Robinson Jugate, lithographed tin, from 1926-campaign 20-30

Stevenson, Our next President Adlai Stevenson, red, white, and blue, 1 3/4" 10-14

Taft, celluloid, multicolor 35-40

Taft/Sherman Jugate, gray and white 100-140

Truman, Inauguration, January 20, 1949, red, white and blue with gray photo, 1 3/4" 18-22

Wilkie, "If I were 21 I'd Vote for Wilkie," green and white, 1 1/4" 6-9

Willkie, white and black with shoulder length portrait, wording "For President" at top 18-22

Wilson/Marshall Jugate, celluloid, black and white, "Win with Wilson and Marshall," 7/8" 32-40

Theodore Roosevelt and Fairbanks jugate, $30-$40; Franklin Roosevelt and Garner jugate, $140-$160. — Items courtesy of Pastimes Antiques.

Scrimshaw

Scrimshaw is artwork done on bone. It can be carved or painted. Carved scrimshaw, which seldom has any painted decoration, is mostly in the nature of little trinkets, boxes, pins, or forks, for example. Painted scrimshaw is done directly on the tooth or bone. It is accomplished by scratching the design into the surface with needles, then working India ink into the scratches. Whalebone is the most commonly found material, followed by walrus tusk. Occasionally a low-grade ivory such as whale tooth is used.

The age, size, artistic quality, subject matter, and state of preservation all go into determining the value of scrimshaw. Beware of fakes made from polymers. See "Fakeshaw" by Stuart Frank, Kendall Whaling Museum, 1993. Also beware of various endangered species laws. Differences in federal and state regulations make this a tricky topic. Check with local authorities before buying or selling scrimshaw.

Schrimshaw teeth. — Photo courtesy of Northeast Auctions.

	AUCTION	RETAIL Low	High
Bellows, sailor-made, inlaid walnut, w. 22"	$ 850	$ 1700	$ 2550
Bookends, pr., engraved colored scrimshaw, h. 9"	2500	5000	7500
Bucket, mid-19th century, bone and mah. staves, dia. 9"	6000	12,000	18,000
Busk, engraved on-board Amer. whaler, c. 1835, 14"	6000	12,000	18,000
Busk, engraved w/ vignettes: strolling lovers, 13"	500	1000	1500
Candlestick-Form Pickwicks, pr., c. 1830, h. 7"	4750	9500	14,000
Coconut-Shell Dipper, w/ star, vine, & spiral motifs, 14.5"	850	1700	2550
Coconut-Shell Dipper, w/ vine motifs, scrimshaw end, 15"	600	1200	1800
Cribbage Board, sailor-made, mah., inlaid w/ ebony, l. 12"	350	700	1050
Cribbage Board, sailor-made, mah., w/ ebony inlay, w. 16"	550	1100	1650
Ditty Box, circular, ht. 2.5", dia. 4.5"	3500	7000	10,000
Double-Block, w/ finely worked rope fitting, 3.25"	1000	2000	3000
Double-Block, w/ rope fitting, 2.5"	325	650	980
Fid, pierced, carved, w/ open-work heart motifs, 6.5"	700	1400	2100
Gavel, ring-turned handle, drum-form mallet, 6.5"	1000	2000	3000
Jagging Wheel, serpent-form whalebone, c. 1845, w. 6".	2100	4200	6300
Jagging Wheel, double, c. 1830, loop handle w/ 2 fists, 9.5" ..	9500	19,000	28,500
Jagging Wheel, stylized whale-form, 8"	1000	2000	3000
Marriage Mantel, w/ 4 colored teeth, ht. 7 2", w. 12.5".	15,000	30,000	45,000

	AUCTION	RETAIL	
		Low	High
Measuring Stick, engraved w/ # 1 - # 23, 24"	$ 600	$ 1200	$ 1800
Measuring Stick, oriental wood w/ scrimshaw inlay, 36"	650	1300	1950
Oval Tray, pierced hearts, mah. base, w. 10"	2400	4800	7200
Parallel Ruler, mah., w. 12"	450	900	1350
Pie Crimper, spatular form, handle w/ pointed tip, l. 4.5"	725	1450	2180
Rolling Pin, mah., acorn-form handles, 18"	950	1900	2850
Rolling Pin, mah., baluster-turned handles, 16.5"	400	800	1200
Rope Seamer, sailor-made, 5.5"	400	800	1200
Sewing Basket, inlaid mah., circular, ht. 3.5", dia. 9"	6500	13,000	19,500
Sewing Basket, c. 1860, flaring hexagonal form, dia. 6"	2300	4600	7000
Straight Edge, sailor-made, tipped w/ scrimshaw, 16"	900	1800	2700
Swift, w/ clenched fist, h. 15"	4500	9000	13,500
Swift, w/ tripod base and cabriole legs, h. 16".	800	1600	2400
Teeth, pr., depicting sailor and sweetheart, h. 6".	2750	5500	8250
Tooth, Amer., 19th century depicting fort and soldier, h. 4.5". ..	650	1300	1950
Tooth, depicting U.S. Brig *Dolphin*, inscribed, 1849, h. 7.5". .	3750	7500	11,250
Tooth, depicting whaleboats & whale, colored, h. 7"	18,000	36,000	54,000
Tooth, Engraved w/ whaling scenes, red highlights, h. 8.5"	8000	16,000	24,000
Walking Stick, fitted w/ baleen rings, 34"	800	1600	2400
Walking Stick, w/ turk's head knot, 33"	750	1500	2250
Wall Pocket, sailor-made, mah., shield form, ht. 8"	1500	3000	4500
Work Box, sailor-made, w/ inlay of lyre and stars, w. 18"	2500	5000	7500

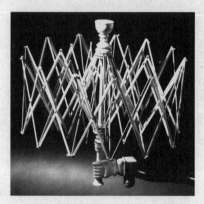

Scrimshaw swift with clenched fist, $4500 at auction. — Photo courtesy of Northeast Auctions.

Shaker Collectibles

The Shakers formed a socioreligious organization in England in 1747. Their doctrines advocated simplicity and celibacy. They were nicknamed "Shakers" because of their devotional dancing in religious services. Ann Lee led a group to America in 1776 and attracted many converts. Known for their fine quality, Shakers made products that symbolized beliefs of purity and utility from the early 19th century to the 20th century. Although the Shakers made furniture for their own use, much was made for commercial sale.

Pieces are worth more if the collector can identify the Shaker community of origin. For the sampling of pieces listed below, the following abbreviations are used: Alfred, Maine = *ALF,* Canterbury, New Hampshire = *CANT,* Enfield, Connecticut = *ENF,* Harvard, Massachusetts = *HAR*, Hancock, Massachusetts = *HAN*, Mt. Lebanon, New York = *MtL,* New Lebanon, New York = *NL,* Pleasant Hill, Kentucky = *PLH,* Sabbathday Lake, Maine = *SDL*, Watervliet, New York = *WVLT.*

Identifying Shaker pieces can be difficult. There are large numbers of fakes and countless reproductions. Note that the famed Shaker oval box with long "fingers" fastening the sides are probably not true Shaker unless the fingers of the lid and the body are pointing the same direction. For further information see *By Shaker Hands*, by June Sprigg. Auctioneers who specialize in Shaker pieces include Willis Henry.

Above: Shaker boxes with finger joints should have the finger on the lid point the same direction as those on the body, as in the examples on the left. Boxes whose finger joints point in opposite direction are rarely Shaker made, as in the examples on the right. Left: Furniture made from highly figured woods, such as this bird's eye maple rocking chair, are worth double or more than plain wood. This example sold for $4500 at auction. — Photos courtesy of Northeast Auctions.

	LOW	HIGH
Apple Peeler, cherry, ALF, c. 1840, len. 26"	$ 1350	$ 2000
Armchair, maple, rush seat, MtL, c.1870, #7	5000	8000
Armchair, maple, tape seat, MtL, c.1870, #3	1200	1800
Basket, ash, 2-handle, initialed, ht. 11"	900	1350
Basket, ash, hickory, rect., hoop handle, PLH, c. 1850, w., 20"	1800	2700
Basket, ash, rect., hoop handle, open weave bottom, signed, w. 14.5"	980	1460
Basket, maple, 2-handle, double-wrapped rim, ENF, c. 1850, dia. 7.5"	1650	2480
Basket, splint, hoop handle, attached lid, signed, HAR, c. 1850, w. 9"	1800	2700
Basket, oak, swing handle, wrapped rim, SDL, c. 1840, dia. 14"	1500	2250
Bench, pine, bootjack ends, HAN, c. 1840, w. 39"	12,000	18,000
Blanket Chest, pine, red paint, cutout base, ENF, c. 1850, w. 41"	2400	3600
Bonnet, linen trimmed, paper label, #5	600	900
Bucket, pine, orig. red paint, ENF, c. 1840, dia. 10"	1350	2000
Bucket, w/ lid, pine, blue paint, MtL, c. 1850, dia. 9.75"	2400	3600
Bureau Box, pine, orig. red stain, molded lid, NL, c. 1830, w. 14.5"	1500	2250
Candle Chest, bootjack ends, SDL, c. 1840, ht. 36", w. 33"	3000	4500
Candlestand, snake leg, orig. finish, NL, c. 1840, ht. 23.5", dia. 16"	8000	12,000
Chair Table, traces of orig. red, CANT, c. 1840, w. 73"	12,000	18,000
Cheese Basket, black ash, ALF, c. 1840, dia. 21"	2400	3600
Cheese Box, orig. green paint, copper nails, pegged, HAN, dia. 16.5"	2550	3820
Child's Chair, maple, orig. yellow stain, spindle back, CANT, c. 1880, ht. 29"	900	1350
Child's Rocking Chair, maple, taped seat, #0, MtL decal, ht. 23"	6000	9000
Child's Side Chair, dark varn., orig. tape, #1, MtL decal, ht. 28"	4500	6750
Child's Tilt Chair, birch, orig. varn., taped seat, ENF, c. 1830, ht. 32"	6000	9000
Clothes Brush, white horsehair, 8.75"	450	680
Clothes Hanger, pine, initialed, NL, c. 1850, w. 17"	200	320
Covered Bucket, pine, orig. red paint, signed "Enfield," dia. 9.75"	3000	4500
Cream Tub, orig. blue paint, wire handles, ENF, c. 1840, dia. 10"	2550	3820
Cutlery Basket, ash, carved medial handle, w. 17"	3300	5000
Desk Box, CANT, c. 1840, w. 18"	3300	5000
Desk Box, chestnut, cherry and pine, orig. red stain, c. 1850, w. 16"	2100	3150
Dipper Ash, orig. cream yellow paint, len. 6.5"	1650	2480
Document Box, pine, orig. blue paint, SDL, c. 1850, w. 6.5"	1650	2480
Dough Box, orig. red paint, cutout handles, WVLT, c. 1840, w. 32"	3300	5000
Dressing Chair, birch, rush seat, double dowel back, MtL, c. 1880	3000	4500
Drop Leaf Table, birch, orig. red paint, CANT, c.1830, w. 45"	33,000	49,500
Dry Sink, pine, refinished, NL, c. 1830, ht. 35", w. 31"	2700	4000
Drying Basket, ash, natural brown, 20" dia.	1800	2700
Drying Basket, black ash, open work, cheese basket design, 2 wrapped handles, 2 runners, c. 1850, ht. 20", dia. 23"	2700	4000
Drying Rack, dark varn., arched foot, NL, c. 1840, ht. 38", w. 24"	1200	1800
Drying Rack, orig. red paint, arched base, WVLT, c. 1850, ht. 55"	3000	4500
Elder's Rocking Chair, serpentine arms, NL, c. 1850	4500	6750
Flax Wheel, oak, maple, signed, complete w/ distaff	900	1350
Folding Drying Rack, orig. salmon paint, 4 part, ENF, c.1840, ht. 60"	3300	5000
Footstool, maple, orig. dark varn., rush seat, #0, decal, MtL, w. 13"	1500	2250
Gathering Basket, ash, swing handle and side handle, w. 18"	3600	5400
Hanger, pine and hickory, CANT, c. 1850	220	340
Hanger, walnut, ENF, c. 1840, w. 12.5"	600	900
Herb Cutter, pine, orig. red stain, dovetailed, wrought-iron chopper, WVLT,		

	LOW	HIGH
c. 1850, w. 29"	$ 1950	$ 3000
Infirmary Screen, light varn., 3 panels, 3 pegs, NL, c. 1850, ht. 80"	2700	4000
Knife Box, canted sides, finger holes, c. 1850, ht. 5", w. 13.25"	900	1350
Land Grant, w. 12"	1350	2000
Medicine Bottle, green, orig. stopper, "New Leb., NY," ht. 9.25"	1720	2500
Milk Tub, pine, orig. blue exterior, c. 1840, dia. 9.5"	1350	2000
Mortar and Pestle, HAR, c. 1830, ht. 4", dia. 3.5"	1650	2400
Music "The Little Shaking Quakers"	1500	2250
Neckerchief Silk, hand-woven, initialed, 1846, sq. 35"	1350	2000
Oval Box, maple, pine, orig. red paint, 3 fingers, PLH, c. 1840, len. 6"	1950	2900
Oval Box, pine, birch, orig. white paint, 5 fingers, c. 1840, len. 12.5"	4500	6750
Oval Box, pine, maple, orig. varn., 3 fingers, SDL, c. 1850, len. 3.25"	1800	2700
Oval Carrier, orig. yellow varn., 2 fingers, CANT, c. 1830, dia. 10"	2700	4000
Oval Gift Box, pine, cedar, natural finish, 3 fingers, dia. 3.5"	2400	3600
Oval Sewing Carrier, maple, clear varn., 4 fingers, satin-lined, fitted, "SDL" trademark, w. 11"...	1200	1800
Oval Sewing Carrier, maple, clear varn., satin-lined, fitted, "SDL" trademark, dia. 7"	1350	2000
Oval Spit Box, maple, pine, yellow stain, 2 fingers, CANT, c. 1840, w. 11"	2700	4000
Pail, pine, orig. paint, wire bail, NL, c. 1820, dia. 6.25"	1000	1500
Peg Rail, pine w/ birch pegs, len. 60"	600	900
Pie Basket, ash, orig. green stain, hinged lid, sq. 12.5"	3000	4500
Poetry, handwritten, "Silent Worship," initialed, Enfield, CT, 1829	600	900
Poplarware Box, satin-lined, orig. "Canterbury Shakers" box, sq. 4.5"	900	1350
Poplarware Box, rect., SDL, blue satin, w. 5.5"	150	220
Revolving Chair, 8 spindles, NL, c. 1840, ht. 27"	15,750	23,000
Rocking Chair, cherry, shawl bar, tape seat, MtL, c. 1870, #7	2700	4000
Rocking Chair, shawl bar, ebony finish, tape seat, MtL, c. 1870, #3	1500	2250
Rocking Chair, maple, black walnut finish, old tape seat, MtL, #5	3900	5850
Rocking Chair, maple, shawl bar, tape seat, MtL, c. 1870, #7	4200	6300
Rocking Chair, maple, stained finish, shawl bar, MtL, c . 1870, #4	1950	2920
Rocking Chair, maple, tape seat, MTL, decal, c. 1900, #7	2700	4000
Round Carrier, pine, maple, HAR, c. 1830, dia. 10.75"	2250	3400
Round Carrier, poplar, maple, orig. green paint, swing handle, dia. 9"	1500	2250
Rug, silk, cotton backing, black border, polychrome field, 24" x 40"	450	680
Sampler, 3 alphabets and numerals, ENF, 10" x 12"	11,000	16,000
Seed Box, pine, label "Fresh Garden Seeds Raised," ht. 5.5", w. 14"	2000	3000
Seed Box, orig. red paint, "Shakers Seeds, Mt. Leb.," ht. 3.5", w. 23.5"	3900	5800
Seed Carrier, pine, orig. red stain, CANT, c. 1830, ht. 9.5", sq. 10.5"	3000	4500
Sewing Basket, maple, side handles, 15.5" sq.	1350	2000
Sewing Basket, splint, sq. base, fitted lid, MtL, ht. 3.5", sq. 5.75"	2400	3600
Sewing Chest, walnut, c.1860, ht. 31", w. 40"	12,750	20,000
Sewing Desk, butternut, pine, birch, orig. paint, signed, SDL, w. 30"	100,000	160,000
Sewing Desk, pine, old varn., 5 drawers, c. 1830, w. 22.5"	9750	14,000
Sewing Stand, orig. red stain, 1 drawer, HAN, c. 1850, w. 22"	3000	4500
Sewing Stand, maple, chestnut, birch top, dark varn., tapered leg, CANT, c. 1840, w. 15.5"..	10,000	15,750
Shovel Birch, dark varn., ENF, c. 1850, len. 36"	2700	4000
Side Chair, cherry, orig. varn., tilters, split reed seat, #3	1650	2500
Side Chair, maple, mustard yellow paint, taped seat, ALF, c. 1830, ht. 41"	2700	4000
Side Chair, maple, orig. varn., cane seat, tilters, CANT, c. 1840, ht. 41" ...	18,000	27,000

	LOW	HIGH
Side Chair, maple, walnut stain, tape seat, MtL, c.1870, #3	$ 1800	$ 2700
Side Chair, tiger maple, orig. finish & tape, tilters, NL, c. 1830, ht. 41"	6300	9500
Sister's Cape, wool, mother-of-pearl buttons, initialed, len. 32"	680	1000
Sister's Cloak, blue wool, satin, labeled "Enfield, N.H.," len. 56"	900	1350
Sister's Shawl, wool, stripe border, fringe, SDL, 64" sq.	900	1350
Sorting Table, oak, tray top, NL, c. 1860, w. 76"	6600	10,000
Sorting Table, poplar, oak, brown stain, sawbuck base, flat stretchers, HAR, c. 1860, ht. 29", w.17.5"	1800	2700
Spice Chest, 13-drawer, walnut, WVLT, c. 1850, ht. 17", w. 17"	2400	3500
Spool Rack & 6 Spools, cherry, orig. varn., horn spindles, thimble holder ht. 5", dia. 5"	5250	7500
Spoolholder, orig. varn., tomato pincushion, thimble holder, dia. 5.5"	1500	2250
Stand, 1 drawer, cherry, CANT, c. 1840, ht. 27", w. 17"	5100	7500
Stand, 1 drawer, cherry, pine, MtL, ht. 27.5", w. 20"	2800	4000
Stand, 1 drawer, cherry, poplar, ENF, c. 1840, ht. 27.5", w.18"	9000	14,000
Stand Up Desk, lift lid, dovetailed drawer, shelf, ht. 51", w. 28"	3900	5850
Storage Basket, ash, rect. bottom, oval rim, NL, c. 1860, ht. 13" w. 37"	1000	1580
Storage Box, maple burl, HAN, c. 1850, ht. 8.25", w. 16"	3600	5400
Storage Box, orig. brown paint, WVLT, c. 1840, ht. 7.5", w. 15.5"	2700	4000
Stove, iron, canted sides, straight legs, NL, c. 1840, ht. 19", len. 29"	1800	2700
Straw Press, cherry, varn. finish, mortise & pegged, threaded knobs, ALF, c. 1830, ht. 18", w. 13"	2400	3600
Swift, maple, orig. mustard paint, ht. 21"	1350	2000
Tailoring Stick, cherry, MtL, c. 1840, len. 36"	3600	5400
Tall Basket, maple, ash, flared top, ENF, c. 1850, ht. 29", sq. 17"	4200	6300
Tall Clock, wooden works, paper dial, dated "1835," ht. 80", w. 17"	50,000	100,000
Triple Hanger, butternut, pine, MtL, c. 1840, ht. l9.5"	1000	1500
Triple Hanger, walnut stain, init., PLH, c. 1850, ht. 6.25", w. 14"	1350	2000
Trustee's Desk, fall-front lid, inner compartments, 2 drawers, ALF, c. 1840, ht. 46.5", w. 37.5"	6000	9000
Wash Table, pine, orig. blue-gray paint, tapered leg, arched ends, separate drying rack, SDL, c. 1840, ht. 32.5", w. 28.5"	8000	12,000
Washstand, pine, refinished, 1 drawer, dovetailed, gallery w/ cup-holders, CANT, c. 1850, ht. 39.5", w. 19"	2850	4000
Washstand, traces of orig. paint, 2 paneled doors, orig. threaded knobs, ENF, c. 1840, ht. 35", w. 32.5"	9750	14,000
Wool Basket, carved double handles, ht. 13", w. 27.5"	1650	2400
Wool Wheel, weathered finish, initialed, SDL, c. 1830,	1000	1580
Work Stand, 1 drawer, turned leg, WVLT, c. 1830, ht. 21", w. 16"	2700	4000
Work Stand, 3 drawer, turned legs, SDL, c. 1840, ht. 27", w. 31"	10,000	15,000
Work Table, new paint over orig. red, turned legs, WVLT, c. 1820, ht. 26", w. 42"	1650	2500
Work Table, pine, birch, red base, scrub top, tapered round legs, CANT, c. 1820, ht. 28", w. 63"	5250	7500
Work Table, pine, maple, orig. red finish, turned leg, ALF, c. 1820, ht. 28", w. 34"	4200	6300
Work Table, pine, oak, red stain finish 1 drawer, chamfered legs, SDL, c. 1860, ht. 27.5", w. 20.5"	1000	1500
Yarn Winder, maple, clock reel, CANT, c. 1839, ht. 37"	1650	2400

Ship Models

There are four main types of ship models. *Wright's models* (*W*) were made by a shipwright (a ship builder) as a working model for an actual ship. *Sailor's models* (*S*) were made while the sailor served on a ship. *Collector's models* (*C*) are made after the ship was constructed, often after it ceased to exist, using photographs or drawings in books. *Kit models* (*K*) are built from components and directions furnished in a commercially sold kit.

Wright's models are the most desired and expensive. Sailor's models may be crude, but they are often highly regarded. The value of a collector's model is determined by age, size, intricacy of detail, and state of preservation. Models of steamships are generally not as valuable as sailing vessels.

Half Hull of the American steamship "Jos. Comstock," 8 feet, $650 at auction. — Photo courtesy of Northeast Auctions.

	AUCTION	RETAIL Low	RETAIL High
America's Cup "J" Boat, 1934, glazed case, w. 17.5", *C* ...... $ 1000		$ 2000	$ 3000
Bone Ship, Amer. Barkentine, c. 1830, rigged, case 27.5", *S* ... 15,000		30,000	45,000
Builder's Half-Hull of Amer. Steamship, w. 96", *W* 650		1300	2000
Sailing Ship, planked, w. 40", *C* 1700		3400	5000
Shadowbox Half-Hull of 7-Mast Schooner, w. 44", *W* 2600		5000	8000
Shadowbox Half-Hull of Amer. Ship, w. 33", *W* 1300		2500	4000
Ship in a Bottle, *Old Ironsides*, len. 4", *K* 100		150	250
Whale Boat, Amer., fitted w/ whaling equip. and sail, w. 24", *S* . 4500		9000	13,000

Tools

Handtools of the 18th, 19th, and 20th centuries often represent fine craftsmanship and engineering. Values vary with quality, rarity, and also usability. Many craftsmen prefer the high quality of some antique tools over those now available. Watch out for missing parts.

"Good" pieces show wear but no damage and are still capable of use. "Best" pieces are in perfect condition with superior quality manufacture. For further information see *The Antique Tool Collector's Guide to Value*, by Ronald S. Barlow.

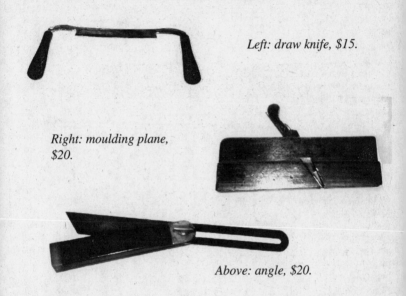

Left: draw knife, $15.

Right: moulding plane, $20.

Above: angle, $20.

Right: folding rule, $90.

	GOOD	BETTER	BEST
Adz	$ 15	$ 40	$ 100
Anvil, Jeweler's	10	30	75
Anvil, Bench	15	30	100
Boring Machines	75	120	200
Auger, Handled	20	50	100
Axe, Mortising	30	40	60
Axe, Ice	10	20	40
Axe, Hewing	30	60	100
Axe, Kent	15	30	50

	GOOD	BETTER	BEST
Axe, Cooper's	$ 20	$ 35	$ 75
Brace	10	30	100
Brace (18th century)	75	150	300
Brace (Sheffield)	60	100	300
C-Clamp, 4"	5	8	15
C-Clamp, 8"	10	15	30
Calipers	10	20	60
Chisel (wood carving)	8	15	30
Chisels (set of 14)	100	200	400
Clamp, Violin	10	20	30
Clamp, Floor	25	40	80
Clamp, Mitre Jack	15	25	45
Cobbler's Bench	100	200	500
Compass, Woodworker's, 8"	5	10	25
Compass, Drafting	5	10	30
Draw Knife	10	15	30
Drill, Bow	150	250	600
Drill, Breast	20	40	80
Drill, Hand	10	20	40
Hacksaw	20	30	50
Hammer, Ball Pien	10	20	40
Hammer, Claw	5	15	35
Hand Screw (all wood)	10	20	35
Lathe, w/ Treadle	150	250	500
Level, 6"	8	15	30
Level, 15"	15	40	75
Marking Gauge	15	30	80
Plane, Badger	10	30	80
Plane, Block	10	40	120
Plane, Compass	15	40	150
Plane, Moulding	10	20	40
Plane, Horn	30	80	200
Plane, Jack	20	35	80
Plane, Jointer	25	45	120
Plane, Plow	25	80	250
Plane, Rabbet	10	30	80
Plane, Smoothing	25	50	175
Pliers	5	15	30
Plumb, 5"	10	18	40
Plumb Bob	15	40	80
Router (Hand)	15	40	80
Saw, Bow	50	100	200
Saw Set (Sharpener)	20	40	60
Screwbox	30	50	150
Screwdriver	8	15	30
Sextant	100	250	500
Sextant (boxed)	150	300	750
Sharpening Stone (hard Arkansas)	10	20	50
Shears	8	15	25
Spokeshave	10	20	50
Square (all steel)	10	15	35

	GOOD	BETTER	BEST
Square (rosewood)	$ 15	$ 20	$ 50
Surveying Compass	50	100	250
Tool Chest (Machinist's)	75	125	200
Trammel	30	60	120
Vise, Bench	50	90	180
Vise, Swivel	50	80	120
Whetstone, Turning Wheel	40	80	150
Wrench (wooden handle)	10	20	40

Stanley Gage Self Setting Plane

Buckeye Self Setting Plane

Stanley Scrub Plane

Lakeside Tongue and Groove Plane

Stanley Rabbet Plane

Stanley Rabbet Plane and Fillister

Stanley Dowel Turner

Stanley No. 45 Combination Plane

Stanley No. 55 Universal Plane

Weathervanes

The most valued weathervanes are those handmade of sheet copper before 1850. These are quite rare. In the 19th and early 20th centuries factory workers made weathervanes of copper hammered in iron molds. Important makers include: Cushing and White of Waltham, MA. and the J. Howard Company of East Bridgewater, MA. Many reproductions have been made from original molds.

Values listed below are for fine examples for auction (A), semi-antique reproduction (S-R), and retail (R).

Clockwise from upper left: rooster, ht. 22", $1500 at auction; "Hambletonian" horse, len. 26" $1000 at auction, horse with jockey, len. 29", $3250 at auction; marsh bird, ht. 38", $5250 at auction; cow, len. 13", $3000 at auction. — Photo courtesy of Northeast Auctions.

	A	S-R	R
Capt. Ahab w/ Telescope, sheet-copper, 19th c., h. 20"	$ 900	$ 500	$ 2400
Cow, cast iron & copper full bodied, w. 27"	3000	1000	8000
Gamecock, full-bodied molded, ptd. highlights, h. 23"	1500	800	4000
"Hambeltonian," full-bodied copper, A.L. Jewell, w. 29"	2000	1100	5400
"Hambeltonian" Horse, copper, W.A. Snow & Co., w. 26"	1000	550	2700
Horse, Rochester Ironworks, cast iron, mid-19th c., w. 36"	9000	1500	24,000
Horse and Rider, red ptd. sheet iron, 19th c., w. 52"	1000	450	2700
Indian Archer, Berks Co., PA, ptd. sheet iron, c. 1880, h. 25" ...	850	450	2300
Jockey & Running Horse, copper, J.W. Fiske, #515, w. 30"	3600	1700	9000
Locomotive &Tender, ptd. copper, gilt, c. 1890, w. 62"	21,000	3500	56,000
Marsh Bird w/ raised leg, full-bodied copper, h. 38"	5250	1800	14,000

	A	S-R	R
Mountain Boy, copper and gilt, on stand, w. 38"	$ 1000	$ 550	$ 2700
Peafowl, full-bodied copper, old patina, h. 29"	4250	1000	11,400
Peafowl, gilt copper full-bodied, h. 18"	1250	650	3300
Pig, copper gilt full-bodied, L.W. Cushing, c. 1883, w. 36"	16,500	1500	44,000
Quill-form, copper, w. 36"	1700	935	4500
Quill-form, copper, on stand, w. 36"	3500	1925	9400
Rooster, carved wood, gray paint, h. 12"	750	412	2000
Rooster, cast iron, h. 23"	1500	825	4050
Rooster, full-bodied molded copper, h. 19"	1700	935	4500
Rooster, full-bodied molded copper, h. 22"	1500	825	4000
Running Horse, copper full-bodied, w. 26"	1000	550	2700
Running Horse, gilt copper, green patina, w. 31"	2900	1600	7500
Running Horse & Jockey, full-bodied copper, w. 29"	3250	1750	8000
Running Horse, J. Harris and Son, full-bodied copper, w. 28"	850	468	2200
Schooner w/ metal sails and rigging, ptd. , c. 1910, w. 35"	400	220	1000
Steeplechase Horse, copper, A.L. Jewell, c. 1860, w. 30"	13,000	2500	35,000
Steer, molded copper and cast iron, w. 29"	1300	715	3500
"The Smuggler," full-bodied copper, w. 29"	350	192	900
Touring Car, copper, E.G. Washburn, c. 1912, w. 28"	12,000	2500	32,000
Trotting Horse, copper, gilt, J. Howard, mid-19th c., w. 20"	6000	1500	16,000
Uncle Sam w/ Donkey Cart, silhouette, sheet-metal, w. 33"	1900	1000	5000

Autographs

The personal mark of the famous and revered has always attracted collectors. The following abbreviations are used: *ALS* -Autograph Letter Signed (a letter hand written by the person who signed it), *LS* -Letter Signed (a letter typed or written out by another person), *DS* -Document Signed (a signed document), *PhS* -Photo Signed, *Cut Sig.*-Cut Signature (a signature cut from a letter, autograph book, or other source).

We have divided this section into Artists, Authors, Entertainment Figures, and Presidents.

Artists

	ALS		Cut Sig.	
	Low	High	Low	High
Benson, Frank W.	$ 36	$ 46	$ 8	$ 12
Ceilini, Benvenuto	7500	12,000	700	900
Cezanne, Paul	800	1400	60	80
Chagall, Marc	340	400	44	56
Church, Frederick S.	220	280	24	30
Corot, Camille	170	200	34	44
Crulkshank, George	200	300	24	34
DaVinci, Leonardo	70,000	120,000	3500	4500
Degas, Edgar	750	1100	120	150
Eastlake, Sir Charles L.	170	200	16	20
Gauguin, Paul	1300	1700	44	56
Gibson, Charies Dana	100	140	14	20
Gifford, R. Swain	16	20	4	8
Landseer, Sir Edwin	44	54	6	10
Lawrence, Sir Thomas	240	300	12	16
Lear, Edward	350	450	24	28
Leslie, C.R.	80	100	8	12
Matisse Henri	280	380	40	60
Michelangelo, Buonarroti	30,000	44,000	2500	3200
Modigilani, Amedee	1400	2000	140	200
Monet, Claude	140	200	24	30
Pissarro, Camille	280	380	50	66
Raphael, Sanzlo	70,000	120,000	3500	5000
Rembrant van Riyn	150,000	300,000	8000	12,000
Remington, Frederick	1000	1800	60	100
Renoir, Pierre A.	700	1000	120	170
Rossetti, Dante G.	500	700	60	80
Rouault, George S.	300	400	50	70
Rubens, Peter Paul	18,000	24,000	1400	2000
Sargent J S.	220	300	24	30
Sully, Thomas	220	300	24	30
West, Benjamin	340	400	24	30
Whistler, James A.M.	240	320	34	44
Wyeth, N. C.	140	200	14	20

Marc Chagall

Authors

Authors' letters have always been a favorite of collectors. But just like the novels and poems they wrote, content counts! A letter refusing a dinner invitation is worth a fraction of a letter discussing alternative endings of a play.

Examples: Harris, Melville, Wolfe, Lowell, Eliot, and Hemingway

	LS		ALS	
	Low	High	Low	High
Alcott, Louisa May	$ 500	$ 700	$ 1000	$ 1400
Alger, Horatio	60	80	400	550
Bryant, William C.	150	190	300	380
Burnett, Frances H.	34	44	60	70
Burroughs, John	70	100	150	200
Curtis, George W.	28	36	32	40
Dana, R.H., Jr.	84	106	200	300
Davis, Richard H.	16	20	28	36
Fiske, John	20	28	24	30
Hale, Edward E.	28	36	44	56
Harris, Joel C.	200	300	600	800
Hawthorne, Nathaniel	3000	4000	4000	6000
Hemingway, Ernest	3000	7000	6000	10,000
Hubbard, Elbert	36	46	70	80
Irving, Washington	2000	3000	6000	8000
Kilmer, Joyce	350	450	800	1000
Longfellow, H.W.	300	360	500	600
Lowell, James R.	90	120	240	320
Melville, Herman	7500	12,000	9000	14,000
Mencken, H.L.	150	200	200	400
Money, Christopher	80	110	120	160
O'Neill, Eugene	1600	4000	3000	4500
Pierpont, John	60	80	120	160
Porter, W.S. (0. Henry)	1600	2000	1600	2000
Sikes, William W.	24	44	60	70
Stockton, Frank	80	100	170	220
Stoddard, R.H.	60	80	120	160
Stowe, H.B.	280	340	800	1100
Tarkington, Booth	350	450	500	700
Taylor, Bayard	80	100	160	200
Thoreau, Henry D	2400	3000	3500	4500
Thorpe, Thomas B.	80	100	160	200
Wolfe, Thomas	800	1400	2400	3200

Entertainers

Who signed that photo? As big stars received more requests for signed photos than they could supply themselves, they (or their studios) hired secretaries to sign photos for them. In the case of Jean Harlow, her mother signed most of the photos picturing this star.

Photo of Jean Harlow signed by her mother, "Mama Jean" Harlow.

| | SIGNED PHOTO | | PLAIN SIGNATURE | |
	Low	High	Low	High
Alda, Alan	$ 14.00	$ 22.00	$ 3.00	$ 4.50
Allen, Gracie	70.00	100.00	8.00	11.00
Allen, Steve	2.30	3.70	1.00	1.50
Allen, Woody	7.50	12.00	2.00	4.00
Allyson, June	4.80	6.60	1.00	1.40
Altman, Robert	8.00	11.00	1.60	2.00
Ameche, Don	4.30	6.00	1.00	1.50
Andress, Ursula	5.80	10.00	1.00	1.50
Andrews, Julie	2.90	4.50	1.00	1.40
Arden, Eve	4.60	5.80	1.00	1.50
Arkin, Alan	5.70	9.00	1.00	1.50
Arness, James	2.90	4.40	1.00	1.50
Arthur, Beatrice	4.50	6.00	1.00	1.60

	SIGNED PHOTO		PLAIN SIGNATURE	
	Low	High	Low	High
Arthur, Jean	$ 4.60	$ 6.00	$ 1.00	$ 1.60
Astin, John	2.00	3.80	1.00	1.50
Bacall, Lauren	13.00	21.00	2.30	4.00
Backus, Jim	3.00	4.50	1.00	1.50
Ball, Lucille	9.40	13.60	1.00	1.40
Ballard, Kaye	3.60	5.00	1.00	1.60
Balsam, Martin	3.00	4.60	1.00	1.60
Bancroft, Anne	6.00	9.00	1.00	1.40
Bardot, Brigitte	23.80	31.00	3.00	4.30
Barr, Roseanne	9.00	12.00	2.00	3.00
Barry, Gene	4.50	6.00	1.00	1.50
Barrymore, Drew	6.00	9.00	1.00	1.50
Bartholomew, Freddie	6.00	9.00	1.00	1.50
Bates, Alan	6.00	8.00	1.00	1.60
Bates, Kathy	4.00	7.00	1.00	1.50
Baxter, Anne	2.90	4.70	1.00	1.50
Bean, Orson	2.90	4.00	1.00	1.50
Beatty, Warren	7.40	10.00	1.60	2.00
Bel Geddes, Barbara	3.00	4.40	1.00	1.50
Bellamy, Ralph	4.70	6.00	1.00	1.60
Belushi, Jim	5.00	8.00	1.00	1.50
Belushi, John	270.00	350.00	40.00	50.00
Benny, Jack	50.00	75.00	7.00	11.00
Bergen, Candice	6.00	9.00	1.00	1.50
Bergman, Ingmar	14.40	22.50	1.60	2.30
Bergman, Ingrid	80.00	120.00	9.00	13.00
Berle, Milton	7.50	11.50	1.60	2.00
Bernardi, Hershel	3.00	4.40	1.00	1.60
Bill Cosby	12.00	15.00	3.00	5.00
Bishop, Joey	3.00	4.40	1.00	1.60
Bisset, Jacqueline	4.50	6.00	1.00	1.50
Bixby, Bill	4.50	6.30	1.00	1.40
Black, Karen	2.80	4.50	1.00	1.60
Blair, Linda	7.00	12.00	1.50	2.50
Blondell, Joan	3.00	4.40	1.00	1.50
Bloom, Claire	8.50	13.40	1.60	2.00
Blyth, Ann	2.80	4.30	1.00	1.60
Bogarde, Dirk	4.50	6.00	1.00	1.60
Bogart, Humphrey	180.00	250.00	18.00	26.00
Bogdanovich, Peter	14.40	21.30	1.60	2.30
Boone, Richard	15.70	22.00	1.60	2.30
Booth, Shirley	7.00	10.00	1.50	2.40
Borge, Victor	4.40	6.00	1.00	1.50
Borgnine, Ernest	4.40	6.00	1.00	1.50
Bosley, Tom	3.00	4.50	1.00	1.50
Boyer, Charles	14.00	22.00	1.60	2.70
Boyle, Peter	4.50	6.00	1.00	1.60
Branagh, Kenneth	5.00	8.00	1.00	1.50
Brando, Marlon	30.00	47.40	4.00	7.50
Brazzi, Rossano	3.00	4.30	1.00	1.50

	SIGNED PHOTO		PLAIN SIGNATURE	
	Low	High	Low	High
Brenner, David	$ 3.00	$ 4.50	$ 1.00	$ 1.50
Bridges, Beau	3.00	4.50	1.00	1.40
Brolin, James	2.50	4.00	1.00	1.50
Bronson, Charles	6.30	9.00	1.00	1.50
Brooks, Mel	7.00	11.00	1.00	1.40
Brynner, Yul	4.50	5.70	1.00	1.50
Bujold, Genevieve	4.40	6.00	1.00	1.60
Burnett, Carol	4.00	6.00	1.00	1.40
Burr, Raymond	4.50	6.00	1.00	1.50
Burstyn, Ellen	5.00	8.00	1.00	1.50
Burton, Richard	65.00	100.00	7.00	12.00
Buttons, Red	3.00	4.70	1.00	1.50
Buzzi, Ruth	3.00	4.40	1.00	1.50
Caan, James	7.40	10.00	1.50	2.00
Cabot, Sebastian	5.30	9.00	1.00	1.50
Caesar, Sid	4.50	6.00	1.00	1.40
Cagney, James	25.00	35.00	4.70	7.00
Caine, Michael	4.40	5.80	1.00	1.50
Calhoun, Rory	2.90	4.70	1.00	1.50
Cantor, Eddie	60.00	85.00	12.00	15.00
Cardinale, Claudia	9.00	12.00	1.50	2.30
Carlisle, Kitty	7.80	3.70	1.00	1.50
Carney, Art	4.50	6.00	1.00	1.50
Caron, Leslie	6.00	9.00	1.00	1.60
Carradine, David	10.00	15.00	1.50	2.00
Carradine, John	4.70	5.70	1.00	1.50
Carrey, Jim	12.00	15.00	3.00	5.00
Carson, Joanna	10.00	14.00	1.40	2.30
Carson, Johnny	5.00	9.00	1.50	2.00
Caruso, Enrico	300.00	375.00	25.00	50.00
Cassavetes, John	3.00	4.50	1.00	1.60
Cavett, Dick	3.00	4.60	1.00	1.60
Chamberlain, Richard	6.00	9.00	1.00	1.50
Chaney, Lon	85.00	125.00	15.00	20.00
Chaplin, Charles	110.00	150.00	8.00	14.00
Charisse, Cyd	6.00	8.00	1.00	1.50
Chase, Chevy	4.00	6.00	1.00	1.50
Christie, Julie	7.00	10.00	1.50	2.00
Clapton, Eric	11.00	13.00	2.00	4.00
Close, Glenn	5.00	8.00	1.00	1.50
Cobain, Kurt	200.00	275.00	40.00	50.00
Coburn, James	4.00	6.00	1.00	1.40
Coca, Imogene	7.00	10.00	1.00	1.40
Coco, James	2.50	4.00	1.00	1.60
Cohan, George M.	70.00	100.00	14.00	20.00
Colbert, Claudette	14.00	22.00	3.00	4.00
Collins, Joan	3.00	4.40	1.00	1.50
Collins, Phil	4.00	6.00	1.00	1.50
Connery, Sean	4.80	6.30	1.00	1.50
Connors, Chuck	4.70	6.00	1.00	1.40

	SIGNED PHOTO		PLAIN SIGNATURE	
	Low	High	Low	High
Connors, Michael	$ 3.00	$ 4.70	$1.00	$ 1.50
Conrad, Michael	3.00	4.50	1.00	1.50
Conrad, Robert	3.90	5.50	1.00	1.50
Conway, Tim	2.00	3.80	1.00	1.50
Coogan, Jackie	6.00	8.70	1.00	1.60
Cook, Barbara	3.00	4.50	1.00	1.60
Cooper, Gary	60.00	90.00	4.30	7.00
Cooper, Jackie	4.50	5.70	1.00	1.60
Copperfield, David	6.00	8.00	1.00	1.50
Cosby, Bill	3.00	4.40	1.00	1.50
Crabbe, Buster	23.00	38.00	3.00	5.00
Crane, Bob	2.90	4.80	1.00	1.40
Crawford, Cindy	6.00	8.00	1.00	1.50
Crawford, Joan	118.00	165.00	18.00	26.00
Crenna, Richard	3.00	4.50	1.00	1.40
Cronyn, Hume	4.70	6.00	1.00	1.40
Culp, Robert	2.90	4.40	1.00	1.50
Curtis, Jamie Lee	4.00	6.00	1.00	1.50
Curtis, Ken	3.00	4.40	1.00	1.50
Cusack, John	3.00	5.00	1.00	1.50
Cushing, Peter	4.70	5.70	1.00	1.40
Daltry, Roger	9.00	12.00	2.00	4.00
Dangerfield, Rodney	3.00	4.70	1.00	1.50
Danner, Blythe	4.70	5.80	1.00	1.60
Darby, Kim	3.00	4.50	1.00	1.60
Darren, James	4.30	6.00	1.00	1.40
Davis, Bette	20.00	30.00	4.40	7.00
Davis, Ossie	4.50	6.30	1.00	1.50
Day-Lewis, Daniel	6.00	8.00	1.00	1.50
Dean, James	250.00	350.00	30.00	40.00
Dee, Sandra	4.50	5.70	1.00	1.50
DeHaviland, Olivia	14.50	23.40	2.30	3.00
Delon, Alain	6.30	9.00	1.00	1.40
DeLuise, Dom	2.80	4.70	1.00	1.60
Deneuve, Catherine	6.00	9.00	1.00	1.40
De Niro, Robert	10.00	15.00	1.40	2.30
Dennis, Sandy	7.50	10.00	1.00	1.60
Denver, Bob	4.50	6.00	1.00	1.50
Depp, Johnny	7.00	10.00	1.00	1.50
Derek, Bo	15.00	25.00	3.00	4.70
Derek, John	7.80	10.00	1.60	2.30
Dewhurst, Colleen	7.50	10.00	1.00	1.60
Dey, Susan	3.00	4.50	1.00	1.50
Dickinson, Angie	4.50	5.80	1.00	1.40
Dietrich, Marlene	25.00	45.00	5.80	10.00
Diller, Phyllis	3.00	4.60	1.00	1.50
Donahue, Troy	4.30	6.30	1.00	1.60
Douglas, Kirk	4.40	5.80	1.00	1.60
Douglas, Mike	6.00	8.50	1.00	1.50
Downs, Hugh	3.00	4.50	1.00	1.50

	SIGNED PHOTO		PLAIN SIGNATURE	
	Low	High	Low	High
Dreyfuss, Richard	$ 7.00	$ 10.00	$ 1.00	$ 1.50
Duke, Patty	4.80	5.70	1.00	1.50
Dunaway, Faye	7.00	10.00	1.50	2.00
Duncan, Sandy	3.00	4.70	1.00	1.50
Dunne, Irene	6.30	9.00	1.00	1.40
Durante, Jimmy	13.00	19.80	2.00	4.50
Durbin, Deanna	11.70	14.90	2.00	3.60
Duvall, Robert	10.00	15.70	1.50	2.30
Eastwood, Clint	15.00	21.40	1.50	2.30
Ebsen, Buddy	3.00	4.50	1.00	1.40
Eden, Barbara	4.40	6.00	1.00	1.40
Falk, Peter	6.00	9.00	1.00	1.50
Farrow, Mia	10.00	14.40	1.50	2.00
Fawcett, Farrah	12.40	19.00	2.00	3.80
Faye, Alice	3.00	4.50	1.00	1.50
Feldman, Marty	10.00	15.70	1.60	2.30
Feldon, Barbara	3.00	4.50	1.00	1.60
Fellini, Federico	14.50	24.00	3.00	5.40
Ferrer, Jose	4.50	6.00	1.00	1.40
Ferrer, Mel	4.50	5.50	1.00	1.50
Ferris, Barbara	7.00	10.00	1.00	1.50
Field, Sally	2.30	3.50	1.00	1.50
Fiennes, Ralph	3.00	5.00	1.00	1.50
Finney, Albert	4.30	6.00	1.00	1.50
Fisher, Carrie	9.30	12.30	1.00	1.40
Fitzgerald, Geraldine	6.00	9.00	1.00	1.50
Fonda, Bridget	4.00	6.00	1.00	1.50
Fonda, Henry	40.00	50.00	3.00	4.50
Fonda, Jane	10.00	16.00	1.50	2.00
Fonda, Peter	7.50	10.00	1.00	1.60
Fontaine, Frank	3.00	4.50	1.00	1.40
Fontaine, Joan	7.00	10.00	1.00	1.40
Fontanne, Lynn	20.00	30.00	3.90	6.00
Forsythe, John	2.90	4.40	1.00	1.50
Fosse, Bob	3.00	4.30	1.00	1.50
Foster, Jodi	5.00	7.00	1.00	1.50
Foxx, Redd	3.50	6.00	1.00	1.40
Franciosa, Tony	2.90	4.30	1.00	1.60
Francis, Arlene	2.90	4.40	1.00	1.50
Franciscus, James	3.00	4.50	1.00	1.40
Freeman, Morgan	10.00	15.00	2.00	4.00
Frost, David	3.00	4.30	1.00	1.50
Funt, Allen	2.00	3.50	1.00	1.50
Gable, Clark	400.00	500.00	125.00	190.00
Gabor, Eva	4.50	5.80	1.00	1.50
Gabor, Zsa Zsa	4.30	6.30	1.00	1.50
Garbo, Greta	700.00	1000.00	275.00	350.00
Gardenia, Vincent	2.90	4.40	1.00	1.60
Gardner, Ava	12.40	15.80	1.50	2.40
Garner, James	3.50	5.80	1.00	1.50

Left: Autographed "Gone with the Wind" script with signatures of the entire movie cast sold for $13,200 at auction; Right: "The New Wizard of Oz Book" with the paw prints of Toto on the introduction, sold for $20,900 at auction. One-of-a-kind rarities of cultural icons are worth vastly more than the sum total of the signatures involved. — Photo courtesy of Christie's East.

	SIGNED PHOTO		PLAIN SIGNATURE	
	Low	High	Low	High
Garson, Greer	$ 9.00	$ 11.90	$ 1.40	$ 2.30
Gaynor, Janet	11.00	15.40	1.60	2.30
Gaynor, Mitzi	3.00	4.30	1.00	1.40
Gazzara, Ben	2.90	4.80	1.00	1.60
Gentry, Bobbie	6.00	9.00	1.00	1.40
Gere, Richard	10.00	15.00	1.50	2.00
Gingold, Hermione	4.40	5.70	1.00	1.50
Gleason, Jackie	4.00	5.70	1.00	1.40
Gobel, George	5.80	9.50	1.00	1.60
Goddard, Paulette	9.00	12.00	1.60	2.40
Godfrey, Arthur	15.00	25.00	3.00	4.60
Goodman, John	8.00	10.00	1.00	1.50
Gordon, Gale	3.00	4.70	1.00	1.60
Gordon, Ruth	6.00	9.40	1.00	1.50
Gould, Elliott	4.30	6.00	1.00	1.50
Goulding, Ray	2.00	3.50	1.00	1.50
Graham, Martha	15.00	25.00	1.50	2.30
Granger, Farley	3.00	4.70	1.00	1.40
Granger, Stewart	3.00	4.40	1.00	1.40
Grant, Cary	15.50	22.70	2.30	3.80
Grant, Hugh	7.00	9.00	1.00	1.50
Grant, Lee	3.00	4.40	1.00	1.50
Graves, Peter	3.00	4.50	1.00	1.60
Greene, Lorne	4.50	5.70	1.00	1.50
Grey, Joel	4.50	6.00	1.00	1.50
Griffin, Merv	5.80	9.00	1.00	1.50

	SIGNED PHOTO		PLAIN SIGNATURE	
	Low	High	Low	High
Griffith, Andy	$ 4.70	$ 6.00	$ 1.00	$1.60
Guardino, Harry	3.00	4.40	1.00	1.50
Guinness, Alec	14.50	21.00	3.00	4.40
Hackett, Buddy	3.00	4.50	1.00	1.60
Hackett, Joan	3.00	4.00	1.00	1.60
Hackman, Gene	3.00	4.70	1.00	1.50
Hagen, Uta	4.40	6.00	1.00	1.50
Hagman, Larry	13.30	18.80	1.50	2.50
Hale, Barbara	3.00	4.50	1.00	1.50
Hall, Arsenio	2.00	4.00	1.00	1.50
Hall, Monty	2.00	3.50	1.00	1.40
Hanks, Tom	10.00	15.00	2.00	4.00
Harlow, Jean	500.00	600.00	50.00	75.00
Harris, Julie	8.00	10.00	1.00	1.50
Harris, Richard	7.00	10.00	1.00	1.50
Harrison, George	170.00	250.00	40.00	60.00
Harrison, Rex	4.50	6.00	1.00	1.50
Hartman, David	3.00	4.50	1.00	1.50
Hawke, Ethan	8.00	10.00	1.00	1.50
Hawn, Goldie	6.00	9.30	1.00	1.50
Hayes, Helen	8.00	10.00	1.60	2.30
Hayworth, Rita	15.00	22.30	3.00	4.50
Heatherton, Joey	4.50	5.70	1.00	1.50
Henderson, Florence	2.80	4.30	1.00	1.40
Hendrix, Jimi	250.00	350.00	30.00	50.00
Hepburn, Audrey	4.50	5.80	1.00	1.50
Hepburn, Katharine	20.00	40.00	3.00	5.80
Heston, Charlton	9.50	12.50	1.40	2.30
Hitchcock, Alfred	25.00	35.00	1.50	2.70
Hoffman, Dustin	7.40	10.00	1.00	1.40
Holbrook, Hal	4.30	6.00	1.00	1.40
Holden, William	45.00	60.00	1.00	1.40
Holder, Geoffrey	3.00	4.30	1.00	1.60
Holliman, Earl	2.80	4.40	1.00	1.40
Holly, Buddy	200.00	300.00	30.00	45.00
Holm, Celeste	4.50	6.30	1.00	1.50
Hope, Bob	6.30	9.00	1.50	2.30
Hopkins, Anthony	8.00	10.00	1.00	1.40
Hopper, Dennis	7.00	10.00	1.00	1.50
Howard, Trevor	4.50	6.30	1.00	1.60
Hudson, Rock	7.00	10.00	1.00	1.50
Hunt, Linda	2.90	4.50	1.00	1.50
Hunter, Holly	6.00	8.00	1.00	1.50
Hunter, Kim	4.70	5.80	1.00	1.50
Hurt, William	4.00	6.00	1.00	1.50
Huston, John	12.00	15.00	1.50	2.30
Huston, Walter	30.00	50.00	4.60	7.80
Hutton, Betty	6.30	8.80	1.00	1.60
Hutton, Lauren	3.00	4.30	1.00	1.60
Hynde, Chrissie	10.00	15.00	2.00	4.00

	SIGNED PHOTO		PLAIN SIGNATURE	
	Low	High	Low	High
Ireland, John	$ 3.00	$ 4.50	$ 1.00	$ 1.40
Jackson, Glenda	7.00	10.00	1.00	1.50
Jackson, Kate	4.50	6.00	1.00	1.60
Janssen, David	23.00	28.50	3.00	4.30
Jeffreys, Anne	3.00	4.40	1.00	1.40
Jessel, George	15.00	23.50	1.50	2.70
John, Elton	10.00	15.00	2.00	4.00
Johns, Glynis	3.00	4.40	1.00	1.60
Johnson, Van	4.50	5.80	1.00	1.50
Jolson, Al	100.00	125.00	15.00	22.00
Jones, Dean	3.00	4.50	1.00	1.60
Jones, Shirley	4.70	6.00	1.00	1.40
Jones, Tommy Lee	8.00	10.00	1.00	1.50
Joplin, Janis	175.00	250.00	30.00	45.00
Kahn, Madeline	9.40	12.50	1.60	2.30
Kaplan, Gabe	4.50	5.80	1.00	1.50
Kaye, Danny	13.00	9.00	1.50	2.30
Kazan, Elia	12.00	15.30	2.30	3.70
Keach, Stacy	6.00	9.00	1.00	1.50
Keaton, Diane	7.00	10.00	1.00	1.40
Keaton, Michael	7.00	9.00	1.00	1.50
Keeler, Ruby	11.00	14.00	1.60	2.00
Keitel, Harvey	5.00	7.00	1.00	1.50
Keith, Brian	4.40	5.80	1.00	1.40
Kellerman, Sally	7.70	10.00	1.00	1.50
Kelly, Grace	200.00	350.00	7.80	11.40
Kennedy, George	3.00	4.50	1.00	1.40
Kerr, Deborah	6.00	9.30	1.00	1.50
Keyes, Evelyn	2.90	4.30	1.00	1.50
Kiley, Richard	4.50	6.30	1.00	1.40
King, Alan	3.00	4.50	1.00	1.60
Klugman, Jack	6.00	9.00	1.00	1.50
Knots, Don	3.00	4.50	1.00	1.60
Korman, Harvey	2.90	4.50	1.00	1.50
Kramer, Stanley	10.00	13.40	1.50	2.30
Kristofferson, Kris	8.00	12.00	1.00	1.50
Kubrick, Stanley	15.00	22.00	1.40	2.00
Lamarr, Hedy	45.00	75.00	6.00	10.00
Lamas, Fernando	14.00	17.50	1.40	2.90
Lancaster, Burt	12.30	15.70	1.50	2.00
Lanchester, Elsa	6.00	9.50	1.00	1.50
Landau, Martin	4.50	6.00	1.00	1.60
Landon, Michael	4.30	6.00	1.00	1.50
Lang, K.D.	6.00	8.00	1.00	1.50
Lange, Hope	2.90	4.30	1.00	1.50
Lange, Jessica	5.00	7.00	1.00	1.50
Langella, Frank	6.00	8.50	1.00	1.40
Lansbury, Angela	3.00	4.70	1.00	1.60
Lasser, Louise	8.00	11.00	1.00	1.60
Laurie, Piper	3.00	4.00	1.00	1.60

	SIGNED PHOTO		PLAIN SIGNATURE	
	Low	High	Low	High
Lavin, Linda	$ 6.00	$ 7.50	$ 1.00	$ 1.50
Lawford, Peter	6.00	8.50	1.00	1.50
Lawrence, Vicki	3.00	4.30	1.00	1.60
Leachman, Cloris	4.40	6.30	1.00	1.60
Learned, Michael	4.40	6.00	1.00	1.50
Lee, Bruce	115.00	150.00	40.00	60.00
Lee, Christopher	4.70	5.70	1.00	1.40
Leigh, Janet	6.00	9.30	1.00	1.60
Leigh, Jennifer Jason	6.00	8.00	1.00	1.50
Lemmon, Jack	9.30	12.00	1.50	2.30
Lennon, John	350.00	500.00	50.00	75.00
Leno, Jay	4.00	5.00	1.00	1.50
Letterman, David	4.00	5.00	1.00	1.50
Lewis, Jerry	2.90	4.50	1.00	1.50
Lewis, Shari	4.40	6.00	1.00	1.50
Liberace	11.50	16.50	1.50	3.00
Linden, Hal	4.50	6.30	1.00	1.50
Linkletter, Art	3.00	4.40	1.00	1.40
Lipton, Peggy	3.00	4.50	1.00	1.50
Little, Richard	3.00	4.70	1.00	1.50
Lockhart, June	2.90	4.30	1.00	1.50
Lollobrigida, Gina	15.50	21.40	1.50	2.00
Lombard, Carole	150.00	225.00	14.00	22.00
Longet, Claudine	12.00	14.70	1.50	2.00
Loren, Sophia	25.00	34.00	2.90	4.70
Louise, Tina	2.90	4.70	1.00	1.60
Love, Courtney	12.00	15.00	1.00	1.50
Lovett, Lyle	5.00	7.00	1.00	1.50
Loy, Myrna	14.00	23.50	1.60	2.00
Lucas, George	8.00	10.00	1.00	1.50
Lunt, Alfred	18.40	30.00	3.00	6.00
Lupino, Ida	5.70	8.80	1.00	1.40
MacGraw, Ali	12.00	14.80	1.60	2.00
MacLaine, Shirley	14.00	21.50	1.40	2.30
MacMurray, Fred	12.40	14.70	1.40	2.40
Madonna	75.00	100.00	5.00	10.00
Majors, Lee	7.30	10.00	1.00	1.50
Malden, Karl	2.90	4.80	1.00	1.50
Malkovich, John	4.00	6.00	1.00	1.50
Marceau, Marcel	22.50	29.80	3.00	4.30
Margolin, Janet	2.90	4.50	1.00	1.40
Marshall, E.G.	4.70	6.30	1.00	1.40
Martin, Dick	3.00	4.30	1.00	1.50
Martin, Ross	3.00	4.50	1.00	1.50
Marvin, Lee	6.30	9.50	1.00	1.50
Marx, Groucho	70.00	100.00	7.40	12.70
Mason, Jackie	3.00	4.70	1.00	1.40
Mason, James	4.70	6.00	1.00	1.50
Mason, Pamela	2.90	4.60	1.00	1.50
Massey, Raymond	6.00	8.50	1.00	1.50

	SIGNED PHOTO		PLAIN SIGNATURE	
	Low	High	Low	High
Matthau, Walter	$ 6.00	$ 9.50	$ 1.00	$ 1.50
Mayo, Virginia	3.00	4.40	1.00	1.50
McCartney, Paul	250.00	350.00	35.00	50.00
McCrea, Joel	7.40	12.00	1.50	2.90
McDowall, Roddy	4.00	6.00	1.00	1.50
McGavin, Darren	3.00	4.40	1.00	1.50
McGoohan, Patrick	6.00	8.50	1.00	1.50
McMahon, Ed	2.30	3.50	1.00	1.50
McQueen, Steve	38.00	50.00	7.40	11.70
Meadows, Audrey	2.90	4.70	1.00	1.50
Meadows, Jayne	3.00	4.30	1.00	1.50
Meara, Anne	3.00	4.50	1.00	1.50
Mercouri, Melina	7.30	10.00	1.60	2.00
Meredith, Burgess	7.50	10.00	1.50	2.00
Merrill, Dina	6.00	8.70	1.00	1.50
Midler, Bette	10.00	14.00	1.60	2.40
Milland, Ray	5.70	9.00	1.00	1.40
Mitchum, Robert	5.50	9.00	1.00	1.60
Monroe, Marilyn	600.00	900.00	50.00	100.00
Montalban, Ricardo	3.00	4.50	1.00	1.40
Montand, Yves	4.50	6.00	1.00	1.50
Montgomery, Elizabeth	2.90	4.50	1.00	1.40
Montgomery, George	3.00	4.70	1.00	1.50
Montgomery, Robert	2.80	4.70	1.00	1.40
Moore, Demi	4.00	6.00	1.00	1.50
Moore, Mary Tyler	4.50	6.40	1.00	1.40
Moore, Roger	8.00	10.00	1.50	2.30
Moreau, Jeanne	4.50	6.00	1.00	1.50
Moreno, Rita	4.50	6.00	1.00	1.50
Morgan, Henry	4.50	6.00	1.00	1.50
Morley, Robert	3.00	4.30	1.00	1.40
Morrow, Vic	3.00	4.30	1.00	1.50
Morse, Robert	3.00	4.40	1.00	1.60
Mostel, Zero	18.00	24.50	2.40	3.70
Murphy, Eddie	5.00	7.00	1.00	1.50
Murphy, George	18.40	26.50	3.00	4.70
Murray, Anne	4.50	6.00	1.00	1.50
Murray, Arthur	7.50	10.00	1.00	1.40
Nabors, Jim	2.90	4.40	1.00	1.50
Neal, Patricia	11.70	15.50	1.50	2.00
Neeson, Liam	4.00	6.00	1.00	1.50
Neill, Sam	3.00	5.00	1.00	1.50
Newhart, Bob	2.90	4.70	1.00	1.50
Newman, Paul	15.40	22.00	1.40	2.40
Newmar, Julie	7.50	12.70	1.00	1.50
Nichols, Mike	12.40	14.40	1.50	2.00
Nicholson, Jack	10.00	13.50	1.50	2.00
Nimoy, Leonard	15.00	23.50	2.30	3.90
Niven, David	28.40	47.00	4.50	7.50
Nolan, Lloyd	4.50	6.30	1.00	1.50

	SIGNED PHOTO		PLAIN SIGNATURE	
	Low	High	Low	High
Nolte, Nick	$ 3.00	$ 4.50	$ 1.00	$ 1.60
Novak, Kim	7.70	10.00	1.50	2.00
O'Brian, Hugh	2.90	4.70	1.00	1.40
O'Brien, Edmund	3.00	4.70	1.00	1.50
O'Brien, Margaret	4.50	6.00	1.00	1.50
O'Connell, Helen	4.30	6.00	1.00	1.60
O'Connor, Carroll	5.70	9.00	1.00	1.50
O'Hara, Jill	2.90	4.50	1.00	1.40
O'Hara, Maureen	4.30	6.30	1.00	1.50
O'Neal, Patrick	3.00	4.70	1.00	1.40
O'Neal, Ryan	6.30	7.00	1.00	1.50
O'Neal, Tatum	9.40	12.00	1.00	1.40
O'Sullivan, Maureen	4.30	6.30	1.00	1.40
O'Toole, Peter	7.80	10.00	1.00	1.50
Oakie, Jack	6.30	9.00	1.00	1.50
Oberon, Merle	9.00	11.40	1.00	1.60
Olivier, Laurence	17.00	28.00	3.00	4.40
Osmond, Donny	3.00	4.00	1.00	1.50
Osmond, Marie	4.50	7.00	1.00	1.60
Paar, Jack	2.80	4.30	1.00	1.50
Pacino, Al	10.00	13.40	1.50	2.00
Page, Geraldine	4.30	6.00	1.00	1.50
Palance, Jack	4.40	6.00	1.00	1.40
Papp, Joseph	7.50	10.00	1.00	1.50
Parker, Eleanor	7.70	10.00	1.00	1.40
Parker, Fess	6.00	9.30	1.00	1.50
Parker, Suzy	2.90	4.40	1.00	1.50
Parks, Bert	2.90	4.40	1.00	1.50
Parsons, Estelle	4.50	5.70	1.00	1.60
Parton, Dolly	12.40	16.00	1.60	2.70
Pearl, Minnie	6.30	9.00	1.00	1.50
Peck, Gregory	12.40	17.00	1.40	2.40
Peppard, George	4.70	6.00	1.00	1.50
Perkins, Anthony	2.80	4.50	1.00	1.50
Perrine, Valerie	7.30	11.00	1.00	1.50
Pfeiffer, Michelle	10.00	14.00	1.50	2.00
Pickford, Mary	22.00	30.00	3.00	4.30
Pidgeon, Walter	4.70	6.00	1.00	1.50
Pitt, Brad	6.00	9.00	1.00	1.50
Pleasance, Donald	7.80	10.00	1.00	1.40
Pleshette, Suzanne	4.40	5.80	1.00	1.50
Plimpton, George	4.40	6.30	1.00	1.50
Plowright, Joan	3.00	4.40	1.00	1.60
Plummer, Christopher	7.30	10.00	1.00	1.60
Poitier, Sidney	7.00	10.00	1.40	2.30
Polanski, Roman	15.00	22.50	2.30	3.80
Ponti, Carlo	15.00	25.00	1.00	1.60
Powell, Jane	3.00	4.40	1.00	1.50
Powell, William	15.00	23.50	1.50	2.40
Powers, Stephanie	2.80	4.70	1.00	1.40

	SIGNED PHOTO		PLAIN SIGNATURE	
	Low	High	Low	High
Preminger, Otto	$ 11.80	$ 14.80	$ 1.40	$ 3.00
Prentiss, Paula	4.30	5.80	1.00	1.50
Presley, Elvis	500.00	800.00	75.00	150.00
Preston, Robert	4.40	6.00	1.00	1.60
Prinz, Freddie	74.90	104.80	12.00	17.00
Provine, Dorothy	3.00	4.50	1.00	1.50
Prowse, Juliet	4.60	6.30	1.00	1.60
Pryor, Richard	15.50	22.30	1.50	2.50
Quinn, Anthony	9.40	12.00	1.40	2.30
Raft, George	12.30	15.30	1.40	3.00
Raitt, Bonnie	8.00	10.00	1.00	1.50
Raitt, John	4.40	6.00	1.00	1.50
Randall, Tony	2.90	4.40	1.00	1.40
Ray, Aldo	3.00	4.30	1.00	1.50
Raye, Martha	8.50	12.40	1.50	2.30
Redford, Robert	9.00	12.50	1.50	2.40
Redgrave, Lynn	7.70	10.00	1.00	1.50
Redgrave, Michael	8.70	11.30	1.50	2.00
Redgrave, Vanessa	14.30	21.50	3.00	4.30
Reed, Donna	3.00	4.70	1.00	1.40
Reed, Rex	2.40	3.70	1.00	1.50
Reilly, Charles Nelson	3.00	4.50	1.00	1.50
Reiner, Carl	4.30	6.00	1.00	1.50
Reiner, Rob	5.70	8.00	1.00	1.60
Remick, Lee	4.40	6.30	1.00	1.50
Reynolds, Burt	14.00	22.00	3.00	5.00
Richardson, Natasha	4.00	6.00	1.00	1.50
Rickles, Don	2.90	4.30	1.00	1.40
Rigg, Diana	8.50	12.50	1.00	1.50
Rivera, Chita	3.00	4.70	1.00	1.50
Robards, Jason Jr.	7.50	10.00	1.00	1.50
Robbins, Tim	7.00	10.00	1.00	1.50
Roberts, Julia	5.00	7.00	1.00	1.50
Robertson, Cliff	3.00	4.50	1.00	1.40
Rogers, Ginger	11.80	14.00	1.50	2.30
Romero, Cesar	2.80	4.50	1.00	1.50
Rooney, Mickey	4.30	6.00	1.00	1.50
Ross, Katharine	2.90	4.40	1.00	1.60
Roundtree, Richard	3.00	4.70	1.00	1.40
Rowan, Dan	4.50	6.30	1.00	1.50
Rowlands, Gena	3.00	4.00	1.00	1.50
Rule, Janice	3.00	4.70	1.00	1.50
Rush, Barbara	4.50	5.70	1.00	1.50
Russell, Jane	7.80	11.00	1.00	1.50
Russell, Ken	8.00	11.00	1.00	1.40
Ryder, Winona	6.00	8.00	1.00	1.50
Sahl, Mort	3.00	4.50	1.00	1.50
Saint, Eva Marie	5.80	8.70	1.00	1.50
Sainte Marie, Buffy	9.00	13.00	1.00	1.50
Sales, Soupy	3.00	4.30	1.00	1.40
Sarandon, Susan	6.00	8.00	1.00	1.50

	SIGNED PHOTO		PLAIN SIGNATURE	
	Low	High	Low	High
Sarrazin, Michael	$ 9.00	$ 12.00	$ 1.00	$ 1.50
Savalas, Telly	7.80	10.00	1.00	1.50
Saxon, John	2.80	4.50	1.00	1.40
Schell, Maria	4.30	6.00	1.00	1.40
Schiffer, Claudia	7.00	10.00	1.00	1.50
Schwarzenegger, Arnold	17.00	25.00	2.00	3.50
Scott, George C.	15.00	25.00	1.60	2.30
Scott, Randolph	5.80	9.00	1.00	1.50
Seberg, Jean	3.00	4.70	1.00	1.50
Segal, George	4.50	5.70	1.00	1.60
Sellers, Peter	23.70	30.00	4.00	7.70
Sharif, Omar	9.00	12.00	1.00	1.60
Shatner, William	4.30	5.70	1.00	1.40
Shaw, Robert	3.00	4.50	1.00	1.60
Shearer, Norma	12.50	15.00	1.50	2.30
Shepard, Sam	4.00	6.00	1.00	1.50
Shepherd, Cybill	12.00	15.00	1.00	1.60
Shields, Brooke	30.00	47.00	7.40	12.00
Shriver, Maria	2.00	4.00	1.00	1.50
Signoret, Simone	4.40	6.40	1.00	1.50
Silvers, Phil	4.50	6.00	1.00	1.60
Simmons, Jean	2.90	4.50	1.00	1.60
Simon, Carly	6.00	8.00	1.00	1.50
Skelton, Red	5.80	8.70	1.00	1.50
Snipes, Wesley	6.00	8.00	1.00	1.50
Sommer, Elke	12.00	14.40	1.40	2.30
Sorvino, Paul	9.50	11.90	1.00	1.60
Sothern, Ann	4.50	5.80	1.00	1.50
Spacek, Sissy	2.90	4.50	1.00	1.50
Spielberg, Stephen	8.00	10.00	1.00	1.50
St. James, Susan	3.00	4.50	1.00	1.60
St. John, Jill	4.50	5.80	1.00	1.40
Stack, Robert	4.70	6.00	1.00	1.50
Stallone, Sylvester	17.00	25.70	2.30	3.80
Stamp, Terence	4.70	6.00	1.00	1.50
Stanwyck, Barbara	8.00	10.00	1.00	1.50
Stapleton, Maureen	4.50	6.30	1.00	1.60
Starr, Ringo	150.00	200.00	25.00	35.00
Steiger, Rod	7.00	10.00	1.00	1.50
Stevens, Connie	3.00	4.70	1.00	1.50
Stewart, James	10.00	14.00	1.40	2.30
Stockwell, Dean	3.00	4.30	1.00	1.60
Stone, Milburn	6.40	10.00	1.50	2.70
Storch, Larry	3.00	4.40	1.00	1.50
Strasberg, Lee	20.00	30.00	3.00	4.30
Strasberg, Susan	4.50	6.00	1.00	1.50
Streisand, Barbra	15.00	20.00	2.00	3.50
Stritch, Elaine	2.90	4.40	1.00	1.50
Struthers, Sally	8.70	12.30	1.50	2.30
Sullivan, Barry	2.90	4.50	1.00	1.50

	SIGNED PHOTO		PLAIN SIGNATURE	
	Low	High	Low	High
Sutherland, Donald	$ 8.70	$ 12.30	$ 1.50	$ 2.00
Swanson, Gloria	25.00	45.00	4.50	8.00
Swit, Loretta	13.00	21.90	2.00	4.00
Tandy, Jessica	6.00	7.70	1.00	1.50
Tate, Sharon	150.00	250.00	14.00	22.00
Taylor, Elizabeth	35.00	50.00	4.30	7.50
Taylor, Kent	3.00	4.30	1.00	1.50
Taylor, Rod	3.00	4.50	1.00	1.60
Temple, Shirley	15.00	20.00	2.00	3.50
Thomas, Danny	4.30	6.00	1.00	1.50
Thomas, Marlo	6.30	7.30	1.00	1.40
Thomas, Richard	4.70	5.80	1.00	1.50
Thompson, Emma	5.00	7.00	1.00	1.50
Thurman, Uma	6.00	8.00	1.00	1.50
Tierney, Gene	5.80	7.50	1.00	1.50
Tilly, Jennifer	3.00	5.00	1.00	1.50
Todd, Richard	2.90	4.50	1.00	1.60
Tomlin, Lily	4.30	6.00	1.00	1.60
Torn, Rip	2.90	4.50	1.00	1.50
Townsend, Pete	9.00	12.00	2.00	4.00
Travolta, John	17.00	24.00	3.00	4.70
Trevor, Claire	4.40	6.40	1.00	1.50
Tucker, Forrest	3.00	4.70	1.00	1.40
Turner, Lana	15.00	20.00	2.00	3.50
Twiggy	40.00	60.00	6.00	9.00
Tyson, Cicely	4.50	6.30	1.00	1.50
Uggams, Leslie	2.50	4.50	1.00	1.50
Ullman, Liv	11.00	15.00	1.50	2.00
Ustinov, Peter	4.70	6.00	1.00	1.60
Vaccaro, Brenda	3.00	4.80	1.00	1.50
Valentino, Rudolph	400.00	500.00	35.00	50.00
Van Cleef, Lee	9.00	12.00	1.00	1.50
Van Doren, Mamie	4.30	6.00	1.00	1.50
Van Dyke, Dick	6.00	8.70	1.00	1.40
Van Peebles, Mario	3.00	5.00	1.00	1.50
Vance, Vivian	6.00	7.00	1.00	1.50
Vandervere, Trish	4.70	6.00	1.00	1.50
Vaughn, Robert	4.40	5.70	1.00	1.60
Vereen, Ben	2.90	4.70	1.00	1.60
Vigoda, Abe	3.00	4.70	1.00	1.60
Voight, Jon	8.00	11.00	1.00	1.50
Von Sydow, Max	4.40	6.00	1.00	1.50
Waggoner, Lyle	3.00	4.50	1.00	1.40
Wagner, Lindsay	3.00	4.50	1.00	1.50
Wagner, Robert	8.80	14.50	1.50	2.30
Walker, Clint	2.90	4.50	1.00	1.50
Wallach, Eli	6.00	9.40	1.00	1.40
Walston, Ray	4.30	6.00	1.00	1.50
Warden, Jack	2.90	4.30	1.00	1.50
Warner, David	4.40	6.00	1.00	1.40

	SIGNED PHOTO		PLAIN SIGNATURE	
	Low	High	Low	High
Waters, Ethel	$ 6.00	$ 9.00	$ 1.00	$ 1.50
Waterston, Sam	3.00	5.00	1.00	1.50
Wayans, Damon	5.00	7.00	1.00	1.50
Wayne, David	3.00	4.50	1.00	1.50
Wayne, John	50.00	75.00	6.00	9.00
Weaver, Dennis	3.00	4.30	1.00	1.60
Webb, Jack	3.00	4.30	1.00	1.50
Weissmuller, Johnny	12.00	18.00	2.00	4.40
Welch, Raquel	11.70	15.80	1.60	2.00
Weld, Tuesday	3.00	4.50	1.00	1.60
Welk, Lawrence	2.80	4.40	1.00	1.50
Welles, Orson	12.00	14.00	1.60	2.30
West, Adam	4.50	5.80	1.00	1.50
West, Mae	44.50	59.70	4.50	7.00
White, Betty	2.90	4.40	1.00	1.50
Whitman, Stuart	2.90	4.50	1.00	1.60
Whitmore, James	4.50	6.00	1.00	1.50
Widmark, Richard	3.00	4.40	1.00	1.50
Wiest, Dianne	4.00	6.00	1.00	1.50
Wilde, Cornel	4.50	6.00	1.00	1.60
Wilder, Billy	7.00	10.00	1.00	1.50
Williams, Cindy	4.30	5.80	1.00	1.50
Williams, Esther	2.80	4.50	1.00	1.50
Williams, Robin	8.00	10.00	1.00	1.50
Willis, Bruce	6.00	8.00	1.00	1.50
Wilson, Flip	3.00	4.30	1.00	1.60
Winfrey, Oprah	4.00	6.00	1.00	1.50
Winkler, Henry	14.00	22.00	2.80	4.60
Winters, Jonathan	3.00	4.50	1.00	1.50
Winters, Shelley	4.50	6.00	1.00	1.60
Withers, Jane	3.00	4.40	1.00	1.50
Wood, Natalie	50.00	70.00	7.50	12.50

Cut signatures of Curly Howard and Larry Fine of "Three Stooges" fame brought $1870 at auction. — Photo courtesy of Christie's East.

	SIGNED PHOTO		PLAIN SIGNATURE	
	Low	High	Low	High
Woodward, Joanne	$ 4.50	$ 6.00	$ 1.00	$ 1.60
Worley, Jo Anne	2.90	4.30	1.00	1.50
Wray, Fay	9.00	11.00	1.00	1.40
Wyatt, Jane	3.00	4.30	1.00	1.40
Wyler, William	4.40	6.00	1.00	1.50
Wyman, Jane	8.50	14.00	1.50	2.50
Wynn, Ed	35.00	50.00	4.50	7.50
Wynn, Kennan	2.90	4.50	1.00	1.60
Wynter, Dana	3.00	4.50	1.00	1.50
York, Dick	2.90	4.40	1.00	1.50
York, Michael	7.50	10.00	1.00	1.50
York, Susannah	5.70	9.50	1.00	1.40
Young, Alan	4.30	6.00	1.00	1.50
Young, Gig	8.00	12.00	1.50	2.00
Young, Loretta	6.00	7.50	1.00	1.50
Young, Robert	4.00	6.30	1.00	1.40
Youngman, Henny	4.70	6.00	1.00	1.50
Zanuck, Daryl	12.50	14.00	1.50	2.40
Zimbalist, Efrem, Jr.	4.75	5.50	1.00	1.50

Ralph Bellamy   *Oprah Winfrey*

Presidents

Presidential letters and autographs are among the most valuable. George Washington, like many men of his era, was a prolific writer. His autograph letters are often offered at auction (notably Swann Galleries in New York City). Dwight Eisenhower, however, rarely took a pen to hand for more than a signature. An Eisenhower ALS is often worth more than a Washington ALS! Also beware of auto-pen. This automatic signing device became entrenched in the White House in the early 1960s. It has signed a vast majority of letters coming from the presidents since that time.

	ALS		LS	
	Low	High	Low	High
Washington, George	$ 20,000	$ 30,000	$ 20,000	$ 30,000
Adams, John	10,000	20,000	6000	10,000
Jefferson, Thomas	20,000	30,000	16,000	24,000
Madison, James	4000	8000	3000	5000
Monroe, James	5000	7000	2000	4000
Adams, John Q.	3000	7000	600	1000
Jackson, Andrew	6000	12000	2000	4000
Van Buren, Martin	2000	4000	800	1600
Harrison, William H.	3000	6000	1200	1800
Tyler, John	2000	4000	1000	1600
Polk, James K.	2000	6000	1000	1600
Taylor, Zachary	2000	4000	1200	1800
Fillmore, Millard	1200	2000	600	1000
Pierce, Franklin	1600	3000	1200	1600
Buchanan, James	1000	3000	600	1000
Lincoln, Abraham	16,000	24,000	6000	10,000
Johnson, Andrew	2000	6000	1600	2400
Grant, U.S.	4000	10,000	1000	3000
Hayes, R.B.	1000	1600	200	400
Garfield, James	800	1200	600	1000
Arthur, Chester A.	3000	5000	600	1000
Cleveland, Grover	400	4000	400	3000
Harrison, Benjamin	800	1600	400	800
McKinley, William	400	800	300	500
Roosevelt, Theodore	1000	6000	600	2000
Taft, William H.	400	800	300	500
Wilson, Woodrow	1000	4000	400	1200
Harding, Warren G.	600	1000	400	800
Coolidge, Calvin	1000	3000	300	500
Hoover, Herbert	1000	6000	200	600
Roosevelt, Franklin	1200	2400	400	800
Truman, Harry	1600	4000	300	500
Eisenhower, Dwight	4000	8000	400	800
Kennedy, John F.	6000	12,000	1200	6000
Johnson, Lyndon	2000	6000	200	400
Nixon, Richard M.	4000	8000	200	400
Ford, Gerald	1600	2400	400	800
Carter, James	2000	3000	300	500
Reagan, Ronald	1500	4000	200	800
Bush, George	1000	1500	200	500
Clinton, William	1000	1500	200	400

Sincerely,

Richard Nixon
actual signature

Richard Nixon
auto-pen signature

	DS		PhS		Cut Sig.	
	Low	High	Low	High	Low	High
Washington, George	$ 8000	$ 16,000	—	—	$ 2000	$ 4000
Adams, John	2000	6000	—	—	1600	2400
Jefferson, Thomas	4000	8000	—	—	2400	3600
Madison, James	1000	1600	—	—	600	1000
Monroe, James	800	1200	—	—	600	1000
Adams, John Q.	600	1000	—	—	200	400
Jackson, Andrew	800	1400	—	—	600	1000
Van Buren, Martin	600	1000	—	—	300	500
Harrison, William H.	1000	1600	—	—	200	400
Tyler, John	800	1200	—	—	160	240
Polk, James K.	800	1400	—	—	200	400
Taylor, Zachary	1000	1600	—	—	300	500
Fillmore, Millard	300	500	—	—	200	400
Pierce, Franklin	800	1200	—	—	200	400
Buchanan, James	400	800	—	—	300	500
Lincoln, Abraham	4000	8000	$ 12,000	$ 20,000	3000	5000
Johnson, Andrew	800	1600	3000	5000	400	800
Grant, U.S.	800	1400	1000	1600	500	700
Hayes, R.B.	400	600	600	1000	300	500
Garfield, James	400	800	2000	3000	200	400
Arthur, Chester A.	600	1000	1200	1800	300	600
Cleveland, Grover	300	500	600	900	200	300
Harrison, Benjamin	400	600	2000	3000	300	500
McKinley, William	300	500	1200	1800	200	300
Roosevelt, Theodore	600	1000	800	1200	300	500
Taft, William H.	300	500	800	1200	200	300
Wilson, Woodrow	600	1000	800	1200	300	500
Harding, Warren G.	200	400	400	800	200	300
Coolidge, Calvin	200	400	300	500	100	300
Hoover, Herbert	200	400	200	400	100	300
Roosevelt, Franklin	300	500	600	1000	200	400
Truman, Harry	200	400	400	800	200	400
Eisenhower, Dwight	200	400	400	800	300	500
Kennedy, John F.	1600	2400	1000	1800	800	1200
Johnson, Lyndon	200	300	200	600	200	400
Nixon, Richard M.	200	300	200	400	100	200
Ford, Gerald	200	300	200	400	100	200
Carter, James	200	300	100	300	100	300
Reagan, Ronald	1000	1400	300	500	200	400
Bush, George	200	300	200	300	100	300
Clinton, William	200	300	200	300	100	200

John Adams   *J. Q. Adams.*

Above left: John Adams. Above right: John Quincy Adams.
Below left: Chester A. Arthur. Below right: Jimmy Carter.

Above left: Grover Cleveland. Above right: Dwight Eisenhower.
Below left: Gerald Ford. Below right: Ulysses S. Grant.

Above left: Warren G. Harding. Above right: Benjamin Harrison.
Below left: William Henry Harrison. Below right: Rutherford B. Hayes.

Above left: Herbert Hoover. Above right: Andrew Jackson.

Above left: Thomas Jefferson. Above right: Andrew Johnson.
Below left: Lyndon B. Johnson. Below right: John Kennedy.

Above left: Abraham Lincoln. Above right: James Madison.
Below left: William McKinley. Below right: James Monroe.

Above left: Ronald Reagan. Above right: Franklin Roosevelt.
Below left: Theodore Roosevelt. Below right: Zachery Taylor.

Above left: Harry Truman. Above right: John Tyler.
Below left: George Washington. Below right: Woodrow Wilson.

Books, Magazines, and Other Published Material

Bibles

Johann Gutenberg printed the first typeset Bible in 1455. Since then, the Bible has been reprinted more than any other book. Some collectors buy only rare Bibles of the 15th and 16th centuries. Others specialize in miniature Bibles (12mo, 24mo, or 32mo), or Bibles translated into exotic languages.

Almost everyone has an old family Bible, but most 19th-century examples are worth about $50; most 18th-century examples are worth around $100. However, there are many valuable Bibles. A selection is listed below. The first figure represents what you might expect to pay at auction (A); the next two figures represent the range, from low (L) to high (H), of the retail trade. For an extensive listing of Bibles sold at auction consult *American Book Prices Current*, edited by Katherine and Daniel Leab, at American Book Prices Current, Box 1236, Washington, CT 06793.

	A	L	H
1500: Paris, T. Kerver for 1. Parvi & 1. Scabeller, (Latin)	$ 600	$ 1000	$ 1400
1510: [New Test.] Paris, (Latin)	1100	2000	2600
1511, 5 June: Venice, Lucantonio Giunta, (Latin)	300	500	700
1513, 3 Sept.: Lyons, J. Sacon for A. Koberger, (Latin)	550	900	1300
1515, 12 Jan.: Lyons, J. Sacon for A. Koberger, (Latin)	700	1245	1650
1521: Lyons, J. Sacon for A. Koberger, (Latin)	850	1513	2000
1526, 6 Nov.: Paris, Widow of T. Kerver, 2 pts. in 1, (Latin)	200	355	470
1538: Basel, H. Froben & N. Episcopius, (Latin)	750	1335	1770
1539: London, J. Byddell for T. Barthlet, (Eng.)	15,000	26,000	35,000
1540: Antwerp, A. Goinus, (Latin)	230	410	500
1541–42: Paris, R. Estienne, (Latin)	20,000	35,000	47,000
1541: [Great Bible] London, E. Whitchurch, 6th ed., (Eng.)	2800	5000	6600
1541: London, R. Grafton, 5 pts., (Eng.)	800	1400	1800
1542: Biblia Sacra, Lyons, (Latin)	650	1100	1500
1545: Paris, R. Estienne, (Latin)	300	500	700
1549: London, T. Raynalde & W. Hyll, (Eng.)	1500	2700	3500
1549: London, T. Raynalde & W. Hyll, 2 pts., (Eng.)	850	1500	2000
1550: [Great Bible ver.] London, E. Whytchurche, (Eng.)	1400	2500	3300
1553: Newe Test. of Our Lord Jesus, London, R. Jugge, (Eng.)	2800	5000	6600
1554: Geneva, Jean Crespin, (French)	1100	2000	2600
1555: [Paris], R. Estienne, (Latin)	200	355	470
1558: Lyons, Guillaume Rouille, 16mo, (Latin)	175	300	400
1564: Catholische Bibell, Koln, Heirs of Quentel, (German)	750	1335	1800
1566: Frankfurt, (Latin)	550	970	1300
1567: Antwerp, Plantin, (Latin)	400	710	950
1567: Lyons, (Latin)	180	320	420

	A	L	H
1573: Basel, Petrus Perna, 2 vols. in 1, (Latin)	$ 350	$ 600	$ 825
1573: [New Test.] Paris, J. Kerver, 16mo, (Latin)	400	710	950
1582: [1st Ed. of Douai New Test.] Rheims, J. Fogny, (Eng.) ..	850	1500	2000
1583: [Geneva ver.] London, C. Barker, (Eng.)	750	1300	1770
1585: London, C. Barker, 2 pts., (Eng.)	1600	2840	3775
1585: [New Test.] London, Henricus Middletonus, (Latin)	110	200	250
1587: Venice, Hieronymus Polus, (Latin)	160	300	370
1589: [New Test.] London, Deputies of C. Barker, (Eng.)	900	1600	2100
1591: Basel, (Latin)	200	355	470
1592: London, Christopher Barker, (Eng.)	120	200	280
1595: [Bishops' Bible] London, Deputies of C. Barker, (Eng.) ...	450	800	1000
1597: [Geneva ver.] London, Deputies of C. Barker, (Eng.)	450	800	1000
1599: [Geneva ver.] London, Deputies of C. Barker, (Eng.)	325	500	750
1600: [2d Ed. in Eng. of Douai New Test.] Antwerp, (Eng.)	275	500	650
1600: Tuebingen, Gruppenbach, (Latin)	1000	1780	2400
1600: London, R. Barker, (Eng.)	400	710	945
1600: [Bishops' Bible] London, R. Barker, (Eng.)	500	900	1200
1600: [Geneva ver.] London, R. Barker, (Eng.)	375	650	900
1600: London, R. Barker, (Eng.)	300	535	700
1649: London, Companie of Stationers, (Eng.)	175	300	400
1650-51: The Holy Bible, London, (Eng.)	400	710	945
1653: [New Test.] London, John Field, 2 vols., 24mo, (Eng.) ...	625	1000	1475
1657: Cambr., John Field, 16mo, (Eng.)	100	170	230
1659-60: Cambr., 2 vols., (Eng.)	1800	3200	4200
1660: Cambr., John Field, 3 vols.,(Eng.)	1200	2100	2800
1660: London, Henry Hills & John Field, (Eng.)	2000	3560	4700
1669: Sainte Bible, Amst., Elzevir., 4 pts. in 2 vols., (French) ...	200	350	470
1672-79: L, (Eng.)	100	170	235
1674: Cambr., J. Hayes, (Eng.)	120	200	280
1692: [Luther's ver.] Nuremberg, (German)	700	1200	1650
1696: New Test. of Our Lord Oxford Univ., 12mo, (Eng.)	130	230	3000
1697: Venice, N. Pezzana, (Latin)	200	355	470
1700: Antwerp, P. Mortier, 2 vols., (French)	1000	1780	2400
1700: Nuremberg, J. L. Buggel, (German)	1000	1780	2400
1700: Frankfurt, (German)	5000	9000	12,000
1700: Leipzig, (German)	80	140	200
1711: Lueneburg, Stern, (German)	950	1600	2200
1715: Oxford, John Baskett, (Eng.)	100	170	250
1716-17: ["Vinegar" Bible] Oxford, J. Baskett, 2 vols., (Eng.) ...	2000	3500	4700
1716: Edin., James Watson, 12mo, (Eng.)	100	170	250
1716: Oxford, John Baskett, 2 vols., (Eng.)	2500	4500	6000
1719: Edin., 12mo, (Eng.)	75	150	177
1723: Oxford, John Baskett, 2 vols., (Eng.)	300	500	700
1726: Amst., (Spanish)	425	750	1000
1735: London, 3 parts in 1 vol., (Eng.)	600	1000	1400
1736: Nuremberg, Endters, (German)	170	300	400
1747: Nuremberg, (German)	650	1100	1500
1748: Venice, 2 vols., (Latin)	150	267	355
1750-51: Oxford, (Eng.)	200	355	470
1753: London, T. Baskett & Assigns of R. Baskett, (Eng.)	2500	4500	6000
1762: Oxford, Baskett, 2 vols., 12mo, (Eng.)	800	1400	1800

	A	L	H
1763: Germantown, PA, C. Saur, (German)	$ 250	$ 445	$ 590
1768: Biblia; die gantze Heilige Schrifft, Nuremb., (German)	600	1000	1400
1769-71: Birm., Baskerville, (Eng.)	100	180	250
1771-72: Birm., John Baskerville, 2 pts. in 1 vol., (Eng.)	400	700	945
1777: Biblia; die gantze Heil. Schrift, Wernigerode, (German)	175	300	400
1788: Birm., Pearson & Rollason, 2 vols. in 1, (Eng.)	350	623	825
1788: [New Test.] Trenton, (Eng.)	750	1335	1770
1790: Phila., 2 vols. in 1, (Eng.)	5500	9000	12,000
1791: Dublin, 2 vols., (Eng.)	600	1000	1400
1791: The Holy Bible, Phila., W. Young, 2 vols., 12mo, (Eng.)	3400	6000	8000
1791: Trenton, Isaac Collins, (Eng.)	150	260	350
1792: NY, T. Allen, (Eng.)	275	500	640
1792: Self-Interpreting Bible, NY, Hodge & Campbell, (Eng.)	120	200	300
1794: New Hieroglyphical Bible for Children, Bost., W. Norman, 1st Amer. Ed. 18mo, (Eng.)	350	600	820
1795: Holy Bible Abridged, Bost., S. Hall, 32mo, (Eng.)	300	500	900
1795: London, 4 vols., (Eng.)	400	700	900
1795: London, Thomas Bensley, 2 vols., (Eng.)	375	675	900
1796: Curious Hieroglyphick Bible for the Amusement of Youth, London, R. Bassam, 12mo, (Eng.)	160	280	375
1800: London, T. Bensley, 1st Macklin Ed., 6 vols., (Eng.)	3200	5000	7500
1800: London, T. Macklin, 6 vols., (Eng.)	500	890	1100
1836: [New Test.] London, S. Bagster, (Eng.)	200	350	475
1837: Cambr., Pitt Press, 2 vols., (Eng.)	6000	10,000	14,000
1837: [New Test.] London, S. Bagster, (Eng.)	750	1335	1770
1846: The Illuminated Bible, NY, (Eng.)	200	355	475
1848: London, W. Pickering, trans. by J. Wycliffe, (Eng.)	400	710	900
1848: [New Test.] London, (Eng.)	600	1000	1400
1850: Oxford, 4 vols., (Eng.)	1500	2700	3500
1856: Genesi, Park Hill, OK, Mission Press, (Cherokee)	200	350	470
1856: Iu Otoshki, New Test., trans. into Ojibwa, NY, 8vo	120	200	280
1858: London, illus. by D. Roberts, (Eng.)	700	1200	1600
1862-60: London, Eyre & Spottiswoode, illus. by Frith, (Eng.)	900	1500	2800
1866: Tours, illus. by G. Dore, 2 vols., (French)	130	200	300
1876: Hartford, trans by J. E. Smith, (Eng.)	50	80	100
[1900]: London, Grolier Soc., 1 of 1000, 14 vols., (Eng.)	80	140	180
1910-11: London, Ballantyne Press, 1 of 750, 3 vols., (Eng.)	225	400	530
[1934-36]: New Test., London, illus. by E. Gill, 4 vols., (Eng.)	350	600	825
[1934]: Bost, R. H. Hinkley, 1 of 488, 14 vols., (Eng.)	200	350	470
[1934]: Holy Bible, Bost., R. Hinkley, 1 of 500, 14 vols., (Eng.)	750	1300	1770
1941: [New Test.], NJ, St. Anthony Guild, 1 of 1000, (Eng.)	120	210	280
1949: Cleveland, 1 of 975, designed by B. Rogers, (Eng.)	400	710	950
1953: Oxford, 1 of 25 specially bound, (Eng.)	7500	13,000	17,000
1956: Paris, Teriade, 1 of 275, illus. by Marc Chagall, 2 vols., (French)	30,000	55,000	75,000
1959: NY, Abradale Press, (Eng.)	70	125	165
1961: Paterson & NY, Pageant Books, 1 of 1000, 2 vols., facsimile of Gutenberg Bible, (Latin)	1500	2670	3500
1965: Cleveland, World Publishing Co., facsimile of 1st Ed. of King James ver., 1611, (Eng.)	340	600	800
1970: Jerusalem Bible, Garden City, illus. by S. Dali, (Eng.)	65	115	150

Catalogs

Catalogs issued by manufacturers, wholesalers and retail merchants are called trade catalogs. Watch for specialized catalogs which pertain to one subject rather than general merchandise catalogs. Sears Roebuck catalogs are some of the most popular. Be aware of reprints.

Since many of the early specimens are rare, allowances are made for their condition. Usually trade catalogs received a great deal of use making it difficult for collectors to find them in excellent condition. "Good" catalogs must be intact, but may show wear and use. "Best" catalogs should not be marked or torn. The covers should not be faded and the spines should be solid.

	GOOD	BETTER	BEST
Bicycles, Tires, Motorcycle & Bicycle Accessories, Edwards & Crist Co., Chicago & Phila., 122 pp., 1923	$ 25	$ 35	$ 50
Blymyer Bells for Churches, Schools, Colleges, Court Houses, Fire Alarms, Factories, Farms, Plantations, Etc., Cincinnati Bell Foundry Co., Cincinnati, 31 pp., 1916	25	30	40
Bottling Supplies & Household Utensils, Consumers Products Co., Brooklyn, N.Y., 20 pp., 1927	10	15	20
Brooms, The Most Modern Broom Manufacturing Plant in the World, Hamburg, Pennsylvania, 28 pp., 1911	10	15	18
Busiest House in America, illus., general merchandise, 640 pp., 1908	75	100	140
Civil Engineers' & Surveyors' Instruments, W. & L.E. Gurley, Troy, NY, 34 pp., 1878	50	75	95
Columbia Bicycles, Pope Manufacturing Co., Hartford, CT, 31 pp., 1897	40	50	65
Counting Machines, W.N. Durant, Milwaukee, 20 pp., c. 1905	25	35	50
Descriptive & Illustrated Catalogue, Iron Cutting Shears, Bolt Forging Machinery, Pawtucket Manufacturing Co., Central Falls, RI, 74 pp., 1892	35	50	63
Florence Home Needle-Work, Nonotuck Silk Co., 96 pp., 1891	15	20	25
Galvanized Patent Stock Trough, Foltz Manufacturing & Supply Co., Hagerstown, MD, 8 pp., c. 1902, price list of livestock troughs	7	10	13
Great Western Gun Works, Catalogue #40, J.H. Johnston Co., Pittsburgh, 64 pp., 1888	55	75	95
Hand-Book & Illustrated Catalogue of the Engineer's & Surveyor's Instruments of Precision, C.L. Berger & Sons, Bost., 212 pp., 1902	45	60	80
Hersey Water Meters, price list, Hersey Manufacturing Co., South Bost., 7 pp., 1908	5	6	8
Hibbard Baskets, Hibbard Basket Works, Lyons, NY, 12 pp., 1900	17	22	30
High Grade Bicycles, Special Catalogue, Cash Buyers' Union, Chicago, 40 pp., 1895	43	55	70
Illustrated Catalogue of Metal Broom Locks & Braces, M. Gould's Son & Co., Newark, NJ, 16 pp., 1908	20	25	30
Jaros Hygienic Wear, I. Jaros, NY, 79 pp., 1890	28	34	40
Keating Bicycles, 1896 Catalogue, Keating Wheel Co., Holyoke, 32 pp	30	37	45
Masonic Ledge Supplies, Catalogue #2, Henderson Ames Co., Kalamazoo, MI, 110 pp., 1905	30	40	50
Photographic Card Stock, A.M. Collins Manufacturing Co., price list, Phila., 47 pp., 1898	30	40	50
Powell Brothers Shoe Co., Spring Catalogue, NY, 49 pp., 1902	14	18	25
Prices Current, Patent Medicines, Proprietary Articles, Plasters, Antiseptic Dressings, Etc., Fuller & Fuller Co., Chicago, 189 pp., c. 1906	20	25	35
Prices Current, Soda Fountain Supplies, Fuller & Fuller Co., Chicago,			

	GOOD	BETTER	BEST
189 pp., c. 1906	$ 30	$ 40	$ 50

Saddlery & Horse Furnishings, Carriage & Sleigh Trimmings, James Bailey
  Co., Portland, ME, 1913, 7" x 10" 35   50   65
Schoenhut's Marvelous Toys, A. Schoenhut Co., Phila., 36 pp., 1904 110   140   175
Vertical Gas, Gasoline, Kerosene & Distillate Engines for All Power
  Purposes, Fairbanks, Morse & Co., Chicago, 32 pp., 1904 12   18   25
Washington Stoves & Ranges, Grey & Dudley Hardware Co., Nashville,
  TN, 110 pp., c. 1918 25   30   40

Sears Roebuck

	GOOD	BETTER	BEST
1897, general catalog, Chicago, IL	$ 225	$ 280	$ 350
1899, general catalog	200	250	320
1900-1910, most editions, food, groceries, tobacco	50	70	120
1902, general catalog #111, 50¢ cover price	145	165	200
1902, general catalog, 1969 reprint (Crown Pub., NY)	10	15	20
1905, general catalog	147	180	225
1906, general catalog	164	200	250
1907, general catalog, 1240 pp.	170	230	265
1908, general catalog, 1232 pp.	200	240	275
1910, general catalog, spring and summer, 1182 pp.	200	250	300
1911-1920, most editions, food, groceries, tobacco	50	60	85
1922, general catalog, spring and summer	140	175	200
1926, general catalog, autumn and winter	124	150	180
1931, general catalog. spring and summer	124	160	193
1944, general catalog, autumn and winter	90	122	150
1947, Christmas catalog	50	68	85
1949, general catalog, autumn and winter	45	60	75
1951, business equipment	10	14	20
1951, Christmas catalog	40	50	62
1955, general catalog, spring and summer	30	40	55
1960, Christmas catalog	20	25	45
1963, general catalog, autumn and winter	15	20	40
1965-75, general catalogs, most editions	10	15	20

Classic Books .

Books were first printed around 1450, although handwritten books date back thousands of years. Many book collectors limit themselves to one or two favorite writers or a favorite subject, since the field of book collecting is vast. A collection is judged on quality rather than quantity. Books with water damage, broken bindings, or missing pages are usually worth almost nothing.

For an extensive listing of books sold at auction consult *American Book Prices Current*, edited by Katherine and Daniel Leab, at American Book Prices Current, Box 1236, Washington, CT 06793. For information on books traded at many flea markets, consult the *Official Price Guide to Old Books*, by Marie Tedford and Pat Goudey, House of Collectibles, Random House, NY.

Values quoted are for First Editions (F), Leather-bound copies (L), Limited Edition Club copies (LEC), Heritage Press copies (HP), and Cloth-bound copies (C).

Right to left: three-quarter leather bindings often used on bound sets; A full leather binding with a gilt embossed crest will usually add several hundred dollars to the value of a 17th century volume; Full leather bindings made by craft guilds of the late 19th century are often not affected by the value of the work they cover.

	F	L	LEC	HP	C
Adams, H., *Education of Henry Adams*	$ 3750	$ 26	$ 80	$ 13	$ 10
Aeschylus, *Oresteia*	—	16	50	8	6
Aesop, *Fables*	—	40	120	16	13
Allen, Hervey, *Anthony Adverse*	500	20	60	10	7
Aristotle, *Politics & Poetics*	—	26	80	13	10
Bacon, Francis, *Essays or Counsels...*	5000	20	60	10	7
Balzac, Honore de, *Droll Stories*	—	33	100	13	10
Baudelaire, Charles, *Flowers of Evil*	—	25	75	12	10
Bellamy, Edward, *Looking Backward*	300	21	65	10	7
Benet, Stephen V., *John Brown's Body*	300	36	110	14	11
Bierce, Ambrose, *Devil's Dictionary*	—	23	70	11	8
Blake, William, *Poems*	—	26	80	13	10
Boccaccio, Giovanni, *Decameron*	—	23	70	11	8
Boswell, James, *Life of Samuel Johnson*	3750	36	110	14	11
Bradbury, Ray, *Fahrenheit 451*	250	36	110	14	11
Bradbury, Ray, *Martian Chronicles*	700	44	140	17	13

	F	L	LEC	HP	C
Brecht, Bertolt, *Threepenny Opera* .... —		$ 23	$ 70	$ 11	$ 8
Browning, E., *Sonnets from the Portuguese* .... —		30	90	15	12
Browning, Robert, *Ring and the Book* .... $ 175		16	50	8	6
Bryant, William Cullen, *Poems* 6250		21	65	10	7
Bunyan, John, *Pilgrim's Progress* .... —		30	90	15	12
Burns, Robert, *Poems* 4750		16	50	8	6
Butler, Samuel, *Erewhon* .... —		30	90	15	12
Caesar, Julius, *Gallic Wars* .... —		28	85	14	11
Camus, Albert, *The Stranger* .... —		33	100	13	10
Casanova, Giacomo, *Memoirs* .... —		25	75	12	10
Cellini, Benvenuto, *Life of Benvenuto Cellini* .... —		33	100	13	10
Cervantes, Miguel de, *Don Quixote* .... —		28	85	14	11
Chaucer, Geoffrey, *Canterbury Tales* .... —		30	90	15	12
Cicero, Marcus Tullius, *Orations and Essays* .... —		16	50	8	6
Clemens, Samuel, *Huckleberry Finn* 1250		36	110	14	11
Clemens, Samuel, *Life on the Mississippi* 450		45	175	18	14
Clemens, Samuel, *Prince and the Pauper* .... —		31	95	12	10
Clemens, Samuel, *Puddin-head Wilson* 500		25	75	12	10
Clemens, Samuel, *Roughing It* 425		26	80	13	10
Clemens, Samuel, *Tom Sawyer* 4000		46	190	18	14
Colette, Sidonie, *Break of Day* .... —		23	70	11	8
Collier, John Payne, *Punch and Judy* 1500		33	100	13	10
Collins, Wilkie, *Woman in White* 3750		16	50	8	6
Confucius, *Sayings* .... —		26	80	13	10
Conrad, Joseph, *Nostromo* 325		23	70	11	8
Crane, Hart, *The Bridge* 2500		18	55	9	7
Crane, Stephen, *Red Badge of Courage* 3000		28	85	14	11
Dante Alighieri, *Divine Comedy* .... —		25	75	12	10
Darwin, Charles, *Descent of Man* .... —		30	90	15	12
Darwin, Charles, ...*Voyage of the HMS Beagle* ... 9,500		31	95	12	10
Darwin, Charles, *On the Origin of Species* 15,000		44	130	17	13
De Quincey, T., *Confessions of an.. Opium-Eater* ... —		23	70	11	8
Defoe, Daniel, *Moll Flanders* .... —		18	55	9	7
Defoe, Daniel, *Robinson Crusoe* 8750		25	75	12	10
Diaz, Bernal, ...*Conquest of Mexico* .... —		30	90	15	12
Dickens, Charles, *Chimes* .... —		47	250	19	16
Dickens, Charles, *A Christmas Carol* 2500		16	50	8	6
Dickens, Charles, *Cricket on the Hearth* 325		33	100	13	10
Dickens, Charles, *Pickwick Papers*, (book) 1500		30	90	15	12
Dickinson, Emily, *Poems* 3250		20	60	10	7
Dodgson, Charles, *Alice... in Wonderland* 3750		54	450	21	17
Dodgson, Charles, *Through the Looking Glass* 688		55	500	22	18
Donne, John, *Poems* 12,500		16	50	8	6
Dostoevsky, Fyodor, *Brothers Karamazov* .... —		26	80	13	10
Dostoevsky, Fyodor, *Crime and Punishment* .... —		20	60	10	7
Dostoevsky, Fyodor, *House of the Dead* .... —		18	55	9	7
Dostoevsky, Fyodor, *Idiot* .... —		21	65	10	7
Dostoevsky, Fyodor, *Possessed* .... —		40	120	16	13
Doyle, A.C., *Adven. of Sherlock Holmes* 2500		30	90	15	12
Doyle, A.C., *Later Adven. of Sherlock Holmes* .... —		20	60	10	7
Dreiser, Theodore, *An American Tragedy* 375		21	65	10	7

	F	L	LEC	HP	C
Dreiser, Theodore, *Sister Carrie*	—	$ 33	$ 100	$ 13	$ 10
Dumas, Alexandre, *Camille*	—	55	500	22	18
Dumas, Alexandre, *Count of Monte Cristo*	—	30	90	15	12
Emerson, Ralph Waldo, *Essays, 1st & 2nd Series*	$ 2500	16	50	8	6
Erasmus, Desiderius, *In Praise of Folly*	—	23	70	11	8
Fielding, Henry, *History of Tom Jones*	3250	18	55	9	7
Fitzgerald, F. Scott, *Great Gatsby*	625	18	55	9	7
Flaubert, Gustave, *Madame Bovary*	—	18	55	9	7
Francis of Assisi, *Little Flowers*	—	23	70	11	8
Franklin, Benjamin, *Autobiography*	500	16	50	8	6
Frazer, James George, *Golden Bough*	250	21	65	10	7
Frost, Robert, *Complete Poems*	—	50	400	20	16
Garcia Marquez, Gabriel, *100 Years of Solitude*	—	23	70	11	8
Gibbon, E., *...Fall of the Roman Empire,* 7 vols	2500	48	250	19	16
Gilbert and Sullivan, *1st Night...*	—	36	110	14	11
Grahame, Kenneth, *Wind in the Willows*	2500	58	700	23	18
Grass, Gunter, *Flounder*	—	48	250	19	16
Graves, Robert, *Poems*	—	18	55	9	7
Grimm Brothers, *Fairy Tales,* (English 1823-6)	3750	28	85	14	11
Hardy, Thomas, *Far from the Madding Crowd*	1500	20	60	10	7
Hardy, Thomas, *Jude the Obscure*	625	26	80	13	10
Hardy, Thomas, *Tess of the D'Urbervilles*	—	30	90	15	12
Hawthorne, N., *House of the Seven Gables*	875	18	55	9	7
Hawthorne, N., *Scarlet Letter*	750	26	80	13	10
Hawthorne, N., *Twice-Told Tales*	—	23	70	11	8

Left: Modern first editions should have their original dust jackets. — Photo courtesy of Phillips Auctioneers. Right: The "First Edition Library" makes excellent reproductions including dust jackets. Make sure that the dust jacket on a first edition is original to that book.

	F	L	LEC	HP	C
Hemingway, E., *For Whom the Bell Tolls* .... $ 375	$ 50	$ 300	$ 20	$ 16
Hemingway, E., *Old Man and the Sea* 375	49	300	19	16
Hesse, Hermann, *Steppenwolf* .... —	20	60	10	7
Homer, *Iliad* .... —	40	120	16	13
Homer, *Odyssey* .... —	47	225	19	16
Hugo, Victor, *Battle of Waterloo* .... —	16	50	8	6
Hugo, Victor, *Notre-Dame de Paris* .... —	45	150	18	14
Hugo, Victor, *Toilers of the Sea* .... —	20	60	10	7
Irving, Washington, *Alhambra* .... 175·	18	55	9	7
Irving, Washington, *Rip Van Winkle* 250	21	65	10	7
James, Henry, *Portrait of a Lady* 1000	16	50	8	6
Joyce, James, *Dubliners* 2000	45	160	18	14
Joyce, James, *Ulysses* 7500	126	4000	50	40
Kafka, Franz, *Metamorphoses* .... —	46	180	18	14
Keats, John, *Poems* 3750	18	55	9	7
Kingsley, Charles, *Westward Ho!* 375	16	50	8	6
Kipling, Rudyard, *Jungle Books* 1000	21	65	10	7
la Fontaine, Jean de, Fables .... —	21	65	10	7
le Sage, Alain-Rene, *Adven. of Gil Blas* .... —	26	80	13	10
Lewis & Clark, *Journals...* 7500	44	125	17	13
Lewis, Sinclair, *Main Street* 188	48	250	19	16
Livius, Titus, *History of Early Rome* .... —	25	75	12	10
London, Jack, *Call of the Wild* 750	31	95	12	10
London, Jack, *White Fang* 325	16	50	8	6
Lytton, Edward, *Last Days of Pompeii* 375	21	65	10	7
Machiavelli, Niccolo, *The Prince* .... —	20	60	10	7
Malory, Thomas, *Le Morte D'Arthur* .... —	40	120	16	13
Mann, Thomas, *Magic Mountain* .... —	26	80	13	10
Marlowe, Christopher, *Four Plays* .... —	23	70	11	8
Marquez, Gabriel (see Garcia Marquez, Gabriel)				
Maugham, W.S., *Of Human Bondage* 175	52	450	21	17
Melville, Herman, *Moby Dick* 15,000	36	110	14	11
Melville, Herman, *Typee* 1250	28	85	14	11
Merimee, Prosper, *Carmen* .... —	21	65	10	7
Miller, Arthur, *Death of a Salesman* 250	50	350	20	16
Milosz, Czeslaw, *Captive Mind* .... —	18	55	9	7
Milton, John, *Masque of Comus* .... —	28	85	14	11
Mitchell, M., *Gone with the Wind* 2000	30	90	15	12
Moliere, Jean, *Tartuffe* .... —	16	50	8	6
Montaigne, Michel, *Essays* .... —	23	70	11	8
More, Sir Thomas, *Utopia* .... —	21	65	10	7
Nietzsche, F., *Thus Spake Zarathustra* .... —	23	70	11	8
Nordhoff and Hall, *Mutiny on the Bounty* 425	30	90	15	12
Omar Khayyam, *Rubaiyat* .... —	30	90	15	12
O'Neill, Eugene, *Ah, Wilderness!* 250	26	80	13	10
Ovid, *Metamorphoses* .... —	36	110	14	11
Paine, Thomas, *Rights of Man* .... —	23	70	11	8
Parkman, Francis, *Oregon Trail* 188	44	130	17	13
Paz, Octavio, *Three Poems* .... —	51	3500	20	16
Pepys, Samuel, *Diary* .... —	30	90	15	12
Plato, *Republic* .... —	25	75	12	10

	F	L	LEC	HP	C
Plato, *Trial... of Socrates* .... —		$ 33	$ 100	$ 13	$ 10
Poe, Edgar A., *Fall of the House of Usher* .... —		49	280	19	16
Poe, Edgar A., *...Arthur Gordon Pym* .... $ 625		16	50	8	6
Poe, Edgar A., *Tales of Mystery...* 250		21	65	10	7
Polo, Marco, *Travels* .... —		25	75	12	10
Porter, William, *Voice of the City...* .... —		46	200	18	14
Prescott, William, *...Conquest of Peru* 300		25	75	12	10
Proust, Marcel, *Swann's Way* .... —		47	225	19	16
Pushkin, Aleksandr, *Golden Cockerel* .... —		44	130	17	13
Rabelais, F., *Gargantua and Pantagruel* .... —		30	90	15	12
Raspe, Rudolph, *...Baron Munchausen* .... —		26	80	13	10
Rimbaud, Arthur, *A Season in Hell* .... —		76	2000	30	24
Rostand, Edmond, *Cyrano de Bergerac* .... —		16	50	8	6
Scott, Sir Walter, *Ivanhoe* 500		16	50	8	6
Shakespeare, William, *Hamlet* .... —		46	200	18	14
Shakespeare, William, *Poems and Sonnets* .... —		46	180	18	14
Shelley, Mary, *Frankenstein* .... —		26	80	13	10
Sheridan, Richard, *Rivals* 375		21	65	10	7
Sheridan, Richard, *School for Scandal* .... —		21	65	10	7
Sienkiewicz, Henryk, *Quo Vadis?* .... —		23	70	11	8
Sinclair, Upton, *The Jungle* .... —		21	65	10	7
Singer, Isaac, *Gentleman from Cracow* .... —		33	100	13	10
Singer, Isaac, *Magician of Lublin* .... —		47	230	19	16
Spenser, Edmund, *Faerie Queene* 20,000		26	80	13	10
Steinbeck, John, *Grapes of Wrath* 1250		53	500	21	17
Steinbeck, John, *Of Mice and Men* 938		18	55	9	7
Stephens, James, *Crock of Gold* 188		25	65	12	10
Sterne, Laurence, *Tristram Shandy* 6250		28	85	14	11
Sterne, Laurence, *A Sentimental Journey* 1000		30	90	15	12
Stevenson, R. L., *Child's Garden of Verses* 750		23	70	11	8

A Portrait of the Artist
as a Young Man
BY
JAMES JOYCE

NEW YORK
B. W. HUEBSCH
MCMXVI

Left: "First American Edition" of a work first published overseas is worth only a fraction of the true first edition. But the Irish author James Joyce's "Portrait of the Artist as a Young Man" was published first in New York, not London. Right: A bookplate of a famous owner will increase the value of a book. — Photo courtesy of Phillips Auctioneers.

	F	L	LEC	HP	C
Stevenson, R.L., *Dr. Jekyll and Mr. Hyde* .... $ 1000		$ 21	$ 65	$ 10	$ 7
Stoker, Bram, *Dracula* 1750		21	65	10	7
Stowe, Harriet B., *Uncle Tom's Cabin* 2000		46	200	18	14
Swift, Jonathan, *Gulliver's Travels* 10,000		33	100	13	10
Tennyson, Alfred, *Idylls of the King* .... —		25	75	12	10
Thackeray, William M., *Henry Esmond, Esq* 625		16	50	8	6
Thackeray, William M., *The Newcomes* 188		20	60	10	7
Thackeray, William M., *Vanity Fair* 2500		26	50	15	12
Thoreau, Henry David, *Cape Cod* 500		21	65	10	7
Thoreau, Henry David, *Walden* 2500		51	400	20	16
Thucydides, *Peloponnesian War* .... —		21	65	10	7
Tolstoy, Leo, *War and Peace* .... —		40	130	16	13
Vergil, *Aeneid* .... —		23	70	11	8
Vergil, *Georgics* .... —		28	85	14	11
Verne, Jules, *From the Earth...* .... —		21	65	10	7
Verne, Jules, *Mysterious Island* .... —		44	130	17	13
Voltaire, Francois, *Candide* .... —		16	50	8	6
Wallace, Lew, *Ben-Hur* .... —		16	50	8	6
Walton, I. & Cotton, C., *Compleat Angler* .... —		45	150	18	14
Warren, Robert P., *All the King's Men* .... —		40	120	16	13
Whitman, Walt, *Leaves of Grass* 15,000		56	700	22	18
Wilde, Oscar, *Lady Windemere's Fan* 350		18	55	9	7
Wilde, Oscar, *Picture of Dorian Gray* .... —		28	85	14	11
Wilde, Oscar, *Salome* 1500		44	130	17	13
Wilder, Thornton, *Bridge of San Luis Rey* 500		26	80	13	10
Wilder, Thornton, *Our Town* 250		25	75	12	10
Williams, T., *A Streetcar Named Desire* .... —		45	150	18	14
Wister, Owen, *The Virginian* .... —		18	55	9	7
Yeats, W.B., *Poems of W.B. Yeats*, 1949 2500		18	55	9	7

Comic Books

Comic book collecting enjoys a huge following. Collectors have actively pursued this area for years but it gained prominence in the early 1990s. There is an endless number of characters and new, exciting books appear each day. The selection below covers a tiny area of the comic book world and concentrates on early, well-known characters. Because comic books (especially early ones) are fragile, condition is crucial to determining value. Grading a comic book is both an art and a science. We suggest you consult the *Overstreet* guide cited below. We list two ranges of prices. The first is loosely described as average condition (what collectors generally refer to as very good). This means the book is intact but shows wear, the color of the paper may be brownish and there may be minor inside creases or a small tear or two. Our second range is excellent, although not near-mint; it is what collectors consider very fine condition. Near mint and, where available, mint-condition books bring considerably more than the values listed below. There are reissues of many books, and some bear a striking resemblance to the original but command only a fraction of the original's price. As in any collecting area, do your homework.

The following listings are organized by publisher with the subhead being the name and date of the series. Each entry includes the issue number, name of the issue, main characters and descriptive information. For more information and extensive listings, refer to *The Overstreet Comic Book Price Guide*, Robert M. Overstreet, Confident Collector, New York, 1995.

Our consultant for this area is Jerry Weist (listed in the back of this book).

D-C/NATIONAL PERIODICAL PUBLICATIONS
ACTION, 1938

	VERY GOOD	FINE
7, Superman (Pep Morgan, Scoop Scanlon), Adventures of Marco Polo, Superman on cover	$ 1400-1600	$ 3400-4000
14, Superman vs. Ultra (Pep Morgan, Chuck Dawson, Clip Carson), Adventures of Marco Polo, Zatara on cover	450-550	1200-1600
17, Superman vs. Ultra, last installment of Adventures of Marco Polo, Superman on cover	550-650	1300-1500
18, Three Aces, begins.	400-450	900-1100
19, Superman vs. Ultra (Chuck Dawson, Clip Carson, Three Aces) Superman on cover	450-550	1000-1200
20, Superman vs. Ultra	450-550	900-1100
22, Last Chuck Dawson, had appeared continuously from #1	250-325	600-700
23, Superman vs. Luthor, Luthor shown w/ red hair initially, first appearance of The Black Pirate. Created by Sheldon Moldoff, this short-lived series ran for only 19 issues and was never regarded as a major feature, but it was superbly illustrated	900-1100	1800-2200
33, Mr. America, origin, created by artist Bernard Bailey	200-250	450-550
37, Superman Charged With Violation of Law, first appearance of Congo Bill, created by Whitney Ellsworth, first appeared as a minor feature in D-C's More Fun Comics for 11 issues, then was dropped. One month later, Action Comics introduced a new series of Congo Bill in which he suddenly became a movie star. The movie serial turned out to be one of the better ones of the 1940s	180-220	400-500
42, Origin of The Vigilante, last Black Pirate, Mr. America uses his cape as a flying carpet for the first time. Vigilante soon became one of D-C's star attractions and he headlined their		

	VERY GOOD	FINE
new entry, Leading Comics, which began as a quarterly publication in January 1942	$ 200-250	$ 575-625
43, The Vigilante vs. The Shade (Billy Gunn)	170-190	375-425
45, The Vigilante, first appearance of Stuff, the Chinatown Kid.	180-220	400-450
46, The Vigilante vs. Rainbow Man	170-190	375-425
51, Superman vs. The Prankster (first appearance)	170-190	380-420
52, Origin of Americommando, cover features montage w/ Superman, Zatara, Congo Bill and The Vigilante	180-200	400-450
56, Americommando vs. Dr. Ito	90-110	200-250
60, Lois Lane, Superwoman	90-110	200-250
64, Superman vs. The Toyman (first appearance)	90-120	275-325
68, Lois Lane, niece Susie is introduced	90-120	280-320

BATMAN (1940)

	VERY GOOD	FINE
2, The Crime Master (Adam Lamb), The Case of the Missing Link (Hackett and Snead, Professor Drake).	$ 1800-2200	$ 4500-5500
3, The Ugliest Man in the World (Carlson, Ugly Horde, Detective McGonicle), The Crime School for Boys (Big Boy Daniels), Batman vs. the Cat Woman, first appearance of Cat Woman in costume, cover: Batman and Robin running toward reader w/ capes flying	1000-1400	2800-3400
4, More Whirlwind Adventures of Batman and Robin, Blackbeard's Crew and the Yacht Society (Thatch), cover: Batman climbing rope ladder	900-1100	2200-2800
5, The Case of The Honest Crook (Smiley Sikes), The Riddle of the Missing Card (Queenie) Diamond Jack Deegan (Clumbsy), cover: Batman weighs fugitives on "scales of justice." Last issue published quarterly, switches to 6 issues per year w/ #6	750-850	1800-2200
6, Suicide Beat (Jimmy Kelly, Fancy Dan, Alderman Skigg)	500-600	1200-1500
7, The Trouble Trap (Linda Page, Commissioner Gordon), The People vs. the Batman (Horatio Delmar, Weasel Venner, Freddie Hill)	550-650	1300-1500
8, The Strange Case of Professor Radium (Professor Rose), Stone Walls Do Not a Prison Make, The Superstition Murders (Johnny Glim),The Cross-Country Crimes (Namtab /Batman)	500-600	1400-1600
9, The Case of The Lucky Law Breaker, The White Whale (Capt. Burly), (Bob Cratchit, Timmy Cratchit)	500-600	1300-1500
10, Sheriff of Ghost Town (Five Aces Frogel), Report Card Blues (Tommy Trent)	550-600	1300-1500
11, Four Birds of a Feather (Buzzard Benny, Joe Crow, Canary, The Penguin), Payment in Full (Joe Dolan)	500-600	1300-1500
12, The Wizard of Words (The Joker), They Thrill to Conquer (Joe Kirk)	400-500	900-1200
13, The Story of the 17 Stones (Rocky Grimes), Comedy of Tears (The Joker)	400-450	900-1100
14, Prescription for Happiness (Pills Mattson), Swastika over the White House (Count Felix, Fritz Hoffner) The Case Batman Failed to Solve	475-525	1000-1200
15, Your Face is Your Fortune (Elva Barr), The Loneliest Man in the World (Dirk Dagner, Tom Wick), The Boy Who Wanted to		

	VERY GOOD	FINE

be Robin (Knuckles Conger, Bobby Deen) .... $ 475-525 $ 900-1100

16, Grade-A Crime (Winthrop, character without first name), Here Comes Alfred, Adventures of the Branded Tree (Squidge, character without first name), The Joker Reforms (Joe Kerswag) ... 800-900   1800-2200

17, Adventure of the Vitamin Vandals (Archie Gibbons), The Penguin Goes a-Hunting, Rogues Pageant (Alfred the Butler) . 220-260   600-700

18, The Secret of the Hunter's Inn (Alfred the Butler, Tweed Cousins), first appearance of Police Stories 220-260   600-700

19, Collector of Millionaires (Ali, Ali's Health Resort), The Case of the Timid Lion (The Joker), Atlantis Goes to War (Emperor Taro, Empress Lanya) 220-260   600-700

20, The Centuries of Crime (Ecla Tate, Swami Meera Kell, The Joker), Bruce Wayne Loses the Guardianship of Dick Grayson (Alfred the Butler, Fatso Foley), The Trial of Titus Keyes (Slick Fingers/George Collins) 220-260   600-700

21, Batman and Robin Whoop It Up in Four Whirlwind Action Stories, The Streamlined Rustlers (Brule, character without first name), His Lordship's Double (Lord Hurley Burleigh C.L.J. Carruthers), The Three Eccentrics (The Penguin), Blitzkrieg Bandits (Chopper Gant, Hannibal B. Brown) 200-250   400-500

47, Special! The Peril-Packed Inside Story of the Origin of Batman (retold), The Chain Gang Crimes (Warden Beltt, Whiskers Mob), cover: Batman as a boy reading *Gotham Gazette* w/ headline "Socialite Thomas Wayne Slain by Mystery Killer!" Thomas Wayne was Batman's father. The Gotham Gazette neglected to mention that Batman's mother was killed at the same time 400-450   900-1100

48, The Thousand Secrets of the Batcave (Wolf Brando), Fowls of Fate (The Penguin), Crime from Tomorrow (Morton, character without first name) 120-160   350-400

49, Scoop of the Century (Jervis Tetch, Vicki Vale), Batman's Arabian Nights (The Crier, Professor Carter Nichols, The Joker) 180-220   400-500

50, The Second Boy Wonder (Waxey Wilson), Lights-Camera-Crime (Vicki Vale, Stilts Tyler, Tom Macon) 120-150   300-350

51, The Stars of Yesterday (Rufus Lane), Pee-Wee the Talking Penguin, The Wonderful Mr. Wimble (Warts) 90-120   275-325

52, Batman and the Vikings (Olaf Erickson, Professor Carter Nichols), The Man With the Automatic Brain (Alfred the Butler), The Happy Victims (The Joker, Mrs. Carlin) 120-160   320-360

57, The Walking Mummy (Andrews, character without a first name, he was a museum curator), The Funny Man Crimes (The Joker) 90-120   275-325

58, The Brand of a Hero (Joaquin Murieta), The State Bird Crimes (The Penguin), The Black Diamond (Bulls-Eye Kendall, Barracuda Brothers, Nitro Nelson). Joaquin Murieta was a real-life desperado of the Old West, here worked into a time-travel piece 90-120   280-330

59, Batman in the Future (Erkham, character without first name), The Man who Replaced Batman (Deadshot/Floyd Lawton, Commissioner Gordon), The Forbidden Cellar (Professor Vincent) . 90-120   275-325

60, The Auto Circus Mystery (Lucky Hooton) 90-120   280-330

	VERY GOOD	FINE

61, The Birth of Batplane II (Boley Brothers),Wheelchair Crime Fighter (Vicki Vale), Mystery of the Winged People (The Penguin) .... $ 90-120 $ 280-330

SUPERMAN (1939)

2, Superman vs. Luthor (first appearance) .... $ 1600-1800 $ 4200-4800
4, Superman vs. Luthor 750-850   2000-2400
10, Superman vs. Luthor 400-450   900-1100
12, Superman vs. Luthor 275-325   700-800
19, Superman Movie Cartoons, redone into book format 220-260   600-700
30, Superman vs. Mr. Mxyztplk, 1st appearance of Mr. Mxyztplk;
    in later issues the name was spelled Mxyzptlk 220-260   600-700
45, Lois Lane, Superwoman (Hocus, Pocus) 90-130   250-300
53, Anniversary Issue, origin retold 375-425   800-1200
54, Superman vs. The Wrecker (first appearance) 90-110   200-250
61, Superman Returns to Krypton, first Kryptonite story 190-210   450-500
76, Guest Appearances By Batman and Robin 200-250   550-650
78, Lois Lane's Meeting with Lana Lang 80-90   180-220
81, Superman's Secret Workshop, discovered by arch-foe Luthor 80-90   180-220
100, Origin Retold, for the second time 200-250   700-800
113, The Superman of the Past, part I 35-45   90-110
114, The Superman of the Past, part II 35-45   70-90
115, The Superman of the Past, part III 25-35   70-90
123, Girl of Steel 25-35   70-90
125, Clark Kent in College 25-35   70-90
127, Return of Titano 25-35   70-90
128, Kryptonite Story 25-35   70-90
130, Krypton Grows Up 25-35   70-90
133, How Parry White Hired Clark Kent 20-25   50-70
135, Lori Lemaris 20-25   50-70
138, Lori Lemaris 20-25   50-70
139, Story of Red Kryptonite 20-25   50-70
140, Superman and the Son of Bizarro 20-25   50-70
141, Superman Returns to Krypton and Meets Lyla Lorry 15-20   40-50
142, Guest Appearances by Batman and Robin 15-20   40-50
143, Return of Bizarro 15-20   40-50
144, Superboy's First Public Appearance 15-20   40-50
145, Great Boo-Boo 15-20   40-50
146, Superman's Life Story 20-25   50-70
147, Superman vs. The Legion of Super Villains (first appearance) .. 18-22   45-60
148, Guest Appearance by Aquaman 18-22   45-55
149, Death of Superman (fantasy) 18-22   45-55
156, Last Days of Superman, w/ appearances by Batman and Robin 8-10   20-25
158, Nightwing and Flamebird 8-10   20-25

FAWCETT
CAPTAIN MARVEL (1941)

19, Cover: Santa Claus riding on Captain Marvel's back, w/ Mary Marvel wording (at upper right): "On sale every third Friday" . $ 70-90 $ 180-220
26, Cover: Captain Marvel soaring skyward against huge American flag, wording "War, Stamps for Victory" 60-70   150-175

	VERY GOOD	FINE

27, Captain Marvel Joins the Navy, cover: Captain Marvel rearing
back to hurl bomb as if it were a football, wording: "This is the
insignia recently adopted by a naval air squadron" (Referring
to the lightning bolt on Captain Marvel's shirtfront) .... $ 60-70 $ 150-175

28, Cover: Captain Marvel standing at attention w/ hands at sides,
receiving medal from Uncle Sam while column of soldiers watch ... 60-70   150-175

31, Captain Marvel in Buffalo, City Saved From Doom; Captain
Marvel Fights His Own Conscience, cover: Captain Marvel in
close-up w/ angel on one shoulder and devil on the other 55-65   140-160

42, Cover: close-up portrait of Captain Marvel in Christmas wreath,
"Season's Greetings" 40-50   90-110

47, Cover: Captain Marvel stands facing old man w/ long beard
who holds scroll. On wall are names Solomon, Hercules, Atlas,
Zeus, Achilles, Mercury,. and "Seventh War Loan, buy stamps
and bonds" 30-40   90-110

60, Captain Marvel Battles the Dread Atomic War, cover: Captain
Marvel in nuclear devastated city, poised to catch falling atomic
bomb 30-40   60-70

70, Captain Marvel and the Horror in the Box, cover: Captain Marvel
peering into box that has a question mark on the lid 28-32   50-60

73, Cover: Captain Marvel speeds past the Woolworth Building in
New York City 28-32   50-60

97, Captain Marvel is Wiped Out, cover: Captain Marvel standing
full-length, a hand w/ an eraser is "wiping out" the drawing. He
exclaims, "Holy moley! What goes on?" 25-30   75-85

104, Mr. Tawny's Masquerade, cover: Mr. Tawny (with cape)
delivering knockout punch Captain Marvel exclaims, "Attaboy,
Mr. Tawny" 20-25   50-60

112, Captain Marvel and the Strange Worrybird, cover: Worrybird
pacing ground w/ dark cloud of gloom over its head, as Captain
Marvel stands by mystified 20-25   50-60

MARVEL COMICS
THE AMAZING SPIDERMAN , (1963)

1, Origin Retold, Spiderman vs. Chameleon (John Jameson),
Fabulous Four, Ditko artwork, Lee stories, inking unknown .. $ 3500-5500 $ 8000-10000

2, Duel to the Death with the Vulture, Uncanny Threat of
the Terrible Tinkerer, Ditko artwork, Lee stories, Duffy
lettering 400-450   1200-1400

4, Nothing Can Stop the Sandman (Betty Brant), Ditko artwork,
Lee stories 200-250   650-750

5 , Marked for Destruction by Dr. Doom (Fabulous Four), Ditko
artwork, Lee stories, Rosen lettering 180-230   500-600

6, Face To Face With The Lizard, Ditko artwork, Lee stories,
Simek lettering 180-220   450-550

7, Return of the Vulture, Ditko artwork, Lee stories, Simek lettering ... 100-150   350-400

8, Living Brain, Spiderman Tackles the Human Torch (Fabulous
Four), Kirby and Ditko artwork, Lee stories, Simek lettering,
Ditko inking 100-150   350-400

9, A Man Called Electro, Ditko artwork, Lee stories, Simek lettering   120-160   380-420

10, Enforcers (Fredrick Foswell, The Ox, Montana, Fancy Dan),

	VERY GOOD	FINE
Ditko artwork, Lee stories, Rosen lettering	$ 100-150	$ 380-420
11, Turning Point (Spiderman, Tracer, Dr. Octopus), Ditko artwork, Lee stories, Rosen lettering 60-80		180-200
12, Unmasked by Dr. Octopus, Ditko artwork, Lee stories, Simek lettering 60-80		180-200
13, Menace of Mysterio, Ditko artwork, Lee stories, Simek lettering ... 80-100		250-300
14, Green Goblin (Hulk, Enforcers, Ox, Montana, Fancy Dan), Ditko artwork, Lee stories, Simek lettering (premium value because of Hulk appearance) 450-550		800-900
15, Kraven the Hunter (Chameleon), Ditko artwork, Lee stories, Simek lettering 80-100		200-250

Little Golden Books

The first twelve Little Golden Books® titles produced in 1942 sold for the bargain price of 25¢ apiece. Early books have a dust jacket and blue binding. Many titles are reprinted for years. The prices below are for first printings, usually called "As." Some books give the date and printing up front. More often the book has a code on the lower portion of the last page squeezed next to the back cover. "A" refers to a first printing, "B" to a second, etc. Prime condition "A" printings command the highest prices. Collectors are a little more willing to accept a later printing on rare or early titles. *A Poky Little Puppy* ® from the 1970s will command a fraction of the price of a first printing. This method of dating a book is a good rule of thumb but the system breaks down on later books. The original price found on the cover is also a way to date a book. Currently titles based on television series are very popular. Books with dolls, puzzles, and games are difficult to find intact; complete examples are worth several times incomplete ones. The prices quoted are for books in excellent condition showing minimal amounts of wear on the covers and pages.

Our consultant for this area is Rebecca Greason owner of Rebecca of Sunny Book Farm and author of *Tomart's Price Guide to Little Golden Books*, Tomart Publications 1991 (she is listed at the back of this book).

 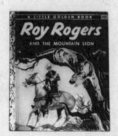 

Clockwise from above left: Rin Tin Tin and Rusty, 1955, #246, $18-$22; Roy Rogers and the Mountain Lion, 1955, #231, $20-$30; Tom and Jerry's Party, 1955, #235, $10-$14; Little Black Sambo, 1948, #57, $85-$125; The Shaggy Dog, 1959, #D82, $15-$22.

	Year	NO.	LOW	HIGH
About the Seashore	1957	284	$ 10	$ 12
Albert's Stencil Zoo, punched	1951	112	20	30
Albert's Stencil Zoo, unpunched	1951	112	50	60
Ali Baba	1958	323	10	15
All Aboard	1952	152	18	22
Animal Stories	1957	5006	8	12
Animals Merry Christmas	1958	329	12	15
Animals of Farmer Jones, w/ dust jacket	1942	11	50	75
Animals of Farmer Jones, without dust jacket	1942	11	12	18
Annie Oakley and the Rustlers	1955	221	20	30
Baby Looks	1960	404	24	30
Benji Fastest Dog in the West	1978	165	8	12
Bible Stories for Boys and Girls	1953	174	7	10
Birds	1958	5011	18	22
Bobby the Dog	1961	440	12	16
Bow Wow! Meow!	1963	523	15	20
Bozo the Clown	1961	446	12	16
Brave Cowboy Bill, w/ puzzle	1950	93	60	80
Brave Cowboy Bill, puzzle missing	1950	93	12	18
Buffalo Bill, Jr.	1956	254	18	22
Bugs Bunny Gets a Job	1952	136	15	20
Bullwinkle	1962	462	18	22
Busy Timmy	1948	50	18	24
Captain Kangaroo	1956	261	18	24
Cars and Trucks	1959	366	10	15
Cave Kids	1963	532	15	18
Charmin' Chatty	1964	554	18	24
Chitty Chitty Bang Bang	1968	581	15	20
Christmas ABC	1962	478	20	25
Christmas Carols	1946	26	12	15
Christmas in the Country	1950	95	12	15
Christopher and the Columbus	1951	103	9	14
Cinderella	1950	D13	18	24
Cinderella's Friends	1950	D17	18	24
Circus Time, dial intact	1955	A2	18	22
Color Kittens	1949	86	18	25
Count to Ten	1957	A6	12	14
Counting Rhymes	1960	361	12	15
Cowboys and Indians	1958	5019	20	30
Dale Evans and the Coyote	1956	253	20	30
Davy Crockett's Keelboat Race	1955	D47	25	30
Day at the Beach	1951	110	30	35
Day at the Zoo	1950	88	18	22
Dick Tracy	1962	497	20	25
Doctor Dan at the Circus, w/ Band-Aids	1960	399	70	90
Doctor Dan at the Circus	1960	399	14	18
Dogs	1957	5008	14	18
Donald Duck and the Mouseketeers	1956	D55	20	30
Donald Duck in Disneyland	1955	D44	15	20
Donald Duck Prize Driver	1956	D49	15	20
Dumbo	1942	D3	30	40

	Year	NO.	LOW	HIGH
Dumbo, w/ dust jacket	1942	D3	$ 60	$ 90
Fish	1959	5023	10	12
Five Little Firemen	1949	301	14	18
Flintstones	1961	450	20	25
Fly High	1971	597	7	10
Four Little Kittens	1957	322	9	12
Four Puppies	1960	405	9	12
Gaston and Josephine	1948	65	18	24
Gene Autry	1955	230	20	30
Giant With Three Golden Hairs	1955	219	15	20
Ginger Paper Doll, uncut	1957	132	75	90
Gingerbread Shop	1952	126	14	18
Golden Book of Birds	1943	13	18	20
Grandpa Bunny	1951	D21	20	30
Gunsmoke	1958	320	25	35
Hansel and Gretel	1954	217	8	12
Happy Birthday, uncut	1949	384	25	35
Hey There, It's Yogi Bear	1964	542	18	24
Hi Ho! Three in a Row	1954	188	25	30
How to Tell Time	1957	285	12	18
Howdy Doody's Animal Friends	1956	252	25	30
J. Fred Muggs	1955	234	12	18
Jamie Looks	1963	522	28	32
Jetsons	1962	500	20	30
Katie Kitten	1949	75	12	18
Lassie and Her Day in the Sun	1958	307	15	20
Leave It to Beaver	1959	347	20	25
Lion's Paw	1959	367	15	20
Little Black Sambo	1948	57	85	125
Little Boy With a Big Horn	1950	100	10	15
Little Eskimo	1952	155	12	15
Little Fat Policeman	1950	91	14	18
Little Golden Book of Uncle Wiggly	1954	148	15	18
Little Golden Holiday Book	1951	109	18	22
Little Indian	1954	202	10	15
Little Man of Disneyland	1955	D46	10	14
Little Yip Yip	1950	75	15	20
Lively Little Rabbit	1943	15	20	30
Lone Ranger and the Talking Pony	1958	310	30	40
Lucky Mrs. Ticklefeather	1951	122	18	22
Lucky Puppy	1960	D89	15	20
Lucky Rabbit	1955	Din7	10	14
Mad Hatter's Tea Party	1951	D23	20	25
Madeline	1954	186	20	30
Make Way for the Thruway	1961	439	12	18
Marvelous Merry Go Round	1950	87	8	12
Maverick	1959	354	18	24
Mickey Mouse and His Space Ship	1952	D29	20	30
Mickey Mouse Christmas Shopping	1953	D33	20	25
More Mother Goose Rhymes	1958	317	10	12
Mr. Ed the Talking Horse	1962	483	20	25

	YEAR	NO.	LOW	HIGH
My Baby Sister	1958	340	$ 12	$ 15
My Christmas Treasury	1957	5003	9	12
My Little Golden Book of God	1956	268	9	12
My Magic Slate Book, intact, w/ pencil	1959	5025	35	40
New Baby	1948	412	15	20
New Brother, New Sister	1966	564	14	18
New Kittens	1957	302	9	14
Noah's Ark	1952	D28	15	20
Noises and Mr. Flibberty Jib	1947	290	20	25
Nursery Rhymes	1948	59	14	18
Off to School	1958	5015	18	22
Once Upon a Wintertime	1948	D12	18	22
Ookpik, the Arctic Owl	1968	579	12	15
Our World	1955	242	8	12
Out of My Window	1955	245	15	20
Pantaloon	1951	114	18	24
Party in Sheriland	1959	360	18	22
Peter Pan and the Pirates	1952	D25	18	22
Pinocchio	1948	D8	20	30
Play Street	1962	484	18	22
Poky Little Puppy w/ dust jacket	1942	8	70	90
Poky Little Puppy, without dust jacket	1942	8	30	40
Prayers for Children	1952	205	8	10
Puss in Boots	1953	137	12	15
Quick Draw McGraw	1960	398	14	18
Raggedy Ann and Andy Help Santa	1979	156	8	10
Rin Tin Tin and Rusty	1955	246	18	22
Ronald McDonald and the Talking Plant	1984		18	24
Rootie Kazootie Detective	1953	150	25	35
Rootie Kazootie Joins the Circus	1955	226	28	36
Roy Rogers and the Mountain Lion	1955	231	25	30
Roy Rogers and the New Cowboy	1953	177	18	25
Saggy Baggy Elephant	1947	385	15	20
Santa's Toy Shop	1950	D16	10	14

Left to right: Gaston and Josephine, 1948, #65, $18-$24,
Pantaloon, 1951, #114, $18-$24.

The Road to Oz, 1951, #144, $20-$30.

	YEAR	NO.	LOW	HIGH
Scuffy the Tugboat	1946	30	$ 20	$ 30
Sleeping Beauty Paper Doll, Uncut	1959	133	90	110
Smokey and His Animal Friends	1960	387	14	18
Smokey the Bear and the Campers	1961	423	14	18
Snow White and Rose Red	1955	228	15	18
Steve Canyon	1959	356	18	24
Supercar	1962	492	25	35
Taxi That Hurried	1946	25	20	30
Tin Woodman of Oz	1952	159	20	30
Tom and Jerry	1951	117	12	18
Tootle	1945	21	15	20
Touche Turtle	1962	474	20	30
Twelve Days of Christmas	1963	526	8	12
Two Little Gardeners	1951	108	10	15
Ugly Duckling	1952	D22	15	20
Ukelele and Her New Doll	1951	102	18	25
Ukelele and Her New Doll, w/ puzzle	1951	102	70	90
Uncle Mistletoe	1953	175	18	22
Up in the Attic	1948	53	15	20
Wagon Train	1958	236	25	30
Waltons, Birthday Present	1975	134	7	10
We Help Daddy	1962	468	10	15
We Help Mommy	1959	352	10	12
When I Grow Up	1950	96	15	20
Where is the Bear?	1967	586	8	10
Winky Dink	1956	266	18	22
Wonders of Nature	1957	293	12	16
Zorro	1958	D68	20	25

Magazines

Magazines are history in the first person. Few things capture the moods of the American nation as the magazines we read. Few things are as American as Life Magazine. But magazines, unlike books, were meant to be read and discarded. Although publishers printed large numbers, readers saved only a small percentage. These saved copies may turn up anywhere, from a church bazaar to the bottom of an auction box lot.

Collectors of magazines want clean, crisp copies. They should not be marked, torn or frayed. Ideally, the best copy is an unread copy.

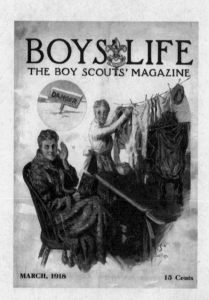

Left: Boy's Life, the Boy Scouts' Magazine, March 1918, $20-$30.

Right: Chess Review, featuring Bogart and Friends, 1943, $25-$35.

	LOW	AVERAGE	HIGH
American Mag., 1950-54	$ 5.00	$ 6.00	$ 7.00
American Mag., 1955, Aug. (Amazing Secret of Walt Disney)	10.00	11.00	12.00
American Mag., 1955-56	3.00	4.00	5.00
American Monthly Review of Reviews, 1900-06	9.00	10.50	12.00
American Monthly Review of Reviews, 1906, July (Olympics)	17.00	18.00	19.00
American Monthly Review of Reviews, 1906, May (Earthquake)	20.00	22.50	25.00
American Neptune, 1941-50	4.00	4.75	5.50
Argosy, 1882-90	4.00	4.75	5.50
Argosy, 1891-00	3.25	3.88	4.50
Argosy, 1901-10	2.75	3.38	4.00
Argosy, 1911-20	2.25	2.75	3.25
Arizona Highways, 1955-60	4.00	4.75	5.50
Arizona Highways, 1961-65	3.25	4.13	5.00
ArtNews, 1942, 10/14 (Charles Dana Gibson)	20.00	22.50	25.00
Asia, 1929, Jan.	25.00	27.50	30.00
Association Men (YMCA Publication), 1917	5.00	6.00	7.00
Atlantic Monthly, 1887, June	14.00	15.00	16.00
Atlantic Monthly, 1950-59	2.75	3.00	3.25
Atlantic Monthly, 1960-69	2.00	2.38	2.75
Atlantic Monthly, 1970	1.25	1.63	2.00
Audubon Mag., 1950-55	4.50	5.75	7.00
Audubon Mag., 1956-60	4.00	5.00	6.00
Bandleaders, 1946, June	11.00	12.00	13.00
Baseball Mag., 1923	12.00	14.00	16.00
Baseball Mag., 1955	3.25	3.88	4.50
Beatles Monthly Book, 1965, Mar.	20.00	22.50	25.00
Better Homes and Gardens, 1920-30	6.75	7.88	9.00
Better Homes and Gardens, 1950-60	3.25	3.88	4.50
Better Homes and Gardens, 1961-70	2.25	2.75	3.25
Black Mask, 1921, Nov.	200.00	225.00	250.00
Black Mask, 1925, Mar.	70.00	75.00	80.00
Black Mask, 1926, Feb.	70.00	75.00	80.00
Black Mask, 1927, Apr.	130.00	142.50	155.00
Black Mask, 1927, Feb.	70.00	75.00	80.00
Black Mask, 1928, Aug.	130.00	142.50	155.00
Black Mask, 1930, Jan. (Maltese Falcon)	130.00	142.50	155.00
Black Mask, 1930, Mar.	35.00	37.50	40.00
Black Mask, 1935, Jan.	60.00	65.00	70.00
Black Mask, 1936, May	70.00	75.00	80.00
Boy's Life, 1946-65	3.25	3.88	4.50
Boys' Life, 1948, Feb. (Norman Rockwell)	18.00	19.00	20.00
Boys' Life, 1959, Feb. (Norman Rockwell)	12.00	13.00	14.00
Brigitte Bardot, 1958, one issue only	35.00	37.50	40.00
Brown Book of Boston, 1903-05	7.00	9.00	11.00
Brown Book of Boston 1905, Apr.	17.00	18.00	19.00
Captain Future, 1940-42	15.00	22.50	30.00
Carnival, 1953-54	1.75	2.00	2.25
Cartoon Comedy Parade, 1963	1.00	1.25	1.50
Cartoon Parade, 1962, 1/1	5.00	6.00	7.00
Cartoon Parade, 1962-68	1.00	1.50	2.00
Century Mag., 1887, Oct.	14.00	15.00	16.00

Above left to right: The Etude Music Magazine, August 1932, $4-$6; The Home Garden, July 1920, $3-$5. — Items courtesy of Pastimes. Below left to right: Life, Joe DiMaggio cover, May 1, 1939; Life, Jackie Robinson cover, May 8, 1950; Sports figures on the cover are issues popular with collectors. — Items courtesy of Pastimes.

	LOW	AVERAGE	HIGH
Century Mag., 1892, Feb.	$ 8.00	$ 9.00	$ 10.00
Child Life, 1936	4.00	4.75	5.50
Clic, 1938-40	4.00	5.50	7.00
Collier's, 1902-10	8.00	9.00	10.00
Collier's, 1910-20	5.00	6.00	7.00
Collier's, 1920-60	3.00	4.00	5.00
Collier's, 1937, 11/6 (Mickey Mouse)	40.00	45.00	50.00
Collier's, 1951, 2/17 (Herbert Hoover's Memoirs)	11.00	12.00	13.00
Comedy, 1956-60	1.00	1.25	1.50
Complete Detective, 1938, May, first issue	45.00	50.00	55.00
Complete Photographer, 1941	6.00	7.00	8.00

	LOW	AVERAGE	HIGH
Cosmic Science Fiction, 1941	$ 40.00	$ 42.50	$ 45.00
Cosmopolitan, 1890-99	16.75	20.88	25.00
Cosmopolitan, 1900-10	13.50	16.75	20.00
Cosmopolitan, 1911-20	12.00	14.38	16.75
Cosmopolitan, 1921-30	2.75	6.38	10.00
Country Gentleman, 1853-60	7.75	10.38	13.00
Country Gentleman, 1861-70	6.75	8.88	11.00
Country Gentleman, 1871-80	4.00	5.38	6.75
Dileneator, 1873-80	5.50	6.63	7.75
Dileneator, 1881-90	4.50	5.63	6.75
Doc Savage, 1933, Sept.	175.00	187.50	200.00
Doc Savage, 1935, Jan.	60.00	65.00	70.00
Doc Savage, 1939, Jan.	50.00	55.00	60.00
Doc Savage, 1939-48	20.00	30.00	40.00
Doc Savage, 1944, Dec.	70.00	75.00	80.00
Double Detective, 1937-40	50.00	55.00	60.00
Esquire, 1944-55	14.00	15.00	16.00
Esquire, 1951, Sept. (Monroe)	45.00	50.00	55.00
Esquire, 1956-66	2.00	3.00	4.00
Esquire, 1967-72	1.50	2.50	3.50
Etude, 1900-10	1.35	2.05	2.75
Family Circle, 1950-59	1.00	1.18	1.35
Family Circle, 1960-69	0.75	0.88	1.00
Farmer's Wife, 1928-31	2.00	3.50	5.00
Fawcett Figure Photography, 1954, one issue only	8.00	9.00	10.00
Field & Stream, 1896-1900	2.75	3.38	4.00
Field & Stream, 1901-10	2.25	2.75	3.25
Field & Stream, 1911-20	2.00	2.38	2.75
Field & Stream, 1921-30	1.00	1.88	2.75
Film Stars, Winter, 1953 (Monroe)	45.00	50.00	55.00
Film Weekly, 1931-37	25.00	32.50	40.00
Filmland, 1951-57	10.00	15.00	20.00
Focus, 1951-53	1.75	2.00	2.25
Focus, 1938, Apr.	5.00	6.00	7.00
Focus, 1953, May (Monroe)	20.00	22.50	25.00
Fotorama, 1955-61	1.75	2.00	2.25
Fotorama, July, 1959 (Elvis)	3.50	4.00	4.50
Front Page Detective, 1936-45	8.00	10.00	12.00
Front Page Detective, 1946-56	4.00	6.00	8.00
Front Page Detective, 1957-60	2.00	4.00	6.00
Front Page Detective, 1960-69	1.00	1.50	2.00
Fun House Comedy, 1964	1.00	1.25	1.50
Godey's Lady's Book, 1844-53	5.50	6.63	7.75
Godey's Lady's Book, late 1860s	2.75	3.38	4.00
Good Housekeeping, 1902-20	7.00	8.00	9.00
Good Housekeeping, 1921-28	5.00	6.00	7.00
Good Housekeeping, 1929-39	3.25	3.88	4.50
Good Housekeeping, 1940-49	2.25	2.75	3.25
Good Housekeeping, 1950-61	1.50	1.75	2.00
Good Housekeeping, 1961, Aug. (Caroline Kennedy)	4.00	5.00	6.00
Good Literature, 1907	2.00	3.00	4.00

	LOW	AVERAGE	HIGH
Groove, 1947-49	$ 10.00	$ 11.00	$ 12.00
Harper's Bazaar, 1893	4.00	4.75	5.50
Harper's Monthly, 1850	6.75	7.88	9.00
Harper's Monthly, 1851-55	11.00	15.50	20.00
Harper's Weekly, 1850-59	5.50	6.63	7.75
Harper's Weekly, 1860, 4/21 (Stephen Douglas)	27.50	30.00	32.50
Harper's Weekly, 1860-65	10.00	25.00	40.00
Harper's Weekly, 1865, 11/18 (woodcut, baseball)	50.00	60.00	70.00
Harper's Weekly, 1865, 11/25 (woodcut, Brooklyn Baseball)	50.00	60.00	70.00
Harper's Weekly, 1866-80	2.75	11.38	20.00
Harper's Weekly, 1904, 4/30 (St. Louis Fair)	9.00	11.25	13.50
Harper's Weekly, after 1880	2.00	4.38	6.75
High Society, 1978, Apr. (Monroe)	17.00	18.00	19.00
High Society, 1981, July (Nastassja Kinski)	14.00	15.00	16.00
High Times, No. 1, 1974	80.00	90.00	100.00
Holiday, 1950-55	3.00	4.00	5.00
Hollywood, 1934-43	15.00	20.00	25.00
Hollywood Life Stories, 1952-58	10.00	17.50	25.00
Hollywood Pinups, 1953, No. 1, w/ 3-D glasses	70.00	80.00	90.00
House Beautiful, 1919-29	7.00	8.50	10.00
House Beautiful, 1930-45	4.00	5.00	6.00
House Beautiful, 1946-60	2.00	3.00	4.00
Illustrated Blue Book, 1926-29	25.00	30.00	35.00
Inside Detective, 1936-58	9.00	11.00	13.00
Inside Detective, 1959-70	6.00	7.00	8.00
Inside Detective, 1970, Mar. (Charles Manson)	9.00	10.00	11.00
James Bond 007, 1964, one issue only	50.00	60.00	70.00
Jest, 1951-59	2.50	3.50	4.50
Jet, 1954	3.00	4.00	5.00
Ladies' Home Journal, 1890-10	10.00	13.50	17.00
Ladies' Home Journal, 1911-29	7.00	8.50	10.00
Ladies' Home Journal, 1930-40	3.00	5.00	7.00
Leslie's Weekly, Frank, 1890-99	5.00	7.13	9.25
Leslie's Weekly, Frank, 1900-10	4.75	6.25	7.75
Leslie's Weekly, Frank, 1911-20	4.35	5.18	6.00
Liberty, 1924-30	1.35	1.68	2.00
Liberty, 1931-40	1.00	1.88	2.75
Liberty, 1936-44	4.00	8.00	12.00
Life, 11/9 (Monroe)	19.00	20.00	21.00
Life, 1936	20.00	22.50	25.00
Life, 1936, 11/23	90.00	100.00	110.00
Life, 1936, 11/30	40.00	42.50	45.00
Life, 1937	8.00	12.00	16.00
Life, 1937, 1/4 (FDR)	22.00	24.50	27.00
Life, 1937, 11/8 (Garbo)	32.00	34.50	37.00
Life, 1937, 5/17 (Quintuplets)	40.00	42.50	45.00
Life, 1937, 5/3 (Jean Harlow)	27.00	29.50	32.00
Life, 1938	7.00	10.50	14.00
Life, 1938, 2/7 (Cooper)	20.00	22.50	25.00
Life, 1938, 5/23 (Errol Flynn)	20.00	22.50	25.00
Life, 1938, 6/20 (Valentino)	25.00	27.50	30.00

	LOW	AVERAGE	HIGH
Life, 1938, 7/11 (Shirley Temple)	$ 32.00	$ 34.50	$ 37.00
Life, 1939	6.00	9.00	12.00
Life, 1939, 3/13 (World's Fair)	25.00	27.50	30.00
Life, 1939, 9/11 (Mussolini)	19.00	20.00	21.00
Life, 1940	5.00	7.50	10.00
Life, 1940, 12/9 (Ginger Rogers)	13.00	14.00	15.00
Life, 1940, 7/15 (Rita Hayworth)	13.00	14.00	15.00
Life, 1941	4.00	6.00	8.00
Life, 1941, 1/27 (Churchill)	10.00	11.00	12.00
Life, 1941, 12/8 (MacArthur)	22.00	24.50	27.00
Life, 1942	4.00	5.00	6.00
Life, 1942, 3/30 (Shirley Temple)	12.00	13.00	14.00
Life, 1942, 4/27 (Nelson Rockefeller)	8.00	9.00	10.00
Life, 1943, 7/12 (Roy Rogers)	37.00	39.50	42.00
Life, 1943-45	4.00	5.00	6.00
Life, 1944, 12/11 (Judy Garland)	13.00	14.00	15.00
Life, 1945, 4/16 (Eisenhower)	17.00	18.00	19.00
Life, 1945, 4/23 (Truman)	22.00	24.50	27.00
Life, 1945, 9/3 (MacArthur)	22.00	24.50	27.00
Life, 1946, 2/4 (Hope and Crosby)	11.00	12.00	13.00
Life, 1946, 4/8 (Circus)	13.00	14.00	15.00
Life, 1946-57	3.00	4.50	6.00
Life, 1947, 7/14 (Elizabeth Taylor)	11.00	12.00	13.00
Life, 1948, 11/22 (Truman)	9.00	10.00	11.00
Life, 1948, 9/27 (football player Doak Walker)	8.00	10.00	12.00
Life, 1949, 8/1 (DiMaggio)	11.00	12.00	13.00
Life, 1950, 1/2 (special issue)	11.00	12.00	13.00
Life, 1950, 6/12 (Bill Boyd)	18.00	19.00	20.00
Life, 1952, 4/7 (Monroe)	27.00	29.50	32.00
Life, 1953, 5/25 (Monroe and Jane Russell)	25.00	27.50	30.00
Life, 1953, 6/8 (Roy Campanella)	19.00	20.00	21.00
Life, 1953, 7/20 (JFK and Jackie)	22.00	24.50	27.00
Life, 1954, 4/26 (Grace Kelly)	9.00	10.00	11.00
Life, 1954, 9/15 (Judy Garland)	9.00	10.00	11.00
Life, 1955, 8/22 (Sophia Loren)	5.00	8.00	11.00
Life, 1955, 9/12 (Joan Collins)	8.00	9.00	10.00
Life, 1956, 6/25 (Mickey Mantle)	14.00	15.00	16.00
Life, 1957, 3/11 (JFK)	14.00	15.00	16.00
Life, 1958, 1/6 (Astronaut)	8.00	9.00	10.00
Life, 1958, 12/1 (Ricky Nelson)	11.00	12.00	13.00
Life, 1958, 4/28 (Willie Mays)	11.00	12.00	13.00
Life, 1958-60	2.00	3.00	4.00
Life, 1959, 10/3, 1955 (Rock Hudson)	10.00	11.00	12.00
Life, 1959, 4/20 (Monroe)	19.00	20.00	21.00
Life, 1959, 8/24 (Jackie Kennedy)	11.00	12.00	13.00
Life, 1960, 12/26 (double issue)	19.00	20.00	21.00
Life, 1960-65	2.00	3.00	4.00
Life, 1961, 1/13 (Gable)	4.00	5.00	6.00
Life, 1962, 11/2 (Cuban missile crisis)	4.00	5.00	6.00
Life, 1962, 6/22 (Monroe)	13.00	14.00	15.00
Life, 1963, 11/29 (JFK assassination)	19.00	20.00	21.00

	LOW	AVERAGE	HIGH
Life, 1963, 12/13 (Johnson)	$ 6.00	$ 7.00	$ 8.00
Life, 1963, 12/13 (Kennedy Memorial)	9.00	10.00	11.00
Life, 1963, 8/2 (Koufax)	6.00	7.00	8.00
Life, 1964, 11/6 (Goldfinger)	5.00	6.00	7.00
Life, 1964, 2/21 (Oswald)	6.00	7.00	8.00
Life, 1964, 8/28 (The Beatles)	20.00	22.50	25.00
Literary Digest, 1910-29	0.75	1.00	1.25
Literary Digest, 1920's, w/ Norman Rockwell covers	4.50	5.25	6.00
Literary Digest, 1924	3.00	4.00	5.00
Literary Digest, 1924, 6/25 (Lindberg)	9.00	10.00	11.00
Literary Digest, 1930-38	0.75	0.88	1.00
Look, 1930-38	6.75	8.18	9.60
Look, 1939, 1/3 (Duke of Windsor)	11.00	12.00	13.00
Look, 1939-43	6.00	8.00	10.00
Look, 1940, 9/24 (Charlie Chaplin)	18.00	20.00	22.00
Look, 1944-53	5.00	6.50	8.00
Look, 1954, 12/28 (Lucille Ball)	9.00	10.00	11.00
Look, 1954-56	3.00	5.00	7.00
Look, 1957, 1/8 (20th Anniversary)	8.00	9.00	10.00
Look, 1957-59	2.00	2.50	3.00
Look, 1960-64	1.00	1.75	2.50
Mademoiselle, 1941, Dec. (Christmas issue)	5.00	6.00	7.00
Master Detective, 1929-40	10.00	12.50	15.00
McCall's 1873-1910	6.00	8.50	11.00
McCall's, 1911-20	4.00	6.38	8.75
McCall's, 1921-30	3.75	5.18	6.60
McCall's, 1931-45	3.25	4.63	6.00
McCall's, 1945-55	2.00	3.50	5.00
McCall's, 1956-75	1.00	2.50	4.00
McClure's Mag., 1899-1904	8.00	10.00	12.00
Modern Movies, 1937-38	20.00	23.50	27.00
Modern Priscilla, 1887-99	2.00	2.63	3.25

Left to right: Texas Rangers, $6-$8, — Item courtesy of Pastimes; Playboy, September 1974, $3-$5.

	LOW	AVERAGE	HIGH
Modern Priscilla, 1913-25	$ 3.00	$ 4.50	$ 6.00
Modern Priscilla, 1921-30	4.50	5.25	6.00
Modern Romances, 1937-39	7.00	8.50	10.00
Modern Screen, 1931-39	25.00	35.00	45.00
Modern Screen, 1940-45	22.00	26.00	30.00
Modern Screen, 1943, Jan. (Ronald Reagan and Jane Wyman)	70.00	75.00	80.00
Modern Screen, 1946-53	15.00	17.50	20.00
Modern Screen, 1948, Aug. (Shirley Temple)	27.00	29.50	32.00
Modern Screen, 1953, Oct. (Monroe)	45.00	50.00	55.00
Modern Screen, 1954-59	8.00	10.00	12.00
Modern Screen, 1955, Oct. (Monroe)	37.00	39.50	42.00
Modern Screen, 1959, June (Rock Hudson)	20.00	22.50	25.00
Modern Screen, 1960-64	5.00	6.50	8.00
Modern Screen, 1962, Nov. (Monroe)	25.00	27.50	30.00
Modern Screen, 1964, Dec. (JFK and Jackie)	25.00	27.50	30.00
Modern Screen, 1965-68	2.00	3.50	5.00
Modern Screen, 1969-79	1.00	1.50	2.00
Modern Screen, 1979, June (Elvis)	8.00	9.00	10.00
Motion Picture, 1920 pre	13.60	16.80	20.00
Motion Picture, 1921, Sept.	60.00	65.00	70.00
Motion Picture, 1921-30	20.00	22.50	25.00
Motion Picture, 1931-40	15.00	17.50	20.00
Motion Picture, 1941-50	10.00	12.50	15.00
Motion Picture, 1951-55	7.00	9.50	12.00
Motion Picture, 1955-64	5.00	7.50	10.00
Motion Picture, 1965-70	2.00	3.00	4.00
Motion Picture, 1965-75	1.00	1.50	2.00
Motion Picture, 1971-75	1.00	1.50	2.00
Motion Picture News, 1930 pre	5.50	6.13	6.75
Movie Classic, 1933-42	25.00	35.00	45.00
Movie Classic, 1940-45	20.00	27.50	35.00
Movie Life, 1939-44	25.00	27.50	30.00
Movie Life, 1945-48	20.00	22.50	25.00
Movie Life, 1949-58	15.00	17.50	20.00
Movie Life, 1952, Nov. (Monroe)	45.00	50.00	55.00
Movie Life, 1955, Apr. (Monroe)	40.00	42.50	45.00
Movie Life, 1958, July (Natalie Wood)	25.00	27.50	30.00
Movie Life Yearbook, 1946-66	10.00	17.50	25.00
Movie Mirror, 1934-39	25.00	37.50	50.00
Movie People, 1954, May (w/ 3-D glasses)	60.00	65.00	70.00
Movie Show, 1946-48	20.00	22.50	25.00
Movie Stars Parade, 1944-60	15.00	20.00	25.00
Movie Stars Parade, 1953, Oct. (Monroe)	45.00	50.00	55.00
Movie Story, 1937-49	20.00	27.50	35.00
Movie Story, 1950-onwards	15.00	17.50	20.00
Movie World, 1952-54	14.00	16.00	18.00
Movieland, 1947-60	20.00	35.00	50.00
Movies, 1935-48	20.00	32.50	45.00
Munsey, 1895-1896	7.00	9.00	11.00
National Geographic, 1880, Vol. 1, No. 1	550.00	613.00	676.00
National Geographic, 1880, Vol. 1, No. 2	200.00	262.50	325.00

	LOW	AVERAGE	HIGH
National Geographic, 1888	$ 300.00	$ 400.00	$ 500.00
National Geographic, 1890-94	80.00	115.00	150.00
National Geographic, 1898, Mar.	45.00	52.50	60.00
National Geographic, 1899	25.00	37.50	50.00
National Geographic, 1900-04	20.00	30.00	40.00
National Geographic, 1905-13	13.50	16.75	20.00
National Geographic, 1914-19	5.00	6.50	8.00
National Geographic, 1920-29	2.00	3.00	4.00
National Geographic, 1930-49	1.00	2.00	3.00
National Geographic, 1950-95	1.00	1.50	2.00
National Monthly, 1913-16	4.00	5.00	6.00
Nature, 1920-29	0.75	1.05	1.35
Nature, 1945-46	1.50	1.75	2.00
Nature, prior to 1920	1.00	1.50	2.00
Needlecraft, 1909	1.35	2.93	4.50
Needlecraft, 1910-	1.36	2.68	4.00
Needlecraft, 1920-29	0.75	0.88	1.00
New Movie, 1930-33	30.00	35.00	40.00
Newsweek, 1950-55	2.00	2.63	3.25
Newsweek, 1956-60	1.76	2.26	2.75
Newsweek, 1961-65	1.36	1.68	2.00
Newsweek, 1966-70	1.00	1.18	1.35
Official Detective (13" x 10.5"), 1937-56	6.00	8.00	10.00
Oui, 1972, Oct. (first issue)	20.00	22.50	25.00
Oui, 1973-74	2.50	3.00	3.50
Outdoor Life, 1915-16	7.00	8.00	9.00
Penthouse, 1972-74	4.00	6.00	8.00
People Today, 1954	1.50	2.00	2.50
People's Home Journal, 1902	3.00	4.00	5.00
Peterson's Mag., 1844-59	4.50	5.25	6.00
Peterson's Mag., 1860-65	6.00	7.25	8.50
Photo, 1952, June (1st issue)	3.50	4.00	4.50
Photo, 1952-55	2.00	2.25	2.50
Photo Life, 1958-61	2.00	3.00	4.00
Photo Play, 1919-29	40.00	52.50	65.00
Photo Play, 1930-37	27.00	33.50	40.00
Photo Play, 1938-43	22.00	27.50	33.00
Photo Play, 1944-45	18.00	21.50	25.00
Photo Play, 1946-50	15.00	17.50	20.00
Pic, 1940-45	3.00	5.50	8.00
Pictorial Review, World War I era	2.75	4.13	5.50
Picture Digest, 1956-57	1.00	1.25	1.50
Picture Life, 1954	1.50	2.00	2.50
Picture Play, 1930-38	20.00	30.00	40.00
Picture Show, 1945-49	15.00	17.50	20.00
Playboy, 1954-55	30.00	45.00	60.00
Playboy, 1956	18.00	20.00	22.00
Playboy, 1957-66	10.00	12.50	15.00
Playboy, 1967-75	7.00	8.50	10.00
Playboy, 1976-79	3.00	5.00	7.00
Playboy, Dec., 1953	90.00	100.00	110.00

*Clockwise from above left: TV Guide, Volume 1 No. 1
Lucy's Baby, $600-$1200; New England TV Guide,
December 1952, Gold Medal Awards, $150-200; TV
Guide, Fred and Ethel Mertz, March 1953, $50-$75.
— Items courtesy of Pastimes.*

	LOW	AVERAGE	HIGH
Playboy, Jan., 1954	$ 90.00	$ 100.00	$ 110.00
Popular Mechanics, 1900-10	10.00	15.00	20.00
Popular Mechanics, 1951-53	2.00	2.50	3.00
Popular Mechanics, 1960-69	0.75	1.13	1.50
Popular Science, 1900 pre	20.00	27.50	35.00
Popular Science, 1901-10	20.00	22.50	25.00
Popular Science, 1911-30	15.00	17.50	20.00
Prairie Farmer, 1920-29	1.00	1.50	2.00
Puck, early 1900's	4.00	5.38	6.75
Puck, late 1800s	7.00	11.38	15.75
Pulse, 1954-55	1.50	2.00	2.50
Radio Broadcast, 1929	5.00	6.00	7.00
Radio Craft, 1929, Oct. (first issue)	10.00	11.00	12.00
Radio Craft, 1929-40	3.00	4.50	6.00
Radio Electronics, 1949-52	2.50	3.00	3.50
Reader's Digest, 1930s	0.75	1.05	1.35
Reader's Digest, 1940-60	0.50	0.75	1.00
Redbook, 1950-60	2.00	3.50	5.00
Saturday Evening Post, 1900-07	10.00	13.38	16.75
Saturday Evening Post, 1908-10	8.00	9.00	10.00
Saturday Evening Post, 1911-20	5.00	7.50	10.00
Saturday Evening Post, 1921-30	4.00	5.00	6.00
Saturday Evening Post, 1931-40	2.75	3.38	4.00
Saturday Evening Post, 1933-37 (Norman Rockwell covers)	20.00	25.00	30.00
Science and Mechanics, 1942-56	3.00	5.00	7.00
Scientific American, 1950-60	1.25	1.50	1.75
Screen Album (quarterly), 1951-54	15.00	17.50	20.00
Screen Book, 1929-39	25.00	37.50	50.00
Screen Guide, 1939-45	15.00	22.50	30.00
Screen Guide, 1946-51	8.00	11.50	15.00
Screen Hits Annual, 1949-52	10.00	15.00	20.00
Screen Life, 1941-49	10.00	12.50	15.00
Screen Life, 1950-60	5.00	7.50	10.00
Screen Life, 1961-68	3.00	5.00	7.00
Screen Play, 1936-37	30.00	35.00	40.00
Screen Romances, 1934-38	22.00	31.00	40.00
Screen Stars, 1946-49	12.00	14.00	16.00
Screen Stars, 1950-57	5.00	7.50	10.00
Screen Stories, 1948-55	8.00	11.00	14.00
Screen Stories, 1956-60	5.00	6.50	8.00
Screen Stories, 1961-72	2.00	4.00	6.00
Screenland, 1924-32	20.00	25.00	30.00
Screenland, 1933-39	16.00	19.00	22.00
Screenland, 1940-48	12.00	15.00	18.00
Screenland, 1949-55	7.00	9.50	12.00
Screenland, 1956-65	2.00	4.00	6.00
Scribner's Mag., 1881-1894	8.00	10.00	12.00
Scribner's Monthly, World War I era	0.50	0.63	0.75
Sexology, 1952-67	1.00	1.50	2.00
Silver Screen, 1939-64	10.00	15.00	20.00
Snappy, 1956-60	2.00	2.50	3.00

	LOW	AVERAGE	HIGH
Sports Afield, 1890-1940	$ 3.25	$ 5.00	$ 6.75
Stage, 1935-37	20.00	25.00	30.00
Startling Detective, 1931-39	9.00	11.00	13.00
Startling Detective, 1940-57	4.00	6.00	8.00
Tab, 1952-66	2.00	2.25	2.50
Tab, 1966, Aug. (Sophia Loren)	4.00	5.00	6.00
Theatre, 1910-14	25.00	27.50	30.00
Theatre Mag., 1925-26	20.00	27.50	35.00
Time, 1932-39	6.00	7.00	8.00
Time, 1939, 12/25 (Gone With the Wind)	25.00	27.50	30.00
Time, 1940-59	1.50	2.00	2.50
Time, 1960-66	1.00	1.50	2.00
True Detective, 1924-39	10.00	15.00	20.00
True Detective, 1940-61	8.00	10.00	12.00
TV Guide, 1950	30.00	50.00	70.00
TV Guide, 1951-52	15.00	27.50	40.00
TV Guide, 1953-55	15.00	22.50	30.00
TV Guide, 1956-60	7.00	13.50	20.00
TV Guide, 1961-69	6.00	9.00	12.00
TV Guide, 1970-74	3.00	5.50	8.00
TV Guide, 1975-79	2.00	4.00	6.00
TV Guide, 1980-95	1.00	1.50	2.00
Woman's Home Companion, 1900-10	4.00	5.38	6.75

Above left to right: TV Guide, Lucy and Desi Tackle The Movies, $100-$150; TV Guide, Groucho and George Fenniman, February-March 1953, $100-$125. — Items courtesy of Pastimes.

Newspapers

Valuable newspapers are those with major events in the headlines. One of the most valuable 20th-century papers carries the premature "Dewey defeats Truman" headline. For more information, consult *The Official Price Guide to Paper Collectibles*, published by The House of Collectibles, Random House, NY.

Prices are for whole issues, not just front pages. Front pages alone are worth less than the prices shown. The major papers of the major American cities are the most valuable. Values are given for New York (NY), Chicago (CH), and Washington, D.C. (W). It should be understood that this is for the main city newspapers, such as, *The New York Times*, The *Chicago Tribune* and *The Washington Post*.

	NY	CH	W
Assassinations			
Archduke Francis Ferdinand	$ 30	$ 25	$ 30
James Garfield Shot (still alive)	33	23	27
James Garfield dies of wound	25	22	25
Mahatma Gandhi	12	8	10
John F. Kennedy	50	40	50
Robert Kennedy Shot (still alive)	14	12	13
Robert Kennedy dies of wound	12	8	9
Martin Luther King, Jr.	12	8	9
Abraham Lincoln	500	400	500
Huey Long	16	14	15
William McKinley Shot (still alive)	50	40	50
William McKinley dies of wound	45	40	45
Benito Mussolini	30	20	28
Anwar Sadat	2	1	2
Leon Trotsky	24	18	20
Attempted Assassinations			
Charles de Gaulle	$ 4	$ 3	$ 3
Gerald Ford	2	1	2
Hitler	22	17	19
Franklin D. Roosevelt	11	8	10
Harry S. Truman	8	6	7
George Wallace	7	4	5
Pope John Paul II	2	2	1
Presidential Elections			
1860, Lincoln/Douglas	$ 200	$ 175	$ 200
1864, Lincoln/McClellan	150	135	150
1868, Grant/Seymour	45	30	40
1872, Grant/Greeley	40	25	35
1876, Hayes/Tilden	22	14	20
1880, Garfield/Hancock	22	14	18
1884, Cleveland/Blaine	22	14	20
1888, Harrison/Cleveland	22	14	20
1892, Cleveland/Harrison	22	14	20
1896, McKinley/Bryan	25	12	20
1900, McKinley/Bryan	25	12	20
1904, Roosevelt/Parker	22	14	18

	NY	CH	W
1906, Taft/Bryan	$ 19	$ 11	$ 15
1912, Wilson/Roosevelt/Taft	25	12	20
1916, Wilson/Hughes	19	11	15
1920, Harding/Cox	14	8	11
1924, Coolidge/Davis	10	6	8
1926, Hoover/Smith	10	6	8
1932, Roosevelt/Hoover	25	22	25
1936, Roosevelt/Landon	14	10	11
1940, Roosevelt/Wilkie	14	10	11
1944, Roosevelt/Dewey	14	10	11
1946, Truman/Dewey	14	10	11
1946, "Dewey Defeats Truman"	—	500	—
1952, Eisenhower/Stevenson	10	6	8
1956, Eisenhower/Stevenson	7	4	6
1960, Kennedy/Nixon	25	16	20
1964, Johnson/Goldwater	7	4	6
1968, Nixon/Humphrey	7	4	6
1972, Nixon/McGovern	7	4	6
1976, Carter/Ford	6	3	4
1980, Reagan/Carter	3	2	3
1984, Reagan/Mondale	2	2	2
1988, Bush/Dukakias	1	1	1
1992, Clinton/Bush	1	1	1

Deaths of Celebrities

	NY	CH	W
Jack Benny	$ 6	$ 4	$ 4
Charlie Chaplin	10	6	8
Winston Churchill	14	9	11
Calvin Coolidge	9	6	7
Charles de Gaulle	6	4	5
Edward VII	9	6	7
Adolph Eichmann (Executed)	19	11	15
Dwight D. Eisenhower	7	5	6
Judy Garland	40	27	33
Warren Harding	10	6	8
Adolph Hitler (unconfirmed)	50	40	40
Herbert Hoover	7	4	6
Lyndon Johnson	6	3	4
Nikita Khrushchev	7	4	6
John Lennon	3	2	3
Ethel Merman, *New York Times*	3	2	3
Marilyn Monroe	50	35	40
Elvis Presley	40	35	35
Queen Victoria	40	35	35
Franklin D. Roosevelt	40	27	33
Theodore Roosevelt	19	11	15
William H. Taft	8	6	7
Harry Truman	7	4	6
John Wayne	2	1	2
Woodrow Wilson	14	10	11

	NY	CH	W

News Events

	NY	CH	W
Astronauts Killed in Fire	8	$ 7	7
Atomic Bomb Dropped on Hiroshima	90	70	80
Battle of Little Big Horn	350	280	300
Billy The Kid Slain by Pat Garrett (Note: This was not treated as "front page" news by most newspapers. The lengthier and more prominent the coverage, the more valuable.	120	150	130
Bonnie and Clyde Shot	90	80	85
John Wilkes Booth Slain	100	75	90
Aaron Burr Slays Alexander Hamilton in Duel	$ 260	—	$ 230
Chicago Fire	200	900	200
Coolidge Sworn in After Harding's Death	40	35	40
Coronation of Elizabeth II	13	9	11
D-Day	52	40	46
John Dillinger Shot	60	60	60
Germany Surrenders (World War II)	40	35	35
John Glenn Orbits Earth	20	15	20
Bruno Hauptmann Executed	130	100	100
Hindenberg Explodes	130	100	100
Jesse James Killed	200	170	170
Japan Surrenders	35	30	35
John F. Kennedy Inaugurated	21	20	25
Charles Lindbergh Baby Kidnapped	35	35	35
Charles Lindbergh Crosses Atlantic	150	100	100
Marilyn Monroe Marries Joe Di Maggio	40	30	35
Moon Landing (first, 1969)	25	25	25
Richard Nixon Resigns	21	15	18
Lee Harvey Oswald Slain by Jack Ruby	30	20	23
Pearl Harbor Attacked	50	40	45
Prince Charles/Princess Diana's Marriage	3	2	3
Russian Sputnik Launched	40	30	38
1929 Stock Market Crash	130	100	110
Titanic Sinks	200	150	180
Triangle Shirtwaist Factory Fire	10	6	8
Truman Relieves Gen. MacArthur of Command	30	20	27

Whitman TV Books

Whitman has published books and produced puzzles and games for over fifty years. Their product line includes Little Golden Books and various juvenile series. In the 1950s they started producing books based on TV shows. There are four series of these books under the names of *Authorized TV Adventure, Authorized Edition, Authorized TV Edition*, and *Walt Disney's Authorized Edition*. These designations usually appear on the spine. Unlike earlier Whitman books there are no dust jackets. Instead, they feature-action packed illustrated covers bonded to the boards, covered with a shiny thin plastic finish. Covers feature heroes of classic television shows. Other series appeared in the same style but the TV themes drew the most interest. These books appeal to series collectors and TV memorabilia enthusiasts. When shelved with their covers showing, they form a chronicle of early TV shows. Later covers lacked the protective coating, giving a more muted effect. The same book might appear under different series.

Prices quoted below are for *near mint* to *mint* examples. That means no peeling or lifting of the transparent coating, no broken binders, no torn or crayon scrawled pages. For further reading see the *Yellowback Library*, Yellowback Press, P.O. Box 36172, Des Moines, IA, 50315.

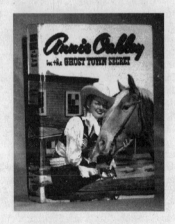

Clockwise from above left: Circus Boy, War on Wheels, 1958, #1578, $12-$18; Annie Oakley, Ghost Town Secret, 1957, #1538, $18-$22; The Rifleman, 1959, #1569, $18-$22.

	LOW	HIGH
Annette, Mystery at Moonstone Bay, 1962, 1537	$ 8	$ 12
Annette, Mystery at Smugglers Cove, 1963, 1574	12	14
Annie Oakley, Danger at Diabolo, 1955, 1549	18	22
Annie Oakley, Double Trouble, 1958, 1538	18	22
Bat Masterson, 1960, 1550	12	15
Beverly Hillbillies, 1963, 1572	10	14
Circus Boy, Under the Big Top, 1957, 1549	12	18
Dale Evans, Danger in Crooked Canyon, 1959, 1506	18	22
Dr. Kildare, Assigned to Trouble, 1963, 1547	5	7
Dr. Kildare, The Magic Key, 1964, 1519	5	7
Dragnet, 1957, 1527	18	22
F Troop, The Great Indian Uprising, 1966, 1544	8	10
Family Affair, Buffy Finds a Star, 1970, 1567	18	22
Flipper, Mystery of the Black Schooner, 1966, 2324	10	12
Fury, Mystery at Trapper's Hole, 1959, 1557	10	15
Garrison's Gorillas, Fear Formula, 1968, 1548	10	15
Gene Autry, Arapaho War Drums, 1957, 1512	18	22
Green Hornet, Disappearing Dr., 1966, 1570	20	30
Gunsmoke, 1958, 1587	18	22
Gunsmoke, Showdown on Front Street, 1969, 1520	6	8
Have Gun Will Travel, 1959, 1568	18	22
Hawaii Five - O, Top Secret, 1969, 1511	6	8
I Spy, Message From Moscow, 1966, 1542	10	14
Invaders, Dam of Death, 1967, 1545	10	15
Land of the Giants, Flight of Fear, 1969, 1516	8	10
Lassie, Forbidden Valley, 1959, 1508	10	14
Lassie, Lost in the Snow, 1969, 1504	6	8
Lassie, Treasure Hunter, 1960, 1552	12	15
Leave It to Beaver, 1962, 1526	18	22
Lucy, The Madcap Mystery, 1963, 1505	15	20
Man From U.N.C.L.E., Gentle Saboteur, 1966, 1541	8	10
Maverick, 1959, 1566	14	18
Mission Impossible, Money Explosion, 1970, 1512	7	10
Mod Squad, The Hideout, 1970, 1517	8	12
Monkees, Who's Got the Button?, 1968, 1539	18	22
Munsters, The Last Resort, 1966, 1567	20	30
Munsters, The Great Camera Caper, 1965, 1510	20	30
Patty Duke, Mystery Mansion, 1964, 1514	10	15
Rat Patrol, Iron Monster Raid, 1968, 1547	10	15
Restless Gun, 1959, 1559	14	18
Rin Tin Tin, Ghost Wagon Train, 1958, 1579	14	18
Ripcord, 1962, 1522	12	15
Roy Rogers, King of the Cowboys, 1956, 1503	15	20
Roy Rogers, Enchanted Canyon, 1954, 1502	18	22
Sea Hunt, 1960, 1541	12	15
Spin & Marty, Trouble At the Triple R, 1958, 1577	10	15
Voyage to the Bottom of the Sea, 1965, 1517	10	12
Wagon Train, 1959, 1567	18	22
Wells Fargo, Danger Station, 1958, 1588	9	12
Wyatt Earp, 1956, 1548	18	22
Zorro, 1958, 1586	18	22

Left to right: Annette, Mystery at Smugglers Cove, 1963, #1574, $12-$14; Mod Squad, The Hideout, 1970, #1517, $8-$12.

Coins

Coins are one of the world's oldest collectibles. Ancient coins from the Roman Empire can still be purchased for $10 or less, but fine examples are worth thousands.

The following ratings are from the American Numismatic Association grading system. For more detailed descriptions, see the _Official A.N.A Grading Standards for United States Coins_, Western Publishing Co., Racine, WI.

Proof—refers to method of manufacture, distinguished by sharpness of detail and usually with brilliant mirror surface. Proof coins are in perfect mint state.

Uncirculated (MS-60)—No trace of wear but may show some contact marks; surface may be spotted or lack some luster.

About Uncirculated (AU-50)—Traces of light wear on many of the high points. At least half of mint luster is still present.

Extremely Fine (EF-40)—Design is lightly worn throughout, but all features are sharp and well-defined. Traces of luster may show.

Very Fine (VF-20)—Shows wear on high points of design. All major details are clear.

Fine (F-12)— Moderate even wear, entire design is bold with pleasing appearance.

Very Good (VG-8)—Well worn; main features clear and bold but rather flat.

Good (G-4)—Heavily worn, design visible but faint in areas. Many details flat.

About Good (AG-3)—Very heavily worn with parts of lettering and date worn smooth.

For further information see _The Handbook of United States Coins_ by R.S. Yeoman for wholesale and auction (selling) values, and _A Guide Book of United States Coins_ by R.S. Yeoman for retail (buying) values.

Half Cents
Liberty Cap Type

	AG-3	G-4	VG-8	F-12	VF-20	EF-40
1794-97	$ 80.00	$ 200.00	$ 325.00	$ 550.00	$ 1000.00	$ 2000.00

Draped Bust Type 1800-08

	AG-3	G-4	VG-8	F-12	VF-20	EF-40
1800	$ 25.00	$ 45.00	$ 60.00	$ 90.00	$ 250.00	—
1803-08	20.00	30.00	40.00	80.00	200.00	—

Classic Head Type 1809-36

	G-4	VG-8	F-12	VF-20	EF-40
1825-35	$ 25.00	$ 35.00	$ 60.00	$ 80.00	$ 300.00

Coronet Type 1840-57

	G-4	VG-8	F-12	VF-20	EF-40
1849-57	$ 35.00	$ 45.00	$ 55.00	$ 75.00	$ 200.00

Large Cents 1796-1807
Draped Bust Type

	G-4	VG-8	F-12	VF-20	EF-40	MS-60
1796-1807	$ 15.00	$ 25.00	$ 45.00	$ 75.00	$ 250.00	$ 650.00

Classic Head Type 1808-14

	G-4	VG-8	F-12	VF-20	EF-40	MS-60
1808-14	$ 15.00	$ 35.00	$ 60.00	$ 100.00	$ 275.00	$ 800.00

Coronet Type 1816-57

	G-4	VG-8	F-12	VF-20	EF-40	MS-60
1816-57	$ 10.00	$ 12.00	$ 18.00	$ 25.00	$ 60.00	$ 250.00

Small Cents
Flying Eagle Type 1856-58

	G-4	VG-8	F-12	VF-20	EF-40	MS-60
1856 ..,.......	$ 2750.00	$ 3000.00	$ 3500.00	$ 3900.00	$ 4250.00	$ 5000.00
1857-58	14.00	15.00	20.00	34.00	75.00	250.00

 Indian Head Type 1859-1909

	G-4	VG-8	F-12	VF-20	EF-40	MS-60
1860-64	$ 5.00	$ 7.00	$ 15.00	$ 22.00	$ 28.00	$ 100.00
1865	5.00	6.00	8.00	17.00	30.00	60.00.00
1866-72	25.00	30.00	45.00	70.00	100.00	200.00
1873-76	12.00	15.00	22.00	35.00	60.00	125.00.00
1877	250.00	300.00	500.00	750.00	1000.00	2000.00
1878	16.00	25.00	30.00	50.00	75.00	150.00
1879	4.00	5.00	7.00	12.00	25.00	60.00
1880-84	2.50	3.00	4.00	7.00	15.00	42.00
1885	4.00	5.00	9.50	15.00`	28.00	65.00
1886-1908	1.25	1.50	2.25	3.75	10.00	32.00

 Lincoln Type (Wheat sheaves) 1909-58

	G-4	VG-8	F-12	VF-20	EF-40	MS-60
1909 v.d.b.	$ 2.00	$ 2.50	$ 3.00	$ 4.00	$ 10.00	$ 100.00
1909S v.d.b.	300.00	350.00	400.00	450.00	475.00	650.00
1909	.50	.60	.75	1.00	2.00	16.00
1916-39	.20	.30	.40	.50	1.00	2.00
1940-42	.15	.20	.30	.40	.75	1.50
1943 (steel)	.20	.25	.40	.75	2.00	4.00
1944-58	.10	.15	.20	.30	.40	2.00

	G-4	VG-8	F-12	VF-20	EF-40	MS-60
Exceptions						
1913S	6.00	7.00	8.00	12.00	25.00	100.00
1914D	80.00	90.00	110.00	175.00	400.00	750.00
1914S	9.00	10.00	12.00	20.00	35.00	165.00
1915S	7.00	8.00	9.00	12.00	25.00	100.00
1922D	5.00	6.00	7.00	10.00	19.00	80.00
1922 (plain)	165.00	240.00	3000.00	500.00	1900.00	4500.00
1924D	10.00	11.00	13.00	20.00	50.00	225.00
1926S	2.00	3.00	4.00	5.00	11.00	100.00
1931D	2.00	2.50	3.50	4.50	7.50	50.00
1931S	32	35.00	37.00	40.00	45.00	65.00
1932	1.50	1.75	2.00	2.50	3.00	—
1932D	.70	.90	1.20	1.75	2.50	15.00
1933	.75	.90	1.25	1.50	2.75	16.00
1933D	1.75	2.00	2.25	3.00	4.00	20.00
1944D (stamped over S)		—	140.00	170.00	750.00	
1955 (double die)—		—	400.00	500.00	1500.00	

Two-Cent Pieces 1864-73

	G-4	VG-8	F-12	VF-20	EF-40	MS-60
1864 (sm. motto)	$ 50.00	$ 65.00	$ 85.00	$ 150.00	$ 225.00	$ 550.00
1864-71	6.00	10.00	15.00	22.00	32.00	85.00
1872	75.00	100.00	150.00	250.00	325.00	750.00

 ### Silver Three-Cent Pieces 1851-73

	G-4	VG-8	F-12	VF-20	EF-40	MS-60
1851-62	$ 12.00	$ 15.00	$ 20.00	$ 30.00	$ 50.00	$ 150.00

Nickel Three Cent Pieces 1865-89

	G-4	VG-8	F-12	VF-20	EF-40	MS-60
1865-74	$ 6.50	$ 7.50	$ 9.00	$ 11.00	$ 18.00	$ 80.00
1875-76	9.00	11.00	14.00	17.00	30.00	160.00
1879-80	50.00	75.00	77.00	80.00	100.00	260.00
1881	6.00	7.00	9.00	12.00	18.00	90.00
1882	65.00	70.00	75.00	85.00	110.00	260.00
1883-87	100.00	150.00	185.00	250.00	350.00	600.00
1888-89	40.00	50.00	60.00	80.00	100.00	260.00

Nickel Five-Cent Pieces
Shield Type 1866-83

	G-4	VG-8	F-12	VF-20	EF-40	MS-60
1866	$ 14.00	$ 16.00	$ 23.00	$ 50.00	$ 90.00	$ 200.00
1867-76	8.00	10.00	11.00	18.00	30.00	100.00
1879-80	250.00	300.00	400.00	450.00	500.00	700.00
1881	150.00	175.00	200.00	260.00	350.00	500.00
1882-83	8.00	10.00	11.00	18.00	30.00	100.00

Liberty Head Type 1883-1913

	G-4	VG-8	F-12	VF-20	EF-40	MS-60
1883-84	$ 7.00	$ 9.00	$ 13.00	$ 22.00	$ 40.00	$ 115.00
1885	180.00	250.00	350.00	450.00	700.00	850.00
1886	50.00	70.00	125.00	175.00	250.00	450.00
1887-96	4.00	5.00	14.00	17.00	32.00	100.00
1897-1912	1.00	1.50	4.00	6.00	20.00	75.00
1912D	1.50	2.00	5.00	10.00	45.00	175.00
1912S	35.00	45.00	65.00	225.00	400.00	600.00
1913 (five known)—	—	—	—	—	—	950,000.00

Buffalo Type 1913-38

	G-4	VG-8	F-12	VF-20	EF-40	MS-60
1914D	$ 25.00	$ 35.00	$ 50.00	$ 70.00	$ 120.00	$ 250.00
1914	5.00	6.00	7.00	9.00	16.00	50.00
1915	2.50	3.00	5.00	7.00	13.00	50.00
1915D	6.00	8.00	17.00	35.00	50.00	200.00
1915S	12.00	16.00	30.00	65.00	125.00	500.00
1916	1.00	1.25	1.75	3.00	7.00	50.00
1916 (double die)	1500.00	3000.00	4000.00	6000.00	8000.00	20,000.00
1921S	15.00	25.00	50.00	300.00	600.00	1200.00
1923-30	.75	1.00	1.50	2.00	6.00	40.00
1923S-26S	.75	.85	1.00	2.00	5.00	40.00
1931S	3.00	4.00	6.00	7.00	10.00	50.00
1934-38	.75	.85	1.00	1.25	2.50	25.00
1937D (3 legs) ..	110.00	175.00	250.00	275.00	400.00	2000.00

Jefferson Type 1938-to date

	G-4	VG-8	F-12	VF-20	EF-40	MS-60
1938-42	$ .05	$ .10	$ .15	$ .20	$ .40	$ 3.00
1939D	.05	4.00	5.00	6.00	9.00	40.00
1939S	.05	.70	.90	1.25	2.50	30.00
1942-45 (silver)	.05	.30	.45	.50	1.00	6.00
1946-52	.05	.10	.15	.20	.40	1.00

Half Dimes
Flowing Hair Type 1794-95

	AG-3	G-4	VG-8	F-12	VF-20	EF-40
1794-95	$ 300.00	$ 600.00	$ 800.00	$ 1000.00	$ 1500.00	$ 2500.00

Draped Bust Type, Small Eagle

	AG-3	G-4	VG-8	F-12	VF-20	EF-40
1796-97	$ 350.00	$ 700.00	$ 800.00	$ 1000.00	$ 2000.00	$ 3000.00

Draped Bust Type, Heraldic Eagle 1800-05

	AG-3	G-4	VG-8	F-12	VF-20	EF-40
1800-05	$ 200.00	$ 500.00	$ 600.00	$ 800.00	$ 1400.00	$ 2000.00
1802	4000.00	8000.00	12,000.00	20,000.00	30,000.00	50,000.00

Capped Bust Type

	G-4	VG-8	F-12	VF-20	EF-40	MS-60
1829-37	$ 13.00	$ 17.00	$ 25.00	$ 50.00	$ 100.00	$ 300.00
1837 (small 5c)	20.00	30.00	40.00	90.00	175.00	2000.00

 Seated Liberty Type 1837-73

	G-4	VG-8	F-12	VF-20	EF-40	MS-60
1837	$ 25.00	$ 35.00	$ 50.00	$ 100.00	$ 225.00	$ 600.00
1838O (no stars)	65.00	100.00	200.00	350.00	550.00	2500.00
1838-73	6.00	8.00	10.00	20.00	50.00	200.00
1844O	60.00	100.00	200.00	350.00	900.00	—
1846	160.00	225.00	350.00	600.00	1200.00	—
1849O	25.00	40.00	75.00	250.00	500.00	—
1852O	20.00	35.00	60.00	150.00	300.00	—
1863	120.00	175.00	225.00	300.00	400.00	750.00
1864	200.00	300.00	350.00	450.00	600.00	1200.00
1864S	25.00	35.00	60.00	100.00	300.00	750.00
1865	200.00	250.00	300.00	350.00	500.00	900.00
1866	125.00	200.00	275.00	350.00	450.00	800.00
1867	250.00	350.00	450.00	550.00	750.00	1250.00
1868	30.00	45.00	70.00	100.00	200.00	400.00

Dimes
Draped Bust Type, Small Eagle

	AG-3	G-4	VG-8	F-12	VF-20	EF-40
1796-97	$ 400.00	$ 900.00	$ 1200.00	$ 1700.00	$ 2500.00	$ 4000.00

Draped Bust Type, Herald Eagle

	AG-3	G-4	VG-8	F-12	VF-20	EF-40
1798-1807	$ 250.00	$ 450.00	$ 650.00	$ 750.00	$ 1200.00	$ 1800.00
1804	450.00	1000.00	1500.00	2500.00	3500.00	7000.00

Capped Bust Type 1809-37

	G-4	VG-8	F-12	VF-20	EF-40	MS-60
1809	$ 85.00	$ 140.00	$ 275.00	$ 450.00	$ 800.00	$ 4000.00
1814	25.00	30.00	50.00	150.00	350.00	1500.00
1820-27	15.00	20.00	35.00	90.00	300.00	900.00
1822	250.00	450.00	750.00	1200.00	2000.00	7000.00
1829-37	12.00	15.00	20.00	50.00	175.00	600.00

Seated Liberty Type 1837-91

	G-4	VG-8	F-12	VF-20	EF-40	MS-60
1837	$ 25.00	$ 40.00	$ 65.00	$ 220.00	$ 450.00	$ 1000.00
1838O	30.00	50.00	90.00	275.00	500.00	2400.00
1838-40	6.00	8.00	12.00	25.00	60.00	350.00
1841-52	5.00	8.00	11.00	20.00	45.00	300.00
1841O	7.00	10.00	15.00	35.00	65.00	1000.00
1843O	35.00	70.00	100.00	200.00	550.00	—
1844	30.00	65.00	90.00	200.00	500.00	2000.00
1845O	15.00	25.00	50.00	200.00	500.00	—
1846	75.00	100.00	140.00	300.00	750.00	—
1849O	10.00	20.00	30.00	100.00	300.00	—
1851O	10.00	15.00	25.00	70.00	170.00	1500.00
1853-73	6.00	7.00	8.00	16.00	40.00	300.00
1875-91	5.00	6.00	7.00	12.00	25.00	175.00
1856S	65.00	100.00	150.00	300.00	600.00	—
1858S	60.00	90.00	125.00	250.00	450.00	—
1859S	65.00	100.00	150.00	300.00	650.00	2500.00
1860O	300.00	500.00	700.00	1200.00	2500.00	—
1861S	25.00	40.00	55.00	125.00	250.00	1200.00
1863	175.00	250.00	350.00	450.00	550.00	1100.00
1863S	20.00	30.00	45.00	75.00	200.00	900.00
1864	160.00	225.00	325.00	450.00	500.00	1000.00
1865	175.00	250.00	350.00	450.00	600.00	1200.00
1866	175.00	250.00	350.00	500.00	650.00	1200.00
1867	250.00	400.00	500.00	650.00	850.00	1500.00
1868S	12.00	17.00	25.00	60.00	150.00	350.00
1870S	150.00	200.00	250.00	350.00	500.00	1500.00
1871CC	500.00	700.00	900.00	1500.00	2500.00	—
1872CC	250.00	400.00	650.00	1200.00	2500.00	—
1873CC	500.00	800.00	1200.00	2000.00	3500.00	—
1873S	15.00	22.00	30.00	60.00	140.00	900.00
1874CC	1200.00	2000.00	3000.00	3500.00	7000.00	—
1878CC	35.00	50.00	80.00	125.00	250.00	700.00
1879	125.00	180.00	225.00	275.00	400.00	700.00
1880	80.00	120.00	160.00	200.00	350.00	500.00
1881	100.00	175.00	190.00	250.00	350.00	550.00
1884S	12.00	18.00	24.00	45.00	65.00	450.00
1885S	250.00	400.00	500.00	750.00	1000.00	3500.00
1886S	20.00	30.00	40.00	60.00	100.00	600.00
1889S	10.00	15.00	20.00	40.00	75.00	400.00

Barber or Liberty Head Type 1892-1916

	G-4	VG-8	F-12	VF-20	EF-40	MS-60
1892	$ 2.50	$ 5.00	$ 10.00	$ 12.00	$ 25.00	$ 125.00
1892O	6.00	9.00	16.00	20.00	30.00	175.00
1892S	25.00	45.00	100.00	125.00	150.00	3550.00
1893O	15.00	20.00	50.00	75.00	100.00	250.00
1893S	7.00	12.00	20.00	30.00	50.00	225.00
1894	8.00	14.00	50.00	80.00	100.00	250.00
1894O	30.00	50.00	125.00	175.00	300.00	1000.00
1894S	—	—	—	—	—	275,000.00
1895	60.00	80.00	200.00	300.00	350.00	600.00
1895O	175.00	300.00	600.00	900.00	1400.00	2500.00
1895S	20.00	35.00	75.00	100.00	120.00	350.00
1896O	42.00	65.00	175.00	200.00	300.00	600.00
1896S	40.00	60.00	150.00	200.00	300.00	600.00
1897-1916	1.50	2.00	4.00	7.00	20.00	100.00
1897O	30.00	50.00	150.00	200.00	300.00	650.00
1897S	8.00	15.00	50.00	75.00	100.00	300.00
1900O	5.00	15.00	50.00	75.00	150.00	500.00
1901S	30.00	50.00	175.00	275.00	350.00	700.00
1902S	3.00	7.00	25.00	40.00	100.00	300.00
1903S	15.00	20.00	50.00	90.00	200.00	375.00
1904S	10.00	14.00	20.00	36.00	65.00	300.00
1909D	3.00	10.00	35.00	60.00	90.00	350.00
1909S	4.00	10.00	40.00	60.00	125.00	400.00
1913S	8.00	15.00	50.00	90.00	175.00	425.00

 Mercury Type 1916-45

	G-4	VG-8	F-12	VF-20	EF-40	MS-60
1916-31	1.50	2.00	3.50	4.50	7.00	50.00
1916D	300.00	500.00	900.00	1500.00	2500.00	4000.00
1921	20.00	40.00	70.00	150.00	350.00	1000.00
1921D	30.00	50.00	90.00	175.00	400.00	1200.00
1925D	3.00	4.00	10.00	30.00	100.00	450.00
1926S	5.00	7.00	15.00	35.00	200.00	1200.00
1927D	3.00	4.00	5.00	15.00	40.00	350.00
1928D	3.00	5.00	7.00	15.00	40.00	300.00
1930S	2.50	3.00	5.00	6.00	15.00	75.00
1931D	4.00	6.00	10.00	20.00	30.00	75.00
1931S	3.00	4.00	5.00	7.00	15.00	50.00
1934-45	.15	.25	.50	.75	1.25	8.00

Roosevelt Type 1946-to date

	G-4	VG-8	F-12	VF-20	EF-40	MS-60
1946-64	$ .10	$ .12	$ .20	$ .25	$ .50	$ 3.00

Twenty-Cent Pieces 1875-78

	G-4	VG-8	F-12	VF-20	EF-40	MS-60
1875-76	$ 50.00	$ 60.00	$ 80.00	$ 110.00	$ 200.00	$ 600.00
1877-78	—	—	—	—	—	(very rare)

Quarter Dollars
Draped Bust, Small Eagle

	AG-3	G-4	VG-8	F-12	VF-20	EF-40
1796	$ 1500.00	$ 3000.00	$ 5000.00	$ 7500.00	$ 10,000.00	$ 15,000.00

Draped Bust, Herald Eagle 1804-07

	AG-3	G-4	VG-8	F-12	VF-20	EF-40
1804	$ 500.00	$ 800.00	$ 1100.00	$ 2200.00	$ 4000.00	$ 7000.00
1805-07	100.00	200.00	300.00	450.00	850.00	2000.00

Capped Bust Type 1815-38

	AG-3	G-4	VG-8	F-12	VF-20	EF-40
1815-28	$ 25.00	$ 45.00	$ 65.00	$ 95.00	$ 250.00	$ 600.00
1831-38 (sm.) ...	15.00	35.00	40.00	50.00	100.00	200.00

Seated Liberty Type 1838-91

	G-4	VG-8	F-12	VF-20	EF-40	MS-60
1838-42	$ 10.00	$ 15.00	$ 25.00	$ 60.00	$ 200.00	$ 1000.00
1843-47	12.00	16.00	20.00	35.00	75.00	600.00
1843O	15.00	25.00	40.00	70.00	200.00	1000.00
1848-53	20.00	35.00	55.00	75.00	150.00	1000.00
1851O	150.00	250.00	400.00	650.00	1000.00	2000.00
1852O	175.00	250.00	400.00	600.00	1200.00	3500.00
1854-55	8.00	11.00	20.00	30.00	90.00	500.00
1855O	35.00	50.00	100.00	200.00	350.00	2000.00
1855S	35.00	50.00	75.00	150.00	275.00	1500.00
1856-65	8.00	10.00	20.00	27.00	55.00	300.00
1856S	30.00	45.00	75.00	150.00	350.00	1400.00
1857S	50.00	80.00	150.00	300.00	500.00	2000.00
1858S	40.00	60.00	100.00	200.00	400.00	—
1859S	75.00	115.00	175.00	275.00	700.00	—
1859O	15.00	25.00	40.00	75.00	100.00	1000.00
1860S	100.00	150.00	300.00	550.00	1500.00	5000.00
1861S	50.00	75.00	150.00	250.00	450.00	2500.00
1862S	40.00	60.00	100.00	250.00	400.00	2000.00
1864S	150.00	250.00	400.00	750.00	1500.00	—
1864	45.00	65.00	90.00	125.00	250.00	900.00

	G-4	VG-8	F-12	VF-20	EF-40	MS-60
1865S	65.00	90.00	130.00	275.00	500.00	2500.00
1867-69	100.00	150.00	200.00	300.00	500.00	2000.00
1866	200.00	250.00	350.00	450.00	650.00	2000.00
1870-73	20.00	30.00	50.00	80.00	150.00	850.00
1870CC	1200.00	2000.00	4000.00	6000.00	8000.00	—
1872CC	300.00	450.00	800.00	1500.00	3000.00	7500.00
1872S	250.00	400.00	650.00	1000.00	2000.00	5000.00
1873-74	12.00	16.00	30.00	60.00	200.00	850.00
1873CC	800.00	1200.00	2000.00	3500.00	6500.00	15,000.00
1875-91	8.00	10.00	20.00	25.00	50.00	300.00
1875CC	50.00	75.00	120.00	200.00	400.00	1500.00
1878S	60.00	120.00	175.00	250.00	400.00	1500.00
1879-88	100.00	115.00	150.00	180.00	250.00	650.00

Barber or Liberty Head Type 1892-1916

	G-4	VG-8	F-12	VF-20	EF-40	MS-60
1892	3.50	5.00	15.00	25.00	50.00	200.00
1892O	4.00	8.00	18.00	32.00	65.00	250.00
1892S	15.00	25.00	40.00	60.00	120.00	400.00
1893-96	4.00	6.00	18.00	35.00	70.00	300.00
1896O	5.00	10.00	45.00	150.00	300.00	750.00
1896S	150.00	250.00	500.00	850.00	1200.00	3000.00
1897-1916	3.00	4.00	15.00	25.00	60.00	200.00
1899S	8.00	15.00	20.00	35.00	75.00	300.00
1901O	15.00	30.00	60.00	140.00	300.00	700.00
1901S	1000.00	2000.00	3000.00	4500.00	6000.00	10,000.00
1909O	8.00	15.00	40.00	100.00	200.00	600.00
1913	10.00	20.00	50.00	150.00	400.00	1000.00
1913S	300.00	500.00	1000.00	2000.00	3000.00	4500.00

Standing Liberty Type 1916-30

	G-4	VG-8	F-12	VF-20	EF-40	MS-60
1917-24	$ 12.00	$ 15.00	$ 18.00	$ 30.00	$ 40.00	$ 200.00
1916	800.00	1200.00	1600.00	2000.00	2500.00	5000.00
1918D	20.00	25.00	35.00	50.00	80.00	450.00
1919D	40.00	70.00	100.00	150.00	250.00	800.00

	G-4	VG-8	F-12	VF-20	EF-40	MS-60
1919S	40.00	60.00	100.00	150.00	300.00	1000.00
1921	50.00	80.00	120.00	175.00	250.00	700.00
1923S	100.00	140.00	180.00	250.00	350.00	750.00
1925-30	3.00	4.00	7.00	15.00	30.00	200.00
1927S	10.00	20.00	50.00	150.00	1000.00	5000.00

 Washington Type 1932-to date

	G-4	VG-8	F-12	VF-20	EF-40	MS-63
1932	$ 1.00	$ 3.00	$ 4.00	$ 6.00	$ 8.00	$ 30.00
1932D	20.00	35.00	45.00	60.00	125.00	800.00
1932S	20.00	30.00	35.00	45.00	65.00	450.00
1934-38	1.00	1.50	2.00	5.00	10.00	50.00
1936D	2.00	5.00	7.00	14.00	35.00	300.00
1937S	1.00	2.50	5.00	10.00	17.00	100.00
1939S	1.00	2.00	4.00	6.00	10.00	60.00
1940D	1.00	2.00	4.00	6.00	12.00	65.00
1941-46	.50	.75	1.00	1.50	1.75	5.00
1947-55	.50	.75	1.00	1.50	1.75	2.00
1949	.50	.75	1.00	1.50	1.75	10.00
1956-64	.25	.25	.50	1.50	1.75	2.00

Half Dollars
Flowing Hair Type 1794-95

	AG-3	G-4	VG-8	F-12	VF-20	EF-40
1794	$ 500.00	$ 900.00	$ 1500.00	$ 2500.00	$ 4000.00	$ 8000.00
1795	250.00	400.00	500.00	800.00	1750.00	4000.00

Draped Bust, Small Eagle

	AG-3	G-4	VG-8	F-12	VF-20	EF-40
1796-97	$ 7000.00	$ 9000.00	$ 12,000.00	$ 15,000.00	$ 22,000.00	$ 35,000.00

Draped Bust, Heraldic Eagle 1801-07

	AG-3	G-4	VG-8	F-12	VF-20	EF-40
1801-02	$ 100.00	$ 200.00	$ 300.00	$ 500.00	$ 900.00	$ 1800.00
1803-07	45.00	100.00	125.00	200.00	350.00	600.00

Capped Bust Type 1807-36

	G-4	VG-8	F-12	VF-20	EF-40	MS-60
1807-08	$ 40.00	$ 85.00	$ 150.00	$ 300.00	$ 750.00	$ 1500.00
1809-36	30.00	45.00	85.00	175.00	400.00	100.00
1836 "50 CENTS"	600.00	750.00	1000.00	1200.00	2000.00	7000.00
1837-38	30.00	40.00	50.00	75.00	200.00	900.00
1838O	—	—	—	—	—	50,000.00
1839O	120.00	160.00	250.00	400.00	650.00	3000.00

Seated Liberty Type 1839-91

	G-4	VG-8	F-12	VF-20	EF-40	MS-60
1839-65	$ 15.00	$ 20.00	$ 35.00	$ 45.00	$ 75.00	$ 450.00
1866-78	13.00	18.00	30.00	40.00	60.00	450.00
1842O (sm. date)	500.00	750.00	1000.00	2000.00	4000.00	—
1848	30.00	40.00	60.00	90.00	150.00	850.00
1850	75.00	100.00	150.00	250.00	450.00	1200.00
1851	75.00	120.00	175.00	300.00	500.00	1500.00
1852	100.00	150.00	250.00	400.00	700.00	1600.00
1852O	40.00	60.00	100.00	150.00	300.00	1000.00
1855S	300.00	400.00	700.00	1200.00	3000.00	—
1857S	25.00	35.00	45.00	100.00	300.00	1300.00
1858S	20.00	25.00	35.00	65.00	140.00	850.00
1862	22.00	30.00	40.00	70.00	100.00	650.00
1870CC	450.00	750.00	1500.00	2500.00	4000.00	—
1871CC	100.00	150.00	250.00	400.00	900.00	4000.00
1872CC	50.00	80.00	150.00	275.00	500.00	2500.00
1873CC	75.00	125.00	200.00	350.00	800.00	4000.00
1874CC	150.00	250.00	400.00	700.00	1200.00	5000.00
1874S	30.00	40.00	60.00	150.00	300.00	1300.00
1878CC	200.00	300.00	450.00	750.00	1500.00	4500.00
1878S	5000.00	6500.00	9000.00	13,000.00	18,000.00	30,000.00
1879-90	110.00	140.00	180.00	240.00	350.00	750.00
1891	20.00	30.00	40.00	60.00	100.00	500.00

Barber or Liberty Head Type 1892-1915

	G-4	VG-8	F-12	VF-20	EF-40	MS-60
1892	$ 13.00	$ 25.00	$ 40.00	$ 75.00	$ 200.00	$ 400.00
1892O	75.00	120.00	170.00	250.00	400.00	800.00
1893S	50.00	75.00	120.00	250.00	350.00	900.00
1893-96	6.00	12.00	40.00	70.00	180.00	450.00
1897-1915	5.00	8.00	25.00	50.00	150.00	400.00
1896S	50.00	75.00	100.00	200.00	350.00	1000.00
1897O	50.00	80.00	200.00	400.00	700.00	1400.00
1897S	70.00	100.00	200.00	350.00	550.00	100.00
1898O	15.00	25.00	70.00	150.00	300.00	650.00
1901S	12.00	20.00	75.00	175.00	450.00	1300.00
1901O	7.00	15.00	40.00	100.00	300.00	1100.00
1904S	10.00	20.00	80.00	200.00	400.00	1200.00
1904O	10.00	15.00	50.00	100.00	300.00	1000.00
1913	15.00	25.00	60.00	175.00	300.00	800.00
1914	18.00	35.00	150.00	275.00	450.00	700.00
1915	16.00	25.00	75.00	200.00	350.00	900.00

Liberty Walking Type 1916-47

	G-4	VG-8	F-12	VF-20	EF-40	MS-60
1916	$ 20.00	$ 30.00	$ 50.00	$ 100.00	$ 150.00	$ 250.00
1916D	12.00	17.00	30.00	65.00	120.00	250.00
1916S	40.00	50.00	100.00	250.00	450.00	800.00
1917-18	5.00	8.00	12.00	25.00	35.00	120.00
1919	12.00	17.00	35.00	120.00	375.00	850.00
1919D	10.00	13.00	30.00	120.00	450.00	2000.00
1919S	10.00	12.00	25.00	100.00	500.00	1700.00
1920-33	6.00	7.00	11.00	20.00	70.00	500.00
1921	50.00	75.00	160.00	450.00	1200.00	2500.00
1921D	65.00	100.00	200.00	550.00	1500.00	2200.00
1921S	15.00	20.00	50.00	400.00	3000.00	7000.00
1934-47	2.50	3.50	3.75	4.00	7.00	25.00
1934S	3.00	3.50	4.50	6.00	25.00	200.00
1938D	15.00	20.00	25.00	50.00	100.00	400.00
1941S	2.50	3.50	3.75	4.00	7.00	85.00

Franklin Type 1948-63

	VG-8	F-12	VF-20	EF-40	MS-60
1948	$ .75	$ 1.00	$ 3.00	$ 5.00	$ 18.00
1948D	.50	.75	2.50	4.50	11.00
1949	.50	.75	2.50	4.50	35.00
1950	.75	1.00	3.00	4.00	35.00
1951	.50	.75	2.50	3.50	11.00
1951D	.50	.75	2.50	3.50	30.00
1951S	.50	.75	2.50	3.50	30.00
1952-63	.50	.60	2.25	3.00	5.00
1952S	.50	.75	2.50	3.50	30.00
1953	.50	.75	3.00	6.00	24.00
1953S	.50	.60	2.50	4.00	12.00

Silver Dollars
Flowing Hair Type 1794-95

	AG-3	G-4	VG-8	F-12	VF-20	EF-40
1794	$ 3500.00	$ 8000.00	$ 11,000.00	$ 17,000.00	$ 25,000.00	$ 42,000.00
1795	400.00	700.00	900.00	1200.00	2000.00	4000.00

Draped Bust, Small Eagle

	AG-3	G-4	VG-8	F-12	VF-20	EF-40
1794-98	$ 300.00	$ 600.00	$ 800.00	$ 1000.00	$ 2000.00	$ 3500.00

Draped Bust, Heraldic Eagle

	G-4	VG-8	F-12	VF-20	EF-40	MS-60
1798-1804	$ 300.00	$ 350.00	$ 450.00	$ 700.00	$ 1300.00	$ 8000.00

Seated Liberty Type 1840-73

	VG-8	F-12	VF-20	EF-40	MS-60
1840-73	—	$ 200.00	$ 300.00	$ 350.00	$ 500.00	$ 2000.00
1846O	—	200.00	250.00	325.00	650.00	4000.00
1850	—	400.00	550.00	800.00	1200.00	4500.00
1851	—	3000.00	7000.00	8000.00	10,000.00	14,000.00
1852	—	1500.00	7000.00	8000.00	10,000.00	17,000.00
1858	—	2500.00	3500.00	5000.00	5500.00	—
1870CC	—	325.00	450.00	650.00	1000.00	4500.00
1870S	—	—	50,000.00	70,000.00	90,000.00	—
1871CC	—	2200.00	3500.00	4500.00	7500.00	20,000.00
1872CC	—	1000.00	1500.00	2500.00	3500.00	15,000.00
1872S	—	300.00	400.00	600.00	900.00	7000.00
1873CC	—	3000.00	4500.00	7500.00	12000.00	27000.00

Trade Dollars 1873-85

	VG-8	F-12	VF-20	EF-40	MS-60
1873-78	$ 65.00	$ 85.00	$ 110.00	$ 150.00	$ 500.00
1879-83 (proof only)	—	—	—	—	1200.00
1884-85 (proof only)	—	—	—	—	very rare

Liberty Head or Morgan Type 1878-1921

	F-12	VF-20	EF-40	AU-50
1878-1921	$ 10.00	$ 12.00	$ 17.00	$ 20.00
1879CC	70.00	200.00	500.00	1200.00

	F-12	VF-20	EF-40	AU-50
1880CC	55.00	80.00	110.00	150.00
1880O	9.00	12.00	22.00	45.00
1881CC	100.00	120.00	130.00	160.00
1882CC	30.00	45.00	50.00	65.00
1883CC	30.00	45.00	55.00	65.00
1883S	13.00	20.00	90.00	350.00
1884S	15.00	35.00	250.00	4000.00
1886O	13.00	18.00	45.00	220.00
1886S	20.00	35.00	50.00	120.00
1889CC	300.00	650.00	2500.00	6500.00
1889S	20.00	30.00	45.00	90.00
1890CC	30.00	45.00	75.00	200.00
1892CC	50.00	80.00	170.00	300.00
1892S	40.00	125.00	1750.00	9000.00
1893	50.00	70.00	140.00	300.00
1893CC	115.00	400.00	700.00	1000.00
1893O	85.00	170.00	350.00	1000.00
1893S	1200.00	2700.00	10,000.00	23,000.00
1894	225.00	350.00	500.00	800.00
1894O	20.00	35.00	125.00	550.00
1895O	100.00	200.00	800.00	8000.00
1895S	175.00	350.00	600.00	1000.00
1896O	12.00	16.00	100.00	650.00
1897O	13.00	17.00	75.00	500.00
1901	25.00	40.00	200.00	1200.00
1903S	55.00	200.00	700.00	2000.00
1904S	35.00	125.00	450.00	850.00

Peace Type 1921-35

	VF-20	EF-40	AU-50	MS-60
1921	$ 30.00	$ 40.00	$ 70.00	$ 140.00
1922-35	8.00	10.00	12.00	25.00
1924S	14.00	20.00	45.00	130.00
1925S	11.00	15.00	25.00	50.00
1926D	10.00	13.00	27.00	45.00
1927	16.00	22.00	35.00	60.00
1927D	14.00	20.00	55.00	120.00
1927S	13.00	18.00	50.00	85.00
1928	100.00	120.00	140.00	175.00

	VF-20	EF-40	AU-50	MS-60
1928S	15.00	18.00	40.00	65.00
1934D	15.00	18.00	40.00	80.00
1934S	40.00	150.00	400.00	1000.00
1935S	12.00	16.00	60.00	100.00

Gold Half Eagle
Classic Head Type

	VG-8	F-12	VF-20	EF-40	AU-50
1834-38	$ 225.00	$ 300.00	$ 500.00	$ 850.00	$ 3000.00

Coronet Type

	F-12	VF-20	EF-40	AU-50
1839-66	$ 400.00	$ 1000.00	$ 2000.00	$ 6000.00
1873	170.00	225.00	500.00	1800.00
1867-77	500.00	1300.00	4000.00	7000.00
1878-1908	130.00	150.00	175.00	200.00

Indian Head Type

	F-12	VF-20	EF-40	AU-50
1908-29 (most)	$ 200.00	$ 225.00	$ 250.00	$ 325.00

Civil War Tokens

	VG-8	F-12	VF-20	EF-40
Copper or Brass	$ 6.00	$ 7.00	$ 9.00	$ 25.00
Nickel or German Silver	22.00	35.00	45.00	75.00
White Metal	27.00	40.00	55.00	85.00
Copper Nickel	35.00	50.00	65.00	100.00
Silver	100.00	150.00	200.00	400.00

Furniture

Antique Furniture

Antique furniture is a tricky field. The collector needs to be a connoisseur of proportions and alterations. Before the middle of the 19th century, cabinetmakers (not carpenters) made furniture by hand. Each piece was unique. The skill of the craftsman and the success of his design are important factors in evaluating furniture. To learn about the proportions and the aesthetics of American Antique furniture, see *The Fine Points of Furniture* by Albert Sack.

Alterations can reduce the value of a piece by over 75%. No collector will sweat over a piece of chipped veneer, but a replaced leg, no matter how skillfully executed, will kill the value of a piece. Also remember that American furniture of the 18th century is more valuable than an otherwise identical English piece.

Abbreviations used in this section: Q.A.-Queen Anne, c. 1720-60, *Chip.*-Chippendale, c. 1750-90, *W. & M.*-William and Mary, c. 1690-1740, *Fed.* -Federal, c. 1780-1820, *Eng.*-English, *Amer.*-American, *Min.*-Miniature, *Mah.* -Mahogany, *CT* -Connecticut, *MA* -Massachusetts, *N.E.*-New England, *PA* -Pennsylvania, *NH*-New Hampshire, *Hpwt.*-Hepplewhite. Note that "Style" implies a reproduction made at a later date.

A Goddard-Townsend three shell knee hole dressing table is the dream of many collectors. This one sold for $125,000 at auction. Knee hole desks from the Goddard-Townsend workshop have sold for over half a million dollars. — Photo courtesy of Northeast Auctions.

	AUCTION	RETAIL	
		Low	High
Apothecary Chest, Early Amer., blue ptd., w. 30"	$ 1600	3200	5600
Armchair, Child's, N.E., black ptd. ladderback, turned legs, ball ft.	600	1200	2100
Armchair, China-Trade, bamboo	200	400	700
Armchair, Country, Q.A.	400	800	1400
Armchair, CT, ladderback, mushroom holds, orig. paint	2300	4600	8000
Armchair, Fed. Style, Martha Washington	500	1000	1750
Armchair, N.E., Pilgrim Century, ladderback, old brown paint	600	1200	2100
Armchair, Pilgrim Century, red ptd., mushroom holds	800	1600	2800
Bed, Cannonball, figured-maple, w. 53"	900	1800	3250
Bed, Cannonball, N.E., red ptd., ht. 46", len. 55"	200	400	700
Bed, Canopy, N.E., Sheraton, birch, w/ arched top, ht. 86", w. 57", len. 78"	4000	8000	14,000
Bed, Hired Man's, old green paint, len. 77", w. 49"	650	1300	2000
Bed, Tall-Post, Amer. tiger maple, w/ acorn finials, ht. 68", w. 55"	950	1900	3000
Bible Box, Pilgrim Century, pine, lunette carving, ptd. crest, w. 27"	4250	8500	14,000
Blanket Box, N.E., ptd. and decorated, w. 43"	4250	8500	14,000
Blanket Box, PA, grain ptd., w. 42"	1200	2400	4200
Blanket Chest, N.E., grain ptd., 2 dr., molded to simulate 4-dr., w. 37"	2000	4000	7000
Blanket Chest, N.E., Pilgrim Century, pine, w. 48"	425	850	1400
Blanket Chest, N.E., Pilgrim Century, w/ bootjack ends, orig. finish, w. 57"	1500	3000	5000
Blanket Chest, PA, eagle-decorated, ht. 30", w. 52"	1000	2000	3500
Bowfront Cabinet on Chest, NH, Fed., inlaid mah., w. 42"	2500	5000	8750
Bowfront Chest, CT, inlaid mah., w/ elaborate figured maple ogee ft., quarter columns, branded "P. Moor" w. 43"	2750	5500	9000
Breakfast Table, cherry drop-leaf, w/ shaped apron, cabriole legs, pad ft., w. 36"	7500	15,000	26,000
Breakfast Table, Eng., mah., Q.A., w/ notched corners, 1 leaf, cabriole legs, pad ft., w. 34"	500	1000	1750
Breakfast Table, N.E., tiger maple, drop-leaf, shaped apron, cabriole legs on pad ft., w. 34"	3100	6000	10,000
Breakfast Table, NY, Classical-Revival, w. 40"	1000	2000	3500
Breakfront, Eng., Sheraton mah., Gothic design, ht. 90", w. 85"	4400	8000	15,000
Bull's-Eye Mirror, Fed. Gilt, w/ applied acorns, dia. 18"	1000	2000	3500
Butler's Tray, Eng., mah., folding, on new stand, w. 29"	600	1200	2100
Butler's Tray, Eng., mah., folding, on new stand, w. 28"	500	1000	1700
Butterfly Table, W. & M., splay leg, vase and ring turnings, w. 39"	2300	4600	8000
Candlestand, Chip., mah., tilting dish top, vase-turned column, cabriole legs, snake ft., dia. 20", ht. 30"	450	900	1575
Candlestand, Chip. Style, mah., dish top, dia. 20", ht. 29"	600	1200	2100
Candlestand, CT, cherry tray top, sq. top, urn-turned standard, cabriole legs on pad ft., w. 17"	1600	3200	5600
Candlestand, CT, cherry tripod, sq. top, w/ backgammon, w. 15"	850	1700	3000
Candlestand, CT, cherry tripod, sq. molded top, notch carved urn standard, cabriole legs and snake ft., w. 15"	2300	4600	8000
Candlestand, CT, River Valley, cherry, sq. top above urn-turned standard on cabriole legs w/ pad ft., w. 16"	550	1100	1925
Candlestand, mah., tilting dish top, dia. 20"	350	700	1225

*Federal candlestand, c. 1800,
$1600 at auction. — Photo
courtesy of Northeast Auctions.*

	AUCTION	RETAIL Low	High
Candlestand, MA, Hpwt., mah., tilt top, w/ cut corner rect. top and spade ft., w. 22"	$ 950	$ 1900	$ 3325
Candlestand, N.E., cherry, porringer top, cabriole legs, w. 15"	600	1200	2100
Candlestand, N.E., cherry, serpentine top, w. 14"	500	1000	1750
Candlestand, N.E., Chip., cherry, oval, w. 22"	400	800	1400
Candlestand, N.E., round, urn-turned column, tripod base w/ cabriole legs on snake ft., dia. 16"	500	1000	1750
Candlestand, N.E., Fed., carved maple, flame-birch inlay, tilting serpentine top, and spider legs, w. 18"	3000	6000	10,000
Candlestand, N.E., Fed., mah., tilt top, spider legs, spade ft., w. 22"	37,000	74,000	130,000
Candlestand, N.E., Hpwt, cherry tilt top, diamond form top w/ banded edge, spider legs w/ spade ft., 17" sq	700	1400	2500
Candlestand, NH, birch, oval, orig. Spanish brown paint, elaborate turned standard w/ cabriole legs on pad ft., w. 20"	1500	3000	5250
Candlestand, NH, Fed., birch, tilt top, inlaid diamond, spider-legs, w. 20"	800	1600	2800
Candlestand, NH, Fed., mah., oval, w. 24"	400	800	1400
Candlestand, NH, Q.A., stained birch elongated cabriole legs, w. 17", ht. 26.5"	4500	9000	15,750
Candlestand, North Shore, MA, mah., tilt top, serpentine-form top, ball and claw ft., w. 20"	2750	5500	9500
Candlestand, Philadelphia, Chip., wal., tilting dish top, tripod cabriole legs, ht. 25", dia. 23"	3000	6000	10,000
Candlestand, simple, tripod	175	350	600
Candlestand, turned X base, black paint, ht. 25"	300	600	1000
Candlestand, Winchester, NH	200	400	700
Canopy Bed, N.E., Sheraton, maple, w. 50"	1400	2800	5000
Card Table, Bowfront, Portsmouth, Sheraton, inlaid mah., w. 38"	3250	6500	11,000
Card Table, Demi-Lune, MA, Hpwt., inlaid mah. taper legs, w. 36"	2100	4200	7250
Card Table, Demi-Lune, Rhode Island, Fed., inlaid mah., sq. fluted legs, w. 36"	4250	8500	14,000

	AUCTION	RETAIL	
		Low	High
Card Table, Eng. Hpwt., inlaid mah., D-form, w. 36"	$ 540	$ 1000	$ 2000
Card Table, Block-Front, mah., w/ 1 dr., cabriole legs, ball and claw ft., w. 34"	1700	3400	6000
Card Table, MA, Sheraton, inlaid mah., Seymour School, w/ bird's-eye maple panels, w. 38"	4000	8000	14,000
Card Table, Serpentine, N.E., Sheraton, inlaid mah., reeded legs, w. 37"	3000	6000	10,000
Carver Armchair, N.E., old surface	4200	8400	14,700
Carver Chair, Pilgrim-Century, MA, maple and oak	6750	13,500	23,000
Center Table, Boston Classical Revival, mah., w/ faceted standard and lotus-leaf plinth, dia. 36"	800	1600	2800
Chest, Amer., Chip., 4 dr., cherry, ogee bracket ft., w. 42"	2000	4000	7000
Chest, Amer., maple and cherry, w/ split-spindle columns, w. 40"	300	600	1050
Chest, CT, Chip., cherry, w/ elaborate scrolled ogee ft., w. 40"	5250	10,000	18,000
Chest, Eng., W. & M. wal., ball ft., w. 38"	1500	3000	5250
Chest, Fed., 4 dr., inlaid wal., bracket ft., w. 41"	700	1400	2450
Chest, N.E., Chip., 4 dr., cherry, molded top, bracket ft., w. 38"	1500	3000	5250
Chest, N.E., Chip., bracket ft., w. 36"	1900	3800	6650
Chest, N.E., Country Q.A., maple, 6 dr., w. 33.5"	2750	5500	9625
Chest, N.E., Hpwt., 4 dr., birch, w/ French ft., w, 39"	2200	4400	7700
Chest, NH, Chip., 6 dr., birch, w. 37"	2700	5400	9450
Chest, NY, Empire, mah., case w/ carved pineapple, acanthus-leaf columns, paw ft., ht. 52", w. 47"	700	1400	2450
Chest, W. & M., paint decorated, 4 dr., w/ applied geometric moldings and ball ft., w. 36"	3700	7400	12,000
Chest-on-Chest, Eng., Chip., mah., ogee bracket ft., ht. 70"	5500	11,000	19,000
Chest-on-Chest, Eng., Hpwt., mah., w/ French ft., ht. 75", w. 45"	2000	4000	7000
Chest on Frame, N.E., maple, cabriole legs, pad ft., ht. 62", w. 36"	4500	9000	15,750
Child's Banister-Back Armchair, N.E., black ptd., yoked crest, rush seat, ht. 23"	400	800	1400
Child's Blanket Box, PA, turnip ft in old finish, w. 27"	950	1900	3325
Child's Country Sideboard, w/ 7 drs. and cupboard, w. 19"	300	600	1000
Child's Table	150	300	525
Chinese 6-Fold Screen, depicting imperial hunt scene, ht. 60"	1750	3500	6000
Chinese carved Rosewood Stand, ht. 51"	450	900	1575
Coffee Table, inlaid w/ Scagliola marble still life, w. 55"	1800	3600	6300
Commode, French, Louis XV Style, carved fruitwood serpentine 2-dr., w. 38"	2900	5800	10,000
Convex Mirror, Fed. Gilt, w/ eagle and candlearms, ht. 48"	1200	2400	4200
Corner Chair, Chip., maple, w/ vase-turned stiles and sq. seat	450	900	1575
Corner Chair, Eng., Chip., mah., w/ pierced splats and sq. legs	900	1800	3000
Corner Cupboard, pine, w/ raised panel door, white enamel, ht. 60"	110	220	385
Corner Washstand, NY, Sheraton, mah., w/ shaped splash back, medial shelf w/ 1 dr., ht. 42"	1000	2000	3500
Courting Mirror, eglomisé panels in elaborate frame w/ whale's-tail crest, ht. 25"	2900	5800	10,000
Cradle, Amer. Pilgrim-Century, pine, w/ orig. red paint	450	900	1575
Credenza, Italian, carved wal., 1 dr. over cupboard door, ht. 35", w. 31"	1100	2200	3850
Cupboard, Scandinavian, green ptd. w/ raised panel doors, dated 1844, ht. 76", w. 58"	2000	4000	7000

Tiger maple greatly increases the value of a piece. — Photo courtesy of Northeast Auctions.

	AUCTION	RETAIL Low	High
Davenport, carved India Trade Sea Captain's, w. 22"	$ 1750	$ 3500	$ 6000
Deacon's Bench, Amer., black ptd., arrowback, gilt, w. 75"	600	1200	2100
Diminutive N.E., Hpwt., cherry 1-dr. Stand, w. 14"	1600	3200	5600
Dining Chairs, 8, Chip. Style, mah., 2 armchairs, sq. molded legs	2000	4000	7000
Dining Chairs, set of 10, Q.A. Style, balloon seats, 2 armchairs	4750	9500	16,000
Dining Chairs, set of 12, carved mah., 2 armchairs	3000	6000	10,000
Dining Chairs, set of 8, Chip. Style, mah., ball & claw ft., 2 arms	1000	2000	3500
Dining Chairs, set of 8, NY, carved mah., Classical Revival, splats Prince of Wales carving	7000	14,000	24,500
Dining Table, Eng. mah., 4-pedestal, d. 54", w. 132"	7000	14,000	24,500
Dining Table, Eng. Q.A., mah., 6-leg drop-leaf, w. 40"	600	1200	2100
Dining Table, Eng. Q.A., mah., 8-leg drop-leaf, ht. 29", w. 56"	1000	2000	3500
Dining Table, Hpwt., mah., 3-part, w/ bowed ends, sq. taper legs, ht. 29", w. 142"	3200	6400	11,000
Dining Table, Irish Q.A., mah., drop-leaf, turned legs pad ft., w. 43"	500	1000	1750
Dining Table, N.E., Country Q.A., maple, drop-leaf, pad ft., w. 47"	1600	3200	5600
Dining Table, N.E., Hpwt., mah., drop-leaf, w. 46"	500	1000	1750
Dining Table, Philadelphia, Sheraton, mah., 2-part, D-form, w/ reeded legs, w. 42" (80" extended)	5750	11,500	20,000
Drop-Leaf Table, N.E., Pilgrim Century, maple, vase turnings, w. 32"	950	1900	3000
Drop-Leaf Table, CT, maple, gate-leg, vase-turned legs, w. 44"	1700	3400	5950
Drop-Leaf Table, PA, Q.A., cherry, cabriole legs, stocking-pad ft., w. 45"	550	1100	1925
Drop-Leaf Table, Rhode Island, Q.A., tiger maple legs, w. 48"	3000	6000	10,000
Etagere, Amer., wal., spool-turned 5-shelf w/ dr., ht. 59"	1400	2800	4900
Etagere, Sheraton, mah., 4-shelf, ht. 61"	3000	6000	10,000
Fancy Side Chair, tiger maple, Sheraton	200	400	700
Farm Table, French, shaped apron w/ 3 drs., ht. 29", w. 77"	1200	2400	4200

	AUCTION	RETAIL	
		Low	High
Footstool, George II Style, needlepoint uph., cabriole legs, w. 21"	$ 400	$ 800	$ 1400
Footstools, pr., Hpwt., mah., w/ sq. tapered legs, w. 13"	200	400	700
Fret Mirror, Chip., ht. 15"	225	450	800
Gate-leg Table, N.E., maple, vase-turned legs, w. 41"	1800	3600	6300
Great Chair, Pilgrim Century, ladderback w/ elongated finials and flat armrests, MA Bay Colony	1600	3200	5600
Handkerchief Table, Eng., Q.A., mah., w/ pad ft., w. 34"	950	1900	3000
Hanging Cupboard, Continental wal., w/ 3 raised panels, centering long door, ht. 29"	650	1300	2200
Hanging Cupboard, Early Amer. grain ptd., ht. 27"	1200	2400	4200
Hanging Glazed Door Cupboard w/ "H" hinges in old red finish, ht. 19", w. 22"	700	1400	2450
Highboy, bonnet-top, Amer. maple, cabriole legs on pad ft., ht. 82"	5250	10,000	18,000
Highboy Base, Salem, Q.A., maple, fan-carved, w. 38"	1400	2800	5000
Highboy, N.E., maple, fan-carved, cabriole legs, ht. 78", w. 40"	4300	8600	15,000
Highboy, N.E., tiger maple, fluted quarter columns, ht. 72", w. 36"	3500	7000	12,000
Highboy, N.E., wal., fan carved bonnet top, ht. 84"	6000	12,000	21,000
Highboy, N.E., wal., cabriole legs on pad ft., ht. 69", w. 37"	3100	6200	10,000
Huntboard, Country, southern pine and pierced tin, ht. 46", w. 47"	1100	2200	3750
Incense Burner, Chinese bronze, decorated w/ scholar and laborers, finial monkey form, ht. 23"	1200	2400	4200
Joint Stool, Eng., Jacobean, carved oak w/ splayed legs, w. 19"	1400	2800	4900
Joint Stool, MA, Pilgrim Century, splay leg, w/ vase and ring turnings, old brown paint, w. 25"	1600	3200	5500
Joint Stool, oak w/ molded top and splayed legs, w. 18"	1000	2000	3500
Knife Box, Hpwt., inlaid mah., ht. 15"	500	1000	1750
Knife Urns, pr., Eng. Regency, carved mah., w/ berry finials, reeding, animal-form masques, ht. 28"	5000	10,000	17,500
Ladderback Side Chair	30	60	100
Lap Desk, exotic oriental wood, w. 15"	150	300	525
Lap Desk, mother-of-pearl inlaid rosewood	125	250	400
Liquor Chest, Dutch, urn-inlaid mah., fitted gilt bottles, w. 10"	1100	2200	3850
Lolling Chair, Amer., inlaid wal	1100	2200	3850
Lolling Chair, MA, Hpwt., mah., barrel-back, attrib. to Lemuel Churchill	4500	9000	15,000
Lolling Chair, North Shore, Fed., mah., school of Joseph Short	2000	4000	7000
Lowboy, Delaware River Valley, Chip., carved wal., elaborate shell-carved dr.	16,250	32,500	56,000
Lowboy, N.E., Q.A., wal., w/ concave carving above shaped apron cabriole legs w/ pad ft., w. 30"	5250	10,000	18,000
Mantel, Vermont, Classical, ptd. and carved pine, ht. 47", w. 65"	850	1700	3000
Miniature Chest, 3-dr., Eng., Hpwt., inlaid mah., ht. 11"	450	900	1575
Miniature Courting Mirror, eglomisé panels, in orig. box, ht. 9"	1800	3600	6300
Miniature Pole Screen, w/ needlework, ht. 17"	125	250	430
Miniature Rocking Tub Chair, Amer. Victorian, carved rosewood, crest elaborately carved, ht. 23"	3900	7800	13,000
Miniature Scrolled-Arm Sofa, Amer. Empire, bolsters, w. 34"	2000	4000	7000
Miniature Sideboard, George IV, carved mah., w. 13"	2200	4400	7700
Miniature Side Chair, wal., Amer. Victorian, ht. 16"	550	1100	1900
Mirror, Adam, giltwood, w/ flower-filled urn, foliate- and swag-			

Left to right: Chippendale mahogany giltwood mirror with carved phoenix, ht. 40"; Chippendale mahogany pier mirror with line inlay and gilt slip, ht. 50"; Chippendale mahogany giltwood mirror with carved shell, ht. 41". — Photos courtesy of Northeast Auctions.

	AUCTION	RETAIL Low	High
decorated crest, ht. 50"	$ 2100	$ 4200	$ 7250
Mirror, Chip., mah., w/ gilt phoenix crest, ht. 51"	3500	7000	12,000
Mirror, Chip., mah., w/ gilt phoenix crest, ht. 48"	1750	3500	6000
Mirror, Chip., wal., w/ pierced and gilt shell, ht. 38"	900	1800	3150
Mirror, Continental Rococo, carved and ptd., ht. 35"	2200	4400	7700
Mirror, Constitution, c. 1920, gilt, ht. 20"	100	200	350
Mirror, N.E., Chip., mah., w/ pierced eagle and carved slip, ht. 36"	650	1300	2275
Mirror, Q.A., w/ 2-part glass and pinwheel carvings, ht. 17"	950	1900	3000
Mirror, Q.A., wal., pierced & gilt shell, 2-part plate, ht. 42"	6600	13,000	23,000
Mirror, Q.A., wal., gilt shell, carved 2-part, ht. 42"	3250	6500	11,000
Mirror, Q.A., wal., w/ 2-part plate, ht. 48"	1800	3600	6300
Mirror, Q.A., wal., w/ gilt shell, ht. 29"	500	1000	1750
Mirror, Q.A., wal., w/ ptd. shell and 2-part plate, ht. 40"	2100	4200	7350
Mirror, Q.A., wal., w/ shaped crest, ht. 25"	700	1400	2450
Mirror, Regency, green and parcel-gilt, carved, drapery, ht. 47"	300	600	1050
Mirror, Venetian Rococo, carved and pierced, yellow ptd. and decorated, ht. 31"	800	1600	2800
Mirror, overmantel, w/ paneled eglomisé border; w/ gilt floral and bamboo molding, ht. 36", w. 48"	100	200	350
Oxbow Slant-Lid Desk, MA, Chip., carved mah., claw ft., w. 42"	4000	8000	14000
Oxbow Slant-Lid Desk, MA, Chip., mah., w. 42"	6250	12,000	21,000
Pembroke Table, Fed., mah., turned, leaf-carved legs, w. 36"	2200	4400	7000
Pembroke Table, Hpwt., cherry, w/ X-stretchers, w. 35"	500	1000	1750
Pembroke Table, Hpwt., inlaid mah., w. 33"	1900	3800	6000

Once considered categorically ugly, the market for quality American Empire pieces has sprung to life within the past 10 years. — Photos courtesy of Northeast Auctions.

	AUCTION	RETAIL Low	High
Pembroke Table, NY, Hpwt., inlaid mah., w/ bellflowers, w. 31".	$ 2800	$ 5600	$ 10,000
Pembroke Table, Rhode Island, Hpwt., mah., w/ bowed ends and 1 dr., taper legs, w. 32"	1400	2800	5000
Pianoforte, Amer. Classical-Revival, ormolu-mounted and stenciled, w. 66"	500	1000	1750
Pier Mirror, Adam gilt, crest w/ urn and griffins, ht. 83", w. 40"	1500	3000	5250
Pier Mirror, Classical, gilt, w/ eglomisé panel of castle, ht. 49"	1700	3400	6000
Pier Mirror, Continental, Neo-Classical, fruitwood, ht. 46"	300	600	1000
Pier Mirror, Fed. giltwood, elaborate crest w/ trophies, ht. 66"	3800	7600	13,000
Pier Mirror, Empire gilt, carved acanthus-leaf spandrels, ht. 60"	700	1400	2450
Pier Table, Amer., ormolu-mtd. carved mah., parcel-gilt, w. 43"	2500	5000	8750
Pole Screen, Fed., inlaid mah., w/ candle shelf, ht. 60"	2000	4000	7000
Roll-top Desk, Victorian, wal., w. 48", w/ swivel desk chair	700	1400	2450
Sawbuck Table, circular, red paint, dia. 22"	400	800	1400
Sawbuck Table, Early Amer., red ptd., ht. 24", L. 34", w. 21"	450	900	1575
Sconce Mirror, Q.A., 2-plate, floral cutting, 1 candlearm, ht. 17"	200	400	700
Secretary Bookcase, Continental, 2-part, w/ arched cupboard doors above slant lid desk over 3 long drs., ht. 84", w. 45"	900	1800	3150
Serpentine Chest, N.E., Fed., mah., attrib. to L. Boardman, Portsmouth, NH, w. 40"	7000	14,000	24,500
Settee, Continental, Biedermeier, fruitwood, w. 60"	600	1200	2100
Settee, Eng. Q.A. Style, double back, needlepoint uph., w. 50"	1500	3000	5250
Sewing Table, NY, Sheraton, mah., Martha Washington, w. 25"	1500	3000	5250
Shaving Mirror, N.E., Fed., mah., 2-dr., w. 17"	250	500	875
Shaving Mirror, NY, Fed., inlaid mah., Bowfront, ht. 22", w. 18"	600	1200	2100
Shelf Clock, MA, inlaid mah., kidney-form dial decorated w/ eagle motif, ht. 32"	1000	2000	3500
Side Chair, banister back, N.E., W. & M.	300	600	1000
Side Chair, Boston, W. & M., carved and turned maple w/ leather seat and back	1700	3400	6000
Side Chair, Country Chip.	175	350	610

Queen Anne side chairs - note the negative space formed between the edge of the splat and the outer vertical stile resembles a bird's head. The shape is far better formed than the similar space on the right hand chair. Although these chairs are otherwise nearly identical, the one on the left is worth twice as much as the one on the right. — Photos courtesy of Northeast Auctions.

	AUCTION	RETAIL Low	High
Side Chair, Country Q.A.	$ 250	$ 500	$ 875
Side Chair, Early Amer., plain	175	350	600
Side Chair, Eng., Q.A., wal., w/ shaped slip-seat, cabriole legs w/ C-scroll knees and pad ft.	350	700	1225
Side Chair, MA, Hpwt., carved mah., shield-back, attrib. to William Fiske	3500	7000	12,250
Side Chair, N.E., 4-Slat, sausage-turned	100	200	350
Side Chair, N.E., banister-back, w/ carved crest, in old Spanish brown	5250	10,000	18,000
Side Chair, N.E., Country Q.A., Spanish ft., in old graining	750	1500	2600
Side Chair, N.E., ladderback, w/ turned finials, in old red paint	100	200	350
Side Chair, N.E., Q.A., mah., oxbow crest w/ carved-shell and block-and-ring turned H-stretcher	5500	11,000	19,000
Side Chair, N.E., sausage-turned 4-slat ladder back, old black paint	300	600	1000
Side Chair, N.E., W. & M., banister back, w/ carved crest, bulbous stretcher	1100	2200	3800
Side Chair, NH, Country Q.A., w/ Spanish ft.	400	800	1400
Side Chair, pr., N.E., Country Chip., Maple	325	650	1100
Side Chair, Philadelphia, Hpwt., carved mah., sq. back w/ urn splat	500	1000	1750
Side Chair, Rhode Island, Country Chip.	250	500	875
Side Chair, Rhode Island, Country Chip., maple	175	350	600
Side Chair, Rhode Island, Q.A., maple, oxbow crest rail above vase splat, cabriole legs w/ pad ft., H-stretcher turned	2000	4000	7000

	AUCTION	RETAIL	
		Low	High
Side Chair, Salem, Hpwt., carved mah., attrib. to S. McIntire	$ 600	$ 1200	$ 2100
Side Chair, Salem, MA, Hpwt., carved mah., shield back, inlaid fan	1750	3500	6000
Side Chairs, Harlequin, set of 8, banister back	2000	4000	7000
Side Chairs, pr., Amer., Country Chip., cherry, w/ rush seats	500	1000	1750
Side Chairs, pr., CT, Chip., cherry w/ heart-pierced splats	2000	4000	7000
Side Chairs, pr., CT, Q.A., each w/ oxbow crest and vasiform splat, slip-seat, cabriole legs w/ pad ft.	3000	6000	9500
Side Chairs, pr., Eng. Q.A., wal., w/ shell-and-tassel-carved knees ...	1400	2800	4900
Side Chairs, pr., N.E., Chip., shell-carved cherry	1800	3600	6300
Side Chairs, pr., Amer., Hpwt., mah	850	1700	2975
Side Chairs, pr., Philadelphia, Fed. carved mah	2500	5000	8750
Side Chairs, pr., Philadelphia, Sheraton mah., Haines-Connelly school, sq. back and reeded legs	4250	8500	14,000
Side Chairs, set of 4, fancy ptd. and decorated Sheraton, rush seats	800	1600	2800
Side Chairs, set of 4, W.& M., cane back, w/ carved crest	1200	2400	4200
Side Chairs, set of 6, Eng., beech, caned, William Morris Style	500	1000	1750
Side Chairs, set of 6, Sheraton, fancy diamond splat rush seat	1000	2000	3500
Side Chairs, set of 6, tiger maple, saber leg, w/ cane seats	1500	3000	5250
Side Table, Continental, wal., stretcher base, w/ dr., w. 28"	1300	2600	4550
Sideboard, Amer., Sheraton, mah., bowfront, w. 61"	7250	14,500	25,000
Sideboard, Eng., Hpwt., inlaid mah., serpentine, ht. 37", w. 78"	900	1800	3150
Sideboard, Eng., Hpwt., mah., bowfront, ht. 36", L. 66"	1800	3600	6300
Sideboard, Eng., Hpwt. Style, mah., ht. 37", w. 57"	2750	5500	9625
Sideboard, Eng., inlaid mah., bowfront, w/ sq. taper legs, w. 70" ...	5500	11,000	19,000
Sideboard, Eng., inlaid mah., demi-lune, ht. 36", w. 84"	800	1600	2800
Slant-Lid Desk, mah., w/ carved fan, ball-and-claw ft., w. 31"	500	1000	1750
Slant-lid Desk, MA, Chip., wal., opening to stepped interior w/ 3 carved shells, w. 40"	6000	12,000	21,000
Slant-Lid Desk, N.E., Chip., cherry, w/ stepped interior and bracket base, w. 36"	900	1800	3150
Sofa, Amer. Classical Revival, carved mah., w. 78"	400	800	1400
Sofa, Amer. Classical Revival, mah., w/ scrolled crest and carved paw ft., w. 84"	700	1400	2450
Sofa, Chip., mah., Camelback, w/ Marlboro legs. L. 87"	3100	6000	10,000
Sofa, Chip. Style, mah., Camelback, w. 72"	350	700	1225
Sofa, French, Louis XVI Style, ptd., w. 84"	300	600	1000
Sofa, mah., Hpwt. Style, small, w. 60"	850	1700	2975
Sofa, NH, Sheraton, mah., w/ bird's-eye maple inlay, w. 74"	1400	2800	4900
Sofa, NY, Classical Revival, carved mah., paw ft., w. 92"	1300	2600	4550
Sofa, Salem, late Fed., mah., scroll arm, acanthus supports, w. 70" ..	825	1650	2800
Sofa, Sheraton, carved mah., w/ rect. back, turned legs, w. 84"	700	1400	2450
Stand, cherry, 1-dr.	250	500	875
Stand, cherry, 1-dr., turned legs	250	500	875
Stand, Early Amer., red ptd., Hpwt., 1-dr., splay legs, 17" sq	1500	3000	5250
Stand, N.E., Hpwt., mah., 1 dr. simulating 2, w. 16"	1900	3800	6650
Stand, N.E., paint decorated Hpwt., 1-dr., w. 21"	300	600	1050
Stand, N.E., Sheraton, 1-dr., old red finish, w. 19"	250	500	875
Stepback Cupboard, OH., cherry, 2-part, w/ arched and gothic panel doors, ht. 83", w. 48"	1500	3000	5250
Stepback Cupboard, PA, 2-part, turned ft., ht. 84", w. 57"	3500	7000	12,250

Three Chippendale mahogany Tilt top tea tables. Each with ball-and-claw feet, c. 1770. These tables brought (left to right) $700, $2700, and $1100 at auction. Note how the piecrust top of the center table more than doubled the value of the piece. — Photo courtesy of Northeast Auctions.

	AUCTION	RETAIL Low	High
Stool, Eng., 3-leg, w/ London label	$ 50	$ 100	$ 175
Stool, W. & M., turned wal., w. 19"	650	1300	2275
Stool, Windsor, splay leg, green paint	350	700	1225
Tall Chest, N.E., Chip., cherry, 6-dr., w. 36", ht. 56"	2000	4000	7000
Tall Chest, N.E., Chip., figured maple, bracket ft., w. 36"	1750	3500	6000
Tall-Case Clock, PA, Chip., mah., w/ swan's neck crest, brass dial engraved "Jos. Ellicott, Buckingham," ht. 93"	2750	5500	9000
Tall-Case Clock, NY, Fed., cherry, bonnet w/ star inlay, ht. 84"	2750	5500	9625
Tall Chest, N.E., maple 6-dr., w. 37"	1750	3500	6000
Tap Table, splay leg, old finish, w. 30"	200	400	700
Tavern Table, Amer., cherry, PA, apron w/ 1 dr., vase-turned legs, ht. 29", w. 51"	1500	3000	5250
Tavern Table, cherry, PA, apron w/ 1 dr. joining sq. legs, box stretchers, ht. 28", top 48" X 34"	1000	2000	3500
Tavern Table, Early Amer., cherry and pine, oval, turned legs w/ button ft., w. 33"	1100	2200	3850
Tavern Table, N.E., Pilgrim Century, w/ vase turnings, old scrubbed finish, w. 38"	1800	3600	6300
Tavern Table, N.E., turned w/ 7 stretchers, w. 37"	2600	5200	9100
Tavern Table, N.E., W. & M., w/ scrubbed top, turned legs, w. 31"	5000	10,000	17,500
Tea Caddy, Eng. Regency mah., sideboard-form, w. 17"	1100	2200	3850
Tea Table, Chip., carved mah., dish top, birdcage on fluted standard, cabriole legs w/ carved knees and ball-and-claw ft., dia. 34"	1100	2200	3850
Tea Table, Chip., carved mah., piecrust tilt top, cabriole legs w/ carved knees and ball-and-claw ft., ht. 28", dia. 34"	2700	5400	9450

	AUCTION	RETAIL	
		Low	High
Tea Table, N.E., Q.A., mah. and maple, rect. w/ checkerboard top, ht. 25", w. 27" .... $ 11,000	$11,000	$22,000	$38,000
Tea Table, Norwich, CT, cherry birdcage, dish top, cabriole legs w/ carved knees and ball-and-claw ft., dia. 48" 3000	3000	6000	10,000
Tea Table, PA, mah., dish top, columnar standard w/ suppressed ball turning on tripod base, dia. 31" 2000	2000	4000	7000
Tester Bed, Fed. Style, mah., w/ acanthus-carved posts, double 650	650	1300	2500
Tester Bed, Amer. Classical Revival, mah., front posts w/ barley twist turning and acanthus-leaf carving, ht. 87", w. 60" 1500	1500	3000	5500
Tester Bed, Amer., Classical Revival, mah., posts w/ pineapple-carved finials, ht. 86", w. 66" 2400	2400	4800	8400
Tilt-top Table, Chip., carved mah., dish top, cabriole legs w/ carved knees, ball-and-claw ft., dia. 31" 700	700	1400	2450
Trunk, China Trade, camphor wood, w. 36" 750	750	1500	2600
Tuck-Away Table, W. & M., vase and ring turnings, w. 38" 5750	5750	11,500	20,000
Washstand, N.E., Sheraton mah., w/ backsplash 400	400	800	1400
Weaver's Stool, blue ptd 75	75	150	300
Windsor Armchair, Sackback, vase turnings 800	800	1600	2800
Windsor, Birdcage Chair, N.E 150	150	300	525
Windsor Chairs, set of 7, Eng., elmwood, incl. 2 armchairs 700	700	1400	2450
Windsor, Comb-Back Armchair, PA, black paint 2000	2000	4000	7000
Windsor, CT, Continuous Arm, old green paint 2200	2200	4400	7700
Windsor, Fanback, pr., CT, w/ fanciful crest rails 2400	2400	4800	8400
Windsor, Fanback Armchair, N.E., vase-turned legs 700	700	1400	2450
Windsor, Sackback, Amer., knuckle-arm, old black paint 1600	1600	3200	5600
Windsor, Sackback Armchair, Early Amer., vase-turned legs 850	850	1700	3000
Windsor, Sackback, N.E., orig. black paint 5250	5250	10,500	18,000
Windsor Side Chairs, set of 6, floral-decorated step-down, bamboo turnings 3500	3500	7000	12250
Windsor, Step-Down, paint-decorated, branded 200	200	400	700
Wing Chair, Eng., Chip., mah., w/ sq. legs, H-stretcher 2000	2000	4000	7000
Wing Chair, Eng., Q.A., carved wal., cabriole legs w/ shell-carved knees and pad ft. 3750	3750	7500	13,125
Wing Chair, Hpwt., mah., sq. molded legs, H-stretcher 3400	3400	6800	12,000
Wing Chair, MA, Q.A., wal., w/ cabriole legs and pad ft., block-and-vase turned H-stretcher 1500	1500	3000	5250
Wing Chair, N.E., Chip., mah. sq. molded legs & H-stretcher 2000	2000	4000	7000
Wing Chair, N.E., Chip., maple, sq. legs w/ beaded edge, H-stretcher 1500	1500	3000	5250
Work Table, Amer. Country Hpwt. drop-leaf, 1 dr., w. 19" 550	550	1100	1925
Work Table, Boston, Classical-Revival, carved mah., 2-dr., w. 23" .. 3400	3400	6800	11,000
Work Table, CT Valley, Sheraton, cherry, 2 dr., w. 18" 1,100	1,100	2200	3750
Work Table, Country Sheraton blue ptd., w/ 1 dr., ring-turned legs, w. 36" 350	350	700	1225
Work Table, MA, Sheraton, mah. and bird's-eye maple, 2 dr., outset corners, "C. Briggs," w. 19" 4250	4250	8500	15,000
Work Table, N.E., Hpwt., mah., 2 dr. 500	500	1000	1750
Work Table, N.E., Hpwt., mah., 2 dr., w. 18" 900	900	1800	3150
Work Table, N.E., Sheraton, mah., 2 dr., turned legs, w. 18" 600	600	1200	2100
Work Table, NY, Classical Revival, carved mah., drop-leaf, 2-dr., paw ft., w. 18" 1400	1400	2800	4900
Work Table, N.E., Hpwt., mah., 2 dr., sq. taper legs, w. 16" 1000	1000	2000	3500

Mission Furniture

The name of Stickley dominates the field of Mission furniture. Those items produced by Gustav Stickley with the "Als ich kann" (As I can) label are generally the most valuable of the "commercial" makers. Unlike much Early American furniture, makers often labeled Mission pieces. Such labels increase value. However, Mission pieces designed by Frank Lloyd Wright, which command exceptional value, are not labeled as such. Original (usually dark) finish is an important point in valuing Mission furniture.

Dover Publications and Turn of the Century Editions have reprinted various catalogs of Mission furniture. For further information see also Bruce Johnson's *Arts and Crafts*, published by House of Collectibles, Random House, NY.

Items are listed under their maker. Prices are given for Refinished and Original Finish. Under each catagory are values for labled (L) and unmarked (UM) pieces. Gallery is abbreviated gal.

Mission furniture is simple and sparse, as this desk and clock. - photos courtesy of Northeast Auctions.

	REFINISHED		ORIG. FIN.	
	L	UM	L	UM
Gustav Stickley				
Armchair, 3 splats, orig. uph. seat, ht. 39.5", w. 24"	$ 400	$ 300	$ 500	$ 400
Armchair, 4 splats, leather seat, ht. 40", w. 24.5"	800	600	1200	1000
Armchair, peaked crest rail over 2 slats, ht. 36.5", w. 27" ...	400	300	500	400
Armchair, spindled high back, through tenons, ht. 48.5", w. 27.5"	6000	5000	10,000	7000
Armchair, V-back crest rail over 5 splats, exposed leg posts, ht. 37.5", w. 26"	500	400	600	450
Armchair, V-back rail over 5 splats, corbels for arms, through tenons, ht. 36", w. 24.5"	400	300	500	400
Armchair, high back, 20 spindles, corbels for arms, through tenons, ht. 49.5"	9000	7000	12,000	10,000
Armchair, spindled high back, spindles for each arm, through tenons, ht. 48.5", w. 27.5"	9000	7000	12,000	10,000
Armchair, high back, sq. cut-outs, continuous arms, box base, w/cut outs, ht. 42.75", w. 32"	5000	4000	7000	6000
Bed, double, maple, inverted V head & foot boards, arched apron, w. 54", len. 75"	4000	3000	6000	5000
Bed, single, inverted V-rail over 3 wide slats, canted				

	REFINISHED		ORIG. FIN.	
	L	UM	L	UM
legs, tapered tops, ht. 43", w. 39" 800		600	1200	1000
Bookcase, 1-door, 16 glass panes, gal. top, ht. 56", w. 36" 4000		3000	5000	4000
Bookcase, 1-door, 16 panes, through tenons, slab sides, gal. top, ht. 56" 3000		2000	3500	2500
Bookcase, 2-door, 8 panes/door, gal. top, ht. 56", w. 48" 4000		3000	5000	4000
Bookcase, 2-door, 12 panes/door, gal. top, ht. 56", w. 54" ..3000		2000	3500	2500
Bookcase, 2-door, 8 panes/door, gal. top, ht. 56", w. 35" 3000		2000	3500	2500
Bookcase, 2-door, 6 panes/door, through & key tenons, gal. top, ht. 44", w. 36" 3000		2000	3500	2500
Bookcase, 2-door, 8 panes/door, gal. top, ht. 55.5", w. 47" 3000		2000	3500	2500
Bookcase, 2-door, exposed tenons, 8 panes per door, gal. top, ht. 56", w. 43" 3000		2000	3500	2500
Bookcase, 2-door, keyed tenons, 6 panes per door, gal. top, ht. 44", w. 36" 3000		2000	3500	2500
Bookcase, open, 4 shelves, through tenons, gal. top, ht. 56", w. 36" 3000		2000	3500	2500
Cellaret, flip top, copper tray under, ht. 43", w. 24" 2000		1500	2500	2000
Chair, cube, wide splat on each side, caned seat 5000		4000	7000	6000
Chair, office, leather back & seat, flat arms, swivel base, orig. leather, w. 21" 2000		1500	2500	2000
Chair, office, revolving base, leather seat, ht. 35", w. 18" 800		600	1200	1000
Chair, office, 11 spindles, flat arms, pedestal base, ht. 40", w. 25.5" 5000		4000	7000	6000
Chair, rabbit ear, keyed-through tenons, black leather inset seat w/brass tacks 800		600	1200	1000
Chair, side, 3 splats, leather seat, 1 front & back rail, orig. leather, ht. 38", w. 17.5" 400		300	500	400
Chair, side, plank seat, 3 graduated slats, beveled top front leg posts, ht. 37.5", w. 18.5" 300		200	400	300
Chairs, 4, ladderback, each w/ 3 slats, leather seat w/ tacks, orig. leather, ht. 37.5" 2500		2000	3500	3000
Chairs, 4, side, each w/ 4 slats, arched lower rail, leather cushion seat, ht. 37" 2500		2000	3500	3000
Chest, 2 dr. over 4 dr., chamfered sides, inverted V back splash, through tenons, ht. 53.5", w. 33" 5000		4000	7000	6000
Chest, 2 dr. over 4 dr., paneled sides, brass pulls, ht. 48", w. 40" 6000		5000	10,000	7000
Chest, 9 dr., maple, arched apron, wooden pulls, backsplash, ht. 50.5" 5000		4000	7000	6000
China Cabinet, 1-door, 20 panes, paneled back, gal. top, ht. 66.5", w. 35.5" 9000		7000	15,000	12,000
China Cabinet, 1-door, glass sides, through tenons, gal. top, ht. 57.5", w. 35" 5000		4000	7000	6000
China Cabinet, 1-door, 9 panes, trapezoidal, butterfly joints, inverted V apron, ht. 65", w. 37" 10,000		7000	20,000	15,000
China Cabinet, 2-door, 2 dr., paneled sides, lower shelf, keyed tenon, ht. 36" 10,000		7000	20,000	15,000

	REFINISHED		ORIG. FIN.	
	L	UM	L	UM
China Cabinet, 2-door, through tenons, 6 panes per door, glass sides, gal. top, ht. 56", w. 51.5" .... $ 5000	$ 4000	$ 7000	$ 6000
China Cabinet, 2-door, 8 panes per door & sides, through tenons, V pulls, gal. top, ht. 64", w. 42" 5000	4000	7000	6000
China Cabinet, 4-door, paneled sides, sloped overhanging top, exposed tenons, ht. 69", w. 42.5" 10,000	7000	20,000	15,000
Costumer, double, 2 tapered legs, posts, copper hardware .. 1000	800	1500	1000
Costumer, single, tapering post, iron hardware, ht. 68" ... 500	400	600	450
Day Bed, 5 splats each side, through tenons, ht. 29", w. 31" 2500	2000	3500	3000
Desk, 2 dr. over shaped lower shelf, wrought-iron V-pulls, ht. 30", w. 40" 800	600	1200	1000
Desk, 2 dr., letter trays, 2 dr. w/copper pulls, lower shelf, ht. 36", w. 40" 2000	1500	2500	2000
Desk, double pedestal, 9 dr., keyed tenons, 4 corner posts, orig. leather top, ht. 30.5", w. 47" 4000	3000	6000	5000
Desk, slant front, 1 dr. w/copper pulls, lower shelf, ht. 39", w. 30" 1000	800	1500	1000
Desk, slant front, fitted interior, 1 dr., platform base, ht. 43.5", w. 30" 1000	800	1500	1000
Desk, 1 dr. over knee-hole shelf, flanked by 4 dr., copper pulls, exposed tenons, ht. 29", w. 42" 1000	800	1500	1000
Dining Chairs, 5, each w/ 3 slats, short corbels, tapered front legs, ht. 37.5", w. 17" 1500	1000	2000	1500
Dining Chairs, 6, each w/ 3 horizontal back slats, double side stretchers 2000	1500	2500	2000
Dining Chairs, 6, each w/ 3 vert. backslats, arched front & side aprons 4000	3000	6000	5000
Dining Chairs, 9, 1 arm, 8 side, each w/ 3 slats, rush seats 2500	2000	3500	3000
Dresser, 2 over 2 dr., maple, arched apron, tapering standards, mirror, w. 48" 2500	2000	3500	3000
Dresser, 4 dr., mirror, butterfly joints, bowed case, copper V-pulls, ht. 66", w. 48" 4000	3000	6000	5000
Dresser, 5 dr., mirror, butterfly joints, 2 over 3 dr., mortise & tenon, ht. 33", w. 46" 6000	5000	10,000	7000
Dresser, 6 dr., reverse V splashboard, paneled sides, wooden pulls, ht. 52.5" 6000	5000	10,000	7000
Dresser, 4 dr., mirror, butterfly joints, ht. 66", w. 48" 2500	2000	3500	3000
Footstool, flared legs extend above leather top, orig. leather, ht. 4.5", sq. 11.75" 500	400	600	450
Footstool, leather top, sq. faceted nails, sq. flared legs, orig. leather, ht. 4.5", w. 12 sq." 500	400	600	450
Footstool, rush top, arched stretchers, sq. form, orig. uph., ht. 18", w. 18.5" 1500	1000	2000	1500
Footstool, uph., arched seat rail, exposed tenons, ht. 15.25", w. 20" 500	400	600	450
Gout Stool, flared legs, leather top, ht. 4.5" 500	400	600	450
Mirror, cheval, maple, arched stretcher, inverted V top, ht. 70", w. 34" 1500	1000	2000	1500

	RÉFINISHED		ORIG. FIN.	
	L	UM	L	UM
Mirror, 3 sections, 4 iron hooks, w. 48" .... $ 1500	$ 1000	$ 2000	$ 1500
Morris Chair, 5 slats for each arm, corbels, side stretcher tenons, shaped top rail, ht. 44", w. 31" 3500	2500	4500	3500
Morris Chair, wide flat arm over 5 splats, caned seat, ht. 38.5" 4000	3000	6000	5000
Morris Chair, bent arm, 18 spindles for each arm, through tenons, ht. 36", w. 24" 9000	7000	12,000	10,000
Morris Chair, bent arm, 5 splat arms, straight apron, through tenons, ht. 40", w. 33" 6000	5000	10,000	7000
Morris Chair, bent arm, corbels & 5 splats for each arm, through tenons, ht. 40", w. 23" 5000	4000	7000	6000
Morris Chair, spindled, adjust. back, spring cushion seat, ht. 38.5", w. 27.5" 6000	5000	10,000	7000
Morris Chair, spindled, ladies flat arm, 7 spindles each side, ht. 38" 4000	3000	6000	5000
Rocker, 3 splats, ht. 38", w. 26" 400	300	500	400
Rocker, 4 slats, ht. 33", w. 18.5" 300	200	400	300
Rocker, 5 splats, corbels for arms, through tenons, ht. 38", w. 28" 400	300	500	400
Rocker, concave crest over 2 slats, ht. 33.25", w. 26" 500	400	600	450
Rocker, V-back, 5 vert. back slats, painted cream color, ht. 37", w. 25" 400	300	500	400
Rocker, V-back w/5 slats, through arm posts, corbels for front arm 500	400	600	450
Rocker, V-top crest rail, 5 vert slats, corbels 400	300	500	400
Rocker, arm, curved crest over 3 splats, flat arms, orig. leather & tacks, ht. 38.5" 400	300	500	400
Rocker, arm, child's, 3 slats, ht. 25", w. 18" 300	200	400	300
Rocker, sewing, 4 slats, leather seat fits into side stretcher, wide seat rail, ht. 33" 400	300	500	400
Rocker, spindled, 11 spindles in back, open arms w/ corbels under, uph. seat, ht. 36", w. 26" 2000	1500	2500	2000
Vanity, maple, 2 dr. w/mirror, arched apron, w. 36" 4000	3000	6000	5000

Quartered Oak Plank Top $16⁸⁵

Solid Oak Top 45 x 28 In. $10⁹⁵

Mission styles were widely copied. Although pieces of furniture may resemble the important makers, their prices do not. The above illustrations came from a Mongomery Ward catalog.

	REFINISHED		ORIG. FIN.	
	L	UM	L	UM

L.&J.G. Stickley

	L	UM	L	UM
Armchair, 4 splats, long corbels, exposed front tenons, ht. 44", w. 27"	$ 300	$ 200	$ 400	$ 300
Armchair, fixed back, short splat back, extended front posts, ht. 32", w. 26.5"	6000	5000	10,000	7000
Bookcase, 1-door, 16 panes, V-board back, keyed tenons, gal. top, ht. 55", w. 30"	4000	3000	6000	5000
Bookcase, 1-door, 16 panes, keyed tenons, gal. top, ht. 55", w. 30"	4000	3000	6000	5000
Bookcase, 1-door, 16 panes, keyed tenons, gal. top, ht. 55", w. 30"	4000	3000	6000	5000
Bookcase, 2-door, 12 panes per door, exposed tenons, gal. top, ht. 56.75", w. 50"	6000	5000	10,000	7000
Bookcase, 2-door, 12 panes per door, keyed through tenons, gal. top, ht. 56.5", w. 49"	6000	5000	10,000	7000
Cellaret, copper slide-out tray, 2-doors w/ copper strap work, ht. 35.5", w. 32"	6000	5000	10,000	7000
Chair, side, 5 splats, arched side rail, leather seat, extended posts, ht. 36", w. 19.5"	500	400	600	450
Chair, arm, 6 splats & 6 for each arm, corbels, cane seat insert, ht. 39.5", w. 28"	400	300	500	400
Chest, 2 dr. over 3 graduated dr., arched backsplash & apron, panel sides, ht. 40", (top) w. 38"	1500	1000	2000	1500
Chiffonier, arched backsplash, 2-doors over 4 graduated dr., splay ft, panel sides, ht. 50, (top) w. 36"	1500	1000	2000	1500
Day Bed, canted posts, 4 splats, ht. 27.75", w. 30"	1500	1000	2000	1500
Desk, 1 dr., keyed tenons on lower shelf	800	600	1200	800
Desk, 1 dr., slatted bookshelf sides, ht. 29", w. 44"	800	600	1200	800
Desk, slant front, fitted interior, 2 dr. over 2 dr., gal. top, ht. 42", w. 42"	800	600	1200	800
Desk, writing, 1 dr., letter slots,	800	600	1200	800
Dining Chairs, 4, each w/ 3 slats, extended posts, 2 side stretchers, 1 front & back, ht. 35", w. 16.5"\	3000	2000	3500	2500
Dining Chairs, 4, each w/ 3 splats, arched front & back stretchers, rush seats, ht. 36"	2500	2000	3500	3000
Dining Chairs, 6, each w/ 3 splats, uph. seats, dbl. side stretcher, ht. 36"	3000	2000	3500	2500
Footstool, box stretcher, ht. 16", w. 14"	400	300	500	400
Footstool, leather top, stretchers, extended posts, orig. leather, ht. 18", w. 19"	500	400	600	450
Footstool, legs extend above tacked orig. leather top, arched apron, 7 spindle sides, ht. 17", w. 18"	3000	2000	3500	2500
Footstool, tacked leather top, arched apron, 7 spindle sides, extended posts, ht. 16", w. 18"	1500	1000	2000	1500
Footstool, uph., arched rail, ht. 16", w. 19.25"	400	300	500	400
Morris Chair, 2 slats for arms, corbels for arms, leather back & seat	1500	1000	2000	1500
Morris Chair, 5 slats on each side, long corbels, exposed tenons, ht. 40", w. 34"	4000	3000	6000	5000
Morris Chair, 5 slats for each arm, long corbels w/				

	REFINISHED		ORIG. FIN.	
	L	UM	L	UM
through tenons, spring seat, ht. 39", w. 34"	$ 1500	$ 1000	$ 2000	$ 1500
Morris Chair, flat arm over 6 slats, wide seat rail, ht. 41", w. 26"	1500	1000	2000	1500
Morris Chair, flat arms, through tenons, leather back & seat, ht. 42", w. 29.5"	1500	1000	2000	1500
Morris Chair, adjust. back, flat arm over 16 spindles, leather seat, ht. 39", w. 36"	2000	1500	2500	2000
Rocker, V-shaped top crest, 5 splats, arched front, side aprons	300	200	400	300
Rocker, cube, 4 back & side slats, slightly higher back, ht. 30", w. 28"	1000	800	1500	1000
Rocker, Morris, flat arm over 6 splats, wide seat rail, ht. 39", w. 25.75"	2000	1500	2500	2000
Rocker, reclining, open arms, through tenons, leather back & seat, ht. 40", w. 24"	800	600	1200	800
Rocker, sewing, 3 slats, leather seat, ht. 30.5", w. 16.5" ..	300	200	400	300

Life Time

Bookcase, 3 dr. over 2-doors, through tenons, ht. 55", w. 48"	$ 1000	$ 800	$ 1500	$ 1000
Chair, cube, ht. 32", w. 28"	800	600	1200	800
Desk, 1 dr., 2 shelves on each side, round pulls, ht. 29", w. 49"	1000	800	1500	1000
Desk, slant front, extended posts, 1 dr. over 2-doors, arched aprons, through tenons	400	300	500	400
Dining Chairs, 5, each w/ 3 splats	800	600	1200	800
Morris Chair, corbels, post tenons, ht. 41", w. 28"	800	600	1200	1000

Limbert

Armchair, cut-out back panel, clip corner arms, sq. cut-outs on side, ht. 41", w. 27.5"	$ 3000	$ 2000	$ 3500	$ 2500
Armchair, high back, 2 crest rails over 4 splats, exposed faceted leg tenons, ht. 40", w. 26"	400	300	500	400
Bookcase, open sided, 1-door, 8 panes, 4 open shelves per side w/cut outs on top, ht. 47.5", w. 33"	6000	5000	10,000	7000
Cabinet, liquor, amethyst glass-lined tray. 1 dr., 2-doors, full gal., ht. 39", w. 31"	2000	1500	2500	2000
China Cabinet, 1-door, 2 panes over 1, arched aprons, plate rack, copper hardware, ht. 60", w. 25"	3000	2000	3500	2500
Desk, 3 dr., wood pulls, arched corbels, shelf w/ through tenons, ht. 29.5", w. 60"	3000	2000	3500	2500
Dining Chairs, 6, each w/ splat cut-outs in top rail, arched apron, ht. 37", w. 18"	3000	2000	3500	2500
Footstool, leather top, extended posts, arched apron	700	500	900	700
Footstool, w/ dr., extended posts, leather top w/ tacks, arched aprons, ht. 12.5", w. 18"	500	400	600	450
Hall Chair, keyed tenon, ht. 42", w. 19"	2500	2000	3500	3000
Vanity, arched mirror, 1 dr. over arched apron, through tenons, wood pulls	1500	1000	2000	1500

	REFINISHED		ORIG. FIN.	
	L	UM	L	UM

Roycroft

Bookshelf, vert. slats on back & sides, 4 shelves, ht. 38.5"	$ 3000	$ 2000	$ 3500	$ 2500
Bridal Chest, serpentine sides, keyed tenons centering lift top, copper strapware, ht. 26", w. 36.5"	6000	5000	10,000	7000
Footstool, uph., rect., extended posts, ht. 15", w. 17.75" .	500	400	600	450
Mirror, iron chains from support bar, sq. mirror, ht. 33", w. 29"	1500	1000	2000	1500
Rocker, 4 splats, rounded arms, ht. 37", w. 31"	2000	1500	2500	2000

Stickley Brothers

Armchair, high back, 4 splats, tapering ft, ht. 44", w. 27".	$ 400	$ 300	$ 500	$ 400
China Cabinet, 1-door, 3 over 2 panes, arched apron, through tenons, copper pulls, ht. 56.5", w. 49"	2000	1500	2500	2000
China Cabinet, 2 doors, 2 panes over 1 per door, arched stretcher, gal. top, ht. 54," w. 40"	3000	2000	3500	2500
Desk, bookshelf sides, 1 dr., nickel-washed hardware, ht. 30", w. 38.5"	500	400	600	450
Footstool, gout, leather drop in top, 4 legs w/ through tenons, orig. leather, w. 12", d. 19"	400	300	500	400
Footstool, spindled, 7 spindles per side, ht. 15", w. 20.5" ..	3000	2000	3500	2500
Rocker, rabbit-ear top, leather & tacks on back & seat, curved arms, ht. 39.5", w. 30"	700	500	900	700

Marks of important mission furniture makers, clockwise from above left: Gustav Stickley (2 examples) Rohlfs, Life Time.

Wallace Nutting Furniture

Wallace Nutting's legacy to collectors includes photographs, ironwares, furniture, and an increased public awareness of American antiques. The reproductions of early American furniture are now seriously collected in their own right, occasionally rising to values over and above some examples of the 18th-century originals that they copy.

Nutting's catalog numbers are given in parentheses. When more than one number is given, they refer to two different, but very similar, items with similar values.

	AUCTION	RETAIL Low	High
Armchair, Federal (438)	$ 940	$ 2100	$ 3400
Armchair, Pilgrim (480, 493)	1000	2230	3700
Bed, Low Urn Post (809)	570	1470	2000
Bed, Sheraton, 4-post (846)	2000	4800	7000
Brewster Chair (411)	1440	3260	5000
Butterfly Table (624)	990	2330	3500
Candlestand, Federal (644)	1100	2520	3500
Chest (909, 913, 918, 931)	2500	6000	10,000
Chest, Block & Shell (979)	7000	19,000	27,000
Corner Chair (430)	650	1390	2300
Cupboard, Bookcase (927)	2000	5300	8500
Day Bed (828)	2160	4600	7600
Desk, Chip. Slant Front (701, 729)	4500	8000	16,000
Gateleg Table (621)	1250	2680	4000
Hat Rack (40)	400	960	1400
Ladderback Armchair (490, 492)	900	2090	3250
Ladderback Side Chair (374, 390, 392)	330	820	1100
Library Table (637)	1060	2720	4100
Refractory Table (601)	980	2100	3300
Secretary, Chip. (729)	9000	15,000	23,000
Settle, pine (416)	540	1370	2000
Side Chair, Dutch (361)	690	1590	2600
Side Chair, Federal (338)	600	1000	2700
Side Chair, Spanish Foot (380)	670	1420	2300
Spoon Rack (903)	310	750	1100
Stand, Federal (608)	700	1730	2600
Stand, Windsor Candlestand (17)	960	2000	3200
Stool (101, 102, 110)	200	470	770
Stool, Gothic (292)	220	500	850
Stool, Joined (165)	930	2160	3400
Stool, William & Mary (166, 169)	350	900	1400
Table, William & Mary (653)	920	2270	3500
Tavern Table (613, 660)	1200	2710	4600
Tester Bed, Federal (832)	2850	6300	10,000
Treen Dish (27, 30)	150	350	550
Trestle Table (610, 615)	1200	3000	5500
Tuckaway Table (616)	400	850	1300
Welsh Dresser (922)	2700	5950	9000
Windsor Comb Back Armchair (415)	1210	2900	4300
Windsor Continuous Armchair (401)	1110	2550	4200
Windsor Knuckle Armchair (408)	790	1920	2800
Windsor Slipper Chair (349)	660	1470	2500

Wicker Furniture

Wicker is the general term for pieces made of woven rattan, cane, dried grasses, willow, reed, or related material. The wicker heyday in the United States was from about 1860 to 1930. Cyrus Wakefield and the Heywood Brothers were the best known wicker manufacturers. They later joined to become the Heywood-Wakefield Company. Other companies include American Rattan Company and Paine's Manufacturing Company.

While 19th-century wicker is more valuable, pieces from the 1920s and 1930s are also desirable and easier to find. Natural finish wicker is preferred to painted pieces. For more information on wicker, see *The Official Price Guide to Wicker*, published by The House of Collectibles, Random House, NY

Values quoted are for mid-19th century (M-19), painted mid-19th century (PM-19), late 19th-century (L-19), painted late 19th century (PL-19), early 20th century (E-20), painted early 20th century (PE-20), machine made (M), and painted machine made (PM). Pieces described as ornate have features such as spooling, rolled arms & backs, unusual shapes, weaving between legs, etc. ("Upholstered" is abbreviated as "uph.")

*A fancy upholstered footstool, labled
Haywood & Wakefield, late 19th century.*

	M-19	PM-19	L-19	P-19	E-20	PE-20	M	PM
Armchair, ornate	$ 600	$ 350	$ 550	$ 350	$ 450	$ 350	—	—
Armchair, plain	360	210	350	250	270	200	$ 200	$ 150
Baby Carriage	770	460	670	440	520	410	460	400
Bassinet, all-wicker	—	—	350	230	300	200	—	—
Birdcage	—	—	250	160	200	125	80	50
Boudoir Chair (w/ cushion) ..	300	180	275	180	—	—	—	—
Bread Basket, open top	250	150	200	125	130	100	70	60
Buffet, all-wicker, plain	1000	800	800	500	600	400	—	—
Buffet, ornate	1310	750	1100	750	—	—	—	—
Bustle Bench	600	350	580	380	—	—	—	—
Chair, spider caning	830	500	700	450	—	—	—	—
Chaise Lounge, ornate	1100	700	900	600	—	—	—	—
Chaise Lounge, plain	800	500	600	500	500	450	380	320
Chandelier	330	190	400	200	250	150	—	—
Coffee Table, glass top	—	—	—	—	230	180	150	130
Coffee Table, oak top	—	—	440	300	300	220	190	160

	M-19	PM-19	L-19	P-19	E-20	PE-20	M	PM
Corner Chair, ornate	$ 1430	$ 850	$ 1300	$ 750	—	—	—	—
Corner Chair, plain	1100	700	1000	600	—	—	—	—
Cornucopia	—	—	—	—	$ 40	$ 40	$ 20	$ 20
Crib	850	550	850	550	570	450	—	—
Crib, swinging frame	—	1000	680	850	650			
Desk (2 or more drawers)	1100	850	1000	750	900	700	600	450
Desk, all-wicker	950	600	700	500	560	440	460	400
Desk, oak top	860	510	750	500	600	450	—	—
Desk, w/ shelves	1100	760	950	700	780	610	500	400
Desk Accessories Stand	—	—	60	40	60	40	—	—
Desk Chair	150	90	120	80	100	75	—	—
Dining Chair	—	—	150	100	130	100	90	70
Dining Table	—	—	1250	900	730	570	—	—
Doll Carriage	300	180	300	190	210	160	90	70
Dresser	3400	2000	3000	2500	2600	2000	700	500
Dresser, w/ mirror	4000	2400	3700	2400	3000	2300	—	—
Easel, ornate	470	300	280	200	—	—	—	—
Easel, plain	220	150	200	130	—	—	—	—
End Table, ornate	770	460	500	400	300	230	—	—
End Table, plain	550	300	450	250	230	180	—	—
Etagere, 4 shelves	350	230	280	220	170	130	160	140
Field Basket	150	90	130	90	120	80	90	60
Firewood Holder	270	160	220	135	80	60	—	—
Flower Basket	150	80	120	80	90	70	60	50
Folding Stand	—	—	300	190	260	200	50	30
Footstool, uph.	—	—	200	130	160	120	50	30
Hamper	—	—	—	—	125	75	70	60
Highchair	510	300	530	340	310	240	230	190
Hourglass Chair	—	—	380	250	230	180	150	120
Knitting Basket	100	90	100	75	100	75	50	40
Lamp, Floor, no shade	200	160	180	120	—	—	—	—
Lamp, Floor, plain shade	340	240	300	200	—	—	—	—
Lamp, Floor, ornate shade	720	550	650	500	420	300	400	200
Lamp, Table, no shade	360	200	300	200	170	90	50	40
Lamp, Table, plain shade	300	220	370	240	300	240	150	130
Lamp, Table, ornate shade	450	350	425	325	300	200	180	90
Library Table, all-wicker	1000	800	850	600	520	400	270	220
Library Table, oak top	900	750	800	550	400	380	—	—
Lounge Chair	—	—	550	300	340	260	—	—
Loveseat, ornate	950	560	1170	760	800	600	—	—
Loveseat, plain	800	500	900	600	680	500	430	360
Loveseat, uph. seat	1000	700	1000	680	—	—	—	—
Magazine Rack	—	—	440	300	300	250	—	—
Magazine Stand	300	220	270	200	170	100	75	50
Music Cabinet	270	160	—	—	—	—	—	—
Music Stand	190	110	—	—	380	300	—	—
Ottoman	—	—	200	130	180	140	—	—
Photographer's Chair	1400	850	1300	700	—	—	—	—
Picnic Basket, hinged lid	190	110	180	100	140	100	70	40
Picture Frame, h. 30"	210	120	190	100	150	80	—	—
Plant Stand	330	190	300	150	220	170	90	55

	M-19	PM-19	L-19	P-19	E-20	PE-20	M	PM
Plant Table, ornate	$ 550	$ 320	$ 500	$ 300	$ 310	$ 240	—	—
Plant Table, plain	360	210	300	200	160	120	—	—
Rocker	710	420	790	500	270	210	200	160
Rocker, Child's	420	250	370	240	260	200	150	130
Rocker, Child's, uph.	420	250	350	230	—	—	—	—
Rocker, ornate	740	500	750	500	500	300	180	150
Rocker, plain	310	180	310	200	230	180	—	—
Rocker, Platform, ornate	500	300	550	350	400	300	—	—
Rocker, Platform, plain	450	260	380	250	340	260	—	—
Rocker, uph., w/ pouch	450	260	450	300	360	280	—	—
Settee, ornate	1000	680	1000	680	700	400	—	—
Settee, plain	710	420	820	530	520	400	450	300
Sewing Basket, ornate	270	240	250	200	200	150	—	—
Sewing Basket, plain	190	120	170	100	140	100	—	—
Side Chair, ornate	890	530	800	500	400	200	—	—
Side Chair, plain	600	350	410	270	160	120	110	100
Slipper Chair	510	300	500	320	—	—	—	—
Smoking Stand, ornate	420	250	500	300	300	175	—	—
Smoking Stand, plain	300	180	350	250	200	100	—	—
Sofa, ornate	800	650	800	600	550	430	—	—
Sofa, plain	—	—	640	420	440	340	360	300
Stool, 3-leg	—	—	90	60	60	50	—	—
Stroller	—	—	580	380	500	300	—	—
Swing	—	—	730	480	470	360	—	—
Table, Tilt-top	650	400	750	500	—	—	—	—
Teacart	—	—	580	380	550	430	—	—
Tete-a-Tete Chair	1670	990	1640	1000	1000	700	—	—
Tray, all-wicker	100	60	90	50	75	60	45	30
Tray, glass bottom	—	—	—	—	60	50	30	20
Tray, oak bottom	—	—	90	60	60	50	40	20
Umbrella Stand	270	160	250	150	170	130	—	—
Vanity Bench	270	160	220	120	150	100	—	—
Victrola	—	—	—	—	1560	1220	—	—
Wheelchair	—	—	2000	1300	1500	1000	—	—
Wine Rack	—	—	—	—	60	50	50	40

$8⁹⁵ $9⁹⁵ $10⁹⁵ $12⁹⁵

Wicker rockers, c. 1920s.

Glass

Art Glass

The Victorians' love for trinkets was a driving force behind the development of Art Glass. A middle class with money to spend on beautifying the home financed many designers and craftsmen. The late 19th and early 20th centuries saw the production of much of the finest glass. Many of the firms famous then are still in business today. Some still produce designs of sixty years ago.

For all practical purposes, glass cannot be restored. A chip may be ground down, but this alters the shape and thus the value. A crack cannot be painted the way a skilled porcelain restorer can hide a small defect in pottery or porcelain. Glass can be damaged by water if it is allowed to sit in a vase or bowl for weeks on end.

For further information see *The Official Price Guide to Glassware*, by Mark Pickvet, House of Collectibles, Random House, NY.

	LOW	HIGH
Amberina		
Bowl, hobnailed pattern w/ ruffled edge, ht. 2.75", dia. 4.5"	$ 300	$ 450
Bowl, swirl, deep fluted, cranberry to amber, gold foliate dec., 7.5" x 10.5"	400	600
Bowl, swirl, fluted, rich red to amber, iridescent finish, ht. 4", dia. 8"	200	300
Butter Pat, daisy and button pattern, dia. 2.75"	175	250
Champagne Glass, hollow stem, ht. 6"	300	450
Cruet, Mt. Washington, Venetian Diamond, fuchsia to amber, stopper	450	680
Cylindrical Vase, white enamel dec. of boy carrying a shotgun w/ bird, ht. 6.5"	250	380
Fingerbowl and Underplate, red and fuchsia, ht. 2.5", sgn. "LIBBEY," 1917	750	1150
Footed Toothpick Holder, daisy and button pattern, ht. 3"	350	520
Mug, bulbous, amber handle, ht. 4"	225	340
Pitcher, bulbous, amber to cranberry, applied handle, enamel floral dec. ht. 8"	375	560
Pitcher, diamond quilted, applied handle, red shaded to amber, ht. 7", dia. 4.5"	500	750
Salt and Pepper Shakers, inverted thumbprint, fuchsia, original tops, 1880s ...	450	680
Salt Shaker, baby thumbprint, pewter top	225	340
Toothpick Holder, tri-cornered top edge in diamond pattern, ht. 2.25"	500	750
Tumbler, amber to cranberry, polychrome enamel flowers w/ jewels, ht. 5.5" ..	150	220
Tumbler, cranberry to amberina quilted design, ht. 3"	100	150
Tumbler, deep cranberry to amber, ht. 5.5"	125	190
Tumbler, fuchsia in diamond pattern, ht. 3.75"	125	190
Vase, flower petal top, applied spiral trim, cranberry to amber, ht. 10", dia. 5.5"	250	380
Vase, Libbey, deep cranberry vase tapers to amber stem, ht. 11.5"	600	900
Vase, swirl, fan-form top, cranberry to amber, wishbone feet, ht. 8.5", dia. 6.5"	200	300
Vases, Jack-in-the-Pulpit, pr., cranberry to amber, flowers and leaves in gold, 14.5" ht., 5.5" dia.	700	1050
Whiskey Tumbler, diamond quilted, deep red shaded to amber, belltone, ht. 2.5", dia. 2"	300	450

Argy-Rousseau footed bowl.

	LOW	HIGH

Argy-Rousseau

Bowl, pate-de-verre, red background, molded fruit & foliate design in black & red, sgn., 4.5" dia., c. 1925 .... $ 1800 $ 2700

Bowl, pate-de-verre, expanding cylinder, mottled lavender & green background, molds w/ roses, sgn., 2.5" ht., c. 1925 1500   2250

Covered Box, circular, light amber, orange, & gray, molded leaves, strapwork & stars, red mask on lid, sgn., 6" dia., c. 1925 4000   6000

Bohemian

Bowl, cobalt overlay, cut hobstars & fans, tapered sides, round, 3.5" ht., 12" dia. .... $ 150 $ 220

Cake Plate, amethyst overlay, cut wave design, hobstars & diamonds, notched & scalloped rim, 11.5" dia. 100   150

Cologne Bottle, ruby red, frosting at center, medallion w/ etched scene of deer; w/ stopper, 7.5" ht., 2.5" dia. 350   520

Compote, green overlay, triangles w/ caning, thumb prints & sunburst design, notched & paneled shafts, 6" ht., 7.5" dia. 75   110

Decanter, cobalt w/ bullseye & fan cuts, paneled neck, clear stopper, 12.5" ht. . 125   190

Dish, green overlay w/ 3 cut fans, footed, round. 3.5" ht., 8" dia. 100   150

Vase, amethyst overlay, graduated cut panels, 10" ht. 65   100

Vase, cobalt overlay, trumpet form, cut pinwheels, diamonds & fans, 12" ht. . 175   260

Vase, cobalt overlay, trumpet form, graduated cut panels, 7" ht. 80   120

Bristol

Cologne Bottle, green satin finish, gilt reeded handles, 9.5" ht., 3.5" dia. .. $ 130 $ 200

Lustres, gilt blue glossy & satin fin., each w/ 8 crystal prisms, 10.5" ht., 5" dia. 320   480

Sweetmeat Jar, of pink overlay, silver-plated lid, handle & base rim, white interior, floral dec. of blue & white & enameled duck in flight, 5" ht. 120   180

Vase, flattened oval, enamel bird & flowers, bug dec., 2.5" ht., 4.5" dia. 200   300

Vase, of pink overlay, scalloped cut top w/ gold trim, dec. in blue, white, & orange enameled flowers, white heron in blue dot pattern, 15" ht. 200   300

Burgun & Schverer

Bowl, half-spherical, sawtooth rim, light green streaked w/ red, enamel floral dec., overlaid & carved in clear, gilt, 7" dia., c. 1895 .... $ 4000 $ 6000

Bowl, waisted dome body, brownish-yellow streaked w/ green background, cut w/ wild animals & flowers, 5.5" dia., c. 1895 3000   4500

	LOW	HIGH
Footed Bowl, sawtooth rim, light green, red-streaked background, enameled w/ poppies, grass, clear overlay, w/ carving, gilt, 8", dia., c. 1895	$ 4000	$ 6000
Vase, bulbous body, sawtooth lip, pale yellow, floral enameled in blue & green, clear overlay, applied foliage on neck, gilt, 5.5" ht., c. 1895	2000	3000
Vase, bulbous body, long neck, gray shading to lavender, clear overlay, flora carved, sawtooth neck, gilt, 5.5" ht., c. 1895	2000	3000
Vase, cabinet, baluster, yellow, clear overlay, floral carved, gilt, 5.5" ht., c. 1895	3000	4500
Vase, cabinet, spherical, flaring lip, 3 feet, lavender overlay, cut w/ bleeding hearts & leaves, gilt highlights, 3.5" ht., c. 1895	600	900

Burmese

	LOW	HIGH
Bowl, Bold fluted edge, satin fin., 3", dia. 6"	$ 450	$ 680
Bowl, Diamond Quilted pattern w/ ruffled edge, satin fin., 2.25", dia. 4.5" ..	300	450
Creamer, applied handle & pedestal base, satin fin., 4" ht.	350	520
Cruet, Mt. Washington, acid fin., melon ribbed, undec., 6.5" ht.	1200	1800
Cruet, Mt. Washington, acid fin., ribbed, w/ stopper, yellow handle, 7" ht. ..	1400	2100
Cup & Saucer, applied handle, satin fin., dia. (cup) 3", (saucer) 5"	500	750
Cylindrical Footed Vase, satin fin., 9"	700	1050
Fairy Lamp, acid fin., deep salmon pink to creamy yellow, rare pressed Burmese base, clear inside cup, base marked "Clarke," 5" ht., 7" dia. ...	600	900
Fairy Lamp, acid fin., salmon pink to yellow, on matching ruffed reversible base, clear cup marked "Clarke," 5.5" ht., 7" dia.	750	1120
Footed Rose Bowl, scalloped edge & 3 applied feet, satin fin., 3.5"	325	490
Jack-in-the-Pulpit Vase, crimped edge, acid fin., 9.75"	700	1050
Lemonade Glass, w/ applied handle, satin fin., 5"	400	600
Mt. Washington Bowl, Diamond Quilted pattern w/ folded edge, pinched to basket shape, glossy fin., paper label, 2.75", len. 6.5"	450	680
Mt. Washington Creamer, Diamond Quilted pattern, glossy fin., 4.25"	450	680
Mt. Washington Trumpet Vase, acid fin., 8"	450	680
Muffineer, Mt. Washington, acid fin., white & colored dots form blossoms, attrib. Timothy Canty, 4.5" ht.	1000	1500
Perfume Bottle, branches & pinecones, satin fin., silver cap w/ monogram, 5"	1200	1800
Stick Vase, dec. w/ leaves & blueberries, gold accent stripe, acid fin., 10" ...	1400	2100
Sugar & Creamer Set, Mt. Washington, acid fin., no dec., ht. 3.5" creamer.....	750	1120
Toothpick Holder, acid fin., bulbous w/ square top, dec. w/ brown leaves, white & blue enameled flowers, 3" ht., 2.5" dia.	300	450
Toothpick Holder, acid fin., square top, 2.5" ht., 2.5" dia.	200	300
Toothpick Holder, satin fin., 2.5"	225	340
Toothpick Holder & Undertray, tri-cornered shape, quilted design, satin finish, 2.25" dia. (of undertray) 3.5"	400	600
Tri-footed Vase, pinched top, 3 applied feet & berry pontil, satin fin., 7.25" ..	1000	1500
Tumbler, acid fin., 3.75"	130	200
Tumbler, dec. w/ ivy leaves, gold rim, satin fin., 3.75"	400	600
Vase, acid fin., ribbed, scalloped top, 3.5" ht., 2.5" dia.	225	340
Vase, acid fin., undec., 3.5" ht., 5.5" dia.	350	520
Vase, Mt. Washington, enameled polychrome stylized blossoms & foliage, applied handles, 10.5" ht.	1500	2250
Vase, Mt. Washington, bottle, acid fin., salmon pink to yellow, white enameled mums & green foliage, 6.5" ht., 3.5" dia.	350	520

Cameo vase and lamp.
— Photo courtesy of
Northeast Auctions.

	LOW	HIGH
Vase, Mt. Washington, bulbous base, long neck, dec. w/ sacred ibis, oasis scene in raised gold, 12" ht., 7" dia.	$ 3000	$ 4500
Vase, Mt. Washington, egg form, acid fin., dec. w/ daisies & foliage in 3 shades of gold enamel, designs outlined in raised gold, 9" ht., 4.5" dia.	1000	1500
Vase, Mt. Washington, jack-in-pulpit, acid fin., crimped top, 12.5" ht., 5" dia.	1000	1500
Vase, Mt. Washington, teardrop form, elaborate polychrome & gold floral dec., 10.5" ht., 5.5" dia.	2000	3000
Vase, shiny fin., ruffled top, 3.5" ht., 3" dia.	220	340
Whiskey Tumbler, Mt. Washington, acid fin., diamond quilted, yellow edge, 2.5" ht.	250	380

Cameo

	LOW	HIGH
Bowl, Eng., ribbed, pink on white, acid-cut fish-scales, dec. w/ morning glory vine and butterfly in gold enamel, 7.5" dia., sgn. in enamel	$ 1200	$ 1800
Perfume Bottle, Eng., round, blue ground, dec. w/ carved white blossoms, foliage and butterfly, silver lid, 7.5" ht.	3000	4500
Vase, Eng., 4 layers, white to red to clear to green, depicts raspberries & foliage, 7" ht., 4.5" dia., unsgn.	3000	5000
Vase, sgn. by Michel Paris, translucent, frosted ground, brown cut to yellow, sailing scene, 3 acid cuttings, 8.5 ht., 3.5" dia.	1200	1800

Cased

	LOW	HIGH
Lustres, white, cranberry banding, circular medallions, ptd. flowers, pedestal bases, prisms, 12" ht.	$ 200	$ 300
Perfume Bottle, decorated yellow, gilt clear ball stopper, applied jewels, 5.5" ht., 2.5" dia.	200	300

	LOW	HIGH
Rose Bowl, amethyst, applied flower, branch and leaf, 3.5" ht., 4" dia., rare	$ 300	$ 450
Rose Bowl, pink hobnailed design, crimp top, 3.5" ht., 3.5" dia.	150	220

Coralene

Pitcher, orange glass, amber applied handle, water lilies of white and green leaves in Coralene beading dec., 8.5" ht., 4" dia.	225	340
Lamp Base, satin glass, fern leaf sprays, beaded Coralene of yellow, brass burner, 7.5" ht., 3" dia.	150	220
Vase, seaweed decoration on pale blue diamond quilted mother-of-pearl, coralene blossoms, applied jewel center, 7" ht.	450	680
Vase, seaweed, pink decoration on gold diamond quilted mother of pearl, 6.5" ht.	500	750

Crown Milano

Cracker Jar, Mt. Washington, melon-ribbed, cream ground, floral enamel dec., silverplate lid is sgn., 7" dia.	$ 500	$ 750
Decanter, dec. w/ enamel roses & gold scrolls on neck & stopper, 10" ht., rare early Albertine Crown Milano sign.	1000	1500
Ewer, Mt. Washington, applied handle, color geometric dec., 13" ht., unsgn.	1600	2400
Ewer, Mt. Washington, pastoral dec., 10.5" ht.	2500	3750
Jam Jar, white body, dec. w/ blue & white forget-me-nots, silver-plated lid sgn. Santa Co., sgn. jar, 4" ht.,	350	520
Plate, rose & fired gold scrolling, enameled dots on 3 reserves, 11" dia.	120	180
Rose Bowl, Mt. Washington, all-over dec. of roses, buds, leaves, gold trim, purple numbered pontil	350	520
Salt Shaker, cockle shell, Mt. Washington, white satin body, enamel blossoms, silver-plated top shaped like seashell	375	560
Tray, Mt. Washington, shiny fin., rolled & serrated edges, enamel thistle & foliage dec., outlined w/ raised gold, 9.5" long, 7" w., sgn.	825	1240
Urn, w/ rare crown-shaped lid, raised gold blossom & foliage dec., 16.5" ht., 8" w., 5.5" deep, sgn.	2800	4200
Vase, Mt. Washington, bulbous, cream-colored body w/ slender neck, gold blossoms & jewels covered w/ gold enamel, 12.5" ht., sgn.	800	1200
Vase, Mt. Washington, cone-shaped, enamel floral bouquet dec., 8" ht., sgn.	850	1280
Vase, square-shaped, rounded corners, 2 delicate applied handles, dec. w/ pastel enamels in tiny free-form geometric patterns, 8" ht., unsgn.	750	1000
Vase, Mt. Washington, square w/ rounded corners, applied scroll handles, cream ground, enamel oak leaves & gold acorns, paper label, 8.5" ht.	950	1420

D'argenthal

Bowl, double conical shape, waisted neck & foot, slightly flaring rim, yellow background, overlaid in red, carved w/ roses, & foliage, sgn., 12" dia., c. 1900	$ 1000	$ 1500
Bowl, swollen spherical, undulated rim scalloped, yellow background, overlaid in maroon, cut w/ roses, sgn., 6" dia., c. 1900	600	900
Box, covered, shallow circular shape, dark yellow background, overlaid in brown & umber, cut w/ wildflowers & leaves, sgn., 3.5" dia., c. 1915	400	600
Vase, baluster shape, light yellow background splashed w/ red, overlaid in red, cut landscape of lake, arched bridge, & trees, sgn., 13.5" ht., c. 1910	2000	3000
Vase, baluster shape, turquoise background, overlaid in dark blue, cut w/		

	LOW	HIGH
flowers & leaves, sgn. 7" ht., c. 1900 .... $ 400		$ 600
Vase, cameo, pastoral scene w/ house, trees and chateau in background,		
sgn., 6.5" ht., 4.5" dia. 480		720
Vase, cameo, dark brown floral pattern, sgn., 14" ht., 6" dia. 650		1000
Vase, cylindrical, orange-yellow background, red overlay, floral cut, sgn.,		
11.5" ht., c. 1900 700		1100

Desire Christian

	LOW	HIGH
Bowl, green shading to turquoise, green overlay, carved lily pads, blossoms,		
& flying dragonfly, sgn., 6" dia., c. 1895 .... $ 1200		$ 1800
Vase, bud, compressed sphere, brown shading to olive green, lavender		
overlay, carved w/ milkweeds, leaves, & grass, sgn., 12" ht., c. 1895 .. 3000		4500
Vase, cylinder expanding to neck, spreading foot, gray w/ red background,		
carved w/ 2 orchids & leaves, sgn., 14.5" ht., c. 1895 2000		3000

De Vez

	LOW	HIGH
Vase, acid fin. background, dark green shaded to rose landscape scene in 3		
acid cuttings, sgn., 9.5" ht., 2" dia. .... $ 620		$ 930
Vase, acid fin. background of blue w/ mountain landscape scenes on 3		
detailed acid cuttings, sgn., 11.5" ht., 3.5" dia. 700		1100
Vase, acid fin. background of shell pink w/ navy blue shaded to yellow		
shaded to pink in 3 acid cuttings, mountain scene, sgn., 6.5 ht., 2.5" dia. . 630		940
Vase, bulbous body, long cylinder neck, light pink background, overlaid		
in yellow & blue. cut scene w/ squirrels & mountains, sgn., 13" ht.,		
c. 1900 1100		1650
Vase, cylinder w/ flaring rim & foot, yellow background splashed w/		
orange & green, cut river scene, sgn., 5.5" ht., c. 1910 700		1050
Vase, cylinder shape tapering toward the neck, overlaid in lavender shading		
to pink, cut cartouches enclosing river landscape, sgn., 9.5" ht., c. 1900 ... 800		1200
Vase, elongated pear shape, short cylinder neck, yellow background overlaid		
in dark blue, cut w/ river scene, sgn., 5.5" ht., c. 1910 700		1050
Vase, pear shape, cylinder neck, flared rim, yellow background, overlaid in		
orange & blue, cut river scene, sgn., 6" ht., c. 1910 700		1000
Vase, trumpet, acid-fin. background, blue shaded to rose in 3 acid cuttings,		
bird & foliage, gold-plated brass base w/ leaves, 18.5" ht., 6.5" dia. 2000		3000

Durand

	LOW	HIGH
Plate, flashed ruby w/ white pulled feathers, hatched pontil, underside		
features Bridgeton Pose engraving by Charles Link, 8" dia. .... $ 325		$500
Vase, baluster shape, waisted & flaring neck, flattened circular foot, amber		
iridescence w/ coalescent trails, 8.5" ht., 1901-30 450		680
Vase, bulbous shape, iridescent blue, wide flared neck, 8.5" ht. 225		340
Vase, compressed bulbous, flattened shoulders, waisted & lobed neck,		
flaring rim, blue iridescence, sgn., 8.5" ht., 1905-30 500		750
Vase, compressed sphere base, cylinder neck expanding into trumpet shape,		
green background, undulating bands in amber iridescence, sgn., 12" ht.,		
1905-30 1800		2700
Vase, compressed spherical body, lobed neck, blue, 8.5, ht. 500		750
Vase, compressed spherical, trumpetlike neck, short circular foot, blue		
iridescence, sgn., 9.5" ht., 1905-30 450		680

	LOW	HIGH

Vase, conical, iridescent gold leaf & vine design, flared rim, 7" ht. .... $ 350 $ 520

Vase, cylindrical, flaring rim, circular base, amber dec. w/ coalescent
    interlacing designs, 8.5" ht. 1000   1500

Vase, cylindrical, iridescent platinum King Tut pattern, narrow mouth,
    5" ht. 300   500

Vase, cylindrical, scalloped rim, opalescent glass, w/ hearts & vines,
    11" ht. 1000   1500

Vase, baluster, blue iridescent, amber iridescent foot, sgn., 14.5" ht. 450   680

Vase, cylindrical, swollen shoulders, silvery blue, sgn., 6.5" ht., 1905-20 .. 450   680

Vase, elongated ovoid, waisted neck, flaring rim, blue iridescent, overlay
    clinging heart vine, 10.5" ht., 1905-1930 450   680

Vase, ovoid, flaring neck, iridescent blue, sgn., 10.5" ht., 1905-25 600   900

Vase, urn form, blue iridescent, w/ white heart & vine overlay, 7.5" ht.,
    1905-25 600   900

Le Verre Francais

Vase, cameo, ovoid, waisted neck, flaring rim, mottled pink background,
    cut daisies, lavender to amethyst overlay, 4.5" ht., c. 1925 .... $ 400 $ 600

Vase, cameo, trumpet form, mottled orange & yellow background, cut
    bouquets in bright orange to deep purple, sgn., 18.5" ht., c. 1920 400   600

Vase, compressed spherical tapering to trumpet-form neck, green background,
    overlaid in mottled orange, brown, & green, carved w/ flowers w/ honey-
    comb pattern around the base, 16.5" ht., c. 1920 800   1200

Vase, cylinder w/ tapering waisted neck, orange overlay shading to green
    & turquoise, cut w/ blossoms & leaves, honeycomb design on neck,
    26" ht., c. 1930 1000   1500

Vase, spherical, w/ cylinder neck, yellow background, cut in flowers &
    tendrils in blue & orange, sgn., 12" ht., c. 1925 500   750

Loetz

Biscuit Jar, iridescent purple shaded to black, swing handle, silverplate
    lid, 9" ht. .... $ 150 $ 220

Bowl, bulbous w/ waisted base & neck, flaring rim, magenta background,
    silvery blue designs of ripples, 10" dia., c. 1900 925   1400

Bowl, circular, green iridescent, fluted, 7.5" dia. 200   300

Bowl, ovoid, crimped lip & sides, oil-spotted yellow background w/ blue
    striations, 10.5" long, c. 1900 900   1350

Bowl, ovoid, silvery amber iridescent background, amber iridescent wave
    pattern, ruffled neck, unsgn., c. 1900 350   520

Lamp, iridescent cylinder, in bronze stand circling body, triangular base,
    body in salmon w/ amber & silvery blue oil spots, 19.5" ht., c. 1900 650   980

Lamp, melon-form base, silvery blue oil spots, helmet-shaped shade in
    avocado green, both w/ 4 vertical hobnailed band, 11" ht., c. 1900 1200   1800

Vase, baluster body, amber iridescent background, loops & trails in orange,
    blue, & amber iridescent, 6.5" ht., c. 1900 800   1200

Vase, baluster, flaring lip, spreading base, iridescent orange, rose spotting
    around foot, 8.5" ht., c. 1900 400   600

Vase, baluster, triangular mouth, orange oil spots, loops & swirls in silvery
    blue & iridescent amber, 8.5" ht., c. 1900 400   600

Vase, bulbous, cylinder neck, everted rim, orange background, lavender
    feathering, blue iridescent oil spots, silver overlay, 10.5" ht., c. 1900 900   1350

	LOW	HIGH
Vase, blue & green, iridescent pinched shoulder & ruffled collar, Loetz		
Austria etched on bottom, 7" ht.	$ 600	$ 900
Vase, purple, wide lip on top, unsgn., 6.5"	400	600

Mary Gregory

	LOW	HIGH
Box, cobalt, round, hinged lid, ormolu feet, white enamel dec. girl w/ bird,		
5" ht., 5.5" dia.	400	600
Box, emerald green, puffy shape, lift-off lid, white enamel dec. depicts		
girl, 3" ht., 3.75" dia.	1250	1800
Box, lime green, hinged lid, white enamel dec. depicts boy, 1.5" ht.,		
2.5" dia.	150	220
Box, patch, round, green, white enamel dec. girl, hinged, 1.5" ht., 2.5" dia.	150	220
Box, sapphire blue, round, hinged lid, white enamel dec. depicts girl,		
2.75" ht., 3.5" dia.	160	240
Plate, cobalt, white enameled dec. depicts girl w/ butterfly net, ormolu		
compote stand, 3 rings hang from holder, 6.5" dia.	150	220
Tumbler, cranberry, white enamel dec. depicts girl, 4.5" ht., 2.5" dia.	75	110
Vase, covered, cobalt, white enamel dec. w/ girl & flower basket, 14" ht. ..	325	500
Vase, cranberry, white enamel dec. depicts boy w/ hat, 7.5" ht.	125	200
Vase, sapphire blue, scalloped top, white enamel dec. depicts boy w/		
goblet, plated brass base w/ woman's-head handles, 14.5" ht., 3.5" dia.	250	380
Wine Bottle, cranberry, white enamel dec. depicts girl w/ bouquet, clear		
bubble stopper, 9" ht., 3.5" dia.	175	260

Moser

	LOW	HIGH
Box, amethyst, applied salamander feet & lid, enameled flowers, hinged,		
4.5" ht.	$ 600	$ 900
Decanter, w/ stopper, clear to green, sgn., 8" ht.	175	260
Ewer, gold over crystal, enameled polychrome flowers & leaves, pedestal		
base, 5.5" ht., 2.5" dia.	150	220
Jug, enameled decorations, strap, twig handle, sgn., 9.5" ht.	75	110
Juice Glass, cranberry, polychrome and gilt enamel leaves & acorns, 4" ht. ..	150	220
Tumbler, cranberry glass w/ gold enameled flowers and colored bees,		
3.75" ht.	175	260
Tumbler, crystal shades to blue, engraved w/ grouse and landscape, cut		
and gilt enamel dec., 5" ht., 3" dia., sgn.	350	520
Vase, decorated opaque pink to clear, applied scroll feet, gold filigree,		
enameled eagle, oak leaves, insect, applied acorns, 7" ht., 7" dia.	1500	2250
Vase, opalescent pink to clear, crimped glass handles burnished w/ gold,		
parrot and foliage in relief gilt polychrome enamel, 7.5" ht., Moser sgn ..	850	1280
Vase, multicolored enameled grape leaves and bee w/ applied yellow and		
red grape bunches, 4 applied feet of amber rosette, 5.5" ht., 2.5" dia.	350	520
Wine Glass, light ruby, elaborately decorated, 5" ht.	300	450

Mother-of-Pearl Satin Glass

	LOW	HIGH
Basket, pink color, Herringbone pattern and pleated top, applied handle,		
5.25"	$ 250	$ 380
Ewers, pr., each w/ applied, frosted thorny handle, Diamond Quilted pattern,		
ruffled edges, 6.75" ht.	200	300
Rose Bowl, blue color, Herringbone pattern, pleated rim, 3.5"	175	260
Rose Bowl, gold/amber color in Diamond Quilted pattern, 2.5"	200	300
Salt, raspberry color, Teardrop pattern, pewter shaker top, 3.5"	275	410

	LOW	HIGH

Tumbler, deep rust shaded to pink, Diamond Quilted pattern, applied
flowers, 4" .... $ 150 — $ 220

Tumbler, amber in Coinspot pattern, 3.5" .... 120 — 180

Tumbler, pink in Diamond Quilted pattern, 4" .... 120 — 180

Tumbler, blue in Diamond Quilted pattern, 4" .... 120 — 180

Vase, pink in Coinspot pattern, ruffled edge, 9" .... 275 — 400

Vase, butterscotch drapery pattern over melon ribbed body, ruffled top,
8.25" . ... 325 — 500

Muller Freres

Bowl, inverted cone, flaring rim, overlaid, carved, and enameled in flurogravure, harvest scene, sgn., 6.5" ht., c. 1900 .... $ 2000 — $ 3000

Ewer, inverted cone, applied C-scroll handle, frosted green background,
overlaid, carved, and enameled blossoms and leaves, sgn., 19" ht.,
c. 1900 .... 2000 — 3000

Vase, baluster form, frosted blue background, carved overlay, enameled
in flurogravure, winter scene w/ dogs & pheasant, sgn., 9" ht., c. 1900 .. 800 — 1200

Vase, double gourd form, purple background, cameo carved, sgn., 6.5" ht. . 350 — 520

Vase, bulbous, waisted neck, lobed lip, orange background, overlaid in
black, cut landscape, sgn., 4.5" ht., c. 1910 .... 700 — 1050

Vase, cameo, storks w/ frosted yellow and gold, 7.5" ht. .... 1450 — 2200

Vase, cylinder, applied serpentine handle, green background, enameled
berries and leaves, sgn., 10.5" ht., c. 1910 .... 1000 — 1500

Vase, frosted pink background, w/ red roses, sgn., 7.5" ht., 3.5" dia. .... 1200 — 1800

Opalescent

Bowl, diamond quilted light green shaded to pink, ruffled, pewter frame,
17.5" ht., 11.5" dia. .... $ 350 — $ 520

Bowl, flashed rainbow, fluted edge, decorated w/ enamel floras, 5" ht. ...... 500 — 750

Ewer, striped white shaded to green, Vaseline applied leaf and handle,
appliquéed flowers in pink, 8.5" ht., 3" dia. .... 250 — 380

Fairy Lamp, amber swirl, sgn. Clarke base, pyramid shade, 3.5" ht., 3.5" dia. . 200 — 300

Fairy Lamp, blue swirl satin finish, light blue glass cup and candle cup,
matching square ruffled base, rare, 6.5" ht., 5.5" dia. .... 750 — 1120

Fairy Lamp, pink and white frosted swirl decoration, dome shape, sgn.
Clarke candle cup, sq. ruffled vase, 5.5" ht., 6" dia. .... 750 — 1120

Fairy Lamp, pressed glass, blue embossed rib design, sgn. Clarke base,
3.5" ht., 2" dia. .... 300 — 450

Vase, Jack-in-the-Pulpit, fluted w/ purple edge, 7" ht., 4" dia. .... 150 — 220

Vase, white opalescent Monot Stumpf, pink shaded to white, fan shape,
belltone, 7" ht., 6.5" dia. .... 450 — 680

Vase, white opalescent Monot Stumpf, pink shaded to striped white, pantin
ruffled fan shape, belltone, 7.5" ht., 7.5" dia. .... 400 — 600

Water Tumbler, cranberry, 10-row hobnailed, 3.5" ht., 2.5" dia. .... 250 — 380

Water Tumbler, decorated peach, white flowers have gold leaves and centers,
4" ht., 2.5" dia. .... 150 — 220

Water Tumbler, lavender, 8-row hobnailed, 3.5" ht., 2.5" dia. .... 225 — 340

Orrefors

Beaker, flaring neck, 4 ball feet set on flattened dome base, clear, etched
jungle scene, sgn., 10.5" ht., c. 1930 .... $ 600 — $ 900

	LOW	HIGH

Bottle, elongated dome stopper, light green, clear, decorated internally w/ sea grass and starfish in maroon, sgn., 6.5" ht., c. 1938 .... $ 800 $ 1200

Bottle, thick-walled, clear, cartouche w/ dove, sgn. 6.5" dia., c. 1940 1500   2250

Bottle, thick-walled, stepped interior, green garlands and air bubbles in walls, sgn., 6.5" dia., c. 1940 400   600

Bottle, flaring, blue-tinted background, engraved scene of women and dolphin, scalloped border engraved around the rim, 8.5" long, c. 400   600

Bottle, octagon, light gray, cut w/ nudes and foliage, sgn., 11.5" c. 1928 ... 450   680

Bowl, cylinder w/ expanding neck, cut w/ hunting scenes, sgn., 8.5" w., c. 1927 500   750

Overlay

Bowl, shaded pink, fan shape w/ amber applied edging, hobnailed at top, 7.5" ht., 9.5" dia. .... $ 300 $ 450

Fairy Lamp, candy striped in pink, matching candle cup, embossed, pink rib dome shade, clear applied feet ruffled base, 3 parts, 5.5" ht. 475   700

Fairy Lamp shade, dark green, sgn. Clarke base, 4.5" ht., 4" dia. 170   260

Finger Lamp and Chimney, blue, shaded, clear reeded applied handle, pink and white enameled flowers and gold color foliage, 5.5" ht., 4.5" dia. 175   260

Finger Lamp and Chimney, pink shaded, clear handle, red roses trimmed in green and dots of white, 6" ht., 5" dia. 225   340

Finger Lamp and Chimney, satin, lemon yellow, embossed shell and leaf, frosted reeded applied handle, 5" ht., 3.88" dia. 250   380

Finger Lamp, blue, shaded, clear resided, applied handle, embossed design, 6" ht., 4.5" dia. 235   350

Goblet, white on crystal, dainty multicolor floral decoration, white cut to clear and outlined in gold in places, Continental 240   360

Hand Lamp and Chimney, shaded chartreuse green, clear reeded applied handle, scroll decoration in beige, 5" ht., 3.5" dia. 190   280

Rose Bowl, diamond quilted, rose satin cut velvet, 8-crimp top, white interior, 3.5" ht., 3.5 dia. 280   420

Rose Bowl, shaded blue w/ embossed swirl rib design, 8-crimp top, white interior, 5" ht., 6" dia. 250   380

Table Lamp, mushroom shape shade has pink embossed flowers w/ ruffled top and clear chimney, white interior, silver-plated base, 17.5" ht., 6" dia. 400   600

Vase, Jack-in-the-Pulpit, amber-edged ruffled top, pink and white applied flowers w/ amber leaves on cream, white interior, 6.88" ht., 6.5" dia. ... 250   380

Vase, Jack-in-the-Pulpit, cranberry-edged, white background, 7.5" ht., 6" dia. 200   300

Vase, Jack-in-the-Pulpit, decorated blue, w/ multi-colored, enameled flowers, branches and butterfly, decorated blue interior, 5.5" ht., 4.5" dia. 200   300

Vase, Jack-in-the-Pulpit, green, white background, applied feet, 7" ht., 5" dia. 175   260

Vase, Jack-in-the-Pulpit, purple, ruffled top, white background, 7.5" ht., 6" dia. 175   260

Vase, Jack-in-the-Pulpit, purple shaded to lavender, ruffled, 7.5" ht., 6" dia. . 175   260

Vase, Jack-in-the-Pulpit, shaded green, clear applied feet, scalloped edges, 6.5" ht., 5.5" dia. 175   260

Vase, Jack-in-the-Pulpit, shaded maroon, white background, ruffled edging,

	LOW	HIGH
7" ht., 6.5" dia.	$ 200	$ 300

Vase, pink, large applied crystal flower and branch, crystal around base, white interior, 8.5" ht., 4.5" dia. .... 200 — 300

Vase, silver floral leaves and swag etched over green, narrow, flaring neck, pear shape, 5" ht. .... 80 — 120

Vases, white w/ enameled blue flowers, clear applied edge, ruffled top, ormolu handled holder, pink interior, 12.5" ht., 7" dia. .... 360 — 540

Water Tumbler, overlay shaded pink, w/ satin blue and white flower & green leaves, gold trim, white interior, 4.5" ht., 3 dia. .... 220 — 330

Overshot

Fairy Lamp, amber embossed swirl, sgn. Clarke base, 3.5" ht., 2.5" dia. .. $ 200 — $ 300

Fairy Lamp, cranberry, embossed hobnailed design, sgn. Clarke base, 4" ht., 3" dia. .... 225 — 340

Fairy Lamp, cranberry, embossed ribs, sgn. Clarke base, 3.5" ht., 3" dia. ... 235 — 350

Fairy Lamp, opaque yellow, w/ embossed swirl pattern, sgn. Clarke base, 3.5" ht., 2" dia. .... 250 — 380

Pitcher, ruffled, pink and white spatter glass, bulbous 3-way top, clear reeded applied handle, 7.5" ht., 5.5" dia. .... 250 — 380

Peachblow

Bowl, New England, flared scalloped rim, 2.5" ht., 5.5" at widest point .. $ 700 — $ 1100

Cruet, Wheeling, deep red shading to cream at base, clear amber faceted handle, reeded handle, 6.5" ht. .... 1100 — 1650

Pitcher, Wheeling, shiny finish, exquisite color, applied amber handle, 9.5" ht. .... 1000 — 1500

Toothpick Holder, ruffled rim, cylindrical shape, 2.5" ht. .... 110 — 160

Toothpick Holder, wild rose color w/ ruffled top edge, paper label, "N. E.G.W./Wild Rose/PATd/MARCH 2, 1886," 2.5" ht. .... 525 — 800

Toothpick Holder, glossy finish, 2.75" ht. .... 200 — 300

Tumbler, Gunderson, w/ applied floral decoration, 3.75" ht. .... 70 — 100

Tumbler, New England, shiny finish, wild rose upper half, 3.5" ht. ...... 350 — 520

Vase, bulbous, gold & silver butterfly on gold & silver background, w/ blue trim, 4.5" ht., 4.5" dia. .... 250 — 380

Vase, hummingbird on gold & silver background, narrow neck, 10.5" ht., 6" dia. .... 435 — 650

Vase, Mt. Washington, trumpet (lily), acid finish, pink shaded to blue, rare, 6.5" ht., 2.5" dia. .... 800 — 1200

Vase, New England, Wild Rose, satin finish, double gourd, red shading to white, 7" ht., 1880s .... 500 — 750

Vase, satin finish, ribbed pear design, narrow neck, 9" ht. .... 75 — 110

Vases, rose shaded to cream, Japanese-style blossoming branches, slender necks, pr., 7" ht. .... 200 — 300

Water Pitcher, Wheeling, finest color. square top, applied amber handle, 10" ht. .... 1000 — 1500

Pomona

Fluted Bowl, second grind, w/ a Rivulet pattern in blue stain, 2.75" ht., 5" dia. .... $ 150 — $ 220

Fluted Bowl, second grind, in a cornflower decoration, 2" ht., 5.25" dia. ..... 70 — 100

	LOW	HIGH
Juice Glass, first grind, delicate hobnailed interior, tapered, 3.5" ht.	$ 120	$ 180
Lemonade Pitcher, first grind, cylindrical, blue-tinted cornflowers, 12" ht. .	1200	1800
Pitcher, New England, first grind, miniature, sq. top	150	220
Spooner, second grind, inverted Thumbprint w/ red stemmed blueberry decoration & crimped base, 5" ht.	150	220
Tumbler, first grind, spray of pansies & butterfly, 3.75" ht.	175	260
Tumbler, New England, second grind, cornflower staining	100	150
Water Carafe, New England, second grind, cornflower staining	225	340
Water Set, pitcher & 6 tumblers, first grind, pitcher is 6.5" ht.	900	1350
Water Tumbler, New England, blue cornflower pattern, 2nd grind, 3.5" ht.	250	380

Quetzal

	LOW	HIGH
Bowl, shallow, flaring lip, iridescent, sgn., 11.5" dia., 1901-25	$ 600	$ 900
Dish, circular shape, 2 ribbed handles, iridescent, 5.5" dia., 1901-25	250	380
Light Shade, flower form, scalloped, flared rim, iridescent yellow, sgn., 5.5" ht., c. 1900	300	450
Vase, elongated baluster, domed foot, yellow background, green feather designs, amber iridescence, 19.5" ht., c. 1901-25	2000	3000
Vase, Jack-in-the-Pulpit, thin stem, flattened circular foot, opalescent, amber iridescent, striated green feathering, sgn., 10.5" ht., 1901-25	3000	4500
Vase, ovoid body, vertical lobbing, cylinder neck, flaring lip, opalescent background, green & amber iridescent draping, 6.5" ht., 1901-25	2500	3750
Vase, pear shape, amber iridescent. overlaid in silver, chased w/ flowers & leaves, strapwork, sgn., 8.5" ht., 1900-1920	1200	1800

Satin

	LOW	HIGH
Bowl Vase, dec. yellow web w/ prunus blossoms & butterfly in heavy gold, 3.5" ht., 4.5" dia.	$ 350	$ 520
Bride's Bowl, overlay of pink, white on bottom, maroon flowers, green, yellow & lavender leaves, frosted, ruffled edging, gold trim, 4.5" ht.	270	400
Ewer, overlay of dec., shaded pink. applied frosted handle, enameled flowers, 3 petal top, white interior, 7" ht., 3 " dia.	110	160
Ewer, overlay of dec., shaded pink. applied frosted handle, enameled flowers, foliage of gold, white interior, 8.5" ht., 4.5" dia.	140	210
Ewer, overlay of dec., shaded pink, frosted, applied handle, enameled flowers, 9.5" ht., 3.5" dia.	120	180
Rose Bowl, embossed flowers of rose shaded to pink, white interior, 8-crimp top, 3.5" ht., 4" dia.	130	200
Rose Bowl, overlay of blue diamond quilted cut velvet, 4-crimp top, white interior, 3.5" ht., 3.5" dia.	175	260
Rose Bowl, overlay of dec. blue, flowers w/ butterfly, petal applied feet, 4-crimp top, white interior, 5.5" ht., 4.5" dia.	150	220
Rose Bowl, overlay of dec. light blue, applied frosted feet, enamel daisies w/ red jewel, 8-crimp top, white interior, 4.5" ht., 4.5" dia.	150	220
Vase, overlay of diamond-quilted rose-cut velvet, white interior, ruffled, 7.25" ht., 3.5" dia.	200	300
Vases, pr., overlay of dec. rose shaded to pink, w/ white enameled flowers, gold foliage, white interior, 57" ht., 4.5" dia.	220	330
Water Tumbler, dec. shaded pink overlay, enameled flowers & leaves, white interior, 4.5" ht., 3" dia.	150	220

Spatter

	LOW	HIGH
Box, cased glass, egg-shaped, dec. yellow, 3 applied feet in clear gold, branches & leaves of gold & white, floral dec., bluebell-shaped, 7.5" ht., 4.5" dia. .... $ 250 $ 380

Finger Lamp & Chimney, peach w/ white & brown spatter, applied handle, 6.5" ht., 4.5" dia. 130 200

Jar, yellow, forget-me-nots in blue, applied final, 6.5" ht., 3.5" dia. 75 110

Vase, Jack-in- the-Pulpit, ruffled, diamond quilted, green, white & peach, 9.5" ht., 5.5" dia. 80 120

Water Tumbler, green & white embossed swirl, 3.5" ht., 2.5" dia. 60 90

Stevens and Williams

Fairy Lamp, satin finish, striped green & white, sgn. Clarke, 5.5" ht., 4" dia. .... $ 200 $ 300

Plate, Pastil, blue, fleur-de-lis, sgn., 7.5" dia. 40 60

Vase, Arbor, frosted cranberry w/ opaque white, frosted, reeded applied handles & pedestal foot, ruffled top, 6.5" ht., 3.5" dia. 140 200

Vase, green rib design, pinched floral form, 6" dia. 35 50

Vase, overlay amber applied edging around ruffle, off-white opaque w/ amber branches w/ multicolored flowers & leaves, pink interior, 6.5" ht., 3.5" dia. 150 220

Vase, overlay, amber handle & branch on white background w/ amber plum, pink, & amber leaf, square top in pink, amber edging, 8" ht., 3.5" dia. 125 190

Webb blue cameo vase, $750 at auction. — Photo courtesy of Northeast Auctions.

Webb

Fairy Lamp, acid fin., dome on sgn. Clarke candle cup .... $ 350 $ 520

Fairy Lamp, acid fin., gold dec. Aladdin shape, green Tunnecliffe pottery base, shade dec. w/ red flowers & green leaves, base marked "Clarke," 6.5" ht. 1100 1650

Rose Bowl, miniature, acid fin., crimped top, dec. w/ red berries, green & brown leaves, unsgn., 2.5" ht., 2.5" dia. 450 680

Vase, acid fin., flower petal top, salmon pink to yellow, polychrome dec. leaves & berries, 3.5" ht., 3.5" dia. 500 750

Vase, acid fin., fluted top, embossed striping, 3.5" ht., 3" dia. 400 600

Vase, acid fin., ruffled top & base, 4.5" ht., 2.5" dia. 300 450

Vase, acid fin., ruffled top, salmon pink to yellow, polychrome dec. flower

	LOW	HIGH
& leaves, unsgn., 4.5" ht., 2.5" dia.	$ 450	$ 680
Vase, acid fin., ruffled top, widely flared, ball shape body, unsgn., 3.5" ht. ..	400	600
Vase, acid fin., salmon pink to yellow, dec. w/ foliage & red buds, unusual shape, 4.5" ht., 2.5" dia.	450	700
Vase, bulbous, acid red background w/ white floral dec., narrow neck, bulbous shoe, 5.5" ht.	675	1000
Vase, bulbous, cylinder neck, peach shading, overlaid in white, cut w/ poppies & leaves, 7.5" ht., c. 1895	4000	6000
Vase, bulbous, long cylinder neck, greenish background, overlaid in white & pink, cut morning glories & leaves, stylized coils around neck, 8.5" ht., c. 1890	4000	6000
Vase, Peachblow, glossy, rose red & pink w/ raised gold prunus & bird decoration, cream lining, 9" ht., 4" dia.	400	600
Vase, Peachblow, satin, rose & pink w/ floral & butterfly decoration in heavy gold, cream lining, 8" ht., 3" dia.	375	560
Vase, Peachblow, two applied handles, raised gold, green, & silver decoration w/squirrels, grapes & grape vines, 10" ht.	450	650
Vase, Queen's, acid fin., bottle, salmon pink to yellow, enamel ivy leaf dec., sgn. Thos. Webb Queen's Burmese Ware, 7.5" ht., 4.5" dia.	1200	1800
Vase, Queen's, acid fin., flower petal top, salmon pink to yellow, dec. w/ leaves & berries, sgn. Thos. Webb Queen's Burmese Ware, 2.5" ht., 3.5" dia.	600	900
Vase, Queen's, acid fin., flower top, frosted edge, salmon pink to yellow, pine cone enameled dec., sgn. Thos. Webb Queen's Burmese Ware, 5.5" ht., 3.5" dia.	750	1250
Vase, ruffled top & bulbous base, satin fin., 3.75"	175	250

Avon Bottles

David Hall McConnell founded The California Perfume Company in New York City at the end of the 19th century. The firm changed its name to Avon in 1939. A pioneer in home sales, most people recognize the company's figural decanters produced in the late 1960s to the early 1980s. Prices are based on bottles in mint condition in original boxes of excellent to near mint condition. For further reading see *Avon Bottle Collector's Encyclopedia*, written and published by Bud Hastin, and *The Official Price Guide to Bottles, Old and New*, published by The House of Collectibles, Random House, NY.

Top left to right: Tug-A-Brella, 1979, $7-$9; Sea Trophy, 1972, $8-$12. Bottom left to right: Straight 8, 1969, $5-$7; '55 Chevy, 1975, $8-$12.

	LOW	HIGH
Aladdin's Lamp, 1971	$ 8	$ 10
Alaskan Moose, 1974	7	9
American Eagle, 1971	5	7

	LOW	HIGH
American Eagle Pipe, 1974	5	6
American Schooner, 1972	7	9
Army Jeep, 1974	4	6
At Point Irish Setter, 1973	4	6
Atlantic 4-4-2 Locomotive, 1973	6	8
Avon Calling Candlestick Phone, 1969	8	12
Avon Calling Wall Phone, 1973	8	10
Betsy Ross, 1976	4	6
Betsy Ross, white on white glass, 1976	8	10
Big Mack Truck, 1973	7	9
Big Rig Tractor Trailer, 1975	8	12
Black Volkswagon, 1970	6	8
Blood Hound Pipe, 1976	4	6
Blue Volkswagon, 1973	6	8
Blunderbuss Pistol 1780, 1976	8	10
Bucking Bronco, 1971	6	8
Buffalo Nickel, 1971	5	7
Bugatti '27, 1974	8	12
Buick Skylark '53, 1979	10	12
Bulldog Pipe, 1972	6	7
Cable Car, 1974	7	9
Calabash Pipe, 1974	6	7
Canada Goose, 1973	7	9
Cannonball Express 4-6-0 Locomotive, 1976	5	7
Casey's Lantern, 1966	45	55
Catch-a-Fish, 1976	7	9
Cement Mixer, 1979	12	14
1876 Centennial Express Train, 1978	7	9
1926 Checker Cab, 1977	7	9
'55 Chevy, 1975	8	12
Chief Pontiac Car Mascot, 1976	7	9
Collector's Pipe, 1973	4	5
Colt Revolver 1851, 1975	8	10
Corncob Pipe, 1974	4	6
'37 Cord, 1974	6	8
Corvette Stingray '65, 1975	4	6
Country Kitchen (Rooster), 1973	4	6
Country Store Coffee Mill, 1972	4	6
Country Vendor, 1973	8	12
Covered Wagon, 1970	4	6
Cuper Cycle II, 1974	5	7
Dear Friends, 1974	8	10
Defender Cannon, 1966	8	12
Derringer, 1977	6	8
Dolphin (American), 1968	8	10
Dueling Pistol 1760, 1973	7	9
Dueling Pistol II, 1975	7	9
Dune Buggy, 1971	7	9
Dutch Pipe, 1973	6	7
Electric Charger, 1970	4	6
Electric Guitar, 1974	5	7

	LOW	HIGH
Extra Special Male (U.S. Mail Jeep), 1977	$ 4	$ 6
Faithful Laddie Collie, 1977	5	6
Ferrari '53, 1974	4	6
1910 Fire Fighter, 1975	6	8
First Volunteer Fire Pumper, 1971	8	12
Flower Maiden, 1973	5	7
Fly-a-Balloon, 1975	6	8
'36 Ford, 1976	6	8
1973 Ford Ranger Pickup Truck, 1978	5	7
Fragrance Hours (tall case clock), 1971	5	7
French Telephone, 1971	15	20
Garden Girl, 1975	7	9
Gas Pump, 1979	7	9
Gavel, 1967	8	10
General 4-4-0 Locomotive, 1971	7	9
Gold Cadillac, 1969	8	10
Golden Rocket Early Locomotive, 1974	7	9
Gone Fishing Boat, 1973	8	12
Greyhound Bus (1931), 1976	7	9
Harvester Tractor, 1973	8	12
Haynes Apperson 1902, 1973	6	8
Highway King, 1977	8	12
Homestead (Cabin), 1973	4	5
Indian Head Penny, 1970	5	7
Island Parakeet, 1977	4	6
Jaguar, 1973	6	8
Jeep Renegade, 1981	5	8
Kodiak Bear, 1977	5	7
Leisure Hours Clock, 1970	6	8
Leisure Hours Clock Miniature, 1974	4	5
Library Lamp, 1976	4	6
Longhorn Steer, 1975	6	8
Majestic Elephant, 1977	8	10
Mallard Duck, 1967	8	10
Maxwell '23, 1972	6	8
1936 MG, 1974	6	8
Mini-Bike, 1972	5	7
Model A, 1972	5	6
Mustang '64, 1976	4	6
Old Faithful St. Bernard, 1972	5	7
Open Golf Cart, 1972	7	9
Packard Roadster, 1970	6	8
Pepper Box Pistol (gold), 1982	7	9
Pheasant, 1972	8	10
Pheasant Reissue, 1977	7	9
Philadelphia Derringer, 1980	8	10
Pierce Arrow '33, 1975	6	8
Pipe Dream, 1967	6	8
Pipe Full (brown), 1971	4	5
Pipe Full (green), 1972	4	5
Pony Express, 1971	6	8

	LOW	HIGH
Pony Express Rider Pipe, 1975	$ 5	$ 7
Pony Post, 1972	5	7
Pony Post Miniature, 1973	3	5
Pony Post Tall, 1966	7	9
Quail, 1973	6	8
Rainbow Trout, 1973	7	9
Red Sentinel Firetruck, 1978	10	12
Revolutionary Cannon, 1975	4	5
Rio Depot Wagon, 1972	6	8
Road Runner, 1973	5	7
Roaring Twenties Fashion Figure, 1972	7	9
Rolls Royce, 1972	7	10
Royal Siamese Cat, 1978	5	7
Scimitar, 1968	18	22
Scottish Lass, 1975	5	7
Sea Maiden (Mermaid), 1971	6	8
Sea Trophy Swordfish, 1972	8	12
Short Pony, 1968	5	6
Side Wheeler, 1971	4	6
Silver Duesenberg, 1970	8	12
Skater's Waltz, 1979	7	9
Skip-a-Rope, 1977	6	8
Snoopy Surprise, 1969	8	10
Snow Mobile, 1974	7	9
Spanish Senorita, 1975	7	9
Spirit of St. Louis Airplane, 1970	9	12
Stage Coach, 1970	5	7
Stanley Steamer, 1971	6	8
Station Wagon, 1971	8	10
Sterling Six II, 1973	4	6
Sterling Six Silver, 1978	5	8
Stock Car Racer, 1974	5	7
Straight 8, 1969	5	7
Studebaker '51, 1975	4	6
1914 Stutz Bearcat, 1974	7	9
Super Cycle, 1971	5	7
Sure Catch Fishing Lure, 1977	5	6
Sure Winner Race Car, 1972	6	8
Swinger Golf Bag, 1969	8	12
Ten Point Buck, 1973	6	8
The Camper, 1972	8	12
The Thomas Flyer 1908, 1974	7	9
Thomas Jefferson Hand Gun, 1978	8	10
Thunderbird '55, 1974	5	6
Touring T, 1969	6	8
Touring T Silver, 1978	5	8
Triumph TR-3, 1975	4	6
Twenty Paces Dueling Set, box, red lining, 1967	30	40
Twenty Paces Dueling Set, rare raised gun sight, 1967	70	90
Uncle Sam Pipe, 1975	5	6
Vantastic, 1979	6	8

	LOW	HIGH
Viking Discoverer Ship, 1977	$ 12	$ 15
Viking Horn, 1966	12	15
Volcanic Repeating Pistol, 1979	6	8
Volkswagon Love Bus, 1975	8	10
Volkswagon Rabbit, 1980	3	5
Western Boot, 1973	4	5
Wild Mustang Pipe, 1976	5	7
Wild Turkey, 1974	7	9
Wilderness Classic (Running Stag), 1976	8	10
Winnebago Motor Home, 1978	8	10

Bottles

Many types of bottles found on the collectible market include: ale and gin, beer, cosmetic, bitters, crocks, cure, food, ink, medicine, mineral water, poison, pontil, soda and spirits. Because of their collector appeal, flasks, fruit jars, and Hutchinson bottles are listed separate sections.

Left to right: Dr. Kilmer's Swamp Root Remedy, $25-35; Old Mill Stream Whiskey, $18-22; 7-Up Quart Bottle, $5-7.

	LOW	AVG.	HIGH
Bitters			
Baker's High Life, The Great Nerve Tonic on back, pt. .... $ 34		$ 46	$ 58
Baxter's Mandrake, Lord Bros. Prop., amethyst, 6.5" 22		32	42
Begg's Dandelion Bitters, stoppered, amber, 7.5" 46		50	55
Caroni, pt., amber 22		32	45
Celery & Chamomile on label, sq., amber, 10" 24		34	43
Compound Calisaya Bitters, tapered top, sq., amber, 9.5" 33		38	42
Dr. Boyce's Tonic label, sample size, 12 panels, aqua, 4.5" 20		26	31
Dr. E. Chyder Stomach Bitters, N.C., amber, 10" 35		42	50
Fer-Kina Galeno on shoulder, beer-type bottle, brown, 10.5" 21		27	33
The Bitters Pharmacy on label, clear, 4.5" 5		10	15
Cure			
Dr. Taylor's Sure Chill Cure, ring top, aqua, 5.5" .... $ 10		$ 17	$ 24
Twenty-Four Hour Cure Guaranteed, ring top, clear, 5" 18		22	26
Veno's Lightning Cough Cure, double ring top, aqua, 7.5" 15		20	25
While's Quick Healing Cure, amber, 6.25" 12		18	24
Wood's Great Peppermint for Coughs & Colds, clear, 6.5" 15		20	25

	LOW	AVG.	HIGH

Food

Joslyn's Maple Syrup, eight sides, round lip, aqua, 8" .... $ 10	$ 18	$ 25
Nut House, figure of house, store jar, ball shape, clear 15	30	45
Peppermint, marble in neck, aqua 7.5" 23	25	27
Planters, same in back, sq., glass top, peanut nobs, clear 65	75	85
Red Snapper Sauce Co., Memphis, 6 sides, clear, 9.5" 19	25	30
Warsaw Pickle Co., aqua, 8.5" 14	18	22

Ink

Angus & Co., cone, aqua, 3.5" .... $ 10	$ 13	$ 16
Arnold's, round, clear or amethyst, ... 15	19	23
Billing a Co., Banker's Writing Ink, aqua, 2" 35	45	55
S & B, pottery bottle, tan, 7.5" 16	18	22

Medicine

B & P, amber, Lyons Powder on shoulder, 4.5" .... $ 6	$ 8	$ 10
Balsam of Honey, pontil, aqua, 3.5" 50	60	80
Batemans Drops, vertical, cylindrical, amethyst, 5.5" 6	9	12
Borax, clear, 5.5" 28	32	36
Brown Sarsaparilla, aqua, 9.5" 13	17	21
Brown's Instant Relief for Pain, aqua, embossed, 5.5" 7	9	11
Burnett, clear, 6.5" 16	21	25
Dr. Barkman's Never Failing Liniment, light green, 6.5" 11	14	17
F. Brown's, aqua, 5.5" 11	14	17
Medicine, T.B. Barton, clear or amethyst, 4.5" 7	10	13

Mineral

Adam W. Young, Canton, Ohio, graduated collar, aqua, 9.5" .... $ 15	$ 17	$ 19
San Francisco Glass Works, tapered neck, blob top, green, 7" 25	35	45
Saratoga Spring, honey amber, 9.5" 50	70	90
Shasta Water Co., Mineral Water Co., 10.5" 12	18	25
Mineral, UTE Chief of Mineral Water, U.T. on base, purple, 8" 10	16	20
Veronica Mineral Water on shoulder, sq., amber, clear, 10.25" 17	20	28
Weller Bottling Works, Saratoga, N.Y., blob top, aqua 17	23	30

Poison

Baltimore, MD printed on bottom, amber, 3" .... $ 7	$ 8	$ 9
DPS, skull & cross, cross on 4 sides, ring top, cobalt 18	22	26
Eli Lilly & Co., Poison printed on panels, amber, 2" 12	18	24
F.S. & Co. on base, Poison vertically, ringtop, amber, 2.5" 15	25	35
R.C. Millings Bed Bug Poison, Charleston, clear, 6.5" 25	35	45
Rat Poison printed on round bottle, clear or amethyst, 2.5" 35	45	55
Tincture Iodine printed under skull & crossbones, sq., amber 13	18	23
Triloids printed on 1 panel, Poison on another, cobalt, 3.5" 14	20	25
Wyeth Poison, round ring base and top, cobalt, 2.5" 15	25	30

Pontil

Bake's Dr. printed, tapered top, pale aqua, 5" .... $ 40	$ 60	$ 80
Balsam of Honey printed, round bottle, ring top, aqua, 3" 40	50	60
Brown's, F., Ess. of Jamaica Ginger, Phila., oval, aqua, 5.5" 20	30	40
Cannington Shaw & Co., St. Helens, beading on shoulder 20	35	50

	LOW	AVG.	HIGH
Cooke's Carmine Ink printed, bell shaped, ring top, aqua, 1.5"	$ 30	$ 35	$ 40
Pontil, Dolby's Criminate printed, round, light ring top, 3.5"	40	50	60
Harrison's Columbia Ink printed, round, ring top, cobalt, 4.5"	70	85	100
Hoover, Phila., 12 panels, ring top, light green	40	50	60
Snuff, label, flare top, beveled corners, olive amber, 4.5"	25	35	45

Spirits

	LOW	AVG.	HIGH
Acker Merrall, label, A9 on bottom, amber, 11"	$ 15	$ 22	$ 29
Belle of Nelson, label, whiskey, M.M. on bottom, clear, 12"	12	19	26

Above: 19th century bottle with elaborate stands are often worth thousands of dollars. — Photo courtesy of Northeast Auctions.

Cambridge Glass

The Cambridge Glass Co., located in Cambridge, OH, chiefly produced cut glass. During the 1920s and 1930s, it maintained a near monopoly on the manufacture of cut glass tableware. The glassware listed here has come to be known as "elegant" Depression glass.

Most Cambridge elegant Depression glass was unmarked. A triangle, a "C" inside, or "Near-cut" appears on some pieces.

	GREEN	CRYSTAL	BLUE	YELLOW	PINK
Almond Bowl, 2.5"	$ 43	$ 40	$ 40	$ 90	$ 80
Berry Bowl, 10"	47	48	45	75	75
Bonbon Bowl, handles, 5.5"	44	43	51	80	75
Bread & Butter Plate, 6.25"	17	17	18	34	32
Celery Tray, 11"	47	40	48	85	77
Cereal Bowl, bell form, 6"	32	35	31	60	56
Cereal Bowl, flat rim, 6"	26	27	25	50	45
Comport, 7"	80	82	81	125	100
Cream Soup, with liner	42	46	48	65	65
Creamer, footed	43	40	40	87	83
Creamer, scalloped edge	40	37	37	80	70
Cruet, handle, stopper, 6 oz.	104	92	97	150	150
Cup	27	28	28	44	43
Dinner Plate, 9.5"	43	42	47	90	70
Grill Plate, 10"	39	37	37	73	65
Mayonnaise Dish, liner & ladle	85	80	82	135	130
Pickle Tray, 9"	50	50	43	85	80
Plate, handles, 7"	42	47	47	57	65
Salad Plate, 8.5"	28	30	30	50	45
Sauce Boat, with saucer	95	90	90	185	160
Saucer	8	7	8	14	14
Service Tray, handles, 13"	83	82	86	150	115
Sugar, footed	38	38	38	81	78
Sugar, scalloped edge	36	38	36	84	80
Vegetable Bowl, oval, 9.5"	50	53	55	95	90

Carnival Glass

The turn-of-the-century craze for iridescent art glass spawned the birth of Taffeta, or Carnival glass, in 1905. Using mass production and new chemical techniques, Carnival glass was widely produced toward the end of the Art Nouveau period. Tastes changed, however, ushering in the streamlined Art Deco period. Though produced until 1930, by 1925 Carnival glass was sold by the trainload to fairs and carnivals and given out as prizes. (Hence, the name Carnival glass.) Since the 1970's, Carnival glass has become a desired collectible. For further information see *The Official Price Guide to Glassware*, by Mark Pickvet, House of Collectibles, Random House, NY.

Patterns are given after each of the following entries.

	GREEN	MARIGOLD	BLUE	AMETHYST
Bowl, dia. 7" - 8.5", Acorn- Fenton	$ 30	$ 25	$ 30	$ 30
Bowl, 7" - 9", Apple Blossom-Dugan	42	37	42	42
Bowl, flat, dia. 10", Chrysanthemum-Fenton	50	35	50	—
Bowl, ftd, dia. 10", Chrysanthemum-Fenton	50	35	50	—
Bowl, Detroit, Elks-Fenton	330	—	330	330
Bowl, Parkersburg, Elks-Fenton	360	—	360	360
Candy Dish, Beaded Cable-Northwood	35	25	35	35
Plate, dia. 9", Acorn- Fenton	300	125	300	300
Plate, dia. 8.5", Apple Blossom-Dugan	70	48	70	70
Rose Bowl, Beaded Cable-Northwood	52	35	52	52
Tumbler, Banded Drape-Fenton	—	18	30	30
Water Pitcher, Banded Drape-Fenton	—	72	190	190

A selection of Carnival glass items including a molded grape pitcher (lower left). — Photo courtesy of George Kerrigan Photography.

Cut Glass

Cut glass features deep prismatic cutting in elaborate, often geometric designs. Developed during the 16th century in Bohemia, it remained popular until the invention of molded pressed glass in America about 1825. It enjoyed a revival during the Brilliant Period of cut glass in America from 1876-1916. The edges are sharp, refracting light clearly. It is thicker and heavier than most blown glass. Round shapes have a distinct bell tone when struck; however, if shaped like Massachusetts, it may sound like a diving helmet.

Making cut glass required patience and talent. Master craftsmen blew the finest 35-45% lead crystal or it poured into molds producing a shaped piece called a blank. These blanks measured from .25"-.5" thick, necessary for the deep cutting which distinguished this glass from later periods. The resulting product was exceedingly heavy. Cutting and polishing required four steps. First, the desired pattern was drawn on the blank with crayons or paint. Next, the deepest cuts were made by rough cutting, pressing the blank on an abrasive cutting wheel lubricated by a stream of water and sand. In the third step, the rough cuts were smoothed with a finer stone wheel and water. Finally, the craftsman polished or "colored" the piece on a wooden wheel with putty powder or pumice to produce the gleaming finish.

The prices here are for American cut glass made between 1880 and 1920. They represent an average range for the forms listed. Prices for some highly collected makers (e.g. Libbey and Hawkes) may go for much higher, depending on the piece. For further information see *The Official Price Guide to Glassware*, by Mark Pickvet, House of Collectibles, Random House, NY.

Clockwise from above left: two footed compotes; one quart pitcher; footed two-part punch bowl; scalloped edge punch bowl.

	LOW	AVG.	HIGH
Basket, handled, 10"	$ 430	$ 455	$ 480
Bell	120	180	240
Bonbon, diamond shape, 6"	120	160	200
Bonbon, covered, 4.5"-5.5"	160	200	240
Bowl, 9"	110	185	260
Carafe, 10"	120	170	220
Celery Tray	80	145	210
Celery, upright	60	80	100
Champagne Glass	40	60	80
Claret Glass	50	75	100
Cologne Bottle, w/ stopper, 6"	60	150	240
Compote, 7"	80	120	160
Compote, 10"	140	200	260
Cordial Glass	50	55	60
Cream & Sugar	120	165	210
Cruet, 6"	60	95	130
Decanter, pt.	160	200	240
Decanter, pt., handled	200	240	280
Decanter, 1 qt.	400	600	800
Decanter, handled, 1 qt.	600	800	1000
Dish, cheese, covered	320	400	480
Dish, ice cream, 6"	220	270	320
Dish, shell form, 6"	160	200	240
Dish, sq., 8"	120	160	200
Dish, 4 section, 9"	160	200	240
Dish, 7"-8"	60	110	160
Finger Bowl	30	40	50
Fruit Bowl, 8"	80	120	160
Glass, water	40	50	60
Goblet	50	70	90
Inkwell, crystal	40	60	80
Jar, powder, covered, 4.5"-5.5"	120	160	200
Jar, tobacco, sterling top, 7"	160	200	240
Jug, whiskey, stoppered	280	340	400
Knife Rest, ball ends	40	50	60
Lemonade mug	50	55	60
Lamp base, 17"	480	600	720
Lamp, mushroom shade, 18"	600	800	1000
Mug	30	45	60
Nappy, 5"	50	65	80
Nappy, 8"	120	155	190
Nappy, handled, 5"	60	80	100
Pitcher, 1 pt.	120	155	190
Pitcher, 2 qt.	160	240	320
Pitcher, 1 qt. or 3 pt.	140	190	240
Platter, ice cream, oval, 13.5"	170	260	350
Powder Puff Box, covered, 4.5"-5.5"	80	100	120
Punch Bowl, on foot (2 part), 14"-15"	1200	1500	2000
Punch Bowl, single piece, 12"	290	505	720
Relish Dish, 7"	80	120	160
Salt, open, 2.5"	30	40	50
Shakers	80	120	160

Depression Glass

Colored glassware was machine-made during the late 1920s and early 1930s. The glass was available in ten-cent stores, given away at filling stations, and theaters, and used for promotional purposes. There are over eighty Depression glass clubs that sponsor shows, with attendance in the thousands.

For more information on Depression glass see Mark Pickvet, *The Official Price Guide to Glassware*, (House of Collectibles, Random House, NY) and Gene Florence, *Depression Glass*.

ADAM	PINK	GREEN
Bowl, 4.75"	$ 17	$ 16
Bowl, 5.75"	48	36
Bowl, 7.75"	25	26
Bowl, 9", w/ lid	60	100
Bowl, oval, 10"	25	32
Butter Dish, w/ lid	80	390
Cake Plate, 10" ftd.	20	28
Candlesticks, 4" pr.	87	117
Coaster, 3.25"	26	10
Cream/Sugar	35	40
Cup/Saucer	32	30
Grill Plate, 9"	10	18
Jar, Candy, w/ lid, 2.5"	86	100
Lamp	272	245
Pitcher, 8", 1 qt.	42	56
Plate, 6"	6	6
Plate, 7.75" sq.	13	15
Plate, 9" sq.	25	25
Platter, 11.75"	17	20
Relish Tray, 8"	15	20
Salt/Pepper, 4" ftd.	66	110
Sherbet, 3"	28	37
Tumbler, 4.5"	28	25
Tumbler, 5.25"	70	50
Vase, 7.5"	247	50

AMERICAN SWEETHEART	PINK	WHITE	RED	BLUE	CREMEX
Bowl, 6"	$ 16	$ 15	—	—	—
Bowl, 6"	—	—	$ 250	$ 320	$ 15
Bowl, 9"	28	55	—	—	—
Bowl, 9"	—	—	300	355	58
Bowl, 18"	—	400	—	—	—
Bowl, 18"	—	—	1100	1270	—
Chop Plate, 11"	—	15	—	—	—
Cream/Sugar	25	10	—	—	—
Cream/Sugar	—	—	195	242	226
Cup/Saucer	17	15	—	—	—
Cup/Saucer	—	—	135	173	—
Pitcher, 2 qt.	560	—	—	—	—
Plate, 6"	—	—	—	25	—
Plate, 6"-7"	3	5	—	—	—
Plate, 8"	12	11	—	—	—

	PINK	WHITE	RED	BLUE	CREMEX
Plate, 8"	—	—	70	115	—
Plate, 9"-10"	20	10	—	—	—
Plate, 9"-10"	—	—	110	155	—
Platter, 12" rd.	15	15	—	—	—
Platter, 12" rd.	—	—	200	220	—
Platter, oval, 13"	30	50	—	—	—
Platter, oval, 13"	—	—	—	—	—
Salt/Pepper, ftd.	400	340	—	—	—
Server, 15.5"	—	250	—	—	—
Server, 15.5"	—	—	370	520	—
Server, 3-tier	—	260	—	—	—
Server, 3-tier	—	—	740	840	—
Sherbet, 4" ftd.	15	23	—	—	—
Sherbet, 4.25" ftd.	—	—	—	—	—
Soup Bowl, 4.5"	43	50	—	—	—
Soup Plate, 9.5"	50	60	—	—	—
Tumbler, 3"-4", 5-9 oz.	61	—	—	—	—
Tumbler, 4.5", 10 oz.	90	—	—	—	—
Vegetable, oval, 11"	45	50	—	—	—

ANNIVERSARY	CRYSTAL	PINK
Bowl, 5"	$ 2	$ 5
Bowl, 9"	12	10
Butter Dish, w/ lid	42	80
Cake Plate, w/ lid	17	23
Candlestick, 5" pr.	23	
Cream/Sugar, w/ lid	13	25
Cup/Saucer	5	11
Dish, 3-ftd.	5	12
Jar, Candy, w/ lid	31	48
Pickle Dish, 9"	5	11
Plate, 6.25"	2	3
Plate, 9"	6	8
Relish Tray, 8"	8	11
Server, 12.5"	8	12
Sherbet, ftd.	5	8
Soup Plate, 7.5"	6	15
Vase, 6.5"	11	16
Wall Pocket	16	25
Wine Glass, 2.5 oz.	8	16

AURORA	DARK BLUE	PINK
Bowl, 4.5"	$ 17	$ 15
Bowl, 5.5"	8	6
Creamer, 4.5"	15	10
Cup/Saucer	15	10
Plate, 6.5"	6	5
Tumbler, 4.75", 10 oz.	16	12

BLOCK OPTIC	GREEN	YELLOW	PINK
Bowl, 4"-5"	$ 10	$ 20	$ 10

	GREEN	YELLOW	PINK
Bowl, 7"-9"	$ 22	$ 30	$ 17
Butter Dish, w/ lid	66	75	—
Butter Tub, open	40	60	—
Candlesticks, low, pr.	60	70	—
Comport, 4" w.	20	40	—
Cream/Sugar	31	32	27
Cup/Saucer	21	23	16
Goblet, 9 oz.	27	28	21
Grill Plate, 9"	10	23	17
Ice Bucket	40	50	—
Jar, Candy, w/ lid	50	68	56
Mug	45	—	—
Pitcher, 7"-8", 2 qt.	70	80	—
Pitcher, 8.5", 3 qt.	45	47	—
Plate, 6"	2	3	2
Plate, 8"	5	7	5
Plate, 9"-10"	21	46	27
Salt/Pepper	43	95	85
Server, center handle	61	65	—
Sherbet, 3"-5"	11	15	10
Tumbler, 5-10 oz.	21	25	25
Wine Glass, 4.5"	27	21	—

BUBBLE, BULL'S EYE, PROVINCIAL DK. GREEN		LT. BLUE	DK. RED
Bowl, 4"-5"	$ 10	—	$ 12	$ 7
Bowl, 8"-9"	12	—	15	—
Cream/Sugar	21	—	50	—
Cup/Saucer	6	—	6	10
Grill Plate, 9.5"	—	—	16	—
Pitcher, 2 qt., w/ lip	—	—	—	58
Plate, 6.75"	2	—	5	—
Plate, 9.5"	8	—	7	10
Platter, oval, 12"	20	—	16	—
Server, 2-tier	—	—	—	25
Soup Plate, 7.75"	—	—	13	—
Tumbler, 6-12 oz.	—	—	—	12
Tumbler, 16 oz.	—	—	—	25

CAMEO, DANCING GIRL, BALLERINA GREEN	YELLOW	PINK	CRYSTAL
Bowl, Cereal, 5.5"	$ 38	$ 36	—	$ 10
Bowl, Cream Soup, 4.75"	70	—	—	—
Bowl, Sauce, 4.25"	—	—	—	7
Bowl, 7"-8"	45	—	$ 180	—
Bowl, 3-ftd., 11"	65	100	35	—
Butter Dish w/ lid	225	1000	—	—
Butter, open, 3" ht.	175	—	680	280
Cake Plate, 10", 3-ftd.	22	—	—	—
Cake Plate, 10.5", flat	110	—	—	—
Candlesticks, pr., 4"	100	—	—	—
Comport, 5" w.	20	—	252	—
Cookie Jar, w/ lid	63	—	—	—

	GREEN	YELLOW	PINK	CRYSTAL
Cream/Sugar, 3"-4"	$ 46	$ 31	$ 167	—
Cup/Saucer	21	15	122	$ 15
Decanter, w/ stopper, 10"	140	—	—	240
Goblet, 3.5"	300	—	—	—
Goblet, 4"-6"	50	—	222	—
Grill Plate, 10"-11"	12	11	—	57
Jam Jar, w/ lid, 2"	150	—	—	160
Jar, Candy, w/ lid	100	82	600	—
Pitcher, 5.75", 1.5 pt.	223	293	—	—
Pitcher, 6", 1 qt.	65	—	—	—
Pitcher, 8.5", 56 oz.	56	—	1700	520
Plate, 6"	5	3	77	3
Plate, 7"-8"	13	5	30	6
Plate, 8.5" sq.	38	140	—	—
Plate, 9"-10"	18	11	53	50
Platter, closed handles, 12"	25	22	—	—
Relish Tray, 7.5" ftd., 3-part	36	93	—	—
Salt/Pepper, pr.	80	—	860	—
Server, center handle	3200	—	—	—
Sherbet, 3"	17	25	42	—
Sherbet, 5"	38	37	85	—
Soup Plate, 9"	45	—	—	—
Tumbler, 3 oz., ftd.	70	—	130	—
Tumbler, 5.25", 15 oz.	68	—	150	—
Tumbler, 6.38", 15 oz., ftd.	400	—	—	—
Tumbler, 9-11 oz., flat	41	45	125	13
Vase, 5.75"	200	—	—	—
Vase, 8"	25	—	—	—
Vegetable, oval, 10"	23	35	—	—

CHERRY BLOSSOM	PINK	GREEN	DELPHITE
Bowl, 4.75"	$ 12	$ 16	$ 15
Bowl, 5.75"	36	35	—
Bowl, 8.5"	22	25	55
Bowl, 2-handled, 9"	10	25	20
Bowl, 10.5", 3-ftd.	56	65	—
Butter Dish, w/ lid	88	115	—
Cake Plate, 3-ftd., 10.25"	23	20	—
Coaster	15	16	—
Cream/Sugar	45	50	75
Cup/Saucer	22	25	25
Grill Plate, 10"	—	66	—
Grill Plate, 9"	30	30	—
Mug, 7 oz.	265	230	—
Pitcher, 7"-8" 1 qt.	52	75	100
Pitcher, 8", 42 oz.	52	67	—
Plate, 6"	7	7	15
Plate, 7"	20	25	—
Plate, 9"	18	10	17
Platter, 13"	51	55	—
Platter, oval, 11"	20	33	48

	PINK	GREEN	DELPHITE
Platter, oval, 9" .... $ 1000		—	—
Salt/Pepper, scalloped 1700		$ 1000	—
Server, 10.5" 18		22	$ 23
Sherbet 16		20	20
Soup Plate, 7.75" 63		65	—
Tumbler, 3.75", 4 oz. 18		20	25
Tumbler, 4"-5", 8-9 oz. 26		35	—
Tumbler, 5", 12 oz. 58		70	—
Vegetable, oval, 9" 28		30	65

CUBE, CUBIST	PINK	GREEN
Bowl, 4.5" .... $ 7		$ 8
Bowl, 6.5" 12		18
Butter Dish, w/ lid 75		85
Coaster, 3.25" 6		8
Cream/Sugar, w/ lid, 3" 28		30
Cup/Saucer 10		13
Jar, Candy, w/ lid, 6.5" 35		45
Pitcher, 8.75", 3 pt. 215		245
Plate, 6" 3		3
Plate, 8" 5		7
Powder Jar w/ lid, 3-ftd. 20		25
Salt/Pepper, pr. 42		45
Sherbet, ftd. 8		11
Tumbler, 4", 9 oz. 50		65

ENGLISH HOBNAIL	PINK
Ashtray .... $ 30
Bowl, 2-handled, 8" 62
Bowl, 4"-5" 17
Bowl, 6" 17
Bowl, 8" 27
Candlesticks, 3.5" pr. 42
Candlesticks, 8.5" pr. 73
Candy, w/ lid, 3-ftd. 90
Celery Dish, 9"-12" 30
Cigarette Box 40
Cologne Bottle 45
Cordial Glass, 1 oz. 26
Cream/Sugar 48
Cup/Saucer 20
Cup/Saucer, Demitasse 47
Decanter, 20 oz., w/ stopper 92
Egg Cup 43
Goblet, 6.25", 8 oz. 30
Grapefruit, 6.5" flange 22
Lamp, 6.25" 82
Lamp, 9.25" 185
Marmalade, w/ lid 58
Nappies, 11"-12" 57
Pitcher, 1 qt. 215

	PINK
Pitcher, 1.5 pt.	213
Pitcher, 2 qt., straight	300
Plate, 10"	35
Plate, 5"-7"	6
Plate, 8"	13
Relish Tray, 8"-12"	28
Salt/Pepper, pr.	125
Sherbet	20
Shot Glass	20
Soup Bowl	25
Tumbler, 5-13 oz.	25
Vase	120
Wine Glass, 2-5 oz.	22

FIRE-KING	JADEITE		TURQUOISE BLUE	
	Low	High	Low	High
Bowl, 4"-5"	—	—	$ 4	$ 5
Bowl, 5"-6"	$ 2	$ 4	—	—
Bowl, sq., 4.75"	5	8	—	—
Bowl, sq., 7.38"	10	15	—	—
Cream/Sugar	—	—	8	12
Cream/Sugar, w/ lid	11	16	—	—
Cup/Saucer	3	5	—	—
Cup/Saucer	—	—	4	5
Cup/Saucer, sq.	5	8	—	—
Mixing Bowl, 1-2 qt.	—	—	4	6
Mixing Bowl, 3-4 qt.	—	—	8	12
Mug, 8 oz.	—	—	5	7
Plate, 10"	—	—	5	7
Plate, 6"-9"	—	—	4	5
Plate, 7.75"	3	5	—	—
Plate, 9"	5	7	—	—
Plate, sq., 8.38"	5	8	—	—
Plate, sq., 9.25"	6	9	—	—
Platter, 12"	6	9	—	—
Relish Tray, 3-part	—	—	6	8
Soup Bowl, 6.5"	—	—	4	6
Soup Plate, 7.5"	5	7	—	—
Vegetable, 8"	—	—	8	10
Vegetable, 8.25"	6	9	—	—

FLORINTINE (#2)	GREEN	YELLOW	PINK	BLUE
Bowl, 4.5"	$ 15	$ 16	$ 20	—
Bowl, 5.5"	33	25	43	—
Bowl, 6"	20	23	38	—
Bowl, 8"	26	31	31	—
Bowl, 9"	31	—	—	—
Butter Dish, w/ lid	150	—	210	—
Candlesticks, 2.75" pr.	52	—	83	—
Candy Dish w/ lid	125	165	215	—
Coaster, 3.25"	15	22	27	—

	GREEN	YELLOW	PINK	BLUE
Coaster, 3.75"	$ 23	—	$ 25	—
Coaster, 5.5"	25	—	47	—
Comport, 3.5" ruffled	20	$ 10	28	$ 75
Cream/Sugar, w/ lid	55	—	60	—
Cream Soup, 5"	15	15	23	55
Cup/Saucer	13	—	16	—
Custard Cup	73	—	115	—
Gravy Boat, w/ stand	—	—	115	—
Grill Plate, 10.25"	11	—	15	—
Parfait, 6"	35	—	70	—
Pitcher, 6.25", 1.5 pt., cone ft.	—	—	150	—
Pitcher, 7.5", 1.75 pt., cone ft.	32	—	32	—
Pitcher, 7.5", 1.5 qt.	75	160	245	—
Pitcher, 8", 4.75 pt.	125	320	280	—
Plate, 6", Sherbet	5	—	7	—
Plate, 6.25", indented	22	—	30	—
Plate, 8.5"	10	10	12	—
Plate, 10"	18	22	18	—
Platter, oval, 11"	17	18	10	—
Relish Tray, 10"	22	26	28	—
Salt/Pepper, pr.	56	—	65	—
Sherbet, ftd.	10	—	13	—
Soup Plate, 7.5"	—	—	86	—
Tumbler, 3"-4", 5-9 oz.	16	11	26	87
Tumbler, 5", 12 oz.	35	—	48	—
Vegetable, oval, 9" w/ lid	56		75	—

FLOWER GARDEN	GREEN	YELLOW	PINK
Candlesticks, 4" pr.	$ 83	$ 98	$ 150
Candlesticks, 8" pr.	150	160	235
Candy, w/ lid, 6"-7.5"	167	180	265
Candy, w/ lid, heart-form	—	540	800
Cologne Bottle, 7.5"	—	300	330
Comport, 3" ht.	28	35	45
Comport, 5"-7" ht.	90	116	135
Cream/Sugar	—	210	—
Cup/Saucer	—	163	—
Plate, 7"-8"	26	30	43
Plate, 10"	55	52	73
Platter 10"-12"	70	100	135
Powder Jar, 6"-7.5", ftd.	111	137	200
Server, center handle	80	100	135
Tumbler, 7.5 oz.	155	—	—
Vase, 6.25"	126	150	180
Vase, 10.5"	—	172	246

FOREST GREEN	GREEN	
	Low	High
Ashtray	$ 4	$ 5
Bowl, 5"-7.5"	7	10
Cream/Sugar	10	15

	GREEN	
	Low	*High*
Cup/Saucer	$ 5	$ 8
Mixing Bowl	8	12
Pitcher, 1.5 pt.	18	22
Pitcher, 3 qt.	25	35
Plate, 6.5"	2	3
Plate, 8.5"	5	7
Plate, 10"	10	15
Platter, rect.	15	20
Punch Bowl, w/ stand	25	35
Punch Cup	2	3
Tumbler, 5-10 oz.	4	6
Vase, 4"-9"	5	7

FORTUNE	PINK	CRYSTAL
Bowl, 4"-5"	$ 6	$ 7
Bowl, 8"	15	14
Candy Dish, w/ lid	25	22
Cup/Saucer	10	8
Plate, 6"	5	4
Plate, 8"	10	8
Tumbler, 3.5"-4"	7	6

GEORGIAN	GREEN	CRYSTAL
Bowl, 4.5"	$ 5	$ 7
Bowl, 5.75"	20	25
Bowl, 6.5"	50	70
Bowl, 7.5"	50	65
Butter Dish, w/ lid	75	100
Cream/Sugar, 3", w/ lid	40	50
Cream/Sugar, 4", w/ lid	100	115
Cup/Saucer	12	17
Plate, 6"	4	5
Plate, 8"	7	10
Plate, 9"	20	25
Platter, 11.5"	60	75
Sherbet	10	12
Tumbler, 4", 9 oz.	45	55
Tumbler, 5.25", 12 oz.	80	120
Vegetable, oval, 9"	60	75

HOBNAIL	PINK	CRYSTAL
Bowl, 5"-7"	$ 7	$ 5
Cup/Saucer	6	6
Cream/Sugar	12	10
Decanter, w/ stopper, 1 qt.	25	—
Goblet, 10-13 oz.	10	—
Pitcher, 1 pt.	22	—
Pitcher, 1.5 qt.	40	33
Plate, 6"	2	2
Plate, 8.5"	5	3

	PINK	CRYSTAL
Sherbet	$ 5	$ 5
Shot Glass	6	—
Tumbler, 3-15 oz.	8	—

HOLIDAY	PINK	CRYSTAL
Bowl, 5"	$ 10	$ 12
Bowl, 8.5"	25	30
Bowl, 11"	80	110
Butter Dish, w/ lid	50	60
Cake Plate, 10.5", 3 ftd.	75	100
Candlesticks, 3" pr.	75	100
Chop Plate, 13.75"	100	120
Cream/Sugar, w/ lid, ftd.	30	40
Cup/Saucer	12	18
Pitcher, 4.75", 1 pt.	70	90
Pitcher, 6.75", 3 pt.	40	50
Plate, 6"	5	7
Plate, 9"	15	20
Platter, 10.5"-11.5"	17	22
Sherbet	8	12
Soup Plate, 8"	35	45
Tumbler, 4", 10 oz.	35	40
Tumbler, 6", ftd.	100	120
Vegetable, oval, 9.5"	20	25

LORAIN	CRYSTAL	GREEN	YELLOW
Bowl, 6"	$ 37	$ 40	$ 75
Bowl, 7.25"	55	60	75
Bowl, 8"	100	115	185
Cream/Sugar	37	40	48
Cup/Saucer	22	25	28
Plate, 5.5"	7	9	11
Plate, 8"	13	15	18
Plate, 10"	46	50	58
Platter, 11.5"	28	30	52
Relish Tray, 8", 4-part	25	27	30
Sherbet, ftd.	25	28	36
Tumbler, 4.75", 9 oz. ftd.	28	30	30
Vegetable, oval, 10"	47	55	70

MADRID	AMBER	PINK	GREEN	BLUE
Ash Tray, 6" sq.	$ 220	—	$ 130	—
Bowl, 8"-9.5"	22	$ 33	25	$40
Butter Dish, w/ lid	87	—	115	—
Cake Plate, 11.25"	16	16	27	—
Candlesticks, 2.25" pr.	28	23	—	—
Coaster (hot dish)	45	—	50	—
Console, low, 11"	10	13	—	—
Cookie Jar, w/ lid	52	45	—	—
Cream/Sugar, w/ lid	50	—	65	130
Cream Soup, 4.75"	16	—	—	—

	AMBER	PINK	GREEN	BLUE
Cup/Saucer	$ 13	$ 15	$ 17	$ 27
Gravy Boat, w/ stand	1600	—	—	—
Grill Plate, 10.5"	15	—	25	—
Jam Dish, 7"	20	—	23	35
Lazy Susan, w/ 7 dishes	800	—	—	—
Mold	15	—	—	—
Pitcher, 5.5", 1 qt.	40	—	—	—
Pitcher, 8", 2 qt.	55	60	175	175
Plate, 6"	5	6	5	11
Plate, 7.5"	15	15	13	23
Plate, 9"	10	11	12	23
Plate, 10.5"	45	—	47	80
Platter, oval, 11.5"	10	15	21	20
Relish Dish, 5"	10	10	10	13
Relish Tray, 10.25"	15	15	18	—
Salt/Pepper, pr.	65	—	90	168
Sherbet	11	—	13	16
Soup Plate, 7"	15	—	18	20
Tumbler, 4"-5.5", 5-12 oz.	27	10	42	33
Tumbler, 4", 5 oz., ftd.	36	—	50	—
Tumbler, 5.25", 10 oz. ftd.	33	—	40	—
Vegetable, oval, 10"	20	10	25	36

MISS AMERICA	CRYSTAL	PINK	GREEN	RED
Bowl, 4"-6"	$ 11	$ 18	$ 13	—
Bowl, 8", curved in rim	57	83	—	$ 500
Bowl, 8.75", straight deep	37	62	—	—
Butter Dish w/ lid	240	600	—	—
Cake Plate, 12"	26	40	—	—
Celery Dish, 10.5"	13	25	—	—
Coaster, 5.75"	17	27	—	—
Compote, 5"	18	30	—	—
Cream/Sugar	25	46	—	450
Cup/Saucer	18	32	28	—
Goblet, 4"-6", 3-10 oz.	20	65	—	265
Grill Plate, 10.25"	12	22	—	—
Jar, Candy, w/ lid, 11.5"	70	143	—	—
Pitcher, 8", 2 qt.	60	130	—	—
Plate, 5.75"	5	10	8	—
Plate, 8.5"	10	21	13	100
Plate 10.25"	15	28	—	—
Platter, oval, 12.25"	18	27	—	—
Relish Tray, 8.75", 4-part	15	21	—	—
Relish Tray, 11.75", round divided	20	200	—	—
Salt/Pepper, pr.	42	71	430	—
Sherbet	11	17	—	—
Tumbler, 4", 5 oz.	21	57	—	—
Tumbler, 4.5", 10 oz.	21	30	22	—
Tumbler, 5.75", 14 oz.	37	72	—	—
Vegetable, oval, 10"	18	25	—	—

MODERNSTONE

	COBALT	AMETHYST	FIRED COLORS
Ashtray, 7.75"	$ 140	—	—
Bowl, 5"	21	11	$ 2
Bowl, 6.5"	62	43	$ 5
Bowl, 8.75"	38	32	10
Butter Dish, w/ lid	100	—	—
Cheese Dish, w/ lid	250	—	—
Cream/Sugar	25	20	10
Cream Soup, 5"	10	17	—
Cup/Saucer	17	15	5
Custard Cup	18	15	—
Plate, 6"	6	5	1
Plate, 7"-8"	8	8	3
Plate, 9"	15	11	6
Plate, 10.5"	27	21	6
Platter, oval, 11"-12"	47	25	12
Salt/Pepper, pr.	48	46	23
Sherbet	13	12	6
Shot Glass	23	—	—
Soup Plate	60	57	7
Tumbler, 5-9 oz.	25	26	8
Tumbler, 12 oz.	85	60	—

MOONSTONE

	OPALESCENT
Bowl, 5"-7"	$ 12
Bowl, 9.5" crimped	22
Bowl, cloverleaf	15
Bud Vase, 5.5"	16
Candleholder, pr.	25
Cream/Sugar	10
Cup/Saucer	15
Goblet, 10 oz.	25
Jar, Candy, w/ lid, 6"	30
Plate, 6"	5
Plate, 8"	13
Plate, 10"	25
Powder Box, w/ lid, 4.75"	28
Relish Tray, 8"	12
Soup Plate, 8"	13
Sherbet, ftd.	10

OVEN GLASS-FIRE-KING

	BLUE	
	Low	High
Baker, 1 pt.	$ 6	$ 8
Baker, 1 qt.	8	12
Baker, 1.5 qt.	15	20
Baker, 2 qt.	18	25
Bowl, 4"-5.5"	15	25
Casserole, 1-4 pt., w/ knob lid	18	25
Casserole, 1 qt., pie plate lid	22	28
Casserole, 1.5" qt., pie plate lid	25	30
Casserole, 2 qt., pie plate lid	30	35

	BLUE	
	Low	High
Casserole, 10 oz., tab handle lid	$ 20	$ 25
Custard Cup, 5-6 oz.	5	7
Hot Plate, tab handles	18	22
Leftover, w/ lid, 5"-9"	13	25
Loaf Pan, 9"	20	25
Measuring Cup, 8 oz., no spout	50	65
Measuring Cup, 8 oz., w/ spout	20	25
Measuring Cup, 16 oz.	20	25
Mug, 7 oz.	30	35
Nurser, 4-8 oz.	18	25
Pie Plate, 8"-9.5"	15	20
Pie Plate, 10.5" juice saver	60	75
Roaster, 8.75"	40	50
Roaster, 10.5"	60	75
Table Server, tab handles	18	22
Utility Bowl, 7"-10"	17	22
Utility Pan, 8" x 12.5"	10	15

OLD FLORINTINE (#1)	GREEN	YELLOW	PINK	BLUE
Ashtray, 5.5"	$ 28	$ 45	$ 42	—
Bowl, 5"	12	10	15	$ 25
Bowl, 6"	15	20	22	—
Bowl, 8.5"	25	37	36	—
Butter Dish, w/ lid	180	225	170	—
Coaster/Ashtray, 3.75"	23	26	35	—
Cream/Sugar, w/ lid	47	55	53	—
Cream/Sugar, ruffled	65	—	77	130
Cup/Saucer	13	10	17	100
Grill-Plate, 10"	12	16	10	—
Pitcher, 6.5", 1 qt., ftd.	50	65	65	900
Pitcher, 7.5", 1.5 qt., flat	60	233	140	—
Plate, 6"	5	6	6	—
Plate, 8.5"	10	15	15	—
Plate, 10"	17	25	26	—
Platter, oval, 11.5"	16	21	25	—
Salt/Pepper, ftd.	55	60	76	—
Sherbet, 3 oz. ftd.	10	15	16	—
Tumbler, 3"-4", 5 oz. ftd.	10	25	23	—
Tumbler, 10-12 oz. ftd.	33	30	30	—
Tumbler, 5.25", 9 oz.	—	—	82	—
Vegetable, oval, 9.5", w/ lid	57	60	65	—

PATRICIAN	AMBER	PINK	GREEN
Bowl, 5"	$ 12	$ 17	$ 13
Bowl, 6"	28	28	20
Bowl, 8.5"	47	28	20
Butter Dish, w/ lid	110	356	162
Cookie Jar, w/ lid	96	—	475
Cream/Sugar, w/ lid	65	95	92
Cream Soup, 4.75"	16	25	28

	AMBER	PINK	GREEN
Cup/Saucer	$ 16	$ 22	$ 23
Grill Plate, 10.5"	15	15	16
Jam Dish	25	36	45
Pitcher, 8", 2.25 qt.	110	135	125
Plate, 6"	11	7	8
Plate, 7.5"	18	21	17
Plate, 9"	13	12	12
Plate, 10.5"	10	25	45
Platter, oval, 11.5"	10	18	21
Salt/Pepper, pr.	72	100	82
Sherbet	12	15	13
Tumbler, 4"-5.5", 5-14 oz.	35	37	35
Tumbler, 5.25", 8 oz., ftd.	47	—	66
Vegetable, oval, 10"	20	25	27

PATRICK	PINK	YELLOW
Bowl, 9", w/ handle	$ 35	$ 30
Bowl, 11"	35	32
Candlesticks, pr.	45	40
Candy Dish, 3-ftd.	50	45
Cheese Set	55	50
Cream/Sugar	35	30
Cup/Saucer	18	15
Goblet, 4"-5"	25	20
Goblet, 6", 10 oz.	35	32
Plate, 7"-8"	10	8
Sherbet, 4.75"	22	20
Tray, 11"	37	35

PRINCESS	GREEN	PINK	YELLOW
Ashtray, 4.5"	$ 92	$ 95	$ 115
Bowl, 4.5"-5"	30	25	36
Bowl, 9" octagon	35	26	110
Butter Dish, w/ lid	92	120	700
Cake Stand, 10"	23	21	—
Candy Dish, w/ lid	62	70	—
Coaster	37	83	125
Cookie Jar, w/ lid	65	75	—
Cream/Sugar, w/ lid	50	46	40
Cup/Saucer	18	17	16
Grill Plate, 9"	16	11	10
Pitcher, 6", 1 qt.	61	46	825
Pitcher, 7.5", 1.5 pt. ftd.	700	685	—
Pitcher, 8", 2 qt.	56	58	90
Plate, 6"	10	6	7
Plate, 8"	13	11	12
Plate, 9"	31	20	10
Plate, 11.5"	18	13	15
Platter, 12"	22	18	48
Relish Tray, 7.5", divided	31	21	81
Relish Tray, 7.5", plain	100	—	185

	GREEN	PINK	YELLOW	
Salt/Pepper, pr.	$ 70	$ 53	$ 73	
Sherbet, ftd.	22	21	42	
Tumbler, 3"-4", 5-9 oz.	35	28	32	
Tumbler, 5.25", 10-13 oz.	40	26	30	
Tumbler, 4.75", 9 oz. sq. ftd.	83	70	—	
Tumbler, 6.5", 12.5 oz. ftd.	92	65	126	
Vase, 8"	36	28	—	
Vegetable, oval, 10"	28	25	60	

SANDWICH	CRYSTAL	AMBER	RED	DK GREEN
Bowl, 5"	$ 5	$ 5	$ 16	$ 13
Bowl, 6.5"	11	10	31	37
Bowl, 7"-8"	12	—	51	70
Bowl, 9"	26	—	—	—
Butter Dish, w/ lid	50	—	—	—
Cookie Jar, w/ lid	55	51	—	27
Cream/Sugar, w/ lid	28	—	58	61
Cup/Saucer	5	12	13	27
Custard Cup, w/ liner	16	—	—	5
Pitcher, 2 qt.	66	—	275	—
Plate, 7"	12	5	—	—
Plate, 9"	17	10	61	—
Plate, 12"	13	15	—	—
Punch Bowl, w/ stand	40	—	—	—
Punch Cup	5	—	—	—
Sherbet	11	—	—	—
Tumbler, 3-5 oz.	10	—	—	—
Tumbler, 9 oz.	10	—	5	—
Tumbler, 9 oz. ftd.	27	40	—	—

SANDWICH	PINK & GREEN	BLUE	RED	
Bowl, 4"-6"	$ 6	—	$ 2	
Bowl, 6" hex.	—	$ 12	—	
Bowl, 8"-10"	26	—	70	
Butter Dish, w/ lid	280	267	—	
Candlesticks, 3.5" pr.	25	—	—	
Candlesticks, 7" pr.	66	—	—	
Cream/Sugar	26	—	130	
Cruet, 6.5 oz., w/ stopper	—	212	—	
Cup/Saucer	12	15	47	
Decanter w/ stopper	140	—	—	
Goblet, 9 oz.	25	—	60	
Pitcher, 2 qt.	145	—	—	
Plate, 6"-7"	5	7	9	
Plate, 8"	8	12	11	
Plate, 10"-13"	21	—	—	
Server, center handle	45	—	—	
Sherbet, 3.25"	10	11	—	
Tumbler, 3-8 oz., ftd.	22	—	—	
Tumbler, 12 oz., ftd.	42	—	—	
Wine Glass, 3", 4 oz.	28	—	—	

SHARON	AMBER	PINK	GREEN
Bowl, 5"	$ 10	$ 10	$ 13
Bowl, 6"	18	23	20
Bowl, 8.5"	7	28	35
Bowl, 10.5"	25	35	38
Butter Dish, w/ lid	75	60	115
Cake Plate, 11.5"	26	30	70
Candy Dish, w/ lid	61	50	186
Cheese Dish, w/ lid	275	900	—
Cream/Sugar	28	31	43
Cream Soup	28	48	53
Cup/Saucer	20	21	25
Jam Dish, 7.5"	45	150	55
Pitcher, 2.5 qt.	160	160	533
Plate, 6"	6	6	8
Plate, 8"-10"	18	23	21
Platter, oval, 12.5"	10	23	25
Salt/Pepper, pr.	53	55	93
Sherbet	15	16	35
Soup Plate, 7.5"	38	42	40
Tumbler, 4"-7", 9-15 oz.	40	40	80
Vegetable, oval, 9.5	16	26	25

SHIPS	BLUE	PINK
Cup/Saucer	$ 33	—
Cocktail w/ Stir	30	—
Cocktail Shaker	33	—
Ice Tub	40	—
Pitcher, 2.5 qt.	55	—
Plate, 6"	17	—
Plate, 9"	26	—
Shot Glass	48	—
Tumbler, 5-12 oz.	13	$ 22

TWISTED OPTIC	PINK
Bowl, 5"	$3
Bowl, 7"	10
Candlesticks, 3" pr.	18
Cream/Sugar	15
Cream Soup, 4.75"	10
Cup/Saucer	6
Jar, Candy, w/ lid	25
Pitcher, 2 qt.	28
Plate, 6"-7"	3
Plate, 8"	5
Server, center handle	20
Server, 2-handle	10
Sherbet	7
Tumbler, 4.5", 9 oz.	8
Tumbler, 5.25", 12 oz.	11

Flasks

Glass flasks have a broad body and narrow neck, usually for alcoholic beverages, often fitted with a closure. Flask collectors search for examples from the early 1800s through the early 1900s. Before 1810, few glass containers were manufactured. Flasks with portraits of presidents or other politicians are highly sought. Many have been reproduced. Color is also an important consideration.

For an extensive listing and identification system of flasks, see *American Bottles and Flasks* by Helen McKearin and Kenneth Wilson.

	LOW	AVG.	HIGH
A.G.W.L. on bottom, saddle flask, amber, .5 pt.	$ 30	$ 40	$ 50
All Seeing Eye, star and eye in center, under it A.D., verso star w/ arms, Masonic emblem, under it G.R.J.A., pontil, sheared top, amber, pt.	500	550	600
Anchor Flask, double ring, amber or clear, .5 pt.	60	75	90
B.P. & B., yellow green, .5 pt.	100	125	150
Baltimore Glass Works, aqua, verso w/ wheat sheaves, .5 pt.	375	425	500
Calabash, hunter and fisherman, aqua, qt.	100	125	150
Chapman, Balt., MD, soldier w/ gun, verso w/ dancing girl, sheared top, aqua, pt.	375	400	425
Clasped Hands-Eagle Flask, c. 1875, deep golden amber, .5 pt.	260	300	340
Clasped Hands-Eagle Flask, c. 1875, Union 13 stars, clasped hands, eagle above banner, "E," Wormer & Co., Pittsburgh, aqua, qt.	200	240	280
Clasped Hands-Flask, c. 1870, w/ eagle and banner, above oval marked Pittsburgh, Pa., verso w/ cannon to left, flag & cannonballs, aqua, pt.	183	206	230
Delicate powder blue, .5 pt.	90	100	110
Dog, verso w/ uniformed man on horse, pontil, sheared top, aqua, qt.	280	315	350
Double Eagle, aqua, pt.	300	350	400
Double Eagle, beneath unembossed oval, sheared top, pontil, amber, 6.25"	80	90	100
Double Eagle (eagles lengthwise), open pontil, olive green	250	275	300
Double Eagle, light green, pt.	240	260	280
Double Eagle, Stoddard, N.H., olive or amber, pt.	250	265	280
Duck Flask, picture of a duck in water, under duck Swim, above duck Will You Have a Drink, aqua, pt.	325	350	375
Eagle and stag, aqua, .5 pt.	350	410	470
Eagle and tree, aqua, pt.	175	200	225
18 diamond quilted flask, green, 6.5"	230	260	290
Flora Temple, aqua, pt.	400	450	500
Flora Temple, handle, puce or amber, pt.	450	490	530
Florida Universal Store Bottle, clear, pt.	13	17	20
For Pike's Peak, old rye, aqua, pt.	70	85	100
For Pike's Peak, verso w/ man shooting at deer, aqua, 9.5	70	85	100
Franklin & Franklin, aqua, qt.	263	304	345
G.H.A., Concord, N.Y. 1865, aqua, .5 pt.	46	54	63
Gen. MacArthur and God Bless America, purple or green, .5 pt.	26	33	40
Girl for Joe, girl on bicycle, aqua, pt.	160	180	200
Granite Glass Co., verso w/ Stoddard, N.H., sheared top, olive, pt. ...	300	350	400
Guaranteed Flask, clear or amethyst, 6.5"	12	18	24
Guaranteed Full, clear, 6.5"	15	20	25
History Flask, label, aqua, side panels, 7.5"	30	40	50

	LOW	AVG.	HIGH
Iron, pontil, double collared, pt.	$ 80	$ 90	$ 100
Isabella, G.W., sheaf of wheat, pt.	150	190	230
Jenny Lind Lyre, aqua, pt.	240	290	340
L.C. & R. Co. on bottom, eagle in a circle, verso plain, clear, .5 pt.	85	100	115
Legendary Grandfather, broken swirl pattern, reddish amber	250	300	350
OH. Frank, Pat'd Aug. 6,1872, all on bottom, circular-shaped flask, 2 circles in center, verso plain, wide rib on sides, ring neck, aqua, pt.	90	115	140
OH. Frank, Pat'd. Aug. 6th 1879, under bottom, 2 circles in center reverse plain, ring top, ribs on sides	80	100	120
Pike's Peak, man w/ pack and cane walking to left, verso eagle w/ ribbon in beak on oval panel, aqua, pt.	225	275	325
Pitkin type, light green, pt.	110	130	150
Pittsburgh, double eagle, aqua, pt.	65	78	90
Pittsburgh, PA., in raised oval circle at base, w/ eagle, verso w/ eagle, aqua applied ring at top, pt., 7.5"	80	100	120
Pottery flask, man and horse, same on verso, pt.	600	700	800
Railroad Flask, c. 1830-48, amber, pt.	345	415	475
Ravenna Glass Works, in 3 lines, ring top, yellow green, pt.	300	340	380
Ravenna Glass Works Star Flask, c. 1860, Ohio, aqua, pt.	350	375	400
Ravenna, in center, anchor w/ rope, under it Glass Company, ring top, aqua, pt.	300	340	380
Ravenna Travelers Companion, pontil, amber, qt.	500	625	750
Spring Garden, in center, anchor, under it Glass Works, verso w/ log cabin and tree to right, ring top, aqua, .5 pt.	300	340	380
Springfield G.W. and Cabin, aqua, .5 pt.	130	160	190
Stag and tree, aqua, pt.	140	160	180
Star Cornucopia Flask, star, circle on shoulder, amber, saddle flask, .5 pt. .	20	30	40
Stoddard, double eagle, Granite Glass Co., Stoddard, N.H. .... pontil, golden amber, pt.	200	250	300
Will You Take a Drink? Will a Duck Swim? aqua, pt.	320	360	400
Willington Eagle Flask, c. 1872, bright green, pt.	230	250	270
Willington Eagle Flask, c. 1872, olive amber, .5 pt.	200	250	300
Willington Glass Co., West Willington, Conn., verso w/ eagle, shield and wreath, on shoulder Liberty amber, pt.	220	260	300
Winter and Summer Flask, trees and birds: Summer and Winter, tapered top aqua, qt. and pt.	250	300	350
Zanesville City Glass Works, in oval panel, verso plain, ring top, amber ..	230	260	290

Left to right: modern reproduction; Masonic elements are prized.

Fostoria

Founded in Fostoria, OH in 1887, Fostoria continues to produce at their Moundsville, WV, factory. Many of their glassware lines are considered as "elegant" Depression-era glass and are avidly sought by collectors.

Fairfax	GREEN	CRYSTAL	BLUE	YELLOW	PINK
Ashtray	$ 33	—	$ 36	$ 25	$ 35
Bonbon Dish	27	—	34	20	30
Bowl, ftd., 11.5"	37	—	43	26	37
Bowl, oval, 10.5"	45	—	60	33	48
Bread & Butter Plate, 6"	7	—	8	5	7
Cake Plate, handles, 10"	25	—	33	25	30
Candy Dish, w/ lid, 3 section	70	—	87	60	66
Cereal Bowl, 6"	23	—	29	19	23
Cigarette Box	48	—	66	40	47
Claret Goblet, 4 oz.	43	—	50	37	40
Coaster, 3.5"	7	—	10	5	7
Cocktail Goblet, 3 oz.	38	—	40	33	38
Compote, 7"	35	—	40	30	38
Cordial Goblet, .5 oz.	56	—	57	43	58
Cream Soup	24	—	27	20	23
Creamer, ftd.	15	—	19	10	15
Cruet, ftd., handle	200	—	240	170	210
Cup, ftd.	11	—	16	9	10
Dinner Plate, 10.5"	50	—	50	40	47
Finger Bowl, 4.5" x 2"	23	—	26	20	25
Fruit Bowl, 5"	12	—	18	10	12
Grill Plate, 10.5"	25	—	33	19	24
Ice Bucket, metal handle	64	—	77	55	63
Luncheon Plate, 9.5"	15	—	18	14	14
Mayonnaise Dish	22	—	28	17	20
Mayonnaise Ladle	27	—	38	27	29
Oyster Cocktail, ftd., 5.5 oz.	26	—	30	18	25
Parfait, ftd., 6.5 oz.	26	—	36	25	28
Pitcher, ftd., 48 oz.	320	—	360	250	325
Platter, oval, 15"	83	—	90	66	83
Relish Tray, 2 section, 8.5"	25	—	27	17	23
Relish Tray, 3 section, 11.5"	34	—	44	25	33
Relish Tray, 3 section, round	27	—	30	20	27
Sauce Boat	55	—	66	48	57
Saucer	4	—	6	4	4
Sherbet, low, 6 oz.	27	—	23	23	26
Sherbet, tall, 6 oz.	25	—	30	26	27
Soup Bowl	29	—	30	24	26
Sugar, ftd.	12	—	22	9	13
Tray, handled 11"	40	—	55	34	44
Tumbler, ftd., 12 oz.	30	—	40	30	33
Tumbler, ftd., 9 oz.	25	—	33	24	25
Tumbler, ftd., 5 oz.	20	—	26	3	20
Tumbler, ftd., 2.5 oz.	20	—	29	20	20
Water Goblet, 10 oz.	33	—	40	30	34

June	GREEN	CRYSTAL	BLUE	YELLOW	PINK
Ashtray	—	$ 47	$ 65	$ 67	$ 67
Baking Dish, egg shape, len. 9"	—	60	100	150	80
Bonbon, stemmed	—	23	19	43	36
Bouillon Bowl, pedestal foot w/ underplate	—	20	67	46	50
Bowl, dia. 10"	—	46	76	64	63
Bread & Butter Plate, dia. 6"	—	10	14	13	12
Cake Plate, handled, dia. 10"	—	46	93	68	78
Canapé Plate	—	18	30	25	26
Candlesticks, pr., ht. 2"	—	55	87	67	70
Candlesticks, pr., ht. 3"	—	67	87	78	76
Candlesticks, pr., ht. 5"	—	—	100	83	90
Candy Jar, w/ lid, capacity 2 cups	—	120	290	200	225
Candy Jar, w/ lid, capacity 6 cups	—	90	300	154	280
Celery Dish, len. 11"	—	40	76	65	70
Centerpiece Bowl, oval, len. 11"	—	40	85	63	90
Cereal Bowl, dia. 6"	—	30	50	56	45
Cheese & Cracker Set	—	45	80	60	85
Chop Plate, dia. 12"	—	40	83	70	70
Condiment Bottle, ftd., w/ stopper	—	280	600	450	600
Comport, dia. 5"	—	60	60	45	60
Comport, dia. 6"	—	75	135	110	115
Comport, dia. 7"	—	94	165	115	130
Comport, dia. 8"	—	114	180	125	150
Cordial Cup	—	40	100	63	83
Cordial Cup Saucer	—	14	24	17	19
Cordial Glass, stemmed	—	74	130	119	116
Creamer, collar base	—	44	66	45	60
Creamer, pedestal foot	—	34	43	35	30
Cup, pedestal foot	—	29	54	40	43
Decanter, w/ glass stopper	—	550	1000	840	845
Dessert Bowl, handled, dia. 8"	—	76	120	85	116
Dinner Plate, dia. 9"	—	20	36	44	28
Dinner Plate, dia. 10.5"	—	46	80	67	73
Fan Vase, pedestal foot	—	150	260	180	190
Finger Bowl	—	35	66	48	47
Fruit Bowl, dia. 5"	—	22	43	35	33
Mayonnaise Compote	—	58	97	60	70
Mint Dish	—	28	57	43	50
Nappy, flat, dia. 7"	—	20	40	33	30
Nappy, pedestal foot, dia. 6.5"	—	22	40	30	34
Oil Cruet, pedestal foot	—	317	900	550	730
Oyster Plate	—	40	58	40	43
Parfait Glass	—	37	66	84	50
Pitcher	—	—	900	657	650
Platter, dia. 11"	—	70	100	85	90
Platter, dia. 15"	—	110	245	165	200
Relish Dish, 2 comp., len. 8.5"	—	30	53	44	50
Sugar Bowl, small w/ lid	—	45	64	43	58
Tray, loop handle, dia. 11"	—	50	100	65	74
Tumbler, ht. 3.5"	—	43	74	63	67
Tumbler, ht. 5"	—	30	50	40	40

June	GREEN	CRYSTAL	BLUE	YELLOW	PINK
Vase, ht. 7.5"	—	$ 70	$ 400	$ 185	$ 190
Water Glass, stemmed	—	38	55	43	60
Whipped Cream Bowl, large	—	140	280	210	250
Whipped Cream Bowl, small	—	35	50	40	43
Whiskey Tumbler, 2.5 oz.	—	40	88	67	60
Wine Glass, stemmed	—	40	100	80	77

Trojan	GREEN	CRYSTAL	BLUE	YELLOW	PINK
Ashtray, large	—	—	—	$ 54	$ 53
Bonbon Bowl	—	—	—	25	25
Bouillon Bowl, ftd.	—	—	—	30	30
Cereal Bowl, dia. 6"	—	—	—	33	37
Compote, ht. 6"	—	—	—	40	45
Creamer, ftd.	—	—	—	30	35
Dinner Plate, dia. 10.5"	—	—	—	55	54
Finger Bowl, w/ liner	—	—	—	46	43
Grill Plate, dia. 10"	—	—	—	50	50
Luncheon Plate, dia. 8.5"	—	—	—	25	23
Mayonnaise Bowl, w/ liner	—	—	—	50	56
Parfait	—	—	—	50	50
Pitcher	—	—	—	475	450
Platter, dia. 12"	—	—	—	57	60
Platter, dia. 15"	—	—	—	83	90
Relish Dish, dia. 6.5"	—	—	—	25	23
Relish Dish, 3 section	—	—	—	47	45
Saucer	—	—	—	16	16
Sherbet, ht. 4.5"	—	—	—	38	36
Sugar Bowl, ftd.	—	—	—	33	33
Tray, dia. 11", center handle	—	—	—	53	55
Tumbler, ht. 4.5"	—	—	—	40	38
Tumbler, ht. 5.5"	—	—	—	29	30
Tumbler, ht. 6"	—	—	—	40	38
Vase, ht. 8"	—	—	—	115	110
Whipped Cream Tub	—	—	—	150	130

Versailles	GREEN	CRYSTAL	BLUE	YELLOW	PINK
Ashtray	$ 44	—	$ 57	$ 53	$ 45
Bonbon Bowl	25	—	30	23	24
Bouillon Bowl	35	—	46	33	37
Bread & Butter Plate, dia. 6"	8	—	10	8	8
Cereal Bowl, dia. 6"	40	—	50	43	38
Chop Plate, dia. 13"	60	—	70	67	58
Compote, ht. 6"	44	—	60	55	46
Compote, ht. 7"	45	—	67	60	48
Creamer, ftd.	30	—	40	30	30
Decanter	270	—	380	290	280
Demitasse Cup & Saucer	40	—	93	64	44
Finger Bowl, w/ liner	38	—	56	48	23
Fruit Bowl, dia. 5"	28	—	34	26	29
Ice Bucket	166	—	158	150	123
Lemon Bowl	20	—	27	24	19

Versailes	GREEN	CRYSTAL	BLUE	YELLOW	PINK
Luncheon Plate, dia. 8.5"	$ 15	—	$ 20	$ 20	$ 15
Mayonnaise Bowl, w/ liner	66	—	90	85	75
Parfait	50	—	60	53	47
Pitcher	500	—	700	600	475
Platter, dia. 12"	63	—	80	65	60
Platter, dia. 15"	85	—	125	100	85
Relish, dia. 8.5"	67	—	80	70	60
Sauce Boat & Underplate	93	—	120	75	84
Saucer	8	—	10	7	8
Soup Bowl, dia. 7"	50	—	56	50	50
Sugar, ftd.	29	—	40	28	30
Tray, dia. 11", center handle	40	—	64	46	40
Tumbler, ht. 4.5", 5 oz.	43	—	45	46	40
Tumbler, ht. 5.25", 9 oz.	40	—	50	40	40
Tumbler, ht. 6", 12 oz.	45	—	50	50	44

Fruit Jars

The Mason jar was produced by John Landis Mason in the early 1800s. One of Mason's innovations was a zinc lid which provided greater air tightness.

Nineteenth-century fruit jars for home canning are collected, especially those with the manufacturer's name or a decorative motif printed on the jar. Before 1810, few glass containers were manufactured.

	LOW	AVG.	HIGH
Anchor Mason's, patent 3 lines, sheared top, Mason seal, qt., clear	$ 35	$ 45	$ 55
Atlas EZ Seal, 3 lines in circle, sheared top, lightning seal, qt., aqua or light blue	14	17	22
Atlas EZ Seal, all in 3 lines, under bottom Atlas E-Z seal, aqua, pt., clear or aqua	2	3	4
Atlas Improved Mason, c. 1890, glass lid, metal screw band, aqua or green	8	11	13
Atlas Mason's Patent, c. 1900, zinc lid, olive green, qt.	18	24	30
Atlas Mason's Patent Nov. 30, 1858, zinc lid, olive green, 2 qt.	20	25	35
Atlas Mason's Patent Nov. 30th, 1858, screw top, olive green, qt.	20	25	36
Atlas Mason's Patent, screw top, green, qt.	4	5	13
Atlas Special, c. 1910, screw top, clear or blue	6	8	13
Baker Bros., c. 1865, wax sealer, groove ring, green or aqua, pt.	30	38	45
Ball, Vaseline glass, screw top, pt., qt.	6	8	12
Ball, c. 1890, screw top, green, 3 sizes	7	9	13
Ball, in script, Ideal, wire top clamp, clear, 3" or 4.5"	6	7	10
Ball, in script, Ideal in back, Pat. July 14, 1908, wire top clamp, green or clear, 3 Zs	5	7	9
Boyd Mason, c. 1910, zinc lid, olive green, pt., qt.	6	8	10
Boyd Perfect Mason, zinc lid, green, 112 pt., pt., qt.	4	5	9
Boyd's Genuine Mason, bottom in diamond "IG Co.," sheared top, Mason seal, qt., aqua	3	5	7
Braun Safetee Mason, zinc lid, aqua	4	6	8
Brelle Jar, glass lid and wire clamp, wide mouth, clear, qt.	20	25	30
Brighten, c. 1890, glass lid, wire clamp, clear, amber or amethyst, qt.	76	88	100
Geo. D. Brown & Co., c. 1875, glass lid, heavy metal clamp, green, qt.	60	70	85
The Burlington, c. 1880, zinc band, clear or aqua, qt.	70	93	100
Decker's Iowana, glass lid and wire ball, clear, qt.	3	5	7
Dexter, c. 1865, zinc band with glass insert, aqua, qt.	32	40	55
Diamond Fruit Jar, glass lid and full wire bail, dear, qt.	3	4	6
Dictator DDI, Holcomb Patented Dec. 14th, 1869, wax seal, blue, qt.	80	100	130
Dillon, c. 1890, wax seal, round, aqua, qt.	10	13	16
Dominion, c. 1886, zinc band and glass insert, round, clear, qt.	75	100	120
Dominion Widemouth Special, zinc lid, round, clear, qt.	4	6	8
Doolittle, The Soft Sealer, glass lid, wide mouth, clear, qt.	50	65	90
Droy Ever Seal, glass lid and full wire bail, clear or amethyst, qt.	3	5	7
Economy, metal lid and spring wire clamp, amethyst, pt., qt., 2 qt.	3	5	7
Economy Trade Mark, clear or amethyst, qt.	3	4	5
E.G.Co. (monogram) imperial, clear, qt.	8	10	15
Electric, glass lid and wire bail, round, aqua, qt.	10	13	16
Electric Fruit Jar, c. 1915, glass lid and metal clamp, round, aqua, qt.	86	100	85
Electroglas N.W., clear, qt.	3	4	5
Empire, in Maltese cross, clear, qt.	6	10	14
Empire, c. 1860, glass stopper, deep blue, qt.	50	75	100
The Empire, c. 1866, glass lid with iron lugs to fasten it, aqua, qt.	60	70	90

	LOW	AVG.	HIGH
Erie Fruit Jar, c. 1890, screw top, clear, qt. .... $ 80		$ 100	$ 120
Erie Lightning, clear, qt. 21		26	31
Eureka, c. 1884, wax dipped cork, extended neck, aqua, pt. 36		45	61
Eureka, Pat. Feb. 9th, 1864, Eureka Jar Co., Dunbar, WV, c. 1870, aqua, qt. . 14		18	26
Everlasting Improved Jar, c. 1904, in oval, qt. 15		19	24
Everlasting Jar, c. 1904, glass lid and double wire hook fastener, round green, pt., qt., 2 qt. 15		19	24
Excelsior, c. 1885, zinc screw band and glass insert, aqua, qt. 50		60	70
Gilberds Improved Jar, c. 1885, glass lid and wire bail, aqua, qt. 40		55	70
Gilberds Jar, c. 1884, glass lid and screw band, aqua, qt. 60		75	90
Glassboro, c. 1890, trademark, zinc band and glass insert, light to dark green, 3 sizes 15		20	25
Glassboro Improved, c. 1880, wide zinc screw band and glass insert, aqua or pale green, qt. 16		19	26
Glenshaw G. Mason (G in square), clear, qt. 3		4	5
Glone, glass lid, metal neck band, top wire bail and bail clamp, amber, green or clear, qt. 12		15	17
Gleeker, Pat. 1911, Other Pending Sanitary, aqua, qt. 13		15	18
H. & D., c. 1915, glass top, metal band 4		6	8
Haines, c. 18820, glass lid and iron clamp, green, qt. 39		53	68
Haines Improved, c. 1870, glass lid and top wire bail, aqua green, qt. 150		200	240
Hamilton Glass Works, green, qt. 15		17	27
Hansee's Place Home Jar, pat. Dec. 19, 1899 under bottom, aqua, 7" 42		50	80
Harris, c. 1860, metal lid, ground top, deep green, qt. 125		165	200
Harris Improved, c. 1875, glass lid and iron clamp, green, qt. 44		56	79
E.C. Hazard & Co., Shrewsbury, N.J., wire clamp, aqua, qt. 10		13	15
Hazel, glass lid and wire bail, aqua, qt. 12		15	19
Hazel-Atlas Lightning Seal, full wire bail and glass lid, green, qt. 7		8	13
Hero, with cross and lightning at top, green, qt. 27		31	37
The Heroine, wide zinc screw band and glass insert, light green, qt. 27		33	38
The High Grade, zinc screw-on top, clear 20		25	30
Holme's Railroad Mills, amber, 7.5" 13		16	19
Holmes Railroad Mills, amber, qt. 13		15	20
The Improved Hero, glass top, metal band, green, Pat'd Nov. 26, 1867 15		19	25
Kerr Economy Trade Mark, Chicago on base, metal lid and narrow clip band, clear or amethyst, pt., qt. 2		3	4
Kerr Wide Mouth Mason, clear, .5 pt. 15		20	25
KG, in oval, wire clamp, clear, qt. 2		4	6
The Kilner Jar, zinc screw band and glass insert, clear, qt. 2		4	6
King, full wire bail and glass lid, clear or amethyst, qt. 10		13	16
Kinsella True Mason, c. 1874, zinc lid, clear, qt. 6		8	10
Kline, Pat Oct. 27, 1863, a on glass stopper, aqua, qt., with jar 100		122	200
Kline A., c. 1863, glass fitted lid and clamp, aqua, qt. 26		30	35
Lectric, in oval, glass lid, ground top, medium green, qt. 8		9	13
Lightning Trade Mark, Reg. U.S. Pat. Office, Putnam 4 on bottom, lid w/ dates, aqua, pt. 2		4	6
Lightning Trade Mark, Putnam 199 on bottom, aqua, 2 qt. 6		8	10
Lightning Trade Mark, Putnam 199 on bottom, aqua, wire and lid, pt. 6		8	10
Lightning Trademark, glass top, round, aqua, 8" 7		10	13
Lightning Trademark, glass top, round, Putnam on base, aqua, qt., 2 qt. 6		10	14
Lightning Trademark, glass top, round, Putnam on base, amber, pt., qt., 2 qt. 16		21	26

	LOW	AVG.	HIGH
Lightning, Putnam 824 under bottom, sheared top, aqua	$ 8	$ 10	$ 15
Lindell Glass Co., c. 1870, wax sealer, amber, qt.	70	85	100
Lockport Mason, zinc top, aqua, 2 qt.	5	8	11
Lockport Mason, Improved, zinc screw band, glass insert, aqua, qt.	4	5	6
Lorillard & Co, on base, glass top, metal clamp, amber, pt.	12	15	20
Lorillard & Co., sheared top, amber, 6.5"	11	13	16
Lustre R.E. Tongue & Bros. Co. Inc. Phila., in circle or shield, wire clamp, qt.	6	8	11
Mason's, swirled milk glass, 7.5"	75	100	125
Mason's CG, Patent Nov. 30, 1858, zinc lid, green, qt.	5	6	10
Mason's-C-Patent Nov. 30th 1858, green, 7"	11	13	15
Mason's Improved Butter Jar, sheared top, aqua, 2 qt.	10	13	16
Mason's Improved, ground top with zinc lid, qt., blue	7	14	20
Mason's Improved, zinc screw band and glass insert, aqua or green, pt.	10	13	17
Mason's Keystone, c. 1869, zinc screw band and glass insert, aqua, qt.	15	20	25
Mason's "M" Patent Nov. 30th 1858, green, 7"	5	7	10
Mason's, under it "M" Patent Nov. 30th 1858, screw top, aqua, qt.	12	16	22
Mason's Patent 1858, zinc lid, amber or green, pt.	15	18	25
The New Perfection, clear or amethyst, 2 qt.	11	13	33
Pat, glass stopper, green, qt.	48	60	75
Pat, glass stopper and wire bail, aqua, qt.	29	40	45
Peerless, wax dipped cork, green, qt.	60	75	90
The Penn, metal cap and wax seal, green, qt.	30	40	50
Peona Pottery, metal top and wax seal, glazed brown stoneware, qt.	16	19	25
Perfection, double wire bail and glass top, clear, qt.	36	42	50
Perfect Seal, full wire bail and glass top, clear, qt.	4	5	7
Perfect Seal in shield, Made in Canada, clear, qt.	2	3	4
H.W. Pettit, Weaville N.H., under bottom, ground top, aqua, qt.	7	11	15
The Goragas Pierie Co., Phila., Royal Peanutene, sheared top, clear, qt.	9	12	15
Pine Deluxe Jar, full wire bail and glass top, clear, qt.	4	6	8
Pine (P in square) Mason, zinc top, clear, qt.	4	5	6
Porcelain Lined, zinc top, aqua, qt.	15	20	25
Porcelain Lined, zinc top, green, 2 gal.	12	16	22
Potter & Bodine Philadelphia, in script, glass top and clamp, aqua, qt.	80	100	120
Premium Ceffeyville Kas., wire ring and glass top, clear or amethyst, qt.	15	18	23
Premium improved, glass top and side wire clips, clear, qt.	15	18	25
Presto, screw-on top, clear	3	4	5

Heisey Glass

A partnership including George Duncan and Daniel C. Ripley established the A.H. Heisey Glass Co. in the 1860s in Newark, OH. It manufactured cut and pressed glasswares. Heisey Glass is high quality. Many patterns are called "elegant Depression glass."

The Heisey Collectors of America, Inc. publishes *The Heisey News,* a newsletter with information on patterns, history of Heisey, and advertisements. Address: Box 27, Newark, OH 43055.

Ipswich Pattern	GREEN	CRYSTAL	BLUE	YELLOW	PINK
Bowl, ftd., dia. 11", floral	—	$ 14	$ 250	—	—
Candlestick, h. 6"	$ 145	73	—	$ 130	$ 100
Candy Jar, w/ lid	240	39	—	190	140
Cocktail Goblet, 4 oz.	—	10	—	—	—
Cocktail Shaker, w/ strainer	440	140	—	340	240
Creamer	32	14	—	28	22
Cruet, w/ stopper, ftd., 2 oz.	85	48	—	75	65
Finger Bowl, w/ underplate	40	14	—	34	25
Goblet, Champagne, 5 oz.	—	10	—	—	—
Goblet, 10 oz.	—	14	—	—	—
Pitcher, 2 qt.	400	95	300	190	140
Plate, sq., dia. 8"	25	15	—	26	22
Sherbet, 4 oz.	20	8	—	20	17
Sugar Bowl	30	15	—	36	27
Tumbler, curved rim, 10 oz.	28	8	—	27	24

Lariat Pattern	GREEN	CRYSTAL	BLUE	YELLOW	PINK
Ashtray, 4"	—	$ 5	—	—	—
Basket, ftd., 10"	—	125	—	—	—
Bowl, 4"	—	14	—	—	—
Bowl, 12"	—	15	—	—	—
Bowl, 13"	—	18	—	—	—
Bowl, flat, 8"	—	13	—	—	—
Buffet Plate, 21"	—	33	—	—	—
Cake Plate, rolled edge, 12"	—	18	—	—	—
Candlestick, 2 candles	—	11	—	—	—
Goblet, 9 oz.	—	10	—	—	—
Goblet, blown, 10 oz.	—	12	—	—	—
Salad Plate, 7"	—	7	—	—	—
Salad Plate, 8"	—	8	—	—	—
Salt/Pepper, pr.	—	140	—	—	—
Server, 2 handles, 14"	—	28	—	—	—
Saucer	—	3	—	—	—
Sherbet, low, 6 oz.	—	4	—	—	—

Octagon Pattern	GREEN	CRYSTAL	BLUE	YELLOW	PINK
Basket, #500, 5"	$ 78	$ 48	—	$ 83	$ 68
Bonbon Dish, #1229, 8"	11	4	—	9	7
Bowl, 6.5"	14	10	—	15	13
Cheese Dish, 2 handles, #1229, 6"	11	4	—	9	7
Hors d'oeuvre Plate, #1229, 13"	29	14	—	24	19
Plate, 6"	9	3	—	7	5

Old Sandwich Pattern	GREEN	CRYSTAL	BLUE	YELLOW	PINK
Ashtray	$ 35	$ 5	$ 40	$ 20	$ 30
Beer Mug, 12 oz.	240	24	270	195	185
Beer Mug, 18 oz.	290	28	320	245	220
Bowl, oval, ftd., 12"	68	25	—	58	46
Bowl, round, ftd., 11"	58	24	—	46	39
Compote, 6"	78	26	—	74	68
Cup	16	7	—	13	11
Decanter, w/ stopper	175	60	320	165	155
Finger Bowl	18	6	—	15	12
Goblet, 4 oz.	20	9	88	18	15
Goblet, 3 oz.	19	8	—	16	14
Oyster Cocktail Goblet, 4 oz.	12	3	—	10	9
Parfait	24	8	—	19	14
Pilsner Glass, 8 oz.	33	10	—	28	23
Pilsner Glass, 10 oz.	36	13	—	30	26
Pitcher, 2 qt.	125	55	—	120	115
Pitcher, ice lip. 2 qt.	130	63	—	125	120
Plate, sq., 6"	13	4	—	10	8
Plate, sq., 7"	15	4	—	14	10
Plate, sq., 8"	17	6	—	15	12
Salt/Pepper, pr.	58	28	—	48	38
Saucer	14	6	—	12	10
Tumbler, 12 oz.	26	9	—	21	16
Tumbler, ftd., 12 oz.	26	9	—	21	16
Tumbler, 5 oz.	19	3	—	14	11

Pleat and Panel Pattern	GREEN	CRYSTAL	BLUE	YELLOW	PINK
Bouillon Bowl, 2 handles, 5"	$ 11	$ 5	—	—	$ 9
Bouillon Underplate, 6.5"	7	2	—	—	5
Bowl, 4"	9	4	—	—	7
Bowl, 6.5"	11	4	—	—	9
Cheese & Cracker Set, 10.5"	34	19	—	—	29
Compote, w/ lid, ftd., 5"	54	24	—	—	44
Creamer, institutional	14	4	—	—	9
Cruet, w/ stopper, 3 oz.	34	16	—	—	29
Cup	14	4	—	—	9
Goblet, Champagne, 5 oz.	11	4	—	—	9
Jelly Bowl, 2 handles, 5"	11	5	—	—	9
Lemon Bowl, w/ lid, 5"	15	9	—	—	13
Marmalade Jar, 4.5"	16	6	—	—	11
Nappy, 4.5"	8	4	—	—	7
Nappy, 8"	16	9	—	—	14
Plate, 8"	11	4	—	—	9
Pitcher	65	30	—	—	50
Pitcher, ice lip	75	40	—	—	60
Plate, 8"	7	2	—	—	5
Platter, oval, 12"	34	18	—	—	29
Sandwich Plate, 14"	29	14	—	—	24
Saucer	5	2	—	—	4

Provincial Pattern	GREEN	CRYSTAL	BLUE	YELLOW	PINK
Ashtray, sq., 3"	—	$ 11	—	—	—
Bonbon Dish, 2 handles, 7"	$ 29	9	—	—	—
Buffet Plate, 18"	—	24	—	—	—
Butter Dish, w /lid	—	55	—	—	—
Candleholder	—	14	—	—	—
Candelabra, 3 candles	—	34	—	—	—
Candy Box, w/ lid, tooled, 5.5"	220	60	—	—	—
Iced Tea Tumbler, ftd., 12 oz.	39	14	—	—	—
Plate, 7"	—	9	—	—	—

Insulators

Insulators are glass figures used to attach electrical wires to poles from 1844 (for telegraph lines) into the 20th century. Color, age, and design determine value. Threadless insulators are older, rarer, and usually more valuable than threaded ones. Clear glass is most common. Colors, including green, milk white, amber, amethyst, and cobalt blue are more valuable.

	LOW	AVG.	HIGH
A.G.M., amber, 3.5" x 2.5"	$ 18	$ 27	$ 36
A.T. & T. Co., aqua, single skirt, 2.5" x 3.5", c. 1900	11	15	17
A.T. & T. Co., aqua, two-piece, 2.5" x 3.5"	7	10	13
A.T. & T. Co., green, single skirt, 2.5" x 3.5"	8	13	18
Ages, clear amethyst, 3.25" x 2.5"	18	22	26
American Insulator Co., aqua, double petticoat, 4" x 3.5"	15	19	21
Armstrong, amber 4" x 3.5"	15	19	21
Armstrong, No. 5, clear, double petticoat, 3.5" x 3.5	7	10	13
A.U. Patent, green, 4.5" x 2.5"	45	50	55
B. & O., aqua, 4" x 3.5"	45	50	55
B.F.G. Co., aqua, 4" x 3.5"	60	70	80
B.G.M. Co., clear amethyst, 3.5" x 2.5"	28	33	40
Barclay, aqua, double petticoat, 3" x 2.5"	27	33	40
Boston Bottle Works, aqua, 4.5" x 3"	60	70	80
Brookee, Homer, aqua, 3.5" x 2.5"	31	42	43
Brookfield, No. 36, aqua, green, 4" x 3.5"	18	22	26
Brookfield, No. 45, aqua, green, 4.5" x 3.5"	10	13	16
Brookfield, No. 55, aqua, green, 4" x 2.5"	15	20	25
Brookfield, No. 83, aqua, green, 4" x 3.5"	25	35	45
Brookfield, dark olive green, double petticoat, 3.5" x 4"	11	14	17
B.T. Co. of Canada, clear, amethyst, 3.5" x 2"	20	30	40
B.T. Co. of Canada, aqua, green, 3.5" x 2.5"	15	20	25
C. & P. Tel. Col., aqua, green, 3.5" x 2.5"	14	18	21
C.E.L., amethyst, 4.5" x 2.5"	20	22	24
C.E.N., amethyst, 3.5" x 2.5"	55	60	65
C.G.I., clear, amethyst, 3.5" x 2.5"	30	35	40
Cable, aqua, green, 4.5" x 3.5"	30	38	46
California, aqua, green, 3.5" x 2.25"	34	38	42
California, CK-1 82, purple, double petticoat, 3.5" x 4"	11	13	15
Canadian Pacific, clear, amethyst, 3.5" x 2.5"	20	24	28
Castle, aqua, 4" x 2.5"	65	70	75
Chester, aqua, 4" x 2.25"	70	80	90
Columbia, aqua, green, 3.5" x 4"	57	47	67
Derflinger, T.N.I., aqua, green, 4" x 3.5"	25	30	35
Dominion No. 9, amber, aqua, and clear, 3.5" x 2.5"	4	7	10
Duquesne, aqua, green, 3.5" x 2.5"	45	50	55
Dwight, aqua, 4" x 3"	46	56	66
E.C. & M. Co., green, 4" x 2.5"	36	41	46
Electrical Supply Co., aqua, green, 3.5" x 2.25"	40	50	60
Folembray, No. 221, olive green, 2.25" x 3.5"	54	62	73
Gayner, 36-190, aqua, 3.5" x 3.5"	16	17	20
Gayner, green, double petticoat, 3.5" x 4"	35	37	42
H.G. Co., amber, double petticoat, 3.5" x 3.5"	19	22	25
H.G. Co. Petticoat, aqua, green, 3.5" x 3.5"	8	10	12

	LOW	AVG.	HIGH
Hawley, aqua, 3.5" x 2.5"	$ 20	$ 25	$ 30
Hemingray, No. 7, aqua, green, 3.5" x 2.5"	4	7	10
Hemingray, No. 8, aqua, green, 3.5" x 2.5"	20	23	26
Hemingray, No. 9, aqua, single skirt, 2.5" x 3.5"	25	30	35
Hemingray, No. 16, green, single skirt, 2" x 4"	5	7	9
Hemingray, No. 19, aqua, double petticoat, 3.5" x 3"	40	50	60
Hemingray, No. 25, aqua, green, 4" x 3.5"	21	24	30
Hemingray, No. 95, aqua, green, 3.25" x 2.25"	50	55	60
Hemingray Beehive, green, double petticoat, 3.5" x 4.5"	25	31	34
Hemingray Petticoat, cobalt blue, 4" x 3.5"	45	50	55
Hemingray Transportation, green, 4.5" x 3.5"	35	40	45
Isorex, clear, black, green, blue, 5.5" x 3.5"	7	9	13
Jeffery Mfg. Co., aqua, 3.25" x 2.5"	44	54	64
Jumbo, aqua, 7.5" x 5.5"	30	37	44
Knowles Cable, aqua, green, 4" x 3.25"	46	51	56
Fred M. Locke, No. 14, aqua, 4.25" X 3"	32	38	46
Fred M. Locke, No. 21, aqua, green, 4" x 4"	8	10	12
Lynchburg, No. 10, aqua, green, 3.5" x 2.5"	10	15	20
Lynchburg, No. 31, aqua, green, 3.5" x 2.5"	10	14	19
Lynchburg, No. 44, 4" x 3.25"	8	10	12
Maydwell, No. 9, clear, aqua, 3.25" x 2.5"	7	11	15
Maydwell, No. 9, clear, single skirt, 2.25" x 3.5"	7	9	11
Maydwell, No. 16, amber, 4" x 2.5"	7	10	13
Maydwell, No. 20, white milk glass, 3.25" x 3.5"	32	37	42
McLaughlin, No. 9, green, single skirt, 2.5" x 3.25"	17	19	26
McLaughlin, No. 18, amber, aqua, green, 3.25" x 2.25"	8	11	15
McLaughlin, No. 19, aqua, 3.5" x 3.5"	4	7	9
McLaughlin, No. 42, aqua, 4" x 3.25"	7	12	15
McLaughlin, No. 82, aqua, 3.25" x 3.25"	11	14	17
Mershon, aqua, 5" x 5.5"	45	50	55
Monogram H.I. Co., aqua, 4.5" x 3.5"	30	34	40
N.E.G.M. Co., aqua, green, 3.5" x 2.5"	22	23	26
N.E.G.M. Co., aqua, 3.5" x 3.5"	26	32	35
N.E.T. & T. Co., aqua, green, 3.25" x 2.5"	7	10	13
N.E.T. & T. Co., blue, 3.5" x 3"	17	23	26
Noleak, aqua, green, 4" x 4"	45	50	55
O.V.G. Co., aqua, 3.5" x 2.5"	10	15	20
O.V.G. Co., aqua, green, 3.5" x 2.5"	18	20	25
Peffingel Anderson Co., aqua, 4" x 2.5"	26	31	34
Pony, blue, 3.5" x 2.5"	33	37	38
Postal, aqua, green, 4.5" x 3.5"	21	25	29
Pyrex, carnival glass, 3" x 3.5"	18	19	25
SIT. & T. Co., aqua, green, 3.5" x 2.5"	20	25	30
Santa Ana, aqua, green, 4.5" x 4.5"	43	47	55
Standard, clear, amethyst, 3.25" x 2.5"	18	23	26
Star, aqua, single skirt, pony, 2.5" x 3.5"	11	14	17
Sterling, aqua, 3.5" x 2.5"	22	26	27
T.C.R., aqua, 4" x 3.5"	17	23	29
T.H.E. Co., aqua, 4" x 3.5"	41	47	56
Thomas, brown pottery, 2.5" x 1.5"	8	12	15
Transportation, No. 2, aqua, 4.5" x 2.5"	30	34	38

	LOW	AVG.	HIGH
U.S. Tel. Co., aqua, 3.5" x 2.25"	$ 20	$ 23	$ 26
V.M.R. Napoll, aqua, green, 4" x 2.5"	19	22	27
W.F.G. Co., clear, amethyst, 3.5" x 2"	19	21	25
W.G.M. Co., clear, amethyst, 3.5" x 2.5"	35	36	46
W.V., No. 5, aqua, 4.5" x 2.5"	25	30	35
Westinghouse, aqua, green, 3.5" x 2.5"	35	40	45
Whitall Tatum, amber, 3.5" x 3.5"	20	25	30

Above left to right : Whitall Tatum, amethyst, $15-$22; Corning Carnival glass, $15-$22; dark blue porcelain, $10-$15. Below left to right,: Diamond Pony , deep amethyst, $14-$22; beehive, straw color, $16-$22; threadless, $60-$80.

Lalique

René Lalique (1860-1945), began his career as a jeweler in Paris and by 1900 had become one of the world's most celebrated Art Nouveau designers. He began to manufacture glass in 1910. Many regard him as the best glass designer of the 20th century. The company is still in business under the direction of René Lalique's granddaughter Marie-Claude Lalique. Most items produced before Rene Lalique's death in 1945 are marked *R. LALIQUE*, while later pieces are marked *LALIQUE*. Collectors focus on the earlier period, especially pieces in color and rare models. Many fakes and forgeries exist. They are often crude and easily recognizable. When examining Lalique never let a signature authenticate the object, let the object authenticate the signature.

Prices are for items in pristine condition, meaning no cracks, chips, stains, or restorations. We have shortened signatures of many of the following pieces; in addition to the *Lalique* or *R. Lalique* there may be a model number or the word *FRANCE*. The following terms refer to the signature of an item and are abbreviated: *en.*-engraved, *m.*-molded, *st.*- stamped, *stc.*-stenciled, *whc.*-wheel cut.

Our consultant for this area is Nicholas Dawes, collector, dealer, and author of *Lalique Glass,* Crown, NY, 1986. He is listed in the back of this book. The Lalique Collector's Society can be reached at 400 Veterans Blvd., Carlstadt, NJ 07072, 1-800-CRISTAL. For information on fakes, see *A Guide to Fraudulent Lalique*, by Alice Bley and Carol Glaze.

	LOW	HIGH
Ashtray, Cygne, clear & frosted w/ swans, en. *Lalique*, ht. 9 cm., c. 1960 .. $ 200		300
Ashtray, Jamaique, deep amber glass, whc. R. LALIQUE, dia. 14 cm., c. 1928	500	700
Ashtray, Deux Zephyrs, gray w/ two putti, stcl. R. LALIQUE, dia. 8 cm., c. 1913	300	500
Ashtray, Dindon, opalescent green w/ turkey, en. *R. Lalique*, dia. 12 cm., c. 1925	700	900
Ashtray, Moineau, green w/ sparrow, en. *R. Lalique*, dia. 12 cm., c. 1925 ..	700	900
Ashtray, Simone, clear & frosted flowerhead, en. *R. Lalique*, dia. 9.8 cm., c. 1929	250	350
Auto Mascot, Coq Houdan, clear & frosted glass rooster, whc. R. LALIQUE, ht. 22.5 cm., c. 1929	3000	5000
Auto Mascot, Longchamp, clear & frosted horse's head, m. R. LALIQUE, ht. 15.5 cm., c. 1929	6000	8000
Auto Mascot, Tete, D'Aigle, clear & frosted eagle head, m. R. LALIQUE, ht. 10.7 cm., c. 1928	1500	2000
Bookends, Hirondelle, clear & frosted, w/ swallows, stcl. LALIQUE, ht. 16 cm., c. 1965	400	600
Bowl, Bulbes, opalescent, stcl. R. LALIQUE, dia. 20.5 cm., c. 1935	300	500
Bowl, Montigny, opalescent w/ stylized flowerheads, m. R. LALIQUE, dia. 30 cm., c. 1928	800	1200
Bowl, Perruches, opalescent mint green w/ parakeets, stcl. R. LALIQUE, dia. 24.5 cm., c. 1913	6000	8000
Bowl, Poissons, opalescent w/ fish, stcl. R. LALIQUE, dia. 23.9 cm., c. 1921	400	600
Box, aluminum, sepia patina, for Roger et Gallet, st. LALIQUE, c. 1922 ..	150	200
Box, Chantilly, clear & frosted, sepia patina w/ deer, m. R. LALIQUE, dia. 8.5 cm., c. 1924	500	700
Box, Coquilles, clear w/ green patina, m. R. LALIQUE, dia. 7 cm., c. 1920 ..	500	700
Box, Epines, clear & frosted, blue patina, en. *R. Lalique*, dia. 6 cm., c. 1920..	300	500

	LOW	HIGH

Box, Quatre Papillons, clear & frosted glass, w/ 4 moths, m. LALIQUE
DEPOSE, dia. 8 cm., c. 1911 .... $ 600 ... $ 800

Box, Vallauris, clear & frosted, en. *R. Lalique*, dia. 14 cm., c. 1928 .... 500 ... 700

Brooch, Deux Aigle, blue reflecting clear glass & gilt metal w/ eagles, st.
LALIQUE, 9.6 cm. .... 700 ... 900

Brooch, Dos a Dos, clear & frosted glass & gilt metal, w/ two crouching
nudes, st. LALIQUE Poincon, ht. 3.5 cm., c. 1913 .... 800 ... 1200

Brooch, Feuilles, amber reflecting glass & gilt metal, w/ leaves, st.
LALIQUE Poincon, ht. 4.3 cm., c. 1919 .... 800 ... 1200

Brooch, Trois Marguerites, clear glass & gilt metal, gray patina, st.
LALIQUE Poincon, dia. 3.3 cm., c. 1912 .... 300 ... 500

Candlesticks, Dahlia, clear & frosted, in two parts, stcl. R. LALIQUE,
ht. 4.5 cm., c. 1934 .... 700 ... 900

Carafe, Cotes Plates, clear w/ vertical ribs, m. LALIQUE, ht. 24 cm.,
c. 1919 .... 300 ... 500

Champagne Glass, set of 6, w/ angels, en. *Lalique*, ht., c. 1970s .... 800 ... 1200

Clock, clear & frosted, w/ naiades, en. *R. Lalique*, ht. 11.3 cm., c. 1926 .. 1000 ... 1500

Clock, deux Colombes, opalescent, w/ lovebirds, whc. R. LALIQUE, ht.
22.2 cm., c. 1926 .... 4000 ... 6000

Clock, Moineaux, clear & frosted, w/ sparrows, m. R. LALIQUE, ht.
15.5 cm., c. 1924 .... 1000 ... 1600

Frame, Bleutes, clear & frosted, stcl. R. LALIQUE, ht. 24 cm., c. 1926 .. 3000 ... 4000

Goblet, Marienthal pattern, amber glass, en. *R. Lalique*, ht. 10 cm.,
c. 1930 .... 150 ... 200

Letter Seal, Faune, clear & frosted glass, stcl. R. LALIQUE, ht. 7.4 cm.,
c. 1931 .... 1200 ... 1600

Letter Seal, Tete d'Aigle, black glass eagle head, en. *R. Lalique*, ht. 7.8 cm.,
c. 1911 .... 800 ... 1200

Pendant, Graines, blue glass, en. *R. Lalique*, ht. 5 cm., 1920 .... 1000 ... 1500

Perfume bottle, clear & frosted, w/ stars, for Worth, m. LALIQUE, ht.
13 cm., c. 1950 .... 150 ... 250

Perfume Bottle, Duncan, clear & frosted, w/ three nudes, stcl. LALIQUE,
ht. 19 cm., c. 1950 .... 300 ... 500

Perfume Bottle, frosted, sepia patina, for La Belle Saison by Houbigant,
m. R. LALIQUE, ht. 14 cm., c. 925 .... 2000 ... 3000

Perfume Bottle, green glass snuff bottle for Le Jade by Roger et Galle,
m. R. LALIQUE, ht. 8 cm., 1926 .... 3000 ... 4000

Perfume Bottle, Violette, clear w/ blue enamel, bushel of violets for
Violette by Gabilla, m. R. LALIQUE, ht. 8 cm., c. 1925 .... 3500 ... 4500

Plate, annual, Hibou, en. *Lalique*, 1971 .... 100 ... 150

Plate, annual, Deux Oiseux, en. *Lalique*, 1965 .... 1200 ... 1600

Plate, Campanules, opalescent w/ tulips, stcl. R. LALIQUE, dia. 31.5 cm.,
c. 1932 .... 600 ... 800

Plate, Chiens, clear, sepia patina, w/ dogs, en. *R. Lalique*, dia. 21 cm.,
c. 1914 .... 300 ... 500

Plate, Fleurons, opalescent, stcl. R. LALIQUE, dia. 26.5 cm., c. 1933 .... 400 ... 600

Stautuette, Chrysis, clear & frosted glass, female nude, en. *Lalique*, ht.
14.5 cm., c. 1965 .... 300 ... 500

Statuette, Deux Danseuses, clear & frosted glass, 2 dancers, en. *Lalique*,
ht. 25 cm., c. 1965 .... 1000 ... 1500

Statuette, Suzanne, opalescent glass, on illum. bronze base, m. R.

	LOW	HIGH
LALIQUE, ht. 23 cm., c. 1925	$ 15,000	$ 20,000
Tray, Pissenlit, clear & frosted w/ dandelion leaves, m. VDA, dia. 19.5 cm., c. 1921	600	800
Vase, Archers, deep amber w/ male archers, en. *R. Lalique*, ht. 26 cm., c. 1921	5000	7000
Vase, Ceylan, opalescent, sepia patina, w/ parakeets, whc. R. LALIQUE, ht. 25 cm., c. 1924	4000	6000
Vase, Coupe Cabrera, clear & blue, tapering form, en. *Lalique*, ht. 9 cm., c. 1955	400	600
Vase, Ferrieres, cased green, florettes, en. *R. Lalique*, ht. 17 cm., c. 1929 ...	3500	4500
Vase, Mimosa, clear & frosted, gray patina, m. R. LALIQUE, ht. 17 cm., c. 1921	1200	1600
Vase, Ondines, clear & frosted w/ sea nymphs, en. *Lalique*, ht. 23 cm., c. 1965	1000	1500
Wine Cooler, Riquewihr, clear & frosted, sepia patina, en. *Lalique*, ht. 12.5 cm., c. 1949	500	700

Lalique vases from the 1920s. — Photo courtesy of Nicholas Dawes.

Pressed Glass

Small, crude objects and feet for footed bowls were first hand-pressed in England in the early 1800s, but pressing glass with machinery appears to have originated in America. Glass companies began producing pressed glass in matching tableware sets during the 1840s.

Although identification of pieces is mainly by pattern name, there is some confusion in this area. Most of the original names have been discarded by advanced collectors who have renamed the pattern in descriptive terms. Manufacturers' marks are exceedingly rare and there are few catalogs available from the period before 1850. By studying the old catalogs that do exist, along with shards found at old factory sites, some sketchy information has been provided. But because the competition quickly copied patterns, absolute verification of the manufacturer is impossible.

Earlier pieces contain many imperfections: bubbles, lumps, impurities, and sometimes cloudiness. Reproductions pose a problem to the beginning collector. Two popular patterns, Bellflower and Daisy and Button, have been reproduced extensively. With careful, informed scrutiny, collectors can detect the dullness and lack of sparkle characteristic of remakes. If the reproduction was made from a new mold (formed from an original object), the details will not possess the clarity and precision of the original article. For further information see *The Official Price Guide to Glassware*, by Mark Pickvet, House of Collectibles, Random House, NY.

	LOW	AVG.	HIGH
BAKEWELL BLOCK			
Celery	$ 105	$ 120	$ 135
Champagne Glass	100	115	130
Cream/Sugar, w/ lid	285	300	315
Decanter	135	150	165
Spooner	60	75	90
Tumbler	85	100	115
Whiskey Tumbler, handle	135	150	165
Wine	65	80	95
CANADIAN			
Butter Dish, w/ lid	$ 75	$ 90	$ 105
Celery	50	65	80
Compote, high, w/ lid	75	90	105
Compote, low	65	80	95
Cordial Glass	45	60	75
Cream/Sugar, w/ lid	145	160	175
Goblet	65	80	95
Jam Jar	60	75	90
Pitcher	115	130	145
Plate, 6.5"	45	60	75
Plate, 7.5"	85	100	115
Sauce, flat	15	25	35
Sauce, ftd.	20	35	50
Spooner	45	60	75
Wine Glass	65	80	95
DIAMOND THUMBPRINT			
Butter Dish, w/ lid	$ 210	$ 225	$ 240
Cake Stand	310	325	340
Celery	225	250	275

	LOW	AVG.	HIGH
Champagne Glass	$ 275	$ 300	$ 325
Compote, ftd., scalloped edge	45	60	75
Cream/Sugar, w/ lid	375	425	475
Decanter, no stopper, 1 pt.	85	100	115
Decanter, w/ stopper, 1 qt.	185	200	215
Goblet	450	500	550
Honey Dish	10	25	40
Sauce Boat	10	15	30
Spooner	105	120	135
Tumbler	135	150	165
Waste Bowl	85	100	115
Water Pitcher	400	500	600
Whiskey Tumbler, handled	300	350	400
Wine Glass	275	300	325
Wine Jug, places for holding glasses	1000	1200	1400

FLUTE

	LOW	AVG.	HIGH
Ale Glass	$ 20	$ 35	$ 50
Bottle, bitters	30	45	60
Bowl, scalloped edge	25	40	55
Candlesticks, pr.	45	60	75
Champagne Glass	15	30	45
Compote, open, dia. 8"	30	45	60
Cream/Sugar	65	80	95
Decanter, 1 qt.	50	65	80
Egg Cup, single	15	25	35
Egg Cup, double	20	35	50
Goblet	15	30	45
Honey Dish	15	25	35
Lamp	85	100	115
Mug	25	40	55
Pitcher	65	80	95
Salt, ftd.	10	25	40
Sauce, flat	10	20	30
Tumbler, 8 oz.	15	30	45
Whiskey, handled	15	30	45
Wine	15	30	45

LEE

	LOW	AVG.	HIGH
Celery Dish	$ 135	$ 150	$ 165
Champagne Glass	185	200	215
Cream/Sugar, w/ lid	360	375	390
Decanter	85	100	115
Goblet	185	200	215
Tumbler	135	150	165

MINERVA

	LOW	AVG.	HIGH
Butter, w/ lid	$ 150	$ 175	$ 200
Cake Plate, dia. 12"	135	150	165
Compote, w/ lid	85	100	115
Cream/Sugar, w/ lid	175	200	225
Goblet	90	110	130

	LOW	AVG.	HIGH
Jam Jar, w/ lid	$ 115	$ 140	$ 165
Pickle Dish, oval, "Love's Request is Pickles"	50	65	80
Pitcher	150	175	200
Plate, tab handled	85	100	115
Platter, oval	65	80	95
Relish Dish, 3-part	40	55	70
Sauce, flat	25	40	55
Sauce, ftd.	30	45	60
Spooner	50	65	80

PICKET

	LOW	AVG.	HIGH
Butter, w/ lid	$ 100	$ 120	$ 140
Celery	65	80	95
Compote, high, w/ lid	75	90	105
Compete, low	55	70	85
Cream/Sugar, w/ lid	145	160	175
Goblet	65	80	95
Jam Jar	50	65	80
Pickle Dish, w/ lid	45	60	75
Pitcher	85	100	115
Salt	15	30	45
Spooner	20	35	50
Toothpick	45	60	75
Tumbler	50	65	80
Wine Glass	30	45	60

SCROLL

	LOW	AVG.	HIGH
Butter	$ 30	$ 45	$ 60
Celery	35	50	65
Compote	20	30	40
Cream/Sugar, w/ lid	50	65	80
Egg Cup	35	50	65
Goblet	10	20	30
Pitcher	45	60	75
Relish Bowl	15	30	45
Salt	10	25	40
Sauce, flat	10	15	20
Sauce, ftd.	15	30	45
Spooner	15	30	45
Wine Glass	20	30	40

Pressed glass footed pitcher,
$150-$200.

Steuben Glass

Steuben Glass Company produces some of the finest crystal in the world today. Founded in 1903 in Corning, NY, it has always concentrated on fine art glass. The Corning Glass Works purchased the company in 1918. Steuben pieces are marked with either the letter "S" or the entire name "Steuben" scratched neatly and in tiny letters on the underside of the base. The model number is usually scratched there as well.

Many famous designs are still in production. The prices listed include the current retail price when new (*new*), the price of a "second-hand" but perfect condition piece (*perf*), and the value if the piece has a small scratch (*sm scr*). Also, the size and model number are given after each entry.

	SM SCR	PERF	NEW
Apple, 4", 7874	$ 70	$ 140	$ 340
Archaic Bowl, 11.5", 8586	330	650	1575
Archaic Vase, 9.75", 8585	350	700	1695
Archaic Vase, tall, 13", 8584	490	950	2375
Arctic Fisherman, 6.5", 1023	800	1500	3850
Arcus, 5", 0217	800	1500	3850
Athena Candlestick, 6", 8687	50	90	225
Balloon Rally, 10.25", 0361	2880	5520	13800
Bear Hand Cooler, 2.5", 5521	30	60	150
Bull Hand Cooler, 2.5", 5524	30	60	150
Butterfly, 8", 0085	2980	5750	14300
Calyx Bowl, 9.5", 8115	80	140	360
Candy Dish, Ram's Head, 5", 7936	130	260	640
Cat Hand Cooler, 2.5", 5520	30	60	150
Cat Nap, 3", 8704	50	90	225
Celestial Bowl, 8.25", 8563	90	170	425
Christmas Tree, 6.25", 8498	120	220	560
Chronos Bowl, 7.5", 8706	70	140	350
Close to the Wind, 8", 1068	880	1600	4200
Cut Vase, 6.5", 0098	820	1500	3950
Deep Flower Bowl, 10", 8091	170	320	795
Deep Pillar Bowl, 9", 8346	200	380	950
Eagle, 4.25", 8496	70	140	340
Eagle, 5.5", 8304	150	280	710
Eagle, 12", 8130	150	300	740
Eagle Hand Cooler, 2.75", 5519	30	60	150
Elephant, 7.5", 8128	170	330	825
Elusive Buck, 7.25", 0503	1500	3000	7500
Equinox Bowl, 9.5", 8517	180	350	875
Excalibur, 8", 1000	650	1240	3100
Fawn, Woodland, 4.75", 8640	60	120	300
Flower Vase, 8.5", 7913	110	210	525
Folded Bowl, 7.25", 8707	40	80	200
Folded Bowl, med., 9", 8708	60	120	300
Fox, 3.25", 8582	40	70	185
Framed Bowl, 16", 8631	3300	6400	16000
Framed Vase, 8.5", 8632	2250	4400	11,000
Framed Vase, tall, 16.5", 8630	2700	5000	13000
Frog Hand Cooler, 2.5", 5510	30	60	150

	SM SCR	PERF	NEW
Galaxy, 3.5", 8395	$ 160	$ 300	$ 780
Gander, 5.25", 8358	70	140	350
Gazelle Bowl, 6.75", 0053	4750	9000	23,000
Glass House, 3.5", 8633	90	180	450
Goose, 4", 8344	70	140	350
Handkerchief Vase, 9.5", 8618	130	250	625
Handkerchief Vase, sm., 7", 8703	50	90	225
Heart, Point Down, 3.5", 8376	90	170	420
Heart, Point Up, 4", 8377	90	170	420
Heart Pendant, 1.75", 1105	580	1100	2800
Heart Throb, 3.25", 8566	80	160	405
Heart to Heart, 2.5", 8626	40	70	185
Hellenic Urn, 9.5", 8592	190	375	925
Heritage Flared Vase, 12", 7706	150	300	725
Highball, 6.5", 7923	60	110	275
Horse Head, 5", 7779	60	120	310
I Love Hope Cube, 2", 8713	60	120	300
Ice Bear, 6", 1022	790	1500	3800
Ice Hunter, 6.25", 1033	860	1600	4150
Juliet Vase, 5.25", 8629	40	80	195
Lighthouse, 8.5", 1159	450	860	2150
Lion, 9.5", 1126	500	960	2400
Low Teardrop Candlestick, 4.5", 7995	100	200	500
Lyre Vase, 7.75", 8113	90	160	410
Menorah, 9.5", 8682	750	1500	3650
Moby Dick, 11.25", 0055	4900	9400	23,500
Monkey Hand Cooler, 2.75", 5526	30	60	150
Monument Valley, 8.75", 0358	900	1750	4300
Moravian Star, 2.5", 8625	90	180	450
New York, New York, 17", 0353	6250	12,000	30,000
Nut Bowl, 6", 8345	50	100	245
Old Fashioned Glass, 3.5", 7933	50	100	240
Owl Hand Cooler, 2.5", 5516	30	60	150
Peach, 3", 8600	60	110	275
Penguin, 3.5", 8295	40	80	195
Peony Bowl, 12.75", 8101	230	450	1100
Pillar of Friendship, 6.5", 8581	160	300	760
Pisces, 2.75", 8620	40	70	185
Porpoise, 9.25", 8126	120	230	580
Prelude & Fugue, 6", 1160	610	1100	2950
Puppy Love, 2.75", 8524	40	70	185
Pyramid Block, 3.5", 8413	80	160	400
Quail, 5.5", 8533	90	170	435
Rabbit Hand Cooler, 2.75", 5523	30	60	150
Rising Star, 4.25", 8621	180	340	850
Rooster Hand Cooler, 3.25", 5527	30	60	150
Rose Vase, 11.5", 8090	150	300	740
Rosebud Necklace, 2", 1116	330	640	1600
Sailboat, 6.5", 8570	120	230	575
Saturn Paperweight, 5.5", 8609	100	190	475
Scallop, 3.5", 8572	40	80	195

	SM SCR	PERF	NEW
Scroll Candlestick, 4.75", 8735	$ 50	$ 100	$ 250
Seashell, 3.5", 8552	60	120	310
Seawave Vase, 8", 8550	110	220	540
Ship's Decanter, 10", 7912	270	520	1300
Shore Bird, 8.25", 8303	90	180	440
Snail, 3.25", 7982	40	80	210
Snow Pine, 4.25", 8611	110	210	525
Spiral Bowl, 7", 8060	80	150	375
Spiral Vase, 6.5", 8058	80	150	365
Star of David, 2.5", 8686	80	140	360
Star Stream, 5.25", 8567	120	220	560
Star-Spangled Banner, 6", 8623	330	640	1600
Stardust Bar Glass, 4.125", 8579	70	130	320
Stardust Decanter, 9.5", 8580	260	500	1250
Starfish, 4.75", 8622	40	80	195
Strawberry Pendant, 2", 1104	230	440	1100
Sunflower Bowl, 10", 8530	90	170	420
Sunflower Bowl, large, 15.5", 8531	200	380	950
Swan, Curved Neck, 7.5", 8484	110	210	515
Swan, Straight Neck, 6.5", 8483	110	210	515
Teardrop Candlestick, 8.75", 7792	140	270	675
Trout & Fly, 8", 1002	450	860	2150
Turtle Hand Cooler, 2.5", 5514	30	60	150
Twist Bowl, 8.75", 8501	90	170	420
Twist Bowl, large, 13.5", 8569	180	340	840
Twist Bud Vase, 8", 8499	60	120	295
Twist Candlestick, 6", 8502	130	240	600
Whirlpool Vase, 11", 8087	190	360	900
Wren, 3", 8603	40	70	185

Right: Beaver, $125 at auction.

Left: Ashtray, $150 at auction.

Waterford Crystal

Waterford Glass House produced Waterford, the most famous Irish glass, from 1783 until 1850. Craftsmen cut blanks by a revolving iron wheel combined with sand and a water trickle. They then polished them with a soft powder. Waterford items are marked "Penrose Waterford." The color of Waterford is whiter than other Irish glass, though it is often mistakenly thought to have a blue tinge.

Americans imported Waterford from 1790 to 1850. Popular import items were decanters, glasses, lamps, chandeliers, candlesticks, and candelabra. However, the characteristic Waterford items, most often associated with Ireland and Irish glass, include covered vases and jars for food, large serving bowls, oil and vinegar bottles, glasses, jugs, and salts.

A new company was started at Waterford in the late 1940s. Along with a variety of fine cut-glass items, they also make copies of original Waterford pieces. This period produced the Waterford crystal listed here.

	LOW	AVG.	HIGH
Bowl, fruit, spiked diamond panels flank cut fans in reserves, notched rim, cut crescents, signed, 3.5" ht., 8" dia.	$ 200	$ 250	$ 300
Bowl, fruit, spiked diamonds w/ panels and thumbprints, tapered sides, signed, 4.5" ht., 12" dia.	250	280	310
Bowl, fruit, tapered sides, cut vesicas on sides and base, round, 3.5" ht., 8" len.	150	200	250
Bowl, fruit, tapered sides, cut stars within a sq. design, notched rim, round, signed, 4" ht., 7.5" dia.	100	150	200
Bowl, notched diamonds, notched and paneled edge, star-cut design on base, oblong shape, signed, 4.5" ht., 13.5" long	120	160	200
Bowl, salad, cut diamond design, notched edge. star-cut base on tapered base, signed. 4.5" ht., 10" dia.	160	220	280
Bowl, salad, marquise shape w/ daisy and button motif, flared rim, cylindrical, signed, 3.5" ht., 9" dia.	150	200	250
Bowl, salad, slanted sides, cut zigzag vesicas, star-cut design on base, round signed, 4" ht., 8.5" dia.	120	160	200
Bowl, wide diamond-cut band, pinwheel cut in pedestal base, signed, 3" ht., 10.5" dia.	150	200	250
Candlesticks, star-cut design on bases, 6" ht.	100	150	200
Compote, spiked diamond band, cut fans around scalloped rim, star-cut design on base, 5.5" ht., 5.5" dia.	120	160	200
Compote, spiked diamond band w/ thumbprint band, round, notched rim, notched base, signed, 6" ht., 7.5" dia.	225	275	325
Compotes, pair, notched thumbprint, lid has spiral finials, base is 6-sided, 14.5" ht.	300	400	500
Decanter, cut diamonds w/ sunburst design, thumbprints, notched neck, star-cut design stopper, signed	140	180	220
Decanter, paneled neck, base has cut sawtooth band, signed, 11.5" ht.	150	200	250
Dish, round-shape spiked diamond bands, ball finial, star-cut design on base, signed, 6" ht., 6" dia.	100	140	180
Dishes, pr., star design in center, 3.5" dia.	75	100	125
Jar, marmalade, pedestal base, 6" ht.	100	150	200
Jar, star-cut design on lid, cut crosses and panels, signed, 5.5" ht.	150	200	250
Mug, notched sides, 4.5" ht.	45	60	75
Mugs, marquise shapes alternate w/ cane design in reserves, star-cut design on base, signed, set of 4, 4.5" ht.	200	250	300

	LOW	AVG.	HIGH
Napkin Ring, cut-diamond pattern	$ 50	$ 75	$ 125
Vase, cut-diamond design, cylindrical shape, 6" ht.	75	100	125
Vase, cut-diamond panels w/ tapered sides, cylindrical shape, 10" ht.	120	160	200
Vase, fine panels of double-shield-form notching, cylindrical shape, signed, 8" ht.	80	120	160
Vase, trumpet shape, grid design formed from cut vesicas, starburst design on base, signed, 10" ht.	200	250	300

Household Items

Advertising Memorabilia

Successful advertising draws people to a store or a product. Artists who design advertisements compete with thousands of other images that bombard consumers. Advertisements must get attention, inform and allure. Advertising often reflects the views and desires of society at a given time. Antique advertising has been an active collecting area for years. Andy Warhol and others blurred the boundry between commercial art and fine art. People recognized that dynamic advertising is good art. In 1990 a Campbell's Soup sign depicting the American flag sold for over $90,000 (no connection to Warhol). Although similar examples have since sold for less, it focused attention on the field and attracted a larger audience.

The diversity of advertising is astounding. Collectors can concentrate on eras, products, companies, signs, tins, trade cards, watches, premiums, dolls, figural displays, toys, etc. In recent years interest has increased in post-World War II advertising. Adding these collectors to the pre-war collectors creates a huge and growing market. The prices listed below are for items in excellent or better condition. Although some wear is expected on older items it should not be substantial or interfere with the visual appeal of the item. Condition for newer items are near mint. The other section in this book that contains advertising and promotional material is Toys and Other Playthings. For further reading see *Hake's Guide to Advertising Collectibles* , Ted Hake, Wallace Homestead, Radnor, PA, 1992; *Advertising Character Collectibles*, Warren Dotz, Collector Books, Paducah, KY, 1993; *Huxford's Collecting Advertising*, Sharon & Bob Huxford, Collector Books, Paducah, KY, 1993.

	LOW	HIGH
A & P Spoon/Coffee Measure, yellow plastic, 1950s	$ 3	$ 4
Alka Seltzer Calendar, 1942	40	60
Ambassador Scotch Pitcher, white, 1960s	8	10
American Agriculturist Sign, embossed tin, 1920s, 6.5" x 13"	25	35
Annheuser Busch Tray, oval, factory scene, 1900, 18" x 15"	2000	3000
Armstrong Tire Ashtray, clear, round, red decal, 1950s, dia. 5.75"	10	15
Arrow Trailer Rentals Sign, embossed U.S. map, 1940s, 14" x 18"	60	90
Aunt Jemima & Chef Potholder Hangers, 1948, ht. 11"	30	40
Aunt Jemima Breakfast Club Mirror, round, 1935	45	65
Aunt Jemima Plastic Syrup Pitcher, 1950s, ht. 5"	45	65
Axelrod the Basset Hound Plastic Bank, 1960s, ht. 8"	30	40
Ayers' Cherry Pectoral Trade Card, girl on front, ailments on back	3	5
Ayers' Sarsaparilla Trade Card, 2 women w/ children & dog on front	3	5
Bacardi Rum Ashtray, white china, 1960s, dia. 4.5"	8	12
Baranger Studios Automaton, The Seven Dwarfs, 1940s, ht. 18"	2000	3000
Barnum's Animal Crackers Sign, commemorative tin, 1979, dia. 4"	6	8
Bear Brand Hosiery Cardboard Box, 1915, 5" x 7"	70	90
Beck's Brewing Tray, picture of a buffalo, 1950s, dia. 13"	50	70
Beefeater Gin Figural Composition Display, 1960s	80	100
Bell Plastic Telephone, 1950s, len. 7"	40	50
Bert and Harry Piel Metal Statue, 1955, ht. 9"	50	75
Bert and Harry Piel Vinyl Store Display, 1965, ht. 11.5"	40	60
Bickmore Shaving Cream Die-Cut Cardboard Sign, man shaving, 1940s	80	100
Big Boy Nodder, 1965, ht. 8"	100	150

	LOW	HIGH
Blatz Beer Display, 3 baseball players, 1968, ht. 11"	$ 100	$ 150
Blatz Beer Bar Display, 3 baseball players, 1960s, ht. 16"	150	200
Borden's Milk Truck, 1940s, len. 9"	300	500
Bromo Seltzer Tip Tray, 1930s	60	90
Bud Man Ceramic Beer Stein, 1989, ht. 8.5"	20	30
Budweiser Ashtray, glass, round, 1950s, dia. 5"	8	10
Budweiser Beer Booklet, 20 pp., 1965, 5" x 7"	7	9
Budweiser Sign, plastic w/ light-up bottle, 1960s, 5" x 12"	40	70
Buffalo Pitts Calendar, Indian and Buffalo, 1911	300	400
Bull Dog Malt Liquor Decal, 1940s, sq. 7"	8	10
Bull Durham Bullfighters Sign, cardboard, 1920s, 14" x 22"	500	800
Bunny Bread Sign, red & white embossed tin, 1940s, 3.5" x 28"	60	90
Burma Shave, set of 3 wooden signs, 1930s, 10" x 3.5"	300	500
Burt Parkes Spiedel Watch Band Animated Display, 1950s, ht. 21"	800	1000
C.I. Heed & Co. Trade Card, telephone series, testimonials on reverse	6	10
Calumet Baking Powder Thermometer, can and child, 1920s, ht. 21"	300	500
Camel Cigarettes Ashtray, round tin, logo in center, 1950s, dia. 3.5"	8	12
Camel Cigarettes Booklet "Know Your Nerves," 1934, 3" x 4"	10	15
Camel Cigarettes Calendar, 1963	18	22
Campbell Kid Silverware, 3 piece set, 1940s	35	45
Canadian Club Sign, for a ceiling fan, round, 1930s, dia. 7"	30	40
Carnation Milk Tip Tray, 1930s	45	75
Ceresota Flour Match Safe, boy slicing bread, 1915, ht. 5.5"	200	300
Charlie the Tuna Telephone, 1980s, ht. 10"	60	80
Charlie the Tuna Vinyl Squeeze Doll, 1975, ht. 7.5"	40	50
Cherry Smash Porcelain Syrup Dispenser, 1910, ht. 16"	800	1400
Chesterfield Cigarette Tin, 1940s	15	20
Chevrolet Motor Cars Calendar, 1920, ht. 14.5"	300	500
Chivas Regal Ashtray, Wade china, triangular, 1950s, len. 11.5 "	8	12
City Club Crushed Cubes Tobacco Upright Pocket Tin, 1935, ht. 4.5"	175	225
Clanky Chocolate Syrup Container, 1965, ht. 10"	25	35
Colonel Sanders Plastic Bank, 1965, ht. 12.5"	30	40
Colonel Sanders Plastic Nodder, 1965, ht. 7"	70	90
Columbia Bicycles Trade Card, cyclists at night, 1910	15	20
Corbys Stir Container, plastic, 1950s, ht. 6"	20	25
Coronet Waiter VSQ Brandy Store Display, 1955, ht. 19"	125	175
Crackle Puppet, 1984, ht. 4"	8	12
Cream of Kentucky Heart-Shaped Thermometer, plastic, 1950s, ht. 10.5"	45	65
Crest Sparkle Telephone, 1980s, ht. 11"	20	30
Dandy Bread Door Handle, metal, loaf and slices, 1940s, 3" x 13"	45	65
De Laval Cream Separator Figural Match Holder, 1915, ht. 6.5"	120	180
De Soto Auto Banner, red, gold, and black fringed silk, 1951, 38" x 66"	500	800
Diamond Dyes Tin & Wood Case, children, girl w/ camera, 1910, ht. 30"	700	1300
Dino the Dinosaur Green Plastic Bank (Sinclair), 1965, len. 4"	18	22
Dino the Dinosaur Inflatable Toy, 1965, ht. 12"	20	30
Dino the Dinosaur Soap, in original box, 1964, len. 3 1/2"	8	12
Dobbins' Soap, 6 Trade Cards, Shakespeare's "Six Ages of Man"	20	25
Dr Jayne's Expectorant Poster, 1895, 13.5" x 29"	500	800
Dr Mile's Remedies Calendar, girl and boy, 1908	300	500
Dr Pepper Bottle Opener, cast iron, 1930s	20	30
Dr Pepper Calendar, 1950	25	45

Clockwise from above left: Eveready Safety Razor Clock, $2000-$3000; Cherry Smash Porcelain Syrup Dispenser, c. 1910, $800-$1400; Anheuser Busch Tray, c. 1900, $2000-$3000; E. Robinson's & Sons Beer Tray, c. 1895, $400-$600. — Photos courtesy of James D. Julia, Inc.

Above: Gold Dust Die-Cut Double -Sided Hanging Banner, c. 1900, $5000-$7500. — Photo courtesy of James D. Julia Auctioneer.
Right: Texaco Fire Chief Helmet, plastic, 1960s, $70-$90.

	LOW	HIGH

Dr Pepper Key Holder, 1930s, len. 2" .... $ 10 ... $ 15

Dr Pepper Thermometer, bottle and clock, "10, 2 and 4," 1930s, ht. 17" .... 200 ... 300

Dr Pepper Tin Sign, red and white, 1950s, 6" x 18" .... 50 ... 70

Dutch Boy Figural String Holder w/ Bucket, 1915, 13" x 30" .... 2000 ... 2500

Dutch Boy Cardboard Sign, "wet paint" picture of boy, 1930s, 6" x 9" .... 80 ... 120

E. Robinson's & Sons Beer Tray, factory scene, 1895, dia. 13.5" .... 400 ... 600

E.R. Durkee & Co. Spices Wooden Box, elephants & India, 1895, 12" x 7" ..... 60 ... 80

Elsie The Cow China Mug, (Borden), 1940, ht. 2.75" .... 35 ... 45

Elsie the Cow Lighted Dial Electric Clock, 1948, dia. 14" .... 300 ... 400

Elsie the Cow Vinyl Bank, 1970s, ht. 9" .... 60 ... 80

Equitable Life Insurance Calendar, 1904 .... 100 ... 150

Ernie the Keebler Elf Vinyl Squeeze Doll, 1975, ht. 7" .... 12 ... 15

Esky *Esquire Magazine* Cardboard Display, 1960s .... 100 ... 150

Esso Glass Bank, 1940s, ht. 5" .... 30 ... 40

Esso Oildrop Red Plastic Bank, 1960s, ht. 7" .... 70 ... 90

Esso Tiger Pitcher & 6 Glasses, 1950s .... 50 ... 75

Esso Tiger Plastic Bank, 1960s, ht. 8.5" .... 30 ... 40

Eveready Safety Razor Clock, man shaving dial, 1915, ht. 28" .... 2000 ... 3000

Eveready Cat Plastic Bank, 1972, ht. 6" .... 25 ... 35

Falstaff Beer Pocket Protector, 1960s .... 4 ... 6

Falstaff Beer Tray, Sir Falstaff holding bottle and tray, 1940s, dia. 12" .... 60 ... 80

Firestone Tire Ashtray, Texas Central Expo, 1936 .... 20 ... 30

Florida Orange Bird Plastic Bank, 1972, ht. 5" .... 18 ... 22

Florida Orange Bird Plastic Nodder, 1972, ht. 7" .... 20 ... 30

Ford Gramophone/Postcard, Car, Santa, & R. Clooney, 1956 .... 8 ... 12

Ford Tractor Sign, Masonite, 1940s, 11" x 21" .... 30 ... 50

Fred Fossil Resin Statue Store Display .... 75 ... 125

Freese's Cementing Glue Trade Card, 1 vertical ill., 1885 .... 6 ... 10

Funny Face Walkers, 1970, ht. 3" .... 60 ... 80

General Electric Radio Wooden Jointed Drum Major Figure, 1935, ht. 18" .. 1000 ... 1500

General Electric Refrigerator-Form Clock, 1930s, ht. 9" .... 100 ... 150

Glenfiddich Pitcher, black, 1970s .... 8 ... 12

Gold Dust Die-Cut Double-Sided Hanging Banner, 1900, len. 15.5" .... 5000 ... 7500

Grape Nuts Tin Sign, girl and Saint Bernard, 1910, 20" x 30" .... 1000 ... 1500

Hall's Vegetable Sicilian Hair Renewer Trade Card testimonials on reverse,
　　portrait of girl on front .... 6 ... 10

Hamm's Bear Ceramic Bank, 1980, ht. 11" .... 15 ... 20

Hammer's Ice Cream Tray, 1920s .... 50 ... 70

Happy Foot Composition Store Display, 1950, ht. 12" .... 300 ... 500

Harry Hood (Milk and Juice) Vinyl Figure, 1970s .... 60 ... 80

Hazard Smokeless Powder Calendar, boy and dog, 1910, 17" x 17" .... 180 ... 220

Heinekin Dutch Boy w/ Bottle Figural Display, 1960s, ht. 15" .... 80 ... 120

Heinz Vinegar Sign, bottle and salad, 1910, 12" x 22" .... 150 ... 200

Helping Hand Clock, 1985, ht. 6" .... 25 ... 35

Hines Cognac Bottle Store Display, 1940s, ht. 20" .... 25 ... 35

Hires Root Beer *Magic Story* Booklet, 1934 .... 10 ... 15

Hires Root Beer Tray, 1910 .... 200 ... 300

Hires Root Beer Mug, boy w/ mug, "Join Health and Cheer," 1900 .... 150 ... 250

Hires Root Beer Syrup Dispenser, hourglass shape, 1912, ht. 14" .... 400 ... 600

Hires Root Beer Thermometer, bottle shape, 1930s, ht. 7" .... 100 ... 150

Hires Root Beer Tin Chalkboard, 1940s, 10" x 20" .... 180 ... 220

	LOW	HIGH
	LOW	HIGH
His Man Figural Cologne Bottle, 1960, ht. 6"	$ 40	$ 60
Hody's Peanut Butter Tin Pail, kids on peanut seesaw, 1925, ht. 3.5"	150	200
Honey Moon Tobacco Upright Pocket Tin, 1935, ht. 4.5"	200	250
Horseford's Self-Raising Bread Preparation Trade Card, 1900	3	5
Hotpoint Wooden Jointed Figure, 1938, ht. 15"	800	1200
Hoyt's Cologne Trade Card, picturing large frog, 1883	3	5
Hoyt's German Cologne Paper Sign, boy & girl writing on wall, 1895, 20" x 29"	1000	1500
Hush Puppy Dog Bank, 1970s, ht. 8"	25	35
Icee Bear Vinyl Bank, 1970s, ht. 8"	25	35
Iron Fireman metal Figural Ashtray, 1940s, ht. 5"	70	90
Ivory Soap Cardboard Sign, little girl washing dolls' clothes, 1915, 17" x 24"	800	100
Jersey Cream Blotter, children, 1920s, 4" x 9"	20	30
Jersey Cream Tray, 1915, dia. 12"	150	200
Johnnie Pfeiffer Plaster Store Display, 1955, ht. 8"	60	80
Johnny Walker, Man in Top Hat Store Display, 1950s, ht. 16"	100	150
Jolly Green Giant Sprout Vinyl Squeeze Doll, 1975, ht. 6.5"	15	25
Jolly Green Giant Vinyl Squeeze Doll, 1975, ht. 9.5"	30	40
Jumbo Trade Card, P.T. Barnum's circus elephant	6	10
Kellogg's *Funny Jungleland Moving Pictures Book*, 1930s, 6" x 8"	35	55
Ken-L-Ration Cat and Sugar & Creamer, plastic, 1955, ht. 3"	25	35
Kool-Aid Dancing Pitcher Man, 1990, ht. 9"	20	30
Kool-Aid Pitcher Man Mechanical Bank, 1970, ht. 7"	30	50
Labatt's Figural Vinyl Display, 1960s	50	70
Lamb Knit Figural Store Display, 1930s, ht. 15"	400	600
Latest Novelty Trade Card, Secret Motto Ring, engravings of ring in corners, 1870s	15	20
Little Sprout Talking Stuffed Doll, 1970s	30	50
Lovell & Covel Candies Tin Pail, house, 1925, ht. 3"	120	200
Lovell & Covel Candies Tin Pail, Little Red Riding Hood, 1925, ht. 3"	90	150
Lovell & Covel Candies Tin Pail, Peter Rabbit, 1925, ht. 3"	180	220
Lucky Strike Cardboard Sign, 1935, 13.5" x 18"	100	150
Lucky Strike Cigarette Tin, 1930s	25	35
Mack Bulldog Hood Ornament, 1965, ht. 3"	20	30
Mammoth Brand Peanuts, 10 lb. can, 1925, ht. 11"	250	350
Maryland Club Mixture Upright Pocket Tobacco Tin, building in circle, 1918, ht. 4"	300	400
McCormick Paper Calendar, 1911, 13" x 20"	150	250
Menehune of Hawaii Plastic Bank, 1972, ht. 9.5"	40	60
Menita Bread Tin Sign, The Lone Ranger, 1948, 24" x 36"	400	600
Michelin Man (Bibendum) Plastic Ashtray, 1935, ht. 4.5"	90	110
Michelin Man (Bibendum) Vinyl Statue, 1980, ht. 14"	30	40
Miller High Life Tip Tray, 1940s, len. 4"	30	40
Miss Curity Plastic Store Display Figure, 1955, ht. 19"	100	150
Mobil Double-Sided Pegasus Gas Globe, 1920s, dia. 18"	300	400
Moxie Horse/Rider Wheeled Vehicle, 1920s, 6" x 9.5"	1200	1800
Mr. Bubble Plastic Figural Bank, 1970s, ht. 7"	35	45
Mr. Clean Plastic Figural Bottle, 1960s, ht. 12"	80	100
Mr. Clean Vinyl Doll, 1960s, ht. 8"	150	200
Mr. Peanut Peanut Butter Maker, 1970s, ht. 12.5"	35	45
Mr. Peanut Store Display, plastic head, top hat lid, 1970s, ht. 12.5"	50	75

Above left to right: Pipe Major upright pocket tin c. 1935, $250-$350; Times Square Tobacco upright pocket tin, c. 1935, $250-$350. — Photo courtesy of James D. Julia Auctioneer. Rocket Brand Needles Case, c. 1948, $12-$15.

Right: Diamond Dyes Tin & Wood Case, $700-$1300. — Photo courtesy of James D. Julia, Inc.

Above left to right: Aunt Jemima's Needle Book, c. 1930, $20-$30; New England Mince Meat diecut trade card, c. 1900, $18-$22.

	LOW	HIGH
Mr. Peanut Wooden Jointed Doll, 1930s, ht. 9"	$ 300	$ 400
Mr. Tomato Talking Alarm Clock (Heinz), 1980s, ht. 9.5"	200	250
Mr. Wiggle Rubber Hand Puppet (Jello), 1965, ht. 6"	70	90
Nature's Remedy-Vegetine The Blood Purifier Trade Card, girl	3	5
Neco Wafers Paper Sign, 1925, 12" x 20"	200	400
Old Angus Scotch Whiskey Figural Display, 1960s, ht. 14"	80	100
Old Crowe Plastic Store Display, 1965, ht. 5.5"	20	30
Old Dutch Cleanser Booklet, 1930s, 3" x 6"	9	12
Old Milwaukee Beer Sign, plastic, woman in Victorian clothing, 1960s, 15" x 22"	25	45
Opia Cigar Tip Tray, woman in veil, 1910, dia. 4.25"	150	250
Orange Crush Cardboard Sign, pinup girl, 1950s, 12" x 15"	40	60
Orange Crush Sign, 1940s	70	90
Orange Crush Tray, oval w/ Diana and stags, 1930	100	150
Pabst Blue Ribbon Beer Tray, "Finest Beer Served Anywhere," 1940s, dia. 13"	30	40
Pabst Blue Ribbon Store Display, motorist in horseless carriage, 1950s	60	80
Page's Glue Trade Card, humorous, men stuck to bench w/ maker's product, printed by Bufford, 1890	10	15
Palmolive Soap Mirror, Dionne Quintuplets & doctor	30	50
Patton's Ice Cream Tray, oval logo, glass & dish of ice cream, 1920s, sq. 13.5"	90	140
Pepsi-Cola Bottle Opener cast iron, 1930s	12	18
Pepsi-Cola Can Bank, 75-year commemorative, 1973	8	12
Pepsi-Cola Tin Sign, "America's Biggest Nickel's Worth," 1930, 10" x 30"	300	500
Pepsi-Cola Embossed Tin Sign, "Here's Health," 1920, 28" x 20"	300	500
Pepsi-Cola Tip Tray, Pepsi Lady, blue, 1908, 4" x 6"	600	900
Philco Transistor Man Figure, 1960s, ht. 5"	60	80
Pizza Hut Pete Plastic Bank, 1970s, ht. 7.5"	25	35
Planters Peanut Jar, raised peanuts on sides, 1910, ht. 13"	300	400
Ponds Extract Co. Trade Card, cures on reverse, 1900	3	5
Pop Puppet, 1984, ht. 4"	8	12
Poppin' Fresh Telephone, 1985, ht. 14"	70	90
Poppin' Fresh Vinyl Squeeze Doll, 1975, ht. 6.5"	6	8
Prince Albert Tobacco Upright Pocket Tin, 1960s, ht. 4.5"	8	10
Punchy Hawaiian Punch Plastic Telephone, 1980, ht. 11"	80	120
Putnam Dyes Tin Cabinet, horses and riders, 1920s, 19" x 15"	120	180
Quaker Oats Figural Plastic Mug, 1970s, ht. 4"	18	22
Quik Bunny Plastic Mug, 1980s, ht. 4.5"	7	9
R.C.A. Nipper Dog Store Display, 1920s, ht. 36"	800	1200
R.C.A. Radiotron Wooden Jointed Doll (M. Parrish design), 1935, ht. 16"	900	1400
Raid Bug Clock Radio, 1980s, ht. 7"	80	120
Raid Bug Plastic Telephone, 1980s, ht. 9"	90	130
Raid Bug Remote Control Robot, 1980s, ht. 12"	150	250
Raid Bug Wind-Up Walking Toy, 1980s, ht. 4"	30	40
Rainer Beer Tray, woman in ruffled hat, 1903, dia. 13"	300	500
Red Goose Plaster Statue, 1945, ht. 5"	30	40
Red Goose Shoes Figural String Holder, 1920s, ht. 28"	2000	2500
Reddy Kilowatt Lightning Bolt Plastic Statue, 1950s, ht. 6"	150	200
Reddy Kilowatt Wooden Jointed Figure, 1950s, ht. 12"	350	450
Rheingold Metal Stir Container, 1950s, ht. 8"	25	35
Rising Sun Stove Polish Trade Card, delivery boy stealing kiss from housewife, 1890s	6	10

	LOW	HIGH
Riverside Tires, owl and tire plaster statue, 1960s, ht. 5"	$ 75	$ 95
Ronald McDonald Cloth Doll, 1970s, ht. 16"	18	22
Ronald McDonald Plastic Telephone, 1985, ht. 10"	60	80
Rough On Rats Trade Card, E.R. Wells, "A Box Will Keep Your House Free"	8	12
Royal Baking Powder Booklet "Making Biscuits," 1927	10	15
Royal Baking Powder Booklet, "Comical Cruises of Captain Cooky", 1926	25	35
Rumford Baking Powder booklet, 1920s	8	12
Scrubbing Bubble Toy Brush, 1990, ht. 3"	4	6
Seagrams Figural 7 (Seven Crown) Lamp, plastic, 1950s	25	35
Seagrams Seven Crown Bottle Store Display, 1940s, ht. 18.5"	30	40
Sears & Roebuck Tip Tray, lady and city scene, 1920s	60	80
Shakey Pizza Chef Ceramic Bank, 1970s, ht. 6"	30	40
Sinclair Motor Oils Paper Sign, dinosaur, 1940s, 28" x 42"	200	300
Sir Walter Raleigh Smoking Tobacco Canister, 1950s	12	18
666 Liquid Medicine Fan, 2 children on horse, 1935	25	35
Smokey the Bear Plastic Bank, 1970s, ht. 8"	25	35
Snap Puppet, 1980s, ht. 4"	8	12
Sparkle Plastic Telephone, 1980s, ht. 11"	30	40
Speedy Alka-Seltzer Button, 1960s, dia. 1.25"	30	40
Speedy Alka-Seltzer Figural Display, 1970s, ht. 8"	300	400
Speedy Alka-Seltzer Vinyl Squeeze Toy, 1960s, ht. 5.5"	175	225
Spuds MacKenzie Plastic Lamp, 1980s, ht. 15"	70	120
Squires Pig Tin Sign, 1920s, 20" x 24"	600	900
Squirt Bottle Opener, cast iron, 1930s	20	25
Squirt Ceramic Bank, 1950s, ht. 8"	150	200
Squirt Composition Store Display, 1950s, ht. 13"	350	450
Stork Club Wooden Display Vase, 1950s, ht. 7.5"	150	250
Stroh's Bohemian Cardboard Sign, top-hatted man, 1910, 15" x 32"	200	250
Sunoco Blue Gas Globe, 1935, dia. 16"	200	300
Sure Shot Tobacco Counter Tin, Indian w/ bow, 1915, 10" x 15"	400	600
Tagament Tommy Figure, 1985, ht. 5"	20	30
Tappan Chef Painted Plaster Figure, 1955, ht. 8"	50	75
Tarrant's Seltzer Aperient Trade Card, little girl & sewing basket, cures on reverse	3	5
Texaco Fire Chief Helmet, plastic, 1960s	70	90
Texaco Oil Can Bank, 1 qt., 1970s	15	20
The Campbell Kids Chef Rubber Squeeze Doll, 1950, ht. 7"	60	80
Tiger Brand Chewing Tobacco Counter Cannister, 1900, ht. 12"	200	300
Times Square Tobacco Upright Pocket Tin, 1935, ht. 4.5"	250	350
Tony the Tiger Vinyl Squeeze Doll, 1975, ht. 7.5"	35	45
Trix Rabbit Vinyl Squeeze Doll, 1977, ht. 9"	30	40
Trout-Line Burley Cut Tobacco Upright Pocket Tin, 1925, ht. 3.75"	300	400
Tydol Oil Man License Plate Holder, 1935, ht. 7"	40	50
Union Metallic Cartridge Co. Calendar, boy w/ shotgun, 1901, 13" x 26"	800	1300
Uniroyal Naugahyde Nauga Stuffed Doll, 1960s, ht. 10"	25	35
Utica Club Tray, Lady's Hand Holding a Glass of U.C., 1940s, dia. 12"	50	70
Wards Vivovim Bread Thermometer, smiling toddler, 1915, ht. 21"	200	300
Waterbury Watch Co. Trade Card, multi-panel cartoon story, 1884	20	25
Weiner Mobile, pop-up Oscar, 1955, ht. 4.5"	150	200
Weiner Mobile, no pop-up Oscar, 1980, ht. 4.5"	10	15
Westinghouse Tuff Guy Plaster Statue, 1950s, ht. 4.5"	75	100

	LOW	HIGH
Whistle Soda Tin Blackboard, adorned w/ gnomes, 1915, 20" x 27"	$ 250	$ 350
White Horse Whiskey Ashtray, figural horse head, 1930s	70	110
White Rock Mineral Water Sign, tin, 1910, 4" x 12"	180	220
White Rock Tip Tray, 1920s	60	90
Wiedmann Brewing Rookwood Stein, raised eagle design, 1930s, ht. 5"	150	250
Wieland's Lager Tin Tray, Indian princess, 1900, dia. 13"	500	700
Willie the Kool Penguin Plaster Statue, 1955, ht. 4.5"	90	130
Willimantic Thread Trade Card, pictures Brooklyn Bridge, Forbes Lith. Co.	10	12
Worcester Salt Trade Card, in the form of eyeglasses w/ eye holes at center		
1885	15	20
World's Largest Fruithouse Trade Card, tall building, 1885	10	15
Wrigley's Gum Streetcar Sign, Wrigley arrow boy, 1920s, 10" x 20"	100	150
Yeast Foam Poster, little girl, tin-rimmed, 1920s, 10" x 14"	100	150
Yuengling Brewery Calendar, 1903, 20" x 27"	700	900

Below left to right: Bert Parks Spiedel Automated Store Display, $800-$1000; Chocolate Worm Cakes Tin, c. 1910, $80-$120. — Items courtesy of Bill Alberta.

Baskets

There are several types of basket construction. Wickerwork, the most common and widely used technique, is an over and under pattern. Twining is similar; two strands are twisted as they are woven over and under, producing a finer weave. Plaiting gives a checkerboard effect in either a tight weave or left with open spaces. Twill work is similar, but with a diagonal effect achieved by changing the number of strands over which the weaver passes. Coiling is the most desirable weave for the collector. This technique has been refined since its conception around 7000 BC. Fibers are wrapped around and stitched together to form the basket's shape. Most of these pieces were either used for ceremonial purposes or for holding liquids, since these tightly woven containers were leak proof.

Baskets are easy to care for but a few basic rules must be followed: Never wash an Indian basket, especially baskets made of pine needles, straw, grass or leaves. Dust them gently using a soft sable artist's brush. Willow, oak, hickory and rattan baskets may be washed in a mild solution of Murphy's Oil Soap and dried briefly in a sunny location. Baskets continuously exposed to the sun will fade.

*Nantucket lightship basket,
5" x 10", $ 700- $ 900.*

	LOW	AVERAGE	HIGH
Apache burden, 2.5" x 2.5"	$ 50	$ 65	$ 80
Apache burden, rawhide bottom, plain, ht. 11.5"	575	700	825
Apache burden, geometric pattern, tin cones, 6.5" x 5"	110	125	140
Apache coiled storage, geometric motifs, ht. 12.5"	1300	1650	2000
Apache coiled storage, flaring rim, animals and human figures, ht. 16.5"	1300	1500	1700
Apache coiled, flat base, dark brown with snowflake motif, dia. 8.5"	570	745	920
Apache grain barrel, geometric design with human figures, 10" x 11"	700	840	980
Apache plaque, geometric design, 16" x 5"	1000	1200	1400
Apache miniature, star design, 5.5" x 1"	290	380	470
Apache tray, dia. 10.5", c. 1895	200	260	320
Apache wedding, dia. 13", c. 1880	60	80	100
Bannock berry, 8" x 8.5"	100	135	170
Buttocks, tightly woven splint, dia. 7"	260	315	370
California, tightly woven, light brown, diamond motif, dia. 5.5"	300	330	360
Caushatta effigies, pine cones and needles, Crawfish, 9" x 6.5"	50	60	70
Crab, 6" x 5"	50	60	70
Alligator, 9" x 2.5"	50	60	70
Turtle, 6.5" x 3"	50	65	80

	LOW	AVERAGE	HIGH
Cheese, splint	$ 250	$ 300	$ 350
Cheese shaker, round, dia. 12"	440	500	560
Chehalis, geometric and cross design, 4.5" x 6.5"	350	450	550
Chemehuevi, two concentric geometric bands, 11.5" x 2"	700	850	1000
Clothes, round with two handles	150	185	220
Cowlitz lidded, 3" x 4.5"	150	210	270
Drying, New England, 30" x 48", shallow rim, c. 1850	600	800	1000
Field, oak splint, c. 1885	190	275	360
Havasupi coiled, triangle design, dia. 11.5"	330	365	400
Hopi coiled, rect. body, rain cloud and thunder motif, 5.25"	210	260	310
Hopi corn sifter, spiral design	160	195	230
Hopi coiled bowl, floral design, dia. 9.5"	170	235	300
Hopi coiled plaque, dia. 14.5", c. 1930	190	255	320
Hopi tray, mythological motif, dia. 11"	140	200	260
Japanese, tightly woven circular, dia. 7.5"	100	125	150
Karok, oval, bottom inverted, 10" x 7"	190	260	330
Klamath tray, dia. 14", c. 1900	390	455	520
Laundry, oak splint, 1910	100	125	150
Lilooet, 12.5" x 16"	300	350	400
Maidu tray, dia. 8.5"	120	145	170
Makah, zigzag designs, dia. 7"	100	135	170
Mandan, wood splint, circular	320	380	440
Mission tray, dia. 12"	500	650	800
Miwok, dia. 7", c. 1900	400	500	600
Modoc cap, diamond design, dia. 6"	200	250	300
Nantucket lightship, 5" x 10"	700	800	900
Navajo wedding, dia. 10"	225	300	375
Nootka whaler's hat, 10.5" x 10.5"	460	510	560
Paiute coiled, exterior is beaded, dia. 5"	320	385	450
Paiute lidded, ht. 10", c. 1900	150	200	250
Paiute water jar, horsehair handles, 5.5" x 7.5"	140	195	250
Panamint, reverse diamond design, 10.5" x 4"	550	700	850
Papago, geometric design, dia. 13"	160	200	240
Papago plaque, concentric square design, dia. 15"	240	290	340
Papago waste paper, men and dogs motif, dia. 10"	190	230	270
Pima bawl, dia. 16"	470	615	760
Pima coiled, flaring body, human figures, dia. 11.5"	500	635	770
Pima coiled, shallow, crosses in the field, dia. 9.5"	220	275	330
Pima grain barrel, geometric design, dia. 11"	800	1000	1200
Pima plaque, dia. 11"	325	400	475
Porno, decorated with feathers, dia. 12"	350	425	500
Sewing, wicker	110	125	140
Skokomish berry, 7" x 8"	210	240	270
Splint collecting, tightly woven, 8" x 9"	100	135	170
Splint cradle, hooded, c. 1820, 19" x 8"	175	225	275
Splint hickory, open handles	100	130	160
Splint, oval, wooded handles	280	325	370
Splint, back pack	120	220	320
Split, oak buttocks	100	130	160
Split, oak buttocks, large	110	215	320
Tlingit, geometric design, dia. 6"	560	680	800

	LOW	AVERAGE	HIGH
Tlingit, dia. 5", c. 1880	$ 600	$ 700	$ 800
Tlingit lidded, 4.5" x 6.5"	800	900	1000
Tlingit twined spruce root, cylindrical, zigzag dec., dia. 5"	700	800	900
Tulare, step pattern, squaw stitch, dia. 7.5"	240	330	420
Tulare, rattlesnake design	210	235	260
Tulare coiled, flat base, rattlesnake bands, dia. 14.5"	2200	2600	3000
Washo, tightly woven, band design, dia. 7"	160	200	240
Washo, geometric design, dia. 7"	130	170	210
Washo coiled trinket, polychrome, dia. 4.5"	220	270	320

Beer Cans

Beer cans are a relatively new phenomena. Krueger Brewing Company in Richmond, VA introduced them in 1935. Called flat tops because of the shape of the can top, a beer can opener and instructions on its use were initially given to purchasers free of charge. America learned quickly. Cone tops or crowntainers appeared shortly afterward from the Jos. Schlitz Co. The advantage of the cone top was that small breweries could produce them on a bottling production line and avoid investing in expensive equipment. They were not as popular with consumers and by the 1960s they were virtually extinct. The next innovation, pull tabs or tab tops, eliminated the need for openers.

There are a variety of ways to collect beer cans. Hobbyists collect full cans or empties. Collectors can concentrate on specific themes such as brand, state, region or tops.

The following prices are for mint examples opened or unopened. Rust, dents and scratches decrease the value of a beer can. Each entry below begins with the name brand and a description, followed by the type of top, the number of ounces, and the brewery name. Many colors are abbreviated throughout, such as wt. for white, bl. for blue, blk. and met. for metallic. Other abbreviations used are: CT cone top, FT flat top, and TT tab top.

Many firms produced the same product in other states or licensed others to produce it. This leads to confusion. For detailed information see *The Official Price Guide to Beer Cans,* Bill Mugrage, House of Collectibles, Random House, NY, 1993. He is listed in the back of this book. The guide suggests to check older, full cans periodically to make sure they are not leaking and, if you want to drain a full can, open it from the bottom where it can't be seen. Mr. Mugrage also dispels the myth about the value of Billy Beer. He states that any of the five different versions of Billy Beer are worth $2-$3 each, not hundreds of dollars as rumored. The collector's club is The Beer Can Collectors of America, 747 Mercus Court, Fenton, MO 83026.

	LOW	HIGH
A-1 Pilsner, wt. label w/ red "A-1," gold frame, FT, 12 oz., Arizona	$ 50	$ 70
Acme Bock Beer, wt., goat/red shield, FT, 12 oz., Acme	380	420
Acme Light Dry Beer, yel., wt. band, FT, 12 oz., Acme	35	45
Altes Lager, silver & blk. crowntainer, CT, 12 oz., Tivoli	80	100
American, red, wt., bl. & gold, name/ bl. script, CT, 12 oz., Am.	90	140
Banner Extra dry, wt. & red, "Prem. Beer" in bl., FT, 12 oz., Cumberland	15	20
Bantam Ale, squat, wt. & lt. grn., FT, 8 oz., Gobel	30	40
Bartels Pure, wt. & red, man w/ beard, FT, 12 oz., Lion	70	90
Bavarian Jay Vee, bl. & wt., FT, 12 oz., Grace	90	120
Bavarian's Old Style, wt., gold & red, name/ gold lettering, CT, 12 oz., Bav.	80	100
Becker's Best, silver w/ blk. lettering, FT, 12 oz., Becker	90	110
Becker's Uinta Club, silver, bl. & red, bronco, CT, 12 oz., Bker	120	160
Ben Brew, yel. & gold, "100% Grain Beer," CT, 12 oz., Franklin	90	120
Blk. Dallas Malt Liq., bl. & blk., evening skyline, TT, 12 oz., Walter	30	40
Buccaneer Beer, gold, wt., pirate, FT, 12 oz., Gulf	180	220
Budweiser, "Tab Top," TT, 16 oz., Anh.-Busch	4	6
Budweiser Malt Liquor, TT, 16 oz., Anh.-Busch	50	70
Buffalo Brew, orange house, FT, 12 oz., Cold Spring	2	3
Burger, wt. & dark red, no outline name, FT, 12 oz., Burger	12	18
Burgermeister Prem., cream, red & gold, gold bands, FT, 12 oz., Warsaw	5	9
Cascade, "King Size" near top, TT, 16 oz., Blitz Weinhard	12	15
Cee Bee, red & wt., TT, 12 oz., Colonial	12	18
Coal Cracker Beer, multi-color, TT, 12 oz., Yuengling	3	5
Country Club, wt., red, & gold, FT, 12 oz., Goetz	20	30
Drewry's Malt Liq., red, grn,. & wt., "A Man's Drink," FT, 12 oz., Drewry	700	900

	LOW	HIGH
Gerst 77 Beer, met., gold, red, wt., CT, 12 oz., Gerst	$ 180	$ 220
Highlander Prem., red & wt., revised ver., FT, 12 oz., Missoula	12	18
Hillman's Superb, bl. & gold, FT, 12 oz., Empire	60	80
Hof-Brau, red & wt., name/ gray, bl. lettering, TT, 12 oz., Maier	8	12
Hofbrau, cream wt. & red, German inn, FT, 12 oz., Hofbrau	18	22
Hoffman House, wt., brn. & red, FT, 12 oz., Walter	4	7
Holiday Special, wt. & brn. w/ bl. bands top & btm., FT, 12 oz., Potosi	12	18
Kingsbury Real Draft, wt., brn. & red, wood grain, TT, 12 oz., Kingsbury	8	10
Knickerbocker Nat., wt. w/ red & bl. ribbons, bl. lettering, TT, 7 oz., Ruppert	10	15
Koehler, dk. bl. & wt., orange trim name, TT, 12 oz., Erie	3	5
Koenig Brau, gold & wt., TT, 12 oz., Koenig Brau	8	10
Krueger, yel., red, & wt., "Lt. Lager" in blk., FT, 12 oz., Krueger	40	60
Lucky Lager, pale bl. & gold, name curved, TT, 12 oz., Lucky Lager	5	7
Lucky Malt Liquor, TT, 16 oz., Lucky Lager	30	40
Maier Select, red, wt., & bl., bl. leaf near top, TT, 12 oz., Maier	40	60
Malt Duck, purple & wt., TT, 12 oz., National	40	60
Manheim, red & wt., TT, 12 oz., Reading	9	12
Meister Brau, wt., gold, & red, red band at top, FT, 12 oz., Peter Hand	8	12
Mile Hi, red, wt., & bl., Colorado mountains, FT, 12 oz., Tivoli	40	60
Miller Select, red, wt., & bl.,1/4 moon in bl. medallion, FT, 12 oz., Miller	50	60
Milwaukee Prem., wt., red, & gold, FT, 12 oz., Waukee	15	20
Milwaukee's Best, bl. & wt., stein, FT, 12 oz., Gettelman	18	22
Mitchell's Prem., red, wt. & bl., FT, 12 oz., Mitchell	100	150
North Star XXX Beer, bl., wt., silver star, FT, 12 oz., Schmidt	25	35
Old Milwaukee, red & wt., dk. printing on shield, FT, 12 oz., Schlitz	5	7
P.O.C. Pilsner Beer, maroon, gold label, CT, 12 oz., Pilsner	90	110
Pabst Bl. Ribbon, gold, wt., & bl., slogan above gold band., FT, 12 oz., Pabst	8	12
Pabst Bl. Ribbon, red, wt., & bl., FT, 12 oz., Pabst	8	10
Pearl Beer, wt., bl, TT, 12 oz., Pearl	8	12
Penguin Extra Dry, wt., bl., FT, 12 oz., Horlacher	12	18
Pfeiffer's, gold, wt., & red, horizon. striping, FT, 12 oz., Pfeiffer	8	12
Pickwick Ale, gold, blk., & wt., FT, 12 oz., Haffenreffer	100	150
Piel's, gold, silver, & blk., name/ wt., FT, 12 oz., Piel's	10	15
Primo Hawaiian, met. gold, wt., map, TT, 12 oz., Jos. Schlitz	18	22
Prinz Brau Beer, "Anniversary Offer," TT, 12 oz., Prinz Brau	20	30
Rainer Ale, grn., gold label, TT, 12 oz., Rainer	12	18
Senate Beer, red, brn. trim, FT, 12 oz., C. Heurich	200	250
Sick's Select Beer, met. maroon, yel., 6 globe, FT, 12 oz., Sick's	60	80
Stag, "Half Quart" large wt. letters. near top, TT, 16 oz., Carling	5	7
Stallion XII, gold, wt., & red. illus. of horse, TT, 12 oz., Gold Medal	80	100
Stand. Cream. Ale, grn., wt., & gold, TT, 12 oz., Std. Rochester	15	20
Standard Dry Ale, bl., wt., & gold, TT, 12 oz., Eastern	5	7
Stegmaier Bock, brn. & wt., "Truly Brewed," TT, 12 oz., Stegmaier	2	3
Stegmaier Gold Medal, gold & wt., TT, 12 oz., Stegmaier	2	3
Sunshine Vitamin D, brn. & wt., CT, 12 oz., Schlitz	60	80
Topaz (crowntainer), silver, red stripes near bottom, CT, 12 oz., Koller	100	150
Topper Draught (gal.), CT, 64 oz., Standard	40	50
Tropical Prem., brn. & wt. "Taste Tells," CT, 12 oz., Florida	350	450
Viking Draft Beer, brn., blk., FT, 12 oz., Spearman	380	420
Wagner's Gambrinus, gold & multi, CT, 12 oz., Wagner	120	160
Wiedemann, (crowntainer), CT, 12 oz., Wiedemann	80	120
Winchester Malt Liquor, TT, 16 oz., Walter	15	20

Boxes

During the 18th and 19th centuries, Americans used boxes as utilitarian items. They made specialized boxes for a wide variety of purposes, from containers for food to storage of wedding dresses. Small boxes, for trinkets, matches or cigarettes, are some of the most collectible.

	LOW	AVG.	HIGH
Apple Box, footed, smoked finish	$ 500	$ 575	$ 650
Apple Box, pine, painted, 11" x 8.5"	100	140	180
Ballet Box, maple, oblong, sliding top	210	240	270
Band Box, hunter shooting deer	1000	1300	1500
Band Box, man and woman with flowers on lid	2250	3000	3750
Band Box, oval, painted, schoolhouse, flowers and trees on lid, 9" x 6"	2500	3250	4000
Book-shaped Box, inlaid colored wax hearts, stars	50	75	100
Book-shaped Box, Pennsylvania German, painted wood	90	155	220
Book-shaped Box, with name and dated 1861	600	720	840
Box, Wilcox, quadruple plate, scrolls, pointer dogs, lock lion's paw feet, 9" x 5"	340	370	400
Brass Box, covered with leather, shape of coffin	100	120	140
Bride's Box, German, oval, c. 1875	420	490	560
Bride's Box, oval, painted couple, floral motif, w. 18"	680	805	930
Bride's Box, painted flowers, dark green, c. 1817	520	600	680
Candle Box, cherry, carved, scalloped arch	750	835	920
Candle Box, geometric design, carved, ht. 8"	190	235	280
Candle Box, pine, sliding lid, red border, ht. 14"	730	815	900
Candle Box, tin, hanging, round	320	400	480
Cigar Box, coromandel, brass fittings. mid 19th century	350	415	480
Cigarette Box, cloisonné, cylindrical, unmarked	120	170	220
Cigarette Box, green, Lenox wreath mark, Lenox	50	60	70
Cigarette Box, pink daisy design, 4.5", Southern Potteries	10	15	20
Cigarette Box, ribbing, relief apple blossom design, Lenox wreath mark	60	70	80
Cigarette Box, "Wavecrest," forget-me-nots, "Cigarettes," ht. 4"	480	540	600
Cigarette Box, white with Lenox Rose trim, Lenox wreath mark	80	95	110
Cigarette Box, white w/ Ming trim, Lenox wreath mark	90	100	110
Coin Box, oak, changer, c. 1823	500	550	600
Collar Box, man's, with drawer, black with red lining	20	25	30
Cookie Box, round with lid and handle, Pennsylvania Dutch design	560	650	740
Cutlery Box, triple compartments, walnut, 8" x 16"	150	150	150
Deed Box, wood, carved	160	185	210
Desk Box, mahogany, compartments for writing tools and ink, 5" x 4.5" x 14"	480	560	640
Desk Box, painted rod, slant lid, w. 17.5"	220	245	270
Dome Top Box, bird motif, w. 10"	900	1000	1100
Glove Box, coromandel, gilt brass with green stones inlaid	130	155	180
Glove Box, covered with wallpaper	160	200	240
Hat Box, covered with bird motif wallpaper	270	315	360
Hat Box, wooden, original finish and hardware, c. 1880	210	245	280
Herb Box, oval, original paint and lid	550	615	680
Jewelry Box, plated silver, cherubs playing, 8" x 6" x 3"	210	270	330

	LOW	AVG.	HIGH
Lacquer Box, octagonal, Oriental designs, c. 1840 .... $ 540		$ 610	$ 680
Lap Desk, brass inlaid, walnut, w. 15" 270		330	390
Lunch Box, oval, c. 1880 75		100	125
Lunch Box, tin, Art Deco design, nursery characters 80		100	120
Match Box, shaped like treasure chest, acorn finial, 3", Willets Manufacturing Co. 70		90	110
Match Box, wooden, carved, ht. 5" 60		75	90
Miniature Box, antique Satsuma, rect., children and swans dec., 3.5", c. 1790 600		650	700
Pantry Box, 2-fingered round, dia. 3" 210		260	310
Pantry Box, 3-fingered oval, painted red 250		300	350
Pantry Box, oval, 2-fingered, c. 1820 280		330	380
Pantry Box, Scandinavian Bentwood 210		270	330
Pantry Box, varnished, dia. 10" 50		70	90
Pantry Boxes, 5 graduated, round, painted 370		420	470
Pill Box, sliding lid, dovetailed 40		50	60
Pottery Box, square with Lion of Lucerne figure, Bennington .. 220		235	250
Salt Box, Pennsylvania Dutch design, 2 compartments, open ... 350		385	420
Salt Box, pine, dovetailed, open, hanging 160		185	210
Salt Box, walnut, dovetailed, slant lid, hanging 270		325	380
Seed Box, 6 compartments, sliding lid 270		325	380
Shaving Box, brush 90		100	110
Snuff Box, Austrian silver gilt, musical, 3", hallmarked Vienna, c. 1828 4000		4750	5500
Snuff Box, French tortoiseshell, musical, sectional comb, 3", c. 1810 2000		2750	3500
Snuff Box, horn, acorn-shaped, screw on top, 1.5" 50		65	80
Snuff Box, Mauchline ware, boxwood, w. 3.5" 90		120	150
Snuff Box, pewter 70		85	100
Snuff Box, treenware, dia. 2.5" 30		40	50
Spice Box, cherry, 9 drawers, original, ht. 1.5" 310		335	360
Spice Box, curly maple, twelve drawers, brass pulls 540		675	810
Spice Box, oak, 8 drawers, wooden pulls, hanging 160		200	240
Spice Box, pine, 8 drawers, porcelain pulls, hanging 190		225	260
Spice Box, tin, 8 drawers, painted black 190		220	250
Spice Box, walnut, 2 drawers, carved back, dovetailed 560		655	750
Stamp Box, brass, footed, covered 80		95	110
Stamp Box, pewter, hinged top 150		165	180
Stamp Box, sterling with enameled lid, chair and finger ring 50		65	80
Tea Caddy, imitation tortoise shell, green, English, c. 1820 450		525	600
Tea Caddy, Marquetry, English, c. 1780 1000		1450	1900
Tin Box, brass rings, hand embossed arch and bullseye, c. 1880 .:. 60		75	90
Tobacco Box, Pennsylvania Dutch design, ht. 19" 120		130	140
Tool Box, child's, with tools, c 1930 80		100	120
Tool Box, oak, modern 50		60	70
Tramp Art Box, footed, geometric design, hinged top, 14" x 15" .. 340		385	430
Tramp Art Wall Box, small 60		85	110
Trinket Box, Art Deco, woman on cover, 6.5", Fulper Pottery .. 380		400	420
Trinket Box, painted, one drawer 575		700	825
Trinket Box, papier mache and antique sulfide, 2.5", c. 1790 ... 680		770	860
Trinket Box, rect., hand painted red roses with gold trim, 2" x 4", Lenox mark 140		155	170

British Royalty Memorabilia

The popularity of the British Royal family has generated a wide variety of commemoratives, from inexpensive tourist trinkets to fine porcelain. As the prestige of the current generation of royalty has faded, prices have leveled off, even if the subject of the commemorative item remains untouched by scandal.

	LOW	AVG.	HIGH
Ashtray, King Edward VIII, Edward's head and flags, Paladin china, 4.5"	$ 10	$ 15	$ 20
Box, King George VI and Queen Elizabeth, king, queen, 2 princesses, tin, 5" x 4" x 3"	20	25	30
Box, Prince Albert, impressed head of prince, round, brass, 2.5"	30	40	50
Cover Jar, Queen Victoria, cover shaped like Victoria's head, milk glass, 8"	90	105	120
Covered Jar, Queen Elizabeth II, Coronation 1953, cream pottery, coat of arms, 5"	60	75	90
Cup, King Edward VII and Queen Alexandra, Coronation 1902, enamel, 3.5"	60	75	90
Cup, King George V and Queen Mary, Coronation 1911, king, queen, Prince of Wales, enamel	80	90	100
Cup, King George V and Queen Mary, Coronation 1911, portraits of royal couple, Royal Doulton	70	85	100
Cup, King George V and Queen Mary, Silver Jubilee, king, queen, flags, green glass, handle	40	55	70
Cup, King George VI and Queen Elizabeth, family portrait, Spode, 3.5"	40	60	80
Cup, Queen Elizabeth II, Coronation 1953, double handle	40	50	60
Cup, Queen Victoria, scroll design with portrait of queen, palace, enamel	70	80	90
Finger Bowl, King George V and Queen Mary, Coronation 1911	60	75	90
Mug, King Edward VII and Queen Alexandra, Coronation 1902, Royal Doulton, 4"	60	75	90
Mug, King Edward VIII, color portrait, lion, unicorn, flags, ribbon, china, 3"	30	35	40
Mug, King Edward VIII, Coronation 1937, Edward's head, 3.5"	40	50	60
Mug, King Edward VIII, family motto, crown, oak branches, tapered, 3.5"	40	55	70
Mug, King Edward VIII, official design," May 1937 Coronation of King Edward VIII," 4.5"	40	60	80
Mug, King Edward VIII, picture of king, Wedgwood, 3.5"	40	50	60
Mug, King George VI and Queen Elizabeth, king and queen in gold frames, flags, crown, china,	10	20	30
Mug, Queen Elizabeth II, Coronation 1953, Copeland Spode, handle, 3.5"	20	35	50
Mug, Queen Elizabeth II, Coronation 1953, portrait of queen, 3.5"	40	55	70
Mug, Queen Elizabeth II, official design, Johnson Brothers, glazed pottery, 3.5"	20	35	50
Mug, Queen Elizabeth II, photo in frame, lion, unicorn, flags, handle, 3.5"	20	30	40
Mug, Queen Elizabeth II, photo of queen, Tucson bone china, handle, 3.5"	40	50	60
Mug, Queen Elizabeth II, picture of queen on front, coat of arms			

	LOW	AVG.	HIGH
on back, green, handle, 3"	$ 10	$ 20	$ 30
Mug, Queen Elizabeth II, picture of queen on front, coat of arms on back, pink, handle, 3"	10	15	20
Mug, Queen Elizabeth II, raised head of queen, white glazed pottery, handle, 3.5"	20	35	50
Mug, Queen Elizabeth II, Royal Albert bone china, handle, 4.5"	50	60	70
Mug, Queen Elizabeth II, Silver Jubilee, photo of queen, handle, 3.5"	30	40	50
Mug, Queen Elizabeth II, Silver Jubilee, portrait, Royal Worcester fine porcelain, 3.5"	40	50	60
Picture, Queen Victoria, figure and flowers in enamel, black glazed redware, 6"	140	155	170
Pierced Dish, King George VI and Queen Elizabeth, 5"	40	50	60
Pitcher, King Edward VII and Queen Alexandra, 25th wedding anniversary, flat sided	90	100	110
Pitcher, King Edward VII and Queen Alexandra, flow blue, 7"	140	160	180
Pitcher, King George V and Queen Mary, clear and frosted glass, 4"	40	55	70
Pitcher, Queen Victoria, 50th Anniversary, picture of queen, sayings, white, flat sided, 5"	130	145	160
Plate, King Edward VII and Queen Alexandra, portrait of Edward, scalloped border, flow blue, 9"	50	60	70
Plate, King Edward VII, photograph of Edward, fleur-de-lis border, glass, 7"	30	40	50
Plate, King Edward VIII, Edward's head with crown, flags, square, 8.5"	20	35	50
Plate, King George V and Queen Mary, picture of royal couple, coat of arms, 6"	40	55	70
Plate, Queen Alexandra, photograph of Alexandra, fleur-de-lis border, glass, 7"	30	40	50
Plate, Queen Elizabeth II, large painted crown, bright colors on white china, 5.5"	10	15	20
Plate, Queen Elizabeth II, oak leaves, acorns, portrait, square	30	45	60

Cameras

Louis Daguerre invented the first commercial camera in 1839. For the next thirty years nearly all cameras were for professional studios. During the 1870s amateur photography bloomed. The cameras of the late 19th century were generally large and bulking box cameras and bellows cameras. But strange and sometimes bizarre novelty cameras also appeared, including cameras designed in the forms of pocket watches, canes, and even neckties. In 1888 the Eastman Dry Plate and Film Company introduced the first commercially available roll film camera, the Kodak. It followed with the no. 1 Kodak the next year. Soon the Eastman Kodak Company came to dominate the American market. The hundreds of various cameras produced under the Kodak name outstrip any other maker's production record.

Collectors want cameras that are complete and in working order. Some allowance is made for the fragility of leather bellows and rubber parts. For further information see *The Official Price Guide to Collectible Cameras* and *Camera Collecting*, by Jason Schneider.

	LOW	HIGH		LOW	HIGH
Adox 35	$ 50	$ 75	Bellieni Jumelle	$ 225	$ 400
Adox Adrette	60	100	Belplasca	500	650
Agfa Antar	10	20	Benson Street	190	340
Agfa Isolette	50	70	Bentzin Planovista	1400	2300
Agfa Karat 36	40	85	Bentzin Primarflex	225	345
Agfa Selecta-M	115	170	Berning Robot I	125	200
Aires Penta 35	70	100	Bischoff Detective	1000	1400
Ansco Cadet Flash	5	10	Blair Hawkeye Baby	200	350
Ansco Craftsman	55	95	Blair Kamaret	500	800
Ansco Dollar	20	30	Bolsey 8	200	350
Ansco Folding No. 1	10	25	Bolsey Jubilee	45	70
Ansco Karomat	40	75	Bolsey Reflex	450	650
Ansco Photo Vanity	1200	2000	Boston Bulls-Eye	65	100
Ansco Rediflex	10	15	Boyer Altessa	155	250
Ansco Regent	40	65	Brack Field	270	415
Ansco Viking	15	25	Brooklyn	285	430
Anthony Buckeye	60	90	Bullard (folding plate)	175	300
Anthony Novelette	300	500	Burke & James Grover	100	185
Argus A	25	30	Burke & James Press	100	200
Argus A2	20	30	Busch Pressman	250	400
Argus AF	30	50	Busch Verascope F40	500	700
Argus Argoflash (AA)	35	50	Butcher Cameo	35	60
Argus Autronic 35	35	65	Butcher Carbine No. 2	15	25
Argus C	35	55	Butcher Carbine Reflex	150	250
Argus K	200	400	Butcher Midg No. 0	30	65
Arnold Karma	455	700	Camel Model II	120	180
Arrow	15	20	Canon 7	200	300
Astraflex	220	300	Canon 7-S	325	500
Balda Baldalette	45	70	Canon Canonet	55	95
Beck Frena	150	250	Canon Dial-35	55	100
Beck Frena Deluxe	550	900	Canon II-B	170	270
Beier Precisa	45	75	Canonet	60	90
Belca Belplasca	400	600	Carmen Pygmee	175	280
Belca Beltica	35	65	Century 35	40	70
Bell & Howell Dial 35	85	150	Certo Certonet	35	50
Bell & Howell Foton	700	1000	Certo Dolly	65	90

	LOW	HIGH
Chase Magazine	$ 140	$ 200
Chevron	200	365
Ciro-flex	30	45
Clarus MS-35	50	90
Clix 120	5	10
Close & Cone Quad	150	200
Columbia Pecto No. 1A	100	150
Compact Graflex	250	375
Conley Junior	20	40
Conley View	150	225
Contessa Citoskop	350	600
Contessa Donata	55	80
Contessa Duchessa	165	300
Contessa Miroflex	300	500
Contessa Nic 63	35	55
Corfield Periflex	225	320
Cornu Ontobloc	55	90
Cornu Reyna II	35	50
Coronet Vogue	100	150
Cosmic 35	35	60
Dallmeyer Speed	360	600
Dan-35	80	130
Darling 16	250	350
Daydark Tintype	120	185
Detrola 400	350	600
Detrola Model B	25	35
Devin Tri-Color	685	960
Devry QRS Kamra	65	95
Dossert Detective	1400	2000
Dover 620A	15	25
Durst 66	70	100
Durst Automatica	140	200
Durst Duca	130	215
Eastman .... (see Eastman Kodak section)		
Ebner	300	440
Echo 8	315	500
Elop Elca	95	150
Encore Deluxe	25	50
Ernemann Bob 0	40	70
Ernemann Bob I	45	70
Ernemann Liliput	85	140
Ernemann Reflex	225	400
Expo Easy-Load	80	150
Expo Police	275	400
Expo Watch	120	200
Feca	45	80
Feinwerk Mec 16	65	100
Ferrania Rondine	30	55
Finetta 99	165	300
Flash Bantam	45	65

	LOW	HIGH
Foth Derby Model l	$ 55	$ 85
Fuji Lyra	50	85
Fuji Mini	100	170
Galileo Condor 1	160	200
Galileo Gami-16	350	500
Garland (wet plate)	2000	3000
Gemflex	400	645
Genie	650	1000
Genos Rapid	15	20
Goerz Ango	150	260
Goerz Tengor	45	65
Goldeck-16	185	275
Goldmann Field	180	270
Graflex 1A	120	200
Graflex 22	45	70
Graflex Auto	150	240
Graflex Compact	230	370
Graflex Fingerprint	120	220
Graflex Naturalist's	3000	5000
Graflex Press	330	570
Hadds Mfg. Co. Foto-Flex	10	20
Hare Tourist	690	1245
Homer 16	20	50
Horsman Eclipse No. 3	270	430
Houghton Klito	85	135
Houghton Midget	65	85
Hüttig Atom	230	365
Hüttig Lloyd	65	125
Ica Icar	45	70
Ica Juwel Universal	315	500
Ica Maximar	65	125
Ica Nelson 225	55	90
Ica Periscop	50	70
Iso Duplex	180	280
Japy Pascal	900	1400
Jeanneret Monobloc	200	330
Jem Jr.	10	15
Jos-Pe Tri-Color	3000	5000
Joux Alethoscope	230	400
Kalart Press	150	250
Kalimar A	30	45
Kameret Jr. No. 2	15	25
Kenflex	30	45
Kent	10	30
Keystone Street Camera	220	320
Kilfitt Mecaflex	600	1000
Kodak .... (see Eastman Kodak section)		
Krauss Eka	1300	2000
Krauss Photo Revolver	2500	4000
Krauss Polyscop	200	350
Krauss Rollette	95	145

	LOW	HIGH
Kullenberg Field	$ 250	$ 400
Kunick Petie	65	100
Lancaster Kamrex	200	330
Le Reve	240	385
Leidolf Lordox	45	70
Leitz Leica I(A) Luxus	20,000	35,000
Leitz Leica I c	285	450
Leitz Leica IIIc K-Model	820	1225
Leitz Leica IIIf	160	245
Leitz Leica M2	360	665
Leonar	45	75
Leroy Minimus	240	430
Liebe Monobloc	200	330
Life-O-Rama III	20	30
Lilliput Detective	3000	5000
Lizars Challenge	200	300
Lumiere Box No. 49	10	30
Lumiere Luminor	45	65
Lure	5	10
Madison l	30	40
Mamiya 6	60	100
Mamiyaflex	100	160
Manhattan Wizard A	350	560
Manhattan Wizard B	95	150
Marion Soho Reflex	400	600
Marvelflex	25	35
Mason Harvard	100	175
Mazo Field	250	450
Meridian	235	400
Mick-A-Matic	30	55
Midas	125	175
Mimosa I	250	400
Minolta 16	20	45
Minolta 35	100	150
Minolta A	35	60
Minolta Six	85	145
Minox A	80	150
Minox III Gold Plated	2500	3500
Minox (orig.)	500	800
Miranda G	100	175
Monroe Model 7	150	250
Montanus Montiflex	125	175
Monti Monte Carlo	30	40
Monti Monte-35	25	30
Moore Aptus Ferrotype	400	650
Murer Express	135	240
Nagel Junior	25	40
Nagel Ranca	250	450
National Graflex	200	300
Naturalist's Graflex	3000	5000
Negel 18 (Recomar)	90	135

	LOW	HIGH
Nescon 35	$ 25	$ 45
Nettel Deckrullo	225	345
Nettel Sonnet Tropical	800	1400
Nikon F	180	300
Nikon Nikkorex	90	140
Nikon S	170	250
Nikon SP	600	900
Nishida Westar	40	65
Olympus 35	50	85
Olympus Pen	85	115
Olympus Pen FT	175	300
Ompex16	125	175
Orion (box)	75	125
Orion Rio Tropical	700	1000
Phoba Diva	40	60
Photak Foldex	10	20
Photo-Porst Hapo 35	30	45
Photrix Quick B	25	35
Pignons Alpa 6	220	370
Pignons Bolsey	345	525
Pipon Self-Worker	280	460
Plaubel (folding plate)	50	70
Plaubel Makina	300	475
Plaubel Roll-Op	300	440
Polaroid J33	15	20
Polaroid J66	10	15
Polaroid Model 110 (Pathfinder)	70	100
Polaroid Model 180	300	450
Polaroid Model 210	10	25
Polaroid Model 80 (Highlander)	10	20
Polaroid Model 800	15	25
Polaroid Model 900	15	20
Polaroid Model 95 (Speedliner)	25	40
Polaroid SX-70 Deluxe (orig.)	45	80
Pontiac Folding	75	100
Pontiac Lnyx	70	110
Popular Pressman (SLR)	130	235
Pouva Start	25	30
Premium (plate box)	250	400
Putnam Marvel	200	350
Raaco	120	225
Rajar No. 6	30	45
Ray No. 1	70	100
Rectaflex Standard	200	300
Regal Miniature	10	15
Rex Kayson	50	80
Richard Glyphoscope	130	200
Richard Homeos	2500	3500
Ricoh Golden-16	150	200
Ricoh-35	20	50
Ricohflex	30	40

	LOW	HIGH
Riken Steky	$ 55	$ 95
Rilex Press	180	315
Robra	30	65
Rochester Favorite	200	300
Rochester Pocket Poco	50	80
Rochester Poco King	200	300
Royer Savoyflex	85	150
Royet Reyna Cross III	35	75
Rubix 16	155	225
Ruthine	30	45
Sabre	10	15
Saint Louis	200	300
Sanderson Regular	260	400
Schleissner Bower	30	45
Scovill Detective	600	900
Seneca Busy Bee	75	125
Seneca Chautauqua	60	90
Seneca Uno	20	50
Seroco Delmar	30	70
Shew Eclipse	320	500
Shew Xit-Day	200	360
Sida Extra	60	125
Signal Corps Signet-35	165	255
Simmon Omega 120	270	500
Simons Sico	2000	3000
Simplex Pockette	40	80
Sinclair Una	300	450
Spartaflex	15	25
Spartus 35	10	20
Spartus Spartaflex	15	30
Speed Candid Perfex	65	120
Speed-O-Matic	45	70
Spiegel Elf	15	25
Steineck ABC	500	800
Steinheil Detective	975	1500
Sunart Folding View	145	255
Sunart Junior	50	80
Taiyodo Koki Beautyflex	30	45
Takahashi Gelto D III	90	130
Thornward Dandy	75	100
Thowe Field	200	300
Thowe Folding Plate	40	65
Tower Type 3	160	240
Tropical Clarissa	1500	2500
Tropical Heag	800	1200
Turret Panoramic	1000	1500
Ultra Fex	25	40
Universal Buccaneer	25	35
Universal Twinflex	30	60
Utility Cariton	10	15
Vive No. 1	100	165

	LOW	HIGH
Vive Tourist	$ 100	$ 150
Voigtländer Perkeo I	40	75
Voigtländer Virtus	225	330
Vokar l	100	170
Walker Takiv	1500	2500
Wanaus View	225	375
Wardflex	35	55
Welta 2-Shutter camera	170	240
Welta Superflekta	500	800
Welta Trio	25	40
Welta Weltaflex	35	55
Wenka	300	450
Western Cyclone Jr.	45	60
White Realist 35	35	55
White Realist 45	150	250
Whittaker Micro-16	45	75
Whittaker Pixie	50	70
Wilca Automatic	650	900
Windrow	10	20
Wing New Gem	1500	2000
Wirgin Gewirette	75	100
Zeiss Bebe	55	80
Zeiss Contarex EE	225	400
Zeiss Contax I	800	1200
Zeiss Contax II	175	300
Zeiss Ikoflex I	135	225
Zeiss Ikoflex II	65	125
Zeiss Ikonta Super A	200	300
Zeiss Kolibri Night	1200	1800
Zeiss Piccolette	200	300
Zeiss Sirene	65	100
Zeiss Tenax I	100	150

$9⁹⁵

Rexo Camera

$17²⁵

Folding Ansco Camera

Eastman Kodak

	LOW	HIGH		LOW	HIGH
Anniversary Camera	$ 16	$ 30	Kodak Six-16 Special	$ 50	$ 80
Automatic 35	35	50	Kodak Six-20	40	70
Baby Brownie	7	10	Kodak Super Six-20	1200	1800
Bantam f3.9 RF	30	50	Kodet Folding No. 4	500	800
Bantam Flash	40	63	Kodet No. 4	300	500
Bantam RF f3.9	35	50	Medalist I	150	250
Beau Brownie	60	100	Monitor Six-16	30	50
Brownie Baby	8	10	Motormatic 35	50	75
Brownie (box) No. 0	20	45	Nagel Junior	26	40
Brownie (box) No. 1 Improved	50	80	Petite	150	200
Brownie (box) No. 1 (orig.)	750	1000	Pony II	10	30
Brownie (box) No. 2	10	16	Pony IV	15	25
Brownie (box) No. 2A	10	14	Premo Cartridge No. 00	50	70
Brownie (box) No. 2C	10	15	Premo Cartridge No. 2	15	25
Brownie (box) No. 3	10	16	Premo No. 12	40	60
Brownie Folding No. 2	26	40	Premo Senior	100	150
Brownie Holiday	6	9	Premoette No. 1	43	60
Bullet No. 2	60	90	Recomar No. 18	80	120
Bullet No. 4	100	150	Regent	300	500
Bulls-Eye No. 2	30	60	Retina Automatic I	150	200
Cirkut No. 10	2500	3500	Retina I	74	135
Cirkut No. 5	800	1200	Retina III C	150	260
Cirkut Outfit No. 6	800	1500	Retina Reflex	100	150
Daylight Kodak A	1200	1800	Retina Reflex III	115	170
Daylight Kodak B	600	1000	Retina Reflex IV	150	250
Ektra	600	1000	Retinette IA	50	80
Eureka No. 2	79	136	Signet 30	35	50
Falcon No. 2	73	120	Special Kodak No. 1A	50	70
Flexo No. 2	39	60	Speed Kodak No. 1A	213	300
Flush Back Kodak No. 3	60	114	Star Premo	57	100
Folding Kodak No. 4A	66	100	Super Kodak Six-20	1200	1800
Gift Kodak	85	133	Tourist	14	20
Girl Scout Kodak	120	200	Tourist II	14	20
Hawkette No. 2	20	50	Vanity Kodak	100	150
Hawkeye Cartridge No. 2	10	16	Vanity Kodak Ensemble	1000	1500
Hawkeye Film Pack No. 2	15	25	Zenith Kodak No. 3	200	300
Hawkeye Vest Pocket	25	50			
Jiffy Kodak Six-16	19	30			
Jiffy Kodak Vest Pocket	16	20			
Kodak 35	20	36			
Kodak 35 Rangefinder	25	40			
Kodak Automatic 35	36	50			
Kodak Junior No. 1	20	35			
Kodak No. 1	1000	1500			
Kodak No. 2	500	700			
Kodak No. 3	500	800			
Kodak (orig. model)	3000	4500			
Kodak Reflex Model I	50	75			
Kodak Senior Six-16	40	60			

Kodak Brownie.

Clocks

The types of clocks listed in the selection below include swing clocks in which the clock mechanism itself is imbedded in the pendulum held by a statue. Banjo clocks have a round face, a tapering neck and a square pendulum base. Calendar clocks show the date as well as the time. Carriage clocks are small, intricate clocks generally about four to five inches high, usually with glass sides. Regulator clocks are precise clocks generally with long pendulums but no bells. Statue clocks combine a clock with a bronze or gilt figure. Kitchen clocks are designed for a shelf and are generally upright with ornate decoration from its edges. Ogee clocks are tall, rectangular clocks framed by a convex and concave molding. Novelty clocks are usually small, inexpensive and in whimsical shapes.

The clocks in this section represent the collectible clocks of the late nineteenth and early twentieth centuries. These represent the first factory produced clocks of the United States which are still frequently seen at auctions and flea markets.

When buying a clock at auction, always factor in the cost of repair. Even if the clock was working during exhibition, by the time it has been moved from display to storage to you, it is often not. Be sure to check for all parts (pendulum, weights, etc.) both before you bid and when you pick it up. Buying from a dealer may cost more money, but can often save on headaches.

	LOW	AVG.	HIGH
Acme China, c. 1900, Ansonia	$ 60	$ 75	$ 90
Acme Crystal Regulator, c. 1910, Ansonia	280	340	400
Actor Kitchen, c. 1890, E.N. Welsh	260	315	370
Africa Kitchen, c. 1890, Ansonia	200	240	280
Alarm, c. 1900, Jerome	140	160	180
Alarm, c. 1960, Lux & Keebler	10	15	20
Alaska Kitchen, c. 1890, Ansonia	240	270	300
Albatross Cabinet, c. 1900, New Haven	260	320	380
Alpine Kitchen, c. 1890, W.L. Gilbert	210	260	310
Angel Swing No. 2, c. 1875, F. Kroeber	1300	1600	1900
Animated Alarm, c. 1890, F. Kroeber	440	535	630
Animated Alarm, c. 1940, Lux & Keebler	240	305	370
Animated Novelty, c. 1910, Mueller & Son	1460	1650	1840
Ansonia Lever, c. 1900, Ansonia	250	280	310
Arab Cabinet, c. 1900, New Haven	310	375	440
Arab Connecticut Shelf, c. 1890, Ansonia	170	210	250
Arcadian Connecticut Shelf, c. 1890, Ansonia	190	235	280
Archer Statue, c. 1910, W.L. Gilbert	440	500	560
Art Nouveau, c. 1910, Seth Thomas	110	140	170
Art Nouveau Novelty, c. 1910, Ansonia	140	175	210
Astronomical No. 74 Mercury Pendulum, c. 1915, E. Howard	25,000	30,000	35,000
Astronomical Regulator, c. 1890, F. Kroeber	20,000	24,000	28,000
Astronomical Regulator, c. 1900, Ansonia	10,000	13,000	16,000
Astronomical Regulator No. 22, c. 1900, E. Howard	15,000	17,500	20,000
Astronomical Regulator No. 47, c. 1900, E. Howard	19,000	23,000	27,000
Astronomical Standing, c. 1900, E. Howard	22,000	24,000	26,000
Attila Statue, c. 1890, Ansonia	690	840	990
Austria Kitchen, c. 1890, Ansonia	240	280	320
Austrian Calendar, c. 1900, New Haven	800	1015	1230
Automobile, c. 1920, New Haven	70	85	100
Avon Kitchen, c. 1900, New Haven	230	295	360
Aztec Mission, c. 1910, Seth Thomas	490	590	690

*Above, left to right: acorn clocks are a rare form, $4000-$8000.
— Photo courtesy of Northeast Auctions; kitchen clocks are easier to
find, $200-$400. — Photo courtesy of George Kerrigan Photography.*

	LOW	AVG.	HIGH
Baghdad Regulator, c. 1900, Ansonia	$ 1100	$ 1300	$ 1600
Banjo, c. 1880, E. Howard	3000	3500	4000
Banjo, c. 1890, Waltham	2000	2400	2800
Banjo, c. 1920, E. Ingraham	240	285	330
Bank Regulator, c. 1880, Ithaca Calendar	5300	6720	8140
Banker's Inkstand, c. 1880, Ansonia	410	495	580
Barbara Wall Regulator, c. 1890, New Haven	800	960	1120
Baronet Crystal Regulator, c. 1910, Ansonia	540	635	730
Baseball, c.1890, F. Kroeber	510	630	750
Baseball Pendulum, c. 1940, Lux & Keebler	260	310	360
Bee Drum Alarm, c. 1890, Ansonia	70	80	90
Beehive Shelf, c. 1880, E.N. Welsh	180	215	250
Beehive Shelf, c. 1880, Jerome	220	280	340
Beehive Shelf, c. 1900, New Haven	100	120	140
Bisque Novelty, c. 1890, Ansonia	140	160	180
Black Cat Pendulum, c. 1940, Lux & Keebler	280	345	410
Black Mantle, c. 1890, E.N. Welsh	140	160	180
Black Wood Mantle, c. 1900, E. Ingraham	150	185	220
Black Wood Mantle, c. 1900, New Haven	150	165	180
Blackbird Kitchen, c. 1890, Ansonia	300	355	410
Boar Hunter Statue, c. 1890, Ansonia	540	665	790
Bouquet Novelty, c. 1900, New Haven	190	250	310
Brass Mantle, c. 1890, F. Kroeber	510	620	730
Brass Novelty, c. 1890, Ansonia	140	160	180
Brass Novelty, c. 1890, F. Kroeber	340	415	490
Brass Plaque, c. 1890, F. Kroeber	260	330	400
Brest Crystal Regulator, c. 1910, Waterbury	220	250	280
Bronze and Iron, c. 1900, Mueller & Son	190	245	300

	LOW	AVG.	HIGH
Bronze Mantle, c. 1900, Ansonia	$ 540	$ 640	$ 740
Brooklyn Figure Eight Regulator, c. 1910, Ansonia	2300	3000	3700
Bullfight Alarm, c. 1900, New Haven	290	340	390
Cabinet, c. 1880, F. Kroeber	390	505	620
Cabinet, c. 1890, E.N. Welsh	130	155	180
Cabinet, c. 1890, Seth Thomas	260	335	410
Cabinet, c. 1890, Waterbury	230	275	320
Cabinet, c. 1900, E. Ingraham	180	195	210
Cabinet, c. 1900, W.L. Gilbert	240	285	330
Cabinet, with mirrored sides, c. 1880, F. Kroeber	380	465	550
Calais Crystal Regulator, c. 1910, Waterbury	600	750	900
Calendar Alarm, c. 1900, Waterbury	130	155	180
Calendar, c. 1880, F. Kroeber	350	400	450
Calendar, c. 1900, Jerome	2200	2500	2800
Calendar, double dial, c. 1890, Waterbury	1000	1250	1500
Calendar Eclipse Regulator, c. 1900, E.N. Welsh	700	790	880
Canada Kitchen, c. 1890, Ansonia	220	255	290
Capital Kitchen, c. 1910, Seth Thomas	290	345	400
Capital Regulator, c. 1900, Ansonia	1100	1400	1700
Captain Kitchen, c. 1900, New Haven	300	335	370
Carlos Calendar, c. 1890, Ansonia	400	500	600
Carpenter Iron Novelty, c. 1890, Ansonia	220	265	310
Carriage, c. 1890, F. Kroeber	260	335	410
Carriage, c. 1890, Seth Thomas	140	165	190
Carriage, c. 1890, Waterbury	190	225	260
Carriage, c. 1900, E.N. Welsh	100	120	140
Carriage, c. 1900, New Haven	240	285	330
Carriage, c. 1900, W.L. Gilbert	200	250	300
Cast Iron Character, c. 1900, Mueller & Son	300	330	360
Cavalier Statue, c. 1900, Waterbury	270	330	390
Character, c. 1900, Mueller & Son	260	315	370
Checkmate Carriage, c. 1890, F. Kroeber	360	400	440
Chicago Kitchen, c. 1890, Ansonia	280	335	390
China, 13", c. 1900, New Haven	300	355	410
China, 6", c. 1900, New Haven	100	115	130
China Novelty, c. 1890, Ansonia	100	120	140
China Novelty, c. 1900, Seth Thomas	100	120	140
Christine Kitchen, c. 1900, New Haven	250	295	340
Cinderella Kitchen, c. 1900, New Haven	260	290	320
Clifton Regulator, c. 1910, Ansonia	350	435	520
Colby Crystal Regulator, c. 1910, Ansonia	340	400	460
College Kitchen, c. 1910, Seth Thomas	260	305	350
Colorado Kitchen, c. 1890, Ansonia	290	330	370
Comet Carriage, c. 1910, Ansonia	270	315	360
Connecticut Shelf, c. 1875, W.L. Gilbert	300	360	420
Connecticut Shelf, c. 1890, F. Kroeber	220	245	270
Connecticut Shelf, c. 1890, Seth Thomas	190	225	260
Connecticut Shelf, c. 1900, New Haven	260	310	360
Connecticut Shelf Round Top, c. 1880, E. Ingraham	220	250	280
Connecticut Shelf Split Top, c. 1880, E. Ingraham	170	215	260
Connecticut Split Top Shelf, c. 1890, Ansonia	240	275	310

Custom built clocks command high prices. This custom built Chelsea ship's bell brought $5500 at auction. — Photo courtesy of Northeast Auctions.

	LOW	AVG.	HIGH
Conroy Kitchen, c. 1900, New Haven	$ 300	$ 340	$ 380
Cottage Connecticut Shelf, c. 1890, Ansonia	130	160	190
Cottage Shelf, c. 1875, W.L. Gilbert	210	255	300
Cottage Shelf, c. 1880, E.N. Welsh	130	160	190
Cottage Shelf, c. 1880, Jerome	200	240	280
Cottage Shelf, c. 1890, F. Kroeber	190	230	270
Cottage Shelf, c. 1900, E. Ingraham	180	220	260
Cottage Shelf, c. 1900, New Haven	100	125	150
Crystal Palace, c. 1890, Ansonia	800	900	1000
Crystal Regulator, c. 1900, New Haven	690	795	900
Crystal Regulator, c. 1900, W.L. Gilbert	590	670	750
Crystal Regulator, c. 1910, Waterbury	420	520	620
Crystal Regulator, c. 1920, New Haven	440	510	580
Crystal Regulator, c. 1920, Seth Thomas	500	630	760
Cuckoo, c. 1945, Lux & Keebler	220	265	310
Cuckoo Mantle, c. 1890, F. Kroeber	540	680	820
Cuckoo Wall, c. 1890, F. Kroeber	400	480	560
Dauntless Alarm, c. 1880 , Ansonia	260	315	370
Diplomat Crystal Regulator, c. 1910, Ansonia	740	890	1040
Dog House Pendulum, c. 1940, Lux & Keebler	220	245	270
Domestic Alarm, c. 1880, Ansonia	200	240	280
Don Juan Statue, c. 1890, Ansonia	410	495	580
Don Juan Statue, c. 1900, New Haven	420	485	550
Dora Carriage, c. 1880, Ansonia	180	215	250
Double Dial Calendar, c. 1890, New Haven	1500	1750	2000
Drum Alarm, c. 1890, E.N. Welsh	70	85	100
Drum Alarm, c. 1890, F. Kroeber	110	125	140
Drum Alarm, c. 1890, New Haven	70	85	100
Drum Alarm, c. 1900, W.L. Gilbert	100	125	150
Drum Alarm, c. 1900, Waterbury	100	125	150
Drum Alarm, c. 1920, E. Ingraham	60	80	100
Drum Form Alarm, c. 1890, Seth Thomas	100	110	120
Duchess Crystal Regulator, c. 1910, Ansonia	500	585	670
Ebony Kitchen Hanging, c. 1910, Ansonia	610	730	850
Echo Alarm, c. 1880, Ansonia	300	335	370

	LOW	AVG.	HIGH
Electric, c. 1960, Lux & Keebler	$ 10	$ 20	$ 30
Elfrida Calendar, c. 1890, New Haven	1400	1600	1800
Empire Crystal Regulator, c. 1920, Seth Thomas	500	635	770
Empire Shelf, c. 1875, Seth Thomas	730	810	890
Empire Shelf, c. 1880, E.N. Welsh	420	505	590
Enamel Mantle, c. 1890, Ansonia	580	695	810
English Long Drop Regulator, c. 1910, Ansonia	570	695	820
Etruscan, c. 1900, Mueller & Son	220	285	350
Exposition Kitchen, c. 1900, Seth Thomas	270	340	410
Fancy Alarm, c. 1890, F. Kroeber	130	155	180
Fancy Alarm, c. 1900, W.L. Gilbert	140	175	210
Figure Eight, c. 1880, E. Howard	6500	7500	8500
Figure Eight Calendar, c. 1880, New Haven	1450	1600	1750
Figure Eight Calendar, c. 1890, F. Kroeber	1390	1575	1760
Figure Eight Regulator, c. 1890, Waterbury	380	470	560
Figure Eight Regulator, c. 1900, Ansonia	420	500	580
Figure Eight Regulator, c. 1900, E. Ingraham	570	635	700
Figure Eight Regulator, c. 1900, New Haven	520	580	640
Fleet Kitchen, c. 1910, Seth Thomas	290	340	390
Flora China, c. 1900, Ansonia	60	75	90
Floral, c. 1900, Mueller & Son	220	260	300
Floral Painted, c. 1900, Mueller & Son	200	235	270
Flute Player Statue, c. 1900, New Haven	200	240	280
Fulton, c. 1890, Ansonia	260	330	400
Gallery Brass Lever, c. 1875, W.L. Gilbert	140	170	200
Gallery, c. 1880, E. Ingraham	280	330	380
Gallery, c. 1880, E.N. Welsh	150	175	200
Gallery, c. 1880, Seth Thomas	240	280	320
Gallery, c. 1890, F. Kroeber	670	805	940
Gallery, c. 1890, Jerome	360	420	480
Gallery, c. 1890, Waterbury	170	215	260
Gallery, c. 1900, New Haven	170	200	230
Gem Ink Calendar, c. 1890, Ansonia	380	465	550
Gilt Metal Novelty, c. 1900, Ansonia	110	125	140
Gilt Metal Novelty, c. 1910, W.L. Gilbert	130	155	180
Good Luck Alarm, c. 1880, Ansonia	100	120	140
Gothic Connecticut Shelf, c. 1890, Ansonia	260	295	330
Gothic Iron, c. 1890, Mueller & Son	260	315	370
Gothic Shelf, c. 1875, W.L. Gilbert	260	305	350
Gothic Shelf, c. 1900, New Haven	200	240	280
Grandfather, c. 1880, E. Howard	15,000	16,500	18,000
Grandfather, c. 1890, Seth Thomas	3000	3300	3600
Grandfather, c. 1900, New Haven	4000	4500	5000
Grandfather, c. 1910, Ansonia	7000	8500	10,000
Grandfather, c. 1910, Waterbury	3000	4000	5000
Grandfather No. 83, c. 1900, E. Howard	4000	5125	6250
Grecian Mantle, c. 1880, E. Ingraham	320	420	520
Greek Kitchen, c. 1900, Ansonia	270	345	420
Gypsy Kettle, c. 1890, F. Kroeber	290	330	370
Hampshire, c. 1890, Ansonia	290	350	410
Hanging Cottage, c. 1890, Ithaca Calendar	1250	1500	1750

	LOW	AVG.	HIGH
Hanging Kitchen, c. 1900, W.L. Gilbert	$ 420	$ 480	$ 540
Hanging Regulator No. 14, c. 1900, E. Howard	4000	5000	6000
Harlequin Cabinet, c. 1900, New Haven	300	350	400
Hawk Oak Kitchen, c. 1900, W.L. Gilbert	300	325	350
Heartbeat, c. 1930, Lux & Keebler	140	170	200
Helena China, c. 1900, Ansonia	70	80	90
Herald Kitchen, c. 1890, Ansonia	240	295	350
Hunter and Dog Statue, c. 1900, New Haven	600	800	1000
Huron Mantle, c. 1905 , E. Ingraham	330	400	470
Imitation Walnut Kitchen, c. 1900, New Haven	130	165	200
Inca Cabinet, c. 1910, Ansonia	180	210	240
Inkstand Brass, c. 1900, Ansonia	170	205	240
Inkwell Calendar, c. 1880, F. Kroeber	410	515	620
Ipswich Cabinet, c. 1910, Ansonia	180	200	220
Iron Case, c. 1890, Ithaca Calendar	4000	5500	7000
Iron Figural Mantle, c. 1880, F. Kroeber	260	325	390
Iron Mantle, c. 1890, Ansonia	210	250	290
Iron Mantle, c. 1890, E.N. Welsh	200	245	290
Iron Mantle, c. 1890, F. Kroeber	220	240	260
Iron Mantle, c. 1900, New Haven	170	205	240
Iron Novelty, c. 1880, E.N. Welsh	140	170	200
Iron Novelty, c. 1890, Ansonia	100	120	140
Iron Novelty, c. 1900, Seth Thomas	100	125	150
Ivanhoe Statue, c. 1900, New Haven	190	230	270
Japan Kitchen, c. 1890, Ansonia	220	245	270
Kentucky, c. 1890, Ansonia	270	330	390
Kitchen, c. 1890, E.N. Welsh	260	295	330
Kitchen, c. 1890, F. Kroeber	430	485	540
Kitchen, c. 1890, Seth Thomas	240	295	350
Kitchen, c. 1890, Waterbury	190	245	300
Kitchen, c. 1900, E. Ingraham	300	325	350
Kitchen, c. 1900, New Haven	240	280	320
Kitchen, c. 1900, W.L. Gilbert	210	245	280
Kitchen Hanging, c. 1900, New Haven	360	420	480
Kitchen Wall, c. 1890, Waterbury	390	470	550
Kitchen, with mirrored sides, c, 1890, F. Kroeber	560	675	790
La Cette China, c. 1890, Ansonia	400	510	620
La Cruz China, c. 1910, Ansonia	370	420	470
La Nord China, c. 1910, Ansonia	430	485	540
La Sedan China, c. 1910, Ansonia	350	435	520
La Tosca China, c. 1910, Ansonia	430	495	560
Leeds Cabinet, c. 1880, Ansonia	220	255	290
Library, c. 1920, Waltham	210	240	270
Lighthouse, c. 1900, New Haven	420	475	530
Lima, c. 1890, Ansonia	260	335	410
Little Dorrit Alarm, c. 1880, Ansonia	230	290	350
Locomotive Iron Novelty, c. 1890, Ansonia	240	290	340
Lodi Kitchen, c. 1890, Waterbury	170	205	240
Lusitania Novelty, c. 1900, Seth Thomas	270	330	390
Lux Art, c. 1930, Lux & Keebler	140	160	180
Mahogany Mantle, c. 1910, New Haven	70	80	90

	LOW	AVG.	HIGH
Mahogany Mantle, c. 1910, Seth Thomas	$ 130	$ 170	$ 210
Mahogany Mantle, c. 1920, Ansonia	110	130	150
Mahogany Mantle, c. 1920, E. Ingraham	100	115	130
Major Kitchen, c. 1890, New Haven	260	295	330
Mandolin Alarm, c. 1900, New Haven	270	325	380
Mantle Lever, c. 1900, Jerome	300	340	380
Mantle, with mirrored sides, c. 1890, New Haven	460	520	580
Mantle, with mirrored sides, c. 1900, E. Ingraham	390	480	570
Marble Dial Wall, c. 1900, E. Howard	2600	3200	3800
Marble Gallery, c. 1910, New Haven	390	495	600
Marble Mantle, c. 1900, Ansonia	220	285	350
Marquis Crystal Regulator, c. 1910, Ansonia	1000	1200	1400
Maryland, c. 1890, Ansonia	230	285	340
Mayflower Kitchen, c. 1900, New Haven	240	290	340
Mechanical Bird, c. 1880, F. Kroeber	3700	4150	4600
Mechanical Ship, c. 1880, F. Kroeber	3600	4000	4400
Metropolis Kitchen, c. 1890, Ansonia	280	320	360
Mission, c. 1910, Waterbury	370	425	480
Mission Cabinet, c. 1910, New Haven	270	340	410
Mission Kitchen, c. 1910, New Haven	220	250	280
Mission Kitchen Hanging, c. 1910, New Haven	510	615	720
Mission Novelty, c. 1910, New Haven	210	255	300
Mission Octagon Short Drop, c. 1910, New Haven	350	410	470
Mosel Kitchen, c. 1890, Ansonia	240	300	360
Musical Mantle, c. 1890, F. Kroeber	750	1000	1250
Nautical Chronometer, c. 1910, Waltham	600	700	800
Nectar Kitchen, c. 1900, New Haven	250	275	300
Nightingale Alarm, c. 1880, Ansonia	140	160	180
Novelty, c. 1900, Waterbury	170	210	250
Nymph Statue, c. 1910, Seth Thomas	140	160	180
Octagon Gallery, c. 1890, Jerome	250	280	310
Octagon Gallery, c. 1900, F. Kroeber	220	250	280
Octagon Long Drop Regulator, c. 1900, W.L. Gilbert	410	490	570
Octagon Peep-o-Day, c. 1890, Ansonia	50	60	70
Octagon Princess Alarm, c. 1890, Ansonia	50	65	80
Octagon Regulator Short Drop, c. 1900, W.L. Gilbert	320	395	470
Octagon Short Drop, c. 1890, Jerome	330	395	460
Octagon Short Drop Calendar, c. 1900, Seth Thomas	560	645	730
Octagon Short Drop Regulator, c. 1890, F. Kroeber	470	585	700
Octagon Top Calendar, c. 1880, Ansonia	410	480	550
Octagon Top Calendar, c. 1890, W.L. Gilbert	400	485	570
Octagon Top Long Drop, c. 1900, E. Ingraham	340	395	450
Octagon Top Long Drop Calendar, c. 1910, E. Ingraham	500	610	720
Octagon Top Long Drop Regulator, c. 1890, Seth Thomas	530	640	750
Octagon Top Long Drop Regulator, c. 1900, E. Ingraham	500	610	720
Octagon Top Long Drop Regulator, c. 1900, E.N. Welsh	480	580	680
Octagon Top Long Drop Regulator, c. 1900, New Haven	340	415	490
Octagon Top Long Drop Regulator, c. 1910, Waterbury	520	675	830
Octagon Top Regulator, c. 1890, Ansonia	430	525	620
Octagon Top Shelf, c. 1875, W.L. Gilbert	170	215	260
Octagon Top Shelf, c. 1880, E. Ingraham	180	220	260

	LOW	AVG.	HIGH
Octagon Top Short Drop, c. 1900, E. Ingraham	$ 270	$ 320	$ 370
Octagon Top Short Drop Calendar, c. 1900, New Haven	410	475	540
Octagon Top Short Drop Calendar, c. 1910, E. Ingraham	380	490	600
Octagon Top Short Drop Regulator, c. 1890, Seth Thomas	490	585	680
Octagon Top Short Drop Regulator, c. 1900, E. Ingraham	320	370	420
Octagon Top Short Drop Regulator, c. 1900, E.N. Welsh	350	425	500
Octagon Top Short Drop Regulator, c. 1910, Waterbury	400	445	490
Office Calendar, c. 1900, Seth Thomas	3000	4000	5000
Office Ink, c. 1900, New Haven	280	330	380
Ogee Connecticut Shelf, c. 1875, W.L. Gilbert	240	290	340
Ogee Connecticut Shelf, c. 1890, Ansonia	260	320	380
Ogee Shelf, c. 1870, Jerome	280	325	370
Ogee Shelf, c. 1880, E.N. Welsh	300	345	390
Ogee Shelf, c. 1890, E. Ingraham	250	295	340
Ogee Shelf, c. 1890, Seth Thomas	290	320	350
Ogee Shelf, c. 1890, Waterbury	270	320	370
Olympia Statue, c. 1890, Ansonia	700	850	1000
Onyx Mantle, c. 1900, Ansonia	360	440	520
Onyx Mantle, c. 1900, New Haven	250	315	380
Onyx Mantle, c. 1910, W.L. Gilbert	320	400	480
Open Swinging Regulator, c. 1910, Waterbury	1070	1245	1420
Oriole Carriage, c. 1890, Ansonia	170	195	220
Orpheus Statue, c. 1900, New Haven	220	250	280
Papier Mache Shelf, c. 1890, Jerome	270	315	360
Parlor Calendar, c. 1900, Seth Thomas	1280	1590	1900
Parlor Iron, c. 1890, Mueller & Son	160	205	250
Parlor Shelf Regulator, c. 1900, Seth Thomas	540	620	700
Parlor Wall Regulator, c. 1890, F. Kroeber	1000	1200	1400
Parlor Wall Regulator, c. 1890, Seth Thomas	1370	1620	1870
Parlor Wall Regulator, c. 1890, Waterbury	830	1025	1220
Parlor Wall Regulator, c. 1900, Ansonia	640	840	1040
Parlor Wall Regulator, c. 1900, E. Ingraham	880	1120	1360
Parlor Wall Regulator, c. 1900, New Haven	790	985	1180
Parlor Wall Regulator, c. 1900, W.L. Gilbert	1000	1200	1400
Parlor Wall Regulator, c. 1910, Seth Thomas	1100	1300	1500
Pearl Carriage, c. 1900, Ansonia	120	145	170
Pearl Inlaid Papier Mache, c. 1890, Jerome	280	360	440
Pendulum, c. 1930, Lux & Keebler	110	125	140
Pet Alarm, c. 1900, New Haven	280	335	390
Philospher Statue, c. 1890, Ansonia	270	335	400
Pillar and Scroll Shelf, c. 1870, Jerome	560	645	730
Pillar and Scroll Shelf, c. 1880, E.N. Welsh	210	245	280
Pillar and Scroll Shelf, c. 1880, Seth Thomas	270	315	360
Pillar and Scroll Shelf, c. 1900, Seth Thomas	220	260	300
Planet Calendar Alarm, c. 1900, Ansonia	160	190	220
Planet Drum Alarm, c. 1880, Ansonia	180	205	230
Plush Novelty, c. 1890, F. Kroeber	250	305	360
Plymouth Cabinet, c. 1880, Ansonia	200	250	300
Porcelain, c. 1900, F. Kroeber	360	405	450
Porcelain Regulator, c. 1910, Ansonia	1900	2315	2730
Porcelain Statue, c. 1910, W.L. Gilbert	350	400	450

	LOW	AVG.	HIGH
Precision Regulator, c. 1890, Seth Thomas .... $ 14,000	$ 16,000	$ 18,000
Prince Crystal Regulator, c. 1910, Ansonia 900	1100	1300
Princess Drum Alarm, c. 1880, Ansonia 70	80	90
Racket Drum Alarm, c. 1900, Ansonia 80	90	100
Rebecca at the Well Statue, c. 1910, Seth Thomas 250	325	400
Reflector, c. 1910, Ansonia 830	980	1130
Regulator No. 11, c. 1900, Seth Thomas 2000	2500	3000
Regulator No. 19, c. 1910, Seth Thomas 1800	2400	3000
Regulator, small second hand, c. 1890, Seth Thomas 1250	1500	1750
Regulator, small second hand, c. 1900, New Haven 1100	1400	1700
Regulator, with small second, c. 1890, Waterbury 1400	1650	2000
Renaissance Crystal Regulator, c. 1910, Ansonia 1120	1280	1440
Rio Parlor Wall Regulator, c. 1880, Ansonia 1050	1155	1260
Riverdale Cabinet, c. 1910, Ansonia 210	260	310
Rockwood Cabinet, c. 1910, Ansonia 200	245	290
Roman Statue, c. 1900, New Haven 260	335	410
Rome Parlor Shelf, c. 1920, Seth Thomas 260	305	350
Rotary, c. 1890, F. Kroeber 2700	3450	4200
Round Head Regulator, c. 1900, E.N. Welsh 2400	2995	3590
Round Top Connecticut Shelf, c. 1880, W.L. Gilbert 170	200	230
Round Top Long Drop Regulator, c. 1880, W.L. Gilbert 1200	1500	1800
Round Top Long Drop Regulator, c. 1890, F. Kroeber 700	850	1000
Round Top Long Drop Regulator, c. 1890, Waterbury 1250	1500	1750
Round Top Mantle, c. 1900, E. Ingraham 200	235	270
Round Top Shelf, c. 1880, Seth Thomas 160	205	250
Round Top Shelf, c. 1900, New Haven 100	115	130
Round Top Short Drop Regulator, c. 1900, E. Ingraham 320	385	450
Russia Cabinet, c. 1900, New Haven 260	305	350
Saratoga Wall Regulator, c. 1900, W.L. Gilbert 650	780	910
Satellite Carriage, c. 1910, Ansonia 340	415	490
Saxon Statue, c. 1900, New Haven 290	340	390
Senator Kitchen, c. 1900, New Haven 210	245	280
Shannon Kitchen, c. 1900, New Haven 150	185	220
Shaver Alarm, c. 1900, New Haven 290	330	370
Shelf Regulator, c. 1880, Ithaca Calendar 3000	4000	5000
Sled, c. 1890, F. Kroeber 300	400	500
Spring Chronometer, c. 1890, Ithaca Calendar 2000	2400	2800
Spring Statue, c. 1890, Ansonia 800	900	1000
Square Top Regulator, c. 1910, Seth Thomas 1000	1200	1400
Square Top Regulator No. 39, c. 1900, E. Howard 5500	6750	8000
Square Top Short Drop Regulator, c. 1900, New Haven 400	500	600
Square Top Short Drop Regulator, c. 1905, E. Ingraham 250	305	360
Standard Connecticut Round Top, c. 1890, Ansonia 210	245	280
Statue, c. 1890, F. Kroeber 390	460	530
Statue, c. 1900, Mueller & Son 220	260	300
Steeple Connecticut Shelf, c. 1890, Ansonia 200	235	270
Steeple Shelf, c. 1870, F. Kroeber 220	270	320
Steeple Shelf, c. 1870, W.L. Gilbert 220	260	300
Steeple Shelf, c. 1875, Jerome 280	335	390
Steeple Shelf, c. 1880, E.N. Welsh 170	205	240
Steeple Shelf, c. 1890, Seth Thomas 140	165	190

	LOW	AVG.	HIGH
Steeple Shelf, c. 1900, New Haven	$ 160	$ 185	$ 210
Stirrup Novelty, c. 1900, New Haven	280	320	360
Store Regulator, c. 1900, E. Ingraham	500	565	630
Store Regulator, c. 1910, Seth Thomas	460	560	660
Summit Cabinet, c. 1880, Ansonia	230	270	310
Sunlight Alarm, c. 1900, W.L. Gilbert	220	260	300
Sweep Second Regulator "A," c. 1890, E.N. Welsh	4000	5500	7000
Sweep Second Regulator, c. 1890, E.N. Welsh	2000	2500	3000
Sweep Second Regulator, c. 1890, F. Kroeber	6000	8000	10,000
Sweep Second Regulator, c. 1890, Seth Thomas	3000	4500	6000
Sweep Second Regulator, c. 1890, W.L. Gilbert	5000	5500	6000
Sweep Second Regulator, c. 1890, Waterbury	5500	6500	7500
Sweep Second Regulator, c. 1900, New Haven	3800	4600	5400
Sweep Second Regulator, c. 1910, Ansonia	7000	9000	11,000
Swing Arm, c. 1890, Ansonia	3500	4000	4500
Symbol Crystal Regulator, c. 1910, Ansonia	750	1000	1250
Tally Ho Carriage, c. 1880, Ansonia	470	540	610
Teardrop, c. 1890, F. Kroeber	440	555	670
Teardrop Kitchen, c. 1890, Ansonia	430	505	580
Teardrop Kitchen, c. 1890, Seth Thomas	240	280	320
Telephone Pendulum, c. 1940, Lux & Keebler	100	125	150
Tivoli Cabinet, c. 1880, Ansonia	250	290	330
Tomahawk Kitchen, c. 1900, New Haven	250	305	360
Toronto Cabinet, c. 1880, Ansonia	250	285	320
Tourist Carriage, c. 1910, Ansonia	210	250	290
Triumph, c. 1890, Ansonia	450	590	730
Tudor Beehive Shelf, c. 1890, Ansonia	250	295	340
Tunis Cabinet, c. 1890, Ansonia	140	175	210
Turkey Cabinet, c. 1880, Ansonia	200	250	300
Verdi Crystal Regulator, c. 1910, W.L. Gilbert	1100	1250	1400
Victorian Kitchen Barometer/Thermometer, c. 1890, Ansonia	230	285	340
Victory Statue, c. 1900, Seth Thomas	220	245	270
Watch Form. c. 1900, New Haven	200	255	310
Watchmaker's Standing Regulator, c. 1880, E. Howard	5000	6000	7000
Watchman's Wall Regulator, c. 1890, E. Howard	5000	6000	7000
Westminister Chime, c. 1900, New Haven	330	395	460
Westminister Chimes, c. 1910, Seth Thomas	320	410	500
Wheat Sheaf, c. 1900, New Haven	360	430	500
Wood Lever Octagon, c. 1900, New Haven	250	305	360
Woodbine Alarm, c. 1880, Ansonia	180	235	290
Zuni Mission, c. 1910, Seth Thomas	410	480	550

Coca-Cola Collectibles

The first batch of Coca-Cola was created by John Pemberton, an Atlanta pharmacist in 1886. Mr. Pemberton was trying to create a tonic rather than a soft drink. The syrup was soon marketed to Willis Venable, an Atlanta soda fountain manager. As legend has it, a clerk mixed the syrup with soda and an empire was born. In 1894 Joseph Biedenhorn started bottling and distributing Coca-Cola in Vicksburg, MS. Coke became the world's favorite soft drink. With over 100 years of advertisements and promotional material Coke collectors have an incredible breadth of material to draw from. The firm has done a great job in promoting its product. One reason collectors love this material is that by viewing it you can draw a time line of our last 100 years. It begins with the Victorian elegance of the 1890s and travels through two World Wars, the Great Depression, Rock 'n' Roll, the country's struggle with the Vietnam War ("I'd Like to Teach the World to Sing"), to today's sports stars' endorsements. Coke ads are usually very appealing and reflective of their time. Since Coca-Cola is now a global entity, the material grows daily, and there are even Coke boutiques specializing in marketing new Coke clothing and products.

The only cautionary note is that there are also many reproductions and items that are done in the style of an earlier era. Such material is often offered as old with prices far beyond its value. Do your homework and deal with knowledgeable people that stand behind their product. The prices below are based on items in excellent or mint condition.

For further information see *Petretti's Coca-Cola Collectibles Price Guide*, Allan Petretti, Nostalgia Publications, Hackensack, NJ, and *Price Guide to Coca-Cola Collectibles*, Deborah Goldstein Hill, Wallace Homestead, Radnor, PA, 1991. You may also wish to contact The Coca-Cola Collectors Club International, P.O. Box 49166, Atlanta, GA 30359

	LOW	AVG.	HIGH
Ashtray, aluminum, round logo in center, c. 1955	$ 18	$ 20	$ 22
Ashtray and figural bottle match holder, c. 1940	800	900	1000
Ashtray, metal, round, "Things Go Better" on rim, c. 1963	8	9	10
Ashtray, Mexican, painted aluminum, c. 1970	3	4	5
Bank, cap form, c. 1972	12	14	15
Bank, plastic vending machine	80	100	120
Bank, tin bat. operated dispenser, c. 1955	300	400	500
Bingo Card, c. 1940	15	18	20
Blotter, "Delicious and Refreshing," Atlanta Litho., c. 1904	250	300	350
Blotter "Delicious and Refreshing," Edwards, Deutsch & Heitman, c. 1904	80	90	100
Blotter, "Duster Girl" in auto, c. 1904	400	450	500
Blotter, icy style "Cold" Refreshment, c. 1937	15	18	20
Blotter, "Restores Energy and Strengthens Nerves," c. 1906	80	90	100
Blotter, Sprite with bottle top hat, c. 1953	5	6	7
Blotter, Sprite with bottle top hat (Canada), c. 1956	15	18	20
Book Cover, "Always Be Careful," c. 1951	5	6	7
Book Cover, Baseball player, c. 1939	10	13	15
Bookmark, celluloid Valentine, 2" x 2.25", c. 1899	300	400	500
Bookmark, Coke can, c. 1960	4	5	6
Bookmark, Hilda Clark, c. 1900	300	350	400
Bookmark, Lillian Nordica, 2" x 6", c. 1904	400	450	500
Bookmark, little girl with bird house, c. 1904	400	500	600
Bookmark, owl on perch, celluloid, 1.5" x 3.125", c. 1906	500	600	700
Bottle, "Best by a Dam Site," c. 1910	70	80	90
Bottle, Biedenhorn Candy, straight side with label, c. 1910	100	125	150

Clockwise from above left: Sign, Paper, c.1928, $200-$300; Thermometer, c.1941, $300-$400; Driver's Uniform with pants, 1960s $100-$150, — Item courtesy of Jim Glaab's Collector's Showcase; Tray, Serving, oval, "Juanita," 1906, $1800-$2200; Tray, Serving, "Topless" Sold at auction in 1994 for $12,000. — Photos Courtsy of James D. Julia, Inc.

Right: Coca-Cola Sunglasses c. 1970s, $18-$22. — Item courtesy of Jim Glaab's Collector's Showcase.

	LOW	AVG.	HIGH
Bottle, display red or clear, ht. 20", c. 1923	$ 250	$ 300	$ 350
Bottle, Donald Duck, 7 oz., ptd., c. 1948	15	20	25
Bottle Holder Protector, 6-bottle type, c. 1933	30	35	40
Calendar, boy with fishing pole, 12" x 24", c. 1937	300	350	400
Calendar, Garden Girl, 12" x 32", c. 1920	1200	1350	1500
Calendar, girl with glass and bottle, 12" x 24", c. 1939	200	225	250
Cigarette Lighter, Coke bottle logo, c. 1965	18	20	22
Cigarette Lighter, Coke bottle shape, c. 1940	20	25	30
Cigarette Lighter, miniature Coke can, c. 1960	12	15	18
Cigarette Lighter, musical, c. 1960	80	100	120
Clock, Bakelite, red "Drink Coca-Cola," dia. 17", c. 1960	80	100	120
Clock, brass mantle type, c. 1954	200	250	300
Clock, dome style, 3" x 5", c. 1950	400	550	700
Clock, leather, 3.25" x 3.25", c. 1919	500	650	800
Clock, regulator style, Gilbert, c. 1930	600	750	900
Clock, reissue of Betty, c. 1974	30	40	50
Cooler, picnic style, c. 1950	60	70	80
Cut-Outs Toonerville Trolley, uncut, c. 1932	250	300	350
Cut-Outs, Uncle Remus, uncut, c. 1930	300	325	350
Door Pull, bottle shape, c. 1950	100	125	150
Flashlight, bottle shaped plastic, c. 1968	20	25	30
Glass, 5¢ w/ arrow, c. 1905	300	350	400
Glass, flair type, c. 1925	60	70	80
Glass flare type, c. 1905	250	275	300
Glass, home type, red/white diamond	5	6	7
Glass, pewter, c. 1930	300	350	400
Ice Pick and Opener, c. 1940	12	14	15
Key Chain, 50th Anniversary Celebration, c. 1936	8	9	10
Key Chain, amber replica bottle w/ brass chain, c. 1964	15	18	20
Key Chain, car key style, c. 1950	12	14	15
Key Chain, red w/ gold bottle., c. 1955	18	20	22
Knife, pocket, 1 blade & opener, Coke bottle design, c. 1910	200	250	300
Knife, pocket, celluloid key, c. 1940	70	80	90
Knife, pocket, Chicago World's Fair, len. 3.5", 1933	30	35	40
Knife, pocket, "Enjoy Coca-Cola," c. 1970	7	8	9
Menu Board, tin, profile of a woman, c. 1940	200	225	250
Mirror, pocket, "Bathing Beauty," c. 1917	900	1100	1300
Mirror, pocket, Coca-Cola Girl, floral hat turned Right "Drink Delicious Coca-Cola," c. 1914	200	225	250
Mirror, pocket, Coca-Cola Girl, in floral hat turned left "Drink Coca-Cola," c. 1909	200	250	300
Mirror, pocket, " Drink Coca-Cola 5¢," c. 1914	300	400	500
Mirror, pocket, "Elaine" girl with bottle turned right, c. 1917	300	325	350
Mirror, pocket, "Enjoy Thirst," c. 1930	150	175	200
Mirror, pocket, "Garden Girl," c. 1920	300	400	500
Mirror, pocket, Juanita w/ pendant & glass, c. 1909	400	450	500
Mirror, pocket-size, "Relieves Fatigue," c. 1906	400	450	500
Mirror, pocket-size, "St. Louis Exposition," c. 1904	300	350	400
Music Box, cooler, c. 1951	100	125	150
Notebook, brown leather, embossed, c. 1903	160	175	190
Notepad, celluloid-covered, 2.5" x 5", c. 1902	300	350	400

	LOW	AVG.	HIGH
Opener, bone handle knife, c. 1908	$ 150	$ 175	$ 200
Opener, Nashville Anniversary, c. 1952	30	35	40
Opener, skate key style, c. 1935	12	14	15
Opener, "Starr X," c. 1930	8	9	10
Paperweight, Coca-Cola gum, c. 1916	100	125	150
Paperweight, "Coke is Coca-Cola," c. 1948	30	35	40
Pen, ball point w/ telephone dialer	8	9	10
Pen, baseball bat, c. 1940	20	25	30
Pencil Box, 10-piece set, c. 1930	25	32	40
Pencil Holder, celluloid, c. 1910	80	90	100
Pencil Sharpener, plastic, c. 1960	6	7	8
Pencil Sharpener, red metal, c. 1933	18	20	22
Plate, glass and Coke bottle motif, dia. 7.25", c. 1930	125	150	175
Plate, "Vienna Art Nude" in orig. frame, c. 1905	600	700	800
Playing Cards, Airplane Spotter (deck), c. 1943	50	60	70
Playing Cards, Girl with bottle (deck), c. 1909	800	850	900
Pocket Secretary, leather-bound, c. 1920	80	100	120
Postcard, "All Over the World," c. 1913	300	350	400
Postcard, "Duster Girl" driving car, c. 1906	300	350	400
Postcard, girl with clown hat, c. 1909	300	350	400
Postcard, horse and delivery wagon (photo), c. 1900	100	125	150
Postcard, men in speedboat, c. 1913	300	350	400
Postcard, photo of bottling plant, c. 1905	100	125	150
Postcard, school teacher at blackboard, c. 1913	300	350	400
Postcard, truck carrying cases of Coke (photo), c. 1913	100	125	150
Postcards, set of 4 Dick Tracy, orig. package, c. 1942	70	80	90
Record, 45, "I'd Like to Teach the World to Sing," Canada, picture sleeve, c. 1970	18	20	22
Sign, cardboard cutout, couple on bicycle, len. 36", c. 1948	300	400	500
Sign, "Cold Drinks," w/ cups and snowbursts, 14" x 20", c. 1960	20	25	30
Sign, round, metal with bottle, dia. 36", 1955	250	300	350
Toy, Cokebot Robot in orig. box, c. 1980	80	100	120
Toy, fountain dispenser, Chilton, 1965	50	55	60
Toy, Matchbox Lorry, 1960	40	55	70
Tray, change, Betty, girl in bonnet, oval, len. 6", c. 1914	250	275	300
Tray, "Hilda Clark," round, dia. 9.75", c. 1903	3000	4000	5000
Tray, serving, "Olympic Games," 15" x 11", c. 1976	20	25	30
Tray, serving, replica of "Duster Girl," c. 1972	10	13	15
Tray, serving, "Sailor Girl," c. 1940	150	175	200
Tray, serving, "Saint Louis Fair," oval, 10.75", c. 1904	1800	2000	2200
Tray, serving, "Santa Claus," 15" x 11", c. 1973	12	14	15
Tray, serving, "Soda Fountain Clerk," c. 1927	300	400	500
Tray, serving, "Springboard Girl," c. 1939	150	175	200
Tray, serving, "Summer Girl," c. 1921	500	650	800
Tray, serving "Topless," dia. 12.5", c. 1908	*Sold at auction in 1994 for $12,000*		
Tray, TV, candle design, c. 1972	20	25	30
Tray, TV, Thanksgiving motif, c. 1961	30	35	40
Tray, "Two Girls at Car," c. 1942	150	175	200
Wallet, Coca-Cola script, c. 1922	30	35	40
Wallet, Coke bottle emblem, c. 1915	50	60	70
Wallet, embossed coin purse, c. 1906	60	75	90
Watch Fob, bulldog, c. 1925	80	100	120

Doorstops

Figural doorstops are practical sculptures. Designed to keep doors open to aid ventilation, most of the doorstops below were produced in the first half of the 20th century. Unless otherwise indicated, examples are made of cast iron. Prices are given for items in excellent condition with minimal paint wear. Beware of doorstops with sloppy workmanship and grainy finish; they are probably reproductions. Examine items carefully to detect cracks and repaints.

Our consultant for this area is Jeanne Bertoia, author of *Doorstops, Identification & Values*, Collector Books, Paducah, KY, 1993 (she is listed in the back of this book).

Man's best friend is a popular doorstop theme.

	LOW	AVG.	HIGH
Ally Sloper, 11.13" x 6.25"	$ 375	$ 412	$ 450
Aunt Jamima, 13.25" x 8"	325	362	400
Basket of Kittens, 10" x 7"	350	388	425
Bathing Beauties, Hubley, signed "Fish," 10.88" x 5.25"	550	600	650
Bear w/ Honey, full-figure, rare, 15" x 6.5"	750+		
Bear w/ Tree, 7.75" x 4.38"	250	275	300
Bellhop, 8.88" x 4.63"	250	275	300
Bird of Paradise, 13.38" x 7"	325	350	375
Bloodhound, Wedge, 13.75" x 7"	300	325	350
Bloodhound, Wedge, 15.25" x 4.75"	200	238	275
Bobby Blake, Hubley, designed by Grace Drayton, 9.5" x 5.25"	400	438	475
Boston Terrier, Bradley & Hubbard, 9.63" x 11.75"	275	312	350
Boston Terrier Puppy, 7.75" x 8.5"	200	225	250
Boy w/ Hands in Pockets, full-figure, 10.5" x 3.63"	300	325	350
Butler, rare, 12.5", 6"	375	405	435
Cat, full-figure, 11.5" x 7"	325	350	375
Cat on Base, 12.5" x 7.5"	150	188	225
Cat, Wedged, Hubley, 6" x 3"	350	375	400
Clipper Ship, 11" x 13"	50	62	75
Clipper Ship, 12.75" x 13"	40	55	70
Clipper Ship, Wedge, 11.63" x 11.63"	45	60	75
Clown, rare, 11.5" x 5.5"	375	400	425
Cockatoo, full-figure, 14" x 4.5"	175	212	250
Cocker Spaniel, Wedge, VA Metalcrafters, 9" x 7"	100	125	150
Colonial Woman, Littco Products, 10.25" x 6"	150	188	225

	LOW	AVG.	HIGH
Conestoga Wagon, 8" x 11"	$ 100	$ 138	$ 175
Dachshund, marked "No. 8 Taylor Cook 1930 C.," 5.5" x 7.25"	350	388	425
Deco Hunchback Cat, two sided, wedge, 11.75" x 9.13"	300	325	350
Dog & Duck, marked "copyright 1925 by A.M. Greenblatt, Boston, Mass.," 10" x 8.75"	600	638	675
Dolly, Hubley, designed by Grace Drayton, 9.5" x 5.5"	400	438	475
Drum Major, full-figure, solid, 13.5" x 6.5"	350	388	425
Duck, 11" x 6.5"	350	375	400
Ducks, Hubley, 8.25" x 6.25"	300	338	375
Dutch Girl w/ Big Shoes, 9.75" x 9.25"	325	362	400
Elephant, 7.25" x 7.13"	50	75	100
Elephant, Bradley & Hubbard, 10" x 11.75"	200	225	250
English Bulldog, full-figure, 5.75" x 8.5"	125	150	175
Fantail Fish, Hubley, 9.75" x 5.88"	100	138	175
Fawn, marked "No. 6 C. 1930 Taylor Cook," 10" x 6"	175	212	250
Fisherman at Wheel, 6.25" x 6"	125	150	175
Fox Terrier, 10.38" x 10.5"	225	250	275
French Bulldog, Hubley, full-figure, 7.63" x 6.75"	125	150	175
French Girl, Hubley, 9.25" x 5.5"	225	250	275
Geese, Hubley, designed by Fred Everett, 8" x 8"	350	388	425
German Shepherd, full-figure, 9.75" x 13"	125	150	175
Giraffe, Hubley, full-figure, 12.5" x 9"	750+		
Giraffe, wedge, 13.5" x 5.25"	250	262	275
Girl Holding Bouquet, full-figure, 7.63" x 4.75"	175	200	225
Girl Holding Dress, Bradley & Hubbard, 13" x 6.75"	500	550	600
Girl in Canoe, 4.38" x 10"	500	538	575
Girl Kicking Flower, rare, 9.88" x 7.25"	600	638	675
Guitar Player, 11.88" x 7.13"	475	512	550
Horse, full-figure, Hubley, 10" x 12"	100	125	150
Horse Jumping Fence, Eastern Specialty Co., 7.88" x 11.75"	325	362	400
Huckleberry Finn, Littco Products, 12.5" x 9.5"	500	550	600
Hunchback Cat, 10.63" x 7.5"	100	125	150
Imp, 5.25" x 3"	100	125	150
Judy, 11" x 8.88"	450	488	525
Koala, marked "No. 5 Taylor Cook 1930 C.," 9.25" x 5.5"	400	425	450
Large Frog, full-figure, rare, 14" x 7"	750+		
Large Mammy, Green Dress, Hubley, full-figure, 12" x 6"	400	425	450
Large Old Salt, 14.5" x 6.5"	325	350	375
Large Old Salt at Rudder, 14" x 6.75"	400	425	450
Large Putting Golf, Spencer, two-sided, 16.63" x 5.63"	500	538	575
Lil Red Riding Hood, Hubley, Grace Drayton design, 9.5" x 5"	400	438	475
Little Boy w/ Bear, full-figure, solid, 5.25" x 3.5"	150	175	200
Little Girl by Wall, full-figure, solid, 5.25" x 3.25"	150	175	200
Little Girl, full-figure, solid, 4.88" x 3.75"	150	175	200
Little Heiskell Soldier, emb. "Little Heiskell, Hagerstown, MD, 1769," 10.75" x 6"	325	362	400
Little Jester Girl, full-figure, solid, 5.63" x 3.38"	150	175	200
Mary Quite Contrary, Littco Products, 11.38" x 9.63"	650	700	750
Messenger Boy, Hubley, signed "Fish," 10" x 5.38"	450	488	525
Monkey on Barrel, "No. 3 C. 1930 Taylor Cook," 8.38" x 4.88"	350	388	425
Monkey, Wedge, 13.5" x 5.63"	300	338	375

	LOW	AVG.	HIGH
Old Woman, Bradley & Hubbard, 11" x 7"	$ 475	$ 500	$ 525
Olive Picker, Hubley, rare, 7.75" x 8.75"	550	600	650
Ostrich, Wedge, 8.5" x 9"	225	250	275
Owl on Books, 9.25" x 6.5"	475	512	550
Pan and Nymph, very rare, 9.25" x 14"	650	700	750
Parlor Maid, Hubley, signed "Fish," 9.25" x 3.5"	750+		
Parrot in Ring, 8" x 7"	100	138	175
Parrot, marked "No. 4 C. 1930 Taylor Cook," 10.5" x 4.88"	350	388	425
Parrot on Ball, 12.13" x 5.5"	125	150	175
Peacock, 5.63" x 8.25"	150	162	175
Peacock, 6.25" x 6.25"	150	175	200
Peasant Girl, Hubley, 8.75" x 5"	175	200	225
Penguin, full-figure, 10.5" x 5"	275	312	350
Penguin, marked "No. 1 C. 1930 Taylor Cook," 9.5" x 5.25"	500	550	600
Penguin w/ Top Hat, Hubley, full-figure, 10.5" x 3.75"	275	312	350
Peter Rabbit, Hubley, designed by Grace Drayton, 9.5" x 4.75"	375	400	425
Pheasant, Hubley, designed by Fred Everett, 8.5" x 7.5"	250	275	300
Pilgrim Boy, double-sided casting, 8.75" x 5.38"	325	362	400
Pirate Girl, marked "Pirate Girl," 13.88" x 7.25"	250	275	300
Pirate w/ Sack, rare, 11.88" x 9.63"	475	500	525
Pirate w/ Sword, 12" x 5.75"	450	488	525
Police Boy, 10.63" x 7.25"	375	412	450
Policeman, marked "LeMur Light Co., pat. pending," 7.88" x 4"	200	238	275
Polly, Hubley, 8.13" x 5.25"	100	125	150
Punch, 12" x 9"	450	488	525
Puppies in Basket, 7" x 7.38"	325	362	400
Quail, Hubley, designed by Fred Everett, 7.25" x 6.25"	300	338	375
Rabbit by Fence, Albany Foundry Co., 6.88" x 8.13"	325	350	375
Rabbit, wedge, two-sided, Spencer, 11.5" x 8.75"	425	462	500
Rabbit w/ Tophat, 9.88" x 4.75"	375	412	450
Rhumba Dancer, 11.13" x 6.63"	475	500	525
Rooster, 13" x 8.5"	325	350	375
Rooster, 7" x 5.5"	125	150	175
Rooster, Spencer, two-sided, 13.25" x 11"	500	538	575
Safety First Policeman, rare, embossed "safety first," 9.5" x 5.63"	625	662	700
Sailor, 11.38" x 5"	425	450	475
Scottie, Wilton Products Inc., 7.75" x 4.5"	75	100	125
Senorita, 11.25" x 7"	275	300	325
Shorebird, 9.75" x 5.13"	275	312	350
Silhouette Girl, Albany Foundry, 11.25" x 10.25"	475	512	550
Sitting Boston Terrier, full-figure, 6.75" x 6.63"	125	150	175
Sitting Bulldog, full-figure, 6.75" x 7"	150	188	225
Skier, full-figure, 12.5" x 5"	400	438	475
Small Halloween Cat, Wedge, 5" x 4"	125	150	175
Small Mammy, Hubley, full-figure, green dress, 8.5" x 4.5"	175	200	225
Small Mammy, Hubley, full-figure, red dress, 8.5" x 4.5"	150	188	225
Southern Belle, 11.25" x 6"	150	175	200
Spanish Girl, Hubley, 9" x 5"	175	212	250
Spotted Dog, marked "C. 1930 Taylor Cook," 7.75" x 7.88"	450	475	500
Spotted Dog Sitting, full-figure, solid, 5.5" x 6.5"	175	200	225
Spotted Dog Standing, full-figure, solid, 5.5" x 7"	175	200	225

	LOW	AVG.	HIGH
Springer Spaniel, 6.75" x 7"	$ 125	$ 150	$ 175
Squirrel on Log, 11" x 9.5"	225	262	300
Squirrel w/ Nut, Hubley, 8.5" x 7"	275	312	350
St. Bernard, 8" x 10.5"	125	150	175
St. Bernard, full-figure, 6.75" x 10.38"	250	275	300
Stagecoach, Hubley, 11.25" x 5.88"	125	162	200
Star of Texas, 10.5" x 10.25"	275	300	325
Stork, 13.75" x 8.88"	300	338	375
Stork, full-figure, Hubley, 2.25" x 7"	325	362	400
Swallows, Hubley, 8.5" x 7.5"	300	338	375
Swan, Spencer, two sided, 7.88" x 13.5"	500	550	600
Terrier w/ Bushes, marked "copt. 1929 PAL," 8" x 7"	150	162	175
The Constitution, A.M. Greenblatt Studios, c. 1924, 11.75" x 8.5"	100	125	150
The Patrol, full-figure, 8.75" x 3.75"	200	225	250
The Snooper, two sided, 13.25" x 4.5"	400	425	450
Tin Soldier, very rare, 11.75" x 4.5"	350	388	425
Topsy, Wedged, Hubley, 6" x 4"	250	275	300
Tropical Woman, 12" x 6.25"	150	175	200
Turkeys, 6.38" x 5.75"	225	250	275
Whippet, 6.75" x 7.5"	125	138	150
Whistling Jim, Bradley & Hubbard, very rare, 16.25" x 5.5"	750+		
White Cockatoo, 11.25" x 9.5"	275	312	350
Wineman, rare, 9.5" x 7"	550	600	650
Wolfhound, Wedge, Spencer, 6.5" x 3"	175	200	225
Woman w/ Hatbox, 6.75" x 5.25"	100	125	150
Yawning Child, full-figure, 9" x 5"	150	175	200

Holiday Decorations

Holidays are special events, times when we can get together with friends and family, exchange gifts, observe religious rites or dress in outrageous costumes. Collectors of holiday items can chose from a wealth of material. Many collectors focus on one holiday, such as Christmas or Halloween. Others prefer to specialize in a type of item, such as postcards. Whatever the method, displaying your finds is great fun and collecting can be enjoyed year round. For further information we recommend *The Official Price Guide to Holiday Collectibles*, Helaine Fendelman & Jeri Schwartz, House of Collectibles, Random House, NY, 1991; *Halloween in America: A Collector's Guide*, Stuart Schneider, Schiffer Publishing, Atglen, PA, 1995, and *Christmas Revisited*, Robert Brenner, Schiffer Publishing, Atglen, PA, 1986

	LOW	AVG.	HIGH
Christmas Figural Light Bulbs			
Andy Gump, milk glass	$ 30	$ 35	$ 40
Bear w/ guitar, milk glass	26	30	34
Blue bird, milk glass	26	30	34
Clock	26	30	34
Clown, milk glass	40	50	60
Elephant, milk glass	70	80	90
Fish, milk glass	20	25	30
Gingerbread man	30	35	40
Grapes, milk glass	20	25	30
House, milk glass	20	25	30
Humpty Dumpty, milk glass	30	35	40
Lantern	12	15	18
Parrot, milk glass	30	40	50
Pinocchio	30	35	40
Puss N' Boots, milk glass	40	45	50
Santa, painted	60	70	80
Snowman, milk glass	20	25	30
Zeppelin w/ flag	100	120	140
Christmas Greeting Cards			
A Merry Christmas and Happy New Year, children & Christmas tree, c. 1870s	$ 3	$ 5	$ 7
A Merry Christmas to You All, family in snowy woodland, c. 1880	3	4	5
Child in 19th century bonnet	3	4	5
Hail, Day of Joy, Prang, angel kneeling with dove on finger, c. 1870	15	18	21
Here, Open the Door, Kate Greenaway, messenger knocking on door, c. 1880	40	50	60
Here Comes the New Year with Lots of Good Cheer, child, tree & toys, c. 1870	4	6	8
Ice pond, boy putting skates on a girl, fringed & embroidered, German	3	4	5
Merry Christmas & Happy New Year, children in snow, church, c. 1880	4	6	8
Merry Christmas to You All, L. Prang, brown suited Santa, sq.	22	26	30
My Lips May Give a Message, Kate Greenaway, girl holding letter, c. 1880	40	50	60
Pop-up card, ice skating scene, England, c. 1890	18	22	26

	LOW	AVG.	HIGH
Prang's American Third Prize Christmas Card, by C. Coleman, oriental scene	$ 18	$ 22	$ 26
Season's Greetings, card shaped like fan	2	3	4
Season's Greetings, mechanical, boy with flowers, 19th century	14	18	22
Season's Greetings, river & small boat, 19th century	3	4	5
Victorian card, paper lace border surrounds Season's Greeting, c. 1800s	10	13	16
Wishing You a Happy New Year, Prang, folded, girl on front, old man on back, fringed, w/ tasseled cord, c. 1884	15	18	21
Wishing You a Merry Christmas, Prang, fireplace, cat & kittens, sq., c. 1800s	15	18	21
With Best Christmas Wishes, Tuck, girl w/ spray of flowers, c. 1885	12	15	18

Christmas Miscellaneous

	LOW	AVG.	HIGH
Bank, Santa at Chimney, plaster, c. 1950s, ht. 11"	$ 70	$ 90	$ 110
Bank, Santa in Armchair, plaster, c. 1950s, ht. 10"	80	100	120
Button, *Merry Christmas*, Santa with pack in household, litho. tin	20	25	30
Button, *Santa Claus Gave This To Me*, c. 1940s, dia. .5"	10	12	14
Button, Santa reading a book titled Good Boys-Good Girls, dia. 1"	10	12	14
Crèche, papier mache stable made of wood, set of seventeen figures, c. 1930	100	130	160
Decoration, Angel, wax, spun glass wings	45	55	65
Decoration, Snowman, with black stovepipe hat, pipe, red scarf, plastic, c. 1950s, ht. 5"	10	12	14
Decoration, Snowman, with blue cap, red mittens and silver skates, c. 1950s, ht. 5"	12	15	18
Lamp, Figural Santa, hard plastic, c. 1955, ht. 16"	25	35	45
Light, Santa glass globe on tin battery box base, c. 1950	30	40	50
Lights, bells on a string	18	22	26
Plate, child's ABC's, features children and snowman	80	100	120
Snowdome, Figural, Santa & reindeer with dome center, plastic, c. 1950s, ht. 5"	18	21	24
Snowdome, Figural, Santa with dome center, plastic, c. 1950s, ht. 5"	16	18	20
Snowdome, Figural, Snowman with dome center, plastic, c. 1950s, ht. 5"	16	18	20
Tree, Bottle Brush, Japan, c. 1950, ht. 1950	4	5	6
Tree, Feather, German, c. 1910, ht. 18"	200	250	300
Victorian Christmas stocking	80	100	120

Christmas Ornaments

	LOW	AVG.	HIGH
Angel's Face, blown glass, ht. 2.5"	$ 40	$ 50	$ 55
Angel, Dresden	200	250	300
Angel, paper, die-cut, trimmed with tinsel	50	60	70
Baby in Basket, cardboard, Dresden	200	250	300
Baby in Bunting, blown glass, emb. lettering, len. 4"	70	80	90
Ball, amber	20	25	30
Basket, fruit filled, blown glass	30	35	40

	LOW	AVG.	HIGH
Bear w/ Muff, blown glass	$ 60	$ 70	$ 80
Camel, cardboard, Dresden, flat	45	55	65
Camel, Dresden	50	60	70
Canary, blown glass	25	30	40
Carrot, blown glass, embossed detail, c. 1910, len. 4"	40	50	60
Child, milk glass	20	25	30
Church, blown glass	40	50	60
Clown head, blown glass	40	50	60
Cuckoo clock, blown glass, emb. & ptd.	50	60	70
Doll's Head, blown glass, silver & flesh color, glass eyes	80	100	120
Elephant, mercury glass w/ milk glass tusks, ht. 4"	70	80	90
Fish, blown glass	50	55	60
Football Player, milk glass	70	90	110
Foxy Grandpa, blown glass w/ applied legs, ht. 4.5"	150	175	200
Girl's Head, blown glass w/ blown glass eyes, ht. 2.5"	50	70	90
Girl, blown glass	40	60	80
Happy Hooligan, blown glass w/ applied legs, ht. 4.5"	150	175	200
Heart, blown glass, large	40	50	60
Icicle, glass	20	30	40
Kugel, dark blue, grapes w/ metal cap	200	230	260
Lamp	50	70	90
Man in the Moon, blown glass, green, ht. 3"	70	80	90
Monkey Holding Stick, blown glass, ht. 2.5"	100	130	160
Moon, happy/sad full moon faces composition squeeze toy, c. 1890	100	120	140
Ornament, Pocket Watch, blown glass w/ paper face	60	80	100
Peacock, blown glass, brush tail	40	60	80
Pear, pressed cotton	20	25	30
Penguin, blown glass, blue, silver, red, embossed feet	40	50	60
Pinecone, blown glass	15	18	21
Pipe, blown glass	20	25	30
Purse, blown glass, wire rapped	60	70	80
Santa carrying bag of toys, blown glass, ht. 2.5"	60	80	100
Santa Claus, celluloid, white and red, c. 1930s, ht. 4.5"	50	60	70
Santa, celluloid	50	70	90
Santa, w/ plaster face	40	50	60
Scottie Dog, blown glass, yellow & blue	80	90	100
Smiling Snowman, w/ broom, blown glass, c. 1910, ht. 3.5"	50	60	70
Stag, blown glass, blue w/ gold antlers, ht. 3"	40	50	60
Star, Dresden, 2-sided	40	50	60
Swan, blown glass w/ spun glass wings & tail, c. 1900	90	110	130
Teapot	30	35	40
Turkey, blown glass w/ spun glass wings & tail, c. 1900	90	110	130

Christmas Postcards

	LOW	AVG.	HIGH
Postcard, Hold-to-the-Light, Santa Claus	$ 125	$ 138	$ 150
Postcard, Santa in Green, full figure	25	28	30
Postcard, Santa painting sled	10	13	15

	LOW	AVG.	HIGH

Easter

	LOW	AVG.	HIGH
Bunny Mobile, plastic, early style auto, c. 1950s 20		25	30
Candy Container, Easter Egg, red, gold, and white litho. cardboard, c. 1940 20		25	30
Candy Container, Rabbit, pressed cardboard, removable head 90		110	120
Candy Container, Rabbit, pressed cardboard, white, c. 1950s 35		45	55
Egg Cup, figural bunny & egg, plastic, c. 1950s, ht. 3" 3		5	7
Greeting Card, Angels on front, by Whitney, New York, 19th century 4		5	6
Greeting Card, Bible verses, birds, late 19th century 2		3	4
Greeting Card, Booklet, poem, cross with flowers, German 4		6	8
Greeting Card, Child coming out of egg, gold fringed 2		3	4
Greeting Card, Cross on reef in sea, by Carter & Karrick, 19th century 3		4	5
Greeting Card, Cupid with ribbon holding flowers, 19th century 3		4	5
Greeting Card, Floral cross on front, German, 19th century 2		3	4
Greeting Card, Girl climbing out of an egg shell, fringed German, 19th century 5		7	9
Greeting Card, Heads of children in flower pot, 19th century 2		3	4
Greeting Card, Shakespeare's, Heaven Give You Many Merry Days, 19th century 2		3	4
Toy, Rabbit pulling cart, tinplate, Chein 70		80	90

Halloween

	LOW	AVG.	HIGH
Candlesticks, Black Cat & Jack-O-Lantern, pr., plastic, c. 1950, ht. 2.5"15 18		21	24
Costume, Gorilla, w/ gauze mask in original Collegetown Costumes box, c. 1940s 40		45	50
Decoration, Black cat, cardboard fold out, 1950s, ht. 20" 30		35	40
Decoration, Jack-O-Lantern Scarecrow on wheeled base, orange & black plastic, c. 1950s, ht. 5" 20		22	24
Decoration, Jack-O-Lantern Scarecrow, orange plastic w/ black jacket, c. 1950s, ht. 5" 18		20	22
Decoration, Jack-O-Lantern Scarecrow, orange plastic w/ orange & black checked jacket, c. 1950s, ht. 5" 24		27	30
Decoration, Snowman, orange & black plastic, ht. 5" 30		35	40
Decoration, Witch and black cat dancers, accordion fold crepe paper, 1960s, len. 28" 15		17	19
Decoration, Witch, bats & black cat, orange, black and green pressed cardboard, c. 1940s, ht. 18" 45		50	55
Eye Glasses, figural hissing black cats plastic 25		30	35
Game, Whirl-O-Halloween Fortune & Stunt Game, card w/ spinner, 7" x 9" 30		40	50
Hat, orange and black crepe paper 8		10	12
Jack-O-Lantern, cardboard, accordion foldout 1950s, ht. 11" 30		35	40
Jack-O-Lantern, pressed cardboard w/ insert, ht. 8" 100		120	140
Jack-O-Lantern, pressed cardboard without insert, ht. 8" 70		77	85
Lantern, cardboard die-cut with various Halloween scenes over orange tissue paper, c. 1935, ht. 12 45		55	65
Light, Jack-O-Lantern glass globe on tinplate battery-box base, c. 1950 30		40	50

	LOW	AVG.	HIGH
Light, Pumpkin, orange plastic, battery operated, c. 1950s, dia. 2.5" ...... $ 35		$ 40	$ 45
Mask, black cat, paper, round eyes, 11" x 8" 12		15	18
Mask, clown, paper, red, black and yellow, 8" x 9" 12		15	18
Mask, Devil, gauze 15		18	21
Mask, Owl, cardboard with cat and pumpkin band, 12" x 12" ... 30		35	40
Noisemaker, cylindrical shake type, litho. tin, Jack-O-Lanterns & witches, c. 1950, dia. 4" 10		12	14
Noisemaker, paddle type, tinplate litho. w/ Jack-O-Lantern, c. 1940s, len. 10" 26		30	34
Noisemaker, spin type, tinplate litho. w/ black cat motif, c. 1948, dia. 4" 10		12	14
Noisemaker, spin type, tinplate litho. w/ flapper witch and skyscrapers, c. 1940, dia. 4" 15		18	21
Noisemaker, tambourine type, tinplate litho. w/ Jack-O-Lantern, c. 1940s, dia. 30		35	40
Party favor, Basket, black & orange plastic, c. 1950s, dia. 3.5" .. 10		12	14
Party favor, Black Cat, holds lollipop, orange plastic w/ black-striped jersey, c. 1950s, ht. 5" 15		18	21
Party favor, Pumpkin, orange plastic, w/ metal bail, c. 1950s, dia. 3.5" 6		8	10
Postcard, Halloween, signed Clapsaddle 15		20	25
Postcard, Halloween, Tuck 12		14	16
Postcard, Halloween, Winsch 50		58	65

Thanksgiving

	LOW	AVG.	HIGH
Candlesticks, cornucopia shape, ceramic, pair, 3" ...... $ 12		$ 15	$ 18
Candlesticks, pilgrims, ceramic, 2" pair 10		12	14
Candy container, Cornucopia, papier mache, c. 1910 50		60	70
Candy container, Turkey, Composition, c. 1930s 20		30	35
Centerpiece, turkey, Hallmark, c. 1940 12		15	18
Cornucopia, wicker 12		15	20
Platter, decorated w/ Tom Turkey, Japan c. 1935 15		18	21
Postcard, Thanksgiving, signed Brundage 15		20	25
Postcard, Thanksgiving, signed Clapsaddle 8		10	12

Valentine's Day

	LOW	AVG.	HIGH
Easel Valentine, fold back, free standing, c. 1900 ...... $ 15		$ 18	$ 21
German, large ship, mechanical pull down 65		75	85
German, pulldown, children, c. 1915 6		8	10
German, pullout & stand up cottage, c. 1910 12		15	18
German, pullout & stand up steam boiler, c. 1910 12		15	18
German, stand up, little girl holding opening parasol c. 1920 ...... 15 / 6		20 / 8	25 / 10
Gibson Art, paper doll mechanical stand up, little girl holding doll, German 20		25	30
Gibson Girl (from photo), Meek & Son, surrounded by lace, cherub heads, c. 1890 20		30	40
Hat Trimmer, Elton & Co., NY, glum looking woman sewing hat, with verse, c. 1880 22		26	30
Heart Shaped, folder, Tuck, little girl on front 12		14	16

	LOW	AVG.	HIGH
Heart Shaped, lace c. 1905	$ 9	$ 12	$ 15
Hearts Are Ripe, children picking heart shaped apples from tree	3	5	7
Honeycomb, "Cupid's Temple of Love," c. 1928	6	8	10
Maggie & Jiggs, c. 1940	15	18	21
McLoughlin, three layer, silver, white, lace, c. 1880	20	25	30
McLoughlin, three layer, white, gold, lace, c. 1880	10	12	14
Mechanical, various animals, c. 1930	10	12	14
Popeye, c. 1940	15	18	21
Temple of Love, Tuck's Betsy Beauties series, young girl and butterfly	12	14	16
To My Valentine, from Tuck's Innocence Abroad series, two children, verse	12	14	16
Victorian, fold out, paper lace	20	22	24

Various Holidays

	LOW	AVG.	HIGH
Fourth of July, Postcard	$ 5	$ 8	$ 10
Happy Birthday, Greeting Card, blue fringed, floral design, c. 1880	3	4	5
Happy Birthday, Greeting Card, children, 19th century	2	3	4
Happy Birthday, Greeting Card, maroon floral, fringed, 19th century	3	4	5
Lincoln's Birthday, Postcard	8	12	15
Memorial Day, Postcard	5	8	10
Washington's Birthday, Postcard	5	8	10

Ice Cream Molds

Before ice cream producers could send the various shapes of ice cream now offered in the freezer of the corner market, local merchants made their own ice cream and sold it in shapes they pressed into molds themselves. Homemade ice cream also found its way into these molds. Because some pewter contains lead, its is not advisable to continue the practice.

All of the following figural molds are pewter unless otherwise indicated.

Clockwise from the top; heart & Cupid, $30-$40; shamrock, $25-$35; flaming hearts, $25-$35.

	LOW	AVG.	HIGH
Ace of Clubs	$ 25	$ 30	$ 35
Ace of Spades	25	30	35
Airplane	80	100	120
American Flag	40	45	50
Apple	25	30	35
Apple, cast iron	20	25	30
Automobile, cast iron	90	105	120
Ball	20	25	30
Banana	45	50	55
Battleship	80	105	130
Calla Lily	30	35	40
Carnation	30	35	40
Cat	40	45	50
Cheese, porcelain, metal	60	70	80
Chicken	45	50	55
Chrysanthemum	35	40	45
Cupid	35	40	45

	LOW	AVG.	HIGH
Daisy	$ 25	$ 30	$ 35
Doves	30	35	40
Easter Lily	30	35	40
Egg	25	30	35
Engagement Ring	25	30	35
Football	30	35	40
George Washington	50	60	70
Grapes	35	40	45
Harp	35	40	45
Heart	30	35	40
Heart & Cupid Pattern, cast iron	40	45	50
Heart w/ Cupid	40	48	55
Hyacinth	25	30	35
Liberty Bell	40	45	50
Locomotive, cast iron	70	80	90
Mutton Chop	30	35	40
Ocean Liner	60	70	80
Orange	25	30	35
Peach	25	30	35
Pear	25	30	35
Petunia	25	30	35
Potato	25	30	35
Pumpkin	35	40	45
Pumpkin, cast iron	40	50	60
Rose	25	30	35
Rosebud	30	35	40
Santa Claus	70	80	90
Smoking Pipe	30	35	40
Stork w/ Baby	50	60	70
Turkey	50	55	60
Wedding Bell	30	35	40

Horseshoe, $30-$40.

Motion Lamps

Animated motion lamps draw the eye by presenting an illusion of a waterfall, a ship at sea, or a variety of action-packed images. The heat of the light bulb causes the cylinder to revolve inside a painted shade creating the illusion of a moving image. The light of the bulb shining through the shade casts a beautiful glow. The most prominent manufacturers were Scene in Action and National in the 1920s, and Econolite and L.A. Goodman in the 1950s through the 1960s. Prices are guided by condition, availability, and collector demand. Care must be taken to ensure that the original cylinder is inside the lamp because cylinders are not interchangeable. Values are given for lamps in mint condition.

Our consultants for this section are Jim and Kaye Whitaker, owners of Eclectic Antiques. They are listed in the back of this book.

Clockwise from above left: Disney Merry-go-round, red, $250-$350, — Photo courtesy of Eclectic Antiques; Niagara Falls, 1950s, $70-$80; Ko-Pak-Ta Nut machine, 1930s, $250-$300; Ship, L.A. Goodman, 1950s, $85-$95 (showing both sides).

	LOW	HIGH
Airplanes, plastic, Econolite, 1958, ht. 11"	$ 90	$ 100
Antique Cars, plastic, Econolite, 1957, ht. 11"	90	100
Bar is Open, plastic, Visual Effects, 1970, ht. 13"	24	28
Bicycles, plastic, Econolite, 1950s, ht. 11"	85	95
Butterflies, Econolite, 1954, ht. 11"	80	120
Butterflies, cone shape, L.A. Goodman, ht. 9"	90	130
Christmas Tree, red green and blue paper, Econolite, 1950s, ht. 15"	65	75
Ducks, plastic, Econolite, 1950s, ht. 12"	70	90
Firefighters, plastic, L.A. Goodman, 1950s, ht. 11"	90	110
Fireplace, plastic, Econolite, ht. 11"	70	80
Forest Fire, Econolite (Roto-Vue Jr.), 1949, ht. 10"	75	85
Forest Fire, glass, Scene in Action, ht. 9"	100	130
Forest Fire, plastic, Econolite, ht. 11"	70	80
Forest Fire, plastic, L.A. Goodman, ht. 11"	70	90
Fountain of Youth, flat front, Econolite, ht. 13"	80	100
Fountain of Youth, plastic, Econolite, 1950, ht. 11"	75	85
Fountain of Youth, plastic, Econolite (Roto-Vue Jr.), ht. 10"	70	80
Hawaiian Scene, plastic, Econolite, ht. 11"	75	85
Hopalong Cassidy, cylinder style, Econolite (Roto -Vue Jr.), 1949, ht. 10"	250	400
Ko-Pak-Ta Nut Machine, chrome, Roy Stringer Co., 1930s, ht. 15"	250	350
Lighthouse/Ship, plastic, L.A. Goodman, 1950s, ht. 11"	85	95
Marine Scene, glass and white metal, Scene In Action, 1930s, ht. 9"	90	110
Merry Go Round, Disneyland, plastic, red & yellow, Econolite, 1950s, ht. 11"	250	350
Merry Go Round, yellow, Econolite (Roto-Vue Jr.), 1950s, 10"	85	95
Mill Scene, plastic, Econolite, 1950s, ht. 11"	75	85
Miss Liberty, plastic, Econolite, 1950s, ht. 11"	90	120
Niagara Falls, glass, Scene in Action, 1930s, ht. 9"	90	110
Niagara Falls, plastic, L.A. Goodman, 1950s, ht. 11"	65	75
Niagara Falls, plastic, Econolite, 1950s, ht. 11"	70	80
Niagara Falls, Econolite (Roto-Vue Jr.), 1950s, ht. 9"	70	80
Ocean Creatures, plastic, L.A. Goodman, 1950s, ht. 11"	80	90
Op-Art, plastic, Visual Effects, 1970s, ht. 13"	35	45
Pot Bellied Stove, black or silver, Econolite, 1950s, ht. 12"	85	95
Santa & Reindeer, plastic, L.A. Goodman, 1950s, ht. 12"	100	140
Seattle World's Fair, plastic, Econolite, 1962, ht. 11"	90	120
Serenader, flat front, metal, Scene In Action, 1930s, ht. 13"	100	150
Snow Scene, church, plastic, Econolite, 1950s, ht. 11"	75	85
Snow Scene w/ Cabin, plastic, Econolite, 1950s, ht. 11"	75	85
Steamboats, plastic, Econolite, 1950s, ht. 11"	75	85
Trains, plastic, Econolite, 1950s, ht. 11"	75	85
Trains, plastic, L.A. Goodman, 1950s, ht. 11"	75	85
Truck and Bus, plastic, Econolite, 1950s, ht. 11"	95	135
Water Skiers, plastic, Econolite, 1950s, ht. 11"	95	135

Radios

The following section encompasses several areas of radio collecting. Included are early examples from the 1920s, Catalin plastic case radios from the 1930s and 1940s, later Cold War-era radios from the 1950s and 1960s, early transistor radios from the same era, novelty radios and advertising radios.

Catalin are the beautiful marbleized or mottled look radios. They are often mistakenly called Bakelite. Catalin refers to a clear plastic that can be colored, first developed by the Catalin Corporation. The prices of Catalin radios shot up dramatically in the late 1980s to early 1990s. Interest has cooled but they still draw great interest. In the case of Catalin radios many collectors suggest "don't touch that dial" because heat can crack the cases. Catalins have also been known to shrink, crack, and fade.

There are those who prefer the early wooden case models. Many new collectors, however, or those frustrated by Catalin's prices, have turned to what we call the dashboard type radios, due to their ultrasleek "Techno" designs. Others pursue newer advertising radios.

In the following entries, each radio is first listed by make, followed by the type of radio it is in parentheses. (T)-table top [includes wooden cases, Catalin radios, plastic and others], (N)- novelty [includes character and interestingly shaped radios], (P)-portable, (TR)-transistor, (C)-crystal (A)-advertising, (F)-floor models. Next follows a brief description, along with the approximate date of manufacture. All prices are for radios in complete and excellent condition. Radios should also be in working order with the possible exception of some of the plastics (since heat can crack the case).

We suggest these books: *Guide to Old Radios*, David and Betty Johnson, Wallace-Homestead, Radnor, PA, 1989; *The Collector's Guide to Antique Radios*, Marty and Sue Bunis, Collector Books, Paducah, KY, 1995; *Radios, the Golden Age*, Philip Collins, Chronicle Books, San Francisco, CA, 1978; *Radios Redeux*, Philip Collins, Chronicle Books, San Francisco, CA, 1991; *Collector's Guide to Novelty Radios*, Marty Bunis and Robert F. Breed, Collector Books, Paducah KY, 1995.

Clockwise from above left: Admiral tabletop, 1950s, $25-$35; OMS Suburbia with leather case, $25-$35; knight's head novelty radio, 1970s, $30-$40; Air King, $70-$90.

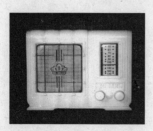 

MAKE	TYPE	DESCRIPTION	DATE	VALUE
Admiral	(T)	brown plastic, gold dial	1950	$ 35-45
Admiral #5Z22	(T)	brown plastic, metal dial	1952	30-40
Admiral #7C65W	(F)	4 knobs	1950	50-80
Admiral #7L12	(TR)	solar powered	1956	120-180
Air Castle #106B	(T)	plastic	1947	70-90
Baseball	(N)	Trophy	1941	800-1000
Bendix #55X4	(P)	plastic, hinged front	1949	50-70
Bowling Ball	(N)	Trophy	1941	500-700
Bulova #670 Bantam	(TR)	jewel decoration	1960	200-300
California Raisin	(A)	California Raisins	1988	30-40
Channel Master #6506	(TR)	pocket	1958	30-40
Charlie McCarthy	(N)	Majestic	1938	900-1200
Charlie the Tuna	(A)	Star Kist Tuna	1970	60-80
Coca-Cola Cooler	(A)	Coca-Cola	1950	600-800
Crosley #538	(T)	wooden slant front	1926	80-100
Crosley X	(T)	wooden	1922	150-200
Crosley VI #VR78	(T)	wooden	1922	100-150
Dahlberg Pillow Speaker	(N)	coin operated	1955	250-350
DeForest #D10	(T)	wooden, loop antenna	1923	400-600
DeForest D6	(T)	wooden, rectangular	1923	900-1100
DeForest #DT600	(T)	wooden, crystal "Everyman"	1923	250-350
Detrola #219 Pee Wee	(T)	plastic (rare colors more)	1940	300-500
Emerson #888·Vanguard	(TR)	pink or blue	1960	80-120
Emerson Patriot #400	(T)	Catalin,	1940	1000-1500
Emerson Tombstone	(T)	Catalin (rare colors more)	1940	1000-1500
Fada #252 Temple	(T)	Catalin (rare colors more)	1940	300-500
Fada #115 Bullet/Streamliner	(T)	Catalin (rare colors more)	1940	600-800
Fada #1000 Bullet/Streamlinr	(T)	Catalin (rare colors more)	1946	600-800
Federal #57	(T)	wooden, 1 dial	1922	400-500
Federal #61	(T)	metal, 3 dials	1923	700-900
Federal #58DX	(T)	metal, "Orthosonic"	1922	400-500
Freshman #SF2	(T)	wooden, 3 dials, "Masterpiece"	1924	90-120
G.E. Clock Radio	(T)	pink plastic	1960	18-22
General Electric #675	(TR)		1956	80-100
Goulden's Mustard Jar	(A)	Goulden's Mustard	1982	30-40
Grand Old Granddad bottle	(A)	Whiskey	1965	45-65
Grebe #CR5	(T)	wooden, 3 dials	1921	400-500
Grebe #MU1	(T)	wooden, "Synchrophase"	1925	150-200
Helping Hand	(A)	Hamburger Helper	1980	30-40
Hitachi #666	(TR)	pocket, red or gray	1958	80-120
Hopalong Cassidy	(N)	Arvin	1950	300-400
Kadette Jewel	(T)	plastic, various models	1935	200-300
Knight's Helmet w/ Crest	(N)		1970	30-40
Lafayette #D140	(T)	ivory plastic deco	1939	90-110
Little Sprout	(A)	Green Giant	1980	30-40
Lone Ranger	(N)	Airline	1951	500-800
Magnavox #TRF5	(T)	wooden, doors	1925	80-120
Manola	(TR)	table red plastic	1958	20-30
Mercedes Auto Grill	(N)		1965	30-40
Mickey Mouse	(N)	brown case	1940	1200-1800
Mork Egg Radio	(N)		1978	30-50

MAKE	TYPE	DESCRIPTION	DATE	VALUE
Motorola	(P)	"V" shield, handle turns	1958	$ 40-60
Motorola	(T)	aqua plastic clock radio	1958	20-30
New World (globe & stand)	(N)	Colonial	1933	800-1200
Philco	(T)	brown plastic, "services" dial	1954	25-40
Philco #525			1929	90-120
Philco #49501	(T)	boomerang Transitone	1949	200-300
Philco #T7	(TR)	black and white	1958	60-80
Philco Cathedral	(T)	wooden	1931	150-200
Polaroid 600 Plus	(A)	Polaroid Film	1980	25-35
Punchy	(A)	Hawaiian Punch	1972	40-60
Raid Bug Clock Radio	(A)	Raid Insecticide	1980	80-120
RCA Radiola X	(T)	wooden	1925	300-400
RCA Aeriola Jr.	(C)		1922	120-180
RCA Radiola 26	(P)	wooden	1925	300-400
RCA #7QBK	(F)		1940	80-100
Regency #TR1	(TR)	white or black, pocket	1954	250-350
Snow White (tan case)	N	Emerson	1938	1000-1500
Sony #TR63	(TR)	pocket	1957	300-400
Spartan #558	(T)	blue mirror, deco	1937	200-3000
Stromberg Carlson Clock Radio	(T)	gray & salmon plastic	1957	20-30
Tide Box	(A)	Tide Detergent	1980	40-50
Tony the Tiger	(A)	Sugar Frosted Flakes	1980	35-45
Toshiba #5TR	(TR)	lacey face plate	1958	150-200
Westinghouse	(A)	aqua plastic, tapering shield	1960	18-25
Westinghouse #H685	(TR)	table top with clock	1959	20-30
Zenith #64	(F)	ornate chest on stand	1919	350-450
Zenith #L515 Clock Radio	(T)	brown, dashboard look	1954	75-100
Zenith Royal #500	(TR)	pocket, black	1956	80-100

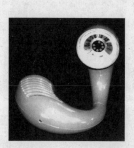

Clockwise from right: Panasonic, 1970s, $18-$22; Zenith dashboard style, $75-$100; Motorola with rotating handle, 1950s, $40-$60.

Wood

While many types of wood items are highly sought after collectibles, this section lists wooden kitchen utensils. Wooden utensils are most commonly made of maple. Other woods used include cedar, pine, hickory, ash and oak. Prices vary depending on item and type of wood.

Burlwood examples are usually worth triple the value (or more!) of plainer grained woods. The greater the burl, the greater the value.

	LOW	AVG.	HIGH
Apple Butter Bucket, bail handle, c. 1850, len. 10"	$ 250	$ 300	$ 350
Apple Butter Paddle, drilled holes, len. 30"	130	160	190
Apple Butter Paddle, paddle stirrer, perforated spatula, len. 60"	110	140	170
Apple Butter Scoop, maple, c. 1850s	500	600	700
Apple Drying Rack, open slats, 3 sided, legged, c. 1870	250	300	350
Apple Parers, clamp, clank, 2 gears, drip board	450	475	500
Apple Peelers, crank handle, 2 size, belt driven gears	380	410	440
Apple Peelers, hardwood gears, c. 1700s	400	500	600
Apple Peelers, wooden with iron gears, 7" x 14"	400	450	500
Bandbox, egg shaped, plain, len. 5"	140	170	200
Barrel, for pickles, staved, 2 concentric wood bands, 12" x 20"	80	115	150
Barrel, nutmeg storage, enameled yellow, dia. 4"	70	95	120
Bread Raiser, lid, tin, len. 12"	100	125	150
Broom, flat, birch splint, bound w/ iron, spindled, maple handle	350	370	390
Broom, oak splint	150	200	250
Bucket, mincemeat, lid, concave, dia. 11"	200	215	230
Bucket, oak, for well	100	140	180
Bucket, sap, dia. 9.5"	310	345	380
Bucket, sugar, floor standing, red	580	635	690
Bucket, sugar, loop handles, lid, flat handle, c. 1890, dia. 5"	380	405	430
Bucket, sugar, stave constructed, enameled, dia. 13"	290	310	330
Bucket, tin top, walnut, "S" shaped legs, dia. 17"	350	370	390
Bucket, water, one piece wood, side handles, rope bail	240	280	320
Butcher's Block, sycamore, decoratively carved	1400	1600	1700
Butter Churn, cylinder type, white cedar, one gallon	160	175	190
Candlestick, adjustable stem, English, c. 1790, ht. 8"	2800	3100	3400
Candlestick, walnut, c. 1760, dia. 6"	680	750	820
Clothes Wringer, crank, handle and roller	40	50	60
Coaster, 18th century, treen, octagonal	500	550	600
Coaster, oak, English, c. 1810, dia. 12"	2500	2750	3000
Coffee and Spice Mill, c. 1760, ht. 9"	2500	3000	3500
Coffee Grinder, 19th century, wooden, French maker	160	200	240
Coffee Grinder, box type	170	210	250

	LOW	AVG.	HIGH
Coffee Grinder, drawer, wooden base	$ 180	$ 200	$ 220
Coffee Grinder, lap, cherry box, brass fittings, crank	200	245	290
Coffee Grinder, lap, oak	170	200	230
Coffee Grinder, lap type, handled, cherry	220	240	260
Coffee Grinder, wood, carved handle	130	170	210
Coffee Mill, hand crank, iron blade, storage box	130	150	170
Colander, wooden, circular, c. 1700s	600	700	800
Cookie Board, carved pattern, walnut, len. 8"	140	165	190
Cookie Board, divided into squares, different molded design, len. 6"	50	70	90
Cookie Board, walnut construction, grape relief design, len. 9"	40	60	80
Lemon Squeezer, 11"	50	65	80
Lemon Squeezer, all wood construction, short handle, ridged press	50	60	70
Lemon Squeezer, hinged, all wood	70	85	100
Lemon Squeezer, hinged, wood frame, wood and ceramic, hinged, press is perforated	60	80	100
Lemon Squeezer, len. 8"	110	140	170
Lemon Squeezer, len. 9"	140	165	190
Lemon Squeezer, on frame, indentation and drain holes, 3 turned legs, c. 1775	290	430	570
Lemon Squeezer, wood and nickel alloy, juicer is perforated	70	90	110
Lemon Squeezer, wood and tin, hinged, perforated	70	85	100
Lemon Squeezer, wooden, on stand, 14" x 9"	240	270	300
Mortar and Pestle, bird's eye maple, early	150	185	220
Muffineer, Tunbridge ware, c. 1790	380	435	490
Noodle Board, wooden circle with paddle handle, len. 24"	180	205	230
Noodle Roller, maple, perforated crank, c. 1840, len. 21"	10	115	220
Noodle Rolling Pin	30	45	60
Nutcracker, 18th century	450	530	610
Nutcracker, bear's head, len. 9"	140	175	210
Nutcracker, large size, c. 1750, 10" long	400	460	520
Nutcracker, wood with iron presses, c. 1650, len. 5.5"	730	805	880
Toddy Stick, early 19th century	40	70	100
Toddy Stick, pestle style, hand carved, turned wood	20	30	40
Washtub, oak slats. natural varnish, len. 23"	160	190	220
Whisk Broom, Fuller Brush Company, len. 8"	90	115	140
Wood Churn, staved, dasher, four gallon capacity	480	565	650
Wood Frame Churn, windmill paddles, side turn handle, ht. 15"	470	520	570
Wooden Box, Shaker	440	485	530
Wooden Shovel, grain	570	640	710
Wooden Wash Bowl, chestnut, c. 1790	280	350	420
Wool Comb, carved handle, len. 13"	30	50	70
Yarn Winder, box-type, spindle suspended on spike over box, 18"	70	90	110
Yarn Winder, duck feet	210	265	320
Yarn Winder, floor model, spindled legs, yard counter, knobbed end	170	220	270
Yarn Winder, maple	220	265	310

Jewelry and Clothing

Belt Buckles

The interest in belt buckles has grown with vintage clothing. They can be found in thrift shops and second-hand clothing stores, as well as in pawn shops, antique shops, and flea markets. For further information see *The Official Price Guide to Antique Jewelry*, by Arthur Guy Kaplan, House of Collectibles, Random House, NY.

	LOW	AVG.	HIGH
Cameo motif, carved lava, gold-plated, c. 1880	$ 350	$ 385	$ 420
Circular motif buckle, beaded edge & slide, sterling, Amer., c. 1898	220	240	260
Cluster motif, pr., rhinestone, white metal, c. 1935	20	30	40
Fan & scroll motif, champleve black & white enamel, gold, 1870	1800	2000	2200
Fancy shape motif, pr., rhinestone, white metal, c. 1935	20	30	40
Oval Etruscan granulation motif, buckle pin, gold, c. 1870	380	415	450
Oval motif, pr., cut steel, c. 1890	60	75	90
Oval motif, paste, silver	600	750	900
Oval wreath motif pr. of buckles, cut steel, c. 1890	40	55	70
Rect. buckle and floral motif slide, floral motif belt, sterling, Amer., c. 1896	120	140	160
Rect. buckle, beaded rim & slide, sterling silver, Amer., 1896	140	170	200
Rect. flower motif pr. of buckles, cut steel, marked: "France", c. 1900	60	80	100
Rect. motif, pr., silver plated, mid 20th	20	35	50
Rect., pr., engraved, sterling , c. 1920	80	115	150
Ribbon and leaf motif, gold, French, c. 1870	1500	1680	1850
Scroll and flower motif, cloisonné and guiliocho enamel, Arts and Crafts, c. 1890	400	460	520
Scroll motif, buckle and button set, translucent green enamel, silver, English, c. 1925	350	425	500
Scroll motif, gold, c. 1890	700	1000	1300
Scroll motif w/ slide, sterling silver, Amer., c. 1898	290	305	320
Scroll motif w/ slide, with beaded rim, sterling, Amer., c. 1896	210	230	250
Shell motif buckle, 2 diamonds, 6 demantoid garnets, gold, c. 1880	2000	2400	2800
Snake motif buckle, enameled, 3 diamonds, gold, c. 1880	2500	3000	3500
Square crescent motif, pr., cut steel, c. 1975	60	70	80
Square motif buckle, seed pearl border, cobalt blue enamel, 14K gold, c. 1920	480	540	600
Square motif buckle, with beaded edge and slide with beaded edge, sterling, Amer., c. 1898	250	270	290
Wide Rect. motif w/ slide, sterling, Amer., c. 1898	140	170	200

Buttons

Buttons are something we use every day but rarely think about. To the collector, however, buttons are tiny treasures full of history, made of wonderful materials and endless variety. Beautiful, small, and for the most part reasonably priced, buttons make an ideal collectible.

Though buttons date back many centuries, button collecting began in this country in the 1930s. In 1938 the National Button Society was formed. Its members wrote many excellent books in the 1940s and '50s.

Collectors look for a wide range of buttons, from 18th-century porcelains, hand painted enamels and carved ivory to mother-of-pearl, black glass and intricate metals. Most buttons available today are 19th or 20th century. They range in price from as little as 25¢ each to several hundred dollars for some of the rarest varieties. Among the more recent buttons attracting attention are Bakelite, Art Deco, and plastic "realistics." Materials include horn, tin, brass, glass, plastic, ivory, porcelain, bone, shell, and sterling. They may be plain or highly decorated. There are many good examples of military buttons from the Civil War and earlier. Picture buttons may depict historical or biblical scenes, heads of famous people, and animals. As with all collectibles, condition is a major factor in the price. Chips, rust or other damage generally make a button uncollectible.

Our consultant for this area is Adam G. Perl, owner of Pastimes Antiques in Ithaca, NY. He is listed at the back of this book.

	LOW	AVG.	HIGH
Black Glass, cameo head	$ 12	$ 15	$ 18
Black Glass, elephant under palm tree	7	9	10
Black Glass, faceted ball, gold foil top	35	40	45
Black Glass, mountain w/ house scene, beaded gilt edge	35	40	45
Black Glass, shape of a slipper	10	13	15
Black Onyx, gold-filled, ball-shaped, 19th century	20	25	30
Black Onyx, w/ 14K gold, ball-shaped, 19th century	60	65	70
Brass, Aesop's Fable, frog and rabbit	30	35	40
Brass, Aesop's Fable, 2 mice	35	40	45
Brass, angry rooster	10	13	15
Brass, cherubs w/ cornucopia and goat	4	5	6
Brass, children playing game, Victorian era	20	25	30
Brass, dancing gypsy girl w/ goat	45	55	65
Brass Disc, bridge and river scene, black and white	75	90	105
Brass, Indian hunter	35	40	45
Brass, mother feeding child, high relief	20	25	30
Brass, rooster standing on wheat shaft	15	20	25
Celluloid, angel head, gold background, gilt rims	35	40	45
Celluloid, Count Fersen, floral brass frame	20	25	30
Celluloid, Duchess of Devonshire, pastel colors	42	48	55
Celluloid, Marie Antoinette	10	13	15
Ceramic, bird, black and white	25	30	35
Ceramic, bird w/ branch in beak, scalloped border	35	40	45
Ceramic, Cupid, scroll design on edge	45	50	55
Cloisonné, birds flying, brass, black & white w/ red background	80	90	100
Enamel, lady riding bicycle, cut steel border	60	65	70
Enamel, lighthouse w/ boat scene	45	50	55
Enamel, maiden, blue and white, diamond paste border	50	55	60
Enamel, portrait of lady, black background, 18th c.	60	68	75
Enamel, rose color scene on wht, emb. scroll border	200	220	240
Enamel, shepherdess, light purple, diamond paste border	45	50	55
Enamel, star shape decorated w/ cut steels	16	21	25

	LOW	AVG.	HIGH
Enamel, w/ seed pearls and 14K gold, lady bug design, 19th century ... $ 550	$ 650	$ 750
Enamel, woman at fountain 55	65	75
Glass, black liberty cap and flag, silver frame, 18th century 55	65	75
Glass, French Revolution motif, copper rim 70	79	88
Glass, molded opaque, brown bird design 25	30	35
Gold, 14K, ball shape w/ ribbing, 19th century 60	65	70
Gold, 14K, button set w/ chain, 19th century 50	55	60
Gold, 14K, engraved collar button, 19th century 30	32	35
Gold, 14K, pearl shape, 19th century 60	65	70
Gold, 14K, scrolled edge design, 19th century 60	65	70
Gold, woven hair under swirls, cartwheel design, 19th century 110	120	130
Gold, woven hair under swirls, cartwheel design, scalloped edge, 19th c. 130	140	150
Gold-filled, ball shape w/ ribbing, 19th century 20	23	26
Gold-plated, dragon 7	10	12
Ivory, carved Royal Salamander 30	35	40
Ivory, cut-out girl and bird, blue background 150	165	180
Ivory, painted cherub in chariot drawn by two horses 90	100	110
Ivory, painted girl and dog chasing butterflies 90	100	110
Ivory, painted lady and dog, silver rim 40	50	60
Ivory, painted Oriental head 35	40	45
Mother-of-Pearl, 14K gold, simple button, 19th century 75	80	85
Oriental, fan design, multicolored, scalloped border 30	35	40
Oriental, floral motif, enameled 35	40	45
Pewter, owl's head 4	5	6
Pierced Brass, Little Red Riding Hood 13	17	20
Porcelain, cherub catching butterflies, pink and white 20	25	30
Porcelain, cupid, scroll design on edge 45	55	65
Porcelain, flowers and butterfly, 18th century 15	20	25
Porcelain, pasture scene w/ children 30	35	40
Porcelain, w/ gold, painted angels, 19th century 500	530	560
Silver, Bacchus, God of Wine, etched design 25	30	35
Stamped Brass, 2 children fighting 20	25	30
Steel, floral design 4	6	8
Turquoise, w/ 14K gold, button set w/ chain, 19th century 95	100	105
Victorian Figure, black glass disc 8	10	12
Wedgwood, classical fig., white on royal blue, gilt rim, 18th century .. 225	250	275
Wedgwood, classical fig., white relief on blue cut steel border, 18th c. .. 250	270	290
Wedgwood, classical figures, white relief on light blue 50	60	70
Wedgwood, floral design, diamond paste border, silver frame 200	225	250
Wedgwood, warrior, copper border, white relief on royal blue 225	250	275

From left to right: Celluloid castle button, $35-$45; lithographed celluloid lady's Head In Profile, $35-$55; pair of floral enamel buttons each, $30-$40; glass bear claw button, $18-$25. — Items courtesy of Pastimes.

Clothing

Vintage clothing is collected by those who wish to add it to their wardrobes as well as by collectors who wish only to display it. Currently, most market activity is in clothes from the 1920s, 1930s, and 1940s. Alterations and construction details are factors in determining price, while skilled workmanship or handmade trims often increase value. Clothing with beadwork is also a good investment.

Vintage clothing requires careful handling. Textiles are perishable: light, humidity, dust, and body oil are potentially harmful. The acids in wood, cardboard, and tissue paper can also hurt clothing. When storing pieces, it is best to wrap items in white sheets and use mothballs. Hang lightweight clothing on padded hangers, and store heavy clothing laid flat.

For further information, contact The Costume Society of America, c/o The Costume Institute, The Metropolitan Museum of Art, New York, NY 10028.

	LOW	AVG.	HIGH
Apron, embroidered, Hungarian, c. 1930	$ 30	$ 45	$ 60
Baby Shoes, hand-stitched satin, moccasin-style lowers, ribbon drawstring through uppers	10	20	30
Baby Shoes, kidskin leather button shoes, 3 buttons on uppers, c. 1880	35	50	65
Baby Shoes, velvet top button on shoes, leather lowers, 5 buttons on uppers, c. 1880	50	75	100
Baby Slippers, white kid Mary Janes, strap, mother-of-pearl button, soft leather sole	30	50	70
Bonnet, for Christening, lace w/ white silk tie ribbons	25	45	35
Coin Purse, nickel-plated metal w/ mother-of-pearl panels, compartments in red leatherette	12	20	28
Dress, black faille damask, cap sleeves, belt, c. 1940	75	90	115
Dress, floor length, horizontal stripes, metallic thread, tiered	60	100	140
Dress, for child, tucked bib, lace trim, embroidered	30	60	90
Dress, handmade traveling dress, c. 1890	200	240	280
Dress, for infant, scalloped collar, embroidered	25	50	75
Evening Bag, Victorian, crochet flowers, metal beads	115	130	145
Evening Bag, Victorian, petit point flowers on silk	100	115	130
Gloves, cotton crochet, c. 1890	14	22	16
Gloves, long, brown suede	20	30	40
Gloves, short, white kid	15	20	25
Gloves, white cotton	8	16	24
Hat, fox fur	15	30	45
Hat, man's beaver top hat, c. 1910	45	65	85
Mantilla, Blonde de Caen lace, cream-colored, c. 1820	120	160	190
Purse, clear crystal beads, white cloth liner, drawstring, beaded decoration, c. 1925	50	60	70
Robe, embroidered silk, Japanese, c. 1890	300	350	400
Shawl, peach silk, bright silk embroidered flowers, c. 1925	250	300	350
Skirt, crocheted, floor length, fringed bottom	30	50	40
Wedding Gown, lace, satin, pearls and white beaded flowers, high neck, cap sleeves, train, c. 1965	100	150	100

Fans

Folding fans were fashionable accessories for women during the 18th, 19th, and even into the early 20th centuries. They used fans not only to show one's social position and wealth, but for coquetry or flirting. In Asia men as well as women utilized them, from the scented fans of the elderly, to the black and red implements of the military. A popular export item (particularly the delicate ivory fans, carved under water and much sought after as wedding gifts), fans served many functions in Asian society.

Craftsmen constructed fans in several ways. The most common method was the insertion of sticks into a pleated piece of material called a "leaf." Leaves were made of silk lace, paper, or even vellum (very thin goatskin). Another type of folding fan was called a "brise." The brise fan was made of wide, overlapping sticks, joined by a ribbon. Nearly all fans of both types have scenes or designs painted on them. Another type, considered quite stylish from the 1870s until about 1910, was the feather fan. Usually made of ostrich feathers, this type is quite perishable.

Beautifully drawn, painted, or inscribed, Asian fans fell into two main structural categories. Women's fans usually did not fold, consisting of a piece of paper glued to a flat bamboo handle. Folding fans, used more extensively in ritual ceremonies, or by high born citizens, were made of paper or silk, with wooden, bamboo, ivory, or mother-of-pearl ribs.

	LOW	AVG.	HIGH
Advertising, Hires Root Beer, 6.5", c. 1930	$ 20	$ 25	$ 30
Advertising, Homer's 5¢ Cigar, 7", c. 1910	20	25	30
Black Net, with sequins	40	55	70
Bride's, lace, hand painted	40	55	70
Bride's, lace, sequins, ivory sticks	70	85	100
Brise, child's, painted, ribbon and floral design	120	140	160
Brise, gilded, painted with three vignettes, loop	240	285	330
Brise, Regency, painted floral design, amber guards	240	255	270
Brise, Regency, painted vase of flowers	70	100	130
Celluloid, carved flower	70	95	120
Celluloid, miniature	80	100	120
Celluloid, Oriental design	40	50	60
Celluloid, sequins, chiffon	80	95	110
Feather, celluloid sticks	90	105	120
Feather, ivory sticks	190	240	290
Feather, painted, c. 1870	190	220	250
Feather, signed Duvelleroy, c. 1865	900	1100	1300
Feather, small, c. 1890	220	250	280
Feather, tortoiseshell sticks	200	215	230
French, painted, carved, signed	150	160	170
French, painted, ivory sticks	310	355	400
French, painted, signed Jolivet, c. 1870	900	1225	1550
French, painted, tortoise sticks, sequins	300	165	30
Garrett Snuff, advertising, paper, c. 1928	30	35	40
George Washington and Cherry Smash, lithographed	40	55	70
Gold edge, pink silk, ebony ribs	50	60	70
Hand painted, floral design, wood	40	50	60
Horn, carved, painted pansies, blue ribbon	180	230	280
Lacquered, black, silver flower	130	145	160
Lacquered, white, silver handle	110	125	140
Marabou feathers, satin, hand painted, 20"	250	280	310

	LOW	AVG.	HIGH
Oriental, bamboo, 7" x 20",1900s, signed Liang Zhuang-chong	$ 900	$ 1100	$ 1300
Oriental, bamboo and birds, 8" x 23", c. 1820-1875, signed by Hezhong	800	1100	1400
Oriental, bird and fruit blossoms, 6" x 18", c. 1820-1865, by Ren Vi	4000	5000	6000
Oriental, blossom, 7" x 21", c. 1820-1875, by Hu Gongshou	900	1100	1300
Oriental, blossoms, 8" x 21", c. 1820-1875, by Hu Gongshou	1000	1300	1600
Oriental, calligraphy, 6" x 21", c. 1620-1665, by Ylin	2000	2300	2600
Oriental, calligraphy, 7" x 20", c. 1820-1895, by Liu Rongsi	800	1100	1400
Oriental, female, 7" x 21", c. 1820-1875, figure preparing to mount horse, by Gu Luo	1000	1315	1630
Oriental, fruit and blossoms, 7" x 21", c. 1820-1875, by Dong Qichang	1160	1485	1810
Oriental, landscape, 7" x 20", 1620-1665, artist unknown	2000	3000	4000
Oriental, landscape, 7" x 20", c. 1720-1795, by Huang Vi	2100	2325	2550
Oriental, landscape, 7" x 20", c. 1820-1890, by Da Jian	600	850	1100
Oriental, landscape, 7" x 21", c. 1820-1875, by Vongbo	1000	1300	1600
Oriental, landscape, 7" x 22", c. 1720-1795, by Fang Shishu	1620	2425	3230
Oriental, magnolia, 6" x 18", c. 1910-1930, by Shao'ang	4000	5000	6000
Oriental, man and youth, 7" x 20", c. 1820-1875, by Fena Ning	900	1100	1300
Oriental, man at table 7" x 20", c. 1820-1875, by Ron Xun	2000	2500	3000
Oriental, mountain scene, 8" x 22", by Juru Bao	800	1050	1300
Oriental, poem, 7" x 22", c. 1620-1665, by Shu Vouzhang	1100	1200	1300
Oriental, poem, 8" x 21",c. 1820-1870, artist unknown	840	1060	1280
Oriental, poem in character, 7" x 20", c. 1620-1685, by Jiang Jie	1400	1700	2000
Oriental, riverscape, 6" x 20", by Shu Youzhang	1000	1500	2000
Oriental, rocks and bamboo, 7" x 21", c. 1890-1910	700	850	1000
Ostrich plume, tortoise shell sticks	80	100	120
Purl sticks, sequin design, 8"	70	80	90
Puzzle, four scones, two-way opening	275	325	375
Satin flower center, carved, ivory sticks	300	335	370
Silk, embroidered, ivory sticks	130	155	180
Silk, hand painted animal figure and books	40	55	70
Silk, hand painted figures and floral designs, original box	130	150	170
Silk, Oriental design, ivory and bamboo	80	95	110
Souvenir Centennial, historical buildings, 12"	175	200	225
Wedding, ivory sticks, lace	120	135	150

Watches

Fine watches contain a varying number of jewels within the mechanism to reduce friction and wear. They improve the accuracy of the watch and hence add to its value. The more jewels contained in the movement, the more valuable the watch.

We abbreviate "jewel" as "j" (e.g., 15j means 15 jewels). American pocket watch movements are described in standard sizes (abbreviated as "s" in this book), ranging from 20s to 0s, 00s, 000s, etc. The most common pocket watch size is 18s, or 1.766". Other popular sizes include 16s (1.7"), 12s (1.566"), 10s (1.5"), 0s (1.166"), and 000s (1.1").

Various fakes are on the market including 24j examples of Illinois and Rockford watches. During the second half of the 19th century, the fledgling Swiss watch industry imitated the better quality American-made pocket watches with deceivingly similar names. They are still not as valuable as the American originals.

For further information, see *The Official Price Guide to Watches*, by Cooksey Shugart and Tom Engle, House of Collectibles, Random House, NY.

Wrist Watches

	LOW	AVG.	HIGH
Alpina, 15j, automatic, waterproof, gold-filled	$ 30	$ 40	$ 50
Alpina, 17j, 18k	200	250	300
American Waltham, 17j, barrel shaped dial, c. 1920, 14k	500	550	600
American Waltham, 17j, cromwell	75	100	125
American Waltham, 17j, oberlin	75	100	125
American Waltham, 17j	100	300	500
American Waltham, wandering minute, jumping hour, 2 windows, c. 1933	700	950	1200
American Waltham, 17j, stan hope	75	100	125
American Waltham, Winfield	75	100	125
American Waltham, Albright, 21j	100	125	150
American Waltham, 21j, Sheraton	125	150	175
American Waltham, 15j, protective grill, c. 1907	1200	1350	1500
American Waltham, 17j, with hackset stainless steel	50	62	75
American Waltham, 17j, curvex	200	450	700
American Waltham, 17j, triangular, Masonic symbols, c. 1950	1800	2150	2500
Angelus, 17j, c. 1943, 18k	700	900	1100
Angelus, same, 14k	400	500	600
Angelus, same, gold-filled	150	200	250
Angelus, 27j, quarter repeater, stainless steel	2500	2750	3000
Aramis, 15j, self-winding, c. 1933, stainless steel	600	750	900
Arbu, 17j, triple date, moon phase, 18k	800	1000	1200
Arbu, 17j, double cronog., stainless steel	200	300	400
Aristo, 17j, cronog., stainless steel	100	162	225
ARSA, 15-17j, moon phase, 18k	900	1050	1200
ARSA, same, stainless steel	300	350	400
Asprey, 16-17j, 9k	200	350	500
Asprey- 15j, duo-dial, 18k	1500	1850	2200
Audemars Piguet, 29j, repeater, c. 1907, 18k	100,000	110,000	120,000
Audemars Piguet, 19j, tourbillon, sundial design, 18k	15,000	16,500	18,000
Audemars Piguet, 36j, octaganal case, triple date, moon phase, 18k	5,000	18,500	22,000
Audemars Piguet, 18j, "Le Brassus," skeletonized, 18k	20,000	22,500	25,000
Audemars Piguet, 17-18j, other skeletonized models, 18k	5000	6750	8500

	LOW	AVG.	HIGH
Audemars Piguet, 17-36j, modern .... $ 1200		$ 2600	$ 4000
Autorist, 15j, lug action 400		900	1400
Ball W. Co., 25j 375		438	500
Baume and Mercier, 17-18j, 14k or stainless steel 400		550	700
Baume and Mercier, 17-18j, 18k, triple chrono. 1200		1900	2600
Benrus, 15-18j, mystery diamond dial, 18k 500		600	700
Benrus, 15j, date, c.1948, stainless steel 50		60	70
Benrus, 15j, c.1950, 14k or gold-filled 100		175	250
Breguet, 21j, skeletonized, 18k, c&b 7000		7500	8000
Breguet, 17j, chronog., triple date, moon phase, stainless steel 8000		9000	10,000
Breguet, 17j, silver dial, Finn model, 18k 1200		1400	1600
Breitling, 17j, chronog., Chronomat, 18k 1500		1600	1700
Breitling, 17j, chronog., Chronomat, 18k, gold-filled 300		400	500
Breitling, 17j, chronog., Chronomat, 18k, stainless steel 250		350	450
Breitling, 17j, chronog., Navitimer, 18k 3000		3300	3600
Breitling, 17j, chronog., Navitimer, 18k, stainless steel 500		600	700
Bueche-Girod, 17j 600		700	800
Bulova, Accutron "spaceview," 14k 400		550	700
Bulova, Accutron "spaceview," 18k 600		700	800
Bulova, Accutron "spaceview," stainless steel 100		175	250
Bulova, diamond dial, rectangular, late '30s-early '40s 200		275	350
Bulova, 17j, duo-dial, c1935, stainless steel 300		350	400
Bulova, 17j, fancy bezel, 14k or gold-filled 100		200	300
Chevrolet, 6j, in form of car radiator, c. 1927, silver 400		500	600
Cheopard, 18j, skeletonized, diamond dial and hands, 18k 4000		4500	5000
Clebar, 17j, chronog., stainless steel 75		88	100
Concord -17j, 14k 125		150	175
Cortebort, 15-17j, gold-filled or stainless steel 50		75	100
Cortebort, 17j, "sport," triple date, moon phase, 18k 1000		1200	1400
Corum, 17j, in form of Rolls Royce car radiator, 18k 1800		2000	2200
Corum, 17-21j, 18k 400		650	900
Croton, 17j, diamond bezel, 14k 700		800	900
Croton, 17j, chronog., stainless steel 100		125	150
Cyma, 17j, 18k 200		250	300
Cyma, 17j, 14k 175		212	250
Cyma, 17j, stainless steel 65		75	85
Daynite, 7j, 8-day movement, stainless steel 250		325	400
P. Ditisheim, 17j, "Solvil," diamond dial, platinum 700		1150	1600
Dome, 25j, triple dates, 18k 500		600	700
Doxa, 17j, chronog., triple dates, moon phase 1100		1300	1500
Doxa, 17j, center sec., w/ or w/out chronog., 14k or stainless steel 100		200	300
Ebel, 21j, chronog., perpetual calendar, 18k 7000		8000	9000
Ebel, 17-18j, chronog. 400		525	650
Ebel, 17j, slide open to wind, silver 200		250	300
Eberhard, 18j, split sec., chronog., 3 reg., 18k 6000		8000	10,000
Eberhard, 17j, tele-tachymeter, c1930, 18k 2500		3000	3500
Eberhard, 17j, chronog., stainless steel 400		500	600
Electra W. Co., 17j,. chronog., silver 500		600	700
Elgin, 17j, rectangular, 14k 200		275	350
Elgin, 15-17j, rectangular, gold-filled 100		120	140
Elgin, 7j, gold-filled 60		130	200

	LOW	AVG.	HIGH
Elgin, 7j, stainless steel	$ 50	$ 65	$ 80
Elgin, 15j, "Official Boy Scout Model," stainless steel	100	138	175
Elgin, same, 7j, stainless steel	50	68	85
Elgin, 15j, round dial, aux. sec., silver	150	188	225
Lord Elgin, 17-21j, stepped case, fancy bezel, gold-filled	100	120	140
Enicar -17j, stainless steel	30	40	50
Eska, 17j, enamel dial, 18k	3000	3500	4000
Evans, 17j, chronog., 2 reg., c. 1940, 18k	300	400	500
Gallet, 15j, autowind, stainless	50	75	100
Gallet, 17j	200	300	400
Geneve, 15j, dual dial	300	350	400
Girard-Perragaux, 39j	300	350	400
Glycine- 17-18j	100	150	200
Grouen, 17j, curvex	200	300	400
Grouen, 17j, double dial	500	600	700
Grouen, 17j, autowind	300	400	500
E. Gubelin, 19j, 18k	400	500	600
E. Gubelin, 25j, triple date	3000	4000	5000
Hamilton, Altair	500	600	700
Hamilton, Clearview	100	150	200
Hamilton, Meteor	200	250	300
Hamilton, Pacer	150	200	250
Hamilton, Skip Jack	70	80	90
Hamilton, Vantage	150	200	250
Hamilton, Victor II	150	200	250
Hamilton, Ventura	1000	1500	2000
Hamilton, Otis, reversible	1200	1500	1800
Hamilton, Bolton	100	150	200
Hamilton, Brock	100	150	200
Hamilton, Dunkirk	300	400	500
Hamilton, Essex	100	150	200
Hamilton, Lee	100	150	200
Hamilton, Midas	300	350	400
Hamilton, Perry	100	125	150
Hamilton, Winthrop	200	250	300
Hamilton, Yorktown	150	175	200
Hampton, 15j	75	125	175
Harvard, 17j	50	100	150
Helbros, 17j	200	250	300
Hydepark, 17j, flip top	400	500	600
Illinois, 17j, Aviator	150	200	250
Illinois, Chieftain	300	400	500
Illinois, Console	300	400	500
Illinois, Jolly Roger	200	250	300
Illinois, Major	200	250	300
Illinois, Picadilly	500	600	700
Illinois, Pilot	150	200	250
Illinois, Speedway	200	250	300
Ingersoll, Radiolite dial	10	20	30
Ingersoll, Grill cover	50	60	70
Ingraham, 7j, Wristfit	5	10	15

	LOW	AVG.	HIGH
International, 17j, 14k	$ 500	$ 750	$ 1000
International, 17j, 18k	800	1000	1200
International, 36j, Da Vinci	6000	7500	9000
Jewel, 15j, dual dial	200	250	300
Kurth, 17j, Certina	30	40	50
Le Coultre, 17j	400	500	600
Le Coultre, 17j, Astronomic	1500	2000	2500
Le Coultre, 17j, Reverso, 18k	6000	7500	9000
Le Coultre, 17j, Reverso, stainless	2000	2500	3000
Lemania, 17j, stainless	50	60	70
Lemania, 17j, chronog., 18k	600	750	900
Lip, stainless	200	300	400
Longines, 17j, Lindberg, 18k	35,000	40,000	45,000
Longines, 17j, Lindberg, silver	8000	9000	10,000
Longines, 17j, Lindberg, nickel	6000	7500	9000
Longines, 17j, chronog.	500	1000	1500
Longines, 17j, diamond dial, 14k	400	500	600
Longines, 17j, flared	400	600	800
Mappin, 15j, dual dial	1000	1250	1500
Meylan, 27j, chronog.	800	1000	1200
Mido, 15j, car radiator	2000	2500	3000
Mido, 17j, multifort	150	200	250
Mido, 17j, chronog.	500	600	700
Minerva, 29j, repeater	40,000	50,000	60,000
Minerva, 17j, chronog., stainless	200	300	400
Minerva, 17j, autowind	70	85	100
Monarch, 7j	50	75	100
Movado, 17j, polypan, elongated	5000	7500	10,000
Movado, Calendarmeto (center opening)	600	750	900
Movado, 15j	400	500	600
U. Nardin, 17j, chronog.	2000	3000	4000
U. Nardin, 29j, Astrolabium	6000	7500	9000
National, 17j	50	100	150
New Haven, 7j	10	15	20
Omega, 17j, Seamaster, 14k	1500	2000	2500
Omega, 17j, Seamaster, stainless	800	1000	1200
Omega, 17j, Flightmaster	6000	7000	8000
Omega, 17j	300	400	500
Orvin, 17j	70	80	90
Patek Philippe, 18j, Gilbert Albert design, 18k	40,000	45,000	50,000
Patek Philippe, 18j, asymmetric, 18k	20,000	25,000	30,000
Patek Philippe, 18j, asymmetric, platinum	30,000	35,000	40,000
Patek Philippe, 18j	4000	5000	6000
Patek Philippe, 18j, flared case	8000	10,000	12,000
Piaget, 18j, $20 gold piece	2000	2250	2500
Piaget, 18j	400	550	700
Record, 17j, 4-dial chronog.	5000	6000	7000
Roamer, 17-23j	30	45	60
Rolex, 26j, Milgauss, stainless	400	500	600
Rolex, 17j, Daytona, 18k	10,000	12,500	15,000
Rolex, 17j, Daytona, stainless	2000	2250	2500

	LOW	AVG.	HIGH
Rolex, 17j, Prince, dual dial, 18k	$ 6000	$ 7500	$ 9000
Rolex, 17j, Prince, dual dial, silver	3000	4000	5000
Rolex, 17j, Prince, dual dial, stainless	2000	3000	4000
Rolex, 26j, Presidential, diamond dial	5000	7000	9000
Rolex, 26j, GMT-Master	4000	5000	6000
Rolex, 26j, Submariner, 18k	6000	7500	9000
Rolex, 26j, Submariner, stainless	600	800	1000
Rolex, 17j, Benvenuto Cellini	1500	2000	2500
Tiffany, 26j, repeater, automaton	8000	10,000	12,000
Tiffany, 15-21j	1000	1250	1500
Universal, 17j, chronog., 18k	2000	3000	4000
Universal, 17j, chronog., stainless	400	600	800
Vacheron, 17j, triple date	5000	7000	9000
Vacheron, 18j, 18k	2000	3000	4000
Zenith, 19j	100	125	150
Zenith, 17j, chronog., 18k	1000	1250	1500
Zenith, 36j, stainless	500	600	700

Pocket Watches

	LOW	AVG.	HIGH
American, 18s, Appleton, Tracy and Co., M#1877-1892	$ 50	$ 100	$ 150
American, 18s, P.S. Barlette, M#1857	200	300	400
American, 18s, Broadway, 7-11j	50	100	150
American, 18s, Crescent Street, 15j, M#1883	100	150	200
American, 18s, Samuel Curtis, 11-15j	2000	3000	4000
American, 18s, Wm. Ellory, M#1857	50	100	150
American, 18s, Export, 7-11j	50	100	150
American, 18s, Paragon, 15j	100	150	200
American, 18s, R.E. Robbins, 13j	100	150	200
American, 18s, Sol, 7-17j	50	100	150
American, 18s, Tourist, 7-11j	50	75	100
American, 16s, Premier, 9-17j	50	75	100
American, 16s, Repeater, 16j	2000	3000	4000
American, 16s, Riverside, 15-19j	50	100	150
American, 16s, 16j, Riverside Maximus	400	500	600
American, 16s, Royal, 15-17j	50	100	150
American, 0s, Royal, 16j	75	100	125
American, 0s, Seaside, 7-15j	100	150	200
Ansonia Clock Co.	40	55	70
Ansonia Sesqui-Centennial	250	300	350
Aurora Watch Co., 18s, 7-11j	100	150	200
Aurora Watch Co., 18s, 15j	200	300	400
California Watch Co., 18s, 11-15j	1000	1500	2000
Cornell Watch Co., 18s	300	450	600
Dudley Watch Co., Masons, 14s	3000	4000	5000
Dudley Watch Co., Masons, 12s	1500	2000	2500
Elgin, 18s, Father Time, 17j	50	100	150
Elgin, 18s, Father Time, 21j	150	175	200
Elgin, 18s, Overland, 17j	100	150	200
E.H. Flint, 18s, 4-7j, 18k	4000	5000	6000
Fredonia, 18s, 7-16j	150	250	350
Jonas G. Hall, 18s, 15j	1500	2000	2500

	LOW	AVG.	HIGH
Hamilton, 18s, 15-21j	$ 150	$ 250	$ 350
Hamilton, 16s, 16-17j	200	300	400
Hamilton, 12s, 17-19j	50	100	150
Hampden Watch Co., 18s, 15-18j	100	150	200
Hampden Watch Co., 16s, 7-15j	50	100	150
Hampden Watch Co., 12s, 7-15j	50	75	100
Hampden Watch Co., 000s, 7-15j	100	150	200
E. Howard and Co., N size (18), I-VIII, 15j	1000	2000	3000
E. Howard and Co., L size (18), V, 15j	1000	1250	1500
E. Howard Watch Co. , 12s, series 6-8	200	300	400
Illinois Watch Co., 18s, Allegheny 11j	50	100	150
Illinois Watch Co., 18s, Baltimore and Ohio RR Special	500	750	1000
Illinois Watch Co., 18s, Bunn, 15j	500	750	1000
Illinois Watch Co., 18s, Bunn Special, 21j	150	200	250
Illinois Watch Co., 18s, Columbia, 11j	75	125	175
Illinois Watch Co., 18s, Currier, 11j	75	125	175
Illinois Watch Co., 18s, Montgomery Ward, 17j	150	175	200
Illinois Watch Co., 18s, The National, 11j	75	100	125
Illinois Watch Co., 18s, Time King, 17-21j	150	225	300
Illinois Watch Co., 16s, Ariston, 11-15j	50	88	125
Illinois Watch Co., 16s, Ariston, 17-19j	150	225	300
Illinois Watch Co., 16s, Ariston, 23j	500	750	1000
Illinois Watch Co., 16s, Ben Franklin, 17-21j	300	450	600
Illinois Watch Co., 16s, Burlington, 15-17j	75	125	175
Illinois Watch Co., 16s, Dispatcher, 19j	50	100	150
Illinois Watch Co., 16s, Getty model, 17-21j	100	150	200
Illinois Watch Co., 16s, Great Northern Special, 17-21j	250	300	350
Illinois Watch Co., 16s, Lakeshore, 17j	100	150	200
Illinois Watch Co., 16s, Railroad King, 17j	200	250	300
Illinois Watch Co., 16s, Sangamo, 21j	150	200	250
Illinois Watch Co., 16s, Santa Fe Special, 17j	150	200	250
Illinois Watch Co., 14s, 7-21j	50	100	150
Illinois Watch Co., 4s, 7-15j	50	88	125
Illinois Watch Co., 0s, 201-204, 11-17j	75	112	150
Ingersoll, Dollar type, Buck	50	88	125
Ingersoll, Dollar type, Climax	40	58	75
Ingersoll, Dollar type, Colby	20	30	40
Ingersoll, Dollar type, Crown	20	30	40
Ingersoll, Dollar type, Defiance	30	45	60
Ingersoll, Dollar type, Ensign	30	40	50
Ingersoll, Dollar type, Escort	20	30	40
Ingersoll, Dollar type, Gotham	15	25	35
Ingersoll, Dollar type, Kelton	15	20	25
Ingersoll, Dollar type, Major	10	15	20
Ingersoll, Dollar type, Patrol	40	50	60
Ingersoll, Dollar type, Pilgrim	40	50	60
Ingersoll, Dollar type, Radiolite	30	40	50
Ingersoll, Dollar type, Saturday Post	150	200	250
Ingersoll, Dollar type, Solar	25	38	50
Ingersoll, Dollar type, Trump	40	50	60
Ingersoll, Dollar type, Uncle Sam	40	50	60

	LOW	AVG.	HIGH
Ingersoll, Dollar type, G. Washington	$ 150	$ 200	$ 250
Ingersoll, Dollar type, Winner	20	30	40
E. Ingraham Co., Autocrat	15	20	25
E. Ingraham Co., Baltimore	10	15	20
E. Ingraham Co., Clipper	20	30	40
E. Ingraham Co., Cub	15	20	25
E. Ingraham Co., Dot	15	20	25
E. Ingraham Co., Laddie	20	30	40
E. Ingraham Co., Overland	30	40	50
E. Ingraham Co., Pilot	30	45	60
E. Ingraham Co., Rex	15	20	25
E. Ingraham Co., St. Regis	15	20	25
E. Ingraham Co., Century	25	30	35
E. Ingraham Co., Sturdy	10	15	20
E. Ingraham Co., Top Notch	40	50	60
E. Ingraham Co., Trail Blazer	150	200	250
E. Ingraham Co., Viceroy	20	30	40
E. Ingraham Co., Zep	150	200	250
Kelly Watch Co., 16s, aluminum	50	100	150
Keystone Standard Watch Co., 18s, 7-15j	75	125	175
Knickerbocker Watch Co., 6-18s	50	75	100
Lancaster, 18s, Comet	150	175	200
Lancaster, Ben Franklin	250	300	350
Lancaster, Malvern	50	75	100
Lancaster, Radnor	100	150	200
Lancaster, Sidney	100	125	150
McIntyre Watch Co., 16s, 21-25j	5000	6000	7000
Melrose Watch Co., 18s, 7-15j	250	350	450
New England Watch Co., Alden	40	50	60
New England Watch Co., Columbian	20	25	30
New England Watch Co., Putnam	70	85	100
New England Watch Co., Tuxedo	20	30	40
Otay Watch Co., 15j	1200	1600	2000
Peoria Watch Co., 18s, 15j	200	300	400
Philadelphia Watch Co., 18s, 11j	150	200	250
Rockford, 18s, Belmont USA	200	250	300
Rockford, 18s, Dome model	150	200	250
Rockford, 18s, Ramsey, 11-15j	100	125	150
Rockford, 18s, 7j	50	100	150
Rockford, 18s, 13j	100	150	200
Rockford, 18s, #825	150	175	200
Rockford, 18s, #835	100	150	200
Rockford, 18s, #870	50	100	150
Rockford, 18s, #910	150	200	250
Rockford, 18s, #950	2000	3000	4000
Rockford, 18s, #170	50	75	100
Rockford, 16s, Peerless	75	100	125
Rockford, 16s, Prince of Wales	300	450	600
Rockford, 16s, 7j	100	150	200
Rockford, 16s, Winnebago	150	225	300
Rockford, 16s, #102	150	175	200

	LOW	AVG.	HIGH
Rockford, 16s, #104	$ 50	$ 60	$ 70
Rockford, 16s, #445	800	1000	1200
Rockford, 16s, #535	200	300	400
Rockford, 16s, #566	150	175	200
San Jose Watch Co., 16s	1500	2000	2500
South Bend, 18s, 15j	100	150	200
South Bend, 18s, Studebaker	200	300	400
South Bend, 18s, #309	75	100	125
South Bend, 18s, #333	100	125	150
South Bend, 18s, #344	300	400	500
South Bend, 18s, #355	1000	1250	1500
South Bend, 16s, 7-9j	50	100	150
South Bend, 16s, #207	50	100	150
South Bend, 16s, #211	50	100	150
South Bend, 16s, #280	100	125	150
South Bend, 16s, #290	200	250	300
South Bend, 16s, #294	300	400	500
South Bend, 12s, Chesterfield	50	100	150
South Bend, 12s, #407	30	45	60
South Bend, 12s, #419	150	175	200
Seth Thomas, 18s, Century	50	100	150
Seth Thomas, 18s, Eagle Series	50	100	150
Seth Thomas, 18s, Edgemere	50	100	150
Seth Thomas, 18s, Keywind	200	300	400
Seth Thomas, 18s, Maidenlane, 17-24j	1000	1500	2000
Seth Thomas, 18s, Henry Molineux	500	1000	1500
Seth Thomas, 18s, #33-#201	50	100	150
Seth Thomas, 18s, #245	1000	1250	1500
Seth Thomas, 18s, #281-382	150	200	250
Seth Thomas, 16s, Centennial	50	75	100
Seth Thomas, 16s, Locust	50	100	150
Seth Thomas, 16s, Republic	50	62	75
Seth Thomas, 16s, #25-336	50	100	150
Seth Thomas, 12s, Republic	50	60	70
Seth Thomas, 12s, #25-328	50	75	100
Seth Thomas, 0s, 7-17j	50	100	150
Trenton Watch Co., 18s, "M" #3-5	50	100	150
Trenton Watch Co., 16s, "M" #1-3	50	88	125
Trenton Watch Co., 12s, Fortuna	50	60	70
Trenton Watch Co., 6s, 7-15j	40	50	60
Trenton Watch Co., 0s, 7-15j	50	60	70
U.S. Watch Co., 18s, Wm. Alexander	200	300	400
U.S. Watch Co., 18s, F. Atherton, 15-17j	250	350	450
U.S. Watch Co., 18s, F. Atherton, 19j	600	900	1200
U.S. Watch Co., 18s, S. M. Beard	250	350	450
U.S. Watch Co., 18s, Centennial Phila.	2000	2250	2500
U.S. Watch Co., 18s, G. Channing	250	350	450
U.S. Watch Co., 18s, J.W. Deacon	200	300	400
U.S. Watch Co., 18s, Fellows	400	500	600
U.S. Watch Co., 18s, Asa Fuller	200	300	400
U.S. Watch Co., 18s, North Star	300	400	500

	LOW	AVG.	HIGH
U.S. Watch Co., 18s, Penna. RR	$ 2500	$ 3000	$ 3500
U.S. Watch Co., 18s, H. Randel	250	350	450
U.S. Watch Co., 18s, Edwin Rollo	200	300	400
U.S. Watch Co., 18s, Rural NY	200	300	400
U.S. Watch Co., 18s, F. Stratton	250	350	450
U.S. Watch Co., 18s, I. H. Wright	200	300	400
U.S. Watch Co., 16s, 15-19j	500	750	1000
U.S. Watch Co., 14s, 7-15j	250	350	450
U.S. Watch Co., 10s, 11-15j	100	200	300
Waterbury Watch Co., Series B-E	200	250	300
Waterbury Watch Co., Series G-H	200	275	350
Waterbury Watch Co., Series I-Z	75	112	150
Waterbury Watch Co., Oxford	50	75	100
Westclox, Boy Proof	40	50	60
Westclox, Bulls eye	15	20	25
Westclox, Country Gentleman	40	50	60
Westclox, Dax	10	15	20
Westclox, Everbrite	20	25	30
Westclox, Explorer	200	250	300
Westclox, Ideal	30	40	50
Westclox, Mark IV	40	50	60
Westclox, Maxim	30	40	50
Westclox, Mustang	40	50	60
Westclox, Smile	25	38	50
Westclox, Vote	25	38	50
Westclox, Zep	200	250	300

Metal

Aluminum

Although aluminum is a basic element on the periodic table, it was extremely difficult to purify. During the 19th century it was a luxury metal. Not until after Charles Hill patented an inexpensive smelting method in 1886 did it become a "practical" metal. Nearly all aluminum wares on the market are 20th century.

For further information see *Collectible Aluminum*, by Everett Grist. Aluminum can be cleaned with soap and water or even paste silver polish. Be gentle in cleaning; aluminum dents and scratches easily. Salt will corrode aluminum.

"Good" pieces are not dented nor heavily scratched. They are simple in form. "Best" pieces have a fine texture, such as a hammered finish, and have a striking visual appearance. This can be very subjective. One collector's treasure is another collector's junk.

Above: The relative prices of aluminum pieces 60 years ago often is the same relationship today. Below left to right: hammered aluminum large serving tray by Cromwell, 11.5" x 18" ,$18-$22; hammered aluminum double handled candy dish by Rodney Kent, len. 14", $10-$15.

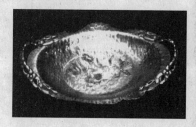

	GOOD	BETTER	BEST
Ashtray	$ 10	$ 20	$ 50
Bar Tray	30	50	70
Basket	15	25	45
Bowl	10	15	45
Box w/ lid	20	40	90
Bread Tray	15	30	50
Breakfast Set	30	50	75
Butter Dish	8	15	20

	GOOD	BETTER	BEST
Cake Stand	$ 12	$ 20	$ 25
Candelabra (pr.)	70	100	160
Candlesticks (pr.)	20	30	50
Candy Dish	10	15	25
Casserole	10	15	20
Cigarette Box	15	30	75
Coaster	2	5	8
Coaster Set	20	30	50
Coffee Urn	40	75	100
Compote	10	20	40
Cream & Sugar	10	18	35
Crumber & Tray	15	20	25
Cup, Collapsible	1	3	8
Cup, Hammered	1	5	10
Folding Server	30	50	80
Fondue Pot	15	20	30
Gravy Boat	10	15	20
Hurricane Lamp (pr.)	20	30	40
Ice Bucket	10	20	40
Lazy Susan	10	15	30
Magazine Rack	60	90	200
Matchbox Cover	10	25	50
Money Clip	5	10	15
Napkin Holder	10	15	30
Notebook Cover	50	100	200
Nut Bowl	15	20	30
Pitcher	20	30	50
Plate (Fancy)	15	30	50
Powder Box	10	15	20
Sandwich Tray	15	30	50
Serving Tray	20	50	80
Silent Butlers	20	30	50
Snack Tray	5	15	25
Teapot	15	20	40
Tidbit	15	30	45
Tray Table	100	200	350
Tray (whimsical shape)	30	50	80
Tumblers	4	8	15
Vase, hammered	20	40	60
Well & Tree Platter	15	25	40

Royal Aluminum struck mark.

Barbed Wire

The first wire fencing was patented in 1853. Western farmers used it on their land to deter cattlemen. Railroads used it in some areas to keep cattle and buffalo off the tracks. Between 1868 and 1900 more than 750 patents were issued for various barbed wire styles. Various types of barbed wire include ribbon wire, double round wire with two points and single round wire with two points.

	LOW	AVG.	HIGH
### Single Round with Two Points			
Bakers Single Strand, c. 1883	$ 6	$ 9	$ 12
Charles O. Rogers, c. 1888	6	9	12
Dobbs and Booth Single line, c. 1875	10	14	17
Gundarson, c. 1881	9	13	17
Half-Hitch, c. 1877	7	12	16
H.M. Rose Wrap Barb, c. 1877	6	10	13
L.E. Sunderland No Kink, c. 1884	6	9	11
Mack's Alternate, c. 1875	21	32	44
Nelson Clip, c. 1876	150	200	250
Putnams Flat Under Barb, c. 1877	30	40	50
R. Emerson, c. 1876	300	350	400
Rose Kink Line, c. 1877	8	12	15
Single Line Wide Wrap Barb, c. 1878	150	200	250
Sunderland Hammered Barb, c. 1884	8	10	11
"Two Point Ripple Wire"	13	18	23
### Double Round with Two Points			
Australian Loose Wrap	$ 8	$ 11	$ 13
Baker's Halt-Round Barb	4	6	8
C. H. Salisbury, c. 1876	28	38	48
Decker Parallel, c. 1884	14	17	20
Figure 8 Barb, Wright, c. 1881	40	50	60
"Forked Tongue," c. 1887	8	12	15
Haish's Original "S," c. 1875	5	8	11
Glidden Barb on Both Lines	9	13,	17
J.D. Curtis "Twisted Point"	4	6	8
J.D. Nadlehoffer, c. 1878	90	110	130
Kangaroo Wire, c. 1876	7	11	14
L.E. Sunderland Barb on Two Line Wire, c. 1884	200	275	350
Missouri Hump Wire Staple Barb, c. 1876	18	22	26
Peter P. Hill Parallel, c. 1876	350	375	400
Rose Barb on Copper Lines, c. 1877	10	14	17
W. Edenborn	8	11	14
W. Edenborn's Locked In Barb, c. 1885	6	9	12
### Ribbon Wire			
Allis Barbless Ribbon and Single Wire, c. 1881	$ 32	$ 42	$ 52
Allis Flat Ribbon Barb, c. 1892	30	42	54
Brinkerhoft's Ribbon Barb, c. 1881	9	13	16
Cast iron Buckthorn	11	17	23
Factory Splice on Thin Barbed Ribbon, c. 1892	80	10	120
F. D. Ford Flat Ribbon, c. 1885	9	13	16
John Hallner's "Greenbriar," c. 1878	3	7	10

Brass

Brass is an alloy of copper and zinc. Early English and Continental pieces are the most valuable. Lighter-weight decorative brassware imported from Asia since the turn of the century often has intricate engraving and tooling, but is less valuable. Objects should be in excellent condition: no dents, no corrosion, even color. Brass may be polished without destroying its value (unlike bronze).

Prices are for items of the late 18th century (L-18), 19th century (19), and early 20th century (E-20).

Above left: Continental eight arm chandelier, $3000 at auction.
Above right: double arm student's lamp, $1000-$3000 retail.
— Photos courtesy of Northeast Auctions.

	L-18	19	E-20
Andirons, Ball-Top, w/ mid-band, pr., ht.14"	$ 1200	$ 325	$ 100
Andirons, NY spire-top, turned standards on spurred cabriole			
legs, ht. 25"	5000	1700	200
Andirons, pr., arched feet, urn finial, ht. 18"	1500	500	200
Andirons, Philadelphia Ball-Top, ht. 18"	600	350	150
Ashtray, ivy leaf form, dia. 5.5"	—	25	10
Ashtray, made from artillery shell, dia. 4.5"	—	45	20
Bellows, wheel driven, len. 24"	2500	1550	500
Bowl, tooled flowers and leaves, dia. 6.5"	100	50	5
Box, oval, pierced hinged lid, 5" x 7"	—	—	5
Breastplate, ht. 18"	—	250	125
Candelabra, 5 arms, ht. 15.5"	45	50	47
Candelabra, pr., each w/ 3 arms, ht. 15"	800	260	145
Candleholders, pr., spiral shaft	—	250	67
Candlestick, mid-drip, 9"	650	150	35
Candlestick, mid-drip, w/ ribbed foot, ht. 7"	—	$ 300	—
Candlesticks, French, stepped octagonal base, pr., ht. 9 "	$ 800	375	$ 50
Candlesticks, heavy, teardrop & saucer turned, sq. base, 9.5" ...	750	380	32

	L-18	19	E-20
Candlesticks, mid-drip, ht. 9".	$ 500	$ 250	$ 35
Candlesticks, octagonal base, engraved w/ grape & vines, Eng., pr., ht. 6"	5000	700	50
Candlesticks, pr., 3"	—	120	10
Candlesticks, petal base, Queen Anne, pr., ht. 8"	1200	400	35
Capstan Candlestick, Continental, ht. 5".	—	450	—
Cigarette Case	—	45	12
Coal Scuttle, w. 18"	300	100	45
Desk Lamp, marble base	500	200	32
Desk Set, 8 pieces, floral scroll design	1000	375	100
Dish, hammered, 4"	—	24	3
Door Knocker, lion, 3.5" x 2.5", marked "C & A"	—	125	22
Fire Fender, D-form wire, w/ rail and finials, w. 50".	—	700	200
Fireplace Fender, Amer., elaborate wire and serpentine, lemon finials, w. 62"	2500	1500	300
Fireplace Tools (broom, poker, shovel)	750	330	125
Firetools, set of 3, Eng., engraved-urn top, w. 30".	2000	400	150
Footman, Eng., w. 13"	700	225	—
Gong, w/ stand & wooden striker, 7"	—	30	8
Incense Burner, pierced lid, 3 feet, ht. 3.5"	—	56	4
Jardiniere, hammered, w. 11.5"	—	225	23
Lantern Clock, Eng., engraved, mah. bracket, ht. 9".	10,000	4,000	—
Lantern, pierced circular, ht. 13".	1500	500	75
Letter Holder, w. 6"	—	75	25
Miniature Andirons, pr., ht. 1.5"	—	100	15
Miniature Candlestick, solid base, ht. 1.5"	—	75	13
Miniature Candlesticks, 1.5"	—	62	10
Miniature Decanter, 1.5"	—	110	18
Monteith Bowl, French, oval, w. 13".	2000	1400	100

Left to right: American Chippendale urn-top andirons, $3250 at auction; New York Federal lemon-top andirons, $2500 at auction; American Federal urn-top andirons, $3000 at auction. — Photos courtesy of Northeast Auctions.

Left: nineteenth century slide candlestick, $100-$200; Right:
Watch for replaced legs on early tinderboxes.

	L-18	19	E-20
Mortar & Pestle, 6"	$ 350	$ 145	$ 45
Mug, 3"	100	50	3
Pig, solid, 4.5"	200	90	25
Pint Measures, ht. 5"	325	250	25
Plate, heavy cast, scalloped rim	200	50	6
Plate, tooled leaf engraving, 4.5"	200	75	4
Platter, pedestal, marked "China," 8"	—	21	18
Sinumbra Lamp, column-form, w/ mushroom shade, ht. 26".	—	1500	250
Spittoon, 6.5" x 4.5"	132	35	33
Steam Gage, Boston, dia. 6"	—	50	25
Student Lamp, Amer., double acorn-form w/ shades, ht. 22".	—	5250	1200
Table Lighter, engraved leaves, 4.5"	—	65	8
Table Top, round, clad, Islamic calligraphy, dia. 24"	—	150	140
Tobacco Box, engraved, Dutch, w. 4"	250	175	—
Tobacco Box, engraved figures, Dutch oval, w. 5".	—	350	—

Seventeenth century candlesticks are heavy and often
unscrew at the base.

Left: Dutch brass tobacco box with a harbor scene, $400 at auction. — Photo courtesy of Northeast Auctions.

Right: Dutch brass and copper tobacco box with a harbor scene, $450 at auction. — Photo courtesy of Northeast Auctions.

	L-18	19	E-20
Tobacco Box, engraved motifs, Dutch oval, w. 6" .... —		$ 450	—
Tobacco Cutter, wheel driven, ht. 10" .... $ 500		325	—
Tongs, claw end, hanging ring, 11" 250		45	$ 16
Tray, 2 handles, engraved peacocks, marked "India," 29" x 8" ... —		—	25
Tray, octagonal, hammered, 15" x 10" .... —		75	14
Trivet, w. 9" .... —		75	—
Vase, bronze birds and flowers, 5" .... —		—	28
Warming Pan, Continental, engraved, w. 43". 600		400	—
Wax Jack, Eng., ht. 6" .... —		400	—
Wax Seal, ... 200		50	12
Whale Oil Lamps, Amer., ht. 9.5" 850		300	—

Bronze

Though bronze sculpture is of ancient origin, most specimens on the market are Victorian and 20th century.

The color and condition of the "patina" is important. Don't clean a bronze sculpture with any highly abrasive cleaner.

Above, left to right: Equestrian Amazon, Classical Female Figure, Irish Setter; see prices below — Photo courtesy of Northeast Auctions. Left: Art Nouveau bronzes like this figure are often made of colored "white Metal," not bronze. — Photo courtesy of George Kerrigan Photogrphy.

	LOW	AVG.	HIGH
Athlete, signed Schmidt Felling, dated 1906, ht. 12".	$ 900	$ 1100	$ 1300
Bull Terrier with Turtle, signed A. Jacquemart, ht. 6", w. 7" ...	3000	3500	4000
Classical Female Figure Holding a Lamp, Henri Dumaiges, dated 1867, ht. 12"..	450	570	690
Eisenhower, bust as general, ht. 15"..	350	425	500
Equestrian Amazon attacked by a tiger, w. 16"	600	750	900
Irish Setter, P.J. Mene, w. 12"	2600	3300	4000
Male, crouching, signed Carl W. Bartlett, dated 1897. ht. 9" ...	5500	6500	7500
Marley Horses, pr., ht. 23"	3500	4250	5000
Massachusetts Governor John A. Andrew, Bronze Statue, Martin Milmore, ht. 21"	2000	2400	2800
Nude Male, full-length, ht. 16"...	700	900	1100
Plaque of woman's head, by Gorham.	1000	1125	1250
Polar Bear, seated, ht. 4"	510	630	750
Setter, P.J. Mene, w. 12"	5000	6000	7000
Swan, w. 17"	900	1100	1300

Chrome

Chrome is a glossy metal used in decorative trimmings on autos and trucks, sailboats, etc. Chrome collectibles include auto items, household objects, and novelties. The Art Deco era used chrome extensively in the 1920s and it has remained popular ever since.

Clean with metal polish recommended for use on chrome. Do not use abrasive tools or steel wool, as these will mar the surface.

	LOW	AVG.	HIGH
Bud Vase, chased, 4.5" cylinder on 3.5" base .... $ 20		$ 25	$ 30
Cocktail Set, shaker w/ 6 flared goblets, h. (goblets) 7" 35		50	75
Cocktail Shaker, footed, etched banding, grape leaf motif, 11.75" . 15		25	45
Cocktail Shaker, grape etching, w/ cap and lid 12		20	35
Cordial Dispenser, clear glass ribbing, chrome plunger, 6 jiggers .. 30		45	70
Cordial Dispenser, keg on pedestal w/ 6 mugs 20		25	35
Farber Cocktail Shaker, w/ 6 glasses, hammered, ht. (glasses) 6.25" .. 35		75	125

Elegant chrome cocktail set in the Art Deco taste.
— Photo courtesy of Phillips Auctioneers

Copper

As the price of the metal itself has risen, so has the price for the well-crafted antiques and collectibles. "Good" examples must be in good condition, with only tiny dents. "Best" examples are undented and well proportioned, and show fine workmanship. All items are 20th century unless otherwise noted.

	GOOD	BETTER	BEST
Cup, w/ handle	$ 55	$ 80	$ 170
Dipper, 19th c.	90	125	275
Dipper (many types)	40	70	190
Egg Poacher, iron handle, for 9 eggs	55	90	245
Egg Poacher, 2 brass handles, for 16 eggs	55	90	245
Evaporating Pan, iron bail handle, ring handles	130	185	360
Funnel, ht. 23"	100	200	300
Funnel, tube-shaped, screen attachment, dia. 8"	55	80	170
Hot Water Bottle, ht. 12"	65	88	170
Hot Water Bottle, egg-shaped, brass cap, unmarked	55	75	150
Hot Water Bottle, bail handle, brass lid, late 19th c.	82	100	200
Hot Water Urn, early 19th c.	480	770	1900
Kettle, apple butter, mid-1800s, dovetail bottom, dia. 25"	730	980	1900
Kettle, apple butter, c. 1890	122	192	475
Kettle, copper, brass, wood handle, 1 gal., Portugal	23	32	68
Kettle, bail handle, iron, swinging, molded lip iron stand	750	975	1800
Kettle, early 19th c.	185	248	475
Kettle, iron bail handle, jelly kettle	98	135	300
Kettle, apple butter, used outdoors, dia. 25"	170	245	500
Kettle, apple butter, used outdoors, dia. 28"	212	285	570
Kettle, 19th c., kitchen, brass knob, ht. 15"	145	200	400
Kettle, mid-19th c., ht. 9"	200	400	1000
Kettle, Early American, dia. 10", ht. 15"	212	300	665
Measure, flared spout, soldered handle, early 19th c., ht. 11"	100	180	400
Measure, 1 qt., handle, brass knob	80	110	225
Measure, pours, sloping edges, 1 pt.	40	55	115
Measure, pours, sloping edges, 1 qt.	40	65	133
Measure set, 1 pt. to 2.5 qts.	275	370	720
Measure set, 19th c., harvest measures	500	1200	3000
Measures, set of 3 for rum, 19th c.	800	1300	2500
Measuring Cups, set of 7, wide-based, marked	2282	3350	7600
Milk Bucket, iron bail, handle, late 19th c.	163	225	475
Milk Churn, 19th c., European, brass ring handles, ht. 32"	1385	2000	4500
Milk Jug	130	178	360
Miniatures, pan, dia. 5", ht. 8"	15	25	60
Miniatures, frying pan, dia. 5", brass handles	20	32	85
Miniatures, kettle, pours, iron bail handle, dia. 3"	15	22	50
Miniatures, wash tub, brass trim and handles, dia. 3"	15	20	50
Mixing Bowl, circular base, 1 handle, dia. 15", ht. 8"	73	108	245
Mixing Bowl, dia. 15", ht. 8"	82	125	300
Mold, bird, pt.	40	70	170
Mold, bundt, qt.	155	210	400
Mold, Easter egg, rabbit	90	125	245
Mold, jelly or pudding, qt.	40	70	170
Mold, jelly or pudding, pt.	40	65	150

	GOOD	BETTER	BEST
Mold, circular base, fruit or floral motif, qt.	$ 40	$ 70	$ 150
Mold, circular base, fruit or floral motif, pt.	20	30	90
Mold, fluted, scroll design at edge, 8"	15	25	45
Mold, pan, iron, handle, hanging eye	240	325	625
Mold, copper handles, dia. 20"	240	325	625
Mold, iron handle, dia. 13"	110	150	285
Pitcher, 2 qt.	65	90	200
Plate, dia. 9"	15	25	75
Pot, hand-crafted, handled, early 19th c., dia. 15"	155	210	418
Pots, iron handles, tin interiors, lids, set of 3, dia. 6", 7", and 8"	40	70	152
Reservoir, from kitchen stove, 19" x 8.75" x 11.5"	20	40	100
Salt Box, w. 7"	82	115	245
Saucepan, covered, brass handle, tin-lined, 1 qt.	82	115	245
Saucepan, covered, handle, tin-lined, 2 qt.	82	115	255
Saucepan, covered, brass handle, tin-lined, 3 qt.	90	135	310
Saucepan, covered, brass handle, tin-lined, 4 qt.	98	140	350
Saucepan, double boiler, 1 qt.	55	70	160

Above left: Turkish coffeepot, $10-$25; 1930s coffeepot, $25-$50; nineteenth century teapot, $500-$1000; nineteenth century mug, $50-$100.

Graniteware

Graniteware is metalware with an enamel coating. It often has a mottled or marbleized appearance. Most graniteware is made for kitchen use. First featured in 1876 at the Centennial Exposition in Philadelphia, graniteware quickly gained popularity. It has been manufactured from the 1870s to the present.

"Good" pieces should have only traces of rust and no more than a few "dings" in the enamel. "Best" pieces should have no rust and no chipping of the enamel.

Right: large blue and white colander, $60-$90.

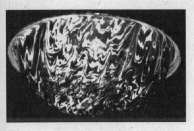

Left: brown/maroon and white dish pan, $40-$60.

	GOOD	BETTER	BEST
Basting Spoon, green/cream mottled	$ 5	$ 15	$ 30
Basting Spoon, light blue, 13.5"	10	25	40
Basting Spoon, blue, pointed bowl, threaded handle	5	10	15
Bathtub, for baby, gray mottled	70	145	225
Batter Bucket, tin lid, handle	45	95	150
Bedpan, gray, odorless tabbed lid	10	20	40
Biscuit Pan	10	25	40
Bowl/Pitcher, blue/white streaked, matched set	45	95	155
Bowl, blue/white swirl, dia. 7"	20	40	75
Bowl, blue, deep	20	40	75
Bowl, blue swirl, dia. 9"	30	60	100
Bowl, cereal, pink w/ cobalt trim, rabbit decoration	10	20	45
Bowl, gray, 2 qt., shallow	10	25	45
Bread Box, white w/ blue swirls, circular, hinged lid	45	95	150
Bread Pan	10	25	40
Bread Raiser, gray mottled, tin lid w/ wood knob, dia. 15"	50	105	170
Bucket, berry, blue/white marbleized swirls, small	10	25	45
Bucket, berry, child's gray, w/ lid, bail handle	55	110	180

	GOOD	BETTER	BEST
Bucket, berry, cobalt/white swirl	$ 53	$ 100	$ 170
Bucket, berry, cobalt diffused	55	110	185
Coffee Boiler, brown/white marbleized, dome lid, 6 qt.	50	120	190
Coffee Dollar, cobalt/white swirl	75	140	230
Coffee Boiler, gray mottled, half-moon shape, 5.5" handle, 9" x 5" x 4.5"	25	50	95
Coffee Boiler, gray, bail handles	35	70	125
Coffee Boiler, navy speckled w/ white, U.S. Navy, wire bail w/ wooden handle, large	20	40	80
Coffee Pot, black/white mottled, 11 qt., dome lid	25	55	90
Coffee Pot, black/white, small...	10	25	40
Coffee Pot, blue/white, slant sides, moss rose decoration	65	130	225
Coffee Pot, blue/white swirl	45	93	150
Coffee Pot, blue/white swirl, gooseneck	65	130	200
Coffee Pot, blue/white swirl, large	55	113	180
Coffee Pot, blue, dome lid	30	60	110
Coffee Pot, blue, large	55	113	183
Coffee Pot, blue swirl	40	80	140
Coffee Pot, blue, tin lid...	40	80	140
Coffee Pot, cobalt swirl, tin lid	45	90	150
Coffee Pot, crystallite/white swirl, goose neck, small	85	160	260
Coffee Pot, crystallite/white swirl, small	30	75	125
Coffee Pot, gray	20	40	80
Coffee Pot, gray, 8 cup, enamel dome lid w/ hollow knob, straight spout	30	60	100
Coffee Pot, gray mottled	30	60	100
Coffee Pot, gray mottled, bail handle	40	80	140
Cup/Saucer, toy, gray	25	55	90
Cup, blue/white swirl	5	10	35
Cuspidor, w/ ironware base, mottled gray	20	45	75
Dinner Bucket, gray, miner's style	65	130	210
Dinner Pail, gray, tin lid, round, striped mottling, wood and bail handle, large	60	120	200
Dinner Plate, red/white marbleized	20	45	75
Dipper, blue/white mottled, white interior, black rim	15	30	50
Dipper, blue/white swirl, 2 qt.	10	25	40
Dipper, blue/white Windsor, marbleized w/ long handle, dia. 5" ...	20	90	125
Dipper, cobalt/white swirl, large	50	110	180
Dipper, cobalt swirl, .5 cup, enamel label: "E.W Morse, Omega" ..	15	30	50
Dipper, gray	10	35	65
Funnel, gray, large	13	33	63
Funnel, gray mottled, canning jar, strap handle, rough edges	5	20	35
Funnel, gray mottled, hollow handle, ht. 5", dia. 4.5"	10	35	65
Funnel, gray mottled, hollow side handle, ht. 7", dia. 5.5"	20	40	70
Funnel, gray mottled, strap handle, ht. 4.5", dia. 3.5"	10	35	65
Funnel, gray, small	10	20	40
Funnel, white w/ black trim, ht. 4"	10	25	30
Grater, cheese, steel handles	35	60	115
Ham Boiler, blue/white, bail handle, oval, white liner, 19" x 9" ..	20	45	75
Heater, kerosene, blue/white mottled, bail handle, ht. 20"	40	100	150
Invalid Feeder, gray, gooseneck spout	10	20	45

	GOOD	BETTER	BEST
Iron, Coleman gas, blue/white swirl	$ 30	$ 60	$ 115
Iron, Coleman, turquoise, nickel over brass tank, nickel over steel base	25	50	85
Kerosene Stove, table top, gray, fancy, ornate nickel-coated trim, includes 1 qt. nickel-plated brass teakettle w/ ornate gooseneck spout and lid, bell-shaped bottom, wood and bail handle, tray w/ raised rim, by George Haller, dia. 11"	350	725	1150
Ladle, black/white mottled, 12"	10	20	30
Ladle, cobalt, 12"	10	20	35
Ladle, cup size	10	20	35
Ladle, dumpling, turquoise/white	30	63	100
Ladle, dumpling, white	10	20	30
Lunch Bucket, gray/white mottled, black rim, miner's style, dia. 24"	50	100	160
Lunch Bucket, white, tin handle and lid	25	50	85
Lunch Pail, gray, 3 piece	70	140	235
Measure, gray, 1 cup	60	120	195
Measure, gray mottling, good old seams, hollow handle, marked: "1 Qt. Liquid"	35	70	115
Measure, gray, qt., handle, wide lip, embossed lines	20	40	70
Mixing Bowl, blue/white marbleized	10	23	40
Mixing Bowl, gray, dia. 8"	5	10	20
Pan, blue, 9"	30	63	100
Pan, blue/white swirl, round, 8"	25	50	90
Pan, blue, round, 8"	25	50	80
Pan, blue, round, 11"	15	30	60
Pan, blue swirl, 11"	20	40	80
Pan, blue swirl, round, 8"	20	40	75
Pan, blue swirl, round, 9"	20	55	95
Rice Ball, gray	160	325	505
Roaster, blue/white mottled	35	75	123
Roaster, brown/white swirl	35	70	120
Roaster, cobalt/white swirl	35	75	125
Roaster, cobalt/white, 3-piece	120	240	380
Roaster, oval, gray, flat side handles, small	20	40	70
Roaster, oval, gray, 2 handles	15	35	65
Roaster, turkey, cobalt swirl	50	105	185
Skillet, aqua/white swirl	73	140	230
Skillet, egg, gray, enamel over iron, 5 eyes, tong handle	75	135	230
Skillet, dark blue/white swirl, dia. 12"	50	100	160
Teapot, robin's egg blue/white speckled, Britannia Metal, hinged cover and spout, fancy handle, Manning-Bowman Co.	145	295	470
Teapot, white/blue speckled	30	75	125
Teapot, white w/ pewter trim	145	290	460
Teapot, wood knob, "S" curve spout	15	35	68

Above: The rust shown on this bundt pan lowers the value to $20-30. Below: Complete sets of matching graniteware are extremely rare and worth approximately 50% more than the individual pieces.

8-Piece Turquoise Blue Enamelware Set
Convex Kettle, 5½ quarts; Preserving Kettle, 5½ quarts; Sauce Pan, 2 quarts; Pudding Pan, 1¾ quarts; Soup Ladle; Basting Spoon, 12 inches; two Pie Plates, 9 inches. Shipping weight, per set, about 18 pounds. **$2**⁷⁹
486 C 770—Complete set................**$2.79**

Ironware

Marked Ironware pieces have greater value. Dates do not always indicate the year made: some dates stand for the year the patent was issued. Oiling or polishing old ironware decreases its value. Many reproductions are made in Indonesia. Careless welding is a sign of modern work or fakery. For further information see *Fabulous But Fake*, by Norman S. Young, Fake Publications, Inc.

"Cast" refers to cast iron, "wrought' to wrought iron. "Good" should have minimal rust and be 100% intact. "Best" pieces should have fine decorative motifs, superior craftsmanship and no rust.

One of a pair of cast iron trig-form pattern benches, length 51",
$3500 at auction. — Photo courtesy of Northeast Auctions.

	GOOD	BETTER	BEST
Andirons, pr., figural, Asian man w/ pipe, Webb, Bost., ht. 12" ..	$ 600	$ 800	$ 1000
Anvil, 100 lb.	100	300	500
Apple Parer, cast, c. 1870	40	55	90
Apple Parer, cast, c. 1900	40	55	90
Apple Parer, cast, F.A. Walker, c. 1870s	29	38	100
Apple Parer, w/ clamp, cast, Simplex Co.	40	55	90
Apple Segmenter, bolt type, cast, patented 1869	38	50	70
Architectural Frieze, boxer silhouette, NY, ht. 25"	2100	2800	3500
Asparagus Buncher, cast, on walnut board	80	200	300
Balance Scales, forged, hook on top, 13"	30	40	75
Basket, fireplace grate, cast, c. 1900, w. 11"	180	240	335
Bathtub, hammered tin alloy, c. 1820	500	800	1200
Bedwarmer, w/ wooden handle, 38"	90	120	150
Bird Spit, wrought, legged w/ hooks and drip pan	135	180	250
Birdhouse, 2-story, Victorian, ht. 14"	1425	1900	2500
Birdhouse, Miller Iron Co., Gothic, octagonal, "pat'd Apr. 14, 1868." ht. 16"	4500	6000	7500
Bookends, bronzed, profile of Lincoln, ht. 4.5"	15	25	50
Boot Scraper, 2 men sawing log, len. 16"	375	500	625
Bowl, cast, dia. 9", w. 3"	75	100	150
Broiler, wrought, for fireplace, 3 legs, dia. 14"	60	80	100
Buffer Tester, pin, w. 17.5"	15	20	38
Butcher Flesh Fork, wrought, w. 15"	30	50	75
Butcher Set, strainer and ladle, wrought, w. 20"	70	100	130
Cabbage Cutter, cast blades on wooden board, w. 33"	45	60	80

	GOOD	BETTER	BEST
Candle Dip, early 19th century	$ 200	$ 400	$ 500
Candleholder, cast, c. 1850, ht. 7.5"	135	180	240
Candleholder, forged, English, c. 1800, ht. 11"	275	300	450
Candleholder, forged w/ spike, wall type, c. 1800, ht. 9"	200	250	400
Candleholder, forged, wall type, c. 1850	135	180	215
Candleholder, wrought, standing double-arm, w/ faceted brass turning, ht: 53"	250	450	600
Chandelier, turned and wrought, 3-branch, ht. 12"	2250	3000	3750
Figure of Uncle Sam, polychrome, c. 1880, ht. 57"	4000	8000	11,000
Hitching Post, youth w/ cap, 19th century, ht. 14"	400	700	1100
Jumping Horse Figure, "Watervliet Iron & Brass Co., NY," w. 66"	900	1200	1500
Lions, pr., American, Recumbent, Mott or Fiske. len. 44"	6000	8000	10,000
Man in a Crescent Moon, ptd., Amer., c. 1900, ht. 10"	4000	5200	6500
Meat Chopper, cast, tin, painted wood, c. 1865	26	34	30
Meat Chopper, cast, w/ crank handle, clamps, c. 1900	17	22	30
Meat Hook, tinned, c. 1890	18	24	30
Meat Slicer, crank handle, clamp-on table type, circular blade	14	18	25
Meat Tenderizer, cast, c. 1892	15	20	45
Pastry Jigger, cast, octagonal, dia. 5.5", c. 1900	10	30	50
Pastry Marker, late 19th century	15	18	30
Pea Huller	56	75	70
Pig-Form Mechanical Bell, len. 6.5"	1200	1600	2000
Planters, pair, oblong, w. 25"	1000	1400	1750
Pot Hook, wrought hook w/ wood handle	17	27	75
Potato Chipper, clamp-on type, crank handle	24	32	44
Raisin and Grape Seeder, c. 1890	42	56	70
Raisin Seeder, cast	24	32	50
Roasting Spit, wrought fireplace, brass finials	300	450	550
Rug Beater, wire, including handle, spade shape, c. 1850	18	30	60
Rug Beater, wire pattern w/ wood handles, c. 1920	10	20	40
Rushlight, ht. 10"; c. 1850	100	200	350
Rushlight, snake head, w. 11", c. 1750	200	350	500
Rushlight, yew pedestal, ht. 8.5", c. 1850	140	250	350
Sausage Stuffer, cast and sheet, gears	45	60	80
Shop Sign of Riding Boot, ptd. cast zinc, Fiske, 1880, ht. 29"	1500	3000	5000
Sugar Cutter, nippers, shears, for snipping cones of sugar	50	100	150
Sugar Devil, for use w/ brown sugar, cut-off hardened lumps	112	150	175
Sugar Nips, late 19th century	19	35	56
Tailors, European origin, mid-19th century, w. 9"	23	30	51
Tallow Dipper, wrought, 18th century, w. 25"	300	500	775
Tenderer Steak, wood, c. 1870	10	15	25
Toaster, 2 slices, 3 legs, handle, w. 17"	202	270	281
Trivet, lacy cast, 6 points and circular motif, mid-19th century	70	100	175
Trivet, letters	30	40	75
Trivet, lyre	52	70	100
Trivet, Maltese emblem	48	64	100
Trivet, Masonic emblem	63	84	150

Above: wrought iron wick trimmer, len. 5",
$20-$40 retail.

Cast zinc retriever, len. 40" , $2700 at auction. — Photo
courtesy of Northeast Auctions.

Pewter

Pewter is a tin alloy, often containing copper. It is usually dark gray and soft, but can be light and shiny, almost resembling silver. Early pewter should not be used for eating, drinking, or storing food, as it often contains lead, which can poison the food.

"Good" examples must be in reasonable condition, without any large dents. "Best" examples are undented and well proportioned, show exceptional workmanship, and usually contain a "touch" or hammered mark of the maker. These marks can be identified by various guides.

Whale oil lamps with rare lenses. — Photo courtesy of Northeast Auctions.

	GOOD	BETTER	BEST
Basin, by Semper Eadam, Boston, dia. 9".	$ 1000	$ 1400	$ 1750
Brunnen Kessel, Swiss, 19th century	300	500	800
Candlestick, 19th century, ht. 12"	40	90	180
Chalice, Continental, 19th century, ht. 8"	75	100	125
Chamberpot, 19th century, dia. 14"	80	120	200
Charger, Eng., 18th century, dia. 18"	712	950	1188
Charger, European, 18th century, dia. 16"	200	250	500
Coffee Urn, Continental, 19th century, ht. 14"	75	100	125
Covered Pot, French, late 19th century	35	50	90
Flagon, Covered, French, late 18th century, ht. 14"	600	800	1000
Flagon, octagonal, ram's head thumb-piece, 19th century, ht. 14".	75	150	225
Flagon, spouted, Continental	250	500	800
Flagon, spouted, French	450	600	750
Flask, octagonal, Continental, 18th century, ht. 13".	750	1000	1250
Fluid Lamp, German, 19th century	375	500	625
Funnel, 19th cent, len. 9"	35	60	90
Glocackenkann Spouted-Flask.	525	700	875
Jug, French, Louis XV style w/ engraved bust	375	500	625
Lamps, pair, Amer. acorn-form, ht. 11".	525	700	875
Lavabo, Continental 2-part	825	1100	1375
Measure, French, 19th century	25	30	50
Measures, set of 7, Eng. bulbous-form, ht. to 5".	375	500	625

Pewter ashtrays in the Art Nouveau style, $25-$50.

	GOOD	BETTER	BEST
Measures, set of 7, French, ht. to 5"	$ 300	$ 400	$ 500
Mess Bowl, 19th century, dia. 8"	20	30	50
Pitcher, French Brocauvin	188	250	312
Plate, Amer., 18th century, dia. 8"	135	180	225
Plate, deep, 18th century, dia. 10"	225	300	375
Plate, European, dia. 10"	50	70	100
Plate, wavy-edge, French, 9"	25	35	60
Platter, Wavy-Edge, French, 12"	60	80	100
Porringer, Continental, 2-handled, dia. 5"	52	70	88
Porringer, Continental, 2-handled, dia. 6"	75	100	125
Porringer, dia. 6"	18	24	30
Soup Plate, 19th century, 8"	20	30	50
Spoon, 19th century	9	12	15
Spouted Flagon, Swiss, Stegkanne-form. ht. 12".	450	600	750
Tankard, dated 1784, ht. 9".	600	800	1000
Tankard, dome top, crenalated lip, by John Will, NY, 1752-66. Jacob's Mark 280, ht.7".	20,000	34,000	42,500
Trophy Cup, armorial, Louis XV style, 19th century, ht. 12"	375	500	625

Much late nineteenth century pewter is "Britainia" metal.

A different maker can mean a very different price. Below left: New York tankard by Frederick Bassett, $20,000 at auction. Below right: New York tankard by Francis Bassett failed to sell at $10,000.

Silver

　　Silver is alloyed with other metals for durability, as pure silver is too soft for most uses. The grade of silver is determined by the amount or percentage of alloy material contained. Sterling silver is 925 parts per 1000 pure (usually stated as .925).

　　The values listed are primarily for easily found items. However, some rare and valuable examples are included for comparison. "Good" examples are considered to be in excellent condition, but without any superlative features. "Best" examples are perfectly proportioned and show exceptional workmanship. Thicker, and therefore heavier, pieces are generally of better quality than light pieces. Although dents can be repaired by a skilled silversmith, it is not cheap. Also beware that a faker can add new marks, new decoration (such as chasing), or even new parts (such as a new base).

Above left: Boston pepper caster by Daniel Parker, 1768, with original bill of sale, $3500 at auction. Above right: Philadelphia soup ladle by Joseph Lownes, c. 1800, $800 at auction.
— Photos courtesy of Northeast Auctions.

	GOOD	BETTER	BEST
Baby Mug, early 19th century, Amer., repoussé	$ 200	$ 270	$ 400
Baby Mug, late 19th century, Eng., engraved	100	180	300
Baby Rattle, mid-19th century, 3" foliate design	200	270	400
Baby Spoon, late 19th century, Amer.	30	40	60
Beaker, Amer., incised rings, by C. A. Burnett, ht. 3", 4 oz.	1800	2380	3500
Bodkin, early 20th century, Eng.	50	70	100
Book Cover, late 19th century	150	180	250
Bookmark, early 20th century, Eng.	50	90	150
Bookmark, late 19th century, Amer.	150	180	250
Boson's Whistle, late 19th century	300	360	500
Bottle Opener, early 20th century	30	50	80
Bottle Stopper, simple form, late 19th century	50	70	100
Bottle Stopper, whimsical form, late 19th century	200	220	300
Buckle, Art Deco, engine turned	100	110	150

	GOOD	BETTER	BEST
Buckle, Art Nouveau, late 19th century	$ 150	$ 220	$ 350
Button Hook, Art Nouveau, late 19th century	75	90	125
Button Hook, repoussé handle, late 19th century	50	70	100
Cake Basket, repoussé	500	760	1200
Calling Card Case, late 19th century, Eng.	200	320	500
Candle Snuffer, mid-20th century	40	50	80
Candlesticks, plain, low, weighted, 20th century	100	160	250
Cane Handle, late 19th century, cast and chased	300	360	500
Christmas Ornament, late 20th century	40	50	80
Cigar Cutter, whimsical shape, late 19th century, Eng.	100	160	250
Cigarette Case, enameled, mid-20th century	200	320	500
Cigarette Case, engraved, early 20th century	100	180	300
Compote, .950-silver, Ball, Black & Co., 30 oz.	1200	1350	1800
Compote, medallion pat., Ball, Black & Co., ht. 10", 22 oz.	1200	1800	2800
Creamer, Amer., by E. Moulton, oval engraved, ht. 5", 5 oz.	900	1080	1500
Creamer/Sugar, Amer., by E. Moulton, 13 oz.	1800	2840	4500
Darning Egg, silver mounts, early 20th century	40	50	80
Ewer, owned by Daniel Webster, by S. Kirk, marine motifs, ht. 11", 42 oz.	10,000	15,750	25,000
Flask, Art Nouveau, repoussé, late 19th century	500	580	800
Flask, engine turned, late 19th century	300	360	500
Flask, engraved, early 20th century	100	180	300
Flask, Tiffany Japanese style, late 19th century	2000	2250	3000
Food Pusher, mid-19th century, Amer.	40	50	70
Frame, Art Nouveau, 7", early 20th century	200	270	400
Frame, repoussé, floral-decorated, late 19th century, 9"	600	720	1000
Frame, undecorated, mid-20th century, 6"	100	180	300
Frame, undecorated, mid-20th century, 9"	200	270	400
Funnel, early 19th century	500	680	1000
Funnel, early 20th century	100	180	300
Glove Stretcher, Amer., late 19th century	50	90	150
Inkstand, Art Nouveau, late 19th century	500	680	1000
Inkstand, Georgian style, late 19th century	400	540	800
Inkwell, late 19th century, Eng., engraved	150	220	350
Judaic Spice Tower, late 19th century, 10"	400	450	600
Letter Opener, engraved handle, mid-20th century	50	70	100
Letter Opener, repoussé handle, late 19th century	100	140	200
Luggage Tag, engraved, late 19th century	50	70	100
Luggage Tag, engraved, mid-20th century	25	40	75
Magnifying Glass, Art Nouveau, late 19th century	300	360	500
Magnifying Glass, engraved, mid-20th century	100	140	200
Matchsafe, enameled, early 20th century	200	270	400
Matchsafe, repoussé, late 19th century	150	220	350
Matchsafe, whimsical shape, late 19th century	400	540	800
Miniature Coffee Pot, 2", Dutch, late 19th century	100	180	300
Miniature Sofa, 3", Eng., early 20th century	100	140	200
Miniature Table, 2", Continental, early 20th century	100	140	200
Miniature Tray, 2.5", mid-19th century, Eng.	300	360	500
Mustache Comb, early 20th century	50	70	100
Napkin Ring, engraved, late 19th century	50	60	75
Napkin Ring, engraved, mid 20th century	10	30	50

Above top row left to right: early American sugar and creamer by Ebenezer Moulton, $800 at auction; early American creamer by Ebenezer Moulton, $500 at auction; Above bottom row left to right: Boston coin-silver keyhole porringer by Robert Evans, $1500 estimate at auction; early American beaker by Charles Burnett, $1000 at auction. Boston coin-silver keyhole porringer by Knight Leverett, $1500. — Photo courtesy of Northeast Auctions.

Tiffany engraved silver letter opener, $30-$50

	GOOD	BETTER	BEST
Napkin Ring, hand-hammered, early 20th century	$ 20	$ 30	$ 50
Napkin Ring, repoussé, mid-19th century	50	70	100
Necessaire, 6 implements, early 20th century, French	200	270	400
Nutmeg Grater, engine turned, cylindrical, early 19th century	400	450	600
Nutmeg Grater, oval, early 19th century	300	360	500
Overlay Glass Cologne Bottle, clear glass, early 20th century	75	100	150
Overlay Glass Cologne Bottle, colored glass, early 20th century .	150	220	350
Overlay Glass Decanter, clear glass, early 20th century	200	270	400
Overlay Glass Pitcher, clear glass, late 19th century	400	450	600
Paper Knife, late 19th century	200	270	400
Pencil, retractable, early 20th century	150	180	250
Pillbox, late 19th century, Eng.	200	270	400
Pin Cushion, animal shape, late 19th century	200	270	400
Pin Cushion, chatelaine type, late 19th century	100	140	200
Place Card Holders, animal shape, set of 4, early 20th century	300	360	500
Place Card Holders, engraved, late 19th century, set of 4	200	270	400
Playing Card Box, early 20th century, Eng.	150	220	350
Porringer, keyhole, coin-silver, K. Leverett, dia. 5.25", 6 oz.	2500	3380	5000
Posey Holder, embossed, late 19th century, Eng.	300	360	500
Posey Holder, filigree, late 19th century, Continental	400	400	500
Posey Holder, paneled, early 20th century	200	270	400
Powder Box, early 20th century, French, engraved	150	220	350
Riding Crop, silver handled, early 19th century	500	680	1000
Ring box, early 20th century, Eng.	50	90	150
Scent Bottle, late 19th century	150	220	350
Seal, for sealing wax, late 19th century	200	270	400
Seal, for sealing wax, mid-20th century	50	90	150
Shoe Horn, engraved, early 20th century	75	100	150
Snuffbox, early 19th century, German	600	720	1000
Snuffbox, late 19th century, Eng.	300	360	500
Soap Case, embossed, late 19th century	100	110	150
Souvenir Spoon, early 20th century	30	40	70
Souvenir Spoon, late 19th century	50	70	100
Spurs (pr.), early 19th century, simple engraved	400	540	800
Spurs (pr.), early 20th century, simple engraved	200	270	400
Stamp Box, late 19th century	150	180	250
Stamp Box, whimsical form, late 19th century	300	360	500
String Holder, late 19th century	300	360	500
Table Bell, late 19th century, Eng.	150	270	450
Talc Shaker, late 19th century	100	140	200
Tankard, Amer., by R. Humphreys, ht. 7", 21 oz.	2500	3380	5000
Tatting Shuttle, late 19th century	50	90	150
Tea Infuser, ball form, late 19th century	75	90	125
Tea Infuser, whimsical form, late 19th century	300	360	500
Tea Infuser, whimsical form, mid-20th century	100	110	150
Tea Strainer, late 19th century	100	110	150
Tea Strainer, mid-20th century	50	70	100
Thimble, chased and engraved, early 19th century	300	360	500
Thimble, engraved, late 19th century	100	140	200
Thimble, engraved, mid-20th century	30	40	50

	GOOD	BETTER	BEST
Thread Holder, reticulated, late 19th century	$ 100	$ 140	$ 200
Toast Rack, early 20th century, Eng.	150	220	350
Tobacco Box, late 18th century, Eng.	500	630	900
Toothbrush Holder, early 20th century	50	70	100
Toothpick, early 20th century	20	30	50
Toothpick Holder, engraved, early 20th century	100	180	300
Torah Finials (pr.), early 20th century	500	580	800
Trophy Cup, 6", engraved, mid-20th century	300	400	600
Vinaigrette, mid-19th century, simple form	150	200	300
Vinaigrette, mid-19th century, whimsical form	500	680	1000
Walking Stick, silver handled, late 19th century	100	180	300
Whistle, penny whistle form, early 20th century	100	140	200
Wine Coaster, mid-19th century	300	360	500
Wine Label, crescent shape, late 19th century	50	90	150
Wine Label, engraved, late 18th century	150	200	300
Wine Taster, early 19th century, Continental	300	360	500
Wine Taster, mid-20th century	100	140	200

Silver Flatware

Silverware includes factory merchandise and products of individual craftsmen. Chief American manufacturers include Gorham, Reed and Barton, Towle, Wallace, Rogers, Oneida, Kirk, and International.

Values are given in two sections. In the first we list a large variety of tableware and serving pieces for a single pattern. Values are for visible worn pieces (W), excellent condition monogrammed pieces (M), and excellent condition pieces with no monogram (E).

In the second section, we list five key pieces for a variety of patterns listed under the name of their manufacturer: Dinner Fork (*DnF*), Dessert Fork (*DsF*), Serving Spoon (*SvSp*), Soup Spoon (*SpSp*), and Teaspoon (*Tsp*).

Versailles Pattern
Gorham - 1898

	W	M	E
Berry Spoon, large	$ 127	$ 135	$ 125
Bouillon Spoon	27	34	27
Carving Fork	67	75	65
Cheese Scoop, large	145	155	145
Citrus Spoon	40	45	37
Cocktail Fork	28	32	25
Cold Meat (Buffet) Fork	112	125	110
Cream Soup Spoon	48	52	47
Cream Soup Spoon, small	37	42	35
Demitasse Spoon	22	27	22
Dessert Spoon	42	47	40
Dinner Fork	47	52	45
Dinner Knife	57	62	55
Fish Fork	40	45	40
Fish Knife	37	45	35
Five O'Clock Teaspoon	15	21	16
Flat Server	30	35	30
Fruit Knife	37	42	35
Gravy Ladle	100	110	95
Ice Cream Fork	40	45	40
Ice Cream Spoon	42	47	40
Iced Tea Spoon	52	57	50
Jelly Server, large	135	145	135
Lettuce Fork	95	100	95
Luncheon Fork	37	42	35
Luncheon Knife	45	50	43
Nut Picks	27	35	25
Olive or Pickle Fork	45	50	45
Pie Server	40	45	40
Salad Fork	47	53	45
Soup Ladle	250	260	250
Steak Knife	37	43	35
Sugar Shell	37	45	35
Sugar Tongs	45	50	45
Tablespoon/Serving Spoon	52	58	50
Teaspoon	21	27	19

	YEAR	DnF	DsF	SvSp	SpSp	Tsp
	Alvin Co.					
Bridal Bouquet	1932	$ 50	$ 37	$ 100	$ 39	$ 41
Chapel Bells	1939	48	34	94	40	38
Chased Romantique	1936	39	33	99	39	32
Chippendale, old	1899	55	47	118	57	43
Francis I	1913	43	32	88	35	33
French Scroll	1953	43	33	89	40	34
Hampton	1911	36	31	80	37	28
Lady Beatrice	1912	33	30	82	32	29
Majestic	1900	60	48	124	54	45
Mastercraft	1937	36	31	89	31	33
Morning Glory	1909	55	46	117	43	46
Raleigh	1902	46	35	100	40	35
Regent	1932	35	30	88	33	27
Romantique	1933	41	30	84	37	24
Shenandoah	1915	36	26	75	29	28
Virginia	1908	31	27	71	33	24
	Dominick & Haff					
Acanthus	1895	$ 39	$ 35	$ 97	$ 43	$ 36
Blossom	1902	84	60	165	53	44
Century, No. 6, engr.	1901	50	38	111	48	37
Charles II	1894	49	43	116	54	36

Gorham "Poppy" pattern. — Photo courtesy of Phillips Auctioneers.

	YEAR	DnF	DsF	SvSp	SpSp	Tsp
Grape	1895	$ 73	$ 57	$ 162	$ 71	$ 46
La Salle, chased	1928	32	27	76	29	30
Louis XIV	1913	39	36	107	45	40
Martha Washington	1926	38	30	82	38	32
Medallion	1907	123	100	297	120	78
Pointed Antique, hammered	1895	35	27	78	36	30
Pointed Antique, No. 2, engr.	1895	32	28	89	37	35
Queen Anne, No. 15, engr.	1910	34	30	82	34	31
Queen Anne, plain	1910	34	25	66	31	20
Queen Elizabeth	1916	38	34	89	40	34
Rococo	1888	56	47	139	56	40

Durgin Division of Gorham

	YEAR	DnF	DsF	SvSp	SpSp	Tsp
Bradford	1909	$ 33	$ 29	$ 77	$ 33	$ 31
Chatham, hammered	1915	32	29	84	33	27
Chatham, No. 4, chased	1915	46	31	97	36	37
Cromwell	1893	58	43	126	56	42
Dauphin	1897	82	70	170	77	50
Empire	1895	117	92	249	111	48
Fairfax, No. 1, engr.	1910	44	37	96	41	33
No. 19-B	1912	36	27	71	31	21

Fessenden & Co.

	YEAR	DnF	DsF	SvSp	SpSp	Tsp
Graeco	1912	$ 51	$ 39	$ 108	$ 50	$ 34
Tulip	1915	101	80	235	93	80

Frank M. Whiting & Co.

	YEAR	DnF	DsF	SvSp	SpSp	Tsp
Antique	1885	$ 48	$ 34	$ 92	$ 36	$ 30
Autumn	1888	39	29	87	35	33
Talisman Rose	1948	38	31	92	35	36
Troubadour	1945	55	45	120	53	34

Frank Smith Silver Co.

	YEAR	DnF	DsF	SvSp	SpSp	Tsp
Adrienne	1919	$ 30	$ 26	$ 71	$ 30	$ 28
Antique	1886	42	31	81	32	29
Cambodia	1916	40	37	105	41	37
Jac Rose	1900	46	39	98	44	34
L. Kraft	1910	49	39	104	43	40
Martha Randolph	1921	41	29	82	33	32
Mayfair	1951	53	40	120	46	40
Mayflower, hand-chased	1918	41	30	79	33	27
Vergennes	1913	33	27	76	33	31

Gorham

	YEAR	DnF	DsF	SvSp	SpSp	Tsp
Andante	1957	$ 54	$ 40	$ 107	$ 45	$ 42
Baronial	1973	79	67	175	74	53
Buckingham	1910	54	47	121	51	38
Cellini	1915	48	38	107	47	39
Chantilly	1895	74	63	159	68	44
Chesterfield	1908	64	47	130	57	40
Chippendale	1890	57	42	124	54	35

	YEAR	DnF	DsF	SvSp	SpSp	Tsp
Classic Bouquet	1972	$ 51	$ 43	$ 125	$ 54	$ 44
Classique	1961	47	39	114	48	38
Clermont	1915	44	35	101	42	36
Colonial Eagle	1960	39	33	95	43	39
Covington	1914	54	38	100	43	32
Cromwell	1900	39	37	96	40	37
Edgeworth	1922	33	29	83	36	27
Florentine	1901	65	55	154	68	40
Gold Tip	1952	38	32	90	39	36
Golden Wheat	1952	51	40	110	44	33
Gossamer, engr.	1966	35	31	83	38	25
Jefferson	1907	32	26	81	36	26
La Scala	1964	79	73	195	85	49
Marie Antoinette	1891	109	84	224	97	66
Medici	1971	82	71	193	82	61
Old Masters	1885	213	174	416	196	118
Paris	1900	135	129	343	150	95
Poppy	1894	80	60	200	100	60
Roanoke	1913	74	70	168	83	47
Rosemont	1915	56	46	126	53	37
Rosette	1868	61	59	155	68	42
Sea Rose	1958	39	30	84	35	31
Sovereign	1968	81	71	187	77	50
Spotswood	1912	55	42	117	52	36
Strasbourg	1897	66	56	143	58	48
Swiss	1870	35	32	81	33	27
Theme	1954	33	26	72	32	24
Touraine	1917	55	46	111	55	34
Villa-Norfolk	1903	41	29	91	32	35

International Silver Co.

	YEAR	DnF	DsF	SvSp	SpSp	Tsp
1810	1930	$ 46	$ 40	$ 107	$ 46	$ 34
Abbottsford	1907	68	51	146	59	43
Alexandria	1915	39	32	85	36	30
Althea	1910	80	61	146	71	42
Andover	1919	36	29	85	38	30
Breton Rose	1954	51	40	116	49	39
Cavell	1923	42	36	104	38	32
Cloeta	1905	101	73	200	92	48
Colonial, hammered	1923	47	40	114	46	35
Continental	1934	36	29	75	34	29
Davenport	1913	37	30	78	36	27
Devonshire	1914	53	40	107	51	34
Diana	1900	67	58	137	69	40
Dorchester, old	1910	38	36	95	45	34
Dresden	1899	55	44	119	52	38
Florence	1903	45	39	102	44	31
Frontenac	1903	125	89	231	105	59
Gadroon	1933	66	50	126	58	44
Governor Warren	1918	34	28	79	35	29
Grande Regency	1969	62	54	145	63	42
Jeanne d'Arc	1905	83	62	161	75	44

	YEAR	DnF	DsF	SvSp	SpSp	Tsp
Lambeth Manor	1952	$ 65	$ 52	$ 142	$ 57	$ 40
Lenox	1929	37	32	92	36	28
Mademoiselle	1964	47	39	104	43	32
Maintenon	1933	58	46	121	50	38
Marathon, old	1909	50	41	106	47	38
May Melody	1952	51	36	105	46	30
Minuet	1925	39	29	80	29	31
Napoleon	1910	36	30	91	37	28
New Margaret	1912	48	41	102	43	34
Patria	1918	37	31	89	38	29
Prelude	1939	72	56	160	69	51
Queen's Lace	1949	60	49	145	61	42
Rosalind, new	1921	38	33	98	42	34
Rosalind, old	1908	53	42	114	45	32
Salem	1928	39	36	99	44	33
Silver Rhythm	1953	36	28	84	35	30
Spring Glory	1941	54	51	133	56	42
Stuyvesant	1916	36	31	84	34	36
Tradewinds	1975	65	50	125	59	43
Trousseau	1935	44	36	92	39	32
Valencia	1965	52	39	107	45	36
Van Dyke	1910	51	38	109	48	38
Wedding Bells	1948	59	42	123	51	40
Wellesley	1912	57	50	140	55	37
Whitehall	1938	64	48	136	60	44
Wild Rose	1948	62	50	131	58	41

Lunt Silversmiths

Adam	1921	$ 48	$ 38	$ 110	$ 45	$ 33
Alexandra	1961	72	54	145	61	52
American Victorian	1941	50	41	122	48	38
Belvedere	1972	57	45	124	52	47
Chatelaine (ex- Enid)	1894	63	51	133	59	38
Colonial Theme	1964	40	35	100	40	28
Coronet	1932	35	28	68	31	22
Early American, engr.	1926	51	44	120	53	37
Early American, plain	1926	37	27	69	32	26
Lace Point	1964	37	28	70	29	23
Rapallo	1968	40	32	83	35	29
Rose Elegance	1958	56	44	113	47	41
Sweetheart Rose	1951	36	27	67	31	21
Tudor	1900	44	35	97	35	35
Verona	1894	67	52	139	65	38
Windsor	1883	27	26	70	30	22

Manchester Silver Co.

Pilgrim	1932	$ 39	$ 30	$ 89	$ 35	$ 33
Polly Lawton	1935	39	29	83	32	33

Mount Vernon Co.

20th Century	1901	$ 47	$ 42	$ 107	$ 47	$ 37

	YEAR	DnF	DsF	SvSp	SpSp	Tsp
Alden	1910	$ 27	$ 23	$ 61	$ 26	$ 18
Angelo	1910	50	42	123	53	42
Harewood, engr.	1915	34	28	79	29	29
Josephine	1899	46	41	101	43	35
Lady Wynn	1913	51	41	106	47	33
Louis XVI	1912	61	47	132	59	41
Mount Vernon (ex-Yale)	1911	31	27	71	30	24
Old South, engr.	1907	34	27	80	33	30
Queen	1898	57	48	126	58	38
Queen Elizabeth	1905	32	29	73	34	25
R.W. Empire	1900	39	35	96	43	33
Round Antique	1900	33	27	70	32	21
Sulgrave	1912	35	26	68	28	23
West Point	1920	31	25	70	28	24
Winthrop	1909	34	29	76	33	30

Oneida, Ltd.

	YEAR	DnF	DsF	SvSp	SpSp	Tsp
Afterglow	1956	$ 59	$ 45	$ 118	$ 50	$ 41
Engagement	1952	47	34	105	39	35
First Frost	1967	39	31	89	32	28
Grand Majesty	1976	72	48	141	58	40
Impresario	1974	44	39	99	40	36
Lasting Spring	1949	36	35	91	42	31
Mansion House	1948	48	37	98	40	34
Reigning Beauty	1953	41	35	100	45	35
Sentimental	1960	43	34	88	36	26
Teramo	1967	31	28	67	28	21
Will 'O' Wisp	1968	32	28	71	30	28

Reed & Barton

	YEAR	DnF	DsF	SvSp	SpSp	Tsp
Burgundy	1949	$ 58	$ 47	$ 129	$ 59	$ 40
Classic Rose	1954	39	34	89	35	29
Fragrance	1941	58	43	131	56	38
French Antique, engr.	1901	35	27	70	30	25
Hepplewhite, engr.	1907	40	29	84	31	26
La Perle, engr.	1902	53	44	110	47	39
La Rocaille	1890	55	42	116	48	35
Lark	1960	35	31	81	33	34
Liberty	1917	33	27	79	30	27
Old Virginia	1973	64	54	161	69	51
Rembrandt	1915	52	39	104	46	37
Riviera	1911	32	26	71	29	27
Silver Sculpture	1954	36	28	80	31	28
Spanish Baroque	1965	55	46	130	56	43
St. George	1918	37	29	88	33	28
St. George, chased	1918	48	33	92	37	34

Samuel Kirk & Son, Inc.

	YEAR	DnF	DsF	SvSp	SpSp	Tsp
Cynthia	1957	$ 41	$ 31	$ 79	$ 36	$ 27
Florentine	1962	35	27	70	32	24
Mayflower	1846	54	46	126	57	44

	YEAR	DnF	DsF	SvSp	SpSp	Tsp
Old Maryland	1850	$ 57	$ 38	$ 113	$ 44	$ 35
Old Maryland, engr.	1936	51	43	115	54	36
Signet, plain	1958	34	27	77	34	23
Skylark	1954	39	29	86	34	28
Winslow	1850	67	50	123	58	33

Schofield Co.

	YEAR	DnF	DsF	SvSp	SpSp	Tsp
Baltimore Rose	1900	$ 67	$ 49	$ 132	$ 44	$ 42
Elizabeth Tudor, plain	1900	25	21	66	25	27
La Rochelle	1890	32	26	74	30	26
Lily	1915	45	37	103	41	31
Mayflower	1915	46	38	109	40	33
Virginia Dare	1915	48	35	104	44	32
Waterford	1915	40	36	100	37	35

Stieff Co.

	YEAR	DnF	DsF	SvSp	SpSp	Tsp
Betsy Patterson, engr.	1979	$ 36	$ 31	$ 79	$ 36	$ 27
Carrollton	1961	47	40	107	48	35
Queen Anne-Williamsburg	1940	64	49	127	54	46
Royal Dynasty	1966	63	48	141	63	52

Towle Mfg. Co.

	YEAR	DnF	DsF	SvSp	SpSp	Tsp
Auvergne	1905	$ 54	$ 37	$ 111	$ 44	$ 30
Chased Diana	1930	45	40	108	45	37
Chippendale	1937	39	27	72	29	24
Danish Baroque	1970	70	58	151	73	50
Empire	1894	48	44	120	50	33
Grand Duchess	1973	77	66	173	80	52
Lady Diana	1929	40	34	103	42	36
Legato	1962	51	43	121	53	40
Louis XIV	1924	40	34	91	38	29
Madeira	1948	43	37	102	37	34
Old Lace	1939	39	30	89	36	33
Peachtree Manor	1957	54	43	117	49	34
Queen Elizabeth I	1970	50	43	114	50	35
Richmond	1901	52	36	96	37	35
Sculptured Rose	1961	39	29	90	33	28
Seville	1926	39	32	88	37	30
Symphony	1931	36	29	86	32	28
Virginia Carvel	1919	41	29	77	33	29
Virginia Lee	1920	37	33	93	36	29

Tuttle Silver Co.

	YEAR	DnF	DsF	SvSp	SpSp	Tsp
Onslow	1929	$ 55	$ 48	$ 133	$ 57	$ 39

Wallace Silversmiths

	YEAR	DnF	DsF	SvSp	SpSp	Tsp
America	1915	$ 37	$ 32	$ 81	$ 34	$ 27
Carnation	1909	71	59	145	65	38
Concord	1926	40	30	85	35	31
Dauphine	1916	64	51	124	58	40
Faneuil	1925	37	36	89	45	31

	YEAR	DnF	DsF	SvSp	SpSp	Tsp
Golden Aegean Weave	1971	$ 88	$ 70	$ 199	$ 88	$ 59
Le Moderne	1926	40	31	91	38	34
Lucerne	1896	89	70	173	77	50
Marie	1895	37	30	84	31	32
Melanie	1959	59	46	121	51	36
Pilgrim	1915	34	30	84	33	25
Princess Anne	1926	40	32	86	36	31
Puritan, hammered	1910	33	31	84	31	24
Putnam	1912	36	29	82	32	27
Rose	1898	57	38	105	48	38
San Juan	1914	43	35	101	40	33
Sir Christopher	1936	105	82	200	91	57
St. George	1878	60	49	128	54	45
Standish	1917	39	30	83	33	32
Still Mood	1963	44	39	104	42	35
Stradivari	1937	81	64	174	70	48
Tipped	1890	42	35	104	39	31
Violet	1904	61	48	120	56	37
Washington	1911	37	31	87	35	32
Waverly	1890	53	38	108	48	40
Windsor	1890	33	27	76	32	29
Wishing Star	1954	39	34	94	44	40

Watson Co. (Wallace)

Mount Vernon	1907	$ 50	$ 46	$ 122	$ 54	$ 33
Colonial Antique	1923	46	32	101	38	38
John Alden	1911	35	31	80	34	31
Lily	1902	113	96	227	105	66
Marlborough	1918	45	33	92	39	31
Queen Louise	1912	47	38	107	44	40
Rochambeau	1919	46	37	105	46	39
Virginia	1911	49	40	105	41	37
Windsor Rose	1940	53	43	127	56	48

Whiting Division of Gorham

Antique, Chased	1880	$ 57	$ 40	$ 112	$ 46	$ 37
Antique Rosette	1885	42	33	99	36	37
Colonial A, engr.	1908	42	36	102	40	32
Dorothy Vernon	1909	57	45	121	53	41
Imperial Queen	1895	77	64	162	69	51
King Albert	1919	41	29	84	37	27
Lady Baltimore	1910	38	30	87	31	31
Lily of the Valley	1885	137	119	304	144	69
Livingston B. chased	1915	34	29	80	33	33
Portland	1913	36	27	75	30	33
Radiant	1895	81	70	177	73	46
Wedgwood	1911	44	35	97	42	35

Tin

Often overlooked, tin collectibles can still be found at many garage sales. "Good" examples must be in good condition, with only small unobtrusive bits of corrosion and only tiny dents. "Best" examples are undented and well proportioned, and show fine workmanship. All items are 20th century unless otherwise noted.

Left: Lithographed biscuit tin, $30-$60.

Right: Nineteenth century tin lanterns, $150-$300.

	GOOD	BETTER	BEST
Mirror-Back Tin Sconce of circular form, c. 1850, ht. 12".	$ 500	$ 1500	$ 3500
Mixing Spoons, perforated bowls, wood handles, c. 1900	10	20	40
Mixing Spoons, set: .5 tsp-2 tbs, Rumford Co.	16	25	60
Mixing Spoons, slotted bowl, bottle opener on handle, advertising slogans	16	25	55
Mixing Spoons, slotted bowl, says "Rumford Cake Mix," c. 1900	16	25	68
Mold, bread or pudding, w. 11"	60	85	190
Mold, fluted edge handle, w. 3"	20	45	106
Mold, for cheese, grape pattern, w. 6"	40	75	190
Mold, ice-cream, c. 1880	40	80	200
Mold, jelly, c. 1890	40	80	200
Mold, lion, w/ base, w. 6"	52	85	213
Mold, pierced tin, heart-form, for cheese, c. 1880	36	52	118
Mold, tubular, c. 1890	20	30	72
Muffin or Cupcake Pan, 12 cups, tin/sheet iron, c. 1890	28	30	80
Muffin or Cupcake Pan, 6 cups, tin/steel alloy, c. 1870	25	40	80
Muffin Pan, 8 cups, push-out function, c. 1910	16	30	50

	GOOD	BETTER	BEST
Muffin Rings, c. 1875	$ 5	$ 10	$ 25
Nurser, tin can, w/ lid, handle, spout	170	245	532
Nutmeg Grater, handmade drum type	35	50	125
Nutmeg Grater, wood handles, c. 1900, 4"	75	145	300
Oven, Biscuit, self-powered w/ charcoal, legs	220	295	570
Oven, Roasting, sits on hearth, w/ spit	260	353	700
Pail, lard, c. 1890, tin, bail handles	65	98	228
Pail, lunch, domed style, w/ dishes, cup	145	203	418
Pail, lunch, rd., handle, 6" dia.	36	55	133
Pail, lunch, w/ cups/dishes	82	115	245
Pail, milk, convex, c. 1890	65	95	200
Pail, milk, rd., late 1800s	55	85	190
Pastry Board, tinned sheet iron, w/ rolling pin	200	350	600
Pastry Board, w/ hanging loop, trough, 18"	100	200	400
Pastry Board, w/ rolling pin cradle, 22" x 18.5"	100	200	400
Pie Lifter, c. 1900	25	35	100
Pie Lifter, shovel type, wood handle, rd.	16	28	76
Pie Lifter, tin w/ wood handle	20	25	60
Pie Lifter, wire tines, heavy tin	16	25	60
Pie Pan, says "Balto. Pie Bakery"	25	38	95
Pie Plate, c. 1880	8	15	42
Pitcher, Water, large globe-form, 8 qt. size, w/ 6 tumblers	60	90	200
Pitcher, Water, sloping sides, flared lip, qt.	40	60	150
Pitcher, Water, sloping sides, hinged lid, qt.	40	75	170
Plate Warmer, bowl-form, legs, handle	145	210	400
Plate Warmer, box-form, legs, handle	120	300	600
Plate Warmer, cylindrical, handle, lid, plate	30	55	100
Popcorn Popper, plain, c. 1890, factory-made	2	38	100
Popcorn Popper, rect., wood handle, c. 1880	82	115	245
Pot Chain, mesh circles for pot cleaning	8	15	38
Pot Chain, mesh circles for pot cleaning, w/ steel scraper	10	18	45
Pot Chain, simple single ring style	5	12	35

Tin roaster

	GOOD	BETTER	BEST
Pot, egg-form, lid w/ hinge	$ 40	$ 63	$ 150
Press, Food, c. 1930, zinc-plated iron	40	63	150
Press, Meat Loaf, tin w/ wood frame, top handle	65	95	200
Press, Wine, perforated tin w/ wood frame, rd.	75	100	225
Pudding Mold, cylindrical, 2 qt., w/ lid	18	26	55
Pudding Mold, cylindrical, 2 qt., w/ lid, scalloped mold	26	38	85
Pudding Mold, oval, scalloped border, 1 qt.	16	25	60
Pudding Mold, oval, serrated rim, 1.5 qt.	23	35	76
Pudding Mold, oval w/ tulip, 2 qt.	28	30	85
Pudding Mold, pan-form, w/ lid, c. 1890	16	25	60
Roaster, black tin, c. 1890	36	50	100
Roasting Oven, swing top, reflector type, w. 11"	163	225	450
Roiling Pin, wood handles	65	95	200
Salt Box, hanging	20	45	100
Salt Box, w/ raised letters, "SALT"	33	40	115
Sander, cylinder, dark finish, 2.5"	25	35	76
Sausage Gun, tapering tube w/ wood plunger	40	72	163
Sausage Gun, tavern size, 4"	100	130	285
Sausage Stuffer, w/ wood press	42	55	115
Scoops, curved handle, 5"	16	25	65
Scrapple Pan, tinned iron, Pennsylvania Dutch	700	1000	2500
Shaker, spice, Norton Brothers, 1890	20	30	65
Shoe Sole Templates, tin, 6 sizes, c. 1920	60	85	185
Sieves, perforated tin, c. 1900	16	28	76
Sifter, says "Kewpie," ht. 3"	40	60	133
Skillet, c. 1880	82	115	245
Skimmer, for candle wax, w/ perforated cover, wood handle	20	30	65
Skimmer, for milk, perforated/stamped, c. 1890s	13	10	45
Skimmer, shallow bowl, wood handle	16	28	76
Skimmer, stamped tin, 19th century	13	10	45
Spice Box, 7, enameled, tray w/ lid	115	160	345
Spice Box, tray, japanned, strap handle	40	70	160
Spice Boxes, 6 sq., w/ tray, nutmeg grater, wood handle	98	135	285
Spice Boxes, 6, w/ tray, wood handle	90	125	250
Steam Cooker, tall cylindrical, hinged lid, handle, dia. 12".	55	85	190
Stove Board, c. 1890	25	42	115
Strainer, cone-form, handle loop	16	25	65
Strainer, hinged to fit various bowls, c. 1870	20	30	75
Strainer, meat pudding, tin, handmade, 2 pcs.	65	92	186
Strainer, perforated bowl w/ wood handle	40	63	150
Sugar Scoop, shovel head, handle strap	23	35	76

Toleware

Toleware is painted tinware. It ranges from the sophisticated forms produced in 18th-century France to the simple pieces from the backwoods of 19th-century America.

When buying toleware, pay attention to condition. Many pieces have flaked off much of their original paint and have been heavily restored or entirely repainted. Dents and rust also lower the value. Early American pieces are often reproduced and sometimes faked. Construction technique is often your best clue. Modern electrical welding is often smoothed out by grinding the surfaces near the weld. Look for modern grinding marks. For further information see *Fabulous But Fake*, by Norman S. Young, Fake Publications, Inc.

Planters are one of the most popular tole items, but beware of causing rust when they are used.

	AUCTION	RETAIL Low	High
Coffin-Form Tray and Sander, Amer., c. 1830, w. 9"	$ 600	$ 1300	$ 1900
Document Boxes, c. 1860, 3 graduated, to 13"	400	740	1300
Lighthouse Coffee Pot, c. 1880, ht. 9"	150	280	500
Tray w/ American Eagle, c. 1890, w. 9"	100	190	330

Early 19th-century Neo Classical French painted mustard yellow toleware with gilt highlights:

	AUCTION	RETAIL Low	High
Biscuit Box, oval, covered	750	1400	2500
Candlesticks, pr., w/ sq. bases.	1000	1800	3250
Chestnut Urns, pr., oval, covered	2800	5200	9000
Condiment Set w/ glass bottles	475	880	1550
Dinner Bell, ht. 7"	100	200	330
Fruit Basket oval, reticulated border	800	1500	2600
Peat Bucket	200	370	650
Rectangular Box, w. 10"	125	230	400
Round Box, dia. 7"	135	250	440
Sauce Boat, reticulated, on secured stand	275	500	900
Tea Kettle, large oval, on reticulated stand.	1300	2400	4000
Tea Urn on burner stand	950	1700	3000
Tray, large oval, w. 26"	800	1500	2500
Tray, oval, w. 18"	1550	2750	5000
Trays, pr., oval, w. 15"	500	900	1600

Above: set of French painted mustard yellow toleware with gilt highlights. All prices are auction results. Top row left to right: teakettle of stand, $1300; large oval tray, $800; oval fruit basket, $800. Middle row left to right: biscuit box, $750; covered chestnut urn (pair), $2800; rectangular box, $150; oval tray, $1550; dinner bell, $125; round box, $150; sauce boat on stand, $275. Bottom row left to right: pair of candlesticks $1000; oval tray (pair), $500; tea urn on stand, $950; condiment set, $475. — Photo courtesy of Northeast Auctions.

Below: The sophistication of the decoration makes a big difference in value. Left: simply decorated tray, 12", $75 retail. Right: ship decorated tray, 18", $2000 retail.

Military Memorabilia

Military memorabilia encompasses items pertaining to all branches of the military. Some hobbyists collect military memorabilia by type of item, for example, badges or swords, while others collect by military branch like the Navy, Army or Air Force. For more information consult *The Official Price Guide to Military Collectibles*, published by House of Collectibles, Random House, NY.

Warning! Federal law prohibits the sale of American military medals. Recently there has been a crackdown at military memorabilia shows.

Top to bottom: Colt M1861 special musket, $2750; New England Kentucky Rifle, by H. Pratt, $2000; Military Kentucky Rifle, c. 1790, by J. Dickert, $7500, Kentucky Rifle, $2000, Kentucky Rifle, c. 1825, $1750; all prices at auction. — Photo courtesy of Northeast Auctions.

	LOW	AVG.	HIGH
ARMOR			
Japanese helmets (Kabuto)	$ 2200	$ 3100	$ 4000
Jingasa	1500	2000	2500
Breastplates, 16th century	5000	6500	8000
17th century	2500	4000	5500
18th-19th century	1500	2000	2500
Reproduction armor (full suits)	5000	9500	14,000
AUTOMATIC PISTOLS			
Colt Military Model 1911 (several variations)	$ 670	$ 1000	$ 1400
Colt Military Model 1911 (North American Arms Co., .45 A.C.P.)	4500	5000	5500
Luger Model 1900	4000	6000	8000
Luger Model 1902	8000	10,000	12,000
Luger Model 1906	2500	3000	3500
Luger Model 1906 (Portuguese Navy, 9 mm)	12,000	16,000	20,000
Luger Model 1906 (Vickers, for Netherlands gov.)	15,000	20,000	25,000
Luger Model 1908	1500	1750	2000
Luger Model 1913	1500	1750	2000
Luger Model 1914	1500	1750	2000
Luger Model 1920	1500	1750	2000
Luger, made by H. Krieghoff	2500	4000	5500
Luger, cutaway models (for demos)	5140	5570	6000

	LOW	AVG.	HIGH
Mausers (Broomhandle models)	$ 1500	$ 2000	$ 2500
Walther Model P.38	800	1400	2000

AVIATION COLLECTIBLES

Propellers (WWI)	$ 1500	$ 1750	$ 2000
Propellers (1930s)	800	1100	1400
Fabric (WWI w/ markings)	800	1100	1400
Instruments (WWI)	270	385	500

BADGES AND OTHER INSIGNIA

German Imperial..	$ 800	$ 1250	$ 1700
Third Reich badges	270	555	840
Note: many fakes			
United States (WWII aviation)	150	225	300
Third Reich armbands	150	275	400
Third Reich cuff titles (sleevebands).....................................	150	425	700
Third Reich cuff title (landwacht)	25	40	55

HELMET PLATES

German Imperial..	$ 150	$ 275	$ 400
British (late 19th century)...	270	385	500
Poland	80	110	140
Russian Imperial	270	385	500
Swedish (late 19th century)	270	335	400
United States (19th century)	150	275	400

BADGES AND OTHER INSIGNIA

Aerial Gunner badge, WWII	$ 100	$ 112	$ 125
Airship Pilot badge, c. 1921, authorized in 1921, dirigible took place			
of balloon	475	500	550
Bombardier badge, WWII	100	115	125
British pilot's wings (WWI)	215	258	300
Combat (Aircraft) Observer badge, WWII	140	158	175
Command Pilot badge, WWII	140	155	170
Flight Surgeon's badge, c. 1943	160	172	185
Japanese pilot's wings (WWII)	160	192	225
Third Reich navy specialty patches	15	28	40

BAYONETS

European Plug Bayonet (early 19th century)	$ 270	$ 555	$ 840
British Enfield Bayonet 1907	65	70	75
British Indian Bayonet..	80	110	140
French (late 19th century)	150	225	300
French Fusil Socket (early 18th century)	800	1100	1400
German Imperial..	80	135	190
Prussian Bayonet Model 1871	270	335	400
British Baker Bayonet	540	620	700
British Brown Bess Socket (19th century)	150	225	300
British Number 4 Mark II Spike	25	32	40
British Martini Henry	150	225	300

	LOW	AVG.	HIGH
Italian (late 19th century)	$ 55	$ 85	$ 115
Japanese Arisaka	80	110	140
Mexican Remington Rolling Block 7 mm Rifle	150	170	190
Russian Imperial (late 19th century)	150	225	300
Siamese (late 19th century)	80	110	140
Spanish Model 1941	60	72	85
Swiss Model 1931	80	98	115
U.S. Bannerman Cadet	160	192	225
U.S. Model 1860	270	335	400
U.S. Model 1942	160	192	225
Dahlgren Bowie Knife	1500	1600	1700
Dahlgren Saber Pattern	270	335	400
Krag	150	160	170
Krag Bolo Blade	215	258	300
Krag Bowie Knife	1500	1600	1700
Ramrod	150	225	300
Ross Model 1905	190	208	225
Socket (19th century)	100	135	170
U.S. (late 19th century)	100	200	300

CIVIL WAR HANDGUNS-UNION

Colt	1500	2750	4000
Remington	1500	2750	4000
Savage and North	4000	5500	7000
Savage Revolving Firearms	1000	1350	1700
Whitney Navy Revolver (first model, Type 1, rare)	1500	2000	2500
Whitney Navy Revolver (second model)	400	900	1400
Whitney Navy Revolver, first model, Type 2-4	1000	1500	2000

CIVIL WAR LONGARMS-UNION

Gwyn and Campbell Carbine	1000	1500	2000
Jenks "Mule Ear" .54 cal.	1500	2000	2500
Remington 1863 Percussion	1500	2000	2500
Joslyn Carbine	1000	1500	2000
Remington Rifled Musket	1000	1500	2000
Sharps Carbines and Rifles	1000	1750	2500
Sharps Coffee Mill Carbine	10,000	15,000	20,000
Sharps and Hankins	1000	1500	2000
Spencer Carbine	1000	1500	2000
Spencer Rifle	1500	2000	2500
Springfield Armory U.S. Rifle Musket	1000	1350	1700

CIVIL WAR HANDGUN-CONFEDERATE

Augusta Machine Works Revolver	$ 5000	$ 8000	$ 11,000
Columbus Firearms Revolver	8000	16,500	25,000
Leach and Ridgon Revolver	4000	6000	8000
Spiller and Burr Revolver	5000	7000	9000
T.F. Coffer Revolver (Types 1-3)	25,000	37,500	50,000

	LOW	AVG.	HIGH

CIVIL WAR LONGARMS-CONFEDERATE

	LOW	AVG.	HIGH
Fayetteville Army Rifles	$ 2500	$ 4750	$ 7000
H.C. Lamb Muzzle Loading Rifle	4000	5500	7000
Morse Carbine (Greenville production)	2500	5250	8000
Morse Inside Lock Musket	5000	9500	14,000
Richmond Armory Carbines	2500	4750	7000
Tallahassee Enfield Pattern Carbine	5000	8000	11,000

EPAULETS

	LOW	AVG.	HIGH
British (early 1800s) Coldstream Guards	$ 540	$ 835	$ 1130
French Officers (early 1900s)	800	900	1000
German (19th century)	350	525	700
United States (Civil War officers)	270	555	840
Unites States (late 19th century)	150	225	300

KNIVES

	LOW	AVG.	HIGH
American Bowie Knife (19th century)	$ 400	$ 550	$ 700
American Bowie Knife w/ silver and ivory trim (19th century)	2500	3250	4000
British Bowie Knife (19th century)	400	550	700
British Trench Knife (WWI)	540	620	700
French Trench Knife (WWI)	270	335	400
German Trench Knife (WWI)	270	335	400
Italian Trench Knife (WWII)	150	180	210
United States Marine Corps KA-BAR fighting/utility knife	150	225	300
United States Trench Knife (WWI)	200	278	355

GORGETS

	LOW	AVG.	HIGH
Bavarian gorget, late 19th century	$ 270	$ 335	$ 400
British officer's gorget, 18th century	540	835	1130
British officer's gorget, 19th century	400	620	840
Nazi political leader's gorget	1000	1350	1700
Nazi SA gorget	1500	1750	2000
Prussian flag bearer's gorget	670	830	990
Prussian officer's gorget, 18th century	2000	2250	2500

HALBERD

	LOW	AVG.	HIGH
British artillery halberd, 18th century	$ 2200	$ 2850	$ 3500
British ceremonial halberd, 19th century	800	1000	1200
German combat halberd, 16th century	800	1100	1400
Swiss combat halberd, 16th century	1000	1350	1700
United States colonial halberd	2500	5250	8000

HEADDRESS

	LOW	AVG.	HIGH
Austrian Dragoon cap, late 19th century	$ 270	$ 335	$ 400
Austrian Field Artillery Officer's cap, early 20th century	270	385	500
Canadian Militia Officer's forage cap, late 19th century	350	400	450
British Officer's patrol cap, late 19th century	400	550	700
British Mounted Police Officer's pillbox cap, late 19th century	370	412	455
French Foreign Legion cap	55	62	70
Bavarian Officer's cap, 19th century	540	835	1130

	LOW	AVG.	HIGH
German Hussar's Officer's cap	$ 540	$ 835	$ 1130
Nazi Infantry Cap	270	385	500
Nazi General Staff Officer's Cap	1500	1750	2000
Nazi Admiral's Visor Cap	4000	5500	7000
Nazi Diplomatic Corps Visor Cap	5000	6000	7000
Nazi Airforce Officer's Visor Cap	270	385	500
Nazi SS Coffee Can Cap	2500	4000	5500
U.S. Enlisted Man's Forage Cap, early 19th century	400	450	500
U.S. Enlisted Man's Fatigue Cap, early 20th century	270	335	400
Austrian Army Grenadier Cap, 18th century	15,000	20,000	25,000
Austrian Army Grenadier Cap, early 19th century	8000	11,000	14,000
British Grenadier's Cap, 18th century	15,000	20,000	25,000
German Officer's Grenadier's Cap, 18th century	20,000	22,500	25,000
Imperial German Grenadier's Cap, late 19th century	5000	9500	14,000
U.S. Officer's Grenadier's Cap, late 19th century	8000	11,000	14,000
U.S. First Guard Other Ranks Grenadier Cap, 19th century	4000	5500	7000
Austrian Officer's Lancer's Cap (Czapka), late 19th century	2200	2850	3500
English Officer's Lancer's Cap, late 19th century	4000	4750	5500
British Other Ranks Lancer's Cap, late 19th century	2200	2850	3500
French Officer's Lancer's Cap, 19th century	2500	4000	5500
French Other Ranks Lancer's Cap, 19th century	1500	2000	2500
Bavarian Officer's Lancer's Cap, 19th century	2500	3250	4000
Bavarian Other Ranks Lancer's Cap, 19th century	1500	2000	2500
Imperial German Lancer's Cap, late 19th century	1000	1350	1700
British Staff Officer's Cocked Hat, early 19th century	1000	1350	1700
Prussian Officer's Black Beaver Hat, early 19th century	800	1100	1400
Prussian Other Ranks Black Felt Hat, late 18th/early 19th century	540	835	1130
U.S. Enlisted Man's Artillery Hat, 19th century	800	1100	1400
U.S. Officer's Tricorn Hat, late 18th/early 19th century	1500	1750	2000
U.S. Officer's Cocked Hat, early 19th century	1500	1750	2000
German Imperial Officer's Busby, late 19th century	5000	6500	8000
German Imperial Other Ranks Busby, late 19th century	2500	3250	4000
British Officer's Fur Busby, late 19th century	800	1100	1400
British Other Ranks Fur Busby, late 19th century	400	550	700
British Royal Scots Bearskin Cap, early 20th century	800	1100	1400
Royal Fusiliers Officer's Racoon Skin Cap, late 19th century	1500	1750	2000
Royal Italian Cavalry Busby, early 20th century	1300	1650	2000
Austrian Hussar Officer's Shako, early 20th century	2150	2775	3400
Austrian Infantry Shako, 19th century	1500	2000	2500
French Officer's Shako, 19th century	1500	2000	2500
Bavarian Shako, 19th century	1500	2000	2500
Prussian Shako, 19th century	1000	1500	2000
Imperial German Infantry Shako, late 19th century	1000	1500	2000
Nazi Police Officer's Shako	540	690	840
British Infantry Officer's Shako, 19th century	2200	2850	3500
Russian Hussar's Shako, 19th century	2200	2850	3500
U.S. Enlisted Man's Shako, 19th century	800	1250	1700

MEDALS
Canada

Efficiency Medal, George VI	$ 150	$ 170	$ 190

	LOW	AVG.	HIGH
Forces Decoration, Elizabeth II	$ 160	$ 192	$ 225
Forces Decoration, George VI	325	362	400
General Service Medal, 1866/1870	1000	1065	1130
General Service Medal, 1870, Red River	2500	3000	3500
Korean War Medal, 1951	100	135	170
Medal of Bravery, instituted 1972, circular medallion w/ maple leaf	435	482	530
Memorial Cross, Elizabeth II	150	170	190
Military Cross, Korea	325	390	455

Germany (Imperial)

Baden Leopold Medal (for service in the Franco-Prussian War) w/ 1870/1871 bar	$ 200	$ 230	$ 260
Baden WWI Honor Medal. Medal inscribed "For Baden's Honor," dated 1914-1910	100	130	160
Bavarian 1870 Cross for Volunteer Nurses	600	720	840
Bavarian Order of Military Merit, 4th Class, w/ swords	360	400	430
Bavarian 10 Year Service Medal	55	62	70
Brunswick Order of Henry the Lion, 3rd Class	1000	1125	1250
Grand Cross to the Iron Cross, 1914	2500	3000	3500
Hesse Order of Philip the Good, 4th Class	525	600	675
Iron Cross, 1st Class, 1870	1100	1200	1300
Iron Cross, 1st Class, WWI, pin back	160	192	225
Iron Cross, 2nd Class, WWI, w/ ribbon	85	115	145
Iron Cross, 2nd Class, 1870 (Franco Prussian War), 25-yr. oak leaf	350	375	400
Saxon Order of Albert, 4th Class, w/ swords, ribbon	370	425	480
Wilhelm I Commemoration Medal	40	55	70
Wurttemberg Medal for Veterans, wars of 1793-1815	230	260	300

SWORDS

Army Foot Artillery sword, Model 1833. Brass scaled grip cast in 1 piece w/ short cross guard w/ plain disk finials. Blade marked w/ American Eagle and "N.P. AMES SPRINGFIELD." American Eagle on pommel, hilt attached to tang of blade by 3 iron traverse rivets	$ 450	$ 488	$ 525

Amerivcan silver hilt sword, c. 1730.

	LOW	AVG.	HIGH

Army Officer's sword, Model 1850. Based on French army model, half-basket hilt, gilt w/ gilt wire-wrapped leather-covered grips. Phrygian helmet pattern pommel, blade single edge and slightly curved, polished black leather scabbard w/ gilt/brass fittings . $ 560 $ 605 $ 650

Army Officer's sword, Model 1902. Generally similar to above, grips are notched on inside for fingers. Full back strap, simple rounded semicap pommel w/ small caspan top, D-shape knuckle guard divides into three parts. Turned down tear shape finial, nickled scabbard 380   438   495

UNIFORMS

Army Air Force Officer's Blouse, U.S. buttons and cuff braid. Officer's U.S. and winged propeller collar insignia. Pilot's silver wings .. $ 140 $ 155 $ 170

Army Enlisted Man's Field Jacket, WWII, so-called "Eisenhower" jacket of stout OD material, 2 pleated pockets. Concealed button front. Embroidered 1st Division patch on left shoulder 60   70   80

Army Enlisted Man's Issue Blouse. WWI, 89th Division, patch on upper left sleeve. Bronze U.S. enlisted device on right collar and Signal Corps device on left side. Single overseas chevron 150   152   155

Marine Corps Enlisted Man's Coat, WWII period. Green coat w/ 4 bronze Marine Corps buttons down front and on 4 pockets. Marine 2nd Division patch on upper left shoulder. Corporal's stripes and 1 enlistment stripe on each sleeve. Red "Ruptured Duck" discharge device on right breast 60   68   75

Marine Sergeant OD Wool Blouse, WWI period. 4 pockets w/ bronze Marine Corps buttons. Blouse has high collar w/ rare collar ornaments incl. disk bearing Marine Corps emblem. Sergeant's chevrons 245   260   275

Music

Records

   Many people who discarded their record collections in the 1980s are buying them back in the 1990s. Collectors feel that the sound quality is richer and more subtle than CDs. People also love the photos and artwork of the covers. The nostalgic appeal of records is very strong; music is often a reminder of happy moments. Many collectors remember records as their first independent purchase as a teenager.

   The following is a cross section of LPs; 45s are not covered. Each entry consists of the performer's name, the title of the LP, the company that produced it, the stock number, and the date. Condition is all important for records; collectors usually grade both the record and the album cover. Scratches on the record that interfere with sound quality can destroy the price of a record. Worn, torn or stained covers also decrease the prices. The prices below are for records in excellent condition with excellent condition covers. That means that the record may have small scratches that can be seen but not heard. The covers should be crisp and clean with only slight wear. Near mint or mint examples will command higher prices than those listed below.

   The world of records is filled with rare variations. Often these are subtle differences such as misspellings. Some people put more value on stereo or mono versions of the same record. In general, the prices below reflect the prices of the more common variations. For further reading see *The Official Price Guide to Records*, Jerry Osborne, House of Collectibles, Random House, NY, 1995 and *Goldmine's Price Guide To Collectible Records*, Neal Umphred, Krause Publications, Iola, IO, 1994.

Above right to left: Harry Belefonte, "Calypso," $22-$28; Jim Reeves, "Best of...," $12-$15. Below right to left: Rick Nelson, "Album Seven," $25-$35; Patti Page, "In the Land of Hi Fi," $25-$35.

VALUE

Acuff, Roy, The Voice of Country Music, Capitol, ST-2276, 1965 .... $ 18-22

Aerosmith, Toys in the Attic, Columbia, JCQ-33479, 1975 12-18

Andrews, Julie, My Fair Lady, Columbia, OL-5615, 1959 10-15

Animals, The Animals, MGM, E-4264, 1964 20-30

Ann-Margret, Bye Bye Birdie, RCA Vic., LOC-1081, 1963 12-18

Archies, The Archies, Calandar, KES-101, 1968 12-15

Arnold, Eddy, Let's Make Memories Tonight, RCA Vic., LPM-2337, 1961 12-15

Autry, Gene, Gene Autry and Champion, Columbia, CL-677, 1955 70-90

Avalon, Frankie, The Young Frankie Avalon, Chancellor, CHL-5007, 1960 20-30

Bachelors, Presenting the Bachelors, London, LL-3353, 1964 10-15

Baez, Joan, In Concert, Vanguard, VRS-9112, 1962 12-18

Bailey, Pearl, Cultured Pearl, Coral, CRL-57162, 1957 20-30

Baxter, Les, Thinking of You, Capitol, T-474, 1954 20-30

Beach Boys, Little Deuce Coupe, Capitol, ST-1998, 1963 20-30

Beach Boys, Surfin' USA, Capitol, ST-1890, 1963 20-30

Bennett, Tony, Blue Velvet, Columbia, CL-1292, 1959 12-18

Berry, Chuck, Berry Is on Top, Chess, LP-1435, 1959 90-150

Berry, Chuck, Golden Hits, Mercury, MG-21103, 1967 12-15

Blues Magoos, Psychedelic Lollipop, Mercury, MG-21096, 1966 15-20

Boone, Pat, Star Dust, Dot, DLP-3118, 1958 15-20

Brewer, Teresa, Music, Music, Music, Coral, CRL-57027, 1956 15-22

Broonzy, Big Bill, Big Bill Broonzy, Folkways, FA-2315, 1957 25-54

Broonzy, Big Bill, Country Blues, Folkways, FA-2326, 1957 25-45

Brown, James, Live at the Apollo, King, KS-826, 1966 25-40

Brown, James, Night Train, King, 771, 1961 200-250

Brown, James, Papa's Got a Brand New Bag, King, 938, 1966 25-40

Browne, Jackson, For Everyman, Asylum, SD-5067, 1973 8-14

Bruce, Lenny, I Am Not A Nut, red vinyl, Fantasy, 7007, 1960 50-90

Byrds, Turn! Turn! Turn!, Columbia, CL-2454, 1965 15-20

Carpenters, Close to You, A & M, QU-54271, 1973 10-15

Cash, Johnny, The Fabulous Johnny Cash, Columbia, CS-8122, 1958 25-45

Chad & Jeremy, Distant Shores, Columbia, CL-2564, 1966 10-15

Charles, Ray, The Genius of Ray Charles, Atlantic, 1312, 1960 15-20

Checker, Chubby, Let's Twist Again, Parkway, P-7004, 1961 25-45

Chiffons, Sweet Talkin' Guy, Laurie, LLP-2036, 1966 35-65

Christy, June, Big Band Specials, Capitol, T-1845, 1962 10-18

Cline, Patsy, Patsy Cline Showcase, Decca, DL-74202, 1961 30-40

Clooney, Rosemary, Swing Around Rosie, Coral, CRL-57266, 1958 18-22

Coasters, Greatest Hits, Atco, 33-111, 1960 25-45

Como, Perry, A Sentimental Date, RCA Vic., LPC-1177, 1956 10-15

Cooke, Sam, My Kind of Blues, RCA Vic., LPM-2392, 1961 20-30

Cortez, Dave (Baby), In Orbit With ..., Roulette, R-25328, 1966 9-12

Creedence Clearwater Revival, Cosmo's Factory, Mobile Fid., MFSL-037 30-50

Crosby, Bing, In a Little Spanish Town, Decca, DL-8846, 1959 12-18

Darin, Bobby, Twist With Bobby Darrin, Atco, 33-138, 1961 20-30

Davis, Skeeter, The End of the World, RCA Victor, LSP-2699, 1962 20-30

Day, Doris, Day in Hollywood, Columbia, CL-749, 1955 10-15

Deep Purple, And the Royal Philharmonic, Tetragrammaton, T-131, 1968 150-250

Denny, Martin, Exotica, Liberty, LRP-3034, 1957 18-25

Diamond, Neil, Greatest Hits, Bang, BLPS-219, 1968 15-20

Drifters, Under the Boardwalk, white cover, Atlantic, 8099, 1964 35-65

VALUE

Elliott, Ramblin' Jack, Country Style, Prestige, PRLP-13045, 1962 .... $ 18-22
Everly Brothers, The Everly Brothers Best, Cadence, CLP-3025, 1969 40-60
Fabian, The Fabulous Fabian, Chanc., CHLX-5005, 1959 40-60
Fisher, Eddie, I'm In the Mood for Love, RCA Vic., LPM-1180, 1955 18-22
Flatt & Scruggs, Foggy Mountain Jamboree, Columbia, CL-1019, 1957 20-35
Flatt & Scruggs, When the Saints Go Marching In, Columbia, CL-2513, 1966........ 10-15
Fleetwoods, Mr. Blue, Dolton, BST-8001, 1959 50-80
Ford, Tennessee Ernie, Spirituals, Capitol, T-818, 1957 15-20
Four Seasons, Born to Wander, Philips, PHS-600-129, 1964 12-15
Four Seasons, Rag Doll, Philips, PHM-200-146, 1964 18-22
Four Tops, Four Tops, Motown, MS-622, 1964 20-30
Francis, Connie, Who's Sorry Now?, MGM, E-3686, 1959 20-30
Franklin, Aretha, The Electrifying ..., Columbia, CL-1761, 1962 25-35
Funicello, Annette, Annette's Pajama Party, Buena Vista, STER-3325, 1964 50-80
Garland, Judy, The Wizard of Oz, Decca, DL-8387, 1957 30-40
Gaye, Marvin, Marvin Gay's Greatest Hits, Tamla, TS-252, 1964 18-22
Gibson, Don, No One Stands Alone, RCA Victor, LSP-1918, 1959 25-35
Gore, Lesley, Boys, Boys, Boys, Mercury, MG-20901, 1964 10-18
Gorme, Eydie, Love Is a Season, ABC-Para., ABCS-273, 1958 12-16
Grateful Dead, American Beauty, Mobile Fid., MFSL-014, 1980 30-50
Grateful Dead, The Grateful Dead, Warner Bros., WS-1689, 1967 30-40
Guy, Buddy, A Man and the Blues, Vanguard, VSD-79272, 1968 10-15
Haley, Bill & His Comets, Rock With Bill..., Essex, LP-202, 1955 250-300
Hendrix, Jimi, Band of Gypsys, Red Label, Capitol, STAO-472, 1970 18-22
Hendrix, Jimi, Pie, Live 'n' Dirty, Nutmeg, NUT-1001, 1978 18-22
Herman's Hermits, Introducing..., MGM, E-4282, 1965 12-18
Hollies, The Hollies-Beat Group, Imperial, LP-9312, 1966 20-30
Holly, Buddy, Buddy Holly, Coral, CRL-57210, 1958 200-300
Hooker, John Lee, Travelin', Vee Jay, LP-1023, 1960 45-65
Horne, Lena, At the Waldorf Astoria, RCA Vic., LSO-1028, 1957 30-40
Ian, Janis, Society's Child, Verve, V-5027, 1967 10-18
Impressions, Keep on Pushing, ABC-Para., ABCS-493, 1964 18-22
Ink Spots, The Ink Spots Greatest, Grand, LP-328, 1959 18-22
Ives, Burl, Down to the Sea in Ships, Decca, DL-8245, 1956 14-18
James, Tommy, I Think We're Alone Now, Roulettte, R-25353, 1967 12-18
Jan & Dean, Little Old Lady From Pasadena, Liberty, LRP-3377, 1964 18-25
Jefferson Airplane, Takes Off, RCA Vic., LSP-3584, 1966 12-18
Jerry & The Pacemakers, Greatest Hits, Laurie, SLLP-2031, 1965 18-25
King, B.B., My Kind of Blues, Crown, CLP-5188, 1961 15-20
King, B.B., Singin' the Blues, Crown, CLP-5020, 1957 40-70
King, Ben E., Greatest Hits, Atco, SD-33-165, 1964 20-30
Kingston Trio, String Along, Capitol, ST-1407, 1960 18-22
Knight, Gladys, Everybody Needs Love, Soul, SS-706, 1967 12-18
Lawrence, Steve & Eydie Gorme, Our Best to You, ABC-Para., ABCS-469, 1964 8-14
Leadbelly, Huddie Ledbetter's Best, Capitol, T-1821, 1962 35-55
Lee, Brenda, This Is Brenda, Decca, DL-74082, 1960 15-20
Lennon, John & Yoko Ono, Sometime in NYC, Apple, SVBB-3392, 1972 20-30
Lewis, Jerry Lee, The Return of Rock, Smash, SRS-67063, 1965 30-40
Liberace, Sincerely Yours, Columbia, CL-800, 1955 12-18
Little Richard, Little Richard, Camden, CAL-420, 1956 100-150
London, Julie, About the Blues, Liberty, LST-7012, 1958 20-30

VALUE

Lovin' Spoonful, Do You Believe in Magic, Kama Sutra, KLPS-8050, 1965 .... $ 18-22

Lynn, Loretta, Hymns, Decca, DL-74695, 1965 15-20

Mancini, Henry, The Mancini Touch, RCA Vic., LSP-2101, 1960 12-15

Martin, Mary, South Pacific, Columbia, OL-4180, 1949 18-25

Mathis, Johnny, Warm, Columbia, CL-1078, 1957 20-30

Mayall, John, Blues Breakers With Eric Clapton, London, PS-492, 1966 18-22

McCartney, Paul, Band on the Run, with poster, Capitol, SO-3415, 1973 18-22

McGuire Sisters, While the Lights Are Low, Coral, CRL-57145, 1957 18-25

Monkees, Papa Jean's Blues, Colgems, COS-101, 1966 25-35

Monkees, Papa Jene's Blues, Colgems, COS-101, 1966 9-14

Monroe, Marilyn, Some Like It Hot, UA, UAL-4030, 1959 40-60

Muddy Waters, Muddy, Brass and Blues, Chess, LPS-1507, 1966 25-35

Nelson, Rick, Ricky, Imperial, LP-9048, 1964 15-20

Nelson, Rick, Ricky Sings Again, Imperial, LP-12090, 1962 75-135

Nelson, Tracy, Deep Are the Roots, Prestige, PRLP-7393, 1965 15-20

Nelson, Willie, And Then I Wrote, Liberty, LRP-3238, 1962 20-30

Orbison, Roy, At the Rock House, Sun, SLP-1260, 1961 300-500

Orbison, Roy, There Is Only One Roy Orbison, MGM, SE-4308, 1965 15-20

Owens, Buck, I've Got a Tiger By the Tail, Capitol, ST-2283, 1965 15-20

Page, Patti, This Is My Song, Mercury, MG-20102, 1955 15-20

Partridge Family, Partridge Family, with photo, Bell, 6050, 1970 10-18

Paul, Les & Mary Ford, Bye Bye Blues, Capitol, T-356, 1955 25-40

Peter, Paul & Mary, In the Wind, Warner Bros., W-1507, 1963 12-15

Pickett, Wilson, In the Midnight Hour, Atlantic, 8114, 1965 20-30

Pitney, Gene, Only Love Can Break a Heart, Musicor, MM-2003, 1962 15-20

Platters, Moonlight Memories, Mercury, MG-20759, 1963 15-20

Preston, Johnny, Running Bare, Mercury, MG-20592, 1960 60-90

Price, Ray, Talk to Your Heart, Columbia, CL-1148, 1958 15-20

Professor Longhair, New Orleans Piano, Atlantic, SD-7225, 1972 15-20

Ramones, Ramones, Sire, SASD-7520, 1976 15-20

Rascals, Once Upon a Dream, Atlantic, SD-8148, 1968 12-15

Redding, Otis, Soul Ballads, Volt, 411, 1965 40-60

Reed, Jimmy, Just Jimmy Reed, Vee Jay, LP-1050, 1962 18-24

Reese, Della, Della, RCA Victor, LSP-2157, 1960 15-20

Reeves, Jim, Jim Reeves Sings, Abbott, LP-5001, 1956 10-15

Reeves, Jim, The Intimate Jim Reeves, RCA Victor, LSP-2216, 1960 20-30

Reynolds, Debbie, Am I That Easy To Forget?, Dot, DLP-25295, 1960 18-22

Rich, Charlie, The Best Years, Smash, SRS-67078, 1966 18-24

Righteous Bros., You've Lost That Loving Feelin', Philles, PHLP-4007, 1965 15-20

Rodgers, Jimmie, Twilight on the Trail, Roulette, R-25081, 1959 15-20

Rogers, Roy, Song Wagon, Golden, GRC-6, 1958 60-80

Rolling Stones, 12 X 5, London, LL-3402, 1965 30-50

Rolling Stones, Flowers, London, LL-3509, 1967 20-30

Rolling Stones, Some Girls, Mobil Fid., MFSL-087 18-22

Rolling Stones, Satanic Maj. Request, 3D, mono, London, NP-2, 1967 90-110

Rolling Stones, Satanic Maj. Request, 3D, stereo, London, NPS-2, 1967 25-35

Ruby & The Romantics, Our Day Will Come, Kapp, KL-1323, 1963 15-20

Rydell, Bobby, Bobby Sings, Cameo, C-1007, 1960 20-30

Sam the Sham & The Pharohs, Wooly Bully, MGM, SE-4297, 1965 18-24

Searchers, Meet the Searchers, Kapp, KL-1363, 1964 15-20

Seeger, Pete, Pete Seeger at Carnegie Hall, Folkways, FA-2351, 1958 15-20

VALUE

Shannon, Del, The Best of Del Shannon, Dot, DLP-25824, 1967 .... $ 18-22
Sharp, Dee Dee, It's Mash Potato Time, Cameo, D-1018, 1962 25-40
Shirelles, Golden Oldies, Scepter, SPS-516, 1964 25-40
Shore, Dinah, Dinah Down Home, Capitol, ST-1655, 1962 12-18
Simon & Garfunkel, Bridge Over Troubled Water, Columbia, CQ-30995, 1973 10-15
Sinatra, Frank, Come Dance With Me, Capitol, SW-1069, 1959 10-15
Sinatra, Frank, Days of Wine and Roses, Reprise, FS-1011, 1964 10-15
Sinatra, Frank, High Society, Capitol, SW-750, 1958 12-18
Snow, Hank, Railroad Man, RCA Victor, LPM-2705, 1963 18-22
Sonny & Cher, Look at Us, Atco, 33-177, 1965 12-15
Sons of the Pioneers, Favorite Cowboy Songs, RCA Victor, LPM-1130, 1955 30-45
Starr, Kay, The Hits of Kay Starr, Capitol, T-415, 1950s 14-18
Statler Brothers, Flowers on the Wall, Columbia, CL-2449, 1966 10-15
Stevens, Cat, Catch Bull at Four, A & M, QU-54365, 1974 10-15
Stone Poneys, The Stone Poneys, Capitol, ST-2666, 1967 20-30
Streisand, Barbra, I Can Get It For You..., Columbia, KOL-5780, 1962 50-80
Supremes, Supremes A' Go-Go, Motown, M-649, 1966 18-22
Taylor, James, James Taylor, Apple, SKAO-3352, 1969 18-25
Temptations, Meet the Temptations, Gordy, GS-911, 1964 20-30
The Band, Music From Big Pink, Capitol, SKAO-2995, 1968 10-15
The Fugs, The Fugs First Album, ESP-Disk, 1018, 1966 20-35
Tubb, Ernest, Ernest Tubb Favorites, Decca, DL-8291, 1956 35-65
Valens, Ritchie, The Original Ritchie Valens, Guest Star, GS-1469, 1963 20-30
Vanilla Fudge, Vanilla Fudge, Atco, 33-224, 1967 12-18
Vee, Bobby, Bobby Vee, Liberty, LST-7181, 1961 25-35
Ventures, Walk-Don't Run, Dolton, BST-8003, 1963 18-24
Wagoner, Porter, The Bluegrass Story, RCA Vic., LPM-2960, 1964 12-18
Wakeman, Rick, Journey to the Center..., A & M, QU-53621, 1975 9-14
Washington, Dinah, In the Land of Hi Fi, EmArcy, MG-36073, 1956 20-30
Watson, Doc, Doc Watson, Vanguard, VSD-79152, 1964 10-15
Weavers, The Best of the Weavers, Decca, DL-8893, 1959 20-35
Wells, Kitty, Kitty's Choice, Decca, DL-78979, 1960s 18-24
Whitman, Slim, Slim Whitman Sings, Imperial, LP-9026, 1958 15-20
Williams, Andy, Under Paris Skies, Cadence, CLP-3047, 1961 8-12
Williams, Hank, Honky Tonkin', MGM, E-3412, 1950 60-90
Winters, Jonathan, A Personal Appearance, Verve, MGV-15027, 1961 15-20
Wonder, Stevie, Stevie at the Beach, Tamla, T-255, 1964 20-30
Yardbirds, Greatest Hits, Epic, LN-24246, 1966 20-30
Young, Faron, Hello, Walls, Capitol, ST-1528, 1961 25-35
Zappa, Frank, We're Only In It For the Money, Verve, D-5045, 1968 50-80
Zappa, Frank, We're Only In It For the Money, Verve, V-5045, 1968 50-80
Zappa, Frank, Weasels Ripped My Flesh, Bizarre, MS-2028, 1970 12-18
Zombies, The Zombies, Parrot, PAR-61001, 1965 25-40

Sheet Music

Sheet music is a musical composition. It was the first way of mass merchandising popular music. Tin Pan Alley originated off-Broadway on 28th Street in New York City. It was the center of American popular music in the late 19th and early 20th centuries. Publishers sought recognition for their songs. They backed shows and employed song pluggers to popularize their music. Waiters often supplemented their wages by belting out tunes.

Condition, rarity, and image establish the value of sheet music. Some collectors want the music, but many others are more interested in the graphics. Sheet music represents a great area for cross-over collecting. It includes themes such as movies, WWI and II, Disney, character and illustration art. Winslow Homer and Norman Rockwell, ("Over There") are a couple of artists that drew covers. Since sheet music was mass produced, most often in huge quantities, it is still relatively inexpensive. It can, however, be fragile, and mint examples are harder to find. Specimens are not always in top condition due to music store stamps, tape marks, staples, binder holes, and ownership signatures. Worn, incomplete copies sell for considerably less than those in mint condition described below.

Garage sales are a good source for sheet music, but be prepared to sort through stacks of material. Dealers that frame sheet music realize that they have a decorative item and reflect that in the price. Sheet music is best stored in unsealed plastic containers designed for paper conservation. If framing, use acid-free backing and make sure the process is reversible, i.e. don't use methods which can damage the sheet music.

Names following the titles listed below are descriptions of the cover; a celebrity's name denotes a photo of that person, "cast" features a group of actors. Sometimes there are different covers for the same composition or similar names for different works.

For further study we suggest *The Sheet Music Reference & Price Guide*, Marie-Reine & Anna Marie Guiheen, Collector Books, Paducah, KY,1995, for composers' and cover artists, names and other information. For history of the business try *American Sheet Music with Prices*, Daniel B. Priest, Wallace Homestead Book Co., Des Moines, IA, 1978.

Left to right: When I'm With You, 1936, $20-$25; Katy Darling, illustrated with an early Winslow Homer lithograph, $300-$500.

	LOW	HIGH
A-Tisket-A-Tasket, 1930	$ 10	$ 15
After Twelve O'Clock, 1932	4	6
Ain't Misbehavin', 1929	6	8
Ain't We Got Fun, 1921	9	12
America I Love You, 1915	35	45
Anchors Away, 1942	6	8
Are You from Dixie, 1915	18	22
Army Air Corps, 1942	8	12
As Time Goes By, Bogart & Bergman, 1941	20	30
Barney Google, 1923	50	80
Bess You Is My Woman, 1935	9	12
Bill Bailey, black couple, 1902	38	42
Blue Moon, 1934	9	15
Button Up Your Overcoat, 1928	4	7
By the Light of the Silvery Moon, 1932	9	12
Cascades, 1904	40	60
Casey Jones, Brave Engineer, 1909	20	30
Chattanooga Choo Choo, 1941	12	18
Chrysanthemum Rag, 1904	40	60
Climb Every Mountain, 1959	6	8
Country Club Ragtime, 1909	45	55
Custer's Last Charge, 1922	40	50
Daisy, 1904	12	14
Danny Boy, 1913	6	8
Dinah, E. Cantor, black face, 1925	20	30
Down by the Old Mill Stream, 1910	7	9
Dream River, 1928	4	6
Easter Parade, cast, 1947	9	12
Easy Winners, 1901	45	65
Edelweiss, Andrews & Plummer, 1959	6	8
Falling In Love Again, Dietrich, 1930	8	10
Forty Second Street, 1932	7	9
Girl from Ipanema, 1943	4	6
Gone with the Wind, 1937	20	30
Goodnight Sweetheart, E. Cantor, 1931	10	15
Great American, Theodore Roosevelt, 1919	40	60
Heartbreak Hotel, Elvis, 1956	40	60
Hello Ma Baby, 1899	40	50
Help, 1969	22	38
Here Comes Santa Claus, Gene Autry, 1947	20	30
Here Comes the Bride, 1912	15	20
Hey Jude, 1968	35	45
Honey Hula, 1921	4	6
How Much is that Doggy in the Window, P. Page, 1952	7	9
Hummingbird , 1955	4	6
I Got Rhythm, 1930	8	10
I'm Dreaming of the Girl I Love, 1912	6	8
If I Only Had a Brain, 1939	30	40
In My Merry Oldsmobile, 1905	25	35
It's a Long, Long Way to Tipperary, 1912	20	30
Jeepers Creepers, 1938	7	9

Above left to right: Aren't You're Glad You're You, 1945, $8-$12; How Strange,1939, $12-$15.

Above left to right: If You're In Love You'll Waltz, 1926, $8-$12; South Of The Border, 1939, $3-$5.

	LOW	HIGH
Lambeth Walk, 1937	$ 8	$ 12
Liberty Bell, 1917	15	25
Looking at the World, Rose Color Glasses, 1926	6	8
Love for Sale, Cole Porter, 1930	8	10
Meet Me in St. Louis, 1935	9	12
Memphis Blues, 1913	10	15
Moon River, A. Hepburn, 1961	6	8
Moxie Fox Trot, 1930	70	90
Now I Lay Me Down to Sleep, 1918	18	22
O Solo Mio, 1923	4	6
On the Street Where You Live, 1956	5	7
Over There, 1917	70	90
Penny Serenade, 1938	4	6
Ragtime Dance, 1906	50	75
Ramblin' Rose, Nat King Cole, 1962	8	10
She'll be Coming Around the Mountain, 1935	4	6
Shortnin' Bread, 1928	30	40
Shrine of St. Cecilia, 1940	3	4
Singing in the Rain, Gene Kelly, 1952	70	90
Someday, 1944	7	9
Someday My Prince Will Come, Snow White, 1937	50	80
Sousa's Grand March, 1895	20	30
Star Dust, 1929	3	4
Summer Place, 1959	4	6
Sunshine on My Shoulders, J. Denver, 1971	3	4
Swanee, Al Jolson, 1932	15	20
Tea for Two, 1940	4	6
Three Coins in a Fountain, cast, 1954	6	8
Time on My Hands, c. 1930, 1930	2	3
Toot-Toot Tootsie, Al Jolson, 1922	18	22
Wait 'Til the Sun Shines Nellie, Bing Crosby, 1942	5	7
White Christmas, cast, 1942	8	12
Who's Afraid of the Big Bad Wolf, 1934	50	80
Who's Sorry Now, Astaire, 1931	6	8
Yankee Doodle Boy, J Jones on phone, 1931	30	50
You are My Sunshine, 1940	5	7
You're a Grand Old Flag, 1933	15	20
Zip-A-De-Doo-Dah, 1941	50	80

Orientalia

Assorted Orientalia

Orientalia refers to objects originating in Asia. Although this could refer to an electronic calculator, the term is usually reserved for items that show the Asian aesthetic in decoration. This chapter is a representative overview; see other chapters in this section for specific areas.

	AUCTION	RETAIL Low	High
Chinese			
Carved White Jade Boat, w. 10"	$ 3000	$ 5250	$ 8500
Celadon Umbrella Stand	350	620	1000
Charger, blue-glazed, gilt, dia. 18"	1600	2750	5000
Cloisonné Planter, w. 5"	130	230	370
Cloisonné Vase, ht. 14"	500	880	1430
Embroidered Coat in floral design, blue satin-stitch floral motifs on dark-blue ground, gray-blue damask lining	175	310	500
Embroidered Coat, polychrome satin and seed-stitch depicting phoenix in sq. medallion	275	480	790
Embroidered Silk Panel depicting dragon, flowers, and birds on orange ground, 225" x 83"	50	90	140
Embroidered Skirt, blue satin-stitch flowers on ivory damask w/ metallic braid, salmon damask facing	200	350	570
Mandarin Coat, blue silk embroidered w/ gold thread depicting imperial dragon w/ Buddhist cloud medallions	1400	2460	4000
Mandarin Robe, Brocade depicting dragon, phoenix, and Buddhist emblems in gold on red ground, w/ peacock-blue lining	800	1400	2300
Mandarin Robe, K'ossu weave on blue black w/ medallions of bats-of-longevity and phoenix, wave-&-cloud motifs	2,000	3520	5720
Peking Glass Vases, pr., red & white	550	970	1570
Scroll Painting depicting tiger on mountain top, within narrow damask border, signed and stamped	50	90	140
Scroll Painting of reindeer under trees, Ching Dynasty, Kaopchi-pei, damask mount, signed and stamped	200	350	570
Silk Embroidered Wall Hanging depicting figures in a pavilion within floral border, 90" x 3"	75	130	210
Spinach Jade Double-Brush Holder w/ beastial figures, ht. 5"	850	1500	2430
Woven Fabric Hanging, K'ossu weave depicting butterflies and flowers on blue-green ground	650	1150	1850
Yellow-Glazed Bulbous Covered Jar, Guanqxu Mark, ht. 12"	1000	1750	3000
Yellow-Glazed Vase w/ incised polychrome lion, ht. 12"	200	350	570
Japanese			
Arita-Ware Blue and White Charger, dia. 14"	$ 550	$ 970	$ 1570
Bronze of Scholar, parcel-gilt, ht. 19"	5000	8800	14,000
Buddhist Garment, depicting storks embroidered on navy silk, orange silk lining printed w/ calligraphy	550	970	1570
Buddhist Garment, Nishiki weave w/ chrysanthemums on brown ground, nishiki shiten of same material	450	800	1300
Buddhist Priest Garment	500	900	1400

	AUCTION	RETAIL Low	High
Buddhist Priest Garment in nishiki weave depicting magnolias on brown ground, kinran shiten same on orange	$ 500	$ 900	$ 1400
Buddhist Priest Robe, Nishiki weave w/ key motif and floral design on deep cream ground, nishiki shiten the same	400	700	1140
Buddhist Priest Robe, Tsuzure weave depicting repeated musical instruments (mako) on cream, tsuzure shiten the same, green lining	350	620	1000
Buddhist Priest Robe, Tsuzure weave w/ leaf and blossom of paulownia leaf, on white ground, Tsurzure shite the same	200	350	570
Ghost Robe From Noh Theater, white gauze fabric w/ stylized bamboo designs in beaten gold, w/ official museum stamp	1600	2800	5000
Imari Bowl, w/ figures	250	440	720
Imari Charger, blue and white	150	260	430
Imari Oval Scalloped Platter, w. 18"	550	970	1570
Imari Vase decorated in red, blue, & gold, ht. 25"	2200	3750	6500
Obi, Nishiki weave depicting chrysanthemums in cerise on orange ground	150	260	430
Print, Court Lady and Attendant, woodblock from "One Hundred Poems" series, Utagawa Kuniyoshi (1797-1861), ht. 13"	350	620	1000
Print, Mt. Fuji, woodblock, within calligraphic border	1200	2000	3500
Print, Oiso-Rain on May 28th, woodblock from "Fifty-three Stations of Tokaido," Ando Hiroshige (1796- 1858), ht. 15"	425	750	1220
Print, Simida in Rainy Weather, Ando Hiroshige (1796-1858), woodblock, 9" x 14", sight	300	530	860
Print, The House By the Lake, Ando Hiroshige (1796-1858), woodblock, ht. 15"	100	180	290
Print, Waterfall At Mino, Ando Hiroshige (1796-1858), woodblock, ht. 15"	350	620	1000
Scroll Painting Depicting a Sage within damask border w/ brocade inset, ht. 38"	500	880	1430
Six-Panel Screen w/ figures in landscape	500	880	1430
Tapestry depicting cocks and wisteria on metallic brown ground within conventional border of nishiki weave, 84" x 54"	1800	3000	5000
Two-fold screen of figures in landscaped setting, ht. 58"	550	970	1570
Umbrella Stand in Imari palette w/ birds and flowers, ht. 28"	400	700	1140

Gentleman's silk coat, late 18th century, $1600 at auction.

Chinese Export Porcelain

The word "china," as in "fine china," derives from the time when all porcelain came from China. Before Europeans learned the secrets of kaolin clay and the firing process, kings and princes spent fortunes (literally) on their porcelain collections. Even after Western entrepreneurs cracked these secrets, merchants imported shiploads of Chinese porcelain for an ever-growing number of dinner services. The Chinese fed this demand with pieces designed for the West. Chinese Export Porcelain (CEP) developed more or less standard designs that crossed the oceans throughout the 19th century. Canton, Nanking, and Fitzhugh are the well-known blue and white designs, while polychrome favorites are Rose Mandarin and Rose Medallion.

Pieces marked "Made in China" date after 1894. Some unscrupulous dealers have ground out this mark. Look for suspicious grinding marks or related flaws on the undersides of pieces. For further information see *Chinese Export Porcelain*, by Peter, Herbert and Nancy Schiffer, Schiffer Publishing, Ltd.

Left: Armorial pieces are among the most prized of Chinese export pieces. The more elaborate the crest, the more valuable the piece.

	AUCTION	RETAIL Low	RETAIL High
Armorial Pieces			
Cups & Saucers, pr., crest of each decorated w/ fawn	$ 750	$ 1400	$ 2500
Deep Plate, Arms of Smith, dia. 9.5"	200	400	700
Deep Plate, reticulated, crested, dia. 11"	900	1700	3000
Hot Water Plate, Arms of Snodgrass, len. 11"	425	800	1400
Mug, Clifford Coat-of-Arms and spearhead border, ht. 7"	3250	6000	10,000
Plate, Arms of Barrington, dia. 9"	750	1400	2400
Plate, Burrell Impaling Raymond, dia. 9"	320	600	1000
Plate, Davis w/ Southerne in Pretence, dia. 9"	1250	2300	4000
Plates, pr., Arms of Parker, dia. 8.5"	700	1300	2300
Soup Tureen, covered, boar's head, matching platter, len. 14"	6250	12,000	20,000
Teapot, crest, ht. 9"	1400	2600	4600

	AUCTION	RETAIL Low	High
Canton			
Circular Dish, 3-piece	$ 1100	$ 2000	$ 3600
Bowls, 2 nested	900	1700	2900
Bulb Tray.	2000	3700	6500
Candlesticks, pr.,	1600	3000	5200
Charger	900	1700	2900
Chop Dish, ftd., len. 14" x 4"	750	1400	2400
Cider Jug, individual	1300	2400	4200
Coffee Pot, strap handle	550	1000	1800
Dome-Top Teapot, ht. 9"	1000	1900	3300
Fruit Bowl, ftd.	1250	2300	4000
Luncheon Plates, 5 rose	350	700	1100
Round Tile	325	600	1100
Sauce Boat and Undertray, double handle	650	1200	2000
Shaped Dish, rose	275	500	900
Shrimp Dish	425	800	1400
Shrimp Dish, rose	450	800	1500
Square Tile	350	700	1000
Tazza, rose	800	1500	2600
Teapot, rare sq., len. 7"	4250	7900	14,000
Trays, pr. of rose-shaped	575	1100	1900
Vases, pr., rose	475	900	1500
Vegetable Dish, lidded, pod finial, len. 12 "	700	1300	2300
Vegetable Dish, oblong, covered	500	900	1600
Vegetable Dish, oblong, open	475	900	1500

Canton blue and white has been exported from China almost continuously since before the American revolution. Eighteenth century pieces are generally higher quality than late nineteenth century ones. Left: a late eighteenth century example. Right: an early 20th century example.

Above left to right: Fitzhugh covered vegtable dish, platter, and plate.

	AUCTION	RETAIL Low	RETAIL High
Fitzhugh			
Cider Jug	$ 1400	$ 2600	$ 4600
Mug	1300	2400	4200
Platter, fitted in custom-made bamboo stand, w. of table 18".	1800	3300	5900
Platter, oval, len. 18"	400	700	1300
Platter, oval, len. 20"	900	1700	2900
Platters, 3 oval graduated, largest 14"	550	1000	1800
Platters, pr., oval, len. 10"	500	900	1600
Salad Bowl, Cut-Corner, len. 10"	8000	14,000	26,000
Sauce Tureen and Undertray, strap handle, len. 7"	2000	3700	6500
Shrimp Dishes, pr., len. 10"	2000	3700	6500
Soap Dish, 3-piece	1000	1900	3300
Soup Plates, pr., orange , dia. 10"	400	700	1300
Soup Tureen & Stand, len. of stand 16"	3600	6700	11,000
Temple Vase	1300	2400	4200
Vegetable Dish, brown covered monogrammed "H." from service made for George Henley, nephew of George Washington	3000	5600	9800
Vegetable Dish, oval, strap handles, berry finial, len. 13"	1000	1900	3300
Vegetable Dishes, pr., oval open, len. 13"	450	800	1500
Vegetable Dishes, rect., lid w/ pod finials, len. 10"	500	1000	2500
Waste Bowl w/ feather edge, dia. 6"	200	400	700
Well & Tree Planter, len. 19"	1600	3000	5200

Nanking covered soup tureen, $1500 at auction. — Photo courtesy of Northeast Auctions.

	AUCTION	RETAIL	
		Low	High

Nanking

	AUCTION	Low	High
Boxed Sweetmeat Set	$ 650	$ 1200	$ 2100
Cider Jug	1000	1900	3300
Creamer	150	300	500
Dinner Service owned by William Gray of Salem, MA, comprising covered tureen and stand, cut-corner salad bowl, sauce tureen, 2 sauce boats w/ stands, 6 platters, 18 soup plates, 18 dinner plates, and 2 deep plates	12,000	23,000	50,000
Hot Water Plate	200	400	700
Mug, "chicken skin" finish	400	750	1600
Platter, oval, len. 19"	500	900	1600
Sauce Boats, pr., strap handle, owned by Wm. Gray of Salem	750	1400	2400
Serving Dishes, pr., shaped	2000	3700	6500
Silver-Form Coffee Pot	2200	4100	7200
Soup Tureen, lidded, owned by Wm. Gray of Salem, len. 15"	1500	2800	4900
Vases, pr., baluster form, "chicken skin" finish	900	1700	2900
Vases, pr., ovoid, "chicken skin" finish	900	1700	2900
Vegetable Dish, covered shaped oval, len. 11"	350	700	1100
Water Bottle	550	1000	1800

Rose Mandarin

	AUCTION	Low	High
Brush Box	$ 850	$ 1600	$ 2800
Covered Bowl, w/ strap handles	475	900	1500
Deep Plate	500	900	1600
Hot Water Plate, border w/ exotic birds & bats, len. 11"	350	700	1100
Punchbowl, elaborate, dia. 11".	3700	7000	12,000
Punchbowl, orange-peel finish, dia. 21"	5500	10,000	18,000
Scalloped-Edge Dish	1000	1900	3300
Shaped Dish, len. 10.5"	400	700	1300
Soup Plates, set of 10, elaborate court scenes, dia. 10".	1900	3500	6200
Teapot and Deep Plate.	800	1500	2600

Rose Medallion

	AUCTION	Low	High
Candlesticks, pr., ht. 6.5"	$ 500	$ 900	$ 1600

Left: Rose Manderine Plate. Right: mug, $350 at auction. — Photos courtesy of Northeast Auctions.

	AUCTION	RETAIL Low	High
Charger, dia. 16"	$ 525	$ 1000	$ 1700
Chop Dish, ftd., len. 14.75"	600	1100	2000
Chop Dish, oval ftd., len. 16"	800	1500	2600
Dome-Top Teapot, ht. 8"	700	1300	2300
Double Gourd Vases, pr., ht. 8.5"	450	800	1500
Garden Barrel, pierced, vignettes of figures, gilt, ht. 19"	2200	4000	7200
Garden Barrels, pr., h. 18 "	5200	9000	17,000
Garden Seat, hexagonal, scenic vignettes & panels, gilt, ht. 18"	2300	4300	7500
Hot Water Plate, w/ knopped lid, len. 11"	675	1300	2200
Octagonal Milk Jug, ht. 6.5"	475	900	1500
Punch Bowl, dia. 16 "	2900	5400	9500
Punch Bowl, ht. 6.5", dia. 14.5"	1200	2200	3900
Razor Box, len. 8"	550	1000	1800
Square Open Dish	350	700	1100
Temple Jar, covered, ht. 18"	1800	3300	5900
Trefoil-Form Tray, len. 11"	450	800	1500
Vase, Ku-Form, dec. w/ figures & botanical motifs, ht. 15"	400	700	1300

Miscellaneous

	AUCTION	RETAIL Low	High
Blue & White Plates, urn dec., pr., dia. 8"	$ 500	$ 900	$ 1600
Blue & White Platter, octagonal, pagoda dec., len. 16"	500	900	1600
Blue & White Porcelain Bowl dec. w/ warriors on horseback, fitted w/ European silver mounts, Kangxi 6 character mark, dia. 10"	2300	4300	7500
Blue & White Saucer, depicting dragon chasing flaming pearl, Chien-Lung Seal mark, dia. 6.5"	2500	4600	8200
Blue & White Saucer, domestic scenes, Chien-Lung Seal mark, dia. 7"	900	1700	3000
Bowl, Imari-style dec., dia. 10".	1200	2200	4000
Charger, Imari-style dec., dia. 15"	1200	2200	4000
Deep Plate centering continental ship, dia. 8"	450	800	1500
Deep Plate w/ Grisaille scene of European children, dia. 8"	175	300	600
Deep Saucer, Docai dec., deer on terrace, reign mark, dia. 6"	850	1600	3000
Famille Rose Bowl, w/ court scene. dia. 10".	450	800	1500
Famille Rose Coffee Pot, w/ side handle. ht. 9".	600	1100	2000
Famille Rose Teapot and Helmet-Form Creamer.	450	800	1500
Garden Seats, pr., celadon ground octagonal, ht. 19".	2000	3700	6500
Garniture Vase, blue urn dec., lidded, ht. 12" .	425	800	1400
Ice Pail & Undertray, sepia landscapes, ht. 7.5".	3100	5800	10,000
Juno & the Peacock Tea Bowl and Saucer	350	700	1100
Mug, Blue & White, ht. 7"	1600	3000	5200
Mug, w/ cornucopia.	450	800	1500
Mug w/ water buffalo.	1000	1900	3300
Orange Sacred Bird & Butterfly Razor Box, l. 7".	900	1700	2900
Plate, Tobacco-Leaf Variant, dia. 9"	850	1600	2800
Platter, sepia dome-top, oval-lidded, len. 14".	800	1500	2600
Reticulated Trays, pr., oval, monogram, len. 8"	2100	3900	6800
Rose Group Plate.	250	500	800
Sauce Tureen and Undertray, scenic medallion, len. 9"	600	1100	2000
Shrimp Dish, Famille-Rose, orange-peel finish, len. 11"	450	800	1500

	AUCTION	RETAIL	
		Low	High
Soup Tureen, w/ pod finial lid and strap handles, w/ undertray .	$ 6750	$ 12,500	$ 22,000
Strainer, Imari-style dec., fitted bamboo turned stand, dia. 14". ..	650	1200	2100
Vegetable Dishes, pr., lidded, w/ strap handles, dec. w/ crest, liners and undertray, len. 15".	12,000	22,000	40,000
Well & Tree Platter, sepia, floral & butterfly motifs, len. 18". ...	600	1100	2000

Left: Batavia ware has a brown exterior and a blue and white interior, It generally sells for 20 -50% less than comparable Canton pieces. Right: high quality blue and white reproductions bring $10-$20 each for small pieces.

Below left: Canton bidet in Sheraton stand, $4250 at auction. Below right: Garden Seat , $1400 at auction. — Photos courtesy of Northeast Auctions.

Cinnabar

Cinnabar is the Chinese carved lacquer. Layers are built up over wood, porcelain, or metal thick enough to carve ornate designs. The color is usually deep red. Although Cinnabar has been made continuously for over 300 years, the majority of the collected pieces currently available date from the turn of the century, as do all pieces listed below.

"Good" pieces may show some wear with some minor flecks of lacquer chipped away. "Best" pieces must be in perfect condition with no chipping or cracks.

Best rectangular vase, 8",
$800-$1000.

	GOOD	BETTER	BEST
Bowl, 4 scenic views, 5.5" sq.	$ 170	$ 250	$ 580
Bowl, pedestal foot, w/ lid, 6" dia.	180	270	550
Bowl, red flower design, black background, w/ lid, 6" dia.	150	270	580
Bowl, scalloped rim, red, 6.5" dia.	150	250	550
Bowl, scenic design, black on red, very shallow, 8" dia.	130	200	450
Box, fan shape, floral and bird design, 15" w.	550	850	1800
Box, floral design, black on red, w/ lid, 6" dia.	200	350	700
Box, flower design, red on green, w/ lid, 6.5" dia.	400	600	1350
Box, melon shape, 6.5" dia.	150	300	700
Box, oblong, carved view, w/ lid, 6.5" w.	200	300	650
Box, scene of playing sports, black on red, w/ lid, 15" dia.	550	800	1900
Cup, flower design, flared rim, 4.5" dia.	270	420	900
Cup, footed, 5.5" dia.	170	270	600
Cup, w/ dragon handles, 4.5" dia.	230	350	800
Dish, overall floral design, 9.5" dia.	280	430	900
Ginger Jar, landscape scene, red on cream, 8.5" ht.	350	530	1130
Hand Mirror, rust-colored landscape, 10.5" w.	200	300	600
Incense Burner, pagoda style, Taoist mask design, 17" ht.	1650	2500	5000
Plate, double dragon design, 12.75" dia.	500	800	1800
Plate, floral scene, red on green, 13" dia.	600	950	2000
Plate, floral scene, w/ ftd. base, 8" dia.	250	380	800
Plate, flower and butterfly scene, 10.5" dia.	330	500	1100
Plate, geometric design, red on black, 8" dia.	150	250	500
Pot, Taoist markings, ftd., 7" dia.	400	600	1250
Screen, floral motif, 70" x 20" panels	6000	12,000	40,000

	GOOD	BETTER	BEST
Screen, floral scene w/ nightingale, ftd. base, 29" ht.	$ 3000	$ 8000	$ 20,000
Smoking set, tray, ashtrays and cigarette box, 11.5" dia.	220	350	750
Stool, Greek key border, floral medallion, 18" ht.	1600	2520	5500
Tray, bird and flower scene, reddish brown, 15" w.	850	1300	2820
Tray, floral and bird, red, yellow and green, 15" w.	800	1250	2600
Tray, flowering tree, 12.5" w.	300	500	1100
Tray, gilded rim, 17" w.	280	450	950
Urn, red flower on black background, 6.5" ht.	100	170	370
Vase, dragon design, green, yellow and red, 15" ht.	1400	2200	5000
Vase, fish shape, red, 7.5" ht.	250	400	900
Vase, floral scene, on porc. body, 6.5" ht.	200	350	800
Vase, Foo dog design, 15" ht.	950	1500	3500
Vase, landscape, on porc. body, 6.5" ht.	250	350	780
Vase, overall dragon design, 12" ht.	350	730	1500
Vase, phoenix bird shape, 8" ht.	600	900	2000
Vase, rect., animal handles, w/ lid, 10" ht.	300	450	1000
Vase, red flowers on black background, 8" ht.	130	200	450
Vase, scenic design, black on red, 8" ht.	150	250	600
Vase, swimming fish scene, 15" ht.	650	1500	3250

Nippon Porcelain

Nippon porcelain resulted from the 1893 American tariff act requiring imports be marked (in English) with the country of origin. "Nippon" was an accepted name for Japan at that time. Nippon ware also represents Satsuma, Noritake, Imari, and other Japanese wares of that period.

The marks most frequently depict an M within a green wreath, and the word "Nippon" printed in curved letters underneath. There are many, many variations, however. By the late 1920s, "Japan" replaced "Nippon." Nippon ware has been faked and reproduced

	LOW	AVG.	HIGH
Bowl, 7" dia., blue, white background, pink, red floral medallions, handles, green M mark	$ 18	$ 21	$ 24
Bowl, 8" dia., enameled, raised chestnut motif, handles, green M mark	32	38	44
Bowl, 9" dia., bisque, walnut motif, green M mark	85	100	115
Bowl, 9" dia., mustard color, hand painted, M wreath, blue mark, gold, jewels, rose motif	60	70	80
Bowl, 9" dia., red, black, figural, scenic, floral motif, unmarked	70	80	90
Bowl, strawberries, leaves and flowers, leaf-shaped handle	375	475	575
Box, 2" ht., blue, gold raised motif, green M mark	110	130	150
Candy Bowl, 6" square, square, beaded, gold rim, blown-out sides, 2 gold handles, floral design	100	125	150
Candy Bowl, scene of palm trees, sailboat, in pastel colors, beaded gold trim, pierced handles	70	85	100
Candy Dish, 7" x 5", oval, hand painted M wreath, green mark, scenic motif, open work handles	60	68	76
Celery Dish, 9" x 4", satin finish, small houseboat w/ sail, w/ floral dec.	35	40	45
Cocoa Set, pot, 6 cups & saucers, lid top and bottom, in turquoise blue w/ sprays of roses	425	500	575
Coffee Set, 9" ht., pot, 5 cups & saucers, demitasse size, M mark	200	250	300
Compote, 3" ht., floral insects, medallion of Chicago Post Office, Oriental China Nippon mark	100	120	140
Compote, 5" x 12", bisque, Indian in canoe, surrounded w/ pictographs	180	220	260
Cookie Server, 10" dia., yellow background, floral motif, gold handle, M mark	30	40	50
Cream/Sugar, painted flowers, leaves, gold trim	65	80	95
Creamer, gold foliage motif, hand painted Nippon mark	15	20	25
Cruets, 6" ht., Oriental garden motif, M mark (pr.)	100	125	150
Cup, 3" ht., gold, grape vine motif, green M mark	21	25	28
Cup & Saucer, multicolored floral motif, Art Nouveau, green M mark	11	13	15
Demitasse Set, pot, 5 cups, saucers, Art Deco, black outline, marked Nippon	175	225	275
Desk Set, 5 pieces, scenic cameos	300	400	500
Dish, 12" x 6", yellow, tan floral motif, green stems, black ribbons, lined in gold, green M mark	14	17	19
Dish, 6" dia., cream background, raised gold, multicolor, M mark	18	22	26
Dish, 7" w., fish shape, mythical bird motif, bordered, unmarked	80	100	120
Dish, 7" x 6", gold background, floral, foliage motif, M mark	35	44	53
Dish, 8" x 6", brown and tan panel, floral motif, gold handle, cover, rising sun mark	65	80	95
Dresser Set, 7" tray, stoppered bottle 3" ht., 2 covered patch boxes, round, trimmed in gold, on white	75	90	105

	LOW	AVG.	HIGH
Egg Cup, white background, blue and amber butterflies	$ 30	$ 40	$ 50
Egg Warmer, 5" dia., green M in wreath	150	175	200
Ewer, 10" ht., bulbous body, band of violets, greens and violets, cabinet item unmarked	250	300	350
Ewer, 12" ht., 1900s, bulbous body, foliate center piece, red and violet	330	380	430
Fruit Bowl, 9" dia., handles, scalloped gold rim, geometric designs, flowers, signed w/ the blue leaf mark	115	135	155
Hat Pin Holder, gold, floral detail on dark blue background	55	66	78
Humidor, 4" ht., bisque finish, trimmed in gold, scene of playing cards	600	750	900
Jar, 4" ht., multicolored floral, gold green M mark	30	37	44
Napkin Ring, satin finish, scene of windmill	90	110	130
Nut Set, bowl, 4 dishes on legs, flowers traced in gold line	50	60	70
Plate, 10" dia., multicolored floral motif, green M mark	25	30	35
Plate, 10" dia., raised gold, red floral motif, pierced handles, marked	85	100	115
Plate, 5" dia., floral motif, Art Nouveau, green M mark	9	11	13
Plate, 6" dia., gold-outlined, oval floral medallions, blue mark	55	64	72
Plate, 7" dia., child holds bouquet, blue M mark	20	24	28
Plate, 7" dia., children playing, elephant motif, hand painted Nippon	27	32	36
Plate, 8" dia., gold raised enamel leaves, vines, oval medallions, green M mark	35	40	45
Platter, 11" dia., autumn scene of lake, path into forest, applied handles	100	125	150
Salt Dip, polychrome floral motif, gold outline, green M mark	20	25	30
Shakers, pr., 2" ht., pink floral, foliage motif, gold handles, rising sun mark	30	38	46
Shakers, pr., designs filled w/ white enamel, salt is open-bowl type	37	46	55
Spoon Holder, floral motif, 2 handles, M mark	60	70	80

Left: Nippon was often sold in large sets.

Right: Gilt triangular planter $30-$60.

Occupied Japan

These are items Japan exported after World War II, when Japan was "occupied" by a foreign country for the first time in its history. The term "occupied" was essential to Japanese economic recovery. Hostile feelings ran high for many years after the war; Americans refused to buy anything with "Made in Japan" as its trademark. Since Japanese exports retained craftsmanship, beauty, and aesthetic symmetry, despite the scarcity of materials and manpower, the trademark "Occupied Japan" assured consumers that they were in no way contributing to the menacing powers of the pre-war era.

	LOW	AVG.	HIGH
Alpine Girl, 4.5" ht., black hat, green dress	$ 9	$ 12	$ 15
Bird, 2" ht., perched on 2 books, polychrome	8	11	14
Bird, 2" x 3", tan body, red head, multicolor wings, black tail	12	15	18
Bird, 3.5" ht., perched on branch, polychrome	12	14	16
Bird, 3.5" x 3", on floral branches, polychrome	11	14	17
Bird, 4.5" ht., perched on stump	15	20	25
Bird, 4.5" x 4.5", cocked head, raised tail, polychrome	22	28	34
Bird, 5" ht., perched on tree stump, leaves on base	14	18	22
Boxer, 3" ht., gray, standing	11	14	17
Boy, 4" ht., carrying bottles and a basket, polychrome	15	20	25
Boy, 4" ht., holding basket, duck at feet, polychrome	11	14	17
Boy, 4" ht., seated on bench w/ violin, polychrome	13	16	19
Boy, 4.5" ht., w/ toy boat, polychrome	10	13	16
Colonial Couple, 3" x 4", on pedestal, lady sitting w/ fan, man in long coat standing	13	17	20
Colonial Couple, 3.5" ht., lady seated w/ musical instrument, man standing	13	17	20
Colonial Couple, 3.5" ht., man holding hat, lady in long skirt	15	19	23
Colonial Couple, 3.5" ht., seated man w/ cape, standing lady w/ ruffled dress, polychrome	16	20	23
Colonial Couple, 4" ht., white, gold trim, lady w/ fan, man w/ book	18	23	27
Colonial Couple, 4.5" ht., dancing, polychrome	20	25	30
Colonial Couple, 4.5" ht., holding hands	20	25	30
Colonial Couple, 4.5" ht., man w/ striped breeches, lady w/ floral skirt, polychrome	20	25	30
Colonial Couple, 4.5" ht., seated lady, man holds hat, polychrome	18	23	28
Colonial Couple, 4.5" ht., seated, man holds rose, lady w/ flower basket, polychrome	20	25	30
Colonial Couple, 4.5" x 3", man stands w/ cape, lady seated	20	25	30
Colonial Couple, 4.5" x 5.5", each w/ musical instrument, polychrome	18	22	26
Crane, 4" ht., blue and yellow outstretched wings	10	13	16
Dog, 2", black spotted, long nose and ears, seated	8	11	13

Oriental Rugs

Oriental rugs older than fifty years have long been collected and used in fine homes throughout the United States. They originated in Persia (modern Iran), Turkey, and the surrounding areas. The following representative examples show prices realized at auction (wholesale) and the corresponding retail range. "Karastan" rugs are machine-made and not collected by anyone we know. All the rugs listed here are hand-woven. European examples from the 19th century are particularly valuable. For further information see the *Official Price Guide to Oriental Rugs*, by Joyce C. Ware, House of Collectibles, Random House, NY.

Left to right: Caucasian Seychor rug, 60" x 42", $3500 at auction; Caucasian Kuba Rug, 35" x 80", $ 2000 at auction. — Photos courtesy of Northeast Auctions.

	AUCTION	RETAIL	
		Low	High
Afghar Rug, 30" x 42"	$ 1300	$ 2600	$ 4000
Afshar Saddlebag, 22" x 19"	125	250	380
Afshar Saddlebag, 24" x 16.5"	1000	2000	3000
Ardebil Design Carpet, 9' 2" x 14', modern, Indian	1900	3800	5700
Baktiari Garden Carpet, signed and dated 1916, 10' x 16'	5000	10,000	15,000
Bidjar Oriental Carpet, medallion on red field, 11' x 19'	28,000	56,000	84,000
Caucasian Karabagh Rug, 41" x 121"	900	1800	2700
Caucasian Kazak Rug, medallion on blue field, 48" x 65"	4400	8800	13,000
Caucasian Kilim Pictorial Rug, horse & riders, 79" x 106"	4250	8500	12,750
Central Asian Yomut Turkoman Rug, 27" x 53"	2100	4200	6300
Chinese Wool Rug, 28" x 54"	150	300	450
Daghestan Scatter Rug, 3' 6" x 4' 11"	1280	2560	3840

*Above left to right: Antique Kazak prayer rug, 53" x 36",
$2000 at auction; Kazak Cloudband rug, 45" x 70" $4500 at
auction. — Photo courtesy of Northeast Auctions.*

*Above: Yomut Turkoman tent hanging, $2100 at auction,
Saddlebag $1000 at auction. — Photo courtesy of
Northeast Auctions.*

	AUCTION	RETAIL	
		Low	High
Ersari Turkoman Camel Bag, 15" x 53"	$ 375	$ 750	$ 1200
Feraghan Rug, medallion on ivory field, 49" x 72"	4500	9000	13,500
Feraghan Rug, Herati design on blue field, 48.5" x 78"	2300	4600	6900
Feraghan Sarouk Rug, w/ floral design, 3' 10" x 6' 3"	1300	2600	3900
French Aubusson Carpet w/ floral sprays , 13' 3" x 17' 4"	14,000	28,000	42,000
French Savonnerie Carpet, w/ floral ground, 14' 4" x 17' 5"	8500	17,000	25,000
Hamadan Jojan Sarouk Design Rug, 6' 8" x 5'	1300	2600	4000
Hamadan Oriental Scatter Rug, 6' 11" x 5' 5"	100	200	300
Hamadan Rug, 6' 4" x 4' 10"	1300	2600	4000

	AUCTION	RETAIL	
		Low	High
Hamadan Runner, red predominant, 2' 6" x 13" .... $ 325		$ 650	$ 1000
Heriz Carpet, w/ medallion on madder ground, 9' 6" x 6' 1800		3500	5500
Heriz Carpet, w/ medallion and spandrels, 10' 11" x 8' 4" 18,000		35,000	55,000
Heriz Rug, w/ stylized tree design, 49" x 59" 1300		2600	4000
Isphahan Silk Rug, w/ central medallion, 8' 6" x 12' 2" 14,500		25,000	45,000
Kajara Carpet, w/ brick red medallion, 9' 2" x 12' 7" 21,000		40,000	65,000
Karaja-Heriz Carpet, medallion on red field, 14' 6" x 25' 25,000		50,000	75,000
Kashan Carpet, blue medallion on floral field, 8' 8" x 11' 9000		18,000	27,000
Kashan Carpet, on ivory field, 8' 6" x 11' 7", modern 1800		3600	5400
Khorassan Rug, w/ military figures, 10' x 11' 7" 6500		13,000	20,000
Kirman Prayer Rug, w/ 3 cypress trees, 4' 1" x 6' 6" 3750		7500	11,250
Kirman Rug, medallion on ivory field, 48" x 72" 1300		2600	4000
Kirmanshaw Carpet, foliate medallion,11' 5" x 21' 2" 7000		14,000	21,000
Kuba Rug, w/ bird motif, 54" x 84" 1500		3000	4500
Kuba Soumak Rug, 48" x 58" 1750		3500	5250
Lori Runner, 59" x 114" 2000		4000	6000
Marasali Shirvan Prayer Rug, 41.5" x 47" 3000		6000	9000
Moteham Kashan Carpet, palmette medallion, 55" x 79" 3000		6000	9000
Northwest Persian Runner, Botek design, 3' 6" x 14' 1400		2800	4200
Oushak Carpet, red medallion, 12' 6" x 15' 11" 4500		9000	13,500

Antique Heriz carpet, 10' 11" by 8' 4", $18,000 at auction. — Photo courtesy of Northeast Auctions.

Satsuma

Satsuma is a cream-colored Japanese pottery, usually with a delicate crackled glaze and elaborately painted and gilt. Although it dates to the 17th century, most pieces seen today are from the 19th and 20th centuries. The following are 19th-century examples.

Above left to right: Large lobbed bowl with thousand-face interior, $2250 at auction; teapot, $650 at auction; charger, $2200 at auction. Below left to right: Large bulbous vase, $700 at auction; thin neck vase, $2000 retail. — Photos courtesy of Northeast Auctions.

	AUCTION	RETAIL Low	High
Cabinet Vase	$ 325	$ 580	$ 880
Cabinet Vase, w/ dark ground	200	360	540
Cabinet Vase, w/ raised dragon	500	900	1350
Large Bulbous Vase	700	1260	1890
Large Charger	450	810	1220
Large Lobed Bowl, w/ Thousand Face interior	750	1350	2020
Plate w/ silver overlay	350	630	940
Ribbed Bowl	450	810	1220
Small Bowl, w/ Thousand Butterflies interior	450	810	1220
Snuff Box, w/ blue ground	1000	1800	2700
Square Koro	850	1530	2300
Teapot	650	1170	1760

Snuff Bottles

Snuff bottles appeared with the growing popularity of snuff in China during the latter part of the 17th century. Originally a practical item, like a cigarette case, craftsmen of all sorts decorated these pieces with greater and greater sophistication. Eventually snuff bottles gained a life of their own. Collected and produced long after the fad of using snuff died out, they are still made today.

Judging snuff bottles is highly subjective. Craftsmanship and beauty are the dominant factors, but rarity of materials also plays a part. Some jade examples are valued almost solely on the quality of the piece of jade, rather than age, craftsmanship, or design.

	LOW	AVG.	HIGH
Agate			
Bird motif, c. 1800s	$ 550	$ 700	$ 850
Brown, flat shape, bat motif, c. 1800s	550	700	850
Brown, gray streaks, round, translucent, c. 1800s	1250	1500	1750
BDuck and young motif, c. 1900s	600	800	1000
Bamboo shape, flat, c. 1900s	1500	1800	2100
Flowering mountain motif, c. 1900s	1000	1250	1500
Hydra, bird motif, c. 1900s	600	800	1000
Monkey on Foo dog motif, c. 1900s	1532	1866	2200
Pale mauve, fisherman, fish motif, c. 1900s	1100	1500	1900
Prawn, crab motif, c. 1900s	700	850	1000
Tan and carnelian, Buddha and bat, 2", c. 1900s	1350	1650	1950
Taoist mask motif, c. 1900s	697	873	1050
Tree, boy, Foo dog motif, c. 1900s	670	800	970
White, duck and lilies motif, c. 1900s	1600	2000	2400
Amber			
Brown, flat sides, rect., trees, rocks, and birds motif, c. 1800s	$ 1200	$ 1500	$ 1800
Brown, pebble shape, c. 1800s	800	1000	1200
Dark yellow, cloud motif, c. 1800s	800	1000	1200
Yellow, streaked gold, knobby texture, c. 1800s	1000	1300	1600
Brass			
Coral, gilt, green glass beads, c. 1900s	$ 2300	$ 3000	$ 3300
Silver inlay, flask-shaped, inscribed, c. 1800s	825	1000	1300
Tree motif, c. 1900s	650	825	1000
Cinnabar			
Floral motif, c. 1900s	$ 230	$ 310	$ 390
Landscape and figurines finely carved, c. 1900s	112	136	160
Cloisonné			
Black background, dragon motif, c. 1900s	$ 90	$ 115	$ 140
Blue, yellow, dragon motif, c. 1900s	100	130	160
Blue, yellow dragon white cloud motifs, c. 1800s	400	500	600
Dark blue background, multicolored floral, vine motif, c. 1900s	400	500	600
Green background, double bottle shape, dragon motif, c. 1900s	600	700	800
Green background, Indian lotus motif, c. 1900s	500	700	900
Turquoise, fish motif, c. 1800s	700	850	1000
Yellow, blue; cloudy, dragon motif, c. 1900s	600	700	800

	LOW	AVG.	HIGH

Coral

	LOW	AVG.	HIGH
Tree shape, c. 1800s	$ 630	$ 780	$ 930
Fish shape, c. 1800s	600	775	950
Bamboo shape, c. 1800s	900	1200	1500

Crystal

	LOW	AVG.	HIGH
Clear, thin black lines, fish motif, c. 1800s	$ 600	$ 750	$ 800
Clear, thin black lines, sq. shape, round edges, c. 1800s	800	1000	1200
Thin, brown hairlines, c. 1900s	1000	1200	1400
Thin gold lines, c. 1800s	900	1200	1500
Thin lines, reclining horse motif., c. 1800s	261	315	370

Enamel

	LOW	AVG.	HIGH
Blue and gray, dragon, wave motif, c. 1800s	$ 1500	$ 2100	$ 2700
Blue, gourd shape, fruit and foliage motif, c. 1800s	687	838	990
Figural, landscape motif, c. 1800s	1800	2300	2800
White, plants and dragonfly motif, c. 1800s	750	1000	1250

Glass

	LOW	AVG.	HIGH
Black, archer, stag motif, c. 1900s	$ 1100	$ 1450	$ 1800
Blue on white, two horses and tree motif, c. 1800s	450	600	750
Blue w/ white flecks, circular, red stopper, c. 1700s	1700	2300	2900
Brown, gold specks, c. 1800s	397	498	600
Brown w/ green overlay of an elephant, c. 1800s	2900	3700	4500
Dark blue, gold specks, c. 1800s	488	629	770
Flattened sides, green, dragon motif, c. 1900s	160	190	220
Gold fleck, flattened form, black metal w/ gold markings and stopper, c. 1900s	120	150	180
Green and red, bottle shape, c. 1800s	1000	1250	1500
Turquoise, multicolored enameled colors, figural mountain motif, c. 1800s	600	800	1000

Jade

	LOW	AVG.	HIGH
Green, flat sides, oval panels, c. 1800s	$ 500	$ 600	$ 700
Streaked brown and white, bat motif, mock handler, c. 1800s	700	800	900
Streaked gray, lion and tree motif, mock handles, c. 1800s	659	839	1020
Streaked green and gray, toad and landscape, c. 1800s	656	788	920
Streaked green and yellow, round, c. 1800s	1300	1600	1900
White, scenic motif, inscribed, c. 1900s	1000	1300	1600
Yellow, streaked beige, double-bottle shape, c. 1800s	1300	1600	1900

Lacquer

	LOW	AVG.	HIGH
Black w/ ivory rim, purse-shaped, c. 1900s	$ 700	$ 850	$ 1000
Brown, green, mother-of-pearl, shore line, water motif, c. 1900s	750	950	1150
Gold and black, c. 1900s	225	300	375
Real gourd, lacquered black, c. 1800s	584	727	870

Malachite

	LOW	AVG.	HIGH
Carved gourds on the front, banded, c. 1900s	$ 220	$ 300	$ 380
Floral motif, c. 1800s	300	375	45

	LOW	AVG.	HIGH

Opal

Green & pink, fish and seaweed motif, 2" ht., 63 carats, c. 1900s ... $ 500	$ 625	$ 750
Green, bird, pine tree motif, 2" ht., 167 carats, c. 1900s 400	500	600
Green, blue fire, eagle motif, c. 1900s 550	700	850
Green fire, gourd shape, c. 1900s 300	400	500
Green, pink fire, fruit shape, branch and leaf motif, c. 1900s 330	400	470
Green, pink, gray, black fish motif, 1" ht., 34 carats, c. 1900s 300	400	500
Pink, fish, seaweed motif, 2" ht., 112 carats, c. 1900s 550	650	750
Pink, gray, black, owl motif, 68 carats, c. 1900s 540	660	780
Pink, green, bird and floral motif, 2" ht., 222 carats, c. 1900s 260	330	400

Porcelain

Blue and white, courtyard scene, 3", c. 1800s .... $ 550	$ 700	$ 950
Blue and white, motif of 2 figures under tree, c. 1800s 500	600	700
Blue and white, scenic motif, c. 1800s 300	400	500
Blue, motif of immortal, sea creature, plum branch, c. 1800s 500	600	700
Blue red white, courtyard motif, c. 1800s 440	545	650
Blue white, dragon motif, c. 1800s 240	300	360
Cream, lions frolicking brocade balls, cream stopper, c. 1800s 1700	2100	2500
Fish lotus, motif, paneled, c. 1800s 500	625	750
Green and white, dragon, cloud motif. ., c. 1800s 600	750	900
Green enamel, yellow background, dragon motif, c. 1800s 550	700	850
Green, red figural motif, red seal on bottom, c. 1800s 400	500	600
Red, dragon motif, seal on base, c. 1800s 280	340	400
Red Foo dog and pup, c. 1900s 400	500	600
Red, warrior motif, c. 1800s 500	640	780
Robin's egg glaze, bird on branch, inscribed reverse, c. 1800s 650	775	900
White glaze, squirrel shape, c. 1800s 500	625	750

Quartz

Pink, flat sides, spade shape, figural, cloud motif, c. 1800s .... $ 300	$ 400	$ 500

Rock Crystal

Clear, crackled, sq. shape, mock handles, c. 1800s .... $ 550	$ 700	$ 850
Clear, flat sides, round, knobby texture, c. 1800s 350	425	500
Clear, sq. shape, basket-work motif, c. 1800s 1500	1900	2300

Silver

Bird motif, c. 1900s .... $ 1000	$ 1200	$ 1400
Coral, turquoise insets, c. 1900s 1170	1525	1880
Jade insets, c. 1900s 1600	1900	2200
Round, red, green, dragon, wave motif, c. 1800s 700	850	1000

Tigereye

Floral tree motif, c. 1800s .... $ 550	$ 700	$ 850
Peapod and vine motif, c. 1900s 500	600	700

Turquoise

Scenic motif, c. 1900s .... $ 600	$ 800	$ 1000
Streaked black, apple shape, c. 1800s 400	500	600

Pottery and Porcelain

J.A. Bauer Pottery

The J.A. Bauer Company started with clay flower pots in 1909. After the introduction of stoneware and art pottery, his company added colored dinnerware in 1930, which it produced until 1962.

Marks-an impressed mark with *Bauer* or a combination of the words *Bauer*, *Los Angeles*, *Pottery*, and *USA*. Many items are unmarked or stamped *Made in USA*.

BAUER   *J.A. Bauer backstamp.*

	LOW	AVG.	HIGH
La Linda (1939-59)			
La Linda appears in at least fourteen colors, some matte, some glossy.			
Butter Dish	$ 45	$ 55	$ 65
Chop plate, 13"	26	28	30
Cookie Jar, plain	55	65	75
Cream/Sugar	20	25	30
Cup	10	13	16
Cup/Saucer, jumbo	25	30	35
Custard	6	8	10
Dish, 5"-6"	9	11	13
Gravy Boat	15	20	25
Pitcher, ball form	35	45	55
Plate, 6"	4	5	6
Plate, 7.5"	7	9	11
Plate, 9"	11	14	16
Platter, 10"-12"	14	17	20
Salt/Pepper	9	11	13
Saucer	3	4	4
Soup Plate, 7"	16	19	21
Teapot, 6 cup	33	38	42
Tumbler, 8 oz.	13	16	19
Vegetable, 8"-10"	21	27	32

	LOW	AVG.	HIGH
Monterey (1936-1945)			
Orange Red and Burgundy are the most desirable of the ten colors.			
Beverage Server, w/ cover	$ 100	$ 120	$ 140
Butter Dish	60	70	80
Cake plate, pedestal	80	90	100
Candleholder	25	30	35
Chop plate, 13"	30	40	50
Coffee Server	32	37	42
Console set, 3-piece	200	240	280
Dish, 6"	11	14	17
Fruit, ftd., 12"	45	54	63
Fruit, ftd., 8"-9"	27	36	44
Gravy Boat	33	38	43
Pitcher, 2 qt.	33	38	42
Plate, 10.5"	26	29	31

	LOW	AVG.	HIGH
Plate, 6"-7.5"	$ 8	$ 10	$ 12
Plate, 9"	13	15	17
Platter, oval, 12"-17"	30	37	45
Relish Tray, 3-piece, 11.5"	42	50	58
Salad, 11.5"	31	36	42
Salt/Pepper	12	16	19
Sauce Boat	38	42	46
Soup Plate, 7"	16	19	21
Teapot, new, 6 cup	45	55	65
Tumbler, 8 oz.	15	18	21
Vegetable, oval, 10.5"	30	38	45
Vegetable, round, 9.5"	25	28	30

Ring (c. 1931)

Ring is the most popular pattern. It is reputedly the line that influenced Homer Laughlin to create Fiesta. The pattern appears in many colors. Black pieces are worth more than the values quoted below.

	LOW	AVG.	HIGH
Baker, Pie, no holder, 9"	$ 20	$ 25	$ 30
Barrel mug, 12 oz	45	60	75
Barrel Pitcher	100	125	150
Batter Bowl, 1-2 qt.	60	80	100
Beating Bowl, 1 qt.	32	38	44
Beating Bowl pitcher, 1 qt.	40	50	60
Beer pitcher	160	180	200
Beer stein	50	60	70
Bowl, nesting, 6"-7"	22	27	32
Bowl, nesting, 8"-9"	31	43	55
Butter Dish	110	130	150
Candlestick, spool	30	35	40
Canister, 4"- 6"	60	80	100
Canister, 6.75"	100	130	150
Carafe, metal handle	35	40	45
Casserole, ind., 5.5"	65	70	75
Casserole, metal holder, 6.5"-7.5"	45	60	75
Casserole, metal holder, 8.5"-9.5"	60	85	110
Chop plate, 12"-14"	42	55	68
Chop plate, 17"	75	90	106
Cigarette Jar	150	180	210
Coffee Pot, 8 cup	120	160	180
Coffee Server, wood handle, 6-8 cup	50	65	80
Custard	8	10	12
Dish, baking, w/ lid, 4"	20	23	26
Dish, fruit, 5"	13	15	17
Egg Cup	65	74	82
Goblet	61	74	86
Gravy Bowl	38	44	50
Jar, Storage, open	15	18	21
Mixing Bowl, 1 gal.	42	48	55
Mixing Bowl, 1 pt.	13	16	19
Mixing Bowl, 1 qt.	20	23	25

	LOW	AVG.	HIGH
Mixing Bowl, 1.5 pt.	$ 16	$ 19	$ 22
Mixing Bowl, 1.5 qt.	22	25	27
Mustard	100	125	150
Pedestal Bowl, 14"	160	180	200
Pickle Dish	16	19	22
Pitcher, 1 qt.	26	30	33
Pitcher, 1.5 pt.	21	25	28
Pitcher, 2 qt.	33	38	43
Pitcher, 3 qt.	42	52	62
Pitcher, ball form	65	75	85
Pitcher, cream, 1 pt.	35	45	45
Pitcher, ice lip, w/ metal handle, 2 qt.	68	80	93
Plate, 10.5"	31	36	40
Plate, 5-9"	12	16	20
Platter, oval, 12"	27	30	33
Platter, oval, 9"	22	24	26
Punch Bowl, 14"	160	180	200
Punch cup	16	19	22
Relish Tray, 5 pc.	36	43	50
Salad, low, 12"-14"	60	75	90
Salad, low, 9"	31	36	41
Salad/Punch, 11"	160	190	220
Salad/Punch, 9"	100	130	160
Saucer, coffee/tea	5	7	9
Shaker, barrel shape	5	7	9
Shaker, low	5	7	9
Shaker, Sugar Bowl	50	60	70
Sherbet	32	38	44
Soufflé Dish	138	150	163
Soup Plate	27	30	32
Teapot, 2-6 cup	50	60	70
Teapot, wood handle, 6 cup	65	75	85
Tumbler, 3-12 oz	11	19	27
Tumbler, barrel shape, w/ metal handle	32	37	42
Vegetable, oval, 8"-10"	26	28	30
Vegetable, oval, divivided	45	55	65

Edwin Bennett Pottery

For ninety years, the Edwin Bennett Pottery Company manufactured a variety of products from stoneware and parianware to majolica and semiporcelain. It is most famous for its Cameo line of dinnerware. The firm opened in 1846 and closed in 1936.

Marks-backstamps include: *Bennett Bakeware* and *Bennett, S-V, Baltimore*, and *II Duce*.

Edwin Bennett backstamp.

	LOW	AVG.	HIGH
Baker, Pie	$ 12	$ 14	$ 16
Bean Pot	16	18	20
Butter Dish	20	23	25
Cake Plate	12	14	16
Cake Server	20	25	30
Canister	39	46	52
Casserole	24	28	32
Casserole	30	35	40
Cream/Sugar	12	14	16
Cup/Saucer	8	10	12
Custard Cup	4	5	6
Dish, 5.5"	2	3	4
Drip Jar	25	28	30
Gravy Boat	12	15	18
Mixing Bowl	20	30	40
Mug, barrel	15	18	21
Pitcher	20	25	30
Pitcher, Syrup	38	44	51
Pitcher, w /lid	38	43	48
Plate, 6"-8"	2	4	6
Plate, 9"	8	9	10
Platter, rect.	10	11	12
Salad Bowl	17	19	21
Salt Box	40	45	50
Salt/Pepper	25	35	45
Soup Plate, 7.5"	8	10	12
Tray	20	26	32
Vegetable	10	11	12

Bennington Pottery

The period of true Bennington was brief, from 1842 to 1858, but this may be deceiving since the output during those sixteen years was heavy. In 1842 Julius Norton (a grandson of the founder) went into partnership with Christopher Fenton. Norton and Fenton set out to duplicate the surface of Rockingham wares. From the original name of "Norton and Fenton," it became "Fenton's Works," then "Lyman, Fenton and Co." Finally, the company used the name "United States Pottery" from 1850 until its collapse in 1858.

The earliest mark of Norton and Fenton, in 1842, was a circular wording of *NORTON & FENTON, BENNINGTON, Vt.* Block lettering was used without any symbol. When the company name changed, after Norton left in 1847, the mark became *FENTON'S WORKS, BENNINGTON, VERMONT* enclosed in a rectangular decorative border. This distinctive mark was set in two styles of lettering with *FENTON'S WORKS* in slanting characters resembling italics. The address was set in standard vertical lettering. The next mark, that of Lyman, Fenton and Co., sat within a plain oval frame and read *LYMAN FENTON & CO., FENTON'S ENAMEL, PATENTED 1849, BENNINGTON, Vt.* This ushered in the era of colored glazes. Within this mark, the year (1849) is very prominently displayed. The United States Pottery Co. era introduced two different marks, both reading *UNITED STATES POTTERY Co., BENNINGTON, VT.* One carries the wording within an oval frame with two small ornamental flourishes; the other is a modified diamond shape composed of decorative printer's type, but without further ornamentation.

Top row left to right: Toby pitcher, $350; "Departed Spirits" book, 9",
$800; figural covered jar, $250, humidor, $600; toothbrush holder,
$100; alternate rib pitcher, $1200; "Departed Spirits" book, 6", $300;
flask, $900. Bottom row left to right: Creamer, $300; pilgrim flask,
$1500; spittoon, $250; candlestick, $ 925; spittoon, $250, cow creamer,
$450, night stick, $500. — Photo courtesy of Northeast Auctions.

	AUCTION	RETAIL	
		Low	High

Flint Enamel "Rockingham" Glazed Pieces

	AUCTION	Low	High
Baking Dish, 1849 mark, len. 9.25" .... $ 200		$ 470	$ 760
"Bennington Battle" Book Flask, ht. 7" 700		1650	2650
"Bennington Battle" Book Flask, ht. 7.5" 700		1650	2650
Book Flask, ht. 5.75" 300		700	1100
Book Flask, ht. 10.5" 1750		4000	6500
Book Flask, ht. 5.25" 300		700	1140
Book Flask, "Departed Spirits," 2 qt. 650		1500	2500
Book Flask, extended spout, rare small 1849 mark, ht. 6" 900		2120	3400
Book Flask, 4 qt., largest size 1600		3500	6000
Book Flask, "Lexington Battle," ht. 7" 600		1420	2250
Candlesticks, pr., ht. 9.25" 725		1700	2750
Candlesticks, pr., ht. 8" 500		1180	1900
Chamber Pitcher, scalloped rib pattern, 1849 mark, ht. 12.75" 750		1750	2840
Chamber Pot, diamond pattern w/ lid 350		830	1330
Chamber Pot, scalloped rib pattern, dia. 9" 600		1400	2300
Circular Baking Dish, 1849 mark, dia. 7" 175		400	660
Coffee Pot, 1849 mark 250		600	950
Coffeepot, scalloped rib pattern, ht. 12" 650		1500	2500
Cow Creamer, complete, lid, len. 7" 350		830	1330
Creamer, tulip & heart pattern, 1849 mark, ht. 6" 300		700	1140
Curtain Tieback, len. 4.5", dia. 4.5" 30		70	100
Curtain Tieback, dia. 4.25" 25		60	90
Cuspidor, Scalloped rib pattern, 1849 mark, dia. 8.25" 100		240	380
Cuspidor, unrecorded Fenton 1849 mark, dia. 9" 450		1000	1700
Cuspidors, graduated set of 3, diamond pattern 175		400	660
"Departed Spirits" Book Flask, ht. 5" 425		1000	1600
"Departed Spirits" Book Flask, ht. 8" 700		1650	2650
"Departed Spirits" Book Flask, ht. 6" 350		830	1330
Doorknob 25		60	90
Early Pitcher, "Norton & Fenton East Bennington VT," ht. 8" 800		2000	3000
Figure of Recumbent Cow, 1849 mark, len. 10" 12,500		25,000	40,000
Foot Warmer, ht. 9" 100		240	380
Goblet, ht. 4.75" 200		470	760
Goblet, ftd., w/ handle, ht. 4.5" 250		590	950
Honey-Colored Coachman Toby, w/ 1849 mark, ht. 10.5" 475		1200	1800
"Hoo Doo King" Book Flask, ht. 5.5" 1300		3000	5000
Lion, ht. 9.5" 10,000		24,000	30,000
Miniature Turk's Head Bowl 250		590	950
Mold, Turk's Head, dia. 6.5" 150		350	570
Mug, ht. 3.25" 60		140	230
Nameplate, len. 8" 125		300	470
Nameplate, framed, Parian letters spelling name, ht. 3.5" 400		940	1520
Oval Picture Frame, 8" x 7" 325		770	1230
Oval Picture Frame, 8" x 9.5" 750		1770	2800
Picture Frame, Rococo,10" x 9" 1600		3780	6000
Picture Frame, Rococo, unusual gray glaze, 9.75" x 10.75" 650		1530	2460
Picture Frame, scalloped or serpentine, 5.75" x 6.75" 150		350	570
Pint Book Flask, "Departed Spirits," w/ exceptional color 700		1650	2650
Pipkin, w/ lid, ht. 7.5" 450		1000	1700

	AUCTION	RETAIL	
		Low	High
Pitcher, 8 panel, molded tulips and hearts, ht. 7"	$ 450	$ 1000	$ 1700
Pitcher, alternate rib, ht. 10.25"	1300	3000	5000
Pitcher, alternate rib, 1849 mark, ht. 10"	900	2000	3400
Pitcher, alternate rib pattern, ht. 6.75"	150	350	570
Pitcher and Bowl Set, 1849 mark	375	900	1420
Pitcher, diamond pattern, ht. 9"	350	830	1330
Pitcher, w/ mask under spout, ht. 8.75"	200	450	750
Pitcher, w/ mask under spout, ht. 9"	50	120	190
Relish Dish, len. 10"	350	830	1300
Seated Toby Creamer, w/ 1849 mark	550	1300	2000
Slop Jar Base, 1849 mark	450	1000	1700
Tile, 1849 impressed mark, 7" sq.	400	940	1500
Tobacco Jar, w/ lid, alternate rib pattern, ht. 6.75"	300	700	1100
Toby Pitcher, vintage handle, ht. 6"	350	830	1300
Toby Snuff Jar, lidded, dark greenish-brown glaze	600	1400	2200
Toby Snuff Jar, w/ 1849 mark	1450	3400	5500
Toothbrush Holder, lidded, alternate rib pattern	500	1200	1900
Tulip Vase, fine and colorful glaze, ht. 10"	600	1420	2250
Wash Bowl, paneled, 1849 mark, dia. 13.5"	475	1120	1800

Parian Pieces

Bust of Dickens, ht. 5"	$ 50	$ 120	$ 190
Bust of girl w/ bird, ht. 5"	50	120	190
Creamer, Bennington-type handle, ht. 4.25"	50	120	190
Doorknob, in rosette pattern	20	50	80
Miniature Vase, hand holding flower, ht. 3"	10	20	40
Pitcher, pond lily pattern, U.S. Pottery ribbon mark, ht. 10"	175	410	660
Pitcher, wild rose pattern, ht. 10"	200	470	760
Porcelain Figural Vase, ht. 7"	100	240	380
Trinket Box, blue & white, len. 5"	30	70	110
Trinket Box, molded flower lid, len. 5.5"	10	20	40
Trinket Box, ribbed pattern, grapes on cover, len. 4"	50	120	200
Trinket Box, sleeping child on lid, len. 4.25"	10	20	40
Vase, molded grapevine pattern, scalloped top, ht. 4.5"	50	120	200
Vase, songbird pattern, blue & white, ht. 4"	25	60	90

Boehm Figures

Edward Marshall Boehm founded a pottery studio in Trenton, New Jersey in 1949. Following Boehm's death, his wife Helen took over the company. In addition to the Trenton studio, Boehm studios started in England in 1971.

Boehm birds are some of the most fragile porcelain ever made. Chipped and broken foliage can be easy to overlook, but the value is considerably less. Current items range all the way from a $20 cup and saucer to a $400 Prince Rudolph's Blue Bird of Paradise.

Boehm birds. - photo courtesy of Northeast Auctions.

	LOW	AVG.	HIGH
Blue Grosbeak	$ 1300	$ 1650	$ 2000
Bobolink	1600	1900	2200
Boxer, large size	1500	1800	2100
Carolina Wrens	7000	9000	11,000
Catbird	2550	2955	3360
Crested Flycatcher	3400	3800	4200
Downy Woodpecker	2100	2300	2500
Fledgling Blue Jay	240	260	280
Fledgling Canada Warbler	2000	2500	3000
Fledgling Goldfinch	300	350	400
Fledgling Magpie	1000	1250	1500
Fledgling Red Poll	260	300	340
Green Jays	7000	8000	9000
Lazuli Bunting Paperweight	180	205	230
Mourning Doves	7000	8000	9000
Nuthatch	360	430	500
Oven-Bird	2000	2400	2800
Parula Warbler	3800	4200	4600
Polo Player	6200	6800	7400
Prothonotary Warblers	600	750	900
Read Runner	6000	7000	8000
Rufous Hummingbirds	3000	3400	3800
Scottish Terrier	600	800	1000
Standing Poodle, apricot-colored	2300	2650	3000
Thoroughbred and Exercise Boy, decorated	10,000	11,500	13,000
Towhee	2970	3300	3630
Tufted Titmice	1500	1900	2300
Varied Buntings	7000	9000	11,000
Whippets	5000	6000	7000

Bookends

Dating back to before either television or the internet, bookends were considered far more a necessity than today. But for those of us who can find no end to our books, these pottery shelf stoppers are well worth their collectors' dollars. Look for bold forms and, as always, beware of cracks and chips.

	LOW	AVG.	HIGH
Atlas, Morton, 5"	$ 30	$ 36	$ 42
Bucking Bronco, Frankoma, 7"	110	130	151
Cactus, Abingdon, 6"	67	86	104
Calla Lily, Royal Haeger, 5.5"	22	26	30
Clydesdale, Frankoma, 5"	300	400	500
Dolphin, Abingdon, 5.5"	20	25	30
Dreamer Girl, Frankoma, 6"	125	150	175
Duck Head, Frankoma, 5.5"	150	175	200
Eagles, Morton , 6"	40	50	59
Elephants, Cliftwood	125	150	175
Fern Leaf, Abingdon, 5.5"	50	60	70
Flying Geese, Shawnee, 6"	30	40	50
Horse Head, Abingdon, 7"	45	60	75
Horse Head, Royal Haeger, 7.5"	27	35	43
Horse, Royal Haeger, 8.5"	30	36	42
Irish Setter, Frankoma, 6"	115	145	175
Leopard, Frankoma, 7"	100	125	150
Leopard, Royal Haeger, 15"	58	73	88
Lion Head, Royal Haeger, 7.5"	28	35	42
Monk, Catalina, 7"	400	500	600
Mountain Girl, Frankoma, 7"	75	100	125
Owl, Van Briggle, 6"	271	340	408
Parrots, Morton , 6"	34	43	52
Quill, Abingdon, 8.25"	70	85	100
Ram, Royal Haeger, 9"	35	43	50
Ram's Head, Royal Haeger, 5.5"	26	32	38
Russian, Abingdon, 6.5"	60	80	100
Scotty, Abingdon, 7.5"	70	90	110
Sea Gull, Abingdon, 6"	50	60	70
Seahorse, Frankoma, 6"	300	400	500
Water Lily, Royal Haeger, 5"	21	27	33
Woodpeckers, Cliftwood, 6.5"	125	150	175

Camark Pottery

The Camark Pottery Company lasted from 1926 (as Camden Art and Tile Company) to 1982, but it produced few pieces for the last decade and a half. Early "Le-Camark" pieces are wheel-thrown and of the hand-decorated line. Most pieces, however, are molded. The most desired are Le-Camark pieces, animal figurals, and pitchers with figural handles. Reproductions, notably the cat with fish bowl ("Wistful Kitten") are on the market.

Marks-most often impressed *CAMARK*.

	LOW	AVG.	HIGH
Bowl, cabbage leaf	$ 6	$ 8	$ 10
Bowl, pumpkin, large	12	15	18
Bowl, pumpkin, small	6	8	10
Bowl, swans	11	15	19
Cream/Sugar, on stand	10	12	14
Dog, miniature	5	6	7
Flower Frog, dancer	18	22	26
Flower Frog, swans	15	19	22
Football, hog on top	12	15	18
Humpty Dumpty	20	25	30
Lion	10	12	14
Pitcher, cat handle	30	40	50
Pitcher, parrot handle	43	56	70

Cookie Jars

Cookie jars may be the most beloved containers in the kitchen. They hold the comforting treat most of us have pursued for years. Cookie jar collecting gained momentum in the early eighties. Sotheby's 1988 auction of the estate of Pop Artist Andy Warhol catapulted figural cookie jars to national prominence. Hearing a cookie jar brought over $20,000 (it was actually for a lot of several jars), people scrambled to their kitchen and attics in hopes of striking gold. As the head of the collectibles department at Christie's, I had to deliver the sobering news to scores of people that their cookie jars were worth considerably less than those of the artist. Following the sale, cookie jar collecting flourished and today many jars command thousands of dollars rather than hundreds.

Collectors can specialize in manufacturers, themes or characters. Many times jars by one firm are referred to by the same name as similar jars by another producer. Make sure you know which jar you are purchasing. Recently, crossover interest from character memorabilia collectors fueled a rapid rise in prices of jars such as the Flintstones series (which has been reproduced), Casper the Ghost, Popeye, and others. Collectors of black memorabilia seek the Mammy cookie jars.

The prices below are for jars in excellent condition, with a minimal amount of paint loss, and no chips or cracks. The amount these faults affect value depends on severity, how it alters the jar's visible appeal, and personal tolerance. Cookie jar collectors are generally more tolerant of paint loss than other collectors, but top condition still brings a premium price. For more information we recommend *The Official Price Guide To Pottery and Porcelain*, Harvey Duke, House of Collectibles, Random House, NY, 1995, and *The Complete Cookie Jar Book*, Mike Schneider, Schiffer, West Chester, PA, 1991.

Left to right: Pig, with cold paint decoration, $50-$70, item courtesy of Cerise Foster, Strawberry, McCoy, $50-$70.

	LOW	HIGH
Alice in Wonderland, Disney, Regal China	$ 2000	$ 3000
Animal Crackers, McCoy	60	80
Apollo, McCoy	900	1200
Apple, yellow, McCoy	40	50
Astronauts, McCoy	500	700
Baby Huey, ABC	1500	2000
Baby Pig, Regal China	400	500

	LOW	HIGH
Ball of Yarn w/ Kittens, ABC	$ 90	$ 140
Bananas, McCoy	80	100
Barnum's Animals, McCoy	300	400
Barrel, ABC	25	35
Baseball Boy, McCoy	200	300
Basket of Eggs, McCoy	40	60
Basket of Fruit, McCoy	45	65
Basket of Strawberries, McCoy	40	60
Basket w/ Dog Lid, McCoy	50	70
Basket w/ Duck Lid, McCoy	50	70
Basket w/ Kitten Lid, McCoy	45	65
Basket w/ Lamb Lid, McCoy	50	60
Bear & Beehive, McCoy	30	40
Bear, Ballerina, Metlox	90	130
Bear, cookies in pocket, cold painted, McCoy	50	70
Bear, Honey, flasher, ABC	100	150
Bear, w/ open eyes, ABC	70	90
Beehive w/ Cat, ABC	45	65
Bell, Liberty, ABC	90	110
Betsy Baker, McCoy	200	250
Big Bird, Calif. Org.	60	80
Bird Feed Sack, McCoy	25	45
Black Cat, McCoy	300	400
Boots, Cowboy, ABC	180	230
Bugs Bunny, McCoy	200	250
Casper, ABC	1000	1500
Chef w/ Spoon, ABC	90	140
Chef's Head, McCoy	80	120
Chick, wearing a beret, ABC	60	80
Chiffonnier, McCoy	50	70
Chipmunk, McCoy	80	120
Christmas Tree, Calif. Org.	200	300
Christmas Tree, McCoy	450	650
Churn, McCoy	180	240
Circus Horse, McCoy	180	220
Circus Tent, Brayton	200	300
Clock, 653, Abingdon	70	100
Clock, Cookie Time, 203, ABC	60	80
Clown Head, Metlox	700	900
Clown in Barrel, tan and white, McCoy	80	120
Clown, on stage, 805, ABC	100	130
Coffee Grinder, McCoy	25	40
Coffee Mug, McCoy	30	40
Coffee Pot, ABC	30	40
Coffee Pot, metal handle, ABC	30	40
Cookie, Girl's Face, glasses, pigtails, Abingdon	80	100
Cookie Box, McCoy	100	150
Cookie Boy, McCoy	180	220
Cookie Jug, dark brown top, white bottom, McCoy	20	25
Cookie Monster, Calif. Org.	40	60
Cookie Truck 2 sizes, ABC	80	100
Covered Wagon, Brush	500	700

	LOW	HIGH
Covered Wagon, w/ lid, McCoy	$ 55	$ 85
Cow, ABC	70	90
Cow Jumped Over the Moon, 806, ABC	800	1000
Cow, Brown, Brush	100	150
Cow, Cat on Back, blue, purple or black, Brush	900	1300
Cowboy, Lane	300	500
Davy Crockett Bust, McCoy	450	650
Davy Crockett, w/ gold, Brush	500	800
Davy Crockett, Boy, ABC	300	500
Davy Crockett, Bust, Regal China	500	700
Davy Crockett, Man, ABC	750	950
Davy Crockett, without gold, Brush	250	350
Dino, Flintstones, ABC	700	900
Dog & Basket, Brush	250	300
Dog in Doghouse, McCoy	180	220
Donald Duck on Pumpkin, Calif. Org.	150	200
Donkey & Cart, Brush	350	450
Drum, McCoy	60	80
Drum, Metlox	100	150
Drum Majorette, ABC	250	300
Duck, McCoy	200	300
Dutch Boy, McCoy	45	55
Dutch Boy, cold painted, ABC	35	45
Dutch Boy, cold painted, Shawnee	80	120
Dutch Girl, Regal China	400	500
Dutch Girl & Boy, McCoy	100	150
Dutch Girl, cold painted, ABC	35	45
Eagle Basket, McCoy	30	40
Ear of Corn, McCoy	100	150
Elephant w/ Beanie, ABC	90	130
Elephant, Whole Trunk, McCoy	300	400
Elephant, w/ ice cream cone, Brush	400	500
Elsie The Cow, barrel, Pottery Guild	250	350
Fat Boy, 495 , Abingdon	300	400
Fish, Brush	400	500
Football Boy, McCoy	200	250
Formal Pig, black coat, Brush	180	220
Fred Flinstone, ABC	1000	1200
Friar Tuck, blue, Red Wing	90	110
Frog, Holiday	25	35
Frontier Family, McCoy	30	50
Frosty the Snow Man, Robinson-Ransbottom	450	650
Goldilocks, Regal China	300	400
Grandma, Brayton	400	500
Granny, ABC	140	180
Granny, Brush	300	400
Granny, McCoy	80	120
Hamm's Bear, McCoy	200	250
Hen on Nest, McCoy	70	90
Hippo, Happy, Bar Jar, 549, Abingdon	300	400
Hippo, Monkey Handle, Brush	500	700

	LOW	HIGH
Hobby Horse, McCoy	$ 100	$ 150
Hocus Rabbit, McCoy	40	50
Honey Bear, yellow, McCoy	80	120
Honeycomb Jar, McCoy	55	75
Horse, Circus, Brush	700	900
Horse, sitting, ABC	700	900
Howdy, Doody-Purinton	700	900
Humpty Dumpty w/ Beanie, Brush	200	250
Humpty Dumpty, in cowboy attire, Brush	200	300
Indian Head, McCoy	250	350
Jack-in-the-Box, ABC	100	150
Jack-O-Lantern, McCoy	400	600
Jack-O-Lantern, 674, Abingdon	300	400
Kangaroo, blue, McCoy	250	300
Kangaroo, tan, McCoy	360	420
Katrina, Dutch Girl, green, Red Wing	150	200
Katrina, Dutch Girl, brown, Red Wing	90	120
Kitten, on beehive, ABC	50	75
Koala Bear, McCoy	75	95
Lady Pig, ABC	90	120
Lamb in Hat, ABC	100	150
Lemon, McCoy	40	60
Leprechaun, McCoy	1000	1300
Lion, Hubert, Regal China	800	1000
Little Boy Blue, w/ gold, Brush	600	800
Little Girl, 693, Abingdon	90	100
Little Miss Muffet, 662, Abingdon	200	250
Little Red Riding Hood, w/ gold, large or small, Brush	700	800
Little Red Riding Hood, without gold, large or small, Brush	400	500
Log Cabin, McCoy	70	90
Lollipops, McCoy	60	80
Ludwig Von Drake, ABC	700	900
Ma and Pa Owls, McCoy	85	105
Mammy, Brayton	900	1200
Mammy w/ Cauliflowers, McCoy	900	1200
Mammy, aqua or yellow, McCoy	500	700
Mammy, cold painted, McCoy	180	220
Mammy, red, Metlox	700	800
Mickey & Minnie turnabouts, Leeds	300	400
Milk Can, McCoy	35	45
Monk, McCoy	35	45
Mother Goose, McCoy	100	150
Mouse, McCoy	35	45
Mugsey the Dog, Shawnee	400	600
Oaken Bucket, McCoy	30	40
Olive Oyl, ABC	1500	2500
Orange, McCoy	45	55
Oscar the Grouch, Calif. Org.	60	80
Owl, white and brown, one eye closed, Shawnee Co.	100	150
Owl, Collegiate, ABC	65	85
Owl, glossy brown, McCoy	30	40

	LOW	HIGH
Peek-A-Boo Bear, Regal China	$ 900	$ 1300
Penguins, kissing, white, McCoy	60	80
Peter Pan, w/ gold, Brush	500	700
Phone, Antique Wall, Cardinal Pottery	45	55
Picnic Basket, McCoy	55	65
Pig, Farmer, ABC	100	150
Pig, Sitting, Brush	400	500
Pig, Smiley, red bandanna, flowers, Shawnee Co.	300	400
Pineapple, McCoy	70	110
Pineappple, Metlox	90	110
Pirates Chest, McCoy	80	100
Popeye, ABC	700	900
Pot Belly Stove, black, McCoy	30	40
Pumpkin Coach, Brush	250	300
Puppy Holding Sign, McCoy	80	100
Puppy, in blue pot, ABC	45	65
Quaker Oats, Regal China	90	130
Rabbit in Hat, ABC	55	75
Raggedy Ann, McCoy	90	110
Red Riding Hood, Hull	300	400
Rooster, McCoy	75	85
Rubble House, Flintstones, ABC	800	1000
Rudolph the Red Nose Reindeer, ABC	600	800
Saddle, ABC	200	300
Sailor Boy, white, Shawnee Co.	90	110
Sandman, Flasher, ABC	250	350
Santa, Winking, ABC	250	350
Schoolhouse Bell, ABC	35	55
Sheriff Pig, Robinson-Ransbottom	120	160
Spaceship, ABC	250	350
Spaceship w/ Spaceman, ABC	650	850
Squirrel on Log, Brush	200	250
Strawberry, '50s, McCoy	50	70
Strawberry, '70s, McCoy	30	40
Swee 'Pea, ABC	2000	3000
Teapot, black, McCoy	45	55
Toby, Regal China	500	700
Tortoise and Hare, Flasher, ABC	500	800
Toy Soldier, ABC	40	50
Train, 651, Abingdon	120	160
Train, Cookie RR, ABC	80	100
Tug Boat, ABC	150	250
Whale, Robinson-Ransbottom	600	800
Windmill, McCoy	100	150
Windmill, 678, Abingdon	200	250
Wise Bird, Robinson-Ransbottom	60	90
Wishing Well, McCoy	30	50
Woodsy Owl, McCoy	100	150
Wren House, McCoy	120	160
Yogi Bear, ABC	400	600

Cronin China

In 1934, the Cronin China Company took over a plant in Minerva, OH. There they produced semiporcelain dinnerware and kitchenware until 1956. The most common mark is a backstamp circular Union mark. Kitchenware is usually marked *Bake Oven* in raised letters in a rectangular box. The following entries are part of the Zephyr pattern (1938) which is known for its angular lines.

     Cronin China backstamp.

	LOW	AVG.	HIGH
Baker, Pie, 9"-10"	$ 12	$ 14	$ 15
Casserole, 7.5"	29	34	40
Casserole, ind., 4.5"	19	22	25
Chop-Plate, lug, 10"-12"	10	12	14
Cream/Sugar	25	29	33
Cup/Saucer	8	10	12
Custard Cup	4	5	6
Dish, 5"-6.5"	2	3	4
Mixing Bowl, 4"-9"	4	12	20
Pitcher, ball form	24	27	30
Pitcher, disk	23	27	30
Plate, 6"	2	3	4
Plate, 9"	8	9	10
Platter, 11"-13"	11	13	14
Salad Bowl, 9"	17	19	20
Salt/Pepper	12	14	16
Soup Plate, 7.75"	8	9	10
Teapot	30	35	40
Vegetable, 9.5"	19	20	21

Crooksville China

The Crooksville China Company manufactured semiporcelain dinnerware and kitchenware from 1902 until 1959. Several backstamps exist.

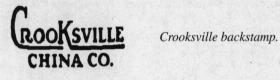

Crooksville backstamp.

	LOW	AVG.	HIGH
Dartmouth (1939)			

Dartmouth has an Art Deco look.

	LOW	AVG.	HIGH
Casserole, 7.5"	$ 21	$ 25	$ 29
Cookie Jar	45	50	55
Cream/Sugar	17	20	23
Cup/Saucer	4	5	6
Gravy Boat	17	18	19
Mixing Bowl, 4"-9"	6	11	15
Pitcher, Syrup	16	19	22
Plate 6"	1	2	3
Plate, 9"-10"	8	11	14
Salt/Pepper	10	14	18
Teapot	16	19	22

Pantry Bak-in Ware (1931)

	LOW	AVG.	HIGH
Baker, Pie, 10"	$ 5	$ 7	$ 9
Bean Pot	14	17	20
Cake Plate	4	5	6
Canister	21	23	24
Casserole, 4"-8"	14	17	20
Coffee Pot, w/ drip	25	30	35
Cookie Jar	16	18	20
Custard Cup	2	3	4
Leftover, 4"-8"	4	7	10
Leftover, oval w/ lid	20	23	25
Mixing Bowl, 6"-12"	5	15	25
Pitcher	19	22	25
Pitcher	8	10	11
Reamer	38	44	48
Teapot	15	18	20
Tray, sq., 9"	4	5	6
Tumbler	8	9	10

Decanters

Ezra Brooks Bottles

Ezra Brooks produces figural bottles with themes from sports and transportation to antiques. The antique series includes an Edison phonograph and a Spanish cannon. Ezra Brooks rivals Jim Beam as one of the chief whiskey companies manufacturing figural bottles.

	LOW	AVG.	HIGH
Alabama Bicentennial, 1976	$ 15	$ 18	$ 20
American Legion, 1971, distinguished embossed star emblem, of WWI, blue and gold, on blue base	38	44	50
American Legion, 1972, City of Chicago, host of the Legion's 54th National Convention	85	100	115
American Legion, 1973, Hawaii, hosted the American Legion's 1973 Annual Convention	15	17	19
American Legion, 1977, Denver	30	34	38
American Legion, 1973, Miami Beach	12	14	16
Amvets, 1974, Dolphin	24	28	32
Amvet, 1973, Polish Legion	22	27	32
Antique Cannon, 1969	8	9	10
Antique Phonograph, 1970, white, black, "Morning Glory" horn, red, detailed in gold	12	14	15
Arizona, 1969, man w/ burro in search of "Lost Dutchman Mine," gold base, "ARIZONA" imprinted	7	9	10
Auburn 1932, 1978, Classic Car	45	50	55
Badger No. 1, 1973, Boxer	20	24	28
Badger No. 2, 1974, Football	24	28	30
Badger No. 3, 1974, Hockey	24	28	30
Baltimore Oriole Wild Life, 1979	53	60	70
Bare Knuckle Fighter, 1971	9	11	12
Baseball Hall of Fame, 1973, Heritage China	22	26	30
Basketball Player, 1974	12	14	15
Bear, 1968	7	8	9
Bengal Tiger Wild Life, 1979	50	55	60
Betsy Ross, 1975	17	20	22
Big Daddy Lounge, 1969, white, green, red	7	8	9
Bighorn Ram, 1973	11	13	15
Bird Dog, 1971	14	17	20
Bordertown, Borderline Club, brown, red, white, club building w/ vulture on roof stopper	7	8	9
Bowler, 1973	8	9	10
Brahma Bull, 1972	17	20	23
Clown, 1978, Imperial Shrine	28	32	38
Club Bottle, 1973, 3rd commemorative, shape of America, each gold star represents the location of an Ezra Brooks Collectors Club	30	35	40
Clydesdale Horse, 1973	15	18	21
Colt Peacemaker, 1969, gun-form flask	6	7	8
Conquistador's Drum & Bugle, 1972	15	18	20
Corvette Indy Pace Car, 1978	62	68	73
Maine Lobster, 1970, lobster shape	28	32	36
Maine Lighthouse, 1971	25	29	32

Man O'War, 1969, race horse in brown & green, gold base, embossed

	LOW	AVG.	HIGH
"MAN-O-'WAR"	$ 14	$ 17	$ 19
M & M Brown Jug, 1975	28	31	34
Map, 1972, U.S.A. Club Bottle	12	14	16
Masonic Fez, 1976	14	17	20
Max, 1976, the hat, Zimmerman	35	41	47
Milady Tank, 1971	22	26	30
Minnesota Hockey Player, 1975	27	30	33
Minuteman, 1975	19	21	23
Missouri Mule, 1972, brown	17	20	22
Moose, 1973	33	36	40
Motorcycle, motorcycle rider and machine, stars 'n stripes helmet, on silver base	12	14	15
Mountaineer, 1971, figure dressed in buckskin, holding rifle, *"MOUNTAINEERS ARE ALWAYS FREE"* trimmed in platinum, one of the most valuable	60	70	80
Mr. Foremost, 1969, bottle-shaped symbol of Foremost Liquor stores,"Mr. Foremost," red, white, and black	13	15	17
Mr. Maine Potato, 1973	9	10	11
Mr. Merchant, 1970, *JUMPING MAN,* whimsical, caricature of shopkeeper, leaping, arms outstretched, yellow, black	12	14	16
Mustang Indy Pace Car, 1979	19	21	22
Nebraska-"Go Big Red", 1972, Heritage China game ball and fan, trimmed in gold	15	17	19
New Hampshire State House, 1970, 150-year-old State House, eagle stopper, gray building w/ gold	15	17	19
North Carolina Bicentennial, 1975	15	18	21
Nugget Classic, golf pin presented to golf tournament participants, gilt finish	12	14	15
Oil Gusher, oil drilling rig, all silver, black stopper as gushing oil	7	9	11
Old Capitol, 1971, shape of Iowa's seat of government as frontier territory, *"OLD CAPITOL, IOWA 1840-1857,"* old dome stopper	23	26	29
Old Ez, 1977, No. 1, barn owl	67	76	86
Old Ez, 1978, No. 2, eagle owl	90	105	120
Old Ez, 1979, No. 3, snow owl	60	70	80
Panda Giant, 1972, Giant Panda ceramic bottle	20	23	26
Penguin, 1972, Heritage China ceramic figural bottle	12	14	16
Reno Arch, 1968, arch shape w/ *"RENO"* embossed, decal of dice, rabbit's foot, roulette wheel, slot machine, etc.	8	9	10
Sailfish, 1971, blue-green, on green "waves" base	11	14	17
Salmon, 1971, Washington King	18	21	24
San Francisco Cable Car, 1968	15	17	19
Sea Captain, 1971, holding pipe, on "wooden" stanchion base	15	17	19
Senator , 1971, cigar-chomping State Senator, stumping on a platform, swallow-tail coat, string tie, gold, black, red, white	17	20	23
Senators of the U.S., 1972, Heritage Ceramic "Old Time" Senator	17	20	22
Setter, 1974	17	21	24
Shrine King Tut Guard, 1979	42	50	58
Silver Saddle, 1973	37	40	44
Silver Spur Boot, 1971, cowboy-boot-shaped bottle w/ silver spur buckled on, *"SILVER SPUR CARSON CITY NEVADA,"* platinum trim	12	14	15

Garnier Bottles

The Garnier Company began producing figural bottles in 1899. Those produced prior to World War II are scarce. Some of the better known include the Cat, 1930; Clown, 1910; Country Jug, 1937; and Greyhound, 1930.

	LOW	AVG.	HIGH
Aladdin's Lamp, c. 1963, silver, 6.5"	$ 50	$ 60	$ 70
Alfa Romeo 1013, c. 1970, red body, yellow seats, black trim, 4" x 10.5"	22	25	28
Alfa Romeo 1020, c. 1969, pale blue body, red seat, black trim, 4" x 10.5"	22	25	28
Alfa Romeo Racer, c. 1969, maroon body, black tires and trim, 4" x 10"	23	25	27
Antique Coach, c. 1970, 8" x 12"	23	26	28
Apollo, c. 1969, Apollo spacecraft, 13.5"	19	21	23
Aztec Vase, c. 1965, "stone," 11.5"	12	14	15
Baby Trio, c. 1963, clear glass, 6.5"	11	12	13
Bandit, figural, c. 1958, 11.5"	15	17	19
Bedroom Candlestick, c. 1967, 11.5"	45	52	58
Bellows, c. 1969, gold and red, 4" x 14.5"	21	25	28
Candlestick, c. 1955, 10.5"	16	19	22
Candlestick, glass, c. 1965, 10"	24	28	31
Cardinal State Bird Illinois, c. 1969, 11.5"	14	17	20
Cat, Black, c. 1962, 11.5"	22	25	28
Chalet, c. 1955, building, 9"	60	67	74
Chimney, c. 1956, 9.5"	80	90	100
Chinese Dog, c. 1965, 11"	20	25	30
Christmas Tree, c. 1956, 11 .5"	85	100	115
Classic Ashtray, c. 1958, clear glass, 2.5"	7	8	9
Clown Holding Tub , c. 1955, 12.5"	22	26	30
Eiffel Tower, c. 1951, 13.5"	22	25	27
Fiat 500, 1913, c. 1970, car, 4" x 10.5"	23	27	30
Flying Horse Pegasus, c. 1958, 12"	70	82	94

Jim Beam Bottles

Jim Beam bottles figural liquor containers were first issued in the 1950s. The company produces a variety of themes including The Executive Series, Regal China Series, and Political Figures Series. Early Beam bottles made before the figural series are also collectible. In 1953, the company produced its first figural decanter. When the decanters sold well, Beam began producing decorative bottles on a large scale.

Jim Bean Bottle
New Hampshire,
$10-$15.

	LOW	AVG.	HIGH
The Big Apple, 1979, apple-form bottle	$ 15	$ 17	$ 19
Ernie's Flower Cart, 1976, wooden cart	30	35	40
Falstaff, 1979, Sir John Falstaff w/ gold goblet, working music box, limited to 1000 bottles	350	400	450
Fantasia Bottle, c. 1971, Regal China w/ presentation case, 16.5"	18	20	22
Fiesta Bowl, c. 1973, football player, Regal China, 13.5"	15	17	18
Figaro, c. 1977, Spaniard w/ guitar, music box plays	450	500	550
Hawaiian Open, c. 1973, golf-ball form, 11"	8	10	12
Hawaiian Open, c. 1974, Golf Classic, Regal China, 15"	8	10	12
Hawaii Paradise, 1978, Hawaiian resort, black stopper, 8.5"	28	34	40
Hemisfair, c. 1968, Lone Star of Texas on tower, Regal China, 13"	8	10	12
Hoffman, c. 1969, liquor store form, Regal China, 9"	6	7	8
Short Timer, 1975, army shoes w/ helmet, 8"	40	50	60
Shriners, 1975, embossed camel, 10.5"	22	26	30
Shriners' Pyramid, 1975, 5"	18	20	22
Tall Dancing Scot, c. 1964, Scotsman in bubble, music box, glass, 17"	18	21	24
Tavern Scene, c. 1959, Regal China, 11.5"	100	113	125
Telephone, 1975, 1907 telephone, Magneto Wallset, 9.5"	100	110	120
Ten-Pin, 1980, bowling pin, 12"	6	7	8
Thailand, c. 1969, elephant in jungle, Regal China, 12.5"	6	7	8
Thomas Flyer 1907, 1976, "Flyabout," luxury car	80	100	120
Volkswagen Commemorative Bottle, 2 colors, c. 1977, Pegs China, 14.5"	46	53	60
Washington State Bicentennial, 1976, patriot drummer, 10"	18	20	22
Waterman, 1980, boatman at helm, in pewter or glazed, 13.5"	230	265	300

Luxardo Bottles

The Luxardo Company has produced wines in the Padua region of Italy since the early 19th century. In 1952, the Hulse Company became their sole American distributor. Under the Hulse influence, the Italian company produced various elaborate decanters for their products. Produced in both glass and ceramics, these bottles are still widely collected.

	LOW	AVG.	HIGH
Apple Figural, c. 1960, yellow apple, green leaves	$ 15	$ 17	$ 19
Assyrian Ashtray Decanter, c. 1961, gray, tan & black	23	27	30
Autumn Wine Pitcher, c. 1958, country scene, handled pitcher	45	50	55
Babylon Decanter, c. 1960, dark green & gold	23	27	30
Baby Amphoras, c. 1956, 6 miniature bottles, set	24	27	30
Florentine Majolica, c. 1956, round-handled decanter, painted pitcher, yellow, dragon, blue wings	32	36	40
Gambia, c. 1961, black princess, on knee w/ tray, gold trim, 10.5"	21	23	25
Opal Majolica, c. 1957, gold handles, translucent opal top, pink base, also used as lamp base, 10"	20	23	26
Penguin, Murano glass figural, c. 1968, black & white penguin, crystal base	36	44	52
Pheasant, red & gold figural, c. 1960, red & gold glass bird on crystal base	34	38	42
Pheasant, Murano glass figural, c. 1960, red & clear glass on crystal base	40	45	50
Primavera Amphora, c. 1958, handled vase, w/ floral design in yellow, green & blue, 9.5"	20	24	28
Puppy, Cucciolo glass figural, c. 1961, amber & green glass	40	45	50

	LOW	AVG.	HIGH
Puppy, Murano glass figural, c. 1960, amber glass, crystal base .... $ 40	$ 45	$ 50
Silver Blue Decanter, c. 1952-55, ptd. silver flowers & leaves 30	36	42
Silver Brown Decanter, c. 1952-55, ptd. silver flowers & leaves 37	42	47
Sir Lancelot, c. 1962, knight in armor, tan-gray w/ gold, 12" 21	25	28
Spring-Box Amphora, c. 1952, African deer, black, brown, 9.5" 21	23	25
Squirrel, glass figural, c. 1968, amethyst squirrel on crystal base 45	50	55
Sudan, c. 1960, handled vase, incised figures, African motif in browns, blue, yellow & gray, 13.5" 20	24	27
Torre Rosa, c. 1962, rose tinted tower of fruit, 10.5" 25	20	35
Torre Tinta, c. 1962, tower of fruit, natural shades 23	27	30
Tower of Fruit, majolicas, Torre Bianca, c. 1962, white & gray tower of fruit, 10.5" 23	27	30
Tower of Fruit, c. 1968, various fruits, 22.5" 23	27	30

Old Commonwealth Bottles

Old Commonwealth is produced by J.P. Van Winkle and Son. Since 1974, the company has produced collector decanters filled with whiskey. Most of the company's decanters are produced in regular and miniature sizes.

	LOW	AVG.	HIGH
Alabama Crimson Tide, 1981, elephant .... $ 55	$ 60	$ 65
Bulldogs, 1982, Georgia 70	80	89
Chief Illini, 1981, Illinois, 2 versions 77	86	95
Cottontail, 1981, rabbit 50	60	70
Coal Miner, 1975, #1, miner w/ shovel 132	150	168
Mini Coal Miner, 1980, #1, miner w/ shovel 62	70	78
Coal Miner, 1976, #2, miner w/ pick 45	50	55
Mini Coal Miner, 1982, #2, miner w/ pick 18	20	22
Coal Miner, 1977, #3, miner kneels 44	59	56
Mini Coal Miner, 1981, #3, miner kneels 19	21	22
Coal Miner-Lunch Time, 1980 52	58	64
Elusive Leprechaun, 1980 54	60	66
Golden Retriever, 1979 46	52	57
Kentucky Thoroughbreds, 1976 43	49	55
L.S.U. Tiger, 1979 69	77	85

Earthenware Pottery

Using less sophisticated kilns and whatever clays were found locally, country potters produced a diverse array of beautiful and imaginative kitchenwares and tablewares. Design and coloration are key in determining values. But a crack or chip puts a major dent in the price.

Delftware is the generic name for the tin-glazed earthenwares made in great numbers in Holland and England during the 17th and 18th centuries. The name comes from the Dutch city of Holland where many of these pieces originated. Do not confuse these pieces with those made by the modern corporation "Delft," whose wares pay tribute to the fine early pieces. The pitchers made in Liverpool, England, often called "Liverpool Jugs," were exported to the United States with many patriotic American themes. Lustreware is decorated in a bright metallic finish, usually having a pink or silvery appearance. Majolica was the tradename used by the Minton Company in England to describe wares that imitated Majolica pieces from the Italian Renaissance. Collectors now use the term to refer to similar pieces made by many English potters of the mid-19th century. Mochaware was decorated in various methods that included finger-painting (to create "earthworm" designs) and spitting a tobacco juice concoction (to create "seaweed" designs). Redware gets its name from the red clay used. Spongeware was decorated with sponges, usually in blue. Yellowware gets its name from the yellow glaze in which it was dipped.

	AUCTION	RETAIL	
		Low	High
Bellarmine			
Jug, salt-glazed, ht. 11"	$ 700	$ 1200	$ 1800
Jug, salt-glazed, ht. 9"	300	500	800

Some Delft plates can be purchased very cheaply at auction. The blue and white Delft plate on the left sold for $60. Continental pottery with a similar look to Delft polychrome wares will sell for similar prices. The continental barber bowl on the right sold for $300 at auction, about what a Delft example should bring.

Above left: Delft handle pot, $550 at auction. Above right modern Delft, $10-$20 retail. Below left: Chinese style blue and white Delft plat, $90 at auction; Delft plate with raised decoration, $100 at auction.

	AUCTION	RETAIL Low	High

Delft

	AUCTION	RETAIL Low	High
Charger, Dutch, blue and white floral decorated, dia. 14"	$ 550	$ 940	$ 1430
Charger, Dutch, w/ polychrome parrot decoration, dia. 13"	850	1440	2210
Charger, Dutch, w/ polychrome parrot decoration, dia. 14"	950	1620	2470
Charger, Dutch, w/ polychrome bird and vase decoration, dia. 13"	1000	1700	2600
Charger, Dutch, w/ polychrome bird and flower-pot motif, dia. 13"	900	1530	2340
Charger, Dutch, manganese and chrome-yellow, dia. 17"	1700	2890	4420
Charger, Dutch, manganese and yellow decorated putti, dia. 14"	950	1620	2470
Charger, Dutch, polychrome	400	680	1040
Charger, Eng., blue and white, dia. 12"	400	680	1040
Cows, pr., w/ milkers, ht. 7"	200	340	520
Cows, pr., w. 8"	150	260	390
Flower Brick, Eng., blue and white, w. 5"	350	600	910
Flower Brick, Eng., blue and white, w. 7"	500	850	1300
Garniture Vase, Dutch, blue and white, fitted as a lamp	310	530	810

Left to right: Dutch Delft manganese and chrome yellow charger, dia. 17", $1700 at auction; pair of Dutch Delft manganese plaques, ht. 11", $1300 at auction. — Photo courtesy of Northeast Auctions.

	AUCTION	RETAIL Low	High
Garniture Vases, set of 5, blue and white, w/ biblical scenes, ht. 10" ...	$ 550	$ 940	$ 1430
Garniture Vases, pr., Dutch, blue and white, covered, ht. 15"	1200	2040	3120
Plaques, pr., Dutch manganese decorated w/ figures & animals, ht. 11" ...	1300	2210	3380
Punch Bowl, Polychrome	450	760	1170
Recumbent Horse, blue and white, w. 6"	1500	2550	3900
Tankard, Dutch, pewter-mounted, ht. 10"	500	850	1300
Tazza, English, blue and white, dia. 7"	450	760	1170
Tobacco Jar, Dutch, blue and white, marked Rappee, ht. 13"	800	1360	2080

Liverpool

Pitcher, w/ Amer. Eagle, ht 8"	$ 300	$ 510	$ 780
Pitcher, w/ Amer. ship & Motto "Seaman's Friend," ht. 12"	850	1440	2210
Pitcher, w/ classical motifs, inscribed "John Nodder," ht. 10"	550	940	1430
Pitcher, w/ Map of Thirteen Colonies, ht. 14"	1200	2040	3120
Pitcher, w/ Masonic emblems, 9"	350	600	910

Lustre

Harrison Campaign Mug, ht. 9"	$ 3750	$ 6500	$ 9750
Sunderland Bridge Jug, ht. 9"	300	510	780
Sunderland Cow Creamer, ht. 5"	100	170	260
Sunderland "Success to the Coal Trade" Pitcher	250	420	650
Tea Set, w/ color transfers of children, on cobalt ground, 38 pcs	300	510	780

	AUCTION	RETAIL	
		Low	High

Majolica

	AUCTION	Low	High
Cheese Dish, Wedgwood	$ 275	$ 470	$ 720
Cheese Dish w/ fern motif	1000	1700	2600
Ewer, w/ gargoyle handle, Minton	1500	2550	3900
Figural Pitchers, pr., Minton	1400	2380	3640
Game Dish, w/ bird cover.	900	1530	2340
Palissy-Type Oval Dish, w/ fish, snake, and other animals, w. 16"	850	1440	2210
Palissy-Type Circular Dish, w/ fish and other animals, dia. 11"	1000	1700	2600
Pineapple Pitcher, Minton	650	1100	1690
Planter, w/ Masques, Minton	600	1020	1560
Strawberry Dish and 12 berry dishes, Wedgwood	950	1620	2470
Syrup Pitcher, w/ motto, Wedgwood	400	680	1040

Mochaware

	AUCTION	Low	High
Bowl, w/ earthworm design on blue, dia. 10"	$ 100	$ 170	$ 260
Bowl, w/ leaf design on russet, dia. 4.5"	700	1200	1800
Caster, knopped w/ cat's eye motif on blue, ht. 6"	550	1000	1500
Chamber pot and bowl, each w/ earthworm decoration, dia. 8"	400	680	1040
Pitcher, w/ earthworm pattern, russet, ht. 7.5"	700	1190	1820
Mug, w/ banding and marbleized design, ht. 6"	800	1360	2080
Mug, earthworm design, gray, ht. 6"	500	850	1300
Mustard Pot, seaweed design, w/ knopped lid, in blue, brown, and mustard, ht. 4"	550	940	1430
Mustard Pot, w/ cat's eye motif, ht. 4"	400	680	1000
Vase, beaker form w/ marbleized decoration, ht. 5"	475	810	1240

Above left to right: Liverpool pitcher "The Betsy," ht. 10", $3700 at auction; fifteen star Liverpool pitcher, ht. 9", $1200 at auction; Lustre mug from William Henry Harrison presidential campaign, $3750 at auction. — Photos courtesy of Northeast auctions.

Left: Slip decorated loaf dish, 14", $3250 at auction. — Photo courtesy of Northeast Auctions.

	AUCTION	RETAIL	
		Low	High

Redware

Deep Dish, brown glazed oblong, w/ alternating serpentine and wavy line motif, the rim plain, 12" x 14"	$ 1800	$ 3000	$ 5000
Deep Dish, circular, w/ crimped rim and yellow slip triple-serpentine motif, dia. 13"	2400	4000	6500
Deep Dish, large brown-glazed oblong, w/ 2 yellow slip stylized evergreens, rim plain, 14" x 16"	2300	3910	6000
Deep Dish, rectangular, w/ coggled rim and brown slip pinstripe motif on yellow ground, 13" x 11"	1700	2890	4420
Deep Dish, dark-brown glazed oblong, w/ plain rim and yellow slip wavy line decoration, 13" x 14"	1000	1700	2600
Deep Dish, glazed & slip-dec., brown slip feather combed, 12" x 15"	1000	1700	2600
Deep Dish, dark-brown glazed circular, w/ yellow slip spiraling and scalloped line, the rim plain, dia. 14"	450	700	1200
Deep Dish, brown glazed, w/ alternating serpentine and wavy line motifs in yellow slip, dia. 15"	2500	4250	6500
Deep Dish, brown-glazed oblong w/ alternating serpentine and wavy lines, w/ plain rim, 12" x 14"	1800	3000	5000

Above left to right: gaudy Dutch teacup; mochaware marbleized bowl.

Below left to right: Mochaware "earthworm" caster, $950; simple polychrome caster, $700; "seaweed" milk jug, $1500; cream pitcher, $800, marbleized caster, $900, marbleized creamer $950. — Photos courtesy of Northeast Auctions.

	AUCTION	RETAIL	
		Low	High
Jug, slip-glazed handled w/ leaf decoration and owner's name, ht. 12"..	$ 350	$ 600	$ 900
Mariner's Jug, English, slip-dec., ht. 11"	850	1400	2200
Mug, ht. 4"	350	600	910
Ovoid Jar, ht. 9"	275	470	720
Plate, w/ slip dec., dia. 11"	225	380	580
Shaving Mug, ht. 4"	375	640	970

Spongeware

	AUCTION	Low	High
Bowl, 1 qt.	$ 100	$ 170	$ 260
Bowl, 2 qt.	200	340	520
Bowl & Pitcher Set	275	470	720
Cookie Jar, 4 qt.	200	340	520
Crock, 2 qt.	100	170	260
Pie Plate	50	80	130
Pitcher, 1 qt.	125	210	320
Pitcher, 2 qt.	150	260	390

Yellowware

	AUCTION	Low	High
Deep Dish, feather combed slip motif & notched rim, 13" x 17"	1200	2040	3120
Deep-Dish, notched rim and brown slip striped design, dia. 13.5"	1100	1870	2860
Deep Platter brown, feathered-combing motif, 16" x 20.5"	2100	3570	5460
Deep Dish, crimped rim and brown-slip stripes, 11" x 13"	1300	2210	3380
Deep Dish, notched rim and combed brown slip design, dia. 13.5"	1000	1700	2600
Deep Dish, notched rim and brown slip feather combed, 13" x 17.5"	1500	2550	3900
Miniature Pot, w/ knopped lid, overall w/ brown polka-dots, ht. 3.5"	1200	2040	3120

Left to right: Redware slip decorated plate, 11", $200 at auction; redware slip decorated deep dish, 13", $650 at auction; redware slip decorated plate, 9", $125 at auction. - photos courtesy of Northeast Auctions. Spongeware pitcher, one quart, $125 at auction.

Fiesta Ware

Fiesta Ware (1936) is a line of brightly colored pottery tableware introduced in 1935 by the Homer Laughlin China Company. Frederick H. Rhead's design with a series of graduated rings was one of the most widely manufactured tablewares of the 20th century.

Colors include red, rose, dark green, medium green, light green, chartreuse, yellow, old ivory, gray, turquoise, and dark blue. Red is the most valuable. Pieces are trademarked in the mold or with an ink hand-stamped mark. Reissued and restyled from the originals in 1986, Fiesta pieces are still available. Prices are for old, not reissued pieces. Medium green is the most valued, follwed by rose, gray, and forrest green.

Clockwise from above left: Fiesta backstamp; small yellow Fiesta pitcher and a sampler of the different sizes and shapes of Fiesta. — Items courtesy of Cerise Foster.

	LOW	AVG.	HIGH
Bowl, serving, 8.5"-9.5"	$ 50	$ 60	$ 70
Cake Server, flat	650	725	800
Candleholder, 3-ftd., pr.	400	425	450
Candleholder, bulb, pr.	90	105	120
Carafe	200	250	300
Casserole	150	175	200
Chop Plate, 13"-15"	50	60	70
Coffee pot	200	250	300
Compote, 12"	140	160	180
Compote, sweets	60	70	80
Cream/Sugar	70	80	90
Cup & Saucer, (Art Deco)	70	80	90
Cup/Saucer	35	45	55
Fruit Dish, 5.5"	25	30	35
Gravy Boat	50	65	80
Grillplate, 10.5"-12"	50	60	70
Marmalade	200	225	250
Mixing bowl, #1-5	90	120	150
Mixing bowl, #6-7	150	200	250
Mug	60	75	
Mustard	180	200	
Pitcher, w/ ice lip	100	125	
Plate, 10"	30	40	50
Plate, 6"-7"	10	13	15
Plate, 9"	15	18	20
Platter, 12.5"	50	65	80
Relish Tray, 5 pieces	200	250	300
Salad, 7.5"	60	75	90
Salad, ftd, 11.5"	250	275	300
Salt/Pepper	30	35	40
Soup Plate, 8.25"	40	50	60
Syrup Pitcher	250	275	300
Teapot	150	175	200
Tray, utility	40	45	50
Tumbler	50	55	60
Water Pitcher (disk)	200	250	300

Figurines

Artisan modeled figurines in pottery and porcelain are a mainstay of the collecting market. Often, the most valuable pieces are not those produced as "limited editions," Quality of design and craft are the most important factors, but condition, rarity and size are also important.

The listings here are by title, followed by maker.

	LOW	AVG.	HIGH
Abigail, Florence Ceramics Co.	$ 90	$ 100	$ 110
Accordion Boy, Ceramic Arts Studio	70	80	90
Adeline, Florence Ceramics Co.	100	110	120
Adonis & Aphrodite, Ceramic Arts Studio	290	325	360
Alden, John, Florence Ceramics Co.	70	80	90
Alice & White Rabbit, Ceramic Arts Studio	60	65	70
Amelia, Florence Ceramics Co.	100	115	130
Amelia in Brocade, Florence Ceramics Co.	340	380	420
Angel, Florence Ceramics Co.	40	45	50
Angels, Kay Finch Ceramics	15	20	25
Anita in Brocade, Florence Ceramics Co.	340	380	420
Ann, Florence Ceramics Co.	50	55	60
Annabel, Florence Ceramics Co.	140	155	170
Arabesque, Ceramic Arts Studio	30	35	40
Archibald the Dragon, Ceramic Arts Studio	70	80	90
Arthur, Brayton Pottery	30	35	40
Asian, Shawnee Pottery	2	5	10
Attitude, Ceramic Arts Studio	30	35	40
Autumn Andy, Ceramic Arts Studio	20	25	30
Baby Black Pegasus, Vernon Kilns	210	235	260
Bald Eagle, 8.5", Cliftwood Potteries	90	100	110
Bali Gong, Ceramic Arts Studio	30	35	40
Bali Hai, Ceramic Arts Studio	30	35	40
Bali Kris, Ceramic Arts Studio	30	35	40
Bali Lao, Ceramic Arts Studio	30	35	40
Balinese Dance Boy & Girl, Ceramic Arts Studio	100	110	120
Ballerina, Florence Ceramics Co.	140	160	180
Ballerina Child, Florence Ceramics Co.	80	90	100
Ballet En Pose, Ceramic Arts Studio	30	35	40
Ballet En Repose, Ceramic Arts Studio	30	35	40
Banjo Girl, Ceramic Arts Studio	40	50	60
Bass Viola Boy, Ceramic Arts Studio	40	50	60
Bear, 2", Morton Pottery Co.	5	10	15
Bedtime Boy & Girl, Ceramic Arts Studio	30	35	40
Berty, Ceramic Arts Studio	80	90	100
Beth, Florence Ceramics Co.	60	65	70
Betsy, Florence Ceramics Co.	80	90	100
Billikin Doll, 11", Cliftwood Potteries	100	110	120
Billikin Doll, 7.5", Cliftwood Potteries	60	65	70
Birthday Girl, Florence Ceramics Co.	120	135	150
Black Girl, Brayton Pottery	220	250	280
Black Girls, Brayton Pottery	150	170	190
Blackamoor, Brayton Pottery	30	35	40
Blackamoor, 7.5", Abingdon Potteries, Inc.	40	45	50

	LOW	AVG.	HIGH
Blossom Girl, Florence Ceramics Co.	$ 60	$ 65	$ 70
Blue Bird, 4.5", Midwest Pottery Co.	15	20	25
Blue Boy, Florence Ceramics Co.	140	160	180
Blue Heron, 11", Midwest Pottery Co.	40	50	60
Blue Jay, 6.5", Midwest Pottery Co.	15	20	25
Bluejay, 2.5", Morton Pottery Co.	5	10	15
Bluejay, 4", Morton Pottery Co.	5	10	15
Blynken, Florence Ceramics Co.	60	65	70
Blythe & Pensive, Ceramic Arts Studio	100	110	120
Bo Peep, Ceramic Arts Studio	30	35	40
Bo Peep's Sheep, Ceramic Arts Studio	20	25	30
Boy and Tiger, Ceramic Arts Studio	40	45	50
Boy Blue, Ceramic Arts Studio	15	20	25
Boy in tuxedo, Florence Ceramics Co.	80	90	100
Boy w/ fiddle, Florence Ceramics Co.	90	100	110
Boy w /Dog, Ceramic Arts Studio	40	45	50
Bride, Florence Ceramics Co.	340	380	420
Bride & Groom, Ceramic Arts Studio	60	65	70
Buffalo, 10", Cliftwood Potteries	240	265	290
Bull Dog, 11", Cliftwood Potteries	90	100	110
Bust, Florence Ceramics Co.	80	90	100
Camel, 2.5", Midwest Pottery Co.	5	10	15
Camel, 8.5", Midwest Pottery Co.	20	25	30
Camille, Florence Ceramics Co.	80	90	100
Canaries, 4.5", Midwest Pottery Co.	30	35	40
Carol, Florence Ceramics Co.	200	220	240
Caroline in Brocade, Florence Ceramics Co.	340	380	420
Cat, 1.5", Cliftwood Potteries	90	100	110
Cat, 5.75", Cliftwood Potteries	40	45	50
Cat, 6", Cliftwood Potteries	40	45	50
Cat, 6", Morton Pottery Co.	10	15	20
Cat, 8.5", Cliftwood Potteries	40	45	50
Cat, angry, 10.25", Kay Finch Ceramics	80	90	100
Cat, contented, 6", Kay Finch Ceramics	40	50	60
Cat, Persian, 10.75", Kay Finch Ceramics	80	90	100
Cat, playful, 8.5", Kay Finch Ceramics	60	65	70
Catherine, Florence Ceramics Co.	140	160	180
Centaur, Vernon Kilns	660	735	810
Centaurette, Vernon Kilns	370	410	450
Chanticleer, 10.5", Kay Finch Ceramics	100	110	120
Charles, Florence Ceramics Co.	90	100	110
Charmaine, Florence Ceramics Co.	70	80	90
Cherub head, 2.75", Kay Finch Ceramics	5	10	15
Chicken, Biddy, 8.25", Kay Finch Ceramics	30	35	40
Chicken, Butch, 8.25", Kay Finch Ceramics	30	35	40
Chinese Boy, Florence Ceramics Co.	40	45	50
Chinese Boy, 7.5", Kay Finch Ceramics	20	25	30
Chinese Boy & Girl, Ceramic Arts Studio	30	35	40
Chinese Couple, Ceramic Arts Studio	15	20	25
Chinese Girl, Florence Ceramics Co.	40	45	50
Chinese Girl, 7.5", Kay Finch Ceramics	20	25	30

	LOW	AVG.	HIGH
Chinese Sitting Girl & Boy, Ceramic Arts Studio	$ 15	$ 20	$ 25
Chipmunk, Ceramic Arts Studio	20	25	30
Choir Boy, Florence Ceramics Co.	50	55	60
Cinderella & Prince, Ceramic Arts Studio	40	45	50
Cindy, Florence Ceramics Co.	50	55	60
Circus Bear, Shawnee Pottery	20	25	30
Clarissa, Florence Ceramics Co.	60	65	70
Claudia, Florence Ceramics Co.	90	100	110
Cocker Dog, 11.75", Kay Finch Ceramics	80	90	100
Coleen, Florence Ceramics Co.	60	65	70
Colonial Boy & Girl, Ceramic Arts Studio	40	45	50
Colonial Lady & Man, Ceramic Arts Studio	40	45	50
Comedy & Tragedy, Ceramic Arts Studio	90	100	110
Court lady, 10.5", Kay Finch Ceramics	30	35	40
Cowboy, Frankoma Potteries	200	220	240
Cowboy on Bronco, 7.5", Midwest Pottery Co.	30	35	40
Cowgirl & Cowboy, Ceramic Arts Studio	50	55	60
Crane, 6", Midwest Pottery Co.	15	20	25
Cuban Child, Ceramic Arts Studio	20	25	30
Cuban Woman, Ceramic Arts Studio	30	35	40
Cynthia, Florence Ceramics Co.	200	220	240
Dancing Dutch Boy & Girl, Ceramic Arts Studio	80	85	90
Dancing Woman, 8.5", Midwest Pottery Co.	20	25	30
David, Florence Ceramics Co.	60	65	70
Deer, 12", Midwest Pottery Co.	30	35	40
Deer, 4.5", Morton Pottery Co.	5	10	15
Deer, 8", Midwest Pottery Co.	15	20	25
Delia, Florence Ceramics Co.	70	75	80
Denise, Florence Ceramics Co.	170	190	210
Diane, Florence Ceramics Co.	90	100	110
Dolores, Florence Ceramics Co.	100	110	120
Donkey, 2", Morton Pottery Co.	30	35	40
Donkey Unicorn, Vernon Kilns	320	355	390
Douglas, Florence Ceramics Co.	70	75	80
Drummer Girl, Ceramic Arts Studio	40	50	60
Duck, 4", Kay Finch Ceramics	5	10	15
Dumbo, Vernon Kilns	120	130	140
Dutch Boy & Girl, Ceramic Arts Studio	15	20	25
Dutch Boy & Girl, sitting, Ceramic Arts Studio	20	25	30
Dutch Love Boy & Girl, Ceramic Arts Studio	30	35	40
Edith, Florence Ceramics Co.	60	65	70
Edward, Florence Ceramics Co.	120	135	150
Elaine, Florence Ceramics Co.	40	45	50
Elephant, Vernon Kilns	320	355	390
Elephant, 17", Kay Finch Ceramics	340	380	420
Elephant, 2.5", Morton Pottery Co.	5	10	15
Elephant, 5", Kay Finch Ceramics	20	25	30
Elephant, 6", Cliftwood Potteries	40	50	60
Elephant, 6.75", Kay Finch Ceramics	40	50	60
Elephant, 7", Cliftwood Potteries	30	35	40
Elephant, 8", Cliftwood Potteries	70	80	90

	LOW	AVG.	HIGH
Elephant, 9", Cliftwood Potteries	$ 40	$ 45	$ 50
Elephant, "GOP/candidate," Morton Pottery Co.	10	15	20
Elisha, Florence Ceramics Co.	90	100	110
Elizabeth, Florence Ceramics Co.	140	155	170
Ellen, Florence Ceramics Co.	70	75	80
Emily, Brayton Pottery	30	35	40
Ethel, Florence Ceramics Co.	60	65	70
Eugenia, Florence Ceramics Co.	170	190	210
Evangeline, Florence Ceramics Co.	50	55	60
Fair Lady, Florence Ceramics Co.	290	325	360
Fall, Florence Ceramics Co.	40	45	50
Fan Dancer, Frankoma Potteries	140	160	180
Fawn, 2.5", Morton Pottery Co.	5	10	15
Female Bust, Midwest Pottery Co.	70	75	80
Female Nude, 11.5", Midwest Pottery Co.	110	125	140
Female Torso, abstract, 10.5", Brayton Pottery	70	75	80
Figaro (Disney), Brayton Pottery	100	110	120
Fighting Cock, 6.5", Midwest Pottery Co.	15	20	25
Fire Couple, Ceramic Arts Studio	180	205	230
Fishing Boy & Farmer Girl, Ceramic Arts Studio	30	35	40
Flame Couple, Ceramic Arts Studio	180	205	230
Flower Girl, Frankoma Potteries	70	80	90
Flute Girl, Ceramic Arts Studio	40	50	60
Frances, Brayton Pottery	30	35	40
Frog, 1", Midwest Pottery Co.	5	10	15
Fruit Girl, 10", Abingdon Potteries, Inc.	90	100	110
Gardener Boy, Frankoma Potteries	90	100	110
Gardener Girl, Frankoma Potteries	70	80	90
Gary, Florence Ceramics Co.	70	80	90
Gay 90s Lady & Man, Ceramic Arts Studio	40	45	50
Gazelle, Shawnee Pottery	40	45	50
Genevieve, Florence Ceramics Co.	100	110	120
Georgia in Brocade, Florence Ceramics Co.	340	380	420
Geppetto (Disney), Brayton Pottery	220	250	280
Geppetto, w/ Pinocchio (Disney), Brayton Pottery	300	335	370
Girl w/ Cat, Ceramic Arts Studio	40	45	50
Girl w/ pail, Florence Ceramics Co.	100	110	120
Godey Lady, 7.5", Kay Finch Ceramics	30	35	40
Godey Lady, 9.5", Kay Finch Ceramics	30	35	40
Godey Man, 7.5", Kay Finch Ceramics	30	35	40
Godey Man, 9.5", Kay Finch Ceramics	30	35	40
Goose, 2", Midwest Pottery Co.	5	10	15
Goose, 2.25", Midwest Pottery Co.	5	10	15
Grace, Florence Ceramics Co.	60	65	70
Grandmother and I, Florence Ceramics Co.	280	310	340
Grandpa Pig, 10.5" x 16", Kay Finch Ceramics	70	80	90
Grumpy Pig, 6", Kay Finch Ceramics	30	35	40
Guitar Boy, Ceramic Arts Studio	40	50	60
Gypsy Girl & Boy, Ceramic Arts Studio	130	145	160
Hansel & Gretel, Ceramic Arts Studio	50	55	60
Hare, Florence Ceramics Co.	90	100	110

	LOW	AVG.	HIGH
Harlem Hoofer, Frankoma Potteries	$ 470	$ 525	$ 580
Harlequin Boy & Girl, Ceramic Arts Studio	140	160	180
Harmonica Boy, Ceramic Arts Studio	40	50	60
Hen, 2.25", Midwest Pottery Co.	5	10	15
Her Majesty, Florence Ceramics Co.	70	75	80
Hiawatha, Ceramic Arts Studio	20	25	30
Hindu Boys, Ceramic Arts Studio	40	45	50
Hippo, Vernon Kilns	320	355	390
Hippo in Tutu, Vernon Kilns	320	355	390
Horse, 2.75", Morton Pottery Co.	5	10	15
Indian Bowl Maker, Frankoma Potteries	90	100	110
Indian Chief, Frankoma Potteries	90	100	110
Irene, Florence Ceramics Co.	50	55	60
Jeanette, Florence Ceramics Co.	70	75	80
Jennifer, Florence Ceramics Co.	130	145	160
Jim, Florence Ceramics Co.	50	55	60
John Kennedy, Jr., Morton Pottery Co.	30	35	40
Jon, Brayton Pottery	30	35	40
Josephine, Florence Ceramics Co.	70	75	80
Joy, Florence Ceramics Co.	50	55	60
Joyce, Florence Ceramics Co.	190	215	240
Julie, Florence Ceramics Co.	70	75	80
Kangaroo, 2.75", Morton Pottery Co.	5	10	15
Kay, Florence Ceramics Co.	60	65	70
King's Jester & Musicians, Ceramic Arts Studio	200	225	250
Kissing Girl & Boy, Ceramic Arts Studio	40	45	50
Kitten, 3.25", Kay Finch Ceramics	5	10	15
Kiu, Florence Ceramics Co.	40	45	50
Kneeling Nude, 7", Abingdon Potteries, Inc.	170	190	210
Lady Diana, Florence Ceramics Co.	140	160	180
Lady Rowena, Ceramic Arts Studio	70	80	90
Lamb, 2.5", Morton Pottery Co.	5	10	15
Lamb, 2.75", Kay Finch Ceramics	5	10	15
Lantern Boy, Florence Ceramics Co.	40	45	50
Laura, Florence Ceramics Co.	100	110	120
Leading Man, Florence Ceramics Co.	140	160	180
Lillian, Florence Ceramics Co.	90	100	110
Lillian Russell, Florence Ceramics Co.	340	380	420
Linda Lou, Florence Ceramics Co.	70	75	80
Lion, 14", Cliftwood Potteries	60	70	80
Lioness, 12", Cliftwood Potteries	60	65	70
Lisa, Florence Ceramics Co.	90	100	110
Little Jack Horner, Ceramic Arts Studio	15	20	25
Lorry, Florence Ceramics Co.	120	135	150
Louis XV, Florence Ceramics Co.	200	220	240
Louis XVI, Florence Ceramics Co.	140	160	180
Louise, Florence Ceramics Co.	100	110	120
Madame Pompadour, Florence Ceramics Co.	200	220	240
Madonna Plain, Florence Ceramics Co.	50	55	60
Madonna w/ Child, Florence Ceramics Co.	70	75	80
Male, abstract, Brayton Pottery	250	280	310

	LOW	AVG.	HIGH
Man in Knickers, 7.5", Morton Pottery Co.	$ 10	$ 15	$ 20
Margot, Florence Ceramics Co.	190	215	240
Marie Antoinette, Florence Ceramics Co.	140	160	180
Marleen in Brocade, Florence Ceramics Co.	340	380	420
Marsie, Florence Ceramics Co.	70	75	80
Martin, Florence Ceramics Co.	170	190	210
Mary & Little Lamb, Ceramic Arts Studio	30	35	40
Matilda, Florence Ceramics Co.	100	110	120
Melanie, Florence Ceramics Co.	70	75	80
Merrymaid, Florence Ceramics Co.	90	105	120
Mexican Boy & Girl, Ceramic Arts Studio	60	65	70
Mikado, Florence Ceramics Co.	140	160	180
Mike, Florence Ceramics Co.	50	55	60
Minnehaha, Ceramic Arts Studio	20	25	30
Miranda, 6.5", Brayton Pottery	30	35	40
Miss Muffet, Ceramic Arts Studio	15	20	25
Modern Dance Woman, Ceramic Arts Studio	60	65	70
Monk, Frankoma Potteries	120	130	140
Mr. Bird, 4.5", Kay Finch Ceramics	15	20	25
Mr. Crow, Vernon Kilns	760	850	940
Mr. Stork, Vernon Kilns	760	850	940
Mrs. Bird, 3", Kay Finch Ceramics	15	20	25
Musette, Florence Ceramics Co.	100	110	120
Nancy, Florence Ceramics Co.	50	55	60
Nita, Florence Ceramics Co.	70	75	80
Nubian Centaurette, Vernon Kilns	370	410	450
Ostrich, Vernon Kilns	680	760	840
Ostrich Ballerina, Vernon Kilns	680	760	840
Our Lady of Grace, Florence Ceramics Co.	50	55	60
Owl, 8.75", Kay Finch Ceramics	30	35	40
Owl, 3.75", Kay Finch Ceramics	15	20	25
Oxen, 3.25", Morton Pottery Co.	30	35	40
Pamela, Florence Ceramics Co.	70	75	80
Parakeet, Florence Ceramics Co.	60	70	80
Parasol, Florence Ceramics Co.	190	215	240
Patricia, Florence Ceramics Co.	90	100	110
Peasant Boy, 6.75", Kay Finch Ceramics	30	35	40
Peasant Girl, Florence Ceramics Co.	60	65	70
Peasant Girl, 6.75", Kay Finch Ceramics	30	35	40
Peasant Woman, Brayton Pottery	30	35	40
Pegasus, Vernon Kilns	370	410	450
Pekinese, 14", Kay Finch Ceramics	80	90	100
Pekingese, Shawnee Pottery	20	25	30
Peter Pan, Ceramic Arts Studio	50	55	60
Pheasant, Florence Ceramics Co.	70	75	80
Pied Piper, Ceramic Arts Studio	30	35	40
Pied Piper Child, Ceramic Arts Studio	20	25	30
Pierrene & Pierrott, Ceramic Arts Studio	80	90	100
Pigeon, Florence Ceramics Co.	70	75	80
Pinkie, Florence Ceramics Co.	140	160	180
Pinocchio (Disney), Brayton Pottery	220	250	280

	LOW	AVG.	HIGH
Pioneer Sam & Susie, Ceramic Arts Studio	$ 40	$ 45	$ 50
Polar Bear, 1.75", Midwest Pottery Co.	5	10	15
Polar Bear, 8.5" x 12", Midwest Pottery Co.	30	35	40
Police Dog, 12", Cliftwood Potteries	80	90	100
Police Dog, 8.5", Cliftwood Potteries	140	160	180
Police Dog, 9", Cliftwood Potteries	40	45	50
Polish Boy & Girl, Ceramic Arts Studio	30	35	40
Pomeranian Dog, 10", Kay Finch Ceramics	80	90	100
Pony, 3.5" x 4.5", Midwest Pottery Co.	5	10	15
Prima Donna, Florence Ceramics Co.	250	280	310
Princess, Florence Ceramics Co.	170	190	210
Priscilla, Florence Ceramics Co.	60	65	70
Puppy, Shawnee Pottery	20	25	30
Rabbit, Ceramic Arts Studio	20	25	30
Rabbit, Shawnee Pottery	20	25	30
Rabbit, 2.5", Midwest Pottery Co.	5	10	15
Rabbit, 3", Morton Pottery Co.	5	10	15
Rabbits, 2.5", Midwest Pottery Co.	20	25	30
Race Horse, 7.25", Midwest Pottery Co.	60	65	70
Rearing Unicorn, Vernon Kilns	320	355	390
Rebecca, Florence Ceramics Co.	100	110	120
Reclining Sprite, Vernon Kilns	150	165	180
Rhett, Florence Ceramics Co.	80	90	100
Road Runner, 8", Midwest Pottery Co.	10	15	20
Roberta, Florence Ceramics Co.	90	100	110
Rooster, 2.25", Midwest Pottery Co.	5	10	15
Rosalie, Florence Ceramics Co.	90	100	110
Rose Marie, Florence Ceramics Co.	90	105	120
Russian Boy & Girl, Ceramic Arts Studio	60	65	70
Sailing Ship, 2", Midwest Pottery Co.	5	10	15
Sally, Brayton Pottery	20	25	30
Sally, Florence Ceramics Co.	60	65	70
Samoan Girl, Gladding, Mcbean	40	45	50
Samoan Mother and Child, Gladding, Mcbean	60	65	70
Santa Claus & Evergreen Tree, Ceramic Arts Studio	20	25	30
Sarah, Florence Ceramics Co.	60	65	70
Sarah Bernhardt, Florence Ceramics Co.	390	440	490
Sassy Pig, 3.5", Kay Finch Ceramics	20	25	30
Satyr, Vernon Kilns	140	160	180
Saxophone Boy, Ceramic Arts Studio	40	50	60
Scandie Boy, 5.25", Kay Finch Ceramics	20	25	30
Scandie Girl, 5.25", Kay Finch Ceramics	20	25	30
Scarf Dancer, 13", Abingdon Potteries, Inc.	170	190	210
Scarlett, Florence Ceramics Co.	140	160	180
Seagull, Ceramic Arts Studio	20	25	30
Shen, Florence Ceramics Co.	110	125	140
Shepherdess & Faun, 11.5", Abingdon Potteries, Inc.	90	100	110
Sherri, Florence Ceramics Co.	140	160	180
Shirley, Florence Ceramics Co.	120	135	150
Sitting Girl & Boy, Ceramic Arts Studio	40	45	50
Sitting Unicorn, Vernon Kilns	320	355	390

	LOW	AVG.	HIGH
Sleeping Kitten, 3.25", Kay Finch Ceramics	$ 5	$ 10	$ 15
Smiley Pig, 6.75", Kay Finch Ceramics	30	35	40
Southern Belle & Gentleman, Ceramic Arts Studio	40	45	50
Spaniel, 6", Midwest Pottery Co.	40	45	50
Spanish Dance Couple, Ceramic Arts Studio	90	100	110
Spring Sue, Ceramic Arts Studio	20	25	30
Sprite, Vernon Kilns	150	165	180
Square Dance Boy & Girl, Ceramic Arts Studio	40	45	50
Squirrel, 2", Midwest Pottery Co.	5	10	15
Squirrel, 2.25", Morton Pottery Co.	5	10	15
St. Francis, Ceramic Arts Studio	80	90	100
St. George, Ceramic Arts Studio	90	100	110
Stallion, 10.75", Midwest Pottery Co.	30	30	30
Stallion, 6", Midwest Pottery Co.	10	15	20
Standing Boy & Girl, Ceramic Arts Studio	40	45	50
Standing Fawn, Ceramic Arts Studio	20	25	30
Stork, 4", Morton Pottery Co.	5	10	15
Stork, , 7.5", Morton Pottery Co.	15	20	25
Story Hour, Florence Ceramics Co.	220	250	280
Sue, Florence Ceramics Co.	50	55	60
Sue Ellen, Florence Ceramics Co.	80	85	90
Sultan & Harem, Ceramic Arts Studio	70	75	80
Summer Sally, Ceramic Arts Studio	20	25	30
Susan, Florence Ceramics Co.	200	225	250
Swan, 2", Midwest Pottery Co.	5	10	15
Swordfish, 4", Morton Pottery Co.	5	10	15
Taka, Florence Ceramics Co.	120	135	150
Teddy Bear, Shawnee Pottery	20	25	30
Temple Dancer, Ceramic Arts Studio	170	190	210
Tiger, 12", Midwest Pottery Co.	50	55	60
Timothy Mouse, Vernon Kilns	200	220	240
Tom Tom the Piper's Son, Ceramic Arts Studio	40	50	60
Torch Singer, Frankoma Potteries	450	500	550
Turkey, 2.5", Morton Pottery Co.	5	10	15
Turtle, 1", Midwest Pottery Co.	5	10	15
Unicorn, Vernon Kilns	320	355	390
Victor, Florence Ceramics Co.	110	125	140
Victoria, Florence Ceramics Co.	200	220	240
Victorian Lady & Man, Ceramic Arts Studio	40	45	50
Virginia in Brocade, Florence Ceramics Co.	340	380	420
Vivian, Florence Ceramics Co.	120	135	150
Wee Chinese, Ceramic Arts Studio	20	25	30
Wee Dutch, Ceramic Arts Studio	20	25	30
Wee Eskimos, Ceramic Arts Studio	20	25	30
Wee French, Ceramic Arts Studio	20	25	30
Wee Indian Boy, Ceramic Arts Studio	10	15	20
Wee Indian Girl, Ceramic Arts Studio	10	15	20
Wee Indians, Ceramic Arts Studio	20	25	30
Wee Scotch, Ceramic Arts Studio	20	25	30
Wee Swedish, Ceramic Arts Studio	20	25	30
Wild Horse, 2.5", Morton Pottery Co.	5	10	15

	LOW	AVG.	HIGH
Wild Turkey, 11.5", Midwest Pottery Co.	$ 40	$ 45	$ 50
Willy, Ceramic Arts Studio	70	80	90
Winged Sprite, Vernon Kilns	150	165	180
Winkie Pig, 3.75", Kay Finch Ceramics	20	25	30
Winney, Ceramic Arts Studio	70	80	90
Winter Willy, Ceramic Arts Studio	20	25	30
Woman in Bonnet, 7.75", Morton Pottery Co.	15	20	25
Woman & Wolfhound, 11", Midwest Pottery Co.	130	145	160
Woodland Fantasy, Ceramic Arts Studio	15	20	25
Wynken, Florence Ceramics Co.	60	65	70
Yorkshire Terrier, 11", Kay Finch Ceramics	80	90	100
Yorky, 5.5", Kay Finch Ceramics	20	25	30
Zulu Couple, Ceramic Arts Studio	100	110	120

Frankoma Pottery

In 1933, while working at the University of Oklahoma Ceramics Department, John Frank started Frank Potteries. By 1938, he had left the university, moved to Sapulpa, OK, and renamed his company Frankoma Pottery. John Frank designed all of Frankoma's dinnerware lines such as Mayan-Aztec (1945), Lazybones, Plainsman (1948), Wagon Wheels (1941), and Westwind. Most are still in production.

Marks-impressed *Frankoma* on the bottom of the piece; some early pieces have *Frankoma* stamped in black. An impressed panther in front of a vase appeared from 1936 to 1938.

Frankoma impressed mark.

	LOW	AVG.	HIGH
Baker, 2qt.-3qt.	$ 18	$ 22	$ 25
Baker, ind.	40	50	60
Bowl, 4.5 qt.	28	34	40
Bowl, 8-20 oz.	5	7	8
Bowl, rd. 1-2 qt.	11	13	15
Butter Dish	10	13	16
Candleholder	28	36	43
Chop Plate, ftd., 15"	13	17	20
Corn Dish	4	5	6
Cream/Sugar, (Art Deco)	10	13	16
Cup/Saucer	10	15	20
Custard Cup	4	6	7
Gravy, 2-spout	11	13	15
Gravy Boat	15	20	25
Horseshoe	13	17	20
Lazy Susan	39	50	60
Mug, 8 oz.-14 oz.	8	10	12
Pitcher, 1-3 qt.	16	20	24
Plate, 7"	6	7	8
Plate, 9"-10"	8	10	12
Platter, oval, deep, 13"	16	21	25
Platter, oval, deep, 17"	23	30	36
Platter, oval, deep, lug, 13"	13	16	19
Platter, oval, shallow, 17"	20	25	29
Platter, rect., deep, 13"-17"	14	20	26
Platter, rect., shallow, 9"-13"	6	9	12
Salad, crescent	4	5	6
Salt/Pepper	7	9	11
Teapot, 12 cup	21	27	32
Teapot, rd. 2-6 cup	12	20	28
Teapot, tall, 2 cup	25	31	37
Teapot, tall, 6 cup	40	50	61
Tray, rect., 9"	6	8	9
Tumbler, 6 oz.-12 oz.	5	6	7
Vegetable, 1 qt.	8	10	12
Warmer	11	15	18

French-Saxon China

The Sebring family of Sebring, OH owned both the French China Company and the Saxon China Company. The bankruptcy of the American Chinaware Company pulled both under in 1932. W.V. Oliver bought the Saxon plant and named his company French-Saxon. It made semiporcelain kitchenware and dinnerware. Royal China bought the company in 1964. The following entries are in the Zephyr pattern. Zephyr (1938) was decorated with decals and in solid colors. The two solid-color lines are called Romany (red, yellow, dark blue, and green) and Rancho (maroon, gray, chartreuse, and dark green). Marks-backstamps included a knight and shield graphic backstamp and a circular Union mark. Romany and Rancho have only their names stamped.

French-Saxon backstamp.

	LOW	AVG.	HIGH
Bowl, 36s	$ 7	$ 8	$ 9
Chop Plate, 13"	9	12	15
Coffee Pot	36	40	45
Cream/Sugar	22	26	30
Cup/Saucer	7	9	11
Dish, 5"-6"	2	3	4
Gravy Boat	15	17	19
Plate, 6"-7"	4	5	6
Plate, 9"-11"	7	8	9
Salt/Pepper	11	15	18
Soup Plate, 7.75"	7	8	9
Vegetable, 8.5"	16	17	18

W.S. George Pottery

In 1903 William S. George bought the East Palestine Pottery Company from the Sebring brothers from whom he had leased the plant. The plant produced his semiporcelain dinnerware for the next half century. The company used many different backstamps; some were unique to their shape.

W. S. GEORGE
MADE IN U.S.A.

backstamp marks

Bolero (mid-1933)

	LOW	AVG.	HIGH
Casserole	$ 18	$ 20	$ 22
Compote	14	16	18
Cream/Sugar	17	19	21
Cup/Saucer	5	6	7
Custard Cup	3	4	5
Dish, lug, 6.5"	2	3	3
Gravy Boat	12	13	14
Pickle Dish	3	5	6
Plate, 6"-8"	2	3	4
Plate, 9"-10"	4	5	6
Platter, 11"-12"	7	8	9
Relish, shell-form	7	8	9
Salt/Pepper	12	16	19
Soup Bowl, w/ lid	11	13	14
Soup Plate	5	6	7
Teapot	29	31	33
Vegetable	10	12	13

    backstamp mark

Georgette (1933)

Georgette is often called "Petal"

	LOW	AVG.	HIGH
Bowl, 36s	$ 5	$ 6	$ 7
Cream/Sugar	16	19	22
Cup/Saucer	5	7	9
Dish, 5"-7"	1	2	3
Gravy Boat	11	12	13
Plate, 6"-8"	4	5	5
Plate, 9"-10"	6	7	8
Vegetable, oval, 9"	11	12	13

	LOW	AVG.	HIGH

Lido (1932)

	LOW	AVG.	HIGH
Bowl, 36s	$ 5	$ 6	$ 7
Butter Dish	19	22	24
Candlestick	18	20	22
Casserole	18	22	25
Cream/Sugar	15	18	21
Cup/Saucer	5	7	9
Dish, 5"-6"	1	2	3
Egg Cup	6	8	10
Gravy Boat	10	12	13
Pickle Dish, 7.5"	4	5	5
Plate, 6"-8"	2	3	4
Plate, 9"-10"	5	6	7
Platter, 11"-13"	6	8	10
Salt/Pepper	12	15	17
Soup Plate, 7.75"	5	6	7
Teapot	33	35	37
Vegetable, 9"	10	12	14

Rainbow (1934)

One variety for this shape is called *Petit Point*, imitating embossed needlework .

	LOW	AVG.	HIGH
Bowl, 36s	$ 5	$ 6	$ 7
Candleholder	21	23	25
Casserole	21	24	27
Compote	16	18	20
Cream/Sugar	15	19	23
Cup/Saucer	5	7	9
Dish, 5"	1	2	3
Egg Cup	7	8	9
Gravy Boat	11	13	14
Plate, 6"-8"	3	4	4
Plate, 9"-10"	5	6	7
Platter, 10"-11"	5	7	8
Relish Tray	7	8	9
Vegetable, 9"	11	13	15

Ranchero

Simon Slobodkin designed this line.

	LOW	AVG.	HIGH
Butter Dish	$ 15	$ 20	$ 25
Casserole	23	27	30
Coffee Pot	30	35	40
Cream/Sugar	19	22	25
Cup/Saucer	6	8	10
Dish, 5"-6"	2	3	4
Egg Cup	8	9	10
Gravy Boat	15	17	18
Plate, 6"-7"	2	3	4
Plate, 9"	6	7	8
Platter	8	10	12
Salt/Pepper	15	17	19
Teapot	20	25	30
Vegetable	12	15	18

Gladding, McBean

The Gladding, McBean & Company started as a sewer pipe manufacturer in 1875. It introduced its famous earthenware Franciscan line of art and dinnerware in 1934. In 1963 the company changed its name to the Interpace Corporation. Wedgwood (England) purchased it in 1979 and continued production until 1986. Franciscanware is now produced in England.

Franciscan Classics was Gladding-McBean's name for the three most popular patterns of embossed, hand painted underglaze dinnerware. These were Apple (1940), Desert Rose (1941), and Ivy (1948). Both Apple and Desert Rose have seen continuous production since the early 1940s.

Marks-various backstamps and decals, including *GMB* in an oval, *F* in a box for Franciscan. Current pieces are backstamped *England*.

Gladding, McBean and Franciscan Classics backstamps.

	LOW	AVG.	HIGH
Apple (1940)			
Batter Bowl	$ 100	$ 125	$ 150
Butter Dish	50	60	70
Candleholder	30	37	45
Casserole, 1.5 qt.	120	135	150
Casserole, ind.	30	40	50
Cheese Server	100	125	150
Chop Plate, 12"-14"	100	125	150
Cigarette Box	120	130	140
Coaster	20	27	34
Coffee Pot	100	120	140
Compote	70	110	150
Cookie Jar	200	225	250
Cream/Sugar	60	80	100
Crescent Dish	30	35	45
Cup/Saucer	21	28	35
Cup/Saucer, 12 oz.	40	45	50
Dish, 5"-6"	18	28	37
Egg Cup	30	35	40
Gravy Boat	34	44	53
Ladle, 10"	70	85	100
Mixing Bowl	80	130	180
Mug, 7-12 oz	33	48	64
Party Plate, rd.	45	50	55
Pitcher, 1 pt - 2.5 qt	50	90	130
Plate, 6"-8"	18	27	36
Plate, 9"-10"	28	38	48
Platter, 12"-14"	80	100	120

	LOW	AVG.	HIGH
Platter, 17"	$ 250	$ 300	$ 350
Porringer	36	44	53
Relish Tray	36	54	73
Salad	122	136	151
Salt/Pepper	59	72	86
Salt/Pepper Mill	218	240	263
Server, 2-tier	84	102	121
Sherbet	35	40	45
Soup Plate	32	41	50
Teapot	100	116	133
Tray, 3-pc.	49	60	72
Trivet	18	26	33
Tumbler, 6 oz.-10 oz	27	40	53
Tureen	300	350	400
Vegetable	52	70	88

Coronado

	LOW	AVG.	HIGH
Butter Dish	$ 27	$ 29	$ 31
Casserole, 10.5"	31	34	36
Casserole, ind., 5.5"	12	16	19
Chop Plate, 12"-14"	18	23	27
Cigarette Box	29	34	38
Coffee Pot	37	40	44
Cream/Sugar	18	21	23
Cream/Sugar, ftd.	27	30	33
Cup/Saucer	6	8	10
Cup/Saucer, 10 oz.	11	15	18
Custard Cup	6	8	9
Dish, 5"-6"	4	7	9
Dish, crescent	9	11	12
Gravy Boat	15	18	20
Nut Dish, ftd.	12	16	19
Party Plate	16	17	17
Pitcher	26	31	36
Plate, 6"-8"	4	6	7
Plate, 9"-11"	9	13	16
Platter, oval, 10"-13"	12	16	19
Platter, oval, 15.5"	27	31	35
Relish Tray, handled	12	14	16
Salad Bowl, 10"	31	32	33
Salt/Pepper	12	16	20
Soup Bowl/Saucer	21	24	27
Soup Plate, 8"	12	14	16
Teapot	70	80	90
Vegetable, 9"-10"	15	19	22

Desert Rose (1941)

	LOW	AVG.	HIGH
Buffet Plate, rd., div.	$ 25	$ 35	$ 45
Butter Dish	43	52	62
Candleholder	23	30	36

	LOW	AVG.	HIGH
Casserole, 1.5 qt.	$ 100	$ 115	$ 130
Casserole, 2.5 qt.	130	150	170
Cheese Server	90	103	116
Chop Plate, 12"-14"	60	80	100
Coffee Pot	80	90	100
Compote	60	90	120
Cookie Jar	175	200	225
Cream/Sugar	60	75	90
Crescent Dish	23	29	35
Cup/Saucer	18	24	30
Cup/Saucer, 12 oz.	35	40	45
Dish, 5"-6"	15	25	35
Egg Cup	25	31	36
Goblet	55	65	75
Gravy Boat	40	50	60
Ladle, 10"	80	90	100
Mixing Bowl	75	110	145
Mug, 7-12 oz.	31	42	52
Party Plate, rd	37	41	45
Pitcher, 1 pt-2.5 qt	30	72	115
Plate, 6"-8"	15	22	29
Plate, 9"-10"	23	32	41
Platter, 12"-14"	58	84	110
Platter, 17"	200	240	280
Porringer	31	38	45
Relish Tray	31	44	58
Salad	100	120	140
Salt/Pepper	47	60	72
Salt/Pepper Mill	175	200	225
Server, 2-tier	72	90	109
Sherbet	32	33	34
Soup Plate	28	36	43
Teapot	75	100	125
Tray, heart form	24	31	38
Trivet	15	22	29
Tumbler, 6-10 oz.	24	34	43
Tureen	215	288	360
Vegetable	44	61	78

Ivy (1948)

	LOW	AVG.	HIGH
Butter Dish	$ 21	$ 24	$ 27
Casserole, 1.5 qt.	46	52	59
Cheese Server	43	49	55
Chop Plate, 12"-14"	27	37	47
Cigarette Box	47	50	54
Coffee Pot	40	48	55
Compote	27	42	56
Cookie Jar	79	88	97
Cream/Sugar	28	34	39
Crescent Dish	10	13	16
Cup/Saucer	8	11	14

	LOW	AVG.	HIGH
Cup/Saucer, 12 oz.	$ 16	$ 18	$ 20
Dish, 5"-6"	7	11	14
Gravy Boat	21	24	27
Ladle	40	44	48
Mixing Bowl	35	50	64
Mug, 7-12 oz.	14	20	26
Party Plate, rd.	16	18	20
Pitcher, 1 pt.-2.5 qt.	13	34	55
Plate, 6"-8"	7	10	13
Plate, 9"-10"	10	15	20
Platter, 12"-14"	26	38	50
Platter, 17"	90	115	140
Relish Tray	13	21	28
Salad	47	54	62
Salt/Pepper	22	28	34
Server, 2-tier	34	40	45
Sherbet	13	15	17
Soup Plate	13	16	19
Teapot	42	48	54
Trivet	7	11	14
Tumbler, 6 oz.-10 oz.	11	16	20
Tureen	100	134	168
Vegetable	20	28	35

Metropolitan (1940)

Morris Sanders designed Metropolitan for its namesake, the Metropolitan Museum of Art. All shapes are square or rectangular.

	LOW	AVG.	HIGH
Butter Dish	$ 24	$ 26	$ 28
Casserole, ind.	20	22	24
Chop Plate, sq., 13"	20	22	23
Coffee Pot	41	46	52
Cream/Sugar	27	32	36
Cup/Saucer	9	12	14
Dish, 5"-6"	4	7	9
Gravy Boat	17	19	20
Pitcher, 1.5 qt	42	45	48
Plate, 10"	10	11	12
Plate, 6"-8"	5	7	9
Platter, rect., 14"	14	15	16
Relish Tray	14	16	17
Salad, 10"	23	25	27
Salt/Pepper	17	20	22
Soup Plate	11	12	13
Teapot	35	41	47
Tumbler	14	16	17
Vegetable, div.	23	31	38

Grueby Potteries

Grueby Potteries operated from 1891 to 1907. After 1907 all Grueby pottery was manufactured and sold under the name of Tiffany. Grueby produced expensive, high quality vases, ornamental wares including statuettes, and decorative tiles. These usually have a factory stamp and an artist's mark: either straight-line or circular.

Grueby incised mark.

	LOW	AVG.	HIGH
Bowl, 4.5", mottled green brown glaze, pressed bulbous form. ...	$ 235	$ 300	$ 345
Bowl, 6.5" x 5" matte blue, thick glaze	435	500	875
Paperweight, 4.5", matte green glaze	180	200	250
Tile, 4", plain, solid color	15	35	65
Tile, 4", windmill design	150	185	220
Tile, 6", grape motif	75	100	125
Tile, 8.5" sq., blue, painted w/ flowers, artist's init.	400	500	600
Tile, Horse, 6.5" sq., blue, painted w/ horse, artist's init.	380	470	560
Tile, Landscape, 4" sq., green and beige, artist's init.	180	225	275
Vase, 10", green, decorated by Erickson, artist's init.	1000	2000	2600
Vase, 11", green, molded w/ leaves.	300	445	500
Vase, 11," matte green glaze, molded bud and leaf, signed	725	824	925
Vase, 12.5", green, cylindrical shape, leaf and bud motif	1000	1200	1400
Vase, 3.5", green, flared neck, rounded lip, thick glaze	195	240	290
Vase, 4.5", green, molded leaf design, bulbous body, artist's init. ...	400	484	564
Vase, 5.5", brown glaze (speckled), flattened spherical form.	400	500	600
Vase, 6.5", green glaze, squared cylindrical neck, artist's init.	590	720	850
Vase, 7", green, ovoid form w/ molded panels, artist's init..	653	780	900
Vase, 7.5", ovoid flask form, pinched neck, dec. by L. Newman..	735	860	1000
Vase, 8", matte green glaze, molded/ buds above leaves, signed ..	350	400	450
Vase, 8", bulbous body, 3 handles, matte glaze, loaf design	950	1275	1500

Hall China

Robert Hall named his 1903 acquisition the Hall China Company, and continued making the semiporcelain dinnerware and toilet ware the old company had produced. After his death, his son experimented with firing the body and the glaze at the same time. He introduced the process in 1911. Hall still makes this vitrified hotel and restaurant ware. In 1920, the famed gold-decorated teapots appeared. In 1931, decal-decorated kitchenware and dinnerware was introduced. Hall reissues many classic designs. All are decorated in solid colors (no decal or gold decoration pieces). Many pieces are in new colors or color combinations.

Early marks read *HALL'S CHINA* in a circular frame, containing a mold or pattern number. *MADE IN U.S.A.* sometimes sat beneath the stamp. Later, a rectangular frame surrounded *HALL'S SUPERIOR QUALITY KITCHENWARE* or *HALL*, with a trademark *R*.

        Hall backstamp.

	LOW	AVG.	HIGH
### *Autumn Leaf (1933)*			
Autumn Leaf was produced in 1933 for the Jewel Tea Co.			
Baker, 9.5"	$35	$44	$53
Bowl, 3.5"	10	13	15
Bowl, 5"	12	15	17
Bowl, 6.5"	19	24	28
Bowl, 8"	24	30	35
Casserole Set, w/ lid, 3 pieces	140	170	200
Casserole, w/ lid, rd.	58	72	87
Coffee Pot, w/ lid, metal insert	85	110	135
Cream/Sugar, ruffled	31	40	48
Cup/Saucer	9	12	15
Custard Cups, set of 6	71	91	111
Dish, 7.5", swirl design	17	21	24
Gravy	18	24	30
Mixing Bowl Set, 6"-9.5"	60	80	100
Pickle Dish	20	24	28
Pitcher, 6"	34	44	54
Pitcher, ice lip	45	60	75
Plate, 10"	12	15	18
Plate, 13", oval	30	40	50
Plate, 6"-7"	5	6	7
Plate, 8"-9"	10	12	14
Salad Bowl, c. 1937	30	35	40
Salt/Pepper, stove	20	24	28
Sauce, 5.5"	12	15	18
Teapot, Newport	150	180	210
Vegetable Dish, 10.5", oval, open	16	21	26
Vegetable Dish, w/ lid	37	46	54

	LOW	AVG.	HIGH

Blue Bouquet (early 1950s)

Blue Bouquet was produced for the Standard Coffee Company, production was discontinued in the mid-1960s.

Item	LOW	AVG.	HIGH
Baker	$ 28	$ 36	$ 45
Bowl, 6"	10	13	15
Bowl, 9"	18	24	30
Cake Stand	23	29	35
Casserole, w/ lid	50	65	80
Coffee Pot	100	125	150
Cream/Sugar	35	44	52
Cup/Saucer	17	21	25
Custard Cup	11	15	18
Fruit Bowl, 5.5"	7	9	10
Gravy Boat	34	42	51
Mixing Bowl, 6"-8.5"	28	35	42
Pitcher	28	36	43
Pitcher, ball form #3	125	175	200
Plate, 6"	5	6	7
Plate, 6.5"	9	12	15
Plate, 9"	10	12	14
Platter, 11"-13"	24	31	38
Salt/Pepper	31	38	46
Soup Plate, 8.5"	19	25	30
Soup Tureen	115	148	181
Tea Tile	92	114	135
Teapot, Aladdin shape	93	113	133
Vegetable Bowl, 9.5"	42	54	66

Cameo Rose (1950s)

Cameo Rose was produced for the Jewel Tea Company.

Item	LOW	AVG.	HIGH
Butter Dish, w/ lid	$ 60	$ 75	$ 90
Casserole, w/ lid, 2 tab handles	50	60	70
Cereal Bowl, 6"	7	9	11
Cream/Sugar	15	18	21
Cup	12	15	18
Fruit Bowl, 5.5"	5	6	7
Gravy Boat	24	30	36
Plate, 10"	9	12	15
Plate, 6.5"	5	6	7
Plate, 8"	5	6	7
Plate, 9.5"	7	9	11
Platter, 11"	20	25	30
Platter, 13"	24	29	34
Relish Dish, 9"	17	21	24
Salt/Pepper Shakers, pr.	23	31	38
Saucer	2	3	4
Soup Plate	12	15	18
Sugar Bowl, w/ lid	20	25	30
Teapot	60	80	100
Vegetable Bowl, oval	20	25	30
Vegetable Bowl, rd., 9"	15	19	23

	LOW	AVG.	HIGH
Crocus (1930s)			
Baker	$ 28	$ 36	$ 44
Bean Pot, w/ lid	100	130	160
Bowl, 5.5"	7	9	11
Bowl, 6"	12	16	19
Cream/Sugar	59	76	94
Cup/Saucer	14	18	22
Custard Cup	7	9	11
Drip Jar	48	58	69
Drip-o-later, china	47	60	72
Gravy Boat	36	44	52
Mixing Bowl, 6"	16	21	26
Mixing Bowl, 7.5"	22	27	32
Mixing Bowl, 9"	28	36	45
Mug	50	60	71
Pie Plate	24	30	35
Pitcher, ball form #3	115	135	155
Plate, 10"	36	46	56
Plate, 6"	7	9	11
Plate, 8.5"	9	12	15
Platter, 11.5"-13.5"	26	34	42
Refrigerator Jar, rect.	48	60	72
Refrigerator Jar, sq.	50	60	70
Salad Bowl, 9"	25	31	36
Server, 3 tier	60	80	100
Soup Plate, 8.5"	20	25	30
Teapot, New York	115	145	175
Tureen, w/ lid	150	185	220
Vegetable Bowl, oval	24	30	36
Mums			
Bowl, 9"	$ 30	$ 36	42
Casserole	68	82	96
Cereal Bowl, 6"	10	13	15
Cream/Sugar	50	60	70
Cup/Saucer	12	15	17
Custard Cup	5	6	7
Fruit Bowl, 5.5"	8	10	11
Plate, 10"	20	24	28
Plate, 6"	5	6	7
Plate, 8.5"	12	15	18
Platter, 11"-13"	34	42	49
Salt/Pepper	25	31	37
Saucer	2	3	3
Soup Plate, 8.5"	15	19	23
Sugar Bowl, w/ lid	21	28	34
Teapot	116	144	172
Pastel Morning Glory (1930s)			
Bean Pot, w/ lid,1 handle	$ 99	$ 120	$ 142
Bowl, 5.5"	10	12	14

	LOW	AVG.	HIGH
Bowl, 6"	$ 12	$ 15	$ 18
Bowl, 9"	24	31	37
Bowl, oval	30	38	46
Casserole, w/ lid, closed tab handles	57	71	85
Cream/Sugar	39	50	60
Cup/Saucer	12	15	18
Drip Jar	34	41	48
Gravy Boat	43	54	65
Pitcher, ball form #3	46	58	70
Plate, 6"	5	6	7
Plate, 8.5"	7	9	10
Plate, 9"	20	25	30
Platter, 11"-13"	36	45	54
Salt/Pepper	36	44	52
Soup Plate, 8.5"	21	28	34

Range Poppy (1933)

Range Poppy was produced for the Great American Tea Company.

	LOW	AVG.	HIGH
Baker	$ 24	$ 30	$ 36
Bean Pot, w/ lid, 1 handle	88	106	123
Bowl, 6"-7.5"	20	25	30
Bowl, 9"-10"	36	45	54
Bread Box, metal	92	118	144
Cake Plate	25	31	36
Canisters, set of 4, metal	71	88	106
Casserole, 11", w/ lid, oval	130	165	200
Casserole, w/ lid, 2 handles, rd.	35	46	57
Casserole, w/ lid, oval, 8"	44	55	66
Coffee Pot	73	92	110
Cream/Sugar	41	54	67
Cup/Saucer	12	16	19
Custard Cup	31	39	47
Drip Jar	32	40	47
Pitcher, ball form #3	33	42	52
Plate 7"	7	9	11
Plate, 7.5"	9	12	14
Plate, 9"	14	18	22
Platter, 11.5"-13.5"	34	45	56
Pretzel Jar, w/ lid	85	108	132
Refrigerator Jar, oval, loop handle	46	59	72
Salad Bowl, 9"	22	28	33
Salt/Pepper	13	16	19
Sifter, metal	36	46	56
Soup Plate, 6.5"	19	24	28
Spoon	70	88	105
Vegetable Bowl, 9.5"	44	54	63

Red Poppy (early 1950s)

Red Poppy was produced for Grand Union Tea Company.

	LOW	AVG.	HIGH
Baker	$ 32	$ 40	$ 48
Bowl, 6"	19	24	29

	LOW	AVG.	HIGH
Bowl, 7.5"	$ 24	$ 29	$ 34
Bowl, 9"	38	44	51
Cake Plate	25	30	35
Cereal Bowl, 6"	10	12	14
Coffee Pot	36	44	51
Cream/Sugar	40	45	50
Cup/Saucer	15	20	25
Custard Cup	7	9	11
Fruit Bowl, 5.5"	7	9	11
Gravy Boat	42	53	64
Pitcher, ball form #3	49	60	70
Plate, 10"	14	18	21
Plate, 7"	7	9	10
Plate, 9.5"	12	16	19
Plato, 6"	2	3	4
Platter, 11"	29	36	43
Platter, 13"	35	45	55
Salad Bowl, 9"	21	27	32
Salt/Pepper Shakers, set	14	18	21
Soup Plate	21	27	32
Teapot, Aladdin shape	72	88	103
Teapot, New York shape	69	90	111
Vegetable Bowl, oval 10"	35	44	53

Rose Parade (1940s)

	LOW	AVG.	HIGH
Baker	$ 24	$ 31	$ 37
Bean Pot, w/ lid, tab handles	72	91	110
Bowl, 6"	19	25	30
Bowl, 7.5"	25	31	36
Bowl, 9"	28	36	44
Casserole, w/ lid, tab handles	37	44	52
Cream/Sugar	30	38	45
Custard Cup	10	12	14
Drip Jar	34	42	49
Pitcher, 5"-7.5"	49	62	76
Salad Bowl, 9"	24	29	34
Salt/Pepper	25	30	34
Teapot, 4-6 cup	41	52	63

Rose White (1940s)

	LOW	AVG.	HIGH
Baker	$ 19	$ 24	$ 29
Bean Pot, w/ lid, tab handles	60	76	92
Casserole, w/ lid, tab handles	44	54	64
Cream/Sugar	27	33	39
Custard Cup	10	12	14
Drip Jar, w/ lid, tab handles	25	30	35
Pitcher, 5"-7.5"	34	43	52
Salad Bowl, 9"	20	25	30
Salt/Pepper	24	30	36
Teapot, 4-6 cup	41	52	64

	LOW	AVG.	HIGH

Royal Rose (1940s)

	LOW	AVG.	HIGH
Casserole, w/ lid	$ 43	$ 56	$ 68
Drip Jar, w/ lid	32	42	52
Mixing Bowl, 6"-8.5"	28	34	41
Pitcher, ball form #3	47	60	72
Salt/Pepper	28	36	43
Teapot	58	72	86

Serenade (1930s)

Serenade dinnerware was produced for the Eureka Tea Co.

	LOW	AVG.	HIGH
Bowl, 5.5"	$ 7	$ 9	$ 10
Bowl, 6"	12	15	18
Bowl, 7.5"	19	25	30
Bowl, 9"	26	33	40
Bowl, 9"	23	28	33
Casserole, w/ lid	48	60	73
Cereal Bowl, 6"	10	12	14
Coffee Pot	37	46	56
Cup/Saucer	10	13	15
Gravy Boat	25	30	35
Plate, 6"	2	3	4
Plate, 8.5"	7	9	11
Plate, 9"	8	10	11
Platter, 11"-13"	31	38	45
Pretzel Jar, w/ lid, tab handles	93	118	143
Salt/Pepper	36	44	53
Soup Plate, 8.5"	18	23	28

Silhouette (1930s)

	LOW	AVG.	HIGH
Baker	$ 25	$ 31	$ 36
Bowl, 6"	15	19	22
Casserole, w/ lid	48	60	73
Coffee Pot, drip.	252	310	368
Cup/Saucer	12	15	18
Drip Jar, w/ lid	25	31	37
Fruit Bowl, 5.5"	7	9	10
Mug	49	60	72
Pitcher	35	45	55
Pitcher, ball form #3	60	75	90
Plate, 6"	14	18	21
Plate, 8.5"	10	13	15
Plate, 9.5"	11	15	18
Platter, 11"-13"	37	44	52
Pretzel Jar, w/ lid, closed tab handles	93	122	150
Refrigerator Jar, w/ lid, rect.	38	46	54
Refrigerator Jar, w/ lid, sq.	50	60	70
Salad Bowl, 9"	20	24	28
Salt/Pepper	19	24	29
Soup Plate, 8.5"	21	28	34
Teapot, New York shape	100	135	170

	LOW	AVG.	HIGH

Springtime

	LOW	AVG.	HIGH
Bowl, 5.5"	$ 7	$ 9	$ 11
Bowl, 6"	160	210	260
Casserole, w/ lid, 2 tab handles	47	60	74
Coffee Pot, drip, china	10	12	14
Cream/Sugar	24	31	37
Cup	12	15	18
Drip Jar, thick	24	30	36
Gravy Boat	37	44	52
Pie Plate	23	31	38
Pitcher, ball form #3	47	58	70
Plate, 6"	2	3	4
Plate, 8.5"	7	9	11
Plate, 9.5"	23	30	37
Platter, 11"	28	34	39
Platter, 13"	30	39	48
Salad Bowl, 9"	21	27	33
Salt/Pepper	35	46	56
Saucer	2	3	4
Soup Plate, 8.5"	17	22	26

Tulip

Tulip was produced for the Cook Coffee Company.

	LOW	AVG.	HIGH
Baker	$ 23	$ 30	$ 37
Cereal Bowl, 6"	9	12	14
Coffee Pot, drip, china	156	192	227
Cream/Sugar	34	42	49
Cup	7	9	11
Custard Cup	7	9	11
Drip Jar	31	40	48
Fruit Bowl, 5.5"	7	9	10
Gravy Boat	35	43	51
Mixing Bowls, set of 3	96	116	137
Plate, 10"	12	15	17
Plate, 6"	2	3	4
Plate, 7"	5	6	7
Plate, 9"	7	9	11
Platter, 11"-13"	32	40	47
Salad Bowl, 9"	18	23	28
Salt/Pepper	19	25	30
Saucer	2	3	4
Soup Plate, 8.5"	20	25	29

Wild Poppy (1930s)

	LOW	AVG.	HIGH
Baker	$ 33	$ 40	$ 48
Bean Pot, w/ lid	75	90	105
Canister	110	140	170
Casserole, oval	24	30	36
Cream/Sugar	14	18	22
Custard Cup	7	9	11
Mixing Bowls, set of 3	50	60	70

	LOW	AVG.	HIGH
Salt/Pepper	$ 23	$ 29	$ 35
Teapot, 4-6 cup	70	85	100

Wildfire (1950s)

Wildfire was produced for the Great American Tea Company.

	LOW	AVG.	HIGH
Baker	$ 19	$ 24	$ 29
Bowl, 9"	19	24	28
Casserole, w/ lid, tab handles	47	60	72
Cereal Bowl, 6"	9	12	14
Coffee Pot	49	59	69
Cream/Sugar	23	31	38
Cup/Saucer	15	18	21
Custard Cup	10	12	14
Drip Jar	23	29	34
Egg Cup	47	61	75
Fruit Bowl, 5.5"	7	9	11
Gravy Boat	24	31	37
Mixing Bowl, large	42	54	66
Mixing Bowl, medium	19	24	28
Mixing Bowl, small	14	18	22
Pie Plate	19	24	29
Plate, 10"	17	21	25
Plate, 6"	5	6	7
Plate, 7"	7	9	10
Platter, 11"	20	25	29
Platter, 13"	24	30	36
Salt/Pepper	37	46	55
Soup Plate, 8.5"	20	24	27
Teapot, Aladdin shape	70	88	105
Tidbit Tray, 3-tier	50	61	72

Yellow Rose

	LOW	AVG.	HIGH
Baker	$ 22	$ 27	$32
Bowl, 5.5"	7	9	11
Bowl, 6"	10	12	14
Casserole, w/ lid	36	45	54
Coffee Pot, drip, Norse shape	76	96	116
Cream/Sugar	29	37	45
Cup/Saucer	10	13	15
Custard Cup	5	6	7
Gravy Boat	25	30	35
Plate, 6"	2	3	3
Plate, 8.5"	7	9	10
Plate, 9"	17	21	25
Platter, 11"-13"	24	30	36
Salad Bowl, 9"	20	24	28
Salt/Pepper Shakers, pr.	35	46	56
Soup Plate, 8.5"	17	22	26

	LOW	HIGH

Hall Teapots

	LOW	HIGH
Airflow	$ 50	$ 70
Aladdin	50	70
Albany	50	70
Automobile	600	750
Baltimore	40	60
Basket	125	175
Basketball	600	700
Birdcage	400	500
Boston	30	50
Cleveland	60	90
Doughnut	300	400
Football	500	700
French	25	35
Globe	70	90
Hollywood	40	60
Hook Cover	30	50
Illinois	200	250
Indiana	225	250
Kansas	250	300
Los Angeles	40	60
Melody	175	225
Moderne	30	50
Nautilus	200	250
New York	20	40
Ohio	175	225
Parade	30	50
Philadelphia	30	50
Rhythm	150	175
Saf-handle	100	150
Sani-Grid	40	60
Star	70	90
Streamline	50	70
Surfside	100	150
Windshield	40	80

Harker Pottery

The Harker Pottery Company began in 1890. In 1931, it bought the E.M. Knowles plant in Chester, WV and closed its own East Liverpool, WV operations. The Chester plant operated until 1972. The Cameoware line and the Hotoven Kitchenware are the favorites. An arrow backstamp is common.

Harker Pottery Co.
East Liverpool, Ohio

Harker and
Hotoven
backstamps.

	LOW	AVG.	HIGH

Hotoven Kitchenware (1926)

Hotoven Kitchenware claimed to be the first decal decorated line of ovenware ever made.

	LOW	AVG.	HIGH
Bean Pot, ind.	$ 4	$ 5	$ 6
Cake Server	14	16	18
Casserole, 7"-9"	17	20	23
Cup/Saucer, 10 oz.	9	10	11
Custard Cup	2	4	6
Drip Jar, Skyscraper	14	16	18
Fork & Spoon	30	50	70
Leftover, paneled	14	16	18
Mixing Bowl, 9"-10"	11	14	17
Pie Plate, 9"-10"	6	8	10
Pitcher	17	20	22
Rolling pin	40	45	50
Scoop	23	26	28
Stack set, 3-4 piece	30	38	47
Tea tile, octagonal	20	22	23
Teapot	29	32	35

Modernage

Modernage pieces have narrow, oval bodys and "lifesaver" finials.

	LOW	AVG.	HIGH
Cake Server	$ 25	$ 28	$ 30
Cake Tray, lug, 11.5"	8	9	10
Casserole, 6"-9"	30	35	40
Cookie Jar	31	34	38
Cream/Sugar	24	28	32
Custard Cup	4	5	6
Drip Jar	13	15	17
Fork & Spoon	30	40	50
Mixing Bowl, 11"	30	33	36
Pitcher	29	40	50
Platter, rd., 11.5"	10	12	14
Teapot	31	36	41

Royal Gadroon backstamp.

	LOW	AVG.	HIGH
Royal Gadroon			

Royal Gadroon pieces have a gadrooned (or lobed) edge.

	LOW	AVG.	HIGH
Chop Plate	$ 12	$ 14	$ 16
Cream/Sugar	23	28	33
Cup/Saucer	10	15	20
Dish, 5"-6"	4	5	6
Dish, w/ lid	12	14	16
Gravy Boat	16	18	20
Pickle Dish	8	10	12
Plate, 6"-8"	4	6	8
Plate, 9"-10"	8	9	10
Plate, sq., 8-9"	6	9	12
Platter, 11"-15"	10	15	19
Salad Bowl	16	18	20
Salt/Pepper	10	13	16
Server, 3-tier	17	20	23
Soup Bowl	8	9	10
Soup Plate, 8.5"	8	9	10
Teapot	30	36	42
Vegetable, 9"	18	20	21

Virginia

Virginia pieces are square.

	LOW	AVG.	HIGH
Bowl, 36s	$ 8	$ 9	$ 10
Casserole	21	26	30
Cream/Sugar	25	29	33
Cup/Saucer	10	14	17
Dish, 5"-6"	2	3	4
Plate, 6"-8"	4	6	8
Plate, 9"-10"	8	9	10
Platter, 11"-14"	10	13	16
Soup, 7.75"	8	9	10
Vegetable, 8.25"	14	15	16

LOW AVG. HIGH

White Clover (1951)

Russell Wright designed White Clover. Some pieces have a cloverleaf decoration, others are a solid color.

	LOW	AVG.	HIGH
Casserole, w/ lid, 2 qt./C	$ 45	$ 49	$ 53
Chop Plate, 9"-11"/C	12	15	17
Clock	90	100	110
Cream/Sugar /C	34	38	42
Cup/Saucer/C	14	16	18
Dish, 5-7"/C	4	7	10
Gravy Boat/C	23	25	26
Pitcher, w/ lid, 2 qt./C	50	55	60
Plate, 11"	20	23	26
Plate, 6"-8"	6	8	10
Plate, 9"-10"/C	9	12	15
Platter, 13.25"/C	24	26	28
Salt/Pepper	26	29	32
Vegetable, 7"-9"	23	35	47

Zephyr

Lidded Zephyr pieces are known with two different finials, a ball knob or a stylized wing finial.

	LOW	AVG.	HIGH
Box, w/ lid	$ 34	$ 38	$ 42
Casserole, 7"-9"	25	31	37
Casserole Tray, 8"-10"	7	8	9
Cookie Jar	25	29	33
Custard Cup	4	5	6
Leftover, rd. 4"-6"	7	12	17
Mixing Bowl, 10"	26	28	30
Salt/Pepper	18	19	20
Serving Bowl, 6"-9"	10	17	24
Stack set, 3-piece	43	46	50
Teapot, 5 cup	35	40	45
Tray, rd., 10"	11	13	15

Head Vases

Head Vases are figural vases most often depicting women and young girls. They were popular in the 1950s and '60s. Ladies with thick eyelashes, long gloves, dangle earrings and elaborate hats capture an exaggerated 1950s' look. Although the U.S. manufactured some vases, Japan produced the majority. Identification is difficult because many were unmarked or had only paper labels.

When handling a head vase be careful not to harm the label, the finish or delicate details such as jewelry. Beware of cracks and chips that decrease value. Watch out for reproductions or new head vases. Interest in head vases has intensified in the last five years and prices have risen accordingly. For further reading see *Head Vases*, Kathleen Cole, Collector Books, Paducah, KY, 1989 and *The Official Price Guide To Pottery and Porcelain*, Harvey Duke, House of Collectibles, Random House, New York, 1995.

Left to right: Woman, black glove and lashes, mkd. "C3282B" Napco, $40-$60; woman, brown gloves and eyelashes, mkd. "4228" Lefton, $60-$80; woman in black lace, dangle pearl earrings, Enesco Imports, $40-$60; — Photo courtesy of George Kerrigan Photography; Items courtesy of Pauline Alberta.

	LOW	HIGH
Barbie, Ceramic Arts Studio, ht. 7"	$ 80	$ 100
Becky, Ceramic Arts Studio, mkd. H306, ht. 5.5"	50	80
Black Man, Ceramic Arts Studio, ht. 8"	80	120
Black Woman, Ceramic Arts Studio, ht. 8"	80	120
Blackamoor in Turban, Royal Copley, ht. 8.5"	50	70
Bonnie, Ceramic Arts Studio, ht. 7"	80	100
Clown w/ patched hat, bow tie, Relpo, ht. 5.5"	40	60
Dutch Girl w/ white hat, hand below chin, Inarco, ht. 5.5"	35	45
Girl, in bonnet, holding bouquet, w/ plaid side bow, Relpo, ht. 5.5"	45	65
Girl, in wide brimmed hat, wall pocket, Royal Copley, ht. 8"	25	35
Girl, w/ closed eyes, applied eyelashes, hat and cut-out bangs, Napco, ht. 6"	30	40
Girl, applied flowers in hair, w/ umbrella, mkd. CN, ht. 5"	28	32
Lotus, large Chinese woman, Ceramic Arts Studio, ht. 8"	90	120
Madonna, in blue and white, praying, Royal Windsor, ht. 8"	25	35
Manchu, Chinese man, Ceramic Arts Studio, ht. 7.5"	90	100
Mei Ling, Chinese woman, Ceramic Arts Studio, ht. 5"	70	90
Svea, Girl w/ pigtail, Ceramic Arts Studio, ht. 6"	60	80

	LOW	HIGH
Sven, boy in hat, Ceramic Arts Studio, ht. 6.5"	$ 60	$ 80
Woman, in black lace, black eyelashes, dangle pearl earrings, Enesco Imports, ht. 5.5"	40	60
Woman, in green hat, pearl necklace, dangle earrings, hand raised, mkd. Napco C3343C, 1958, ht. 4.5"	30	40
Woman, in yellow, wall pocket, roses at bodice & sun bonnet, high lustre finish, ht. 6"	25	35
Woman, w/ closed eyes, painted lashes, honey blond hair, turquoise blouse, molded flower, ht. 6"	25	35
Woman, in green, w/ gold accents, hat, and lashes, ht. 4"	12	18
Woman w/ turban and pearl necklace, Napco, ht. 5"	28	32
Woman, black glove and lashes, pearl necklace, mkd. C3282B Napco, 1956, ht. 5"	40	60
Woman, black hair, applied black lashes, molded hood, Inarco, ht. 6"	40	60
Woman, brown gloves and eyelashes, mkd. 4228 Lefton, ht. 6"	60	80
Woman, brown hair, pearl earrings, necklace and brooch, ht. 7.5"	40	50
Woman, closed eyes, green and gold, applied bow and flowers in hat, ht. 4.5"	20	25
Woman, in blue, molded flower in hair , ht. 6"	15	25
Woman, small, closed eyes, painted lashes, blond hair, blue blouse, flower in hair, ht. 4"	18	22
Woman, wall pocket, lashes, black hair, high lustre, wide brim green hat, ht. 7"	20	25

A.E. Hull Pottery

Begun as a stoneware company, the A.E. Hull Pottery Company moved on to semi-porcelain dinnerware in 1907 with the purchase of the Acme Pottery Co. It slowly added various lines until the late 1930s, when Hull introduced its famous matte-finished pastel art pottery. Production continued through the 1950s when manufacturing operations ceased.

Prices for gilt pieces are higher, glossy pieces somewhat less. The listings include pattern numbers.

Early marks include an impressed *H* in a circle or diamond. Later marks include *Hull*, *Hull Art*, or *Hull Ware* written in block letters or script.

	LOW	AVG.	HIGH
Blossom Flite			

Blossom Flite features multicolored flowers over a basketweave background of high gloss pink with blue lattice decor and green interior, or black decor with pink interior.

	LOW	AVG.	HIGH
Basket, low, T8, 8" x 9"	$ 85	$ 100	$ 115
Basket, T2, 6"	44	50	55
Basket, T4, 8.5"	67	84	100
Bowl, low, handled, T9, 10"	84	100	115
Candleholder, pr., T11	49	60	72
Console Bowl, T10	70	80	90
Cornucopia, T6, 10.5"	75	80	85
Cream/Sugar, T15/16	80	90	100
Ewer, T13, 13.5"	140	170	200
Flower Bowl, T12	60	75	90
Pitcher, T1	30	35	40
Pitcher, T3, 8.5"	70	80	90
Teapot, T14	75	90	105

Bow-Knot (1949)

Bow-Knot is decorated with high-relief multicolored flowers and bows in matte finish on a background of pink with blue, or blue with blue or turquoise.

Basket, B12, 10.5"	600	700	800
Basket, B25, 6.5"	160	175	190
Candleholders, pr., B17	120	140	160
Console Bowl, B16, 13.5"	196	220	245
Cornucopia, B5, 7.5"	70	85	100
Cornucopia, double, B13, 13"	163	169	175
Creamer, B21	80	90	100
Ewer, B1, 5.5"	80	100	120
Ewer, B15, 13.5"	1100	1300	1500
Sugar Bowl, B22	80	90	100
Teapot, B20	300	350	400

Butterfly

Butterfly has pink and blue flowers and butterflies with black that decorate either cream-colored matte with turquoise interiors or glossy all-white pieces.

Basket, B13, 8"	$ 100	$ 110	$ 120
Basket, B17, 10.5"	170	200	230
Bowl, fruit, B16	90	100	110
Bud vase, pitcher shape, B1	56	63	70
Candleholders, pr., B22	70	82	94
Candy Dish, bonbon, B4	33	36	40

	LOW	AVG.	HIGH
Candy Dish, urn shape, open, B6	$ 40	$ 45	$ 50
Console Bowl, 3 feet, B21 ....,	110	135	160
Cornucopia, B12	60	70	80
Cornucopia, B2, 6.5"	27	35	43
Cream/Sugar, B19/20	80	103	126
Ewer, B15, 13.5"	125	143	161
Lavabo set, B24/B25, 16"	160	190	220
Pitcher/Vase, handled, B11	81	94	108
Teapot, B18	150	175	200
Tray, div., B23	100	120	140
Window Box, B8	56	68	81

Calla Lily

Calla Lily is also called Jack-in-the-Pulpit. It has embossed flowers in matte-color combinations with green leaves.

Bowl, 500-32, 10"	$ 140	$ 170	$ 200
Candleholders, pr., 508-39 ....;	135	150	165
Console Bowl, 590-33, 13"	145	180	215
Cornucopias 570-33, 8"	84	94	104
Ewer, 506, 10"	250	315	380

Dogwood

This line has raised dogwood flowers.

Basket, 501, 7.5"	$ 200	$ 250	$ 300
Bowl, low, 521, 7"	90	110	130
Candleholders, pr., 512, 4"	140	170	200
Console Bowl, 511, 11.5"	180	220	260
Cornucopia, 522, 4"	50	62	75
Ewer, 505, 8.5" (marked 6.5")	133	168	202
Ewer, 519, 13.5"	500	620	740
Ewer, 520, 4.75"	85	100	115
Teapot, 507, 6.5"	200	250	300
Window Box, 508, 10.5"	100	125	150

Ebbtide

Ebbtide shows glossy fish and seashell designs on various backgrounds.

Basket, E11, 16.5"	$ 180	$ 200	$ 220
Candleholder, pr., E13, 2.5"	38	44	51
Console Bowl, E12, 15.75"	128	142	156
Cornucopia, E3/E9, 7"-12"	91	104	116
Cream/Sugar, E15/E16	100	122	143
Pitcher Vase, E10, 14"	200	250	300
Pitcher Vase, EA, 8.25"	90	100	110
Teapot, E14	180	200	220

Iris (1940)

Iris has embossed iris flowers on matte-finished bodies.

Basket, 408, 7"	$ 200	$ 240	$ 280
Candleholders, pr., 411, 5"	125	135	145
Console Bowl, 409, 12"	200	220	240
Ewer, 401, 5"	70	80	90

	LOW	AVG.	HIGH
Ewer, 401, 8"	$ 145	$ 160	$ 175
Ewer, 401, 13.5"	350	400	450
Rose Bowl, 412, 4"	80	100	120
Rose Bowl, 413, 7"	100	115	130

Little Red Riding Hood

This was a popular figural line with Little Red Riding Hood and the Wolf.

	LOW	AVG.	HIGH
Bank, 7"	$ 500	$ 550	$ 600
Butter Dish	500	550	600
Canister, blank	750	825	900
Canister, snack	1000	1250	1500
Canister, staples	800	900	1000
Casserole Dish, red handle	1400	1600	1800
Covered Jar, basket in front, 8.5"	400	450	500
Covered Jar, basket on side, 9"	350	400	450
Cream/Sugar, ruffled skirt	510	580	650
Cream/Sugar, side open	257	285	313
Creamer, spout on top of head	180	200	220
Grease Jar, Wolf	800	950	1100
Jar, spice	600	750	900
Matchholder, 5.25" (2 styles)	900	1000	1100
Mustard Jar, 4.5"	500	550	600
Mustard Jar, w/spoon, 5.5"	400	440	480
Pitcher, batter, 5.5"	200	260	320
Pitcher, milk, 8"	323	332	341
Salt/Pepper, 3.5"	60	66	72
Salt/Pepper, 5.5"	120	135	150
Shaker, Sugar Bowl (4 holes on top)	60	78	95
String Holder, 9"	1600	1800	2000
Sugar Bowl, "creeping," hands on table	180	200	220
Teapot	300	350	400

Magnolia [matte] (1946)

Matte Magnolia has embossed magnolia flowers on colored backgrounds.

	LOW	AVG.	HIGH
Basket, 10, 10.5"	$ 190	$ 250	$ 310
Candleholders, pr., 27, 4.5"	80	90	100
Console Bowl, 26, 12.5"	123	129	135
Cornucopias 19, 8.5"	60	65	70
Cream/Sugar, 24/25	80	90	100
Ewer, 14, 4.75"	44	49	54
Ewer, 18, 13.5"	202	230	258
Teapot, 23	122	136	150

Magnolia [glossy]

Glossy Magnolia has embossed magnolia flowers on colored backgrounds.

	LOW	AVG.	HIGH
Basket, H14, 10.5"	$ 200	230	260
Cornucopia, double, H15, 12"	100	110	120
Cornucopia, H10, 8.5"	80	90	100
Cream/Sugar, H21/22	83	98	112
Ewer, H11, 8.5"	88	92	96
Ewer, H19, 13.5"	325	375	425
Teapot, H20	125	135	145

	LOW	AVG.	HIGH

Open Rose

Also called Camellia, this pattern has polychrome roses on pastel matte backgrounds.

	LOW	AVG.	HIGH
Basket, 107, 8"	$ 200	$ 275	$ 350
Basket, 140, 10.5"	550	700	850
Basket, hanging, 132, 7"	180	230	280
Candleholders, dove-shape, pr., 117, 6.5"	160	200	260
Console Bowl, 116, 12"	200	250	300
Cornucopia, 101, 8.5"	97	120	144
Cornucopia, 141, 8.5"	113	137	161
Cream/Sugar, 111/112, 5"	108	140	171
Ewer, 115, 8.5"	145	185	225
Teapot, 110, 8.5"	230	290	351

Parchment and Pine

Parchment and Pine has pine cones on glossy backgrounds.

	LOW	AVG.	HIGH
Basket, S3, 6"	$ 60	$ 75	$ 90
Basket, S8, 16"	100	125	150
Candleholder, pr., S10, 2.75"	40	50	60
Console Bowl, S9, 16"	58	73	88
Cornucopia, S2, 8"	42	54	66
Cornucopia, S6, 12"	70	90	110
Cream/Sugar, S12/13	49	62	74
Ewer, S7, 13.5"	120	150	180
Teapot, S11	70	90	110
Teapot, tall, S15, 8"	117	150	184

Serenade

Serenade has birds on branches.

	LOW	AVG.	HIGH
Basket, bonbon, S5, 6.75"	$ 60	$ 70	$ 80
Basket, S14, 12"	250	320	380
Bowl, ftd. fruit, S15, 11.5"	75	100	125
Candleholder, pr., S16, 6.5"	60	70	80
Casserole, S20, 9"	80	100	120
Cornucopia, S10, 11"	50	60	70
Cream/Sugar, S18/S19	60	70	80
Ewer, S13, 13.25"	250	330	410
Ewer, S8, 8.5"	75	86	96
Pitcher, beverage, S21	100	110	120
Pitcher vase, S2, 6.5"	55	60	66
Teapot, S17	106	119	132
Window Box, S9, 12.5"	50	58	65

Sunglow

Sunglow has flowers, and butterflies and bows (not on all pieces).

	LOW	AVG.	HIGH
Basket, 84, 6.5"	$ 54	$ 60	$ 67
Bowl, 50, 5-10"	22	34	47
Casserole, 51, 7.5"	42	48	54
Cornucopia, 96, 8.5"	63	72	81
Drip Jar, 53	32	38	43
Ewer, 90, 5.5"	35	38	41
Pitcher, 52, 24 oz.	45	48	52
Pitcher, 55, 7.5"	90	100	110
Salt/Pepper, 54	18	21	23

	LOW	AVG.	HIGH

Tokay (1958)

Also called Tuscany, Tokay has embossed grapes and leaves on high-gloss backgrounds.

	LOW	AVG.	HIGH
Basket, 11, 10.5"	$ 70	$ 78	$ 86
Basket, 15, 12"	87	111	135
Bowl, fruit, 7, 9.5"	110	130	150
Candy Dish, w/ lid, 9C, 8.5"	60	70	80
Consolette, 14, 15.75"	110	127	144
Cornucopia, 6-11"	30	45	60
Cream/Sugar, 17/18	80	90	100
Ewer, 13, 12"	200	250	300
Ewer, 21, 16"	300	340	380
Ewer, 3, 8"	60	65	70
Teapot, 16	97	120	143
Urn, 5 , 5.5"	30	35	40

Water Lily

This line has water lilies on pastel backgrounds.

	LOW	AVG.	HIGH
Basket, L14, 10.5"	$ 280	$ 310	$ 330
Candleholder, pr., L22, 4.5"	110	118	125
Console Bowl, L21, 13.5"	171	184	198
Cornucopia, double, L27, 12"	148	162	175
Cornucopia, L7, 6.5"	74	86	99
Cream/Sugar, L19/L20	113	124	136
Ewer, L17, 13.5"	350	400	450
Ewer, L3, 5.5"	67	72	76
Teapot, L18	160	180	200

Woodland Glossy (1950)

	LOW	AVG.	HIGH
Basket, W22, 10.5"	$ 180	$ 220	$ 260
Basket, W9, 8.75"	70	85	100
Candleholder, pr., W30, 3.5"	58	64	70
Console Bowl, W29, 14"	80	90	100
Cornucopia, W10, 11"	58	62	67
Cornucopias, W2, 5.5"	30	35	40
Cream/Sugar, W27/28	62	72	81
Ewer, W24, 13.5"	230	265	300
Ewer, W3, 5.5"	40	45	50
Ewer, W6, 6.5"	58	63	68
Teapot, W26	90	100	110
Window Box, W14, 10"	45	65	85

Hummel Figurines

Hummels are ceramic figurines, usually of children. Berta Hummel, an artist and nun, created the concept and the original designs in 1935. For more information, consult *The Official Price Guide to Hummel Figurines and Plates,* published by The House of Collectibles, Random House, NY.

Each design has a title and a number. We have listed the designs by number, followed by the title. Through 1990, all marks fall into six basic categories (although variations exist): Crown Mark (CM), 1935-49; Full Bee (FB), 1950-56; Stylized Bee (SB); 1956-63; 3-line mark (3-L), 1963-72; Goebel/V (V-G), 1972-79; and Goebel (G), 1979-90. (Since 1991 a "New Crown Mark" is used.)

Above left to right: Crown Mark, Full Bee, Stylized Bee.
Below left to right: 3-line mark, Goebel, Goebel/V.

Below left to right: Goose Girl, #47; Stormy Weather, #71.

	CM	FB	SB	3-L	V-G	G
1, Puppy Love	$ 340	$ 250	$ 170	$ 120	$ 100	$ 80
2/0, Little Fiddler (Brown Hat)	410	250	160	100	110	90
3/I, Bookworm	650	480	270	200	160	130
4, Little Fiddler (Black Hat)	340	210	150	100	80	70
5, Strolling Along	320	190	140	80	90	80
6/0, Sensitive Hunter	370	230	170	100	90	70
7/0, Merry Wanderer	450	320	210	140	100	110
8, Bookworm	460	310	190	140	100	90
9, Begging His Share	440	280	200	110	100	90
10/I, Flower Madonna, white	370	330	120	110	80	80
11/2/0, Merry Wanderer	300	190	140	60	90	70
12/2/0, Chimney Sweep	110	90	80	60	50	40
13/2/0, Meditation	—	180	110	80	80	60
14A & B, Bookworm Bookends	750	610	400	290	210	200
15/0, Hear Ye, Hear Ye	370	210	160	140	110	100
16/2/0, Little Hiker	220	130	100	70	60	50
17/0, Congratulations	310	220	180	150	80	70
18, Christ Child	260	190	130	80	80	—
20, Prayer Before Battle	350	200	160	110	90	70
21/0, Heavenly Angel	200	160	90	60	60	40
22/0, Angel With Birds	180	150	100	60	30	20
23/I, Adoration	630	400	230	200	180	160
24/I, Lullaby	330	270	190	130	100	90
25, Angelic Sleep	440	260	180	100	110	80
26/0, Child Jesus	170	100	70	50	30	20
27/I, Joyous News	560	420	—	—	—	—
28/II, Wayside Devotion	760	420	290	230	190	160
29, Guardian Angel	1570	1190	870	—	—	—
30/0 A &B, Ba-Bee Rings	530	330	180	140	120	90
31, Silent Night With Black Child	5490	—	—	—	—	—
32/0, Little Gabriel	320	180	110	90	—	—
33, Joyful	330	190	150	100	80	70
34, Singing Lesson	400	170	160	100	100	90
35/0, Good Shepherd	150	90	40	30	30	20
36/0, Angel With Flowers	160	90	50	40	30	20
37, Herald Angels	600	280	170	150	100	90
I/38/0, Joyous News With Lute	130	100	70	30	—	—
I/39/0, Joyous News With Accordion	120	90	50	40	—	—
I/40/0, Joyous News With Trumpet	150	90	40	40	—	—
42/0, Good Shepherd	280	250	140	90	—	—
43, March Winds	270	170	90	80	70	60
44A, Culprits	510	390	360	260	210	190
44B, Out of Danger	520	420	340	260	230	190
45/0, Madonna With Halo	200	130	90	70	50	40
46/0, Madonna Without Halo	240	140	100	80	50	50
47/3/0, Goose Girl	310	200	140	90	70	60
48/0, Madonna Plaque	340	150	70	50	70	50
49/3/0, To Market	320	240	150	110	100	70
50/2/0, Volunteers	500	420	180	140	110	100
51/3/0, Village Boy	160	100	190	70	60	40
52/0, Going to Grandma's	490	380	260	130	110	100

	CM	FB	SB	3-L	V-G	G
53, Joyful	$ 260	$ 170	$ 90	$ 70	$ 70	$ 50
III/53, Joyful	300	180	90	70	60	40
54, Silent Night	490	270	240	140	110	90
55, Saint George	840	420	270	170	200	140
56A, Culprits	540	290	170	130	120	90
56B, Out of Danger	540	280	190	140	120	100
57/0, Chick Girl	270	170	120	90	80	60
III/57, Chick Girl	420	420	140	130	100	90
58/0, Playmates	270	190	150	90	80	70
III/58, Playmates	510	450	140	—	100	90
59, Skier	350	270	130	150	120	90
60A & B, Farm Boy and Goose Girl	830	580	420	350	270	230
61A & B, Playmates and Chick Girl	970	650	500	400	300	220
62, Happy Pastime	370	250	200	140	100	90
63, Singing Lesson	270	140	110	80	70	60
III/63, Singing Lesson	470	410	340	110	110	110
64, Shepherd's Boy	400	350	190	140	100	100
66, Farm Boy	350	210	140	90	80	70
67, Doll Mother	470	430	200	180	120	90
68, Lost Sheep	290	230	230	100	—	—
69, Happy Pastime	350	270	140	110	100	70
III/69, Happy Pastime	500	370	340	150	150	90
70, The Holy Child	320	210	130	90	80	70
71, Stormy Weather	750	640	440	340	300	190
72, Spring Cheer	320	200	120	90	70	60
73, Little Helper	300	150	100	80	80	60
74, Little Gardener	310	120	100	70	50	50
75, White Angel	140	90	50	30	30	20
78/0, Infant of Krumbad	210	210	150	—	—	—
79, Globe Trotter	500	390	140	100	100	80
80, Little Scholar	330	220	140	110	80	70
81/2/0, School Girl	270	160	120	80	70	70
82/2/0, School Boy	260	180	110	100	80	50
83, Angel Serenade With Lamb	490	360	360	190	100	100
84/0, Worship	350	250	150	90	80	70
85/0, Serenade	220	150	100	80	60	50
86, Happiness	230	160	110	80	70	70
87, For Father	370	250	150	80	100	90
88/I, Heavenly Protection	460	340	320	240	190	150
89/I, Little Cellist	350	330	140	130	90	90
91/ A & B, Angels at Prayer	230	210	160	60	50	50
92, Merry Wanderer Plaque	350	230	170	120	100	90
93, Little Fiddler Plaque	—	190	170	100	80	70
94/3/0, Surprise	200	190	110	90	80	80
95, Brother	300	220	160	90	90	70
96, Little Shopper	240	140	90	80	70	50
97, Trumpet Boy	230	140	120	90	70	50
98/2/0, Sister	160	100	80	80	60	60
99, Eventide	440	360	200	130	140	130
100, Shrine	5250	4920	—	—	—	—
101, To Market	4800	—	—	—	—	—

	CM	FB	SB	3-L	V-G	G
102, Volunteers	$ 4930	—	—	—	—	—
105, Adoration With Bird	4200	—	—	—	—	—
106, Merry Wanderer Plaque	6700	—	—	—	—	—
107, Little Fiddler Plaque	6700	—	—	—	—	—
109/0, Happy Traveler	230	$ 160	$ 100	$ 80	$ 70	$ 70
110/0, Let's Sing	210	140	100	60	60	50
III/110, Let's Sing (candy box)	510	450	370	150	110	90
111/3/0, Wayside Harmony	260	180	140	90	60	380
II/111, Wayside Harmony (lamp)	—	2630	—	—	—	—
112/3/0, Just Resting	300	170	130	80	70	70
II/112, Just Resting (lamp)	—	3440	—	—	—	—
113, Heavenly Song	3610	2540	2140	—	2500	—
114, Let's Sing	950	970	170	130	80	70
115, Girl With Nosegay	160	90	70	40	30	30
116, Girl With Fir Tree	130	80	80	50	40	30
117, Boy With Horse	120	70	50	30	30	30
118, Little Thrifty	460	330	170	100	90	70
119, Postman	370	230	150	120	90	80
123, Max and Moritz	380	280	130	100	90	70
124/0, Hello	280	240	140	100	80	80
125, Vacation Time	510	330	220	160	120	90
126, Retreat to Safety	450	290	210	150	120	90
127, Doctor	250	180	130	90	80	70
128, Baker	330	170	90	80	80	70
129, Band Leader	340	270	130	130	100	100
130, Duet	440	290	160	120	110	100

Left: Doctor, #127. —Photo courtesy of Jim Glaab's Collector's Showcase. Right: Brother #95.

	CM	FB	SB	3-L	V-G	G
131, Street Singer	$ 290	$ 190	$ 130	$ 90	$ 80	$ 60
132, Star Gazer	350	250	130	120	110	100
133, Mother's Helper	380	210	130	120	110	80
134, Quartet	640	430	250	210	170	140
135, Soloist	220	150	100	80	60	60
136/I, Friends	490	250	140	130	100	90
137, Child in Bed	550	270	130	60	40	30
139, Flitting Butterfly	390	290	170	130	40	40
140, Mail is Here	—	390	250	180	140	140
141/3/0, Apple Tree Girl	290	140	90	80	70	60
142/3/0, Apple Tree Boy	170	140	100	90	50	40
143/0, Boots	350	220	140	110	80	70
144, Angelic Song	320	200	110	90	80	80
145, Little Guardian	200	120	80	90	80	70
146, Angel Duet	160	90	50	40	30	30
147, Devotion	100	40	40	30	30	20
150/2/0, Happy Days	290	180	130	120	100	100
2/I, Little Fiddler (Brown Hat)	670	580	300	300	180	190
2/II, Little Fiddler (Brown Hat)	1700	1480	980	850	800	660
2/III, Little Fiddler (Brown Hat)	2630	1960	1460	880	820	590
2/4/0, Little Fiddler (Brown Hat)	—	—	—	—	—	40
3/II, Bookworm	1450	1230	1180	940	790	640
3/III, Bookworm	2720	2200	1000	950	780	750
6/I, Sensitive Hunter	980	590	220	160	100	90
6/II, Sensitive Hunter	1460	770	420	340	300	190
7/I, Merry Wanderer	990	760	740	260	190	170
7/II, Merry Wanderer	1830	1500	1300	850	670	630
7/III, Merry Wanderer	2620	2100	1150	900	750	680
7/X, Merry Wanderer	—	—	—	—	12,000	12,000
9, Begging his Share, w/ candle holder	—	360	270	120	—	—
10/I, Flower Madonna, brown	770	780	270	180	—	—
10/I, Flower Madonna, blue	370	240	160	130	110	100
10/III, Flower Madonna, white	460	210	200	150	160	160
10/III, Flower Madonna, brown	2860	1910	420	310	—	—
10/III, Flower Madonna, blue	630	400	260	280	250	270
11/0, Merry Wanderer	490	250	200	190	90	70
11/2/0, Merry Wanderer, large	350	200	160	100	90	80
11/0, Merry Wanderer, large	570	240	140	100	80	70
12/I, Chimney Sweep	370	270	130	110	70	70
13/0, Meditation	290	240	190	120	80	100
13/II, Meditation	3110	2620	2140	—	250	190
13/2, Meditation	1990	2000	1780	—	160	160
13/V, Meditation	—	2560	1730	1220	770	680
13/5, Meditation	—	3480	4000	3900	430	420
14A &B-III, Bookworm Bookends	2000	2250	2180	2340	—	—
15/I, Hear Ye, Hear Ye	520	300	200	150	120	90
15/II, Hear Ye, Hear Ye	1000	650	440	310	230	170
16/I, Little Hiker	380	260	150	120	100	80
17/2, Congratulations	6620	—	—	—	—	—
18, Christ Child, white	420	380	290	250	—	—
21/0 1/2, Heavenly Angel	350	250	160	100	90	70

	CM	FB	SB	3-L	V-G	G
21/I, Heavenly Angel	$ 420	$ 300	$ 280	$ 150	$ 100	$ 90
21/II, Heavenly Angel	1140	840	410	320	190	200
22/I, Angel With Birds	500	290	230	—	—	—
23/II, Adoration	—	2100	—	—	—	—
23/III, Adoration	1000	920	750	300	240	160
24/III, Lullaby	1630	1290	560	—	360	250
26/I, Child Jesus	540	330	260	—	—	—
27/III, Joyous News	2210	1830	1000	—	270	100
28/2, Wayside Devotion	470	430	360	250	200	—
28/III, Wayside Devotion	840	660	470	400	260	210
29/0, Guardian Angel	1640	1280	1000	—	—	—
29/I, Guardian Angel	2000	1790	1180	—	—	—
32/I, Little Gabriel	1610	1270	1100	920	—	—
32, Little Gabriel	—	—	—	—	70	60
35/I, Good Shepherd	630	280	140	—	—	—
36/I, Angel With Flowers	360	300	180	90	—	—
III/38/0, Joyous News With Lute	160	100	70	50	40	30
III/38/I, Joyous News With Lute	340	260	160	120	—	—
III/39/0, Joyous News w/ Accordion	120	110	50	40	40	20
III/39/I, Joyous News w/ Accordion	240	210	150	100	—	—
III/40/0, Joyous News w/ Trumpet	120	100	60	50	30	30
III/40/I, Joyous News w/ Trumpet	280	190	160	60	—	—
42/I, Good Shepherd	4800	3400	3000	—	—	—
42, Good Shepherd	—	—	—	—	90	70
45/0/W, Madonna With Halo	60	100	70	60	40	30
45/I, Madonna With Halo	140	110	90	60	40	30
45/1/W, Madonna With Halo	260	180	110	80	80	30
45/III, Madonna With Halo	520	390	150	140	130	90
45/III/W, Madonna With Halo	260	150	120	80	80	80
46/0/W, Madonna Without Halo	60	130	100	90	50	50
46/I, Madonna Without Halo	270	190	120	100	60	60
46/1/W, Madonna Without Halo	160	120	90	70	40	30
46/III, Madonna Without Halo	430	360	260	210	150	100
46/III/W, Madonna Without Halo	300	180	110	100	90	70
47/0, Goose Girl	470	390	170	120	100	90
47/II, Goose Girl	1000	640	400	300	240	220
48/0/W, Madonna Plaque	170	80	—	—	—	—
48/II, Madonna Plaque	680	340	190	130	100	100
48/II/W, Madonna Plaque	1620	1340	—	—	—	—
48/V, Madonna Plaque	1640	1400	960	—	—	—
48/V/W, Madonna Plaque	2000	1200	—	—	—	—
49/0, To Market	480	280	190	150	130	110
49/I, To Market	1460	1100	630	540	—	—
49, To Market	—	—	—	—	290	250
50/0, Volunteers	780	500	310	190	200	140
50, Volunteers	1300	900	—	—	—	—
50/I, Volunteers	1100	830	500	360	240	230
51/2/0, Village Boy	150	160	100	70	60	60
51/0, Village Boy	400	300	190	150	100	100
51/I, Village Boy	760	410	290	—	140	120
52/I, Going to Grandma's	1200	850	680	—	510	230

	CM	FB	SB	3-L	V-G	G
52, Going to Grandma's	$ 1400	—	—	—	—	—
57/I, Chick Girl	470	$ 290	$ 180	$140	$ 110	$ 110
58/I, Playmates	500	290	200	150	110	80
65, Farewell	360	220	130	100	80	90
65/I, Farewell	370	280	150	120	110	—
68., Lost Sheep	540	350	240	250	—	—
68/2/0, Lost Sheep	190	130	110	80	60	60
68/0, Lost Sheep	220	170	160	110	90	80
70, The Holy Child (over 7")	330	260	—	—	—	—
78/I, Infant of Krumbad	210	160	40	30	30	20
78/II, Infant of Krumbad	250	220	40	40	30	30
78/III, Infant of Krumbad	320	190	60	40	40	30
78/V, Infant of Krumbad	490	440	160	120	100	60
78/VI, Infant of Krumbad	750	460	260	190	190	130
78/VIII, Infant of Krumbad	970	750	390	350	280	230
81/0, School Girl	350	180	150	90	80	70
81, School Girl	350	280	—	—	—	—
82/0, School Boy	350	250	160	110	90	90
82/II, School Boy	900	830	400	—	260	190
84/V, Worship	2800	1750	880	870	710	590
85/II, Serenade	910	650	260	220	230	180
88/II, Heavenly Protection	830	750	470	260	240	230
89/II, Little Cellist	940	550	310	290	220	200
94/I, Surprise	460	300	190	120	120	90
94, Surprise	470	270	190	—	—	—
98/0, Sister	180	130	140	90	80	80
98, Sister	340	230	180	—	—	—
109/II, Happy Traveler	520	600	340	290	240	210
109, Happy Traveler	980	710	—	—	—	—
110/I, Let's Sing	210	230	110	100	80	70
110, Let's Sing	380	250	—	—	—	—
111/I, Wayside Harmony	290	190	130	80	80	60
111, Wayside Harmony	440	280	200	140	—	—
112/I, Just Resting	420	250	190	130	100	80
112, Just Resting	520	350	270	140	—	—
124/I, Hello	1000	560	350	—	100	70
136/V, Friends	2000	1720	860	630	570	290
136, Friends	2300	—	—	—	—	—
137/B, Child in Bed	530	350	130	60	—	—
141/I, Apple Tree Girl	440	270	190	130	120	90
141/V, Apple Tree Girl	610	560	420	—	—	—
141/X, Apple Tree Girl	—	—	—	—	13,500	12,000
142/I, Apple Tree Boy	80	440	400	300	70	100
142/V, Apple Tree Boy	—	—	—	610	580	530
142/X, Apple Tree Boy	—	—	—	—	12,000	1330
143/I, Boots	540	360	230	170	150	120
143, Boots	750	490	300	200	—	—
145, Little Guardian, blue flowers	300	170	80	—	—	—
150/0, Happy Days	430	360	190	—	150	130
150/I, Happy Days	120	1000	790	—	530	250
150, Happy Days	260	1170				

Iroquois China

The Iroquois China Company produced hotel ware from 1905 until 1969. The company is best known to collectors today for its Russell Wright and Ben Seibel lines.

	LOW	AVG.	HIGH

Casual China (1946)

Russell Wright designed Casual China. Of the many colors produced, Aqua and Brick Red and Cantaloupe are the most sought. Add a premium for these pieces.

	LOW	AVG.	HIGH
Bowl	$ 30	$ 33	$ 36
Carafe	80	100	120
Casserole, 2-4 qt.	40	55	70
Casserole, 3 qt.-6 qt.	70	85	100
Chop Plate, 14"	32	36	40
Coffee Pot	55	60	65
Cream/Sugar	28	34	41
Cup/Saucer	9	13	16
Cup/Saucer, Art Deco	60	64	68
Dish, 5"-7"	8	9	10
Dutch Oven	85	100	115
Frying Pan, w/ lid	60	70	80
Gravy, w/ lid, old	29	37	45
Mug	60	70	80
Party Plate	30	35	40
Pitcher	78	77	76
Plate, 6"-8"	6	8	10
Plate, 9"-10"	9	11	13
Platter, 12"-14"	18	24	30
Salad Bowl, 10"	26	30	34
Sauce Pan, w/ lid	60	65	75
Shaker, stacking	11	13	15
Soup Plate, 8.5"	21	23	25
Teapot	45	58	72
Vegetable, 8"-10"	22	29	36
Vegetable, div., w/ lid	50	54	58

Casual backstamp.

	LOW	AVG.	HIGH

Impromptu

Impromptu was designed by Ben Seibel.

	LOW	AVG.	HIGH
Butter Dish	$ 17	$ 20	$ 23
Casserole, w/ lid	22	25	28
Coffee Pot	29	31	33
Compote	18	20	22
Cream/Sugar	14	16	18
Cup/Saucer	6	9	12
Gravy Boat	14	16	18
Plate, 6"-8"	2	4	6
Plate, 9"-10"	4	5	6
Platter, 12"-15"	6	9	11
Relish Tray	6	7	8
Salt/Pepper	14	16	18
Soup Plate	7	8	9
Vegetable	9	12	15

Left: Impromptu backstamp. Right Informal backstamp.

Informal

Informal was designed by Ben Seibel.

	LOW	AVG.	HIGH
Butter Dish	$ 18	$ 21	$ 24
Casserole, 2 qt.	23	26	29
Coffee Pot, 9 cup	48	54	60
Cream/Sugar	13	16	19
Cup/Saucer	5	6	7
Dish, 5"-6"	1	2	3
Dutch Oven, w/ lid	23	26	29
Frying Pan, w/ lid	23	26	29
Gravy Boat	14	16	18
Plate, 6"-8"	2	4	6
Plate, 9"-10"	4	5	6
Platter, 12"-15"	7	9	11
Salt/Pepper	14	16	18
Samovar, w/ stand	36	42	48
Sauce Pan, w/ lid	22	26	30
Soup Plate	7	8	9
Soup, w/ lid	13	15	17
Vegetable	9	12	15

James River Pottery

Originally the Hopewell China Co., the James River Potteries' best known designer was Simon Slobodkin. He designed the following pieces. They are part of the Cascade (1935) pattern. Pieces are usually unmarked. Some have an impressed or stamped *JR*..

James River backstamp.

	LOW	AVG.	HIGH
Cream/Sugar	$ 18	$ 22	$ 24
Cup/Saucer	6	8	10
Dish, 6"	1	2	3
Pickle Dish, 11"	6	7	8
Plate, 6"-7"	1	2	3
Plate, 9"-10"	6	7	8
Platter, 12"-14"	8	9	10
Relish Tray	8	10	12
Teapot	20	25	30
Vegetable, rd., 8.5"	14	15	16

Josef Originals

Muriel Joseph George of Arcadia, CA designed Josef Originals Figurines from 1946-82. (The spelling was a printing error on the labels that time did not allow them to correct). In 1982 she sold the company to her long-time partner and representative George Good, but she continued designing figures through 1985. These pieces were produced in California through 1960, when production was moved to Japan. Examples below are from the 1940s through the 1980s. In this time period the girls were all made with black eyes and a glossy finish, the animals with a semigloss finish. Figures are now produced by Applause who purchased the firm in 1985.

Prices are for figurines in perfect condition with no damage. All original figurines are marked on the bottom, either incised or ink-stamped "Josef Originals c" and have a Josef oval sticker with either the California or Japan designation. Beware of copies, which have only a Josef label. Our consultants for this area are Jim and Kaye Whitaker co-authors of *Josef Originals*, and owners of Eclectic Antiques (they are listed in the back of this book).

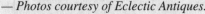

Above left to right: September, "Doll of the Month" series, green dress, ht. 3.5"; Adeline, "Gibson Girl" series, green dress, ht. 6.5". Bottom left to right: Ostrich babies, each, ht. .5", Ostriches large, ht. 5"; Elephant, flower on head, ht. 4.5".
— Photos courtesy of Eclectic Antiques.

LOW HIGH

Josef Originals of California 1946-52

	LOW	HIGH
Autumn Leaf, Asian girl, white dress, black fan up, ht. 4.5"	$ 40	$ 50
Cherry Blossom, Asian girl, white dress, black fan down, ht. 4.5"	40	50
Cho Cho, tall Asian girl, white w/ pink fan up, ht. 10.75"	85	95
Hedy, girl in pink dress w/ hat holding gift, ht. 4.25"	40	50
Little TV Cowboy, large hat, rope in hands, ht. 5.25"	60	70
Mama, blue dress sitting w/ book, ht. 7.25"	70	80
May, "Dolls of the Month," green w/ green jewels, ht. 3.25"	25	35
Pitty Sing (the first Chinese boy), large hat	42	48
Sakura, tall Oriental girl, white dress, w/ pink fan down, ht. 10.75"	85	95
Saturday, "Days of the Week" series, yellow w/ pie, ht. 4"	30	40
Teddy, boy in gray suit holding flowers, ht. 4.25"	40	50
The Prince, boy sitting w/ thumb in mouth, ht. 3.75"	45	55
Wee Ching, Chinese boy w/ dog	35	45
Wee Ling, Chinese girl w/ kitten	35	45

Josef Originals of Japan, 1960-85

	LOW	HIGH
Adeline, "Gibson Girl" series, green dress w/ guitar, ht. 6.5"	$ 80	$ 100
Africa, "Little Internationals," white dress, pink feather, ht. 3.5"	25	35
America, Indian Girl, "Little Internationals," brown dress, feather, ht. 3.5"	25	35
Antonio, barefoot man in brown pants w/ flower basket, ht. 6"	65	75
August, "Birthstone Dolls" series, green dress, green jewel, ht. 3"	16	22
Baby w/ kitten, blue, pink or yellow, each, ht. 3"	28	32
Birthday Girls #1, angel w/ wings, blue dress	22	28
Birthday Girls #14, angel w/ wings, pink dress	25	35
Blue Bird, girl in yellow dress w/ bird on hand, ht. 9"	80	100
Christmas Girl, red dress w/ green front, cape, ht. 6"	25	35
Christmas Girl, white dress w/ pink trim, basket, ht. 6"	25	35
Debby, "First Love" series, pink dress w/ hat, ht. 5"	22	28
"Gigi" series, pink dress, w/ hat, and puppy, ht. 6"	80	100
Happiness Is, boy in bed, puppy	22	28
High Heels, "Sweet 16" series, green dress, ht. 7.5"	80	100
"Housekeepers" series, green dress w/ teapot, ht. 3"	22	28
January, "Doll of the Month" series, rose dress w/ hat, ht. 3.5"	22	28
Jeanne, "Colonial Days" series, lavender dress, ht. 9.5"	80	100
Jill, "Nursery Rhymes," green dress, w/ bucket, ht. 4"	22	28
Lara's Theme Music Box, couple, green suit and rose dress	65	75
Love Rendezvous, girl w/ light blue dress and hat, ht. 9"	80	100
Mary Holding Jesus, white gown, ht. 5"	25	35
Mighty Like a Rose, girl in white dress, pink flower hat, ht. 4"	22	28
New Hat, "A Mother's World" series, blue & yellow dress, hat, ht. 7.5"	80	100
October, "Birthstone Dolls" series, blue dress w/ pink jewel, ht. 3"	16	22
Robin, "Musicale" series, in blue dress w/ harp, ht. 6"	55	65
Russia, "Little Internationals" series, rose dress, white hat, ht. 3.5"	25	35
School Belle, yellow dress w/ apple, ht. 3"	22	28
September, "Doll of the Month" series, green dress, hat, ht. 3.5"	22	28
Shepherd, ht. 3"	22	28
Sweden, "Little Internationals," gray & white dress w/ flowers, ht. 3.5"	25	35
Tammy, "Musicale" series, in pink dress w/ piano, ht. 6"	55	65
The Bridal March Music Box, couple in tuxedo and bridal gown	65	75
The Engagement, "Romance" series, in blue dress w/ ring, ht. 8"	80	100

Animals

	LOW	HIGH
Bees, various poses, each	$ 14	$ 18
Elephant, flower on head, ht. 4.5"	35	45
Frogs, various poses, each	10	14
German Shepherd Dog, ht. 3"	18	22
Hippo, ht. 2.5"	20	25
Mice, various poses and costumes, each	14	18
Monkeys, various poses and costumes, each	14	18
Ostrich Babies, each, ht. .5"	20	25
Ostrich Mama, ht. 5"	40	50
Rabbits, various poses, each	10	14
Siamese Cat, ht. 2"	14	18

Edwin M. Knowles China

Edwin M. Knowles, son of the founder of Knowles, Taylor, Knowles, manufactured his own semiporcelain from 1901 until 1963. There are many different backstamps.

Knowles backstamp.

	LOW	AVG.	HIGH
Deanna (1938)			
Bowl, 36s	$ 7	$ 8	$ 9
Butter, open	15	20	25
Casserole	27	31	34
Chop Dish	14	16	18
Coaster	14	16	18
Cream/Sugar	21	24	27
Cup/Saucer	9	13	16
Dish, 4"-5"	2	3	4
Egg Cup, double	9	11	13
Gravy Boat	14	16	18
Pickle Dish	5	7	9
Plate, 6"-8"	4	6	7
Plate, 9"-10"	7	8	9
Platter, 8"-12"	8	13	18
Salt/Pepper	21	24	27
Soup, coupe	7	8	9
Teapot	27	31	34
Vegetable, 7"-10"	13	15	17
Esquire (1956)			
Esquire was designed by Russel Wright.			
Compote	$ 58	$ 61	$ 64
Cream/Sugar	42	44	46
Cup/Saucer	15	19	22
Dish, 5"-7"	12	14	16
Gravy Boat	36	39	42
Pitcher, 2 qt.	84	94	104
Plate, 6"-7"	9	12	14
Plate, 9"-10"	15	16	17
Platter, 9"-14"	26	31	36
Salt/Pepper	25	32	39
Server, 22"	45	50	55
Teapot	100	110	120
Vegetable	46	58	69

	LOW	AVG.	HIGH

Yorktown (1936)

Yorktown has an Art Deco appearance.

	LOW	AVG.	HIGH
Bowl, 36s	$ 8	$ 9	$ 10
Bowl, coupe, 6"	4	5	6
Butter, open	21	23	25
Candleholder, pr.	24	27	29
Casserole	30	36	41
Chop Plate	12	15	17
Coaster	10	13	16
Cream/Sugar	24	28	32
Cup/Saucer	10	15	20
Custard Cup	4	5	6
Dish, 6"	2	3	4
Gravy Boat	14	16	18
Pickle Dish	6	7	8
Plate, 6"-8"	4	6	8
Plate, 9"-10"	8	9	10
Platter, 8"-12"	11	18	25
Salt/Pepper	24	28	32
Soup Plate	8	9	10
Teapot	40	45	50

Homer Laughlin China

Founded in 1874 as the Laughlin Brothers Pottery, it became the Homer Laughlin China Co. in 1896. Homer's brother, Shakespeare, withdrew in 1877. Homer Laughlin mainly produced semiporcelain. In 1959, vitreous dinnerware and institutional ware lines were introduced. The company is one of the largest still manufacturing today.

Homer Laughlin is most famous for its Fiesta dinnerware (listed separately under Fiesta). The company is also well known because of its dinnerware designed by Frederick Rhead, head designer from 1928 to 1942, and Don Schreckengost, head designer from 1945 to 1960. Laughlin used a variety of backstamps.

HOMER LAUGHLIN

Early Homer Laughlin backstamps.

	LOW	AVG.	HIGH
Americana (1949-56)			
Chop Plate, 13"	$ 18	$ 20	$ 22
Cream/Sugar	30	35	40
Cup/Saucer	12	18	23
Dish, 5"	5	6	7
Egg Cup	22	26	29
Gravy Boat	24	27	29
Pickle Dish	12	13	13
Plate, 6"-7"	4	7	10
Plate, 9"-10"	9	12	15
Plate, sq., 8"	9	14	19
Platter, 11"-13"	13	19	25
Platter, 15"	29	32	35
Soup Plate, 9"	24	25	26
Teapot	40	50	60
Vegetable, 8"-9"	22	34	46
Century (1931)			
Century is an early square shape in dinnerware.			
Butter Dish	$ 75	$ 85	$ 95
Casserole	34	40	46
Cream/Sugar	18	22	26
Cup/Saucer	12	14	16
Dish, 5"	6	7	8
Dish, 6"	12	14	16
Gravy Boat	15	20	25
Pickle Dish	16	17	18
Pitcher, Batter	80	100	120
Pitcher, Syrup	80	88	96
Plate, 6"-7"	6	8	10
Plate, 9"-10"	15	20	25
Platter, 11"-15"	16	23	29

	LOW	AVG.	HIGH
Soup Bowl/Saucer	$ 50	$ 60	$ 70
Soup Plate, 8"	12	14	16
Teapot	75	85	95
Vegetable, 9"	20	22	24

Epicure backstamp.

Epicure

Epicure was designed by Don Schreckengost and glazed in solid colors.

	LOW	AVG.	HIGH
Casserole	$ 42	$ 46	$ 50
Coffee Pot	95	110	125
Cream/Sugar	25	30	34
Cup/Saucer	15	17	19
Dish	12	15	18
Gravy Boat	21	23	24
Plate, 6"-8"	8	10	12
Plate, 9"-10"	12	15	18
Salt/Pepper	20	23	26
Soup Plate	11	14	16

Harlequin (1938)

Similar to Fiesta, it has bright colors, simple shapes and a series of rings, but not on the rim. Pieces were unmarked.

	LOW	AVG.	HIGH
Bowl, 36s	$ 17	$ 20	$ 23
Butter, .5 lb	50	75	100
Candlestick, pr.	80	110	140
Casserole	51	63	75
Cream/Sugar	18	25	31
Cup/Saucer	7	10	13
Cup/Saucer, jumbo	49	58	67
Dish, 5.5"	4	7	10
Dish, 6.5"	16	19	22
Egg cup	9	12	14
Gravy Boat	11	14	17
Jug, 22 oz.	18	22	26
Jug, Ball form	32	38	44
Marmalade	90	105	120
Plate, 10"	17	21	25
Plate, 6"-7"	3	6	9
Plate, 9"	7	9	11
Platter, 10"-13"	17	22	26
Relish Tray, 4-part	160	190	220
Shaker	6	8	10
Soup Plate	11	13	15
Syrup pitcher	160	190	220
Teapot	52	64	75
Tumbler	24	28	32
Vegetable, 9"	13	18	23

	LOW	AVG.	HIGH

Rhythm

Rhythm was designed by Don Schreckengost.

	LOW	AVG.	HIGH
Cream/Sugar	$ 25	$ 29	$ 33
Cup/Saucer	10	14	18
Dish, 5"-6"	4	5	6
Gravy Boat	16	18	20
Pickle Dish, 9"	8	9	10
Pitcher, 2 qt.	50	60	70
Plate, 6"-8"	4	6	8
Plate, 9"-10"	8	9	10
Platter, oval, 11"-15"	15	20	24
Salt/Pepper	12	15	18
Soup Plate, 8"	8	9	10
Spoon rest	130	165	200
Teapot	43	48	53
Vegetable, 9"	17	19	20
Vegetable, w/ lid	30	34	38

Riviera

Riviera was based on the Century design.

	LOW	AVG.	HIGH
Butter Dish	$ 150	$ 165	$ 180
Casserole	135	145	155
Cream/Sugar	34	42	50
Cup/Saucer	25	28	31
Dish, 5"	12	14	16
Dish, 6"	37	44	52
Gravy Boat	31	40	48
Pickle Dish	30	34	38
Pitcher, Batter	145	182	220
Pitcher, Syrup	130	155	180
Plate, 6"-7"	12	16	20
Plate, 9"-10"	30	40	50
Platter, 11"-15"	31	46	62
Soup Plate, 8"	24	28	31
Teapot	150	175	200
Vegetable, 9"	40	45	50

Swing (1938)

Swing has delicate round handles and finials.

	LOW	AVG.	HIGH
Butter Dish	$ 19	$ 22	$ 25
Casserole	31	34	38
Coffee Pot	30	34	38
Cream/Sugar	28	32	36
Cup/Saucer	8	10	12
Egg Cup	10	13	15
Muffin Cover	29	36	42
Plate, 6"-8"	4	5	6
Plate, 9"-10"	8	9	10
Platter, 11"-13"	10	11	12
Salt/Pepper	14	16	18
Soup Bowl/Saucer	25	30	35

	LOW	AVG.	HIGH

Tango

Tango is rare and widely sought.

	LOW	AVG.	HIGH
Casserole	$ 35	$ 45	$ 55
Cream/Sugar	35	45	55
Cup/Saucer	10	13	15
Dish, 6"	6	8	10
Egg Cup	35	45	55
Plate, 6"-7"	6	8	10
Plate, 9"-10"	10	13	15
Platter, 11.5"	16	18	20
Salt/Pepper	17	22	27
Soup Plate	17	19	21
Vegetable, 8"-9"	19	21	23

Wells backstamp.

Wells (1930)

Wells was designed by Frederick Rhead, It has a thin rim and open handles.

	LOW	AVG.	HIGH
Bowl, 36s	$ 11	$ 13	$ 15
Casserole	44	52	60
Coffee Pot	45	53	61
Covered Toast	44	52	60
Cream/Sugar	35	40	46
Cup/Saucer	12	15	18
Dish, 5"	3	5	6
Egg Cup	14	18	22
Gravy Boat	22	25	28
Pickle Dish	9	12	14
Pitcher	58	64	70
Plate, 6"-8"	6	9	11
Plate, 9"-10"	12	14	15
Plate, sq.	11	13	14
Platter, 11"-15"	14	22	30
Soup Bowl/Saucer	39	44	50
Soup Plate	22	26	30
Teapot	52	57	62
Vegetable, rd., 8"-9"	14	16	18

	LOW	AVG.	HIGH

World's Fair/Expositions

	LOW	AVG.	HIGH
Four Seasons Plate	$ 55	$ 60	$ 65
George Washington pitcher, 2"	31	38	44
George Washington pitcher, 5"	52	54	57
Golden Gate Plate	80	86	92
Martha Washington pitcher, 2"	45	51	57
Martha Washington pitcher, 5"	65	70	75
New York World's Fair Plate	120	135	150
Potter's Plate	28	36	44
Vase, 6"-10"	85	90	95
Zodiac Cup/Saucer	85	90	95

Yellowstone

Yellowstone is octagonal.

	LOW	AVG.	HIGH
Bowl, 36s	$ 8	$ 9	$ 10
Butter Dish	20	22	24
Casserole	29	32	34
Cream/Sugar	25	29	33
Cup/Saucer	10	15	20
Dish, 5"-6"	2	3	4
Gravy Boat	17	19	21
Pitcher 1 pt.	12	14	15
Plate, 6"-7"	4	5	6
Plate, 9"-10"	8	9	10
Platter, 9"-12"	11	12	13
Soup Plate, 8.5"	10	12	14
Teapot	30	36	42
Vegetable, 9"-10"	17	19	21

Limoges China

The Sterling China Company changed its name to Limoges early in this century. After WWII, legal action brought by Limoges of France forced the name change to American Limoges. Production halted in 1955. Viktor Schreckengost designed some American Limoges. Limoges is not the same quality dinnerware as the French company of the same name. Don't pay French Limoges prices for American Limoges pieces.

Limoges backstamps.

	LOW	AVG.	HIGH
Casino (c. 1954)			

Casino has the shape of playing card suits, with matching decal decoration.

	LOW	AVG.	HIGH
Cream/Sugar, diamond	$ 20	$ 30	$ 40
Cup, club	10	14	18
Dish, diamond	6	7	8
Plate, spade	9	13	16
Platter, diamond	18	22	24
Saucer, heart	4	5	6

Square

Square has rounded corners and an arrow-head finial.

	LOW	AVG.	HIGH
Butter Dish	$ 15	$ 18	$ 21
Casserole	14	17	20
Cream/Sugar	12	14	16
Cup/Saucer	4	5	6
Gravy Boat	8	10	12
Plate, 6"-7"	2	3	4
Plate, 9"	4	5	6
Teapot	20	22	24

	LOW	AVG.	HIGH
Triumph (1937)			

Viktor Schreckengost designed Triumph with horizontal fluting.

	LOW	AVG.	HIGH
Casserole	$ 20	$ 23	$ 26
Chop Plate, 11"-13"	12	16	20
Coffee Pot	40	45	50
Cream/Sugar	13	15	17
Cup/Saucer	4	5	6
Dish, 5"-6"	1	2	3
Gravy Boat	8	9	10
Plate, 10"-11"	4	5	6
Plate, 6"-7"	1	2	3
Platter, oval, 11"-15"	10	14	18
Salt/Pepper	8	10	12
Soup Plate, 8.25"	10	11	12
Vegetable, rd.,8.75"	15	17	20

Marblehead Pottery

Marblehead Pottery started as a therapeutic resource for invalids. In 1916, it was bought by artist Arthur Baggs. It ceased production in 1936. The wares were heavy and dark. Later, Baggs introduced a cream-colored ware with multicolored decoration and a line of children's pieces.

Backstamps include a sailing ship with a *M* and *P* on opposite sides and a monogram of Arthur E. Baggs.

Marblehead impressed mark.

	LOW	AVG.	HIGH
Bowl, 6", dark blue glaze	$ 35	$ 60	$ 85
Candlesticks, 3", blue glaze, pr.	90	120	150
Pitcher, 4.5", dark blue glaze	50	80	110
Planter, turquoise glaze, artist signed, 1934	300	350	400
Tile, 6.5" x 6.5", brown and yellow glaze, floral motif	200	250	300
Vase, 3.5", bulbous shape, gray matte w/ blue flecks	80	90	100
Vase, 6", black glaze	500	625	750
Vase, 6.5", green glaze	40	65	90
Vase, 7", cylinder shape, tree motif, gray and green glaze, signed	350	450	550
Vase, 7", dark blue glaze	50	80	110
Wall Pocket, blue glaze	50	80	110

Metlox Pottery

Metlox Potteries makes art ware, novelties, and Poppytrail dinnerware. Although solid color wares may date to 1927, decorated wares date from the 1940s through the present.

	LOW	AVG.	HIGH
California Ivy			
Butter Dish	$ 50	$ 55	$ 60
Chop Plate, 13"	30	35	40
Coaster	12	15	18
Coffee Pot	100	120	140
Cream/Sugar	30	35	40
Cup/Saucer	14	18	21
Dish, 5"-7"	11	17	22
Gravy Boat	35	38	41
Mug	22	25	28
Pitcher, 2.5 qt.	50	60	70
Plate, 10"	21	25	28
Plate, 6"-8"	14	17	20
Platter, oval, 9"-13"	33	46	58
Salad Bowl, 11"	34	38	42
Salt/Pepper	14	21	28
Soup Bowl, 5"	8	10	12
Soup Plate, 7"	17	19	21
Teapot	100	125	150
Tumbler, 13 oz.	40	45	50
Vegetable, 9"-11"	40	45	50

Homestead Provincial

Homestead Provincial has American folk art themes using the šame shapes as Rooster.

	LOW	AVG.	HIGH
Bread Server, rect., 9.5"	$ 50	$ 60	$ 70
Butter Dish, rect.	50	55	60
Canister Set, 4-piece	225	250	275
Casserole, hen lid, 1 qt.	57	64	71
Chop-Plate, 12.25"	30	35	40
Coaster, 3.75"	11	14	17
Coffee Pot, 7 cup	100	112	125
Cookie Jar	70	85	100
Cream/Sugar	30	35	40
Cruet	50	55	60
Cruet set, 2-5 piece	100	125	150
Cup/Saucer	16	22	28
Dish, 5"-6"	8	10	12
Egg Cup	23	25	27
Gravy Boat	32	38	43
Lazy Susan, 7-piece	90	115	140
Mug, 8 oz.	16	19	21
Pitcher, 1 qt.-2 qt.	50	60	70
Plate, 10"	23	26	28
Plate, 6"-8"	12	16	20

	LOW	AVG.	HIGH
Platter, oval, 11"-16"	$ 40	$ 55	$ 70
Salad, 11"	34	38	42
Salt/Pepper	14	22	30
Shakers, hen/rooster	45	48	52
Soup Plate, 8"	16	20	23
Tankard, 1 pt.	45	50	55
Teapot	110	125	140
Tumbler, ftd, 11 oz.	110	125	140
Vegetable, 7"-12"	29	39	49
Vegetable, w/lid, 1 qt.	57	62	67

Red Rooster

Red Rooster is a toleware-influenced design; note the "rivets" on the hollowware pieces.

	LOW	AVG.	HIGH
Bread Server, rect., 9.5"	$ 70	$ 80	$ 90
Butter, rect.	60	65	70
Canister Set, 4-piece	200	250	300
Casserole, hen lid, 1.25 qt.	65	75	85
Casserole, ind., hen lid	110	120	130
Chop Plate, 12"	29	32	36
Coaster, 3.75"	14	17	20
Coffee Pot	110	130	150
Cookie Jar	150	170	180
Cream/Sugar	36	43	50
Cruet set, 2-5 piece	100	150	200
Cup/Saucer	21	27	32
Dish, 6"	18	22	25
Egg Cup	29	32	36
Gravy Boat	42	47	52
Jewelry Box	130	145	160
Lazy Susan set, 7-piece	450	500	550
Marmalade	130	150	170
Mug, 8 oz.	28	31	34
Pitcher, 1.5 pt.-2.25 qt.	50	70	90
Plate, 6"-8"	11	18	25
Platter, oval, 9"-16"	40	60	80
Salad, 11.5"	40	47	54
Salt Box	170	185	200
Salt/Pepper	17	26	35
Salt/Pepper Mill	150	160	170
Shakers, hen and rooster	50	60	70
Soup, ind., 5"	11	13	15
Soup Plate, 8"	22	26	30
Tankard, 1 pt.	50	60	70
Teapot	135	155	175
Tumbler, ftd., 11 oz.	140	160	180
Tureen	500	750	1000
Vegetable	40	60	80
Watering Can	70	80	90

Morton Pottery

Morton Pottery expanded into novelties in the late 1930s and continued producing until 1971. Its best-known marks are *Morton* and *USA* incised.

The following entries are from the Woodland pattern, which has a brown and green splatter on yelloware.

	LOW	AVG.	HIGH
Baker, Pie, 9"	$ 80	$ 100	$ 120
Casserole	60	75	90
Coffee Server, 8-cup	70	85	100
Custard Cup	16	21	25
Grease Jar, 3"-4"	30	40	50
Mixing Bowl, 4"-8"	45	60	75
Pitcher	50	70	90
Salt/Pepper	75	100	125
Teapot, 3-9 cup	60	75	90
Vase, bulbous, 11"	100	125	150

Newcomb Pottery

The Newcomb College Art Department in New Orleans began producing pottery for sale in 1896. Newcomb wares carry underglaze designs, picturing subjects from nature.

There are usually five marks on each piece: the mark of Newcomb (a white-on-black vase with the initials *N.C.*, or merely the *N* within the *C*, or *NEWCOMB COLLEGE* spelled out), a potter's mark, an artist's or decorator's mark, a recipe mark, and a registration mark.

       Newcomb impressed mark.

	LOW	AVG.	HIGH
Bowl, 5", painted flowers, applied roses and leaves	$ 130	$ 160	$ 190
Candlesticks, 7.5", pr., trumpet form, matte glaze, c. 1925	450	525	600
Trivet, floral motif, signed	260	310	360
Vase, 4", green, lavender, and rose, high-gloss finish	300	350	400
Vase, 5", polychrome flowers, & leaves, blue ground, signed	700	800	900
Vase, 5", floral motif, bulbous body, matte glaze, signed, 1910	550	600	650
Vase, 5", ovoid, foliate motif, matte glaze, signed, c. 1910	800	900	1000
Vase, 6", moon shining in trees motif, blue ground, signed	1900	2100	2300
Vase, 6", white floral motif, blue background, signed	1000	1100	1200
Vase, 8", floral motif, signed	600	700	800
Vase, 8", beige glaze, dogwood motif, signed, c. 1910	800	1000	1200

Niloak Pottery

Niloak Pottery is old classic redware, influenced by Greek, Roman, and Native American design, but with a striking marbleized texture. Potters threw Niloak ware on a wheel. Many pieces have only an inside glaze. The word "niloak" is kaolin (the chief ingredient in porcelain) spelled backwards. Niloak pottery is completely unlike porcelain. Most successful during the 1920s, the firm survived until 1946.

The pottery had an impressed mark or a circular paper label, reading simple *NILOAK POTTERY*. Paper labels became standard in later years.

ⓃⒾⓁⓄⒶⓀ   *Niloak incised or impressed mark.*

	LOW	AVG.	HIGH
Hywood (1930s)			
Ewer, 10", semi-matte glaze, molded eagle on side	$ 40	$ 70	$ 90
Pitcher, miniature	15	25	40
Vase, matte white glaze, 12"	150	200	230
Vase, 6", applied handles, matte glaze	40	70	95
Vase, 7.5", matte rose glaze	50	80	100
Vase, 8", two handled, scalloped rim, rose to blue glaze	60	90	130
Mission Ware (early 1900s)			
Bowl, 10", earth tone swirls	$ 75	$ 100	$ 130
Matchholder, swirls	40	65	85
Vase, 3.5", swirls	35	60	80
Vase, 4", dark blue, cream and blue swirls	40	68	90
Vase, 4.5", tan and blue swirls	50	75	100
Vase, 5", brown, blue and cream swirls	40	55	80
Vase, 5.5", blue and brown swirls	42	65	85
Vase, 6.5,. blue and white swirls	50	80	110
Vase, 6", bulbous body, flared rim, swirls	63	85	110
Vase, 6", swirls	42	65	85
Vase, 6.5", tan, ivory and blue swirls	70	95	115
Vase, 9", swirls	115	145	175
Vase, 10", swirls	165	200	235

George Ohr Pottery

George Ohr, of Biloxi, Mississippi, designed and manufactured all pieces himself. Ohr pottery is free hand-work, like doodles in clay, all produced between the early 1880s and 1906. Ohr's markings have no set pattern. Most are marked G.E. OHR, BILOXI.

	LOW	AVG.	HIGH
Ashtray, 2.5", brown, w/ shaped rim.	$ 300	$ 375	$ 450
Ashtray, 2.5", brown-green, caved-in sides, high gloss glaze.	800	1000	1200
Bowl, 3.5", beige, squat form w/ cylindrical sides flaring into wide base, crimped lip, ornaments along base rim.	180	220	260
Bowl, 3.5", green and mud-brown, squat design.	320	400	485
Bowl, 4", green, flecked w/ dark brown, circular.	400	500	600
Bowl, 7", shades of brown, V-form, severely crimped sides.	430	525	650
Ink stand, 6.5", artist's palette form, thumbhole and brush.	445	520	650
Pitcher, 5", green mottling, fish form, w/ tail handle.	800	1000	1200
Teapot, 4", brown and green splatter glaze, ovoid bulbous form w/ thumbprint designing, braided handle, disc-type lid.	1000	1200	1400
Vase, 10", blue, cylindrical form widening slightly at bottom.	700	800	900
Vase, 3.5", brown, bulbous form w/ pinched and dented sides.	250	325	400
Vase, 3.5", brown smear glaze, bulbous form, crimped neck.	550	700	850
Vase, 5.5", burnt orange and green glaze, cologne-bottle form, dome-shaped bowl, pinched, funnel-type neck and mouth.	250	325	400
Vase, 5.5", burnt orange and olive glaze, hurricane lamp form w/ bulbous body, wide mouth, applied caterpillar.	700	850	1000

Paden City Pottery

The Paden City Company manufactured semiporcelain dinnerware from 1914 through 1963. It exhibited at the 1938-39 World's Fair. The Caliente line is the favorite of collectors.

BAK-SERV
GUARANTEED
OVEN-PROOF
P. C. P. Co.

Caliente
MADE IN U.S.A.

Paden City backstamps.

	LOW	AVG.	HIGH

Bak-Serve (1931)

Bak-Serve was manufactured exclusively for the Great Northern Products Company of Chicago. The design sported solid Caliente colors and decals.

	LOW	AVG.	HIGH
Carafe	$ 15	$ 20	$ 25
Casserole	15	20	25
Pitcher, ball form	12	16	22
Teapot, Rose Marie	15	20	25

Blue Willow (1937)

Paden City etched its version of the Blue Willow design into the body of seven different items. They glazed it in blue, allowing the design to remain visible.

	LOW	AVG.	HIGH
Bowl, salad	$ 15	$ 17	$ 19
Cup/Saucer	9	13	16
Dish, 5"-6"	3	4	5
Plate, 7"	3	4	5
Plate, 9"	8	9	10
Platter	13	14	15

Caliente

The Caliente line, identified by bright colors on the Elite/Shellcrest shape, was introduced in 1936.

	LOW	AVG.	HIGH
Casserole	$ 22	$ 27	$ 31
Cream/Sugar	19	21	23
Cup/Saucer	6	8	10
Dish, 5"-6"	2	3	4
Gravy Boat	11	13	15
Plate, 6"-7"	3	4	5
Plate, 9"-11"	6	7	8
Platter, oval, 12"-16"	9	12	15
Salt/Pepper	18	21	23
Soup Plate	6	7	8
Teapot	44	48	52
Vegetable, 9"-10"	12	14	16

Pfaltzgraff Pottery

The Pfaltzgraff Pottery Company is the oldest family-owned pottery in continuous operation in America, dating to the early 19th century. The company has operated under the Pfaltzgraff name since 1896. It produced art pottery during the 1930s when it began manufacturing the kitchenware still made today. An embossed or stamped Keystone or Castle mark are most common.

The following entries are from the Country-Time pattern. Ben Seibel designed this pattern to be made in white or solid colors. Sunburst and a fruit and leaf motif appeared on lighter pieces.

  Pfaltzgraff backstamps.

	LOW	AVG.	HIGH
Butter Warmer	$ 35	$ 45	$ 55
Casserole, 2 qt.	40	45	50
Casserole, ind., 12 oz.	20	25	30
Casserole, w/ 2-3 lids	100	120	140
Coffee Pot, 10-cup	45	50	65
Cream/Sugar	26	31	35
Cruet	20	25	30
Cup/Saucer	10	13	16
Gravy Boat	30	35	40
Pitcher, 2 qt	30	35	40
Plate, 8"-11"	10	14	18
Platter, 11"-13"	18	24	30
Relish Tray, 16"	30	35	40
Salad Bowl, 10.5"	20	25	30
Salad Bowl, ind., 6"	12	14	15
Salt/Pepper	23	26	29
Samovar, 28-cup	80	90	100
Tureen, 6 qt	65	75	85

Planters

Are planters the final frontier in figural ceramic collecting? Planter collectors think so, but something new is always being discovered. Collectors boast that planters are the perfect size; they demand less shelf space than cookie jars and display better than the smaller salt and pepper shakers. Shawnee, McCoy, and other firms that produced cookie jars and salt and pepper shakers made many planters. So far, planters don't enjoy the widespread collecting base of cookie jars and salt and pepper shakers. Perhaps people are deterred by the clumps of dirt and flora that cling to many planters. Beneath all that is often a sparkling gem. Be cautious however; cracks, chips, and dull finishes are also found under the grime.

We listed style numbers of the various pieces and the manufacturer when known, and "Japan" under company name for items so identified. Shawnee often marked pieces with "USA," sometimes with a style number.

This attribution is not foolproof because other firms also used the "USA" mark. Many planters had a paper label or are unmarked, so do your homework. We recommend *The Official Price Guide to Pottery and Porcelain*, Harvey Duke, House of Collectibles, Random House, NY, 1995; *Shawnee Pottery*, Jim and Bev Mangus, Collector Books, Paducah, KY, 1995; *McCoy Pottery*, Sharon and Bob Huxford, Collector Books, Paducah, KY, 1991; and *Royal Haeger*, Lee Garmon and Doris Frizzell, Collector Books, Paducah, KY, 1989.

Above left to right: Pot and saucer, button tufted, McCoy, $9-$14; lamb cart, $15-$20; covered wagon, small, Shawnee, $18-$24.

Below left to right: Frog and lilly pad, $9-$12; doe and fawn, McCoy, $32-$38; baby carriage and Lady, blue, Royal Haeger, $28-$34.

	LOW	HIGH
Angel Fish, ht. 3.5", Japan	$ 8	$ 10
Baby Carriage and Lady, blue, ht. 7.5", Royal Haeger	28	34
Bambi, ht. 5.5"	40	60
Basket, bird on handle, Camark	28	32
Basket, Green Leaf, Red Berry, ht. 9", McCoy	30	40
Bed, canopy style, 734, len. 8", Shawnee	70	90
Beetle, w/ metal feet, ht. 3"	15	20
Bird and Flower, raised base, ht. 4"	15	20
Bird in Flight, w/ flowers, ht. 5"	8	10
Bird on Basket, w/ flowers, ht. 6", Shawnee	9	13
Bird on C-shaped Bamboo, ht. 5.25"	7	9
Bird on Log, on metal stand, ht. 7"	22	28
Birds on Double Branches, ht. 5.25"	8	10
Boot, "tooled" design, ht. 6.5", Shawnee	10	15
Bow w/ gold highlights, wall pocket, 534, ht. 3.5", Shawnee	20	25
Bowling Boy, blue, ht. 6", Royal Haeger	25	35
Boy at Stump, 533, Shawnee	8	12
Bulldog & Drum, ht. 3"	18	24
Burro, 673, ht. 4.5", Abingdon	28	32
Burro, blue, ht. 5"	6	8
Burro, Sleeping Man in Sombrero , ht. 5.75"	30	40
Caboose, 553, Shawnee	30	40
Calypso Band, 3 piece, ht. 7.5", Napco	60	90
Cat Playing Sax, 729, Shawnee	30	50
Cat, black, painted eyes, len. 15"	30	40
Chick, w/ cart, 720, Shawnee	15	20
Chick, w/ egg, 730, ht. 3.5", Shawnee	15	20
Chinese Figures Carrying Basket, 537, Shawnee	12	18
Chinese Girl, ht. 7", Royal Copley	25	35
Chinese Man w/ basket & umbrella, 617, ht. 4.5", Shawnee	15	20
Circus Wagon, Shawnee	28	34
Coach, ht. 4.5", Germany	8	10
Coolie & Rickshaw, len. 5", Shawnee	7	9
Covered Wagon, small, 617, ht. 3.5", Shawnee	18	24
Doe and Fawn, ht. 7", McCoy	32	38
Dog Cart, ht. 5", McCoy	25	30
Dog in Cup Wall Pocket, ht. 5"	12	15
Donkey, w/ basket, 722, ht. 5.5", Shawnee	12	15
Donkey, 669, ht. 7.5", Abingdon	35	45
Double Dog Profile, ht. 5"	15	20
Duck and Logs, ht. 3", Occupied Japan	12	15
Dutch Boy and Girl, ht. 6.5"	20	30
Dutch Boy at Wall, ht. 5.5"	12	14
Dutch Girl & Oxcart, ht. 3.5", Japan	12	18
Dutch Shoe, len. 5", Abingdon	30	50
Elephant, Shawnee	20	25
Elephant, small, 759, Shawnee	8	10
Elephant and Leaf, 501, Shawnee	50	70
Fawn, 645, ht. 6.5", Morton	10	15
Fawn, 672, ht. 5", Abingdon	20	30
Fish, Black Bass, ht. 4.5"	20	30

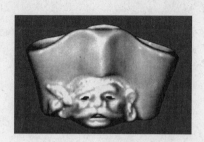

Left: Pirate, Brush, $25-$35.

Above: Calypso band, Napco, $60-$90.

Right: Flamingo and foliage, $30-$40.

	LOW	HIGH
Fish, green & yellow, wall pocket, ht. 8"	$ 30	$ 50
Fish in Swirling Waves, green, ht. 7.5"	18	24
Flamenco Dancers, ht. 9"	30	40
Flamingo & Foliage, ht. 9.5"	30	40
Frog & Lilly Pad, ht. 3.75"	9	12
Gazelle, large, len. 17", Royal Haeger	80	120
Girl and Basket, 534, Shawnee	10	15
Girl in Wide Brim Hat, wall pocket, ht. 5", Royal Copley	18	22
Gondolier, 657, len. 19.5", Royal Haeger	30	50
Horse, large, rearing, ht. 9.5"	25	35
Horses, racing, 883, len. 11", Royal Haeger	30	50
Jalopy, len. 7", Relpro	7	9
Jardiniere, diamond design, len. 7", McCoy	8	12
Jardiniere, green rocky rectangle, ht. 5.75", McCoy	7	9
Jardiniere, green shingled sides, ht. 5.5"	12	15
Jardiniere, oblong, molded berry and leaf, len. 8", McCoy	12	18
Jardiniere, rectangular, pine cone feet, len. 8", McCoy	18	22
Lady, w/ Donkey Cart, ht. 5.5", Japan	15	20
Lamb Cart, ht. 4.5"	15	20
Leopard, 760, Royal Haeger	25	35
Lovebirds on Pine Cone, ht. 4"	20	30
Madonna in Blue, ht. 4.5", Royal Windsor	15	20
Madonna, white, large, 650, ht. 9", Royal Haeger	25	35
Mexican Boy, ht. 5.5", Royal Copley	30	40
Panther, maroon, rocky base, len. 9"	20	25
Pelican on Bamboo Log, len. 9", Japan	60	80
Penguin & Igloo, yellow, ht. 3.25"	8	10
Pheasant, black, gold highlights, len. 17"	20	30
Piano, 528, Shawnee	20	30
Pirate, ht. 3.5", Brush	25	35
Pixie, winged, 536, ht. 4", Shawnee	7	10
Plaid Cat, ht. 5.25", Japan	6	8
Poodle, w/ green square, ht. 7"	15	20
Poodle, yellow, whimsical, ht. 5"	10	14
Pot and Saucer, button-tufted design, ht. 3.5", McCoy	9	14
Rabbit w/ Cabbage, ht. 5"	9	12
Rooster, 501, Camark	18	22
Sad Dog, ht. 4.5"	7	9
Santa & Chimney, ht. 7", Morton	20	25
Shoe & Pup, Shawnee	9	12
Swan, black, ht. 5.5"	8	12
Swan, blue w/ gold floral decoration, ht. 6"	15	20
Three Pigs, Shawnee	8	10
Top Hat, star spangled , ht. 3", Shawnee	7	9
Tragedy & Comedy Mask. on rect., ht. 3.5", McCullogh	10	12
Train Box Car, 552, Shawnee	20	30
Train Engine, 550, Shawnee	50	60
Train Set, 550, 551, 552 , 553, Shawnee	120	180
Train Tender, 551 , Shawnee	25	35
Turkey, ht. 5", Morton	10	15
Turtle, green, len. 7", McCoy	30	40

Left: Pelican on bamboo log, Japan, $60-$80.

Right: Turtle planter, green, McCoy, $30-$40; turtle sprinkler, green , McCoy, $35-$45.

Above: Bowling boy, blue, Royal Haeger, $25-$35; bird on c-shaped bamboo, $7-$9; duck and logs, Occupied Japan, $12-$15.

	LOW	HIGH
Turtle, green sprinkler, len. 9", McCoy	$ 35	$ 45
Violin, len. 17", Royal Haeger	25	35
Wagon Wheel & Cow Skull, ht. 8", McCoy	30	40
Wheelbarrow & Watering Can, ht. 3"	12	15
Wishing Well, ht. 6.5", McCoy	25	35
Wishing Well, Dutch Kids, ht. 5.5", Shawnee	25	35
Wishing Well, green, w/ red painted roof, ht. 8.5"	20	30

Collector's Plates

Collector plates began in 1895 with the Bing and Grondahl Christmas plate. Despite much publicity about increasing values, selling a collection of plates may realize only pennies on the dollar. As with all collectibles, buy what you love because you love it, not as an investment.

The following entries are listed by company name, with collection titles indented under each entry.

Royal Doulton, Kristina and Child, designed by Edna Hibel, 1975, one of 15,000, $30.

	LOW	AVG.	HIGH
Count Agazzi			
Children's Hour Series (animals)1970-73	$ 11	$ 12	$ 13
Easter Series, 1971-73	11	12	13
Famous Personalities Series, 1968-73	8	11	15
Allison and Company			
Late to Party, 1982-83	30	35	40
American Artists			
Horses of Fred Stone Series, 1982-85	65	87	110
Zoe's Cat Series, 1985	25	27	30
American Commemorative			
Southern Landmark Series, 1973-80	45	67	90
American Crystal			
Christmas Series and Mother's Day Series, 1970-73	15	20	25
American Express			
Birds of North America Series, 1978	38	39	40
Four Freedoms Series, 1976	35	36	38
Roger Tory Peterson (bird series), 1981-82	55	57	60
American Heritage			
Celebrity Clown Series, 1982	50	52	55
Craftsman Heritage, 1983	40	41	42
American Rose Society			
American Rose Series, 1975-85	50	95	140
Anna-Perenna			
American Silhouettes Collection, 1981-84	75	77	80
Children of Mother Earth Series (Seasons), 1983	240	245	250
Flowers of Count Bernadotte, 1982-84	75	85	95
Rhythm and Dance Series, 1983	30	31	32

	LOW	AVG.	HIGH
Romantic Love Series, 1979-82	$ 90	$ 95	$ 100
Anri			
Christmas Series, 1971-84	100	150	200
Christmas Series, 1973, Alpine Horn	375	400	425
Ferrandiz Wooden Birthday Series, 1973-74	10	15	20
Mother's Day Series, 1972-76	50	57	65
Antique Trader			
All series	9	11	13
Arabia of Finland			
Christmas Series, 1978-82	50	72	95
Kalevala Series, 1977-85	40	65	90
Kalevala Series, 1976	230	235	240
Arizona Artisan			
All series	15	17	20
Armstrong's/Crown Parian			
American Folk Heroes, 1983-85	35	37	40
Beautiful Cats Series of the World, 1979-82	60	70	80
Butterflies of the World Series, 1978	60	61	62
Oriental Bird Series, 1975-76	400	400	400
All other bird series	50	65	80
Sporting Dog Series, 1980-82	56	56	56
Brantwood Collection			
All series	30	40	50
Braymer Hall			
All series	25	37	50
Briant, Paul and Sons			
All series	80	100	120
Brindle Fine Arts			
Lenore Beran Special Series, 1980	125	127	130
All other series	60	67	75
Bydgo			
Christmas Series, 1969-72	10	10	10
California Porcelain Incorporated			
All series	30	50	70
Canadian Collector Plates			
Children of the Classics, 1982-83	78	78	78
Discover Canada Series, 1979 (Sawmill)	300	350	400
Discover Canada Series, 1980-84	125	137	150
Capo di Monte			
Christmas Series, 1972-76	60	75	90
Mother's Day Series, 1973-76	68	68	68
Carmel Collection			
All series	30	37	45
Carson Mint			
American Has Heart Series, 1980	130	135	140
American Has Heart Series, 1981-83	30	35	40
Old-Fashioned Mother's Day Series, 1979-82	40	60	80
All other series	30	40	50
Castleton China			
All series	35	50	65

	LOW	AVG.	HIGH
Chilmark			
All series	$ 70	$ 80	$ 90
Christian Bell Porcelain			
Age of Steam Series, 1981	250	260	270
Age of Steam Series, 1982-83	90	95	100
Last Spike Centennial, 1986	140	145	150
All other series	45	55	65
Christian Fantasy Collectibles			
All series	50	50	50
Continental Mint			
All series	62	62	62
Crown Delft			
All series	15	22	30
Curator Collection			
Gift Edition, 1982-87	37	37	38
Magical Moments Series, 1981-83	30	45	60
Masterpieces of Impressionism Series, 1980-82	35	42	50
Masterpieces of the West Series, 1980-82	35	50	65
Portraits of American Brides Series, 1987	29	29	30
D'Arceau Limoges			
Cambier Four Seasons Series, 1978-80	100	110	120
Christmas Series, 1975-82	30	37	45
Les Femmes Du Siecle, 1976-79	25	35	45
Lafayette Legacy Series, 1973-75	15	20	25
Les Sites Parisiens de Louis Dali Series, 1979-83	25	27	30
Daum			
Art Nouveau Series, 1979-81	125	150	175
Famous Musicians Series, 1971-72	75	75	75
Four Seasons Series, 1970	150	150	150
David Kaplan Studios			
Fiddler's People Series, 1978-81	60	60	60
Dresden			
Christmas Series, 1971-77	30	40	50
Duncan Royale			
History of Santa Claus, 1985-86	40	40	40
Enesco			
Christmas Collection, 1981-84	40	50	60
Precious Moments Collections, 1980-82	30	30	30
All other series	50	70	90
R.J. Ernst Enterprises			
All series	20	30	40
Escalera Production Art			
Olympiad Triumphs Collection, 1984	60	60	60
Evergreen Press			
Catalina Island Series, 1986-87	39	39	40
Fairmont China			
Famous Clown Series, 1976	500	500	500
Famous Clown Series, 1977-79	75	75	75
Israeli Commemorative Series, 1978	80	85	90
Memory Annual Series, 1977-80	80	85	90
All other series	30	40	50

	LOW	AVG.	HIGH
The Fleetwood Collection			
All series	$ 40	$ 55	$ 70
Franklin Mint			
American Revolution Series, 1976-77	80	80	80
Arabian Nights Series, 1981-82	30	30	30
Audubon Society Series, 1972-73	100	110	120
Bernard Buffet Series, 1973-77	250	262	275
Bicentennial Series, 1973-76	200	205	210
Birds and Flowers of Beautiful Cafe Series, 1981-83	40	40	40
Birds and Flowers of the Orient Series, 1979-80	60	60	60
Butterflies of the World Series, 1977-79	250	262	275
Clipper Ships Series, 1982-83	55	57	60
Country Year Series, 1980-82	55	57	60
Currier and Ives Series, 1977-79	40	45	50
Days of the Week Series, 1979-80	40	42	45
Fairy Tales in Miniature Series, 1979-84	15	17	20
Flowers of the American Wilderness Series, 1978-80	40	42	45
Flowers of the Year Series, 1976-78	50	50	50
Game Birds of the World Series, 1978-80	55	55	55
Grimm's Fairy Tale Series, 1978-79	42	43	45
Hans Christian Andersen Series, 1976-77	50	60	70
International Gallery of Flowers Series, 1980-81	55	57	60
James Wyeth Series, 1972-76	130	155	180
Mark Twain Series, 1977-78	40	45	50
Poor Richard's Series, 1979-81	14	16	18
Robert's Zodiac Series, 1973-80	150	160	170
Norman Rockwell Series, 1970-79	150	175	200
Seven Seas Series, 1976-82	120	120	120
Songbirds of the World Series, 1977-81	55	55	55
Songbirds of the World Miniatures, 1980-83	15	16	18
Woodland Birds of the World, 1980-82	65	67	70
World's Great Porcelain Houses Series, 1981-83	20	22	25
Frankoma Pottery			
Christmas Series, 1965-67	100	150	200
Christmas Series, 1968-87	20	30	40
Teenagers of the Bible, 1973-82	20	25	30
Furstenberg			
Deluxe Christmas Series, 1971-73	45	55	65
All other series	20	30	40
Ghent Collection			
American Bicentennial Wildlife Series, 1976	200	250	300
Christmas Wildlife Series, 1974-78	30	40	50
Mother's Day Series (animals),1975-79	35	37	40
Goebel Collection			
American Heritage Series, 1979-81	100	115	130
Hummel Annual Series, 1971	500	600	700
Hummel Annual Series, 1972-88	80	100	120
Mother's Series (animals), 1975-80	40	57	75
Winged Fantasies Series, 1982-84	50	50	50
Gorham Collection			
Boy Scout Plates Series (Norman Rockwell),1975-80	40	50	60
Charles Russell Series (western), 1981-83	40	45	50

	LOW	AVG.	HIGH
Christmas Series (Norman Rockwell), 1974-87	$ 30	$ 40	$ 50
Cowboy Series, 1980	35	37	40
Moppets (all series), 1973-83	15	17	20
Remington Western Series, 1973-76	30	35	40
Grande Copenhagen			
Christmas Series, 1975-82	30	45	60
Christmas Series, 1983 (Little Mermaid)	100	125	150
Greentree Potteries			
All series	10	17	25
Dave Grossman Designs			
Norman Rockwell (all series)	40	60	80
All other series	30	40	50
Hackett American			
All series	30	45	60
Hamilton Collection			
America at Work (Normal Rockwell), 1984	30	30	30
Children of the American Frontier, 1986-87	25	25	25
Chinese Symbols of the Universe, 1984	90	90	90
Country Garden Calendar (Bing and Grondahl), 1984	55	57	60
Fairy Tales of Old Japan, 1984	40	40	40
Flower Festivals of Japan Series, 1985	50	52	55
Gardens of the Orient Series, 1983	20	20	20
Greatest Show on Earth Series, 1981-82	30	40	50
The Little Rascals, 1985	25	25	25
Majestic Birds of Prey, 1983-84	60	62	65
Noble Owls of America, 1986-87	45	45	45
The Story of Heidi Series, 1981-82	45	47	50
Summer Days of Childhood, 1983	30	30	30
Tale of Genji Series, 1985	45	45	45
Haviland			
Bicentennial Series, 1972-76	40	45	50
Christmas Series, 1970	80	100	120
Christmas Series, 1971-81	40	50	60
French Collection Mother's Day Series, 1973-80	30	40	50
Historical Series (great Americans), 1968-71	70	75	80
1001 Arabian Nights Series, 1979-82	27	50	60
Visit from Saint Nicholas Series, 1980-85	55	60	65
Haviland and Parlon			
Christmas Madonnas Series, 1972-79	50	75	100
Tapestry Series, 1971-82	50	75	100
Heinrich Porzellan			
Flower Fairies Series, 1979-85	30	40	50
Russian Fairy Tale Series, 1980-83	70	95	120
Heirloom Traditions			
All series	35	45	55
Hibel Studios			
Production Series of 500 or less	1000	2000	3000
Production Series of 2000-5000	200	300	400
Production Series 15,000 and over	50	75	100
Historic Providence Mint			
Alice in Wonderland Series, 1986	28	30	32

	LOW	AVG.	HIGH
America the Beautiful Series, 1981	$ 37	$ 38	$ 39
Lil' Peddlers Series, 1986	30	30	30
Vanishing Barn Series, 1983	40	40	40
Hornsea			
Christmas Series, 1979-81	40	45	50
House of Global Art			
American Heritage Series, 1979-81	100	112	125
Dolly Dingle Series, 1982-83	30	30	30
Hoyle Products			
All series	30	45	60
Hudson Pewter			
All series	35	40	45
Hutschenreuther			
Country Birds of the Year, 1983-86	30	30	30
Nibelungen Series, 1986	125	125	125
Enchantment Series (princesses), 1979-82	60	75	90
Glory of Christmas Series, 1982-85	80	90	100
Gunther Granget Series, 1972-78	80	100	120
Gunther Granget Series, 1976 (Freedom in Flight-Gold) .	200	200	200
Hans Achtziger Series, 1979-85	150	200	250
Legend of St. George, 1985	100	100	100
Love for All Seasons Series, 1981-83	125	125	125
Songbirds of North America Series, 1981	60	60	60
Waterbabies Series, 1983-84	45	45	45
Zodiac Series, 1978	125	130	135
Imperial			
America the Beautiful Series, 1969-75	20	21	22
Christmas Series, 1970-81	20	27	35
Incolay Studios			
Great Romances of History Series, 1979-82	65	67	70
Romantic Poets Series, 1977-85	70	80	90
Voyage of Ulysses Series, 1984-86	50	55	60
Christmas Series, 1974-79	75	87	100
International Museum			
Letter Writer's Series, 1982-84	38	39	40
Stamp Art Series, 1979-83	40	60	80
Georg Jensen			
Christmas Series, 1972-76	25	37	50
Svend Jensen			
Christmas/Andersen Fairy Tales Series, 1970-84	40	50	60
Mother's Day Series, 1970-84	30	45	60
Josair			
Bicentennial Series, 1972-76	250	250	250
Kaiser			
Anniversary Series, 1972-83	25	32	40
Christmas Series, 1970-82	20	30	40
Fairy Tale Series, 1982-84	40	45	50
Famous Lullabies, 1985-88	40	45	50
Feathered Friends Series, 1978-81	80	90	100
Happy Days Series, 1981-83	75	75	75
Mother's Day Series, 1971-83	30	45	60

	LOW	AVG.	HIGH
People of the Midnight Sun Series, 1978-83	$ 70	$ 80	$ 90
Traditional Fairy Tales Series, 1983-85	40	40	40
Woodland Creatures, 1985	37	38	40
Yesteday's World Series, 1978-84	70	75	80
Kera			
Christmas Series, 1967-71	15	20	25
Kern Collectibles			
Adventures of the Old West Series, 1981-85	65	70	75
Children's World Series, 1983-84	45	45	45
Companions Series, 1978-81	60	70	80
Leaders of Tomorrow Series, 1980-83	50	50	50
Mother's Day Series, 1976-80	40	45	50
Sugar and Spice Series, 1976-80	80	100	120
This Little Pig Went to Market, 1982-85	40	42	45
King's			
Christmas Series, 1973-76	150	200	250
Flower Series, 1973-77	120	150	180
Edwin Knowles			
American Holidays Series, 1976-84	25	30	35
Annie Series, 1983-86	25	30	35
Biblical Mothers Series, 1983-86	50	65	80
Birds of Your Garden Series, 1985-87	20	25	30
Gone With the Wind Series, 1978-79	150	200	250
Gone With the Wind Series, 1980-85	50	65	80
Frances Hook Legacy Series, 1985-87	20	22	25
Oklahoma Series, 1985-87	20	20	20
Sound of Music Series, 1986-87	20	21	23
Wizard of Oz Series, 1977-80	30	45	60
Konigszelt			
Grimm's Fairy Tales, 1981-87	25	30	35
Hedi Keller Christmas Series, 1979-86	35	40	45
Koscherak Brothers			
All series	50	55	60
KPM			
Christmas Series, 1969-73	200	300	400
Christmas Series, 1974-77	100	150	200
Christmas Series, 1978-80	50	62	75
Lalique			
Annual Series, 1965-76	80	100	120
Lenox			
American Wildlife Series, 1983	65	65	65
Boehm Bird Series, 1970	100	150	200
Boehm Bird Series, 1971-81	50	70	90
Boehm Woodland Wildlife Series, 1973-82	60	80	100
Butterflies and Flowers Series, 1982-85	60	67	75
Christmas Tree Series, 1976-82	50	65	80
Nature's Nursery Series, 1982-86	65	72	80
Lihs Linder			
America the Beautiful, 1975	42	43	45
Christmas Series, 1972-78	30	40	50
Easter Series, 1973-75	30	37	45

	LOW	AVG.	HIGH
Limoges-Turgot			
Durand's Children's Series, 1978-80	$ 35	$ 37	$ 40
Morals of Perrault Series, 1983-85	30	32	35
Lladro			
Christmas Series, 1971-79	40	60	80
Mother's Day Series, 1971-79	40	60	80
Longton Crown Pottery			
Canterbury Tales Series, 1981-82	30	32	35
Jean-Paul Loup			
Christmas Series, 1971-76	500	650	800
Lund and Clausen			
All series	12	15	18
Lynell			
All series	40	50	60
Marmot			
Christmas Series, 1970-76	20	30	40
Mother's Day Series, 1973 (Polar Bear)	100	125	150
Mother's Day Series, 1972-76	25	32	40
President's Series, 1972-73	25	27	30
Mason			
Christmas Series, 1975-80	75	75	75
Meissen			
Annual Series, 1973-80	80	100	120
Metal Arts Company			
All series	25	37	50
Mettlach			
Christmas Series, 1978-80	150	175	200
Michelon			
All series	75	75	75
Mingolla			
Christmas Series (enamel and copper), 1973-77	120	150	180
Four Seasons Series, 1978	150	150	150
Modern Concepts Limited			
All series	25	37	50
Modern Masters			
All series	30	42	55
Moser			
Christmas Series, 1970-83	80	100	120
Moussalli			
Birds of Four Seasons, 1977-79	375	412	450
Newell Pottery Company			
Calendar Series, 1984-86	20	25	30
Noritake			
Annual Series, 1977-80	400	500	600
Christmas Series, 1975-80	50	87	125
Nostalgia Collectibles			
Elvis Presley Collection, 1985	15	15	15
James Dean Collection, 1985	15	15	15
Shirley Temple Collection, 1983-86	35	35	35
Shirley Temple Collectibles (autographed), 1982-83	100	125	150

	LOW	AVG.	HIGH
O.K. Collectibles			
All series	$ 40	$ 55	$ 70
Opa's Haus			
Annual German Christmas, 1978-84	55	57	60
Pacific Art Limited			
· All series	30	45	60
Palisander			
All series	50	57	65
Parkhurt Enterprises			
International Wildlife Foundation Series, 1984	60	60	60
Pemberton and Oakes			
Childhood Friendship Series, 1987-88	20	22	25
Children at Christmas Series, 1981-86	60	70	80
Moments Alone Series, 1980-83	30	37	45
Wonder of Childhood Series, 1982-87	20	35	50
Pickard			
Annual Christmas Plate Series, 1976-81	60	75	90
Children of Mary Cassatt Series, 1983-84	60	60	60
Children of Renoir Series, 1978-80	70	90	110
Legends of Camelot Series, 1982	60	62	65
Let's Pretend Series, 1984-85	80	80	80
Lockhart Wildlife Series, 1970-80	150	200	250
Lockhart Wildlife Series, 1974 (American bald eagle)	600	750	900
Beautiful Women Series, 1981-84	75	75	75
Symphony of Roses Series, 1982-85	90	95	100
Pollerat			
Calendar Series, 1972-73	100	125	150
Christmas Series, 1972-73	350	375	400
Poole Pottery			
Medieval Calendar Series, 1972-77	100	112	125
Porcelaine Ariel			
The Rubaiyat of Omar Khayyam, 1980-82	45	47	50
Greatest Show on Earth Series, 1981-82	30	45	60
Waltzes of Johann Strauss Series, 1981-82	25	27	30
Porcelana Granada			
Christmas Series, 1971-82	15	20	25
Porsgrund			
Christmas Series, 1968	80	100	120
Christmas Series, 1969-83	20	30	40
Easter Series, 1972-77	15	20	25
Father's Day Series, 1971-80	15	20	25
Mother's Day Series, 1970-84	15	20	25
Traditional Norwegian Christmas Series, 1978-82	30	37	45
Ram			
Boston 500 Series (holidays), 1973	30	35	40
Rare Bird			
All series	45	47	50
Raynaud (Limoges)			
All series	40	45	50
Reco International			
Childhood Almanac Series, 1985	30	35	40
Becky's Day Series, 1985-86	25	30	35

Above: Reco International. The high limitation number (25,000) will considerably diminish chances of an increase in value.

	LOW	AVG.	HIGH
Dresden Christmas Series, 1971-77	$ 30	$ 40	$ 50
Dresden Mother's Day, 1972-77	20	25	30
Games Children Play Series, 1979-82	45	50	55
Great Bible Stories Series, 1987	30	30	30
Little Professional Series, 1982-85	40	47	55
Mother Goose Series, 1979 (Mary, Mary)	200	300	400
Mother Goose Series, 1980-86	30	40	50
Sophisticated Ladies Series, 1985-86	30	32	35
Springtime of Life Series, 1986-86	30	30	30
Vanishing Animal Kingdom Series, 1986-87	30	35	40
Reed and Barton			
American Christmas Series, 1976-78	65	70	75
Annual Series, 1972-75	65	65	65
Audubon Series, 1970 (Pine Siskin)	150	175	200
Audubon Series, 1971-77	65	70	75
Christmas Series, 1973-76	65	65	65
Old Fashioned Christmas Series, 1977-81	55	60	65
Currier and Ives Series, 1972-74	80	85	90
Founding Fathers Series, 1974-76	60	65	70
Missions of California Series, 1971-76	60	70	80
Kentucky Derby Series, 1972-74	80	85	90
Rhea Silva Porcelain Collection			
All series	40	50	60
Ridgewood			
Christmas Series, 1975-76	30	35	40
Tom Sawyer Series, 1974	10	12	15
Wild West Series, 1975	15	17	20
River Shore			
Baby Animal Collection, 1979-82	60	80	100
American Songbirds Series, 1985	20	22	25
Lovable Teddies Series, 1985	20	22	25
Rockwell Four Freedoms Series, 1981-82	60	65	70
Rockwell Good Old Days Series, 1982	22	25	28
Signs of Love Series, 1981-83	20	22	25
Vignette Series, 1981-82	20	22	25

	LOW	AVG.	HIGH
Rockwell Museum			
American Families Series, 1979 (Baby's First Step) ..... $ 100	$ 125	$ 150	
American Families Series, 1979-81 30	45	60	
Christmas Collectibles Series, 1979-84 60	75	90	
Classic Plates Series, 1981-82 25	27	30	
A Touch of Rockwell Series, 1984 15	20	25	
World of Children Bas Relief Series, 1982 40	45	50	
Rockwell Society			
American Dream Series, 1985-87 20	22	25	
Christmas Series, 1974-84 30	45	60	
Heritage Series, 1977-78 100	125	150	
Heritage Series, 1979-85 30	45	60	
Mother's Day Series, 1976-78 80	100	120	
Mother's Day Series, 1979-87 30	35	40	
Rockwell Tour Series, 1983-84 20	30	40	
Rockwell's Rediscovered Women Series, 1982-84 25	35	45	
Roman, Inc.			
Cat Series, 1984-85 25	30	35	
Frances Hook Collection, 1982-83 50	62	75	
Lord's Prayer Series, 1986 20	25	30	
Magic of Childhood Series, 1984-85 20	25	30	
Masterpiece Collection, 1979-82 60	80	100	
Sweetest Songs Series, 1986 40	42	45	
Rorstrand			
Christmas Series, 1968 (Bringing Home the Tree) 350	400	450	
Christmas Series, 1969-86 20	35	50	
Father's Day Series, 1971-84 20	30	40	
Mother's Day Series, 1971-84 25	35	45	
Rosenthal			
Christmas Series, 1910 (Winter Peace) 400	500	600	
Christmas Series, 1911-45 200	300	400	
Christmas Series, 1946-47 700	850	1000	
Christmas Series, 1948-70 200	225	250	
Christmas Series, 1971-74 80	100	120	
Classic Rose Christmas Series, 1974-85 100	150	200	
Famous Women and Children Series, 1980-82 300	400	500	
Fantasies and Fables Series, 1976-77 50	65	80	
Lorraine Trester Series, 1975-77 100	110	120	
Nobility of Children Series, 1976-79 120	135	150	
Oriental Gold Series, 1973-79 400	600	800	
Wiinblad Christmas Series, 1971 (Maria and Child) 800	1000	1200	
Wiinblad Christmas Series, 1972-82 200	300	400	
Royal Bayreuth			
Christmas Series, 1972-79 40	50	60	
Mother's Day Series, 1973-82 60	80	100	
Sunbonnet Babies Playtime Series, 1981-82 50	60	70	
Royal Copenhagen			
Christmas Series, 1908 (Madonna and Child) 1500	1750	2000	
Christmas Series, 1909-15 120	135	150	
Christmas Series, 1916-31 80	100	120	
Christmas Series, 1932-39 100	125	150	

	LOW	AVG.	HIGH
Christmas Series, 1940-45	$ 300	$ 400	$ 500
Christmas Series, 1946-56	150	200	250
Christmas Series, 1957-70	100	125	150
Christmas Series, 1971-84	70	85	100
Historical Series, 1975-80	30	45	60
Motherhood Collection, 1982-85	30	40	50
Mother's Day Series, 1971 (American Mother)	100	125	150
Mother's Day Series, 1972-82	30	45	60
National Parks of America Series, 1978-81	70	75	80

Royal Cornwall

	LOW	AVG.	HIGH
Alice in Wonderland Series, 1979-80	40	50	60
Beauty of Bouguereau Series, 1979-80	35	50	65
Classic Christmas Collection, 1978	65	75	85
Leyendecker Classic Collection, 1980	55	60	65
Courageous Few Series, 1982-83	60	62	65
Creation Series, 1977-80	80	115	150
Crystal Maidens Series, 1979	70	75	80
Dorothy's Day Plates Series, 1980-81	50	55	60
Exotic Bird of Tropique Series, 1981-82	45	50	55
Four Seasons, 1978	50	60	70
Golden Age of Cinema, 1978-79	40	45	50
Golden Plates of the Noble Flower Maidens Series, 1982	60	65	70
Impressions of Yesteryear Series, 1982-83	55	60	65
Kitten's World Series, 1979-80	50	60	70
Legend of the Peacock Maidens Series, 1982	70	72	75
Legendary Ships of the Sea Series, 1980-81	50	60	70
Little People Series, 1980-81	30	35	40
Love's Precious Moments Series, 1981	50	55	60
Grandma Moses Memories of America, 1980-81	100	110	120
Memories of the Western Prairies Series, 1983-84	45	50	55
Most Precious Gifts of Shen Lung Series, 1981	45	50	55
Promised Land Series, 1979-80	45	47	50
Puppy's World Series, 1982	45	50	55
Charles Dickens Series, 1980-82	60	62	65
Treasures of Childhood Series, 1979-80	45	47	50
Two Thousand of Ships Series, 1982-84	40	42	45
Windows on the World Series, 1980-82	40	45	50

Royal Delft

	LOW	AVG.	HIGH
Christmas Series (large), 1915 (Christmas Bells)	5000	6000	7000
Christmas Series (large), 1916 (star floral design)	600	700	800
Christmas Series (large), 1916-86	250	350	450
Christmas Series (9"), 1955-58	150	200	250
Christmas Series (small), 1915 (Christmas Star)	2000	3000	4000
Christmas Series (small), 1926-32	250	300	350
Christmas Series (small), 1959-86	120	150	180
Easter Series, 1973-76	150	175	200
Father's Day Series, 1972-76	80	100	120
Mother's Day Series, 1971-76	80	100	120
Space Series, 1957-72	50	75	100
Halley's Comet, 1910	600	700	800

	LOW	AVG.	HIGH

Royal Devon

	LOW	AVG.	HIGH
All series	$ 40	$ 60	$ 80

Royal Doulton

	LOW	AVG.	HIGH
All God's Children Series, 1979-84	70	85	100
American Tapestries Series, 1978-81	70	85	100
Annual Christmas Series, 1983-87	35	40	45
Behind the Painted Mask Series, 1982-83	95	97	100
Beswick Christmas Series, 1972-78	40	55	70
Children of the Pueblo Series, 1983	55	60	65
Commedia Dell'Arte Series, 1974-78	70	75	80
Festival Children of the World Series, 1983	60	65	70
Flower Garden Series, 1975-79	70	80	90
I Remember America Series, 1977-80	70	80	90
Jungle Fantasy Series, 1980-83	80	90	100
Leroy Nieman Special Series, 1980	80	85	90
Log of the Dashing Wave Series, 1976-84	80	100	120
Portraits of Innocence Series, 1980-83	100	150	200
Ports of Call Series, 1975-78	65	77	90
Reflections on China Series, 1976-79	70	80	90
Victorian Christmas Series, 1977-82	40	47	55
Victorian Valentine Series, 1976-84	40	50	60

Royal Grafton

	LOW	AVG.	HIGH
Twelve Days of Christmas Series, 1976-80	20	25	30

Royal Oaks Limited

	LOW	AVG.	HIGH
Love's Labor Series, 1983	50	50	50

Royal Orleans

	LOW	AVG.	HIGH
Coca Cola/Santa Claus Series, 1983-85	55	60	65
Elvis in Concert Series, 1984-85	30	35	40
Famous Movies Series, 1985		15	30
Marilyn Monroe, 1983-85	30	35	40
Nostalgic Magazine Covers Series, 1983	30	35	40
Pink Panther Christmas Series, 1982-85	15	17	20
TV Series, 1983	25	30	35

Royal Tettau

	LOW	AVG.	HIGH
Papal Series, 1971-73	100	150	200

Royal Worcester

	LOW	AVG.	HIGH
Audubon Bird Series, 1977-78	125	150	175
Bicentennial Series, 1972-76	50	65	80
Currier and Ives Series (British produced), 1974-77	100	125	150
Doughty Birds Series, 1972-83		100	200
English Christmas Series, 1979-80	60	65	70
Famous Bird Series, 1976-78	60	65	70
Kitten Classics Series, 1985	25	30	35
Water Birds of North America Series, 1985	50	55	60
Birth of a Nation Series, 1972-76	80	100	120
Currier and Ives Series (American produced), 1974-76	60	65	70

Royale

	LOW	AVG.	HIGH
Christmas Series, 1969-77	30	45	60
Father's Day Series, 1970-77	30	45	60
Game Plates Series, 1972-75	200	235	270

	LOW	AVG.	HIGH
Mother's Day Series (animals), 1970-77	$ 30	$ 45	$ 60
Royale Germania			
Annual Flower Series, 1970-76	300	450	600
Royalwood			
Leyendecker Series, 1978	20	25	30
John A Ruthven			
Moments of Nature Series, 1977-80	35	40	45
Sango			
Christmas Series, 1974-77	30	40	50
Santa Clara			
Christmas Series, 1970-79	30	35	40
Mother's Day Series, 1971-72	30	35	40
Schmid			
Beatrix Potter Series, 1978-80	45	50	55
Berta Hummel Christmas Series, 1971-87	50	65	80
Berta Hummel Christmas Series, 1973 (Nativity)	400	450	500
Berta Hummel Mother's Day Series, 1972-87	25	37	50
Cat Tales Series, 1982-83	40	50	60
Country Christmas Annual Series, 1983-87	45	50	55
Ferrandiz Beautiful Bounty Porcelain Series, 1982	40	45	50
Ferrandiz Mother and Child Series, 1977-79	60	80	100
Golden Moments Series, 1978-81	200	250	300
Music Makers Series, 1981-82	25	27	30
Zemsky Star Series, 1981-82	25	30	35
Prairie Woman Series, 1982	30	35	40
Reflections of Life Series, 1980-81	80	85	90
Schmid Design Series, 1971-80	20	30	40
Disney Annual Series, 1983-86	20	22	25
Disney Christmas Series, 1973-74	200	300	400
Disney Christmas Series, 1975-82	20	25	30
Disney's Mother's Day Series, 1974-82	20	30	40
Nature's Treasures Series, 1974	40	45	50
Paddington Bear Series, 1979-81	15	20	25
Peanuts (all series)	20	30	40
Prime Time (television) series, 1984	25	30	35
Raggedy Ann (all series), 1980-84	15	25	35
Schonfield Gallery			
Clowns Series, 1986	45	50	55
Schumann			
Christmas Series, 1971-75	12	15	18
Imperial Christmas Series 1979-82	80	90	100
Sebastian			
America's Favorite Scenes, 1978-79	70	75	80
Seven Seas			
Christmas Carols Series, 1970-80	15	20	25
Mother's Day Series, 1970-73	20	25	30
New World Series (Christmas), 1970-72	20	25	30
Signature Collection			
Angler's Dream Series (fish), 1983	50	55	60
Baker Street Series, 1983	50	55	60
All other series	30	40	50

	LOW	AVG.	HIGH
Southern Living Gallery			
Game Bird of the South Series, 1983	$ 40	$ 42	$ 45
All other series	35	40	45
Spode			
Christmas Series, 1970-81	30	45	60
Maritime Series, 1980	140	150	160
Sports Impressions			
Baseball Series, 1987	60	92	125
All other series	60	92	125
Sterling America			
Christmas Customs Series, 1970-74	20	25	30
Mother's Day Series (animals), 1971-75	15	20	25
Twelve Days of Christmas Series, 1970-77	20	22	25
Stieff			
Bicentennial Series, 1972-76	45	50	55
Stratford Collection			
All series	35	40	45
Stuart International			
Childhood Secrets Series, 1983	30	35	40
Studio Dante Di Volteradici			
All series	40	50	60
Stumar			
Christmas Series, 1970-78	20	25	30
Mother's Day Series, 1971-78	15	20	25
Egyptian Series, 1977-78	45	50	55
Tirschenreuth			
Christmas Series, 1969-73	15	20	25
Songbirds of Europe Series, 1985-87	20	22	25
Topsy Turvy			
Storybook Series, 1982	15	20	25
U.S. Historical Society			
Annual Historical Series, 1977-78	60	70	80
Annual Spring Flowers Series, 1983-84	125	137	150
Buffalo Bill's Wild West Series	50	55	60
Christmas Carol Series, 1982-87	55	60	65
Great American Sailing Ships, 1983-85	130	140	150
Stained Glass Cathedral Christmas Series, 1978-83	100	125	150
Two Hundred Years of Flight, 1984	45	50	55
Vague Shadows			
Chieftain Series, 1979 (Sitting Bull)	400	500	600
Chieftain Series, 1979-81	100	125	150
Chieftain II Series, 1983-84	60	70	80
Indian Nations Series, 1983	45	50	55
Legends of the West Series, 1982-84	60	65	70
Masterworks of Impressionism Series, 1980-81	30	35	40
Masterworks of the West Series, 1980-81	35	37	40
Nature's Harmony Series, 1982	50	75	100
Pride of America's Indians Series, 1986-87	20	25	30
The Princesses Series, 1981-82	80	90	100
The Storybook Collection, 1980-82	40	45	50
The Professionals Series, 1979	100	110	120

	LOW	AVG.	HIGH
The Professionals Series, 1980-83	$ 30	$ 45	$ 60
The Thoroughbreds Series, 1984	50	65	80
War Ponies Series, 1983-84	80	100	120
Val St. Lambert			
American Heritage Series, 1969-71	200	300	400
Annual Old Masters Series, 1969-72	70	80	90
Veneto Flair			
American Landscape Series, 1979-80	70	75	80
Cat's Series, 1974-76	45	50	55
Children's Christmas Series, 1979-82	65	80	95
Christmas Card Series, 1975-78	40	45	50
Dog Series, 1972-76	40	55	70
Four Seasons Series, 1972-74	80	100	120
La Belle Femme Series, 1978-80	70	75	80
Mother and Child Series, 1981	90	92	95
Valentine's Day Series, 1977-80	60	65	70
Vernonware			
Christmas Series, 1971-79	30	45	60
Corvette Collector Series, 1986-87	25	27	30
Viletta China			
Alice in Wonderland Series, 1980-81	20	25	30
Carefree Days Series, 1982	20	22	25
Christmas Annual Series, 1978-80	45	50	55
Coppelia Ballet Series, 1980-82	25	27	30
Disneyland Series, 1976	80	90	100
Israel's 30th Anniversary Series, 1979	55	60	65
Making Friends Series, 1978-80	40	45	50
Nutcracker Ballet, 1978-80	30	45	60
Portraits of Childhood Series, 1981-83	20	22	25
Rufus and Roxanne, 1980	10	12	15
Seasons of the Oak Series, 1979-80	50	55	60
Unicorn Fantasies Series, 1979-82	50	55	60
Women of the West Series, 1979-80	40	42	45
Waldenburg Porcelain			
All Series	30	35	40
Enoch Wedgwood			
Avon Christmas Series, 1973-79	25	30	35

Left: Russian examples are appearing, but their prices are rarely appreciating.

	LOW	AVG.	HIGH
Bicentennial Series, 1972-76	$ 40	$ 60	$ 80
Blossoming of Suzanne Series, 1977-80	40	50	60
Calendar Series, 1971-88	20	30	40
Children's Story Series, 1971-85	10	15	20
Christmas Series, 1969 (Windsor Castle)	150	200	250
Christmas Series, 1970-87	40	60	80
Eyes of the Child Series	60	65	70
Mother's Day Series, 1971-88	30	40	50
Peter Rabbit Christmas Series, 1981-87	25	27	30
Western Authentics			
All series	30	40	50
Westminster Collectibles			
Holidays Series, 1976-77	35	37	40
Wildlife International			
All series	60	75	90
Zanobia			
All series	30	35	40

Purinton Pottery

Bernard Purinton moved the company from its 1936 home of Wellsville, OH to Shippenville PA in 1941. It remained there until its close in 1959. It is best known for its hand painted slip decoration under the glaze on dinnerware, kitchenware, and novelties.

Marks-script *Purinton* backstamps, *Slip Ware* in block letters sometimes appears. Many pieces are unmarked.

	LOW	AVG.	HIGH
Apple			
Bean Pot	$ 30	$ 40	$ 45
Bowl, 14.5" rect.	70	85	100
Butter Dish	60	90	120
Casserole, 9"	50	70	90
Chop Plate, 12"	45	60	75
Coffee Pot, 8 cup	55	70	85
Cream/Sugar	30	40	50
Cup/Saucer	12	16	20
Dish, 5"-7"	10	12	14
Fruit, 12"	30	40	50
Party Plate, 8.5"	20	25	30
Pickle Dish, 6"	9	12	15
Plate, 6"-8"	10	13	15
Plate, 9"-10"	15	20	25
Platter, 11"-12"	20	30	40
Relish Tray, 3-pc.	30	40	50
Salad, 11"	41	50	60
Teapot, 2 cup	19	24	28
Teapot, 6 cup	40	49	58
Tray, 11"	35	45	55
Vegetable, 8"	25	30	35
Vegetable, div.	40	50	60
Normandy Plaid			
Bean Pot	$ 25	$ 35	$ 45
Butter Dish	60	80	100
Casserole, 9"	40	50	60
Chop Plate, 12"	20	35	50
Coffee Pot, 8 cup	50	70	90
Cookie Jar	50	60	70
Cookie Jar, w/ wooden lid	80	100	120
Cream/Sugar	30	45	60
Cup/Saucer	12	16	20
Dish, 5"-7"	9	12	15
Fruit, 12"	31	39	47
Marmalade	40	50	60
Pickle Dish, 6"	9	12	14
Plate, 6"-8"	9	12	14
Plate, 9"-10"	17	21	25
Platter, 11" - 12"	25	30	35
Relish Tray, 3-pc.	35	40	45
Salad, 11"	40	50	60
Teapot, 2 cup	20	25	30
Tray, 11"	25	32	40
Vegetable, 8.5"	19	24	29

Red Wing Pottery

The Red Wing Potteries, Inc., traces its roots to 1878, although it operated under that name only from 1936 until its close in 1967. The early Red Wing stoneware and the dinnerware produced from the thirties onward are collected. Backstamps often use a wing motif.

Red Wing backstamp.

	LOW	AVG.	HIGH

Bob White (1955)

Charles Murphy designed the Bob White pattern.

	LOW	AVG.	HIGH
Beverage Server, w/ lid	$ 80	$ 90	$ 100
Bread Tray, 24"	60	75	90
Butter Dish	70	80	90
Butter warmer, w/ lid	45	60	75
Casserole, 1-4 qt.	50	75	100
Cocktail Tray	30	45	60
Coffee Cup	20	28	36
Cookie Jar	40	60	80
Cream/Sugar	60	75	90
Cruet, w/ stopper	140	160	180
Dish, 5"-6"	20	30	40
Gravy Boat, w/ lid	45	57	70
Lazy Susan	90	95	100
Mug	58	64	70
Pepper Mill, tall	450	475	500
Pitcher, 1.5 qt.	60	72	85
Pitcher, 3.5 qt.	140	170	200
Plate, 10"	23	26	29
Plate, 6"-8"	11	17	22
Platter, 13"	30	37	44
Platter, 20"	60	80	100
Relish Tray, 3-pc.	40	50	60
Salad Bowl, 12"	58	66	74
Shaker, tall	28	36	43
Soup Plate	28	36	44
Teapot	60	80	100
Trivet	100	105	110
Tumbler	175	200	225
Vegetable	29	44	60
Water Jar, w/ base, 2 gal.	454	532	610

Fondoso (1939)

Belle Kogan designed Fondoso as one of four shapes for Gypsy Trail Hostessware (also Chevron, Reed, and Plain). It appeared in many pastel colors.

	LOW	AVG.	HIGH
Butter Dish, large	$ 35	$ 38	$ 40
Casserole, 8.5"	60	75	90
Chop Plate, 14"	28	34	40
Coffee Pot	40	50	60
Coffee Server	36	44	52

	LOW	AVG.	HIGH
Console Bowl	$ 30	$ 38	$ 46
Cookie Jar	30	50	70
Cream/Sugar, large	60	64	67
Cream/Sugar, small	36	41	46
Cup/Saucer	25	32	39
Custard Cup	23	27	30
Dessert cup, ftd., 4"	11	15	19
Dish, 5"-6"	18	24	30
Mixing Bowl, 5"-7"	14	21	28
Mixing Bowl, 8"-9"	33	44	55
Pitcher, Batter	60	65	70
Pitcher, straight, 1-5 pt.	40	60	80
Pitcher, Syrup	42	50	57
Pitcher, tilt, 2 qt.	57	66	74
Plate, 6"-8"	11	16	21
Plate, 9"-12"	19	27	34
Platter, oval, 12"	30	32	34
Relish Tray	24	32	40
Salad Bowl, 12"	35	40	45
Salt/Pepper	30	37	44
Soup Plate, 7.5"	18	21	24
Teapot	40	50	60
Tray, Batter set	45	50	55
Tumbler, 7 oz.-10 oz.	25	35	45
Vegetable, rd. 8"	25	30	35

Town and Country (1947)

Eva Zeisel designed Town and Country as an irregular, off beat pattern. For example, the plates are slightly higher on one side than the other.

	LOW	AVG.	HIGH
Bean Pot	$ 140	$ 160	$ 180
Casserole	50	65	80
Casserole, ind.	28	33	38
Cream/Sugar	31	36	42
Cruet, w/ lid	37	40	42
Cup/Saucer	22	26	30
Dish, 5"-6"	11	14	17
Mixing Bowl, 9"	70	90	110
Mug	40	50	60
Mustard Jar	41	52	64
Pitcher	50	65	90
Plate, 10"-11"	10	14	18
Plate, 6"-8"	6	9	12
Platter, 9"-15"	26	38	50
Relish Tray, 7"	20	25	30
Salad Bowl, 13"	35	55	75
Salt/Pepper, large	30	45	60
Salt/Pepper, small	20	25	30
Syrup pitcher	50	60	70
Teapot	100	112	125
Vegetable, oval, 8"	30	35	40

Rookwood Pottery

Rookwood manufactured pottery from 1879 to 1967. Its heyday was from 1890-1930. It featured large, bold underglaze painting. Products bore a factory and artist mark. They sometimes bore a clay mark, size mark, and process mark (add 10-30%).

Left: Painted pieces are the most valuable. Above: Unpainted pieces like this bowl are worth $50-$150.

	LOW	AVG.	HIGH
Bookends, 5.5", green, sailing-ship form, initialed, 1936 .... $ 200	$ 250	$ 300
Bookends, 5.5", turquoise, yacht form, signed, 1925 120	160	200
Bookends, 6", green, glazed finish, horse form, signed, 1940 200	260	320
Box, 5", pink, slip-painted floral decoration, signed, 1925 240	300	350
Box, 5.5", modeled grapes, green shades to blue, signed, 1905 250	350	450
Cologne Bottle, 4.5", incised butterfly and vines, signed, 1883 ... 250	450	650
Compote, 8.25", eagle wings form base of bowl, signed, 1923 250	400	550
Creamer, turquoise, matte finish, 1940 20	35	50
Dish, 5", cameo glaze, white flowers, log shape, 1890 150	175	200
Ewer, 5.5", silver overlay, tankard form, floral ptd., init., 1892 .. 1000	1250	1500
Figurine, 4.5", reclining woman on high glaze green mount 90	120	150
Figurine, goat, 6", white, matte finish, signed, 1945 75	100	125
Ginger Jar, 3.5", pink, w/ lid 80	110	140
Honey Jug, 4.5", bisque, intaglio clover design, signed, 1883 180	220	260
Jardiniere, 10.5", orange slip-painted poppies, signed, 1892 1500	1750	2000
Jardiniere, dia. 12", factory glaze, floral painting, signed, 1891 ... 700	830	960
Jug, 6.5", factory glaze, seals of Cincinnati and Ohio, 1888 1000	1200	1400
Plaque, 5" x 9", vellum glaze, seascape ptd., signed, 1919 950	1150	1350
Tray, 10.5", brown matte finish, w/ leaves, acorns & rook, 1922 . 200	250	300
Vase, 12.5", birds and flowers, signed, 1949, factory second 600	1000	1400
Vase, 6", lavender shades, slip-painted pansies, signed, 1904 900	1100	1300
Vase, 6", pink, matte finish, turned, 1923 50	75	100
Vase, 6", pink glaze, lavender floral ptd., signed, 1922 150	200	250
Vase, 6", slip-painted tiger lilies, standard glaze, signed, 1905 850	1000	1150
Vase, 6", white, slip-painted birds and flowers, signed, 1948 700	830	960
Vase, 6.5", Dutch-style slip-painting of man, signed, 1898 5000	6500	8000
Vase, 6.5", purple, slip painted iris and crocus, signed, 1903 1000	1200	1400
Vase, 7", dogwood border, vellum glaze, signed, 1914 400	550	800
Vase, 9", blue glaze, signed, c. 1924 300	450	600

Above: Size and elegance of shape are important factors. The vase on the right is the most valuable of these three. — Photo courtesy of Northeast Auctions.

Right: Typical Rookwood impressed marks. The number of "flames" surrounding the logo varies with the date.

Roseville Pottery

The Roseville factory opened in 1885 in Roseville, OH. In 1902, the factory bought a stoneware plant in Zanesville and made art pottery there until 1954. In 1910, the Roseville arm of the company closed. Roseville called its artware Rozane (from ROseville and ZANEsville). Various lines included: Egypto, Mongol, Woodland, Mara, and Royal. The main line was vases, although water pitchers, jugs, lamp bases and ashtrays were made.

Most of the art pottery is marked Rozane or Rozane Ware, with an artist's mark. Often, a figure of a rose appears within a circle.

Roseville
U.S.A.

Incised mark.

	LOW	AVG.	HIGH
Baby Plate, Juvenile, 8", green, duck in hat & shoes, signed RV ...	$ 70	$ 95	$ 120
Basket, Ixia., shape #346, 10", green	120	160	200
Bookends, Foxglove, shape #10, pink and blue, pr.	85	100	115
Bowl, Carnelian II, 3" x 8", pink w/ green, purple & yellow	40	62	85
Bowl, Imperial I, 9", w/ handle	30	50	70
Candlesticks, Luffa, 4.5", brown w/ original seal, pair	167	208	250
Compote, Carnelian I, 9.5" x 7", pink & blue drip, mkd. RV	50	70	90
Conch, Magnolia, shape #453, 6", brown	40	60	80
Console, Montacello, oval, 13" x 3", blue	160	210	250
Console Set, Florentine, 10" bowl, 2" candleholders, blond, set	100	130	160
Cornucopia, Apple Blossom, shape #321, 6", green	25	44	64
Ewer, Fuchsia, shape #902, 10.5", green and brown	95	122	148
Hanging Basket, Bushberry, green, berries and leaves	75	100	125
Humidor, Old Ivory, 6", blue tint, w/ lid, spherical, no mark	200	245	290
Jardiniere, Bleeding Heart, shape #651, 10", pink	310	370	430
Jardiniere, Jonquil, 9.5" x 7" x 4.5"	350	425	500
Mug, Holland, 4", embossed figure, simple shape, no mark	45	65	85
Mug, Peony, shape #2, 3/2", green	30	50	70
Pitcher, Autumn, 8.5", orange, bulbous, no mark	800	1000	1200
Planter, Bittersweet, shape #828, 10"	30	50	70
Planter, Poppy, shape #336-5, 8.5" x 2.5", pink	40	60	80
Pot, Morning Glory, 5", aqua, 2 handles, bell form, no mark	140	190	240
Soap dish, Colonial, 4", lid, mottled green, spherical, no mark	120	150	180
Sugar Bowl, Persian, 4", lid and 2 handles, 4-sided, no mark	50	70	90
Vase, Azurean, 9", landscape, egg form, narrow neck, no mark	2400	2600	2800
Vase, Dogwood, 10", green, marked RV	90	115	140
Vase, Freesia, shape #117, 6", green	30	50	70
Vase, Fujiyama, flowers, lighthouse shape, marked in ink	1000	1250	1500
Vase, Imperial II, 5.5", yellow, beehive shape, no mark	100	150	200
Vase, Lustre, 10", pink, cylindrical, no trim, paper label, black	60	80	100
Vase, Matt Green, 4" x 5", marked H 1/170/bot 2/2	30	50	70
Vase, Rozane Olympic, 14.5", 3 feet, Chariot of Xerxes, urn shape, cylindrical neck, marked *ROZANE POTTERY* in ink	6000	7000	8000
Wall Pocket, Antique Green Matt, 10", triangular, no mark	150	200	250
Wall Pocket, Rosecraft Vintage, brown w/ fruit and grapevines	90	120	150

Royal China

The Royal China Company's semi-porcelain dinnerware, cookware, and premiums date to 1933. After a series of owners in the 1970s, the plant closed in 1986.

Royal backstamp.

	LOW	AVG.	HIGH

Regal (1937)

Thin fluting charaterizes the Regal pattern.

	LOW	AVG.	HIGH
Cream/Sugar	$ 12	$ 14	$ 15
Cup/Saucer	5	6	7
Plate, 11"	7	8	9
Plate, 6"-8"	5	7	9
Salt/Pepper	10	12	14
Teapot	21	23	25
Vegetable, 9"	7	8	9

Royalty (1936)

Royalty consists of spider-web embossing with decal decorations.

	LOW	AVG.	HIGH
Casserole	$ 20	$ 22	$ 24
Cream/Sugar	12	14	16
Cup/Saucer	5	6	7
Dish, 5"	1	2	3
Gravy Boat	8	9	10
Pickle Dish, 8"	6	7	8
Plate, 6"-8"	4	5	6
Plate, 9"-10"	6	8	10
Salt/Pepper	10	12	14
Teapot	21	23	25

Royal Doulton

Royal Doulton figures are ceramic works of art. Although the English company produces other items, its HN series is the best known. The company was begun in the early 1800s by John Doulton. The HN series was introduced in 1913 and named after Harry Nixon, head colorist at the time.

Besides their figurines, there are many different Royal Doulton collectibles, including Toby jugs, plates, limited editions, and bird and animal figures. Royal Doulton figures are identified by the HN prefix followed by numbers in a chronological sequence. Subjects in this series are highly diverse representing the works of many different artists at different time periods.

The earliest Royal Doulton figures (with the lower HN numbers) are usually the most desirable to collectors. For more information, consult *The Official Price Guide to Royal Doulton*, published by The House of Collectibles, Random House, NY.

Royal Doulton backstamps.

HN#	TITLE	LOW	AVG.	HIGH
HN8	Crinoline	$ 1600	$ 1900	$ 2200
HN19	Picardy Peasant (male)	2300	2700	3100
HN41	Lady of the Georgian Period	2000	2400	2800
HN51B	Spook	1500	1700	2000
HN53	Lady of the Fan	2000	2150	2300
HN60	Shy Anne	2300	2700	3100
HN63	Little Land	2500	2750	3000
HN71A	Jester (1st ver.)	1700	1900	2100
HN78	Flounced Skirt	1800	2000	2200
HN80	Fisherwomen	4700	5100	5500
HN81	Shepherd (1st ver.)	2620	2860	3090
HN83	Lady Anne	3500	3900	4300
HN89	Spooks	2300	2700	3100
HN96	Doris Keene as Cavallini (2nd ver.)	2920	3300	3690
HN304	Lady with Rose	2000	2200	2400
HN306	Milking Time	3200	3500	3700
HN322	Digger (Australian)	1730	2100	2480
HN342	Lavender Woman	2440	2640	2840
HN349	Fisherwomen	3200	3450	3700
HN351	Picardy Peasant (female)	3500	3750	4000
HN352	Gainsborough Hat	2000	2250	2500
HN366	Mandarin (2nd ver.)	3510	3900	4300

HN#	TITLE	LOW	AVG.	HIGH
HN374	Lady and Blackamoor (1st ver.)	$ 3000	$ 3300	$ 3600
HN402	Betty (1st ver.)	3000	3300	3600
HN409	Omar Khayyam (1st ver.)	3500	3900	4300
HN415	Moorish Minstrel	3750	4000	4250
HN419	Omar Khayyam and the Beloved	5400	5700	6000
HN427	One of the Forty (9th ver.)	1400	1600	1800
HN433	Puff and Powder	2300	2500	2700
HN447	Lady with Shawl	5000	5350	5700
HN451	An Old Man	3510	3900	4300
HN460	Mandarin (3rd ver.)	3510	3900	4300
HN471	Katharine	2300	2700	3100
HN493	One of the Forty (10th ver.)	1400	1600	1800
HN500	One of the Forty (13th ver.)	1600	1800	2000
HN510	Child's Grace	4000	4500	5000
HN518	Curtsey	1900	2000	2200
HN519	Welsh Girl	3000	3200	3400
HN537	Bill Sykes	20	90	160
HN545	Uriah Heep (1st ver.)	20	90	160
HN568	Shy Anne	2300	2700	3100
HN575	Falstaff (1st ver.)	1370	1680	2000
HN585	Harlequinade	1000	1150	1300
HN612	Poke Bonnett	1700	1900	2100
HN616	Jester (1st ver.)	1900	2100	2300
HN621	Pan on Rock	3000	3300	3600
HN629	Curtsey	1800	2000	2200
HN630	Jester (2nd ver.)	2300	2500	2700
HN636	Masquerade (male, 1st ver.)	1200	1400	1600
HN637	Masquerade (female, 1st ver.)	1200	1400	1600
HN664	One of the Forty (10th ver.)	1600	1800	2000
HN679	Lady with Shawl	4940	5340	5750
HN680	Polly Peachum (1st ver.)	600	720	850
HN683	Masquerade (male, 1st ver.)	1370	1560	1750
HN687	Bather (1st ver.)	950	1230	1510
HN688	Yeoman of the Guard	890	1020	1150
HN694	Polly Peachum (2nd ver.)	420	540	670
HN695	Lucy Lockett (2nd ver.)	710	840	970
HN702	Lady of the Georgian Period	2300	2700	3100
HN703	Woman Holding Child	2320	2520	2720
HN707	Fruit Gathering	3500	3900	4300
HN708	Shepherdess (1st ver., mini)	1130	1500	1880
HN716	Proposal (lady)	1600	1800	2000
HN718	Lady Clown	3000	3300	3600
HN722	Mephisto	3000	3300	3600
HN746	Mandarin (1st ver.)	3510	3900	4300
HN752	London Cry, Turnips and Carrots	1490	1620	1750
HN763	Pretty Lady	1000	1200	1400
HN775	Mephistopheles and Marguerite	1730	1960	2180
HN786	Mam'selle	1670	1860	2060
HN1213	Boy with Turban	1000	1200	1400
HN1215	Pied Piper	1900	2150	2400
HN1245	Baba	800	1000	1200

HN#	TITLE	LOW	AVG.	HIGH
HN1263	Lady Clown	$ 3000	$ 3300	$ 3600
HN1265	Lady Fayre	700	800	900
HN1275	Kathleen	700	900	1100
HN1278	Carnival	4100	4810	5510
HN1291	Kathleen	950	1080	1210
HN1293	Spanish Lady	1130	1350	1570
HN1299	Susanna	1200	1350	1500
HN1307	An Irishman	3200	3600	4000
HN1330	Sweet Anne	270	390	510
HN1332	Lady Jester (1st ver.)	1840	2100	2360
HN1338	Courtier	3500	4000	4500
HN1341	Marietta	710	840	970
HN1345	Victorian Lady	300	420	540
HN1347	Moira	3510	3900	4300
HN1348	Sunshine Girl	2000	2250	2500
HN1351	One of the Forty (1st ver.)	1430	1660	1880
HN1365	Mendicant	240	340	450
HN1370	Marie (2nd ver.)	50	120	180
HN1379	Fairy	800	1000	1200
HN1389	Doreen	800	1000	1200
HN1395	Fairy	1000	1200	1400
HN1396	Fairy	800	1000	1200
HN1404	Betty (2nd ver.)	1700	2100	2400
HN1418	Little Mother (2nd ver.)	3000	3300	3600
HN1421	Barbara	830	1020	1210
HN1443	Child Study	950	1080	1210
HN1445	Biddy	170	300	420
HN1447	Marigold	540	660	790
HN1460	Paisley Shawl (1st ver.)	540	700	850
HN1461	Barbara	830	1050	1270
HN1471	Annette	480	600	730
HN1479	Chloe	240	330	420
HN1485	Greta	270	380	480
HN1490	Dorcas	800	1000	1200
HN1492	Old Lavender Seller	1000	1150	1300
HN1493	Potter	480	540	600
HN1495	Priscilla	800	900	1000
HN1499	Miss Demure	600	720	850
HN1501	Priscilla	700	850	1000
HN1507	Pantalettes	540	700	850
HN1511	Constance	1430	1660	1880
HN1517	Veronica (1st ver.)	360	450	540
HN1522	Potter	1100	1300	1500
HN1529	Victorian Lady	650	840	1030
HN1534	Fairy	1000	1200	1400
HN1541	"Happy Joy-Baby Boy"	800	1000	1200
HN1549	Sweet and Twenty (1st ver.)	650	870	1090
HN1550	Annette	420	530	640
HN1556	Rosina	800	1000	1200
HN1559	Priscilla	700	850	1000
HN1580	Rosebud (1st ver.)	800	1000	1200

HN#	TITLE	LOW	AVG.	HIGH
HN1598	Clothilde	$ 700	$ 900	$ 1100
HN1599	Clothilde	700	900	1100
HN1629	Grizel	1400	1600	1800
HN1684	Lisette	1300	1550	1800
HN1690	June	480	600	730
HN1691	June	420	530	640
HN1692	Sonia	1200	1350	1500
HN1701	Sweet Anne	300	420	540
HN1711	Camilla	950	1140	1330
HN1730	Vera	1370	1680	2000
HN1743	Mirabel	1430	1660	1880
HN1749	Pierrette (3rd ver.)	1370	1680	2000
HN1752	Regency	1840	2100	2360
HN1755	Court Shoemaker	2440	2760	3090
HN1764	Windflower (1st ver.)	600	760	910
HN1768	Ivy	30	100	180
HN1775	Salome	7500	8500	9500
HN1778	Beethoven	7000	7500	8000
HN1794	This Little Pig	480	600	730
HN1798	Lily	60	140	210
HN1809	Cissie	110	170	230
HN1825	Spirit of the Wind	4100	4500	5000
HN1844	Odds and Ends	950	1140	1330
HN1850	Antoinette (1st ver.)	1250	1500	1750
HN1856	Memories	540	660	790
HN1873	Granny's Heritage	1310	1500	1690
HN1888	BonJour	830	1020	1210
HN1892	Uriah Heep (2nd ver.)	270	360	450
HN1893	Fat Boy (2nd ver.)	300	420	540
HN1906	Lydia	700	900	1000
HN1921	Roseanna	1600	1800	2000
HN1922	Spring Morning	150	240	330
HN1931	Meriel	1790	2040	2300
HN1953	Orange Lady	270	360	450
HN1957	New Bonnet	1730	1960	2180
HN1981	Ermine Coat	210	320	420
HN1987	Paisley Shawl (1st ver.)	210	330	450
HN1997	Belle o' the Ball	300	390	480
HN2000	Jacqueline	480	660	850
HN2007	Mrs. Fitzherbert	710	840	970
HN2013	Angelina	950	1170	1390
HN2018	Parson's Daughter	360	450	540
HN2021	Blithe Morning	120	200	270
HN2027	June	420	540	670
HN2040	Gollywog	240	330	420
HN2041	Broken Lance	480	600	730
HN2046	He Loves Me	180	260	330
HN2056	Susan	330	440	540
HN2069	Farmer's Wife	540	660	790
HN2071	Bernice	950	1080	1210
HN2102	Pied Piper	270	380	480

HN#	TITLE	LOW	AVG.	HIGH
HN2112	Carolyn	$ 300	$ 420	$ 540
HN2136	Delphine	240	340	450
HN2139	Giselle	360	460	570
HN2142	Rag Doll	40	110	180
HN2160	Apple Maid	360	480	600
HN2175	Beggar (2nd ver.)	600	780	970
HN2210	Debutante	300	400	500
HN2215	Sweet April	340	440	540
HN2231	Sweet Sixteen	150	240	330
HN2253	Puppetmaker	450	540	640
HN2255	Tea time	210	280	340
HN2269	Leading Lady	120	210	300
HN2278	Judith	170	240	300
HN2281	Professor	150	240	330
HN2283	Dreamweaver	240	330	420
HN2307	Coralie	170	200	240
HN2309	Buttercup	160	230	300
HN2311	Lorna	120	210	300
HN2314	Old Mother Hubbard	300	400	510
HN2315	Last Waltz	240	300	360
HN2320	Tuppence a Bag	210	280	360
HN2333	Jacqueline	170	240	300
HN2337	Loretta	80	160	240
HN2342	Lucrezia Borgia	1100	1200	1400
HN2349	Flora	270	360	450
HN2356	Ascot	240	300	360
HN2368	Fleur	240	300	360
HN2377	Georgina	50	130	210
HN2385	Debbie	60	140	210
HN2388	Karen	270	340	420
HN2394	Lisa	160	230	300
HN2401	Sandra	170	240	300
HN2425	Southern Belle	200	310	420
HN2427	Virginals	1700	2100	2400
HN2445	Parisian	120	210	300
HN2471	Victoria	210	280	360
HN2475	Vanity	110	200	300
HN2479	Pamela	100	170	240
HN2480	Adele	140	220	300
HN2547	Royal Canadian Mounted Police	240	360	480
HN2700	Chitarrone	800	1000	1200
HN2704	Pensive Moments	120	220	330
HN2710	Jean	50	120	200
HN2729	Song of the Sea	210	290	370
HN2737	Harlequin	1000	1100	1200
HN2757	Lyric	50	120	180
HN2760	Private, Massachusetts Reg., 1778	800	1000	1200
HN2791	Elaine	240	330	420
HN2797	Viola d'Amore	540	660	790
HN2800	Carrie	60	140	210
HN2802	Anna	60	140	210

HN#	TITLE	LOW	AVG.	HIGH
HN2805	Rebecca	$ 480	$ 600	$ 730
HN2807	Stephanie	100	180	270
HN2815	Sergeant, 6th Maryland Reg., 1777	890	1060	1240
HN2818	Balloon Girl	160	230	300
HN2841	Mother & Daughter	110	180	240
HN2845	Private, Connecticut Reg., 1777	830	990	1150
HN2861	Washington at Prayer	2400	2700	3000
HN2877	Wizard	290	360	420
HN2883	H.R.H. Prince of Wales	650	810	970
HN2889	Captain Cook	390	480	570
HN2891	News Vendor (Ltd. Ed., 2,500)	240	330	420
HN2892	Chief	270	340	420
HN2895	Morning Ma'am	160	230	300
HN2910	Lalla Rookh (Ltd. Ed., Ships Figurehead)	830	920	1020
HN2913	Gollum (J.R.R. Tolkien Series)	30	100	180
HN2924	Tom Bombadil	150	240	330
HN2952	Susan	270	340	420
HN2957	Edith	50	130	210
HN2963	It Won't Hurt	30	100	180
HN2974	Carolyn	120	200	270
HN2978	Magpie Ring	50	120	180
HN2989	Genie	110	180	240
HN2995	Julie	40	110	180
HN3048	Tapestry	1400	1600	1800
HN3059	Sophistication	110	180	240
HN3060	Wintertime	180	270	360
HN3075	Tango	140	220	300
HN3078	Dancing Delight	110	180	240
HN3079	Sleeping Beauty	170	240	300
HN3083	Sheikh	110	180	240
HN3105	Love Letter	100	160	230
HN3132	Good Pals	110	180	260
OM8	Patricia	270	380	480
OM9	Chloe	270	360	450
OM16	Pantalettes	300	440	570
OM24	Priscilla	360	450	540
OM28	Patricia	270	380	480
OM29	Chloe	300	390	480
OM85	Maureen	770	900	1030

Salem China

The Salem China Company reached its 100th year in 1968 solely as a distributor. Its semiporcelain dinnerware, famous in the 1930s and 1940s ceased production in 1967.

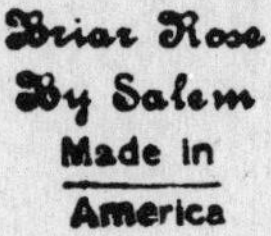

Briar Rose
By Salem
Made in
America

Salem Briar Rose backstamp.

	LOW	AVG.	HIGH

Briar Rose (c. 1930)

J. Palin Thorley designed Briar Rose for the American China Corporation. Salem purchsed the pattern when ACC went bankrupt.

	LOW	AVG.	HIGH
Butter Dish, open	$ 14	$ 16	$ 18
Cake Plate, 10"	5	6	7
Casserole	20	23	26
Cream/Sugar	13	16	18
Cup/Saucer	7	9	11
Dish, 5"-6"	3	4	5
Gravy Boat	11	13	15
Pickle Dish	4	5	6
Plate, 6"-7"	4	6	8
Plate 9"-10"	9	11	13
Platter, 11"-13"	7	9	10
Soup, coupe, 7"	5	6	7
Vegetable, 8"-9"	11	13	15

TRICORNE
By
Salem
U. S. PATENT

Salem Tricorne backstamp.

Tricorne (1934)

Tricorne was an avant garde shape using many angles. Originally produced only in bright red (Mandarin), it later appeared with tamer decals: Polo (pony and rider), Sailing (sailboats), Dutch Petitpoint (boy, and girl), and Bridge (card suits).

	LOW	AVG.	HIGH
Casserole	$ 31	$ 34	$ 37
Compote	18	20	22
Cream/Sugar	25	30	35
Cup/Saucer	13	16	19
Dish, 5"-6"	3	4	5
Nut Dish, 4"	6	7	8
Plate, 5"-6"	3	4	5
Plate, 9"-12"	8	12	14

Salem Victory backstamp.

	LOW	AVG.	HIGH

Victory (1938)

Viktor Schreckengost designed Victory. It appears with many decal motifs: Godey Ladies, Indian Tree, Basket Petitpoint, and Parkway.

	LOW	AVG.	HIGH
Bowl, 6"-7"	$ 6	$ 8	$ 10
Cake Plate, 10"	5	6	7
Candleholder	15	17	19
Casserole	22	28	34
Coffee Pot	30	40	50
Cream/Sugar	12	15	17
Cup/Saucer	6	9	12
Dish, 5"-7"	2	3	4
Gravy Boat	10	12	13
Mustache Cup	16	18	19
Plate, 10"	8	11	13
Plate, 6"-7"	1	3	5
Platter, oval, 11"-13"	7	8	9
Salt/Pepper	13	16	19
Soup Bowl/Saucer	8	10	12
Soup Plate, 8.25"	5	6	7
Vegetable, rd., 8"	10	12	14

Sebring Pottery

The Sebring family established the town of Sebring, OH in 1899. There they consolidated their various business ventures and built the Sebring Pottery to produce semiporcelain dinnerware, etc. Some art ware and kitchenware was made in the 1930s. The name Sebring vanished in the 1943 takeover by National Unit Distributors, although some patterns continued manufacture.

Aristocrat (1932)

	LOW	AVG.	HIGH
Casserole	$ 18	$ 22	$ 25
Coffee Pot	24	29	34
Cream/Sugar	13	15·	16
Cup/Saucer	6	7	8
Plate, 6"-7"	3	4	4
Plate, 9"	5	6	6
Platter, 13"	9	10	10
Salt/Pepper	10	11	12
Soup Plate, 7.5"	5	6	6
Teapot	25	29	32

Gadroon

Gadroon is named for the lobed pattern around each edge.

Casserole, oval	$ 31	$ 36	$ 40
Cream/Sugar	16	20	23
Cup/Saucer	10	13	15
Dish, 5"-6"	2	3	4
Domed cover	29	36	42
Plate, 6"-7"	4	5	6
Plate, sq. 9"	8	9	10
Platter, oval, 11.5"	10	11	12
Soup Plate, 8"	8	9	10
Teapot, 2-4 cup	31	34	38

backstamp mark

Trojan

Trojan is a round version of Doric.

Casserole	$ 21	$ 25	$ 28
Coffee Pot	22	26	30
Cream/Sugar	15	18	21
Cup/Saucer	8	10	12
Dish, 5"-6"	2	3	4
Egg Cup	7	9	11
Gravy Boat	12	14	15
Plate, 6"-7"	2	3	4
Plate, 9"-11"	6	8	10
Vegetable, oval, 9"	12	13	14

Shakers

Salt and pepper shakers are on most dinner tables (very few of us use salt cellars). Although people obtain S & Ps to match table settings, we listed shakers that are considered novelty or figural shakers; some even advertise products. Collectors are drawn to the strange forms and bright colors. Many shakers match a more expensive cookie jar by the same firm such as Shawnee or Regal. Shakers draw collectors not only from the cookie jar field but from the fields of Black Americana, comic character, and advertising memorabilia. With so many shapes and themes, crossover collecting is nearly endless. Collectors talk about sets such as one piece (one container), nodders (which sit in a base and rock back and forth), nesters (which sit inside one another), or huggers (which fit together). (The Huggies in the listing refers specifically to the work of Ruth Van Telligen Bendel.) Sometimes a pair of salt and peppers aren't really a pair but two different forms that share a theme such as a Cow Jumping Over the Moon or a bowling ball and pin. Many times there are other pieces, such as a condiments jar, a tray, or bench, that are required for a complete set. Be alert to reproductions or copies of expensive shakers and missing pieces. Prices listed are for excellent-condition examples-no chips, cracks, or flaking finish.

The shakers below usually range from 1" to 5" in height, so nearly everyone has room for two or three....hundred. Many more common shakers can be purchased for less than $10. For further reading we recommend *The Official Price Guide to Pottery and Porcelain*, by Harvey Duke, House of Collectibles, Random House, New York, 1995; *The Complete Salt and Pepper Shaker Book*, by Mike Schneider, Schiffer, Atglen, PA 1993; and *Salt and Pepper II*, by Helene Guarnaccia, Collector Books, Paducah, KY, 1989.

Left: Plastic Croquet Mallet S & P with steak markers, with original box, $18-$22, without box, $12-$15 . — Item courtesy Jim Glaab's Collector's Showcase.

Right: Plastic soda fountain sodas, $9-$12. — Item courtesy of Cerise Foster

	LOW	HIGH
Alice in Wonderland, Regal	$ 400	$ 600
Aunt Jemima, Uncle Moses, plastic, '50s, ht. 5.5"	20	30
Bert and Harry Piel, '50s, ht. 3.5"	35	45
Black Boy with Watermelon	60	80
Bo Peep & Sailor Boy, ht. 3.25", Shawnee	20	35
Bowling Ball, pin and tray, wooden	10	12
Campbell Kids, plastic, '50s, ht. 4.5"	30	40
Cats, black, wooden, leather ears	6	9
Chanticleers, no gold, small, ht. 3", Shawnee	25	35
Chef & Jemima, Brayton	150	200
Colonel and Mrs. Sanders, plastic, '60s, ht. 4"	60	80
Cow Jumps Over the Moon, len. 5"	25	35
Dachshund, long body, one piece, len. 10", Japan	10	15
Ducks, ht. 3", Shawnee	20	30
Dutch Kids, no gold, ht. 5", Shawnee	40	50
Dutch Shoes, Frankoma	20	30
Elephant, Frankoma	60	70
Elsie and Elmer, ceramic, '50s, ht. 4"	60	80
Fifi and Fido, Ken-L Ration Dogs, plastic, '60s, h. 3.5"	25	35
Fish in base, 3 piece nodder	45	65
Flamingos, one head up, one down	12	18
Flower Pots, no gold, ht. 3.25", Shawnee	18	22
Gingham Dog & Calico Cat, Brayton	35	45
Giraffe, long body, one piece, len. 10", Japan	10	15
Handy Flame, ceramic, '50s, ht. 4"	15	20
Hedge Hog Chefs	10	15
Huggies, Bunny, brown & black, Van Tellingen, Regal	20	30
Huggies, Love Bug, small, Van Tellingen, Regal	70	110
Huggies, Mermaid/Sailor, unpntd., Van Tellingen, Regal	90	140
Huggies, Bear, mkd. Van Tellingen, Regal	20	30
Huggies, Boy/Dog, Van Tellingen, Regal	70	90
Huggies, Duck, Van Tellingen, Regal	30	50
Huggies, Dutch Boy/Girl, Van Tellingen, Regal	35	45
Huggies, Love Bug, large, Van Tellingen, Regal	200	300
Huggies, Mary/Lamb, Van Tellingen, Regal	40	60
Humpty Dumpty, Regal	150	200
Humpty Dumpty Before the Fall, plastic	10	15
Ice Cream Cones, glass and tin, h. 4", Enesco Imports	20	30
Jack and Jill, ht. 5", Shawnee	40	60
Jug, Frankoma	14	18
Magic Chef, ceramic, '50s, ht. 5"	50	70
Magic Chef, plastic, '50s, ht. 5"	30	40
Milk Bottles, Sealtest	20	30
Milk Cans, ht. 3.25", Shawnee	18	22
Monkeys in Tree, ht. 4.5", Dee Bee Imports	6	8
Mount Rushmore	6	9
Mr. and Mrs. Mushroomhead, ht. 6"	8	12
Mr. and Mrs. Snowman, formal attire	10	12
Mr. Peanut, single color, plastic, '50s, ht. 4"	18	22
Mr. Peanut, yellow w/ black top hat	30	40
Mugsey, small no gold, ht. 3", Shawnee	35	55

Left to right: Nesting chickens, $12-$16; swinging monkeys, Dee Bee Imports, Japan, $6-$8.

Above left: Goose that laid the golden egg, $15-$20; Shawnee pigs, 5.5", $70-$90, Shawnee pigs, 3.5", $35-$65. Below: One piece girafee, $10-$15. — Items courtesy Cerise Foster.

	LOW	HIGH
Native Children on Carrots	$ 80	$ 120
Niagra Falls, Maid of the Mist Boat, 3 piece nester	100	150
Nipper & phonograph, plastic, '50s, ht. 3"	25	35
Old Woman who Lives in a Shoe, ht. 4"	15	20
Old Salt & Pepper, his wife, Purinton	100	150
Owls, no gold, ht. 3.25", Shawnee	20	30
Peek-a-Boo, small, Regal	200	300
Peek-a-Boo, large, Regal	400	500
Pigs, Brayton	35	45
President Kennedy in Rocking Chair	40	50
Puss-n-Boots, no gold, ht. 3.25", Shawnee	15	25
"S" and "P" letters, Camark	10	15
7-Up Bottles, glass, '50s	10	12
Skunks with Hats	9	12
Smiley Pigs, blue or red scarves, ht. 5.5", Shawnee	70	90
Smiley Pigs, ht. 3.5", Shawnee	35	65
Smoky the Bear, ceramic, '60s, ht. 4"	20	30
Spot, tall tan and white dogs	8	12
Statue of Liberty, Empire State Building on tray	20	30
Steam Irons, plastic	8	12
Sword Fish, ht. 4.5", Japan	6	8
Tappan Chefs, ceramic, '60s, ht. 4"	20	30
Teepee, Frankoma	25	35
Toaster with removable toast, plastic, ht. 2.5"	10	15
Trylon and Perisphere, plastic	60	90
TV Set, plastic	15	20
Tweedle Dee and Tweedle Dum, Regal	600	800
Willie and Millie Penguin, plastic, '50s, ht. 3"	10	15

 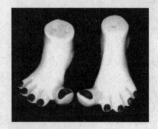

Left to right: Monks by Goebel, $10-$12; feet, $6-$9.
— Items courtesy Cerise Foster.

Shawnee Pottery

The Shawnee Pottery Company produced earthenware art pottery and brightly colored dinnerware and kitchenware from 1937 through 1961.

Marks include an embossed *USA*, and/or *Shawnee*, and/or a shape number. Some pieces are unmarked. Gilt trim is worth more.

The following entries are from the Corn king pattern

	LOW	AVG.	HIGH
Casserole	$ 50	$ 75	$ 100
Cereal Bowl	40	50	60
Cookie Jar	140	160	190
Dish, 6"	10	12	14
Mixing Bowl, 5"-8"	20	30	40
Mug	40	50	60
Pitcher, 1 qt.	80	90	100
Plate, 10"	35	50	65
Platter, 12"	50	60	70
Relish Tray	40	45	50
Salt/Pepper	20	30	40
Teapot, 30 oz.	60	80	100
Tumbler	30	35	40
Utility Jar	40	50	60

Staffordshire

Staffordshire Pottery refers to pottery produced in and around Staffordshire, England, from the mid-18th century through the end of the 19th century. Originally conceived as an affordable alternative to Chinese porcelain, Staffordshire wares are now recognized in their own right. Important makers include Enoch Wood, Ridgway, and Clews. With the development of the transfer decoration process, manufacturers covered dinnerware with scenes of popular landmarks and historical vignettes. "Historical Blue" had its heyday in the second half of the 19th century. Many popular designs are still produced.

Above left to right: Shakespeare, ht. 15", $300-$350; boy on zebra, ht.7.5", $200-$250. — Items courtesy of Valerie Hoyt.

Below left: Lafayette dark blue platter, len. 17", $750 at auction. Below right: Staffordshire blue transfer decorated milk jug, $500-$750.

	AUCTION	RETAIL	
		Low	High
Bird Whistle	$ 450	$ 900	$ 1500
Cheese Dish, Bull's Head	650	1300	2000
Dinner Plate, *Fairmount Near Philadelphia*	175	350	560
Dish Base, vegetable, Mt. Vernon	150	300	480
Dogs, pr., standing, rust-colored	450	900	1440
Figural Bottle of a Dandy	175	350	560
Figural Tobacco Jar of Peasant Woman	275	550	880
Figural Toby, of a Toper	500	1000	1600
Figure of a Judge	250	500	800
Fruit Bowl, dark blue	140	280	450
Luncheon Plate, dark blue	75	150	240
Pitcher, dark blue, *Rebecca at the Well*	425	850	1300
Pitcher, Harlequin & Animal, colored, Elsmore & Foster, h. 9"	700	1400	2240
Plate, *Boston Hospital*, dark blue	225	450	720
Plate, dark blue w/ English scene	80	160	260
Plates, set of 5, *Capitol at Washington*	1600	3200	5000
Platter, floral, dark blue, 16"	175	350	550
Platter, *Don Quixote*	200	400	650
Platter, *Lake George, New York*	2000	4000	6400
Platter, *Landing of Lafayette*	1275	2550	4000
Platter, *Mendenhall*	550	1100	1750
Platter, *Pennsylvania Hospital*	775	1550	2480
Platter, *Sancho Panza and the Duchess*	400	800	1280
Platter, *St. George's Chapel*	200	400	650
Platter, Wilkie Valentine	400	800	1250
Sauce Tureen, *Quadrupeds*	1300	2600	4160
Sauce Tureens, pr., *Lawrence-Mansion* dark blue	200	400	650
Saucer, dark blue	50	100	150
Soup Plate, *Dr. Syntax*, dark blue	150	300	500
Soup Tureen and Ladle, dark blue	950	1900	3000
Tureen, covered, English Derby type, Partridge	950	1900	3000
Whippet	225	450	750

Above: Staffordshire Spaniels are more valuable as pairs. Potteries have produced them almost continuously for the past century and a half. The larger and older the pair, the more valuable. — Items courtesy of Valerie Hoyt.

Stangl Pottery

In 1926, John M. Stangl, acting as president of Fulper, bought the Anchor Pottery Company of Trenton and began manufacturing there as the Stangl Pottery Company. After his death in 1972, the Wheaton Glass Co. purchased and ran the company until 1978.

The following entries are from Colonial Dinnerware line. This line has a fluted shape and carries the shape number 1388 inscribed on the bottom. Ranger (cowboy) pieces are a favorite and worth somewhat more.

	LOW	AVG.	HIGH
Baker, Pie	$ 25	$ 35	$ 45
Baking Shell	14	19	24
Bean Pot	45	55	65
Bean Pot, ind.	20	30	40
Bowl, soup w/ lid	21	27	33
Butter Chip	7	9	11
Candlabra	35	45	55
Candlestick	14	18	22
Carafe, w/ lid, wood handle	40	55	70
Casserole, 5"-8"	30	40	50
Chop Plate, 12"-14"	30	38	46
Cigarette Box, 8.5"	28	35	42
Coaster	10	13	16
Coffee Pot	46	60	75
Compote, 7"	21	26	31
Console Bowl, 12"	38	46	54
Cream/Sugar	26	32	38
Cup/Saucer	16	20	24
Custard Cup	9	12	15
Dish, 6"	12	15	18
Egg Cup	11	14	17
Gravy Boat	22	28	33
Hors d'oeuvres, 9"-12"	27	36	44
Jar, Storage, w/ lid	45	60	75
Mixing Bowl, 5"-14"	30	38	45
Mug	12	15	17
Pitcher, 3"-6"	21	28	34
Pitcher, Ball form	46	58	69
Pitcher, Syrup	27	34	41
Plate, 6"-8"	6	7	8
Plate, 9"-10"	13	17	20
Plate, grill, 10"	17	22	26
Platter, oval, 12"-14"	17	21	24
Relish Tray Dish, 2 pc., 7"	15	19	23
Salad Bowl, lug, 8"-10"	24	32	40
Salt/Pepper	18	23	27
Teapot, 6 cup	50	60	70
Teapot, ind.	28	36	43
Vegetables, oval, 10"	18	23	28

Stoneware Crocks

Although specimens date back to 1641, most thick earthenware crocks were made in the 19th century; those with an interior glaze appeared after 1900. With the introduction of the automatic glassblowing machine in 1903, the use of pottery crocks declined.

Clockwise from above left: early American crock, $200-$400; Dundee Marmalade, $10-$15; reproduction early American crock, 7", $10-$20; stenciled crock with glaze damage on lower right, reducing value by over 50%.

	LOW	AVG.	HIGH
American Stone Ware, blue letters, gray, 13.5"	$ 40	$ 50	$ 60
F.A. Ames Co., Owensboro, KY, flat, tan and brown, 3.5"	50	60	70
Anderson's Weiss Beers, 7.5"	15	19	23
Armour Co., Chicago, jug, pouring spout, white, 7.5"	30	40	50
B. & J. Arnold, London, England, Master Ink, dark brown, 9"	22	26	30
B & H, cream, 3"	40	50	60
Bass Co., NY, cream, 9.5"	25	30	35
Bean Pet, label, light blue, 4.5"	7	9	11
L. Beard, on shoulder, cream and blue, blob top, 8.5"	30	35	40
Bellarmine Jug, c. 1920, w/mask, 2 horseshoe dec. below mask, 13"	45	55	65
Jas. Benjamin, Stoneware Depot, Cincinnati, OH, stencil lettering, 9"	50	60	70
Jas. Benjamin, Stoneware Depot, Cincinnati, OH, stencil lettering, 13.5"	60	70	80
Bitter, label, olive, brown trim, 10.5"	50	60	70
B.B. Bitter Mineral Water, Bowling Green, MO, white, 5 gal., 15"	55	65	75
Black Family Liquor Store, H.P. Black, 1-gal. jug, ivory & dark brown	40	50	60
Black Family Liquor Store, stamped in blue glaze, brown & tan, 1 gal.	30	35	40
Blue Picture Print Ginger Jar, w/ building and junk in sail, 3.5"	30	40	50
Boston Baked Beans, HHH on back, brick color. 1.5"	9	11	13
Boston Baked Beans, OK on back, brick color, 1.5"	9	11	13
Bowers Three Thistles Snuff, cream color w/ blue lettering, 2-3 gal.	60	70	80

	LOW	AVG.	HIGH
Brownings Pale Ale, Lewes, potters mark: Stephen Green's Lambeth ..	$ 20	$ 25	$ 30
Bryant & Woodruff, Pittsfield, Ma. handled jug, blue gray, 7"	40	45	50
Butter, no label, handle, blue-gray decoration, 4"	40	45	50
Butter, no label, blue-gray decoration, 5.25"	29	34	40
California Pop, pat. Dec. 29, 1872, blob top, tan, 10.5"	80	100	120
California Cough Balm, brown, crock jug w/ handle, 3.5"	150	175	200
Cambridge Springs Mineral Water, in 2 lines, 2.5", brown and tan	30	35	40
Canning, inscribed "Hold Fast That Which is Good," dark brown, 6.5" .	36	44	52
Canning, wax sealer, 6"	34	39	44
Canning, wax sealer, reddish brown, 8"	32	38	45
Canning, blue w/ gray decorative design, 8.5"	35	42	48
Canning, mustard color, 7"	28	34	39
Canning, maple leaf design in lid, caramel color, 6"	17	22	25
Canning, wax channel, brown, 8.5"	26	30	34
Canning, reddish brown, green on inside, 6.5"	26	31	36
Canning, crude, brown, 4"	17	21	24
Canning, wax sealer, dark brown, 5.5"	23	29	35
Canning, wax sealer, tan, 5.5"	23	29	34
Canning, wax sealer, mottled gray, 5"	15	18	20
Canning, barrel, dark brown, 5.5"	20	25	29
Canning, lid, star design, dark brown, 8.5"	28	34	40
Canning, dark brown, 7.5"	25	30	35
Canning, tan, 9"	28	32	38
Canning, wax channel, brown, 7.5"	20	25	30

TV Lamps

TV lamps have been described as outrageous forms for subtle lighting. We define TV lamps as those lamps and lamp/planter or lamp/clock combinations that produce an indirect light either shaded by its position within its figural structure or by a screen shade or an inset shade. These lamps serve in many capacities but are now categorized as TV lamps. The need for TV lamps arose from the fear that flickering TV images could harm eyesight if not offset by another source of light. The lamps also allowed 1950s homemakers a means to lessen the intrusiveness of the electronic box. In the early 1950s manufacturers such as Royal Haeger often revamped vases and figural pieces based on pre-war designs. It is not uncommon to see a vase produced in the late 1930s fitted as a lamp in the 1950s (collectors avoid home conversions). As the fifties progressed makers integrated bold and sometimes bizarre themes of fashion and design into TV lamps. They produced lights in the shape of pink poodles, Siamese cats, and flying ducks.

Avoid chipped or cracked examples, especially when these defects detract from the lamp's visual appeal. When using a lamp make sure it is wired properly. One common mistake is using a higher wattage bulb than the lamp's specification. This causes the singe marks sometimes seen on shade screens and cracks around the lighting fixtures of many lamps. Low-wattage low-heat bulbs are recommended. For further reading we recommend *Turned On*, Leyland & Crystal Payton, Abbeville Press, NY, 1989.

Above left to right: Galleon, $40-$50; ship on green wave base, $30-$40. Below: Mallard in flight, $35-$50.

	LOW	HIGH
Antelope & Leaf, brown, green highlights, Royal Haeger, 11" x 17"	$ 30	$ 40
Black King, in maroon & gold (head vase style)	60	80
Blacksmith at Forge, plaster	25	35
Blue Birds, Double, plaster tray, Lane, 11" x 13"	50	75
Cabin Cruiser, metal sails, light-up portholes, 14" x 17"	50	75
Carp, pink, gold accents, 6.5" x 13"	25	35
Cats, Siamese, cut-out eyes, mkd. Kron, Texans Inc., ht. 13"	45	65
Chinese Figures, pr. of lamps w/ pierced gold fixtures, ht. 11"	80	120
Chinoiserie Double Planter, green, brass surround, 7.5" x 11"	18	24
Comedy & Tragedy Mask "Tri-Wonder Lamp," Royal Haeger, ht. 8"	80	100
Cougars, Double, brown & cream, 8" x 11"	30	40
Cowboy Horse, w/ red fiberglass conical shade, 11" x 11"	25	35
Criss-Cross Sides & green shade insert, 7" x 12.5"	60	90
Dancer, Leaping, gold & black plaster, 13" x 15"	40	60
Deer, Porcelain, w/ plaster tray, 13" x 13.5"	45	65
Deer, small running, green, w/ leaf & vine, 5" x 10"	15	20
Doves, white & gold, Royal Fleet Company	20	30
Farm Scene, Vinyl, Cylindrical, pierced gold metal base, ht. 11.5"	15	20
Fawn, white, pink planter, Electrolite, ht. 8"	25	35
Fish, Double, gray & maroon	40	60
Flower in Basket, green, ht. 9"	25	35
Galleon Clock/Lamp, wooden, Gilbrator Precision, 18" x 13"	30	45
Galleon, multicolor, 9.5" x 12"	40	50
Gazelle, Leaping, black, green & cream, Royal Haeger, 10" x 12"	40	60
Gazelle, Leaping, black, swirling base, 11" x 16"	45	65
Gazelles, Leaping Twin, planter, swirl plume base, 11" x 14"	35	65
Horse Head Bust, brown, ht. 14.5"	25	35
Horse Head, Knight Style, gray, cut-out eyes, ht. 14"	45	55
Horse on Rocky Plateau, white, ht. 13"	35	45
Horse, porcelain, on plaster rocky bluff base, Lane, 11" x 13.5"	30	40
Horse, small, black, 5.5" x 10.5"	20	30
Leaf Form, 7" x 12"	25	35
Leaf, green, "triple frond," 5" x 13.5"	25	35
Leopard in Forest, small, w/ green screen, ht. 9"	35	45
Mallard in Flight, planter surround, 11.5" x 14.5"	35	50
Mallard in Flight, planter surround, small, 11" x 10"	30	45
Mare & Colt, brown, 8.5" x 11"	30	40
Mare & Colt, gray, 9.5" x 10"	35	45
Mermaid, w/ deep sea background, 7.5" x 9.5"	90	140
Mountain Lion, Crouching, "chiseled" rock base, 7.5" x 18"	45	65
Nude, Reclining Accordion Player, plaster, screen back, 9" x 14"	70	90
Owl, cut-out eyes, mkd. Kron, Texans Inc., ht. 12"	80	100
Owl, whimsical, Maddux	25	35
Panther on Rock, beige, 9" x 9"	30	40
Panther on Rock, brown & cream, 8.5" x 9"	35	45
Panther, black planter, len. 22"	25	45
Panther, black w/ rhinestone eyes, len. 22"	25	45
Panther, brown planter, len. 22"	25	45
Panther, cut out-eyes, lime green, Royal Haeger, len. 20"	35	45
Panther, leaf & log base, gray base, 9" x 15"	30	40
Panther, leaf & log base, pink & gray base, 9" x 15"	40	50

Above left to right: Mermaid, deep sea screen background $90-$140; nude with accordion, plaster, $70-$90. Below left to right: Owl, cut-out eyes, $80-$100; German Shepherd, plaster, $70-$90.

	LOW	HIGH
Panther, plaster w/ green screen background, 8.5" x 17"	$ 45	$ 65
Panther, small, black w/ gold accents, len. 15"	25	30
Panther, small, green, 5" x 11"	20	30
Panther, small, pink, 6" x 9"	25	35
Panther, white screen, oval base, Royal Haeger	40	60
Pierced Metal, black, inner shade & wire legs, ht. 13"	12	18
Plastic Surround Landscape, ht. 10"	12	18
Poodles, double pink, 10" x 13	80	100
Rooster, Crowing, maroon, ht. 10"	24	32
Sailboat Planter, small, green, ht. 8.5"	15	25
Sailing Ship, gray waves base, ht. 11"	30	40
Sampan, w/ Asian couple, green, gold highlights, 6" x 16"	35	45
Shell, Conch, pink w/ white & gold, Premco, ht. 11"	35	55
Ship, green stylized wave base, 10" x 11"	30	40
Stag, Leaping, green, 11.5" x 10.5	20	30
Stallion, Running, black, yellow, & white highlights, 11" x 15"	40	60
Swan, small, pink w/ plastic rose, ht. 10"	10	15
Swan, white, blue water base, Maddux, ht. 11"	20	30
Tree Trunk, stylized, brown, green, & white, ht. 10"	18	22
Tropical Leaves, Lane, 13.5" x 10.5"	50	70
TV, stylized, metal, porthole w/ scene, 7" x 11"	30	40

Van Briggle Pottery

Artus and Anne Van Briggle founded this arts and crafts pottery in 1901. It dominated the western market with pots and vases of stylized tree limbs, cactus, and other plants. Colors included Mountain Craig (green to brown), Midnight (black), Moonglo (off-white), Persian Rose, Turquoise Ming, and Russet.

The first and most famous mark consisted of the letters AA, the initials of Van Briggle and his wife, Anne. The mark often included the date of production until 1920. These are the most desireable pieces. A stock number often appeared, especially on later pieces. The words "HAND CARVED" are often on pieces with raised decoration.

Van Briggle marks.

	LOW	AVG.	HIGH
Ashtray, 5.25", Indian Girl, rose color, matte, signed	$ 280	$ 335	$ 390
Ashtray, 5.5", rose, spiral interior	30	35	40
Ashtray, 6.5", trapezoid, Turquoise Ming	30	35	40
Ashtray, Female Nude w/ shell, 7", blue, matte , signed	340	370	400
Bookends, pair, rams, red and blue glaze	220	250	280
Bowl, 12" #762, pine cone	90	100	110
Bowl, 12.5", rose glaze, leaf motif	280	350	420
Bowl, #283, 10.5", Moonglo, flower and stem motif, c. 1908	240	280	320
Bowl, 3", acorn form, brown, c. 1915	230	265	300
Bowl, 3", rose, butterfly decor	90	100	110
Bowl, 3.5", rose glaze, cherry, leaf and vine motif	130	140	150
Bowl, 4", fiat, small base, brown, leaf motif, c. 1917	130	145	160
Bowl, 4", red, leaf motif across top, c. 1914	50	55	60
Bowl, 5", plain dec., maroon, signed, c. 1918	180	220	260
Bowl, 5", rose, scalloped rim, flared ends	30	35	40
Bowl, 5.25", green, floral and leaf motif	180	200	220
Bowl, 6", acorn and leaf motif across top	40	50	60
Bowl, 6", flat, yellow, leaf motif, c. 1903	740	845	950
Bowl, 6", rose, swirled ivy motif	50	55	60
Bowl, 8", #22, styled leaves, bronzed, c. 1905	1300	1600	1900
Bowl, 8", #22, styled leaves, yellow w/green on leaves, c. 1917 ...	1800	2000	2200
Bowl, 8", #762, pine cone and branches	50	60	70
Bowl, 8", styled leaves, #22, Turquoise Ming, c. 1902	1000	1200	1400
Bowl, #878, 2", bulbous shape, band of berries and leaves, pink and green, c. 1908	230	260	290
Bowl, #903D, 8.5", frog and dragonfly motif, Turquoise Ming	90	110	130
Candlesticks, 6", pair, rose, double tulip motif	50	55	60
Conch, 9", Turquoise Ming	50	55	60
Creamer, 2", hexagon, Turquoise Ming	20	20	20
Cup, 3.25", six incised panel lines, Turquoise Ming, c. 1917	50	55	60
Figurine, 3", elephant, on base, yellow and brown	50	55	60
Figurine, 4", donkey, Turquoise Ming	40	50	60

	LOW	AVG.	HIGH
Figurine, 4", elephant, rose, triangular ears	$ 110	$ 125	$ 140
Figurine, 4.5", elephant, Turquoise Ming, trunk raised	40	50	60
Figurine, 8", cat, sits on base, long neck	70	90	110
Figurine, 8", detailed girl grinding corn, Turquoise Ming	40	50	60
Figurine, 8.5", rearing horse, on stand, brown	70	80	90
Figurine, 9.5", owl on stump, brown	390	485	580
Jug, "Firewater," 7", #12, yellow, c. 1905	10,000	12,500	15,000
Lamp, 18", flat base, narrow neck, horse motif, red	100	110	120
Lamp, 20", bulbous, Moonglo	70	80	90
Mug, #28B, plain, 5.5", blue, c. 1912	700	800	900
Ornament, 3", oval, angel w/ trumpet, natural glaze, c. 1980	30	35	40
Ornament, 4", "Noel," natural glaze, c. 1978	40	45	50
Paperweight, 3.5", rabbit, green and brown	90	105	120
Paperweight, Rabbit, 2.5", Turquoise Ming, c. 1914	110	125	140
Pitcher, 11", bulbous, Turquoise Ming	70	85	100
Pitcher, 3", Moonglo	30	35	40
Pitcher, 3.5", bulbous, handled, collared neck, Turquoise Ming, ca. 1908	200	240	280
Planter, 12.5", rose shell form	70	85	100
Planter, 9", blue, floral motif	50	60	70
Plaque, 4.5", oval, rise glaze, Indian head design	70	85	100
Plate, 8", #20, stylized poppy, blue, c. 1917	450	475	500
Plate, 8", #20, stylized poppy, green, white, c. 1904	2200	2600	3000
Tile, 6", water lilies, green leaves, Turquoise Ming, c. 1910	950	1120	1290
Vase, 10", #17, white, c. 1916	11,000	13,000	15,000
Vase, 10", Lorelei, #17, maroon, c. 1911	1000	1200	1400
Vase, 10.5", #240, ribbed, handles, green, c. 1910	1080	1195	1310
Vase, 10.5", #240, ribbed, handles, maroon, c. 1915	290	320	350
Vase, 12", 3 head Indian, 12", maroon, c. 1912	350	405	460
Vase, 12", 3 head Indian, brown, c. 1915	2400	2800	3200
Vase, 12.25", urn form, ribs, handles, Turquoise Ming, matte, signed, c. 1920	350	425	500
Vase, 14", #139, Yucca, floral dec., c. 1910	4000	4500	5000
Vase, 14", #139, Yucca, maroon, c. 1904	2000	2200	2400
Vase, 14", #139, Yucca, red flowers, c. 1903	6000	7000	8000
Vase, 2", bulbous body, red, leaf and stem motif, c. 1919	80	90	100
Vase, 2", rose, c. 1918	120	135	150
Vase, 3", bulbous body, blue butterfly motif, c. 1921	110	120	130
Vase, 3", flared rim, feather motif, Turquoise Ming	30	35	40
Vase, 4", rose, c. 1917	210	245	280
Vase, 4", rose, ivy and floral motif	50	55	60
Vase, 4" rose, tulip shaped, scalloped rim	20	25	30
Vase, 4.5", #645, violet floral, white w/green buds, c. 1911	600	700	800
Vase, 4.5", #645, violets & leaves, blue, c. 1908	50	60	70
Vase, 4.5", #645, violets & leaves, green, c. 1918	250	270	290
Vase, 4.5", ivy and floral motif, Turquoise Ming	30	35	40
Vase, 4.5", rose, butterfly motif	110	140	170
Vase, 5", bulbous body, collared neck, green, leaf motif, c. 1908	110	125	140
Vase, 5", rose and green, floral motif, c. 1905	630	700	770
Vase, 5", rose, floral motif	40	50	60
Vase, 5.25", rose, heart shaped, ivy motif	40	50	60

	LOW	AVG.	HIGH
Vase, 5.5", #833, flowers, green, c. 1923	$ 620	$ 670	$ 720
Vase, 5.5", #833, flowers, Turquoise Ming, c. 1930	30	35	40
Vase, 6", #132, flowers, black, c. 1909	2100	2500	2900
Vase, 6", #132, flowers, green, c. 1919	1500	1750	2000
Vase, 6", #132, flowers, rose, c. 1905	1200	1500	1800
Vase, 6", #132, flowers, white flowers, c. 1910	3500	4000	4500
Vase, 6", flowers, bronzed, c. 1915	2250	2500	2750
Vase, #645, violets & leaves, 4.5", brown w/ green, c. 1930	50	60	70
Vase, 7", cylinder shape, collared neck, Turquoise Ming, c. 1916	400	430	460
Vase, 8", bulbous body, narrow neck, handled, red and blue, leaf motif, c. 1920	60	75	90
Vase, 8", floral dec., blue, c. 1986	40	45	50
Vase, 8", floral dec., brown, c. 1970	60	65	70
Vase, 8", floral dec., brown w/ green drip	30	35	40
Vase, 8", floral dec., Moonglo matte white, c. 1965	40	45	50
Vase, 8", floral dec., Turquoise Ming matte, c. 1960	40	45	50
Vase, 8", floral dec., yellow, c. 1989	30	35	40
Vase, 8.5", Moonglo, bird of paradise motif	30	35	40
Vase, 9", open handles, rose color, matte, signed, c. 1920	400	470	540
Vase, 9", rose, flower and leaf motif	100	115	130

Prints, Photographs, and Other Images

Audubon

John James Audubon is a name synonymous with bird pictures. His "Birds of America" series is recognized worldwide. Between 1826 and 1842, Audubon traveled throughout the United States and Canada gathering material to paint this famous work.

Today, experts believe there are less than 200 sets of "Birds of America" actually bound in volumes. The work was engraved by R. Havell and Son in London. There are 435 plates in a complete set. In 1971 an exact facsimile edition of 250 copies was printed in Amsterdam.

We list the original Havel prints, first with a typical auction range; next, a retail price is given (R), followed by retail prices for the later Bien edition (B) and the Amsterdam printing (A). Entries are listed sequentially by plate number, followed by subject. For further information refer to *The Official Price Guide to Collector Prints,* published by The House of Collectibles, Random House, NY.

Above: Plate 260, Fork-tail Petrel.
Below: Plate 224, Kittiwake Gull.

PLATE #	SUBJECT	AUCTION RANGE		R	B	A
1	Turkey Cock	$ 12,000	$ 18,000	$ 37,500	$ 3000	$ 2400
2	Yellow-billed Cuckoo	2500	3500	7500	620	500
3	Prothonotary Warbler	800	1000	2200	200	160
4	Purple Finch	600	1000	2000	150	120
5	Bonaparte's Flycatcher	800	1200	2500	200	160
6	Hen Turkey	10,000	15,000	31,000	2500	2000
7	Purple Grackle	3000	4000	8800	750	600
8	White-throated Sparrow	1000	1500	3100	250	200
9	Selby's Flycatcher	800	1000	2200	200	160
10	Brown Titlark	5000	700	7100	1250	1000
11	Bird of Washington	3000	4000	8800	750	600
12	Baltimore Oriole	3000	5000	10,000	750	600
13	Snow Bird	800	1000	2200	200	160
14	Prairie Warbler	1500	2500	5000	380	300
15	Blue Yellow-backed Warbler	1500	2000	4400	380	300
16	Great-footed Hawk	3000	4000	8800	750	600
17	Carolina Turtle Dove	8000	12,000	25,000	2000	1600
18	Bewick's Wren	800	1000	2200	200	160
19	Louisiana Water Thrush	800	1000	2200	200	160
20	Blue-winged Yellow Warbler	2000	3000	6200	500	400
21	Mockingbird	4000	5000	11,200	1000	800
22	Purple Martin	2000	3000	6200	500	400
23	Maryland Yellow Throat	1200	1800	3800	300	240
24	Roscoe's Yellow Throat	800	1000	2200	200	160
25	Song Sparrow	800	1000	2200	200	160
26	Carolina Parrot	7000	11,000	22,500	1750	1400
27	Red-headed Woodpecker	2000	3000	6200	500	400
28	Solitary Flycatcher	600	900	1900	150	120
29	Towhe Bunting	800	1200	2500	200	160
30	Vigor's Warbler	1000	1000	2500	250	200
31	White-headed Eagle	3000	5000	10,000	750	600
32	Black-billed Cuckoo	4000	5000	11,200	1000	800
33	American Goldfinch	2500	3540	7600	620	500
34	Worm-eating Warbler	1000	1500	3100	250	200
35	Children's Warbler	600	1000	2000	150	120
36	Stanley Hawk	2000	2500	5600	500	400
37	Golden-winged Woodpecker	3000	4000	8800	750	600
38	Kentucky Warbler	800	1200	2500	200	160
39	Crested Titmouse	1200	1800	3800	300	240
40	American Redstart	2000	3000	6200	500	400
41	Ruffed Grouse	4000	6000	12500	1000	800
42	Orchard's Oriole	800	1200	2500	200	160
43	Cedar Bird	2000	3000	6200	500	400
44	Summer Red Bird	2000	3000	6200	500	400
45	Traill's Flycatcher	600	900	1900	150	120
46	Barred Owl	3000	5000	10,000	750	600
47	Ruby-throated Hummingbird	10,000	15,000	31,200	2500	2000
48	Azure Warbler	800	1200	2500	200	160
49	Blue-green Warbler	800	1200	2500	200	160
50	Black & Yellow Warbler	600	900	1900	150	120
51	Red-tailed Hawk	3000	4000	8800	750	600

*Right: Plate 68,
Cliff Swallow.*

*Left: Plate 107,
Canada Jay.*

PLATE #	SUBJECT	AUCTION RANGE		R	B	A
52	Chuck Will's Widow	$ 2000	$ 4000	$ 7500	$ 500	$ 400
53	Painted Finch	2000	3000	6200	500	400
54	Rice Bird	800	1200	2500	200	160
55	Cuvier's Regulus	800	1200	2500	200	160
56	Red-shouldered Hawk	6000	8000	17,500	1500	1200
57	Loggerhead Shrike	1000	1500	3100	250	200
58	Hermit Thrush	800	1200	2500	200	160
59	Chestnut-sided Warbler	1200	1800	3800	300	240
60	Carbonated Warbler	1200	1800	3800	300	240
61	Great Horned Owl	6000	8000	17,500	1500	1200
62	Passenger Pigeon	5000	8000	16,200	1250	1000
63	White-eyed Flycatcher or Vireo	800	1200	2500	200	160
64	Swamp Sparrow	800	1200	2500	200	160
65	Rathbon's Warbler	800	1200	2500	200	160
66	Ivory-billed Woodpecker	4000	7000	13,800	1000	800
67	Redwinged Starling	2000	3000	6200	500	400
68	Cliff Swallow	800	1200	2500	200	160
69	Bay-breasted Warbler	1000	1800	3500	250	200
70	Henslow's Bunting	1200	1800	3800	300	240
71	Winter Hawk	2000	3000	6200	500	400
72	Swallow-tailed Hawk	3000	5000	10,000	750	600
73	Wood Thrush	1000	1500	3100	250	200
74	Indigo Bunting	1200	1800	3800	300	240
75	Le Petit Caporal	1000	1500	3100	250	200
76	Virginia Partridge	3000	5000	10,000	750	600
77	Belted Kingfisher	2000	4000	7500	500	400
78	Great Carolina Wren	2000	2500	5600	500	400
79	Tyrant Flycatcher	1000	1500	3100	250	200
80	Prairie Titlark	1000	1500	3100	250	200
81	Fish Hawk or Osprey	15,000	25,000	50,000	3750	3000
82	Whip-Poor-Will	1540	6600	10,200	380	310
83	House Wren	2000	3000	6200	500	400
84	Blue-gray Flycatcher	800	1200	2500	200	160
85	Yellow-Throated Warbler	800	1200	2500	200	160
86	Black Warrior	2000	3000	6200	500	400
87	Florida Jay	2000	4000	7500	500	400
88	Autumnal Warbler	800	1200	2500	200	160
89	Nashville Warbler	800	1200	2500	200	160
90	Black and White Creeper	700	900	2000	180	140
91	Broad-winged Hawk	4000	6000	12,500	1000	800
92	Pigeon Hawk	1000	1500	3100	250	200
93	Sea Side Flinch	2000	4000	7500	500	400
94	Bay-winged Bunting	600	900	1900	150	120
95	Blue-eyed Yellow Warbler	800	1200	2500	200	160
96	Columbia Jay	2000	3000	6200	500	400
97	Little Screech Owl	2000	4000	7500	500	400
98	White-bellied Swallow	600	900	1900	150	120
99	Cow Pen Bird	800	1200	2500	200	160
100	Marsh Wren	600	900	1900	150	120
101	Raven	2000	4000	7500	500	400
102	Blue Jay	800	1200	2500	200	160

*Left: Plate 324,
Bonaparte's Gull.*

Below: Plate 210, Least Bittern.

PLATE #	SUBJECT	AUCTION RANGE		R	B	A
103	Canada Warbler	$ 800	$ 1200	$ 2500	$ 200	$ 160
104	Chipping Sparrow	700	1000	2100	180	140
105	Red-breasted Nuthatch	600	900	1900	150	120
106	Black Vulture	1000	2000	3800	250	200
107	Canada Jay	1000	1500	3100	250	200
108	Fox Colored Sparrow	800	1200	2500	200	160
109	Savannah Finch	800	1200	2500	200	160
110	Hooded Warbler	500	700	1500	120	100
111	Pileated Woodpecker	10,000	15,000	31,200	2500	2000
112	Downy Woodpecker	1500	2500	5000	380	300
113	Blue Bird	1200	1800	3800	300	240
114	White-crowned Sparrow	600	900	1900	150	120
115	Wood Pewee	600	900	1900	150	120
116	Ferruginous Thrush	1500	2500	5000	380	300
117	Mississippi Kite	1500	2500	5000	380	300
118	Warbling Flycatcher	1500	2500	5000	380	300
119	Yellow Throated Vireo	800	1200	2500	200	160
120	Pewee Flycatcher	500	700	1500	120	100
121	Snowy Owl	25,000	35,000	75,000	6250	5000
122	Blue Grosbeak	800	1200	2500	200	160
123	Black and Yellow Warbler	2000	3000	6200	500	400
124	Green-Black Capped Flycatcher	800	1200	2500	200	160
125	Brown-headed Nuthatch	600	800	1800	150	120
126	White-headed Eagle (young)	2000	4000	7500	500	400
127	Rose-breasted Grosbeak	2000	4000	7500	500	400
128	Cat Bird	800	1200	2500	200	160
129	Great Crested Flycatcher	600	900	1900	150	120
130	Yellow-winged Sparrow	700	1000	2100	180	140
131	American Robin	4000	6000	12,500	1000	800
132	Three-toed Woodpecker	2000	4000	7500	500	400
133	Black Poll Warbler	800	1200	2500	200	160
134	Hemlock Warbler	800	1200	2500	200	160
135	Blackburnian Warbler	1000	1500	3100	250	200
136	Meadow Lark	8000	12,000	25,000	2000	1600
137	Yellow-Breasted Chat	3000	5000	10,000	750	600
138	Connecticut Warbler	1200	1800	3800	300	240
139	Fed Sparrow	800	1200	2500	200	160
140	Pine-creeping Warbler	1000	1500	3100	250	200
141	Goshawk	2000	3000	6200	500	400
142	American Sparrow Hawk	2000	3000	6200	500	400
143	Golden Crowned Thrush	700	1000	2100	180	140
144	Small Green-Crested Flycatcher	1000	1500	3100	250	200
145	Yellow Red Poll Warbler	700	900	2000	180	140
146	Fish Crow	2000	3000	6200	500	400
147	Night Hawk	3000	5000	10,000	750	600
148	Pine Swamp Warbler	600	900	1900	150	120
149	Sharp-tailed Finch	800	1200	2500	200	160
150	Red-eyed Vireo	600	900	1900	150	120
151	Turkey Buzzard	1500	2500	5000	380	300
152	White-Breasted Nuthatch	2000	4000	7500	500	400
153	Yellow-Rump Warbler	1500	2500	5000	380	300

PLATE #	SUBJECT	AUCTION RANGE		R	B	A
154 .... Tennessee Warbler		$ 800	$ 1200	$ 2500	$ 200	$ 160
155 ... Black-throated Blue Warbler		1000	1500	3100	250	200
156 .... American Crow		2000	4000	7500	500	400
157 .... Rusty Grackle		600	900	1900	150	120
158 .... American Swift		500	700	1500	120	100
159 .... Cardinal Grosbeak		5000	7000	15,000	1250	1000
160 .... Black-capped Titmouse		800	1200	2500	200	160
161 .... Caracara Eagle		4000	6000	12,500	1000	800
162 .... Zenaida Dove		800	1200	2500	200	160
163 .... Palm Warbler		800	1200	2500	200	160
164 .... Tawny Thrush		1000	1500	3100	250	200
165 .... Bachman's Finch		1200	1800	3800	300	240
166 .... Rough-legged Falcon		3000	5000	10,000	750	600
167 .... Key West Quail Dove		3000	5000	10,000	750	600
168 .... Fork-tailed Flycatcher		3000	5000	10,000	750	600
169 .... Mangrove Cuckoo		1500	2500	5000	380	300
170 .... Gray Tyrant		800	1200	2500	200	160
171 .... Barn Owl		7000	10,000	21,200	1750	1400
172 .... Blue-headed Pigeon		1200	1800	3800	300	240
173 .... Barn Swallow		2000	3000	6200	500	400
174 .... Olive Sided Flycatcher		800	1200	2500	200	160
175 .... Marsh Wren		600	900	1900	150	120
176 .... Spotted Grouse		3000	5000	10,000	750	600
177 .... White-crowned Pigeon		3000	5000	10,000	750	600
178 .... Orange-crowned Warbler		500	700	1500	120	100
179 .... Wood Wren		800	1200	2500	200	160
180 .... Black Capped Titmouse		800	1200	2500	200	160
181 .... Golden Eagle		4000	6000	12,500	1000	800
182 .... Ground Dove		2500	3500	7500	620	500
183 .... Golden-crested Wren		600	900	1900	150	120
184 .... Mangrove Hummingbird		2000	3000	6200	500	400
185 .... Bachman's Warbler		1000	1500	3100	250	200
186 .... Pinnated Grouse		6000	8000	17,500	1500	1200
187 .... Boat-tailed Grackle		2000	3000	6200	500	400
188 .... Tree Sparrow		700	1000	2100	180	140
189 .... Snow Bunting		800	1200	2500	200	160
190 ..... Yellow-bellied Woodpecker		1200	1800	3800	300	240
191 .... Willow Grouse		3000	5000	10,000	750	600
192 .... Great American Shrike		800	1200	2500	200	160
193 .... Lincoln Finch		1200	1800	3800	300	240
194 .... Canadian Titmouse		500	700	1500	120	100
195 .... Ruby-crowned Wren		800	1200	2500	200	160
196 .... Labrador Falcon		2500	3500	7500	620	500
197 .... American Crossbill		1200	1800	3800	300	240
198 .... Worm-eating Warbler		800	1200	2500	200	160
199 .... Little Owl		800	1200	2500	200	160
200 .... Shore Lark		600	900	1900	150	120
201 .... Canada Goose		4000	6000	12,500	1000	800
202 .... Red-throated Diver		2000	4000	7500	500	400
203 .... Fresh Water Marsh Wren		1000	1500	3100	250	200
204 .... Salt Water Marsh Wren		600	800	1800	150	120

PLATE #	SUBJECT	AUCTION RANGE		R	B	A
205	Virginia Rail	$ 700	$ 1000	$ 2100	$ 180	$ 140
206	Summer or Wood Duck	8000	12,000	25,000	2000	1600
207	Booby Gannet	1200	1800	3800	300	240
208	Esquimaux Curfew	800	1200	2500	200	160
209	Wilson's Plover	500	700	1500	120	100
210	Least Bittern	1500	2500	5000	380	300
211	Great Blue Heron	25,000	35,000	75,000	6250	5000
212	Common Gull	1200	1800	3800	300	240
213	Puffin	2000	3000	6200	500	400
214	Razor Sill	800	1200	2500	200	160
215	Phalarope	600	900	1900	150	120
216	Wood Ibis	10,000	15,000	31,200	2500	2000
217	Louisiana Heron	15,000	25,000	50,000	3750	3000
218	Foolish Guillemar	800	1200	2500	200	160
219	Black Guillemar	1500	2500	5000	380	300
220	Piping Plover	600	900	1900	150	120
221	Mallard Duck	20,000	30,000	62,500	5000	4000
222	White Ibis	3000	5000	10,000	750	600
223	Pied Oyster Catcher	1000	1500	3100	250	200
224	Kittiwake Gull	600	900	1900	150	120
225	Kildeer Plover	500	700	1500	120	100
226	Whooping Crane	10,000	15,000	31,200	2500	2000
227	Pin-tailed Duck	5000	7000	15,000	1250	1000
228	Green-wing Teal	3000	5000	10,000	750	600
229	Scaup Duck	2000	4000	7500	500	400
230	Ruddy Plover	600	800	1800	150	120
231	Long-billed Curlew	10,000	20,000	37,500	2500	2000
232	Hooded Merganser	3000	5000	10,000	750	600
233	Sora or Rail	500	700	1500	120	100
234	Tufted Duck	1500	2500	5000	380	300
235	Sooty Tern	600	900	1900	150	120
236	Night Heron	4000	6000	12,500	1000	800
237	Great Esquimaux Curlew	1000	1500	3100	250	200
238	Great Marbled Codwit	1000	1500	3100	250	200
239	American Coot	1200	1800	3800	300	240
240	Roseate Tern	2000	3000	6200	500	400
241	Black-Backed Gull	1000	1500	3100	250	200
242	Snowy Heron	15,000	25,000	50,000	3750	3000
243	American Snipe	2000	3000	6200	500	400
244	Common Gallinule	800	1200	2500	200	160
245	Thick-billed Murre	600	800	1800	150	120
246	Eider Duck	10,000	15,000	31,200	2500	2000
247	Velvet Duck	2000	3000	6200	500	400
248	American Pied-Bill Dobchick	1500	2500	5000	380	300
249	Tufted Auk	1000	1500	3100	250	200
250	Arctic Tern	2000	3000	6200	500	400
251	Brown Pelican	12,000	18,000	37,500	3000	2400
252	Florida Cormorant	1500	2500	5000	380	300
253	Pomarine Jager	1000	1500	3100	250	200
254	Wilson's Phalarope	700	900	2000	180	140
255	Red Phalarope	800	1200	2500	200	160

PLATE #	SUBJECT	AUCTION RANGE		R	B	A
256	Purple Egret	$ 5000	$ 7000	$ 15,000	$ 1250	$1000
256	Purple Heron	4000	6000	12,500	1000	800
257	Double Crested Cormorant	1500	2500	5000	380	300
258	Hudsonian Godwit	800	1200	2500	200	160
259	Horned Grebe	1200	1800	3800	300	240
260	Fork-tail Petrel	800	1200	2500	200	160
261	Whooping Crane	12,000	18,000	37,500	3000	2400
262	Tropic Bind	2000	4000	7500	500	400
263	Curlew Sandpiper	800	1200	2500	200	160
264	Fulmar Petrel	800	1200	2500	200	160
265	Buff-Breasted Sandpiper	800	1200	2500	200	160
266	Common Cormorant	1000	1500	3100	250	200
267	Arctic Jager	1000	1500	3100	250	200
268	American Woodcock	2000	3000	6200	500	400
269	Greenshank	1200	1800	3800	300	240
270	Stormy Petrel	500	700	1500	120	100
271	Frigate Pelican	2000	4000	7500	500	400
272	Richardson's Jager	600	900	1900	150	120
273	Cayenne Tern	1000	1500	3100	250	200
274	Semipalmated Snipe	800	1200	2500	200	160
275	Noddy Tern	500	700	1500	120	100
276	King Duck	2000	3000	6200	500	400
277	Hutchins' Goose	1500	2500	5000	380	300
278	Schinz's Sandpiper	600	900	1900	150	120
279	Sandwich Tern	1200	1800	3800	300	240
280	Black Tern	600	800	1800	150	120
281	Great White Heron	15,000	25,000	50,000	3750	3000
282	White-winged Silvery Gull	800	1200	2500	200	160
283	Wandering Shearwater	600	800	1800	150	120
284	Purple Sandpiper	600	900	1900	150	120
285	Fork-tailed Gull	800	1200	2500	200	160
286	White-fronted Goose	3000	5000	10,000	750	600
287	Ivory Gull	1200	1800	3800	300	240
288	Yellow Shank	3000	5000	10,000	750	600
289	Solitary Sandpiper	1200	1800	3800	300	240
290	Red-backed Sandpiper	800	1200	2500	200	160
291	Herring Gull	3000	5000	10,000	750	600
292	Crested Grebe	2000	3000	6200	500	400
293	Large-billed Puffin	1500	2500	5000	380	300
294	Pectoral Sandpiper	800	1200	2500	200	160
295	Manx Shearwater	500	700	1500	120	100
296	Barnacle Goose	3000	4000	8800	750	600
297	Harlequin Duck	1200	1800	3800	300	240
298	Red-nicked Grebe	800	1200	2500	200	160
299	Dusky Petrel	600	900	1900	150	120
300	Golden Plover	400	600	1200	100	80
301	Canvasback Duck	600	900	1900	150	120
302	Black Duck	2000	3000	6200	500	400
303	Upland Sandpiper	1500	2500	5000	380	300
304	Turnstone	600	800	1800	150	120
305	Purple Gallinule	2000	3000	6200	500	400

Above: Plate 328, Long Legged Avocet.

Above: Plate 325, Bufflehead.

PLATE #	SUBJECT	AUCTION RANGE		R	B	A
306	Common Loon	$ 1500	$ 2500	$ 5000	$ 380	$ 300
307	Little Blue Hen	10,000	15,000	31,200	2500	2000
308	Greater Yellow Legs	800	1200	2500	200	160
309	Common Tern	2000	3000	6200	500	400
310	Spotted Sandpiper	800	1200	2500	200	160
311	American White Pelican	15,000	25,000	50,000	3750	3000
312	Long-Tailed Duck	1200	1800	3800	300	240
313	Blue-winged Teal	3000	5000	10,000	750	600
314	Laughing Gull	800	1200	2500	200	160
315	Sandpiper	600	900	1900	150	120
316	Black Bellied Darter	3000	4000	8800	750	600
317	Surf Duck	1000	1500	3100	250	200
318	Avocet	1200	1800	3800	300	240
319	Lesser Tern	1500	2500	5000	380	300
320	Little Sandpiper	800	1200	2500	200	160
321	Roseate Spoonbill	8000	12,000	25,000	2000	1600
322	Red-head Duck	2000	4000	7500	500	400
323	Black Skimmer	2000	3000	6200	500	400
324	Bonaparte's Gull	800	1200	2500	200	160
325	Bufflehead	2000	3000	6200	500	400
326	Gannet	3000	5000	10,000	750	600
327	Shoveller Duck	7000	10,000	21,200	1750	1400
328	Long Legged Avocet	1500	2500	5000	380	300
329	Yellow Rail	600	900	1900	150	120
330	Plover	500	700	1500	120	100
331	American Merganser	4000	6000	12,500	1000	800
332	Labrador Duck	1500	2500	5000	380	300
333	Green Heron	3000	5000	10,000	750	600
334	Black-bellied Plover	400	600	1200	100	80
335	Red-bellied Sandpiper	800	1200	2500	200	160
336 .	Yellow Crowned Night Heron	3000	5000	10,000	750	600
337	American Bittern	1500	2500	5000	380	300
338	Bemaculated Duck	3000	5000	10,000	750	600
339	Little Auk	600	900	1900	150	120
340	Stormy Petrel	600	900	1900	150	120
341	Great Auk	2000	3000	6200	500	400
342	Golden-eyed Duck	2000	3000	6200	500	400
343	Ruddy Duck	1500	2500	5000	380	300
344	Long-legged Sandpiper	600	900	1900	150	120
345	American Widgeon	1500	2500	5000	380	300
346	Black Throated Diver	4000	6000	12,500	1000	800
347	American Bittern	1500	2500	5000	380	300
348	Gadwall Duck	2000	3000	6200	500	400
349	Least Water Hen	800	1200	2500	200	160
350	Rocky Mountain Plover	500	700	1500	120	100
351	Great Cinereous Owl	3000	5000	10,000	750	600
352	Black-winged Hawk	800	1200	2500	200	160
353	Chestnut-Backed Titmouse	2000	3000	6200	500	400
354	Louisiana Tanager	2000	4000	7500	500	400
355	MacGillivray's Finch	800	1200	2500	200	160
356	Marsh Hawk	3000	5000	10,000	750	600

PLATE #	SUBJECT	AUCTION RANGE		R	B	A
357	American Magpie	$ 1200	$ 1800	$ 3800	$ 300	$ 240
358	Pine Grosbeak	500	700	1500	120	100
359	Arkansas Flycatcher	800	1200	2500	200	160
360	Winter and Rock Wren	700	1000	2100	180	140
361	Long-tailed Grouse	1500	2500	5000	380	300
362	Yellow-billed Magpie	1500	2500	5000	380	300
363	Bohemian Chatterer	800	1200	2500	200	160
364	White-winged Grossbill	1000	1500	3100	250	200
365	Lapland Longspur	500	700	1500	120	100
366	Iceland Falcon	12,000	18,000	37,500	3000	2400
367	Band-tailed Pigeon	3000	5000	10,000	750	600
368	Rock Grouse	1200	1800	3800	300	240
369	Mountain Mockingbird	1200	1800	3800	300	240
370	American Water Ouzel	600	900	1900	150	120
371	Cock of the Plains	3000	5000	10,000	750	600
372	Common Buzzard	1000	1500	3100	250	200
373	Evening Grosbeak	800	1200	2500	200	160
374	Sharp-Shinned Hawk	800	1200	2500	200	160
375	Lesser Red Poll	800	1200	2500	200	160
376	Trumpeter Swan	3000	5000	10,000	750	600
377	Scolopaceys Courlan	1800	2200	5000	450	360
378	Hawk Owl	1000	1500	3100	250	200
379	Ruff-necked Hummingbird	3000	5000	10,000	750	600
380	Tengmalm's Owl	600	900	1900	150	120
381	Snow Goose	2000	4000	7500	500	400
382	Sharp-tailed Grouse	1200	1800	3800	300	240
383	Long-eared Owl	1200	1800	3800	300	240
384	Black-throated Bunting	700	1000	2100	180	140
385	Bank Swallow	200	1200	1800	50	40
386	Great American Egret	12,000	18,000	37,500	3000	2400
387	Glossy Ibis	3000	5000	10,000	750	600
388	Troopial (Orioles)	500	700	1500	120	100
389	Red-cocked Woodpecker	700	1000	2100	180	140
390	Prairie Finch	600	900	1900	150	120
391	Brant Goose	2000	3000	6200	500	400
392	Louisiana Hawk	1200	1800	3800	300	240
393	Blue-winged Teal	600	900	1900	150	120
394	Buntings and Finches	1000	1500	3100	250	200
395	Audubon's Warbler	800	1200	2500	200	160
396	Burgomaster Gull	1500	2500	5000	380	300
397	Scarlet Ibis	3000	5000	10,000	750	600
398	Lazuli Finch	600	900	1900	150	120
399	Black-throated Warbler	800	1200	2500	200	160
400	Townsend's Finch	600	900	1900	150	120
401	Red-Breasted Merganser	2000	4000	7500	500	400
402	Auks and Guillemots	1000	1500	3100	250	200
403	Golden-eyed Duck	1200	1800	3800	300	240
404	Eared Grebe	800	1200	2500	200	160
405	Semipalmated Sandpiper	600	900	1900	150	120
406	Trumpeter Swan	3000	5000	10,000	750	600
407	Dusky Albatross	800	1200	2500	200	160

PLATE #	SUBJECT	AUCTION RANGE		R	B	A
408	American Scoter Duck	$ 1200	$ 1800	$ 3800	$ 300	$ 240
409	Havell's Tern	1200	1800	3800	300	240
410	Marsh Tern	1500	2500	5000	380	300
411	Common American Swan	12,000	18,000	37,500	3000	2400
412	Violet Green Cormorant	1000	1500	3100	250	200
413	California Partridge	1000	1500	3100	250	200
414	Golden-winged Warbler	600	900	1900	150	120
415	Brown Creeper	1000	1500	3100	250	200
416	Hairy Woodpecker	3000	5000	10,000	750	600
417	Maria's Woodpecker	2000	3000	6200	500	400
418	American Ptarmigan	800	1200	2500	200	160
419	Little Tawny Thrush	500	700	1500	120	100
420	Prairie Starling	800	1200	2500	200	160
421	Brown Pelican, young	8000	12,000	25,000	2000	1600
422	Rough-legged Falcon	1200	1800	3800	300	240
423	Plumed Partridge	1200	1800	3800	300	240
424	Lazuli Finch	500	700	1500	120	100
425	Columbian Hummingbird	1500	2500	5000	380	300
426	California Condor	2000	4000	7500	500	400
427	White-Legged Oyster Catcher	1200	1800	3800	300	240
428	Townsend's Sandpiper	500	700	1500	120	100
429	Western Duck	800	1200	2500	200	160
430	Slender-billed Guillemot	600	900	1900	150	120
431	American Flamingo	20,000	30,000	62,500	5000	4000
432	Burrowing Owl	800	1200	2500	200	160
433	Bullock's Oriole	400	600	1200	100	80
434	Little Tyrant Pewee, 1	400	600	1200	100	80
435	Columbian Water Ouzel	400	600	1200	100	80

Cigar Box Labels

The major types of cigar box labels are inside lids (placed on the inside lid of the box), box end labels (placed on the ends of the box), and box sealers (which seal the lid to the sides). They came into use in the middle of the 19th century. Witsch & Schmitt of New York created many artistic labels. Most collected labels are multicolored stone lithographs dating from the turn of the century.

Labels damaged when removed are usually worthless. In the early 1900s printers often sold unused bands directly to collectors.

Right: The Colonel, inside label. Below left to right: Orlando cigar box displaying inside label; Cremo Cigar box inside label. — Item courtesy of Pastimes.

	LOW	AVG.	HIGH
A Dream, small boy riding bicycle, full colors, 4" x 5.5"	$ 20.00	$ 21.25	$ 25.00
Acropolis, inside lid, 6" x 9", c. 1920	3.00	4.25	5.50
Alcazar, inside lid, 6" x 9", c. 1920	1.00	2.00	3.00
American Twins, twin girls, full colors, 6" x 9", c. 1880-90			
(This brand of cigar was sold by the pair)	40.00	43.00	50.00
Barrister, inside lid, 6" x 9", c. 1895	8.00	9.50	11.00
"Big Five," inside lid, 6" x 9", c. 1935	.20	.25	.30
Blue Bird, inside lid, 6" x 9", c. 1930	1.00	2.00	3.00
Blue Goose, box end label, 4"x 4", c. 1935	.20	.25	.30
Blue Goose, inside lid, 6" x 9", c. 1935	.50	1.00	1.50
Calendar, inside lid, 6" x 9", c. 1905	13.00	15.50	18.00
Castellanos, inside lid, 6" x 9", c. 1930	1.00	2.00	3.00
Castle Hall, inside lid, 6" x 9", c. 1940	.25	.50	.75
Christy Girl, box end label, 4" x 4", c. 1932	.50	1.00	1.50
Christy Girl, inside lid, 6" x 9", c. 1932	2.00	2.50	3.00
College Inn, box sealer, 2" x 3", c. 1910	.25	.50	.75
College Inn, inside lid, 6"x 9", c. 1910	8.00	10.00	12.00
Custom House, inside lid, 6" x 9", c. 1930	3.00	4.00	5.00
Damasco, inside lid, 6" x 9", c. 1900	13.00	15.00	17.00
Diamond Crown, box end label, 2" x 5", c. 1940	.20	.25	.30

	LOW	AVG.	HIGH
Diamond Crown, inside lid, 6" x 9", c. 1940	$ .50	$ 1.00	$ 1.50
Don Alfonso, inside lid, 6" x 9", c. 1905	14.00	15.00	16.00
Don Nieto, box end label, 2" x 5", c. 1940	.20	.25	.30
Don Nieto, inside lid, 6" x 9", c. 1940	.20	.25	.30
Duo Art, box end label, 4" x 4", c. 1930	.25	.50	.75
Duo Art, inside lid, 6" x 9", c. 1930	.25	.50	.75
Edmund Halley, inside lid, 6" x 9", c. 1900	8.00	10.00	12.00
El Escudero, box end label, 4" x 4", c. 1940	.20	.25	.30
El Escudero, inside lid, 6" x 9", c. 1940	.20	.25	.30
El Guardo, inside lid, 6" x 9", c. 1910	4.00	5.50	7.00
Farragut, inside lid, 6" x 9", c. 1905	8.00	10.00	13.00
Fidelity, box end label, 4" x 4", c. 1945	.25	.50	.75
Fidelity, inside lid, 6" x 9", c. 1945	.25	.50	.75
Flor de Franklin, Ben Franklin flying a kite, full color, 3" x 5"	30.00	31.50	35.00
For Cash Only, man buying cigar from female clerk, full color, 6"x 6", late1800s (In the late 1800s many restaurants kept open boxes of cigars at the cashier's desk. Patrons were welcome to take one for free. Better-grade cigars could be purchased. For Cash Only" - wasn't to be mistaken for a freebie.)	40.00	43.00	50.00
Garcia Y Garcia, inside lid, 6" x 9", c. 1937	.50	.80	1.25
Garcia Y Hermanos, box end label, 4" x 4", c. 1920	4.00	5.00	6.00
Garcia Y Hermanos, inside lid, 6" x 9", c. 1920	3.50	4.50	5.50
Lord Vernon, inside lid, 6" x 9", c. 1930	2.00	3.25	4.50
Madrigal, inside lid, 6" x 9", c. 1930	.25	.50	.75
Manila Blunts, inside lid, 6" x 9", c. 1942	.20	.25	.30
Miss Pluck, pictures woman & corset, color, 8" x 9", c. 1885	35.00	37.00	45.00
Moro Light, inside lid, 6" x 9", c. 1938	.50	1.00	1.50
Newport Club, men riding stage past hotel, color, 4.25" x 5.25"	20.00	21.50	25.00
Old Abe, Lincoln in gray and white w/ embossed gold, 7" x 9"	20.00	21.50	25.00
Old Hickory, box end label, 4" x 4", c. 1930	.25	.50	.75
Old Hickory, inside lid, 6" x 9", c. 1930	.50	1.00	1.50
Old Hickory, Andrew Jackson, color, 7" x 8", c. 1930	20.00	26.00	25.00
Our Bird, Lindbergh's airplane *Spirit of St. Louis*, 7" x 9" 1927	25.00	26.00	30.00
Our Fire Laddies, uniformed firemen and engine, color, c. 1880	30.00	33.00	40.00
Our Kitties, box sealer, 2" x 3"	.25	.50	.75
Peace Time, box end label, 4" x 4"	.25	.50	.75
Peace Time, inside lid, 6" x 9", c. 1927	.25	.50	.75
Pearl, inside lid, 6" x 9", c. 1925	3.00	4.50	6.00
Pony Pest, box end label, 4" x 4"	4.00	5.00	6.00
Prima Rosa, inside lid, 6" x 9", c. 1930	2.00	2.75	3.50
Prize Beauty, young girl, c. 1880	4.00	5.75	6.50
Pug, inside lid, 6" x 9", c. 1903	7.00	9.50	12.00
Quaker Quality, box end label, 4" x 4", c. 1934	.50	1.00	1.50
Quaker Quality, inside lid, 6" x 9", c. 1934	.50	1.00	1.50
Red Ball, couple on skates w/ huge red ball, color, 4.25" x 5.25"	30.00	31.50	35.00
Red Dandies, inside lid, 6" x 9", c. 1900	14.00	15.25	16.50
Regal X Ten, inside lid, 6" x 9", c. 1920	3.00	4.50	6.00
Rigoletto, inside lid, 6" x 9", c. 1929	1.00	2.00	3.00
Rolamo, inside lid, 6" x 9", c. 1945	.20	.25	.30
Rosa Moro, inside lid, 6" x 9", c. 1940	.25	.50	.75

Currier & Ives

In 1835, Nathaniel Currier started a lithography company in New York. James Ives joined in 1852 as a bookkeeper. Currier and Ives was unique in its ability to combine artistic talent, skilled craftsmanship, appropriate technology, and merchandising acumen into a successful business enterprise. It employed well-known artists of the day, including Maurer, Palmer, Tait, and Worth. The finest materials were used: stones from Bavaria (where lithography was invented), lithographic crayons from France, and colors from Austria. The firm invented a lithographic crayon, reputed to be superior to all others, and produced a lithographic ink of beef suet, goose grease, white wax, castile soap, gum mastic, shellac, and gas black. Mass distribution and low cost were the keys to success. Uncolored prints sold for as little as six cents each and even large-colored folios sold for no more than three dollars. Prints were sold door-to-door by peddlers and in the streets by pushcart vendors, and even overseas through agents. The firm of Currier and Ives was dissolved in 1907. Although an estimated ten million prints sold, only a small percentage survive today.

Published in various sizes, the prints are commonly grouped into folio sizes shown below:

Very Small: up to approximately 7" x 9"
Small: approximately 8.8" x 12.8"
Medium: approximately 9" x 14" to 14" x 20"
Large: anything over 14" x 20"

The sizes pertain to the image only, not the margin. Often, print owners trimmed the margins of the pictures, so an uncut print is more valuable than a pared one.

Most prints were struck in black and white and then hand colored. Because of this method, different colorings of the same print are found. Folio sizes Very Small, Small, and Medium were completed in this manner. However, the Large folios were sometimes partially printed in color and then finished by hand, usually by only one artist. Many of these prints have been reprinted often. Beware buying a modern calendar print. For further information see *Currier's Price Guide to Currier and Ives Prints*, Kaminski Auctioneers, (800) 344-0760.

Each print is given with its Conningham number (C#), a reference to the checklist by Frederic Conningham, *Currier and Ives Prints*. Over fifty years ago, Mr. Conningham referred to the "Best Fifty" in both the Large Folio size and the Small Folio size. Many of these are still the top valued prints of Currier and Ives, though some have fallen from grace. We've listed these 100 prints with their current retail ranges. C#'s followed by an asterisk are known to appear on more than one composition

Hudson Near Cold Spring, #2977, small, sold at auction for $150. — Photo courtesy of Northeast Auctions.

	C#	LOW	HIGH
The Best Fifty (small folio)			
1. The Express Train 1790*		$ 2000	$ 4000
2. American Railroad Scene-Snowbound 187*		2000	4000
3. Beach Snipe Shooting 445		2500	3000
4. Ice-boat Race on the Hudson 3021		2000	4000
5. Central Park in Winter 953		2000	2500
6. The Star of the Road 5701		600	800
7. The High Bridge at Harlem, N.Y. 2810*		300	500
8. Maple Sugaring, Early Spring in the Northern Woods 3975		1000	1500
9. Shakers Near Lebanon 5475		1500	2500
10. Winter Sports-Pickerel fishing 6747		1200	1800
11. The American Clipper Ship *Witch of the Wave* 115		800	1200
12. Gold Mining in California 2412		1200	1800
13. The Great International Boat Race 2623		1200	1800
14. Wild Turkey Shooting 6677		600	800
15. Perry's Victory on Lake Erie 4754		500	700
16. Washington at Mount Vernon, 1797 6515		400	600
17. The Whale Fishery, "Laying On" 6626		1000	1500
18. Chatham Square, New York. 1020		500	700
19. Water Rail Shooting 6567		600	900
20. The Sleigh Race 5554		1500	2500
21. Franklin's Experiment 2128		600	900
22. Washington Crossing the Delaware 6523*		300	500
23. American Homestead Winter 172		600	900
24. Washington Taking Leave of the Officers of His Army 6547		300	500
25. Steamboat Knickerbocker 5727		500	700
28. Kiss Me Quick! 3349*		400	600
27. On the Mississippi Loading Cotton 4607		1000	1500
28. Bound Down the River 627		800	1200
29. American Whalers Crushed in the Ice 205		1500	2500
30. Dartmouth College 1446*		2000	4000
31. Terrific Combat Between the *Monitor*, 2 Guns, and the *Merrimac*, 10 Guns 5996*		400	600
32. General Francis Marion 2250		400	600
33. Art of Making Money Plenty 275		500	700
34. Hon. Abraham Lincoln 2895		200	400
35. Gen. George Washington (w/ cape) 2261		150	250
36. Black Bass Spearing 543		2000	2500
37. Early Winter 1652		3000	5000
38. Woodcock Shooting 6773*		500	700
39. "Dutchman" and "Hiram Woodruff" 1640		600	800
40. Great Conflagration at Pittsburg. Pa. 2581		600	800
41. Bear Hunting, Close Quarters 446*		1500	2000
42. The Destruction of Tea at Boston Harbor 1571		800	1200
43. Cornwallis is Taken 1258		400	600
44. Landing of the Pilgrims at Plymouth, 11th Dec., 1620 ...... 3435*		300	500
45. The Great Fight for the Championship 2613		300	500
46. Benjamin Franklin 499*		400	600
47. Noah's Ark 4494*		200	400
48. Black Eyed Susan 551		200	400
49. The Bloomer Costume 573*		300	500
50. The Clipper Yacht *America* 1173*		1000	1500

The Best Fifty (large folio)	C#	LOW	HIGH
1. Husking	3008	$ 8000	$ 12,000
2. American Forest Scene- Maple Sugaring	157	10,000	15,000
3. Central Park Winter-The Skating Pond	954	15,000	20,000
4. Home to Thanksgiving	2882	12,000	18,000
5. Life of a Hunter-A Tight Fix	3522	40,000	60,000
6. Life on the Prairie-The Buffalo Hunt	3527	5000	7000
7. The Lightning Express Trains Leaving the Junction	3535*	10,000	15,000
8. Peytona and Fashion	4763	10,000	15,000
9. The Rocky Mountains- Emigrants Crossing the Plains	5196	12,000	18,000
10. Trolling for Blue Fish	6158	8000	12,000
11. Whale Fishery-The Sperm Whale in a Flurry	6627	5000	10,000
12. Winter in the Country-The Old Grist Mill	6738	8000	12,000
13. American Farm Scenes No. 4 (Winter)	136	6000	9000
14. American National Game of Baseball	180	25,000	35,000
15. American Winter Sports-Trout Fishing on Chateaugay Lake	210*	6000	9000
16. Mink Trapping-Prime	4139	8000	12,000
17. Preparing for Market	4870*	3000	5000
18. Winter in the Country-Getting Ice	6737	10,000	15,000
19. Across the Continent-Westward the Course of Empire Takes Its Way	33	12,000	18,000
20. Life on the Prairie-The Trappers Defense	3528	5000	7000
21. The Midnight Race on the Mississippi	4116	5000	8000
22. The Road Winter	5171	15,000	25,000
23. Summer Scenes in New York Harbor	5876	4000	6000
24. Trotting Cracks at the Forge	6169	7000	10,000
25. View of San Francisco	6409	8000	12,000
26. Wreck of the Steamship *San Fransisco* (also known as "Ships Antarctic of N.Y." and "3 Bells")	5492	$ 4000	$ 6000
27. Taking the Back Track "A Dangerous Neighborhood"	5961	5000	7000
28. American Field Sports-Flushed	149	3000	5000
29. American Hunting Scenes-A Good Chance	174	5000	8000
30. American Winter Scenes-Morning	208	5000	7000
31. Autumn in New England-Cider Making	322	10,000	15,000
32. Catching a Trout-"We Hab You Now, Sar"	845	4000	6000
33. Clipper Ship *Nightingale*	1159	4000	6000
34. The Life of a Fireman-The Race	3518	2000	3000
35. Mac and Zachary Taylor-Horse Race	3848	1500	2500
36. New England Winter Scene	4420	6000	9000
37. Rail Shooting on the Delaware	5054	4000	6000
38. Snowed Up-Ruffed Grouse-Winter	5581	5000	7000
39. Surrender of General Burgoyne at Saratoga	5907	2000	3000
40. Surrender of Cornwallis at Yorktown	5906	2000	3000
41. Clipper Ship *Red Jacket*	1165*	5000	7000
42. American Winter Sports-Deer Shooting on the Shettagee	209	6000	8000
43. The Bark "Theoxana"	371	7000	9000
44. The Cares of a Family	814*	2500	3500
45. The Celebrated Horse Lexington	887*	2000	3000
46. Grand Drive-Central Park	2481	3000	4000
47. The Great Fire at Chicago	2615	5000	8000
48. Landscape, Fruit and Flowers	3440	5000	7000
49. The Life of a Fireman-The Metropolitan System	3516	3000	5000
50. The Splendid Naval Triumph on the Mississippi	5659	2000	2500

Fruit Crate Labels

The decorative labels that adorned the sides of wooden fruit crates are popular collectibles. The oldest and rarest date to the 1880s. Rarity and design are the important variables with fruit crate labels. California labels are usually worth more than Florida labels, and orange labels usually have more ornate designs. Label designs changed over the years, and some collectors focus on labels that have undergone design changes.

	LOW	AVG.	HIGH
Aftisaimo, CA, citrus, pictures mountains in pink and blue on a blue sky background, dated 1918, 10" x 11"	$2	$4	$5
Ahtanum, WA, pear, three pears, mountains, stock label #947, pictorial	7	11	14
Airline, CA, citrus, globe with wings, stars in red, white and blue, 10" x 11"	2	4	6
Airship, CA, citrus, pictures commercial airplane, royal blue, 10" x 11"	12	20	28
Ak-Sar-Ben, CA, citrus, picture of oranges on a blue background, 10" x 11"	2	4	6
All American, WA, apple, flag type shield, patriotic appearance, blue background, pictorial	9	14	18
All Year, CA, citrus, black border frames landscape scene, 12.5" x 8.5"	2	3	4
Alpine Orchards, WA, pear, three pears, yellow, red, black background, pictorial	5	8	11
Blue Mountain, WA, apple, silhouette of trees and mountains, two apples in right corner, orange background, blue border	21	26	31
Blue Streak, WA, apple, large red ribbon seal with two red apples, brown border	7	11	15
Blue Tip, CA, citrus, picture of a large feather, 9" x 9"	1	2	3
Blue Winner, WA, apple, cowboy on horseback picking up an apple in a rodeo, blue and white background	6	10	13
Boa Vista Ranch, CA, apple, mountains, orchard and farm house, one red and one golden apple, blue border	3	7	10
Bolero, CA, apple, Spanish dancer with two guitarists, black background	10	14	17
Bounty, CA, pear, bright yellow background, blue and red lettering, blue border	2	5	8
Boy Blue, WA, apple, boy with horn, white lettering	8	12	15
Boy Blue, WA, pear, boy about to blow an old horn, blue background, white letters	6	10	13
Briant, WA, apple, Washington State map, white and blue lettering, blue background	2	5	8
Briskey, WA, apple, snowy scene from Naches Pass, mountains and two red apples, black background, blue border	4	7	10
Broadway, CA, pear, red and black lettering (old) graphic type, gold leaf, blue background, blue-green border	5	8	11
Bronco, CA, citrus, old stone litho of fully dressed cowboy riding a wild horse, very colorful	6	10	13
Brownie's, CA, citrus, pictures Brownies preparing orange juice against a yellow sun and blue background, 10" x 11"	2	5	8
Buckaroo, WA, apple, cowboy breaking a bucking horse, mountains and desert, yellow sky	12	17	21
Buddy, Michigan, broker label, smiling baby, blue background, green border, 1920	8	12	16
Buffalo, CA, apple, angry looking buffalo, red lettering, blue background, green border	7	11	15

	LOW	AVG.	HIGH

Bunting, WA, apple, one red apple, ribbon sash through the center, red lettering, blue background .... $ 7 — $ 10 — $ 13

Butler's Pride, WA, apple, branch with large red apple, white lettering, graphic, blue background .... 2 — 5 — 8

Cal-Flavor, CA, citrus, oranges, blossoms and leaves against a wood grained and black background, 10" x 1I" .... 2 — 5 — 8

Caledonia, CA, citrus, picture of Scotch thistles on plaid background, 10" x 11" .... 1 — 2 — 3

Cambria, CA, citrus, brown border frames a brown eagle and two torches against a blue background, 10" x 11" .... 2 — 5 — 8

Carefree, CA, citrus, pictures a girl with blonde hair laughing against a blue background, 10, x 11" .... 2 — 5 — 8

Carro Amano Arancl, CA, citrus, pictures Italian fruit peddler with a cart full of oranges, 10" x 11" .... 2 — 5 — 8

Chief Joseph, WA, apple, large white arrowhead with Chief Joseph's image in front of it, dressed in full headdress and beads, historic, red lettering, blue background .... 16 — 21 — 25

Cho Paks, WA, apple, trees, mountains, distant orchard scene, blue background .... 19 — 23 — 27

Chore Best, WA, apple, aqua inset with block lettering, blue background .. 2 — 5 — 8

Circle A&F, WA, apple, yellow and black lettering, circle in center with A & F in white loners, black background .... 7 — 11 — 14

Clasen, WA, apple, old litho of orchard homes and Mt, Adams in the background, two red apples on a limb, red lettering, 40 lbs, (old) .... 6 — 10 — 13

Cliff, WA, apple, rock cliffs with raging waterfall, span bridge over water with old sedan driving over it, orchard hills, blue sky and rod lettering, brown border .... 7 — 11 — 14

Clipper, FL, citrus, three-mast schooner, 7" x 7", ... 2 — 4 — 6

Clipper Ship, WA, apple, large sailing ship on the ocean, blue background .... 40 — 45 — 50

Coed, CA, citrus, pictures smiling girl in graduate cap and gown against a purple background, 10" x 11" .... 2 — 5 — 8

Color Guard, WA, apple, blue bottom, yellow lettering, graphic, black background .... 5 — 8 — 11

Columbia Bell, WA, apple, patriotic dressed lady with crown and holding a drawn sword, one red apple, blue and white background .... 7 — 11 — 14

Columbia, WA, apple, mountains, cliffs, Columbia River gorge, farm, houses, orchards, ghostly Statue of Liberty with torch in background (the torch is emitting a light on two large apples), blue background, rare .... 90 — 105 — 120

Congden Refrigerated, WA, apple, first edition label, one red apple frozen in a block of ice, art deco lettering, black background .... 32 — 40 — 48

Congdon Refrigerated, WA, pear, pear frozen in a block of ice .... 9 — 13 — 17

Corona Uly, CA, citrus, white and gold speckled lily against a black background, 10" x 11" .... 3 — 6 — 9

Desert Bloom, CA, citrus, white, blooming yucca with desert greenery and mountains against a blue sky background, 10" x 11" .... 3 — 6 — 9

Dewy Fresh, WA, apple, modern green leaf, fairy in leafy skirt holding a wand, believed to be one of the last labels printed, white and red background, 1958 .... 3 — 7 — 10

Diamond, OR, apple, red diamonds in center with white letters saying Hood River Apples (cartoon of apple head man), green background ... 12 — 17 — 21

Diamond, OR, pear, ML Hood scone, red diamond shipper is apple growers service .... $ 4 $ 8 $ 12

Diamond S, CA, pear, two horse heads, blue diamond 14   17   20

Dinner Gong, WA, apple, one red apple with leaves and stem, black bottom, blue background 2   5   8

Diving Girl, CA, apple, 1920s girl in swimming suit diving into the lake .. 13   19   24

Dixie Boy, FL, citrus, picture of a black boy, 9" x 9" 4   7   10

Don Juan, CA, pear, orchard scene in upper left corner, blue/black/red background 3   6   9

Don't Worry, WA, apple, blond boy holding apple with bite out of it, written white letters, shiny black background 10   14   17

Donnater, TX, citrus, pink grapefruit against a black background, 9" x 9" . 1   2   2

Double A, CA, citrus, train supported by two capital letter As on a trestle, 10" x 11" 2   4   5

Duckwall, OR, apple, stone wall with a very colorful duck in front, red background 32   40   49

Dunbar, OR, pear, cartoon pear skiing down snowy hill, yellow letter, blue sky 6   10   14

Eagle, CA, pear, eagle and two pears, red lettering, blue background, yellow border 8   12   16

Eat One, CA, citrus, pictures arrow pointing to an orange, aqua background, 10" x 11" 2   5   8

Eatmor, WA, pear, 1920s boy in plaid knickers, holding a pear, red lettering, green background, rare 40   53   66

Eatum, WA, apple, one red and one golden apple, yellow letters, graphic type label, blue and black background 2   5   8

El Mejor, CA, citrus, pictures Sunkist orange, 10" x 11" 2   4   5

Emerald Beauty, WA, pear, Spanish lady playing a guitar, rare 38   45   52

Emerald Green, WA, apple, suit of armor head with shield with a large emerald on it, green background 7   10   13

Empire Builder, WA, apple, mountains, large warehouse, trucks, train orchards, large apple covered wagon and four oxen 3   6   9

Empire, WA, apple, evaporated apples, old litho of mountains, orchards and trees 7   11   15

Endurance, CA, citrus, night scene pictures walking camels against a purple and black background, 10" x 11" 12   16   19

Esporanza, CA, citrus, pictures a senorita with a carnation in her hair, wearing a lace mantilla and holding a lace fan against a blue background, 10" x 11" 2   4   5

Exeter, CA, citrus, Tulare Co, map against a multicolored background, 10" x 11" 2   4   5

Fide, CA, citrus, white puppy with black spot against a black background, 12.5" x 8.5" 19   25   30

Fiesta, TX, citrus, girl dressed in gown against a black background, 10" x 11" 1   2   2

Fillmore Crest, CA, citrus, blue border frames three oranges and green leaves against a turquoise background, 10"x 11" 2   4   6

First Blue, WA, apple, photo of three apples, light blue and orange letters, on a yellow sash, blue background 3   6   9

Flavor Crest, treasure chest full of red and golden apples (apple label from New York), blue background 12   16   20

LOW AVG. HIGH

Florida Cowboy, FL, citrus, cowboy astride bucking bronco with diamond
    K brand palm trees in background, 9" x 9" .... $ 6 $ 12 $ 18
Florita, CA, citrus, dancing senorita and two guitarists against a black
    background, 10" x 11" 7   11   14
Flying V, WA, apple, photo of red apple, yellow written letters and a V
    with wings on it, blue background 7   15   22
Foothills, OR, pear, old stone litho of orchard, mountain, river and two
    pears 10   14   17
For The Kids Of Austin, WA, apple, stock label, two red apples and a
    leafy limb, Kiwanis International insignia, tufted yellow, blue
    background 6   10   13
Full O' Juice, CA, citrus, pictures half peeled orange and a glass of
    orange juice, lavender background, 10" x 11" 2   5   8
Galleon, CA, citrus, galleon sailing on the open sea, sky background,
    12.5" x 8.5" 3   6   9
Gladiola, CA, citrus, two gladiola sprays on a gold and tan background,
    10" x 11" 3   6   9
Globes O' Gold, CA, citrus, pictures three oranges, blossoms, leaves,
    10" x 11" 2   3   4
Gold Buckle, CA, citrus, outline of a belt with a gold buckle frames an
    orchard scene against a blue background, 10" x 11" 2   5   8
Gold Circle, CA, pear, gold circle, yellow circle, two pears, graphic,
    blue background 4   8   11
Kentucky Cardinal, KY, apple, three apples and a red cardinal on a
    blossoming apple limb, 1918 stone litho 37   47   57
King David, CA, citrus, king with white beard in royal ropes and
    crown, 10" x 11" 2   5   8
Kings Park, CA, citrus, pictures a waterfall and mountain stream,
    10" x 11" 3   6   9
La Relna, CA, citrus, hacienda scene with Spanish senorita holding a
    black fan against a blue background, 10" x 11 2   3   4
Lake View, WA, apple, two goldens with a red apple between them,
    scene of the Pajaro Valley, old, blue background, green border 12   16   19
Lakecove, CA, pear, barefoot boy with straw hat on, loaning on a tree,
    lake and mountain 12   16   19
Lamb, WA, apple, Lamb's first printing, lamb standing on a hillside
    with orchard mountain background, two red apples hanging over
    its head, blue/black border, 19205 artwork, beautiful 125   150   175
Laurea, CA, citrus, pictures oranges, berries, laurel leaves, blue
    background, 10" x 11" 2   3   4
Laurie, CA, apple, little girl with an apple in each hand, she has a pink
    dress on, blue background, 1930s label, rare 22   27   31
Leavenworth, WA, pear, two green pears with white loners, blue
    background 3   7   10
Legal Tender, CA, citrus, pictures U.S, currency in a $250 bundle
    against a blue and black background, 10" x 11" 2   5   8
Lemonade, CA, citrus, three lemons in foreground, orchard scene in
    background, 12.5" x 8.5" 1   2   3
Lincoln, CA, citrus, portrait of Lincoln with oranges and leaves, 10" x 11" ... 3   6   9
Loch Lomond, CA, citrus, Scottish scene on blue and green plaid

	LOW	AVG.	HIGH
background, 10" x 11"	$ 2	$ 3	$ 4
Loop Loop, WA, apple, Indian chief on a palomino horse, he is picking an apple from the horse's back	21	26	31
Loot of Ventura County, CA, citrus, multicolored, 10"x11"	3	6	9
Lucky Lad, WA, apple, large red apple with image of the 1920s farm boy in front of it, gold letters, black background, green border	110	130	150
Lure, WA, apple, image of a big, largemouth bass hooked on a fish plug, bright red letters, blue border	60	70	80
Luxor, WA, apple, big red Maltese cross with the name Luxor in white on it, blue background	23	27	31
M Brand, WA, apple, big blue M with some kind of gold lance behind it, red background, rare	15	21	26
Nimble, CL, citrus, pictures an orange and blossoms against an orchard landscape, aqua background, 10"x11"	2	3	4
Nob Hill, CA, pear, Metropolitan skyscrapers, autos and street cars	11	15	19
Nuchief, WA, apple, little cartoon Indian chief with an apple in his right hand and a tomahawk in his left, says Apples from Washington State, blue background	8	14	20
Orchard King, CL, citrus, orange, with crown, royal blue background, 10" x 11"	2	3	4
Orchard, OR, pear, old stone litho, Model T truck on a road, orchard and mountains, white background	10	16	21
Oriole, CA, citrus, oriole perched on a branch with orange, blossoms and leaves, black background, 10" x 11"	6	10	13
Orland, CA, citrus, pictures old dam scene, 10" x 11"	9	14	18
Our Pride, WA, apple, parrot sitting on a twig, one red apple, black background, blue border, copy 1923, 40 lbs	11	15	19
Prinoeso, CA, citrus, princess in royal robes and crown jewels, with grapefruits, leaves on a blue background, dated 1911	3	5	7
Pure Gold, CA, citrus, pictures prospector and his mule, blue background, 10" x 11"	2	4	6
Pyramid, Canada, apple, three pyramids with river, palm trees, camel and rider, blue background	23	28	32
Queen Esther, CA, citrus, elegant queen dressed in turquoise gown, golden crown, 10" x 11"	5	8	11
Queen Fruits, WA, pear, 2 pears, old queen in full dross, blue background	23	29	34
Quercus Ranch, CA, pear, orchard, sky, lake mountains and two pears	7	10	13
Rancheria, CA, pear, Indian Chief on horse by a maiden, teepees, black background	5	9	13
Red Bird, CA, citrus, large red eagle, black background, 10" x 11"	2	3	4
Red Label, WA, apple, valley scene with town roads, river and mountains, 2 large red apples in the sky, red border	35	41	47
Red Peak, CA, citrus, landscape scene, 10" x 11"	2	3	4
Red Seal, WA, apple, red ribbon with old time red wax seal, 2 red apples, white letters, green background	4	7	10
Red Star, CA, apple, big red star in the center, red and white letters, black background, red border	9	13	16
Red Streak, WA apple, two drawn apples, one red and one golden, red lightning streak shooting through the label, black background, red border	31	38	46

	LOW	AVG.	HIGH

Red Wagon, WA, apple, cartoon boy pulling a red wagon full of red and golden apples, black background, yellow border .... $ 18 $ 24 $ 28

Red Winner, WA, apple, picture inset of Indian maiden in leather and beads, on a white horse, grassy plains, desert and mountains, red and yellow letters, red and white background 9 13 16

Redlands Best, CA, citrus, four blue arrows pointing to big orange in center, 10" x 11" 4 8 12

Redman, WA, apple, Indian brave, behind him are cave drawings, two red apples and one golden, blue background 9 14 18

Reindeer, CA, citrus, reindeer and grove scene against a yellow background, 10" x 11" 4 8 12

Repetition, WA, apple, three identical boys in front of three identical boxes of apples with the same label on them, black background 23 30 36

Rider, FL, citrus, Jockey in white and green silks astride a brown race horse, 9" x 9" 2 3 4

Rocky Hill, CA, citrus, Indian chief on horse standing on cliff against a blue background, 10" x11" 2 3 4

Rose, WA, apple, two large red roses with thorns and leaves, white letters, blue background 7 12 17

Round Robin, OR, pear, big red robin standing on a hill, old, blue background 18 24 30

Royal Feast, CA, citrus, pictures orange, blossoms, dark blue loaves with two lions in black framed by a black checkered border, 10" x 11" . 2 3 4

Royal Knight, CA, citrus, knight on horseback against a yellow background, 10" x 11" 2 3 4

Sails, WA, apple, large sailing ship in a rough choppy sea, yellow and red letters, blue background, red pen line border, 40 lbs 12 16 20

Sam Birch, OR, apple, one red apple, yellow strip through the label with blue letters on it, blue background 19 23 26

Safe Hit, TX, vegetables, 1920s baseball player hitting a ball, grandstand in the background, 7" x 9" 5 9 12

Sun Smile, CA, pear, smiling face of the sun, blue letters, also a blue anchor, sunburst background 6 10 14

Sun Sugared, OR, pear, photo of an orange pear, black background 2 5 8

Sunshine Ranch, WA, apple, large warehouse with Mt, Adams in the background at sunrise, letters in the orange sky say EAT GOOD APPLES FOR VITAMINS/EAT APPLES FOR HEALTH, blue border 22 28 33

Super Crisp, WA, apple, two and-a-half apples, one red and one golden; orchard, house, hill, writing in the sky, blue border, c, 1948 .... 3 7 10

Super-Pak, WA, apple, blue ribbon in a triangle with the lettering on it, black background 2 5 8

Sure Mark, CA, pear, red stripes, blue background 6 10 13

Surety, WA, apple, stone litho of a steamship in a cove with pine trees, orchards, mountains, red sky with blue letters in the sky, in the corner it says "FROM TREE TO TRADE." a busy red lace type border 11 16 20

Swan, WA, apple, big white swan on the water, orange letters, black background 12 17 22

Sweet Sue, WA, apple, three red apples in the center of the label with an inset in front of them with 19205 lady's face, white letters, brown and green border 19 25 31

	LOW	AVG.	HIGH

Talisman, CA, citrus, three talisman roses against a blue and black background, 10" x 11 .... $ 2 | $ 5 | $ 8

Tasty Treet, WA, apple, three apples, two reds with one golden in the center, blue stripe with white lettering on it, on the tail of the last "t" it says YOUR TASTY TREAT TO HEALTH, black background .... 4 | 7 | 10

Tom Cat, CA, citrus, black and white cat reclining on a pillow, 12 .5" x 8 .5" .... 40 | 60 | 80

Topaz, WA, apple, there is a big topaz in the word topaz where the "O" should be, blue background .... 5 | 9 | 12

Triton, WA, apple, King Neptune sitting on a rock by the ocean holding a spear and an apple, he is wearing a gold crown, the sky is orange and pink, blue and light blue border .... 10 | 15 | 20

Uly, CA, citrus, two white calla lilies, green leaves on a black background, 10" x 11" .... 2 | 5 | 8

Louis Icart Prints

Louis Icart's works demonstrate a mastery of dry point, line etching, aquatint, and their variations. Icart produced up to 500 prints each of over 1,000 subjects. However, his works are scarce, because many have been lost or destroyed.

Most prints bear his hallmark near the edge of the print. His signature is also easily identifiable, although subject to forgery and sometimes found on lithographic reproductions of his prints. Earlier works will have his signature but may not bear the hallmark. Most will, however, bear the stamp of his gallery, an oval shape with the letters EM for "estampe moderne." It is possible to have an original Icart with no hallmark at all, but this is rare. Icart often pulled two editions, one for Europe and one for American distribution. Sometimes the number is preceded by the letter "A" for an American edition, for example "A 75/120." Not all prints were numbered.

Clockwise from above: Before the Raid, $2000; Illusion, $14,000; Melody Hour, $2000; Zest, $3000. — Photos courtesy of Phillips Auctioneers.

	LOW	AVG.	HIGH
After the Raid	$ 1525	$ 2262	$ 3000
Angry Steed	2000	3000	4000
Apache Dancer	1880	3940	6000
Arrival	850	1425	2000
Attic Room	2050	4025	6000
Autumn Leaves	700	900	1100
Backstage	880	1440	2000
Bathing Beauties	1550	2275	3000
Before the Raid	2250	3125	4000
Bird of Prey (w/ eagle)	1900	2950	4000
Bird Seller	925	1462	2000
Black Fan	750	1125	1500
Blue Buddha	1000	1600	2400
Bubbles	2100	4050	6000
Carmen	900	1400	1900
Cassanova	1475	2738	4000
Charm of Montmarte	875	1438	2000
Cinderella	825	1212	1600
Coach, The	825	1312	1800
Conchita	1350	1875	2400
Coursing II	1925	3962	6000
Coursing III	1675	3338	5000
D'Artagnan	1175	2088	3000
Dame Rose	1000	1600	2400
Dancer (Finale)	1000	1600	2400
Date Tree	1000	1600	2400
Dear Friends	2125	4062	6000
December	1175	2088	3000
Defense of the Homeland	2475	4238	6000
Descending Coach	1050	1925	2800
Dollar	700	1250	1800
Don Juan	1625	3112	4600
Dream Waltz	1250	1925	2600
Ecstacy	2300	4150	6000
Embrace	925	1562	2200
Eve (Large Oval)	1300	1850	2400
Fair Dancer	1000	1600	2400
Fashion Early	1225	2212	3200
Faust	1100	1850	2600
Favorite	1575	2988	4400
Feeding Time	1075	1938	2800
Finlandia	1275	2338	3400
Flower Vendor	1025	1812	2600
Follies	1500	2750	4000
Forbidden Fruit	1150	2075	3000
Fountain, The	1400	2500	3600
Four Dears	1475	2738	4000
France de Foyer	1950	3475	5000
French Bus	1375	2488	3600
French Doll	800	1300	1800
Frou Frou	1525	2962	4400

	LOW	AVG.	HIGH
Gatsby 1920s	$ 980	$ 1690	$ 2400
Gay Senorita	1130	1965	2800
Gay Trio	1125	1562	2000
German Eagle	1625	2812	4000
Girl in Crinoline	1650	3325	5000
Golden Veil	1600	2800	4000
Goosed	950	1675	2400
Green Broken Jug	1000	1500	2000
Green Robe	1400	2100	2800
Guardian	1300	2350	3400
Gust of Wind	1425	2312	3200
Happy Birthday	2600	5300	8000
Hop-la	1000	1500	2000
Hydrangas	2500	3750	5000
Illusion	10,000	15,000	20,000
Imprudence	1000	1500	2000
In the Trenches	2200	3300	4400
Intimacy	2800	4200	5600
Japanese Garden	1200	1800	2400
Joan of Arc	900	1350	1800
Joy of Life	6000	9000	12,000
Kiss of the Motherland	600	900	1200
Kittens	3000	4500	6000
Lady of the Camelias	1500	2250	3000
Lassitude	900	1350	1800
Laughing	1800	2700	3600
Leda & the Swan	4600	6900	9200
Lilies	3000	4500	6000
Little Bo Peep	1300	2050	2800
Little Kittens	800	1200	1600
Louise	1200	1800	2400
Love's Awakening	1200	1800	2400
Love's Blossom	2400	3600	4800
Madame Bovery	1100	1550	2000
Meditation	1700	2550	3400
Memories	2200	3300	4400
Mimi	800	1200	1600
Minuet	1200	1800	2400
Modern Eve	1800	2700	3600
My Model	3000	4500	6000
New Friends	1200	1800	2400
Nineteen Thirty	1500	2250	3000
On the Branches	900	1350	1800
Orchids	3000	4500	6000
Papillons	1800	2700	3600
Parasol	900	1350	1800
Parfum de Fluers	2400	3600	4800
Recollections (woman at desk)	600	900	1200
Red Alcove	1080	1940	2800
Red Riding Hood	1200	2200	3200
Reflections Pool	2250	4125	6000

	LOW	AVG.	HIGH
Ritz, The	$ 2000	$ 3500	$ 5000
Salomé	1200	2100	3000
Sappho	1200	2200	3200
Scherazade	1100	1950	2800
Seashell	1800	3300	4800
Secrets or Blue Book	1125	2062	3000
Singing Lesson	1075	1838	2600
Sleeping Beauty	1275	2238	3200
Smoke	1625	2812	4000
Spanish Dancer	1325	2462	3600
Speed (w/ greyhound)	1850	3325	4800
Spilled Apples	980	1690	2400
Springtime	1250	2225	3200
Summer Music	800	1400	2000
Swans	1500	2450	3400
Sweet Mystery	1425	2612	3800
Symphony in Blue	1175	2088	3000
Symphony in White	1500	2550	3600
Tennis	1100	1850	2600
Thoroughbreds	2350	3875	5400
Tosca	1225	2212	3200
Treasure Chest	900	1650	2400
Trenches	2500	3800	5000
Unmasked	1250	2025	2800
Venetian Nights	1150	1975	2800
Venus (companion to Eve)	1500	2450	3400
Victory in the Skies	1575	2688	3800
View of Montmartre	1000	1900	2800

Maps

Maps have a long collecting history. Those listed here are some of the earliest still available on the market. You won't find these in the glove compartment of your car, but we've seen these treasures at estate sales and small auctions throughout the country.

Maps are more valuable with original hand coloring, but beware of old maps with new hand coloring. Tears, stains, poor printing, and trimmed margins all reduce value. Maps of the New World are more valuable than those of Europe, especially those of obscure central European areas. A map is almost always more valuable when sold in the area it depicts. The more important the mapmaker, the more valuable the map.

For an extensive listing of maps sold at auction consult *American Book Prices Current*, edited by Katherine and Daniel Leab, at American Book Prices Current, Box 1236, Washington, CT 06793.

In the following entries, the maker is listed first, followed by the title of the map, the place of publication, the date, and the size. The following abbreviations are used: place of printing not identified-N.p.; London-L; New York-NY. Information given in brackets does not appear printed on the map itself.

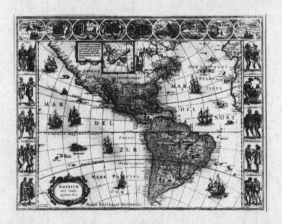

Above: Although all three maps are the same size, by the same maker, and of the same date, the one depicting North and South America is worth twice the value of those depicting Asia and Africa. — Photos courtesy of Phillips Auctioneers

	AUCTION	RETAIL	
		Low	High
Bellin, Jacques N., An Essay of a New and Company Map... of the Globe., The Hague: P. de Hondt, 1750, 492 mm x 680 mm	$ 150	$ 250	$ 500
Bellin, Jacques Nicolas, Carte de la Louisiane et des pays voisins., Paris, [1730], 443 mm x 601 mm	600	1000	2200
Bellin, Jacques N., Partie occidentale de la Nouvelle France ou du Canada.., [Nuremberg], 1755, 425 mm x 535 mm	300	530	1000
Blaeu Willem & Jan, Peru., Amst., [1635], 372 mm x 485 mm	100	150	300
Blaeu, Willem & Jan, Surria, vernacule Surrey., [Amst., 1667], 378 mm x 498 mm	100	125	400
Blaeu, Willem & Jan, Tabula Russiae., [Amst., 1663], 423 mm x 542 mm	100	150	300
Blome, Richard, A Mapp or Generall Carte of the World...., L, [1670 or later], 427 mm x 533 mm	1200	2000	4000
Bonne, Rigobert, Carte des Isles Sandwich., [Paris, c.1785], 232 mm x 343 mm	250	400	800
Bowen, Emanuel, A New and Accurate Map of America, [L, 1748], 353 mm x 445 mm	100	160	300
Bowen, Emanuel, A New Map of Georgia, w/ Part of Carolina...., L, 1748, 363 mm x 475 mm	300	600	1200
Bradley, Abraham, Map of the United States...., [Phila., 1796], 4 sheets, totalling 880 mm x 955 mm	11,000	18,500	37,000
Briggs, Henry, The North Part of America, [L, 1625], 323 mm x 381 mm	4800	8000	16,000
Brion De La Tour, Louis, Mappe monde geo-hydrographique, Paris 1786, 452 mm x 640 mm	170	200	600
Bry, Theodor De, America sive novus orbis respectu Europaeorum...., Frankfurt, 1596. 330 mm x 400 mm	2400	4060	8000
Buache, Philippe, Carte du Golphe du Mexique et des Isles Antilles, Paris, 1780, 500 mm x 940 mm	150	250	500
Burr, David H., Map of New Jersey and Pennsylvania., Wash., 10 July 1839, 2 sheets, tog. 37.5" x 50.5"	450	750	1500
Cantelli Da Vignola, G., Accuratis sima totius Regni Hispaniae...., Amst., [c.1680], 19.5" x 22.75".,	100	200	400
Cantelli Da Vignola, G., Parte Settentrionale delle coste della Francia...., Rome: G. G. de Rossi, 1691. 16.75" x 22.85"	200	350	700
Cary, John, A New Map of Part of the United States...., L, 1811, 450 mm x 506 mm	130	200	400
Chatelain, Henri Abr., Carte de l'Amerique., Amst., 1732-39, 330 mm x 445 mm	500	800	1800
Colton, J. H., Map of the United States of America...., NY, 1854, 32" x 50.5"	100	160	300
Colton, J. H., Map of the U.S....routes of ... Mail Steam Packets...., NY, 1849	750	1250	2500
Colton, J. H., Map of the U.S. the British Provinces, Mexico &c., NY, 1849, 483 mm x 635 mm	500	800	1800
Cook, James, A Draught of Port Royal Harbour...., L: E. Bowen, [1766], 547 mm x 761 mm	3000	5000	10,000
Cook, James, A Draught of West Forida...., L: E. Bowen, [1776], 540 mm x 1,326 mm	6000	10,000	20,000

Above: When detail is lacking because the area was unexplored, the value is increased. — Photos courtesy of Phillips Auctioneers. Below: When detail is lacking because the map maker was trying to save time and space, the value is decreased.

	AUCTION	RETAIL Low	High
De Brahm, William G., A Map of South Carolina and a Part of Georgia, L: Thomas Jefferys, 20 Oct 1757, 1st issue. 4 sheets . 5250		8750	17,500
De Lisl E, Gui Llaume, America Sep tentrionalis, Concinnata..., [Vienna, 1778], 452 mm x 580 mm 400		600	1400
De Lisle, Guillaume De, Carte d Afrique dressee pour l'usage du Roy., Paris, 1722, 482 mm x 622 mm 100		125	400
De Wit, Frederick, Regnum Hungaria...., Amst., [c. 1680], 19" x 23". 150		250	500
Delisle, Guillaume, L Amerique septentrionale, Paris, 1700 [1708], 455 mm x 605 mm 350		560	1000
Eddy, William M., Official Map of San Francisco...., Wash., 1849, 25" x 19" 360		500	1200
Ellicott, Andrew, Plan of the City of Washington...., Phila., 1792, 338 mm x 420 mm 3750		6250	12,500
Ellicott, Andrew, Territory of Columbia., [Phila., 1793-94], 588 mm x 590 mm 5250		8750	17,500
Endasian, Elia, Amerika, [Venice: Monastery of St. Lazar,1787], 553 mm x 724 mm 2600		4300	8800
Evans, Lewis, ... Middle British Colonies in America...., Phila., 1755, 549 mm x 745 mm 800		1300	2800
Evans, Lewis, A Map of Pensilvania, New-Jersey, New-York..., Phila., 1749, 635 mm x 495 mm 21,000		35,000	70,000
Evans, Lewis, A Map of the Middle British Colonies in America...., L, 1776, 595 mm x 978 mm 2800		4600	9400
Faden, William, A Plan of the Town...of Charlestown..., L, 1780, 548 mm x 719 mm 600		1000	2200
Faden, William, Plan of the City and Environs of Quebec, with its Siege and Blockade by the Americans...., L, 1776, 445 mm x 617 mm 750		1250	2500
Faden, William, The Province of New Jersey., [L, 1777], 810 mm x 614 mm 1400		2500	5000
Fer, Nicolas De, La Nouvelle France ou la France occidentale.., Paris, 1718, 4 sheets joined, 991 mm x 1060 mm 18,000		30,000	60,000
Flemming, C., Texas, Glogau, [c.1840-45] 16" x 12.75" 250		400	800
Gascoigne, John, A Plan of Port Royal in South Carolina, [L: Jeffreys & Faden, 1776], 841 mm x 661 mm 15,000		20,000	47,500
Goos, Pieter, Pascaerte van Nieu Yederlandt and Virginies., [N.p., c. l660], 434 mm x 535 mm 1800		3000	6000
Harenberg, I.C., Palaestina seu Terra olim Sancta...., Nuremberg: Heredes Homaniani, 1744, 500 mm x 585 mm 100		200	400
Harrison, John, Map of the City of New-York...., NY, 1852, 24 sections. 2305 mm x 1225 mm 600		1000	2000
Hills, John, A Plan of the Surprise of Stoney Point...., L, 1784, 546 mm x 752 mm 1600		2800	5600
Hills, John, Sketch of the Position of the British Force at Elizabeth..., L, 1784, 666 mm x 551 mm 2400		4000	8000
Holme, Thomas, A Mapp of Ye Improved Part of Pensilvania..., L, [1715], 444 mm x 578 mm 5000		8000	17,500
Homann, Johann B., Amplissimae regionis Mississippi..., Nuremberg, [c.1687] 492 mm x 585 mm 300		500	1000

Above: Historical associations, like this 1852 map of California's gold regions, add to the value of a map. Below: An early map of a current popular vacation destination is far more valuable than an unvisited wasteland. — Photos courtesy of Phillips Auctioneers.

	AUCTION	RETAIL	
		Low	High

Homann, Johann B., Judaea seu Palaestina...., Nuremberg, [1720], 498 mm x 585 mm 100   125   400

Homann, Johann B., Nova Anglia septentrionali Americae..., Nuremberg, 1716, 485 mm x 578 mm 300   500   1000

Hondius, Jodocus, Tartaria., [Amst., l613], 340 mm x 490 mm, hand-colored 100   150   300

Hutawa, Julius, Map of Mexico and California., St. Louis, 1863 . 400   800   1600

Hutchins, Thomas, A New Map of the Western Parts of Virginia, Penn...., L, 1778, 28 sections, tog. 900 mm x 1002 mm 6750   11,000   22,500

Janssonius, Joannes, America noviter delineata. Amst., [c.1650], 14.6" x 19.5". 860   1400   2900

Janssonius, Joannes, Indiae orientalis nova descriptio., Amst., [1630, but 1638 or later], 388 mm x 502 mm. 100   300   600

Janssonius, Joannes, Polus Antarcticus., [Amst., 1645], 440 mm x 495 mm 400   600   1400

Jefferson, T. H., Map of the Emigrant Road From Independence, Mo. to St. Francisco Calif...., NY, 1849, 4 sec., tog. 396 mm x 555 mm 20,000   40,000   95,000

Jefferys, Thomas, A Map of the Most Inhabited Part of New England...., L, 1755, 4 sheets joined as 2. 5600   9300   18,000

Keeler, William J. , National Map of the...United States...., Wash., J.F. Gedney, [1867], 50" x 60" 500   800   1800

Keulen, Gerard Van, Pas Kaart van de Zee Kusten van Virginia, Amst.,[1684], 530 mm x 605 mm 600   1000   2000

Keulen, Gerard Van, Pas-Kaart vande Zee kusten van, Nieuw Nederland anders genaamt Niew York, Amst., [1684 or later], 528 mm x 608 mm 1600   2500   5000

Lawson, J. T., Lawson's Map From Actual Survey of the Gold..., Regions of Upper California...., NY: Dewitt & Davenport. [c.1849], 14.8" x 20.75" 1000   1800   3800

Lotter, Conrad, A Map of the Most Inhabited Part of New England, Augsburg 1776, 674 mm x 552 mm 1200   2000   4200

Lotter, Matthew, A Map of the Provinces of New-York and New-Jersey., Augsburg: M. E. Lotter, 1777. 400 mm x 562 mm 400   600   1400

Lotter, T. C., Pensylvania, Nova Jersey et Nova York...., Augsburg, [c.1748], 570 mm x 500 mm 250   400   800

Lotter, Tobias C., America Septentrionalis, Concinnata..., 452 mm x 580 mm 300   660   1300

Madison, James, A Map of Virginia, formed from surveys, 9 sheets, ea. 585 mm x 875 mm 17,250   30,000   57,000

Mather, W.W., Geological Map of Long & Staten Islands..., NY, 1842, 22.5" x 50.7" 300   500   1000

Melish, John, Map of the United States of America, Phila., [1818] 400   600   1400

Melish, John, United States of America, Phila., 1820. 16.75" x 21" 200   470   900

Mercator, Gerard, Guiana, sive Amazonum regio. Amst., [1636, or later], 375 mm x 485 mm 100   300   600

Mitchell, John, Amerique septentrionale avec les routes..., Villages et etablishements Francois et Anglois, Paris, 1777,

	AUCTION	RETAIL Low	High
8 sheets, tog. 1344 mm x 1938 mm 2250		3750	7500
Mitchell, John, Amerique Septentrionale...., [Paris: Le Rouge, 1756], 8 sheets, each 718 mm x 520 mm 3500		5000	11,000
Moll, Hermann, A General Map of New France...., L, 1703. 8.75" x 13.25" 100		125	400
Moll, Hermann, Map of South America, L, [1720], 22.75" x 37.5" 250		400	800
Montanus, Arnoldus, Guiana sive Amazonum Regio., [N.p., 1671], 11" x 14".. 100		160	300
Montresor, Capt. J., A Map of the Province of New York...., L, 1777, 4 sheets, 757 mm x 967 mm 1800		3000	6000
Montresor, John, A Plan of the City of New-York & Its Environs...., L, [1775], 2d issue, 678 mm x 554 mm 3000		5000	10,000
Mouzon, Henry, An Accurate Map of North and South Carolina, L, 1794, 4 sheets joined as 2, each 534 mm x 1448 mm 1500		2500	5000
Muenster, Sebastian, Altera generalis tabula secundum Ptolemaeum., [Basel?, c.1545, or later], 251 mm x 345 mm . 300		600	1200
Munster, Sebastian, Novus Orbis, [Basel, 1540], 312 mm x 391 mm 2060		3400	7000
Ortelius, Abraham, Aevi veteris typus ..[the Ancient World], Antwerp, 1590 [i.e. 1612], 12.25" x 17.25" 200		300	800
Ortelius, Abraham, Americae sive novi orbis..., [Antwerp, 1570 or later], 420 mm x 554 mm 2250		3750	7500
Ortelius, Abraham, Culiacanae, Americae... Hispaniolae, Cubae...., [Antwerp, 1603], 2 maps on 1 sheet, 14" x 19.5" 450		750	1500
Ortelius, Abraham, Tusciae antiquae typus., [Amst., 1601], 12.75" x 18.75" 100		160	300
Ortelius, Asraham, Hiberniae Britanicas Insulae.., [Antwerp, 1595 or later], 349 mm x 476 mm 360		500	1200
Park, Moses, Plan of the Colony of Connecticut..., 24 Nov1776, 546 mm x 788 mm 9000		15,000	30,000
Randel, John, The City of New York, NY, 1821, 16 parts, 655 mm x 950 mm 1200		2000	4000
Ratzer, Bernard, Plan of the City of New York...., [L, c. 1767], 1st State, 624 mm x 940 mm 6000		10,000	20,000
Ratzer, Bernard, Plan of the City of New York...., Surveyed in the Years 1766 & 1767, L, 1776, 2 sheets, ea. 634 mm x 922 mm 10,000		17,500	35,000
Robert De Vaugondy, Carte de la Virginie et du Maryland...., [Paris], 1755 [or later], 480 mm x 642 mm 250		400	800
Sanson D Abbeville, N., Amerique septentrionale...., [Paris], 1669, 395 mm x 555 mm 400		800	1600
Sanson, Guillaume, Atlantis insula, Paris, 1669, 397 mm x 556 mm 600		1000	2000
Santini, Francois, Carte des Nouvelles Decouvertes..., Venice, [c.1776], 445 mm x 620 mm 100		125	400
Sauthier, C. J., A Chorographical Map of the Province of New York...., L: Faden, 1 Jan 1779, 3 sheets, ea. 610 mm x 1372 mm 2600		4300	8800
Sauthier, Claude J., A Plan of the Operations of the King's			

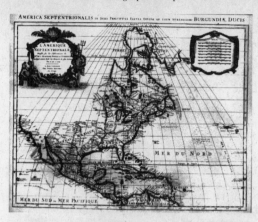

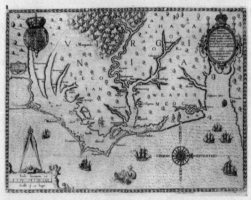

Maps like these depicting colonial America are usually cheaper when purchased in Europe. But they are getting harder and harder to find. — Photos courtesy of Phillips Auctioneers.

	AUCTION	RETAIL	
		Low	High

Army, under the Command of General Sr. William Howe....,
L, 1777, 2d, issue, w/ 3 British ships off "Terry Town,"
758 mm x 552 mm .... 1600 — 2800 — 5600

Schenk, Pieter, America Septentrionalis, Amst, [early 18th c.],
19" x 22.5" .... 100 — 150 — 300

Scull, N. & Heap, G., A Plan of the City and Environs of Phila....,
L: Faden, 12 Mar 1777, 625 mm x 460 mm .... 100 — 200 — 400

Seutter, Matthaeus, Africa juxta navigationes et observationes....,
Augsburg, [1735], 497 mm x 579 mm .... 100 — 125 — 400

Seutter, Matthaeus, Pensylvania, Nova Jersey et Nova York....,
Augsburg, [c. 1735], 580 mm x 500 mm .... 650 — 1000 — 2000

Smith, John Calvin, Colton's Map of the United States, NY,
1852, 36 sections totalling 1,643 mm x 2,071 mm .... 750 — 1250 — 2500

Smith, John Calvin, Map of North America...., NY, 1850. 527
mm x 482 mm plus margins. .... 450 — 750 — 1500

Speed, John, A New and Accurat Map of the World, L, [1626?],
395 mm x 520 mm... 2400 — 4000 — 8000

Speed, John, America, w/ those known Parts in that unknown
Worlde..., L: Bassett & Chiswell, 1626 [but c. 1676], 447
mm x 547 mm.. 2250 — 3750 — 7500

Speed, John, Europ, and the Chief Cities...., L: G. Humble,
1626, 395 mm x 510 mm .... 400 — 600 — 1400

Taylor, Benjamin, A New & Accurate Plan of the City of
New York...., NY, 1797, 625 mm x 978 mm .... 12,000 — 20,000 — 40,000

Tirion, Isaac, Nieuwe Kaart van het Westelykste Deel der
Weerald...., Amst., 1754, 350 mm x 365 mm .... 100 — 150 — 300

Tirion. Isaak, Kaart van het Nieuw Mexico en van California,
Amst., 1765, 12.25" x 13.5" .... 100 — 125 — 400

Visscher, N., Novi Belgii Novaeque Angliae nec non partis
Virginiae...., [Amst, c. 1651 or later], 465 mm x 555 mm .. 2000 — 3500 — 6500

Visscher, Nikolaus, Insulae Americanae in Oceano..., [N.p., c.
1690], 18.25" x 22" .... 360 — 500 — 1200

Vrients, J. B., Serenissimae Reipublicae Genuensis..., Antwerp,
1608, 391 mm x 538 mm .... 100 — 200 — 400

Waghenaer, Lucas J., Caerte vande Zee Custen van Galissien....,
[Leiden, 1586], 325 mm x 508 mm .... 170 — 200 — 600

Wells, Edward, A New Map of the Terraqueous Globe., Oxford,
[c.1700], 14" x 20" .... 250 — 400 — 800

Whitman & Searl, Map of Eastern Kansas, Bost.: J.P. Jewett,
1856, 695 mm x 535 mm .... 400 — 600 — 1400

Willdey, George, Map of North America...., L, [c.1720], 2 sheets,
979 mm x 620 mm.. 1600 — 2800 — 5600

Williams, W., A New Map of the United States, Phila., 1853,
25" x 29.5" .... 150 — 250 — 500

Wytfliet, Jcornelis, lucatana regio et Hondura, [N.p., 1598], 9"
x 11"... 250 — 400 — 800

Young, J. H., The Tourist's Pocket Map of the State of Indiana,
Phila., 1833, 15.75" x 13.25".. 100 — 150 — 300

Maxfield Parrish Prints

Maxfield Parrish illustrated magazines and advertisements for various national companies during the early 1900s. He also created many limited edition prints. There are many reproductions on the market.

Above left and right: Magazine covers need not be complete with the entire magazine, but should be crisp, clean examples. Below: A print incorporated into the design of a box, however, should still be attached to a good condition box. — Photos courtesy of Phillips Auctioneers.

	LOW	AVG.	HIGH
Above the Balcony, knaves and maidens in garden	$ 90	$ 112	$ 135
Air Castles, nude in bubbles	250	300	350
Aladdin and the Lamp, 10" x 12"	160	200	240
Aladdin in Cave of 40 Thieves, 12" x 16.5", on quality paper	190	238	285
Ancient Trees, large oak tree by lake	200	250	300
Argonauts, In Quest of the Golden Fleece	100	125	150
Arizona, landscape of mountain, rich blues, 11" x 13"	100	125	150
Atlas, giant holding up sky	160	200	240
Aucassin Seeks Nicolotte, knight on horse, bookplate SM	56	70	84
Autumn, maiden standing on hilltop	170	212	255
Below the Balcony, knaves and maidens in garden	90	112	135
Bookplate, John Cox-His Book	60	75	90
Brazen, The Boatman, 10" x 12"	160	200	240
Brown and Bigelow Landscape, the village church, 24" x 27"	370	462	555
Cadmus Showing the Dragon's Teeth, 10" x 12"	100	125	150
Canyon, maiden in canyon, 12" x 5"	280	350	420
Circles Palace, maiden standing on porch	100	125	150
Cleopatra, rare, large	800	1000	1200
Community Plate, 11" x 13", 1918	70	85	100
Contentment, large Edison Mazda Calendar	600	800	1000
Dawn, maiden sitting on rock, Mazda print	100	125	150
Daybreak, large size	400	500	600
Daybreak, nude and maiden on porch, small size	200	300	400
Dinkey Bird, nude on swing, 13.5" x 18", 1904	200	300	400
Djer-Kiss Ad, maiden on swing in forest, 10.5" x 14"	100	125	150
Dream Castle in the Sky, 9" x 12"	90	112	135
Dreaming, large size	700	850	1000
Dreaming, nude sitting under oak, medium size	400	500	600
Dreamlight, maid on swing, Edison Mazda Calendar, 9.5" x 20.5", 1925	500	650	800
Duchess at Prayer, illustration for L'Allegro, 10" x 15", 1901	60	75	90
Ecstasy, large Edison Mazda Calendar	1000	1250	1500
Ecstasy, maiden standing on rock, small size	225	300	375
Enchantment, maiden standing on stars at night, 9.5" x 20.5", large	800	1000	1200
Errant Pan, Pan sitting by stream, 6" x 8", small	70	85	100
Evening, nude sitting in lake, 13" x 17"	180	225	270
Evening, nude sitting on rock in lake	250	300	350
Fisherman and the Genie, The, 10" x 12"	150	188	225
Florentine Fete, maidens in garden, 10" x 16"	80	100	120
Garden of Allah, 3 maidens sitting in garden, medium size	200	300	400
Garden of Allah, large Edison Mazda Calendar	500	700	900
Garden of Opportunity, prince and princess	600	800	1000
Garden of Opportunity Triptych, 10" x 13"	120	150	180
Golden Hours, maidens in forest, large Edison Mazda Calendar	720	900	1080
Harper's Weekly, poster	2400	3000	3600
Hilltop, large size, House of Art	920	1150	1380
Hilltop, small size	175	200	225
Hilltop, youths sitting on mountain, medium size, House of Art	420	525	630
His Christmas Dinner, tramp eating dinner	120	150	180
Interlude, maidens in garden playing lutes	240	300	360
Isola Bella Scene, 9" x 10"	52	65	78
Jason and His Teacher Chiron the Centaur, 1910	90	112	135

	LOW	AVG.	HIGH
King of the Black Isles, king on throne, on quality paper, 9" x 11" ..	$ 160	$ 200	$ 240
King's Son, Arab in garden by fountain	100	125	150
Knave of Hearts Book, mint	600	800	1000
Knaves and Maidens, conversing in garden	120	150	180
Lamplighters, Mazda Calendar, 9" x 13", 1924	200	250	300
Lampseller of Baghdad, The, maiden on steps, Mazda Calendar	600	800	100
Land of Make-Believe, The, maiden to garden	60	75	90
Little Princess, princess sitting by fountain	56	70	84
Lute Players, large size, House of Art	750	1000	1250
Lute Players, small size, House of Art	150	175	200
Milkmaid, maiden walking in mountain	60	75	90
Morning, maiden sitting on rock, 13" x 16"	260	325	390
Night Call, bare-breasted girl in surf, 6" x 8"	60	80	100
October-1900, woman w/ fruit draped in her gown, orange moon, 18" x 23"	60	80	100
Old King Cole	700	900	1100
Old Romance, nude sitting in pool, 8" x 8"	110	138	165
Pandora's Box, maiden sitting by large box	160	200	240
Pierrot, clown w/ lute, sky glittering, 1912	240	300	360
Pipe Night, comical men w/ pipes and coffee urns sitting facing each other at table, 9" x 12.5"	70	88	105
Pool of the Villa D'Este, nude lying besides luminous pool, 7.5" x 10.5"	56	70	84
Post Standing, by river in forest	70	88	105
Potpourri, nude in garden picking flowers	100	125	150
Prince, from Knave of Hearts, 10" x 12.5", rare	270	338	405
Prince Goodad, pirates on boat	160	200	240
Prosperina, maiden in the sea, 10" x 12"	160	200	240
Providing it By the Book, 2 gents at table	56	70	84
Queen Guinare, maiden on porch, 10" x 12"	160	200	240
Reveries, Large Edison Mazda Calendar	400	500	600
Reveries, 2 maidens sitting by fountain	90	112	135
Sandman, w/ full moon, 6" x 7.5"	80	100	120
Sea Nymphs, 12" x 14", 1914	110	138	165
Search for the Singing Tree	90	112	135
Seven Green Polls at Cintra, 6" x 8"	70	88	105
Shepherd w/ Sheep, 8.5" x 13.5"	56	70	84
Ship in Ocean, 11" x 13.5"	90	112	135
Sinbad and the Cyclops, 10" x 12"	90	112	135
Sing a Song of Sixpence, 9" x 21"	600	850	1000
Singing Tree, The, 10" x 12"	100	125	150
Stars, House of Art, large size, nude sitting on rock	1000	1200	1400
Stars, House of Art, medium size, nude sitting on rock	500	700	900
Story From Phoebus, 8" x 10", 1901	50	65	80
Sunlit Valley, scenic of river and mountains	270	338	405
Sunrise, Edison Mazda Calendar, rare, large	1000	1250	1500
Sunrise, Edison Mazda Calendar, small	270	338	405
Swifts Ham Ad, Jack Sprat and wife	100	125	150
Turquoise Cup, man sitting in villa	50	65	80
Twilight Had Fallen, 2 figures on beach	60	80	100
Valley of Diamonds, Arab in valley	90	112	135

	LOW	AVG.	HIGH
Venetian Lamplighter, Edison Mazda Calendar, 1924	$ 150	$ 200	$ 250
Villa D'Este, nude sitting by pool	80	100	120
Wails of Jasper, youth and castle, 12" x 14"	150	200	250
Waterfall, large Edison Mazda Calendar	1000	1200	1400
Waterfall, small Edison Mazda Calendar	200	300	400
White Birch, farmer under large birch	90	112	135
Wild Geese, girl on rock, 13" x 16"	260	325	390

Above: A Mazda Lamp advertising display may have replaced lightbulbs, but they must be Mazda bulds identical to the originals. Below: A complete advertising display is worth more than twice the value of either half. — Photos courtesy of Phillips Auctioneers.

Photographs

In the following entries, photographs are listed by subject matter. The values quoted are the average retail price for various types of prints. Daguerreotypes (D) generally average 4" x 3" on silver plates; Tintypes (T) generally average 3" x 2" (these values are not for the thumbnail-size variety); Carte-de-Visites (CdV) average 4" x 2.5" on cardboard; Studio Photos (SP) are about 6" x 4" on cardboard; and Stereopticon Cards (Str) have a double image for observing in one of a variety of viewers.

The value of photographs is determined by age and subject matter. Prints made in the studios of important photographers such as Edward Curtis, Matthew Brady, Alfred Stieglitz, and Carleton Watkins command high prices. Tintypes were invented in 1858 and declined by the 1870s. Stereographs with a revenue stamp on the back date between 1864-66. In 1868, many publishers listed the views in a particular stereographic series by underlining or outlining a card number or title. After 1880, curved stereographs appeared, believed to have a more 3-D quality. Collectors may wish to contact the National Stereoscopic Association, Box 14801, Columbus, OH 43214.

Above left: Dagureotypes are cased to protect the image. Although they can be cleaned, many amatuer attempts have destoyed such photos. Above right: Tiny thumbnail sized tintypes are generally valued only for the album that contains them. Below: Early sporting photos have greatly increased in value.

	D	T	CdV	SP	Str

Historical Events

	D	T	CdV	SP	Str
Chicago Fire of 1871	$ 800	$ 200	$ 40	$ 65	$ 15
Mill Creek Flood of 1874	400	150	—	45	10
San Francisco Earthquake, 1906	—	300	150	250	30
Spanish American War	—	75	25	35	20
World War I	—	—	—	10	6

Landscapes

	D	T	CdV	SP	Str
Death Valley	$ 500	$ 200	—	$ 45	$ 7
France	75	25	$ 10	15	5
House	35	15	5	10	10
Landscape	100	50	—	30	7
Mining Scene	400	200	—	50	10
New York City, landmark	250	75	40	50	10
Niagra Falls	750	175	—	50	10
Street Scene	100	45	—	15	12
Western USA landscape, w/ mountains	200	100	—	50	8
Yosemite Falls	400	200	50	75	30

People and Portraits

	D	T	CdV	SP	Str
Actor / Actress	$ 45	$ 15	$ 7	$ 12	$ 12
African American	200	120	40	55	25
Booth, Edwin	300	75	35	45	20
Booth, John Wilkes	750	500	300	350	200

Left: Stereoscope. Below: Comic scenes are a common subject matter for stereopticon photos.

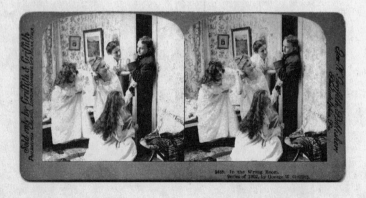

	D	T	CdV	SP	Str
Bryan, William Jennings	$ 300	$ 80	$ 40	$ 55	$ 20
Circus Performer	150	55	25	45	30
Civil War Officer	200	125	35	50	15
Civil War Soldier	175	75	30	50	40
Cowboy	75	25	10	15	9
Edison, Thomas Alva	—	200	75	100	60
Ford, Henry	—	150	50	75	50
Lindbergh, Charles	—	—	75	120	35
Native American	250	150	50	85	25
Nude, woman	250	75	35	50	25
Opera Star	65	25	15	20	15
Portrait of a beautiful woman	40	5	5	10	—
Portrait of a Cat (or other pet)	100	25	10	15	7
Portrait of a Child	50	1	1	1	—
Portrait of a Man	15	1	1	1	—
Portrait of a Woman	15	1	1	1	—
Professional (portrait holding tools, etc.)	100	50	20	30	15
Rockefeller, John D.	—	—	50	75	25
Sporting figure	350	200	35	50	35
Tom Thumb	300	200	75	100	40

Presidents

	D	T	CdV	SP	Str
Arthur, Chester A.	—	$ 75	$ 20	$ 35	$ 35
Buchanan, James	$ 300	100	50	50	20
Cleveland, Grover	—	125	25	50	40
Garfleld, James	—	75	20	35	35
Grant, U.S.	750	175	45	90	45
Harrison, Benjamin	—	65	20	40	35
Hayes, R.B.	—	75	20	35	35
Johnson, Andrew	400	100	50	65	12
Lincoln, Abraham	rare	rare	2000	4000	50
McKinley, William	—	100	25	50	40

Left : Typical Carte-de-visite. Right: Civil War posed camp scenes are not as valuable as battle scenes, but more valuable than simple portraits of unknown soldiers. — Photo courtesy of Phillips Auctioneers.

Wallace Nutting Photographs

At the same time he was reproducing American antique furniture, Wallace Nutting funded his many projects with money earned from selling photographs of quaint scenes. Often signed, these photographs have been collected since their first appearance.

	LOW	AVG.	HIGH
Admiral's Daughter, 13" x 16"	$ 200	$ 245	$ 290
Afternoon in Nantucket, 13" x 16"	400	465	530
Almost Ready, 14" x 17"	340	380	420
Almost Ready, 13" x 16"	260	310	360
Along the River, 12" x 18"	130	160	190
Along the Wall, 11" x 14"	130	150	170
Ancestral Cradle, 14" x 17"	310	360	410
Ancient Treasures, 14" x 18"	280	325	370
Andover Glen, 11" x 14"	110	125	140
Apple Tree Bend, 11" x 14"	130	155	180
April Foliage, 12" x 17"	130	160	190
Arch at the Inn, 11" x 17"	110	135	160
Arlington Hills, 11" x 17"	600	685	770
Around the Bend, 11" x 14"	70	80	90
Around the Cottage End, 11" x 14"	60	70	80
At Canterbury Gate, 14" x 17"	390	445	500
At Leisure, 13" x 16"	130	160	190
At the Landing, 11" x 14"	110	135	160
Autumn Shore, 11" x 14"	100	120	140
Barre Brook, 18" x 22"	130	150	170
Bars Down to Beauty, 11" x 14"	100	120	140
Beautiful Perkiomen, 13" x 16"	200	225	250
Beckoning Road, 15" x 22"	240	285	330
Beech Borders, 12" x 15"	90	105	120
Berkshire Brook, 11" x 14"	50	60	70
Berkshire Curves, 11" x 14"	80	95	110
Berkshire Mere, 11" x 14"	110	125	140
Birch Approach, 13" x 17"	130	155	180
Birch Hilltop, 11" x 14"	80	95	110
Birch Paradise, 13" x 15"	110	130	150
Birch Wood, 14" x 17"	90	100	110
Blooms at the Bend, 10" x 16"	90	110	130
Blossom Cottage, 14" x 17"	130	150	170
Blossom Dale, 12" x 16"	70	85	100
Blossom Drive, 11" x 14"	50	60	70
Blossom Pasture, 12" x 18"	620	725	830
Blossoms at the Bend, 13" x 16"	100	135	170
Bonny Dale, 11" x 14"	160	195	230
Book Settle, 16" x 20"	400	510	620
Bowered, 14" x 17"	260	300	340
Braiding a Rug, 14" x 17"	260	310	360
Brandon Hall, 14" x 17"	280	325	370
Breakfast Hour, 13" x 17"	360	450	540
Broken Waters, 11" x 14"	90	110	130
Brook Ford, 12" x 15"	160	185	210

	LOW	AVG.	HIGH
Button Basket, 11" x 14"	$ 160	$ 180	$ 200
By the Meadow Gate, 11" x 14"	90	100	110
By the Stone Fence, 11" x 14"	60	75	90
Calling on Priscilla, 12" x 15"	130	150	170
Camden Harbor, 14" x 17"	250	320	390
Capri Bay, 13" x 16"	360	420	480
Castle of St. Angelo, 11" x 14"	220	255	290
Chair for John, 13" x 16"	350	405	460
Cherry Blossoms in New York, 13" x 16"	200	250	300
Christmas Jelly, 14" x 17"	280	310	340
Cold Day, 14" x 17"	440	515	590
Comfort and a Cat, 12" x 16"	250	295	340
Connecticut Blossoms, 11" x 14"	110	135	160
Corner in China, 13" x 16"	280	340	400
Corner of the Field, 11" x 14"	110	135	160
Cottage Front, 13" x 16"	210	235	260
Cottage Front, 11" x 14"	110	135	160
Cottage Garden, 13" x 16"	110	135	160
Cottage on the Floss, 13" x 16"	100	135	170
Crossroads in May, 14" x 17"	90	110	130
Dangers of Irish Roads, 11" x 17"	410	505	600
Decked as a Bride, 14" x 17"	70	90	110
Dell Dale Road, 10" x 12"	40	50	60
Dell of Blossoms, 8" x 10"	50	65	80
Devon Arches, 13" x 16"	160	200	240
Divining Cup, 14" x 17"	250	320	390
Dixville Shadows, 14" x 17"	210	250	290
Down the Lane, 13" x 17"	180	210	240
Drying Apples, 14" x 17"	680	785	890
Dublin Curve, 11" x 14"	120	135	150
Durham, 13" x 15"	430	520	610
Dutch Twins, 13" x 16"	250	300	350
Echo Lake Borders, 13" x 16"	150	185	220
Embroidering for Christmas, 14" x 17"	280	320	360
English May, 12" x 16"	110	130	150
Entering the Old Bridge, 11" x 14"	110	130	150
Equinox Pond, 11" x 17"	110	145	180
Evangeline Lane, 13" x 16"	120	140	160
Eventful Journey, 13" x 16"	830	1000	1170
Fair Orchard Way, 12" x 15"	120	135	150
Far Dixie, 9" x 13"	320	375	430
Farm Borders, 12" x 16"	100	115	130
Filling the Oven, 13" x 16"	350	400	450
Fine Effect, 10" x 12"	260	305	350
Fireside Fancies, 13" x 16"	310	385	460
Five 0'Clock, 15" x 22"	270	325	380
Florida Sunrise, 13" x 17"	610	800	990
Flowering Time, 15" x 22"	130	160	190
Flume Falls, 10" x 13"	120	145	170
Forks of the Road in May, 13" x 16"	100	130	160
Formal Call, 11" x 14"	180	215	250

	LOW	AVG.	HIGH
From a Friend, 11" x 14"	$ 260	$ 330	$ 400
From the Hill, 13" x 15"	120	135	150
Garden Gossip, 11" x 14"	120	145	170
Golden River, 11" x 14"	60	80	100
Good Night, 16" x 20"	460	550	640
Grandmother's China, 14" x 17"	190	235	280
Grandmother's Guests, 13" x 16"	150	170	190
Great Wayside Oak, 14" x 17"	240	275	310
Happy May, 16" x 20"	120	140	160
Happy Valley Road, 14" x 17"	140	155	170
Hawthorn Bridge, 13" x 16"	180	220	260
Hawthorn Den, 14" x 17"	190	235	280
Hawthorn Gable, 13" x 16"	230	270	310
Head Waters, 11" x 14"	80	100	120
Hidden Cove, 16" x 20"	140	165	190
High Rollers, 14" x 17"	430	515	600
Highland Brae, 11" x 14"	80	95	110
Home Charm, 11" x 17"	290	330	370
Homestead Blossoms, 14" x 17"	150	175	200
Honeymoon Cottage, 11" x 14"	100	120	140
Honeymoon Drive, 18" x 22"	180	205	230
Hope of the Year, 11" x 14"	110	135	160
In the Old Dominion, 13" x 16"	230	295	360
In Wales, 11" x 14"	120	140	160
Into the West, 8" x 15"	70	80	90
Jane, 12" x 18"	120	145	170
Jersey Blossoms, 11" x 14"	120	145	170
July at Plymouth, 11" x 14"	120	140	160
June Beautiful, 14" x 17"	130	155	180
June Haze, 14" x 17"	170	200	230
June Shadows, 14" x 17"	80	100	120
Killarney Castle, 13" x 16"	180	225	270
Kitchen at Morning, 13" x 16"	310	390	470
La Jolla, 13" x 16"	260	310	360
Lavender Canopy, 11" x 14"	220	280	340
Leaf Strewn Brook, 13" x 16"	70	85	100
Leisurely Errand, 13" x 16"	180	220	260
Letter from the Front, 12" x 16"	150	180	210
Little Homestead, 12" x 18"	110	135	160
Little River, 16" x 20"	210	250	290
Looking Seaward, 10" x 12"	130	150	170
Lure of Home, 10" x 12"	60	75	90
Lure of May, 11" x 14"	80	95	110
Luscious May, 14" x 17"	80	100	120
Luxurious Chamber, 14" x 17"	160	190	220
Maine Coast Sky, 13" x 16"	440	515	590
Maple Sugar Cupboard, 16" x 20"	300	360	420
Mary's Little Lamb, 11" x 14"	240	280	320
May by the Brook, 12" x 16"	110	135	160
May Countryside, 12" x 20"	130	145	160
May Drive, 13" x 16"	110	130	150

	LOW	AVG.	HIGH
Meadow Beauty, 14" x 17"	$ 80	$ 100	$ 120
Merchant's Daughter, 14" x 17"	420	510	600
Midsummer Vale, 11" x 14"	150	185	220
Monument Between Blossoms, 12" x 15"	240	305	370
Morning Among the Birches, 11" x 14"	120	140	160
Morning Duties, 11" x 14"	180	225	270
Morning Errand, 13" x 16"	270	325	380
Mystery Pool, 12" x 15"	180	205	230
New Hampshire Birches, 10" x 12"	50	60	70
New Hampshire Delights, 13" x 16"	120	135	150
New Parasol, 8" x 10"	70	90	110
Newton Autumn, 13" x 16"	170	205	240
Nova Scotia Idyll, 11" x 14"	180	200	220
Ocean Eddies, 11" x 17"	390	480	570
Old Time Gallant, 13" x 16"	420	500	580
Olde Story, 13" x 16"	150	185	220
Olden Time, 13" x 16"	150	170	190
On the Heights, 10" x 16"	270	345	420
Open Gate, 11" x 14"	310	370	430
Orchard Brook, 13" x 16"	70	80	90
Orchard in the Hills, 11" x 14"	90	105	120
Over the Canal, 11" x 14"	110	135	160
Over the Road, 12" x 15"	60	75	90
Pastoral Brook, 11" x 14"	110	135	160
Peep at the Hills, 11" x 14"	90	110	130
Pergola, Amalfi, 14" x 17"	210	235	260
Perkiomen October, 13" x 16"	180	220	260
Petals Above and Below, 11" x 14"	130	150	170
Pilgrim's Daughter, 12" x 15"	270	320	370
Pine Landing, 13" x 16"	110	135	160
Purity and Grace, 16" x 20"	150	180	210
Quilting Party, 14" x 17"	260	305	350
Reception, 12" x 15"	120	135	150
Red, White, and Blue, 11" x 14"	130	160	190
Reeling the Yarn, 11" x 14"	190	220	250
Returning from a Walk, 11" x 14"	100	115	130
River in Maine, 10" x 12"	90	105	120
Rose Gate, 12" x 16"	120	145	170
Rug Pattern, 13" x 16"	190	215	240
Rural Joys, 16" x 20"	140	170	200
Rural Sweetness, 11" x 14"	80	95	110
Sallying of Sally, 14" x 17"	260	320	380
Samoset Fleur De Lis, 13" x 16"	170	220	270
Scottish Stronghold, 13" x 16"	270	325	380
Sea Captain's Daughter, 14" x 17"	260	320	380
Seeking the Shade, 12" x 15"	320	415	510
Shaded Bridge, 11" x 14"	220	250	280
Sheltered Brook, 16" x 20"	200	230	260
Shore Battle, 13" x 16"	240	305	370
Silhouette-Girl Sewing at Rocker, 4" x 4"	40	50	60
Silhouette-Girl Tending Flowers, 4" x 4"	50	60	70

	LOW	AVG.	HIGH
Silver Birches, 10" x 12"	$ 60	$ 80	$ 100
Skirting Lake Como, 11" x 14"	220	255	290
Snow on the River, 10" x 12"	320	380	440
Songs of Long Ago, 13" x 16"	140	170	200
Soul of Harmony, 14" x 17"	350	415	480
Southern Village Street, 14" x 17"	320	385	450
Spanning the Glen, 11" x 14"	100	120	140
Spring Fashions, 11" x 14"	130	150	170
Spring in Sudbury, 13" x 16"	110	135	160
Spring's First Green, 11" x 14"	100	115	130
Springfield Blossoms, 14" x 17"	80	90	100
St. Mary's in May, 13" x 16"	240	295	350
Still River, 15" x 18"	140	170	200
Stitch in Time, 14" x 17"	270	310	350
Stone Bridge, 11" x 14"	80	90	100
Summer Clouds, 11" x 14"	60	75	90
Summer Grotto, 14" x 17"	270	320	370
Summer Ripples, 14" x 17"	140	170	200
Summer Vale, 12" x 15"	80	95	110
Summer Wind, 11" x 14"	100	115	130
Sunkissed Way, 13" x 17"	90	110	130
Swan Cove, 20" x 28"	1280	1520	1760
Swimming Pool, 14" x 17"	100	120	140
Swirling Seas, 18" x 22"	560	675	790
Tea Maid, 13" x 16"	200	250	300
Thanksgiving Goodies, 11" x 14"	240	275	310
Thanksgiving Landscape, 11" x 17"	180	215	250
Tranquil Vale, 11" x 17"	140	170	200
Tunnel of Bloom, 11" x 14"	120	140	160
Under Elm Arches, 16" x 20"	180	210	240
Under the Blossoms, 11" x 14"	190	240	290
Valley in the Pyrenees, 13" x 16"	190	245	300
Valued Customer, 14" x 17"	490	560	630
Vicarage, 13" x 16"	290	345	400
Wadsworth House, 13" x 16"	280	320	360
Walpole Road, 13" x 17"	100	125	150
Washington Cherry Blossoms, 13" x 17"	270	315	360
Wealth of May, 14" x 17"	290	375	460
Weaver, 14" x 17"	280	345	410
Wilder Pond, 13" x 16"	150	175	200
Wilderness Camp, 12" x 18"	200	225	250
Windsor Maid, 14" x 17"	260	320	380
Wissahickon Decorations, 10" x 12"	70	80	90
Woodland Cathedral, 14" x 17"	140	155	170
Work Basket, 13" x 16"	210	250	290
World Beautiful, 11" x 14"	110	130	150

Postcards

Picture postcards in the United States started in 1893 at the Columbian Exposition. By 1910, they were a national craze with nearly a billion cards being sent through the mail. In 1914, the introduction of the folding greeting card began the rapid decline of this "Golden Age" of postcards. While collectors are mainly looking for postcards from this early period, there are many wonderful cards from the 1920s through the present day that are also prized by collectors.

Postcards can be roughly divided into three categories: greeting cards, view cards, and real photo cards. A greeting card is any card designed by an artist. This includes all the holidays (including the popular Halloween and Santa cards), children, animals, advertising, romance, Art Nouveau, etc. Many of the better greeting cards are embossed, highly colorful and beautifully designed. Some of the best-known publishers include Tuck, Winsch, and PFB . Many of these cards are "artist signed," meaning that the artist's name is on the front of the card. Some of the rarer types of greetings include Hold-to-the-Lights and mechanicals.

View cards are pictures of specific places, typically prints made from a photograph. They may be black and white or colored and were usually mass produced. Views are the most widely collected postcards since nearly every city, town, or hamlet in the U.S. can be found on a postcard. Many collectors are interested in how their hometown looked at the beginning of the century. Expositions, transportation (trains, planes, autos, ships), commercial enterprises, and main streets are among the views prized by collectors. Things that have changed little, such as monuments and waterfalls, as well as frequently visited tourist areas (Niagara Falls, Washington, D.C., National Parks, etc.) are common and not very desirable.

The third category, and the one that has shown a meteoric rise in value in the past decade, is the real photo card. A real photo card is simply a photograph printed directly onto a postcard. They are usually black and white, although occasionally colored. The reason for the interest in these cards is their subject matter and scarcity. While the bigger cities had millions of published views, many small towns and villages are represented only on photo postcards. Unidentified views and family portraits have little value, but Main Streets, train stations, commercial enterprises, occupational photos, political and social themes (e.g. suffragettes, labor unions, presidential campaign stops, criminals), postal and photographic history, and any other unique subject matter is of great interest to collectors.

As with all paper collectibles, condition is a major factor in determining value. Prices listed are for mint condition. Even a slight flaw will reduce the value considerably while a serious flaw may render the card uncollectible.

Our consultant for this section is Adam G. Perl, owner of Pastimes Antiques in Ithaca, NY (he is listed in the back of this book).

Left to right: Real Photo, International Stores, $35-$45; Real Photo, Ruins After Fire, Mecklenburg, NY, $50-$65. - items courtesy of Pastimes.

Left to right: Advertising, The Clark Irish Harp, $25-$35; Votes for Women, $45-$50. — Items courtesy of Pastimes.

	LOW	AVG.	HIGH
Advertising, Campbell Kids, horizontal	$ 50	$ 62	$ 75
Advertising, Campbell Kids, vertical	75	88	100
Advertising, Red Star Line, poster style	20	28	35
Antelope Hunting, two-tone, undivided back, Wild West Series, Ridley, artwork by Charles M. Russell	22	25	28
April Fool, signed Hutaf	15	18	20
Austrian Cavalry Patrol Crossing River, Underwood & Underwood, color	7	9	10
Beef Herd on Water, black and white, undivided back, Morris & Kirby	6	7	8
Branding Calves, two-tone, undivided back, Holmes & Warren	5	6	7
Buster Brown and Tige, Resolved: "That Nothing can Stop Us," signed Outcault	10	13	15
Children, signed Clapsaddle	25	28	30
Christmas, children w/ toys	5	6	7
Christmas, Santa in Green, full figure	25	28	30
Christmas, Santa painting sled	10	13	15
Columbian Exposition, 1893, pub. Goldsmith	25	28	30
Fur Canoe, color, undivided back, Wild West Series, MacFarlane	10	12	14
Halloween, signed Clapsaddle	15	20	25
Halloween, Tuck	12	14	16
Halloween, Winsch	50	58	65
Hold-to-the-Light, 1904 St. Louis Expo.	25	28	30
Hold-to-the-Light, Santa Claus	125	138	150
Home Sweet Home, color, undivided back, Tammen	12	14	15
Horse Drawn Double Decker Buses in London's Ludgate Circus, color, Louis Levy divided back	6	7	8
Hudson-Fulton Expo, Redfield Floats	5	6	7
Indian Encampment on River Bank, color, undivided back, Illinois Postcard Co.	5	6	7
Indians, Chief Spotted Tail, color, undivided back, Leighton	5	6	7

	LOW	AVG.	HIGH
Iron Ore Docks of Toledo, color, undivided back, Clinton & Close	$ 7	$ 9	$ 11
Kewpies, signed Rose O'Neill	25	32	40
Levee Scene, color, undivided back, Erker #221	5	6	7
Lewis and Clark Exposition, pub. B.B. Rich	10	13	15
Missouri State Building, color, undivided back, Sun. Post Dispatch (St. Louis), 1900	7	9	11
Oklahoma Building, color, undivided back, Samuel Cupples	7	9	11
Pan-American Expo, 1901, pub. Niagara Env.	15	18	20
Patriotic, Fourth of July	5	8	10
Patriotic, Lincoln	8	12	15
Patriotic, Memorial Day	5	8	10
Patriotic, Washington	5	8	10
Political, Bryan, campaign	15	25	35
Political, Prohibition	35	42	50
Political, Taft, campaign	10	13	15
Political, Teddy Roosevelt, campaign	10	15	20
Political, Teddy Roosevelt, family	5	7	8
Real photo, dry goods store interior	25	30	35
Real photo, girl w/ doll	15	18	20
Real photo, horse-drawn milk wagon w/ adv.	65	70	75
Real photo, Spencer, NY, parade on Main St.	20	23	25
Real photo, train in station, good detail	45	48	50
Red River Carts, color, divided back, Wild West Series, MacFarlane ...	10	12	14
Red Roof Tower at Left of Mountains, German Tyrolean Alps Series, Samuel Cupples	15	18	20
Residence House at Roof Square, German Tyrolean Alps Series, Samuel Cupples	15	18	20
Roper, two-tone, undivided back, Wild West Series, Ridley, artwork by Charles M. Russell	20	23	26
Soulard Market, color, undivided back, Erker #246	5	6	7
Thanksgiving, signed Brundage	15	20	25
Two Crow Papooses, black and white, undivided back, Miller ...	5	6	7
Valentine, The Westmount Club of Montreal, color, divided back	6	7	8
Village Square, German Tyrolean Alps Series, Samuel Cupples	16	18	20
Wabash Freight Station, color, undivided back, Erker #250	6	7	8

Left to right: Advertising, Humorous Swift's Pride Soap, $15-$20; Santa, Sleeping Child silk clothes, $35-$45; — Items courtesy of Pastimes.

Vanity Fair Prints

London's Vanity Fair appeared weekly from 1860 to 1914. Each issue featured a lithograph depicting a satirical portrait of a well-known man or woman. Two of the most famous Vanity Fair artists were SPY (Leslie Ward) and APE (Carlo Pilligrini). In the following entries artist's monograms are given in capital letters. The print should be in excellent condition, with no tears and no browning or "mat burn." For further information refer to *The Official Price Guide to Collector Prints*, published by The House of Collectibles, Random House, NY.

	LOW	AVG.	HIGH
Ambassadors from England, Diplomacy, 1873, unsigned	$ 36	$ 45	$ 54
Ambassadors from England, Siam, 1879, SPY	36	45	54
Americans, An Arbitrator, 1872, unsigned	40	50	60
Americans, Captain, Tanner, Farmer, 1872, unsigned	52	65	78
Americans, President of the New York, 1889, SPY	40	50	60
Americans, The New President, 1913, HESTER	48	60	72
Automobile Devotees, Steam, 1907, SPY	48	60	72
Aviators, The Deutsch Prize, 1901, GEO HUM	160	200	240
Boxers, A Good Lightweight, 1877, SPY	48	60	72
Businessmen and Empire Builders, Manchester, 1875, APE	36	45	54
Businessmen and Empire Builders, Sir Horace, J.P., 1909, SPY	36	45	54
Clergy, A Fashion Canon, 1898, FTD	32	40	48
Clergy, The Chief Rabbi, 1904, spy	70	90	110
Freemasons, The Lord Mayor, 1902, SPY	28	35	42
Game Hunters, Pointers, 1885, SPY	60	75	90
Horse Trainers, Sollie, 1910, HCO	32	40	48
Jockeys, Top of the List, 1906, SPY	80	100	120
Legal, Dick, 1900, SPY	80	100	120
Legal, The Majesty of the Law, 1870, APE	80	100	120
Literary, Waterloo, 1883, T	40	50	60
Music, English Tenor, 1892, LIB	48	60	72
Music, Wagnerian Opera, 1899, WAG	48	60	72
Newspapermen, New York Herald, 1884, NEMO	40	50	60
Orientals, LI, 1896, GUTH	40	50	60
Photographers, East Birmingham, 1902, SPY	72	90	108
Policemen, Criminal Investigation, 1883, SPY	36	45	54
Politicians, A Sticker, 1908, SPY	40	50	60
Politicians, The Kent Gang, 1885, APE	28	35	42
Prime Ministers, The Greatest Liberal, 1869, APE	40	50	60
Red Robe Judges, The Recorder, 1903, SPY	120	150	180
Rowing, Pembroke, 1888, artist, HAY	60	75	90
Royalty, Oh Child, Mayst Thou, 1905, GUTH	40	50	60
Shipping Officials, Plymouth, 1888, SPY	28	35	42
Theater, The St. James's, 1909, MAX	40	50	60
Turf Devotees, Bunny, 1876, SPY	40	50	60
Turf Devotees, Sundown Park, 1891, SPY	40	50	60
Yachting Devotees, Alisa, 1896, MILLER	40	50	60

Toys and Playthings

Baby Rattles

Baby rattles are a universal toy. Almost every culture in the world has its own traditions and superstitions surrounding them. Available examples range from Georgian coral & bells to the plastic ones of today. Rattles can be of gold, silver, ivory, tin, celluloid, paper, and plastic. Collectors must compete with silver collectors and toy collectors for the prime examples, but flea markets, antique shows, and some auctions are still good resources.

Prices give a typical retail range. Our consultant for this section is Marcia Hersey.

Spanish Mermaid rattle. — Photo courtesy of Marcia Hersey.

	LOW	AVG.	HIGH
American, c. 1900, wood "tramp art"	$ 200	$ 250	$ 300
American, c. 1910, tin, painted w/ pony cart	200	250	300
American, c. 1920, celluloid Kewpie doll w/ tennis racquet	120	150	180
American, Gorham, silver rabbit in ring, silver handle	80	95	110
American, silver, man-in-the-moon w/ mother-of-pearl	600	750	900
American, Tiffany, c. 1920, silver and mother-of-pearl	450	550	650
American, c. 1991, wood ice cream sandwich, hand carved	20	20	20
Austrian, c. 1750, adapted silver coin w/ bells	350	450	550
Birmingham, 1807, silver-gilt and coral	550	675	800
Birmingham, 1869, silver w/ mother-of-pearl	300	375	450
Dutch, c. 1850, silver-gilt, carnelian handle	440	550	660
English, 1745, silver w/ stained ivory handle	1600	2000	2400
English George II,1735, silver w/ coral handle	1500	1800	2100
English, silver dog head, ivory handle	500	600	700
French, Art Deco, c.1930, silver w/ ivory ring.	120	150	180
French, c. 1800, gold w/ mother-of-pearl handle	2800	3500	4200
German, c. 1902, silver house, ivory handle	300	400	500
Indian, stuffed cloth, 1980	20	25	30
Italian, tin, painted w/ saint's picture	200	250	300
Japanese, c. 1900, leather and woods	200	250	300
Portuguese, silver fish w/ ivory handle, c. 1940	80	100	120
Russian, c.1900, silver w/ niello (bracelet attached)	900	1150	1400
Spanish, c.1850, silver mermaid	400	500	600

*Left: French gold rattle. Above:
Russian rattle. — Photos courtesy of
Marcia Hersey.*

Other Baby Items	LOW	AVG.	HIGH
Baby Teether, English, 1799, silver and coral, Bateman mark ...	$700	$ 900	$1100
Doll's Rattle, English, c.1910, silver acorn, ivory ring	60	75	90
Doll's Rattle, French, c. 1880, silver gilt w/ ivory handle.	550	650	750

Barbie

Barbie was born in 1959, arriving as a svelte, young woman. Mattel founders Elliot and Ruth Handler had already bought out their partner Harold Matson when they introduced the doll named after their daughter. She was modern and little girls could role play with her, dressing her in countless costumes. Barbie had elegant gowns, mirroring many of the best designers of the day, as well as work togs and casual clothes. They advertised on "The Mickey Mouse Club." Barbie rapidly became the "must have" doll of the baby-boomer area. Ken (named after the Handler's son) and a group of friends soon joined Barbie. The doll is still going strong after thirty-six years. Many adults who adored her as a child now collect her today. Her thirtieth birthday in 1989 was a gala event covered by news services around the world

Collectors look for condition. The most desirable Barbies are pristine examples from the 1950s and '60s. Collectors shy away from much '70s material because there is a perception of inferior quality.

The prices below are based on items in near mint to mint condition. Since the same item can be bought at a variety of locations and prices and many dolls are no longer in their original boxes, we have devised a double range system. The low range (MNP) includes items that are near mint to mint without packaging. The higher-end range (MIP) reflects the prices of near mint to mint items in near mint to mint original boxes. Therefore, prices below are for the best items available; scratched, chipped, or altered are not included. Cut hair, missing clothes, and cracked or stained plastic greatly reduce the price of Barbie. Each entry lists the approximate year of introduction and the item number.

See *The Collectors Encyclopedia of Barbie Dolls and Collectibles*, Sybil DeWein and Joan Ashabraner, and *Doll Fashion Anthology & Price Guide,* A. Glenn Mandeville, Hobby House Press, Grantsville, MD,1994.

	Intro. Yr.	#	MNP	MIP
Barbie and Friends				
Barbie #1, blond	1959	850	$ 1800-2200	$ 3000-4000
Barbie #1, brunette	1959	850	2200-2800	4000-5000
Barbie #2, blond	1959	850	1500-2000	2500-3000
Barbie #2, brunette	1959	850	1800-2400	3000-4000
Barbie #3, blond	1960	850	400-500	700-800
Barbie #3, brunette	1960	850	450-550	800-1000
Barbie #4, blond	1960	850	200-250	400-600
Barbie #4, brunette	1960	850	250-300	500-700
Barbie, bendable legs, rare side flip hairdo	1965	1070	1800-2400	3200-3600
Barbie, bendable legs, American girl hairdo	1965	1070	300-400	700-900
Benefit Performance Porcelain Barbie	1988	5475	90-120	340-420
Barbie, bendable legs, American girl hairdo	1966	1070	300-400	900-1200
Bubble Cut Barbie	1961	850	140-160	250-350
Bubble Cut Barbie	1962	850	140-160	250-300
Color Magic Barbie	1966	1150	650-750	1000-1500
Fashion Queen Barbie	1963	870	100-150	400-500
Francie Twist 'N' Turn, bendable legs	1967	1170	70-90	260-320
Francie, bendable legs, black	1967	1100	300-350	700-800
Francie, bendable legs, white	1966	1130	60-80	200-300
Free Moving Barbie	1975	7270	12-18	50-70

	Intro. Yr.	#	MNP	MIP
Free Moving Ken	1975	7280	$ 10-15	$ 30-40
Gold Medal Olympic Skater Barbie	1975	7262	12-16	75-95
Happy Holidays Barbie, red velvet gown	1988	1703	120-180	380-420
Happy Holidays Barbie, white satin gown	1989	3253	50-70	90-120
Hawaiian Barbie	1977	7470	25-35	70-90
Hawaiian Ken	1978	2960	15-20	30-40
Hispanic Barbie	1979	1292	12-16	50-60
International Barbie, Canadian	1988	4928	8-12	22-28
International Barbie, Eskimo	1982	3898	60-80	120-160
Julia,1 piece nurse outfit	1970	1127	40-60	100-150
Julia, 2 piece nurse outfit	1969	1127	50-80	120-180
Julia, talking	1969	1128	50-80	120-180
Ken, bendable legs	1970	1124	25-35	80-120
Ken, bendable legs,	1965	1020	90-130	200-300
Ken, flocked, crew cut hair	1961	750	50-70	130-180
Ken, painted crew cut hair	1962	750	40-50	100-150
Live Action Barbie, blond	1971	1155	30-50	90-130
Malibu Barbie	1971	1067	12-18	40-50
Midge, bendable legs,	1965	1080	200-250	400-500
Midge, straight legs	1964	860	40-60	140-180
Miss Barbie (sleep-eye)	1964	1060	250-350	700-900
Mod Hair Ken	1973	4224	40-50	90-120
Pink Jubilee Barbie (1200 made)	1989	—	700-900	1400-1800
Quick Curl Barbie	1973	4220	12-18	50-70
Ricky, straight legs	1965	1090	50-60	90-110
Skipper, bendable legs	1965	1030	40-60	90-110
Skipper, straight legs,	1964	950	40-60	90-120
Skipper, straight legs, reissues, pinker skin	1970	950	50-70	120-180
Skooter, bendable legs,	1966	1120	60-80	220-280
Standard Barbie	1967	1190	80-100	280-320
Swirl Pony Tail Barbie	1964	850	200-250	400-500
Talking Barbie	1969	1115	60-80	200-250
Talking Ken	1969	1111	40-60	110-130
Talking P.J.	1969	—	50-70	120-160
Talking Truly Scrumptious	1969	1107	120-160	320-360
Truly Scrumptious, straight legs	1969	1108	100-150	350-450
Twiggy	1967	1185	70-90	220-320
Twist and Turn Barbie	1967	1160	80-100	280-340
Walk Lively Barbie	1972	1182	50-70	120-180
Walk Lively Ken	1972	1184	25-35	60-80

Clothing

Aboard Ship	1965	1631	$ 90-140	$ 200-250
American Airlines Stewardess	1961	984	50-75	140-180
Arabian Knights	1964	874	90-120	200-250
Ballerina	1961	989	40-60	130-160
Barbie in Japan	1964	821	190-220	360-420
Barbi-Q Outfit	1959	962	55-75	140-180

	Intro. Yr.	#	MNP	MIP
Beautiful Bride	1967	1698	$ 300-500	$ 800-1000
Benefit Performance	1966	1667	300-350	600-800
Campus Sweetheart	1964	1616	200-300	400-600
Career Girl	1963	954	60-80	180-220
Cheerleader	1964	876	60-80	140-180
Commuter Set	1959	916	300-400	600-800
Debutante Ball	1966	1666	200-300	400-700
Easter Parade	1959	971	750-950	1500-2000
Gay Parisienne	1959	964	400-600	1200-1800
Gold 'N Glamour	1965	1647	300-400	700-800
Here Comes the Bride	1966	1665	350-400	700-900
Little Red Riding Hood & the Wolf	1964	880	180-220	380-420
Miss Astronaut	1965	1641	300-350	600-700
Modern Art	1965	1625	150-200	280-320
Nighty-Negligee	1959	965	40-50	90-130
Pajama Party	1964	1601	12-18	50-80
Pan American Stewardess	1966	1678	500-700	1500-2000
Poodle Parade	1965	1643	200-250	400-500
Roman Holiday	1959	968	1200-1800	2200-2800
Saturday Matinee	1965	1615	320-380	600-700
Shimmering Magic	1966	1664	450-500	900-1300
Ken Campus Hero	1961	770	20-30	50-70
Ken Country Clubbin'	1964	1400	40-60	90-110
Doctor Ken	1963	793	50-70	90-120
Ken Fraternity Meeting	1964	1408	25-35	60-70
Ken Here Comes the Groom	1966	1426	220-280	450-600
Ken Mr. Astronaut	1965	1415	180-240	400-500
Ken Tuxedo	1961	787	40-60	90-120

Gift Sets and Accessories

	Intro. Yr.	#	MNP	MIP
Barbie and Ken Tennis Gift Set	1962	892	$ 250-350	$ 800-1200
Barbie Beautiful Blues Gift Set	1967	3303	300-350	700-900
Barbie's Sparkling Pink Gift Set	1964	1011	250-350	600-800
Barbie's Wedding Party Gift Set	1964	1017	400-600	1000-1800
Casey Goes Casual Gift Set	1967	3304	300-400	700-900
Fashion Queen Barbie & Ken Trousseau Gift Set	1964	864	250-350	800-1000
Midge's Ensemble Gift Set	1964	1012	300-400	800-1000
Barbie's Sport Plane (Irwin)	1964	—	250-350	550-750

Board Games

Board games are a part of practically everyone's lives. Beginning in the 1840s mass-produced games have offered hours of fun and provided glimpses of their eras. A large number of those listed below are based on television shows, a theme that dominates post-war collecting. There are also examples of card, skill, and target games included. The majority are by American companies.

The following prices are for games ranging from the 1880s to the 1980s. There are differences between post-WWII and pre-war collecting but condition and quality are sought by all collectors. Prices for post-war games are for *near mint complete*. These examples must have no tears, stains, broken corners, or missing pieces. Prices of the pre-war games, particularly before 1920, are a bit more lenient on condition due to age. They reflect examples that are complete with no stains or tears on the box or board image, but may have minor flaws: repaired inner corner or small skirt tears, and some dirt but nothing that affects the illustration.

All dates are approximate. Abbreviations: *AF*-Alderman Fairchild, *AG*-Adventure Games, *AL*-All Fair, *BB-B & B* American Novelties, *G*-Gems, *GB*-Gabriel, *GR*-Gardners, *HB*-Hasbro, *ID*-Ideal, *JS*-J. Spears, *KN*-Knapp., *KR*-Kenner, *L*-Lowell, *M*-Mattel, *MB*-Milton Bradley, *Mc*-McLoughlin, *MX*-Marx, *NG*-National Games, *PB*-Parker Brothers (after 1888), *GP*-George S. Parker (pre-1888), *PR*-Pressman, *RM*-Remco, *SB*-Sudbury, *SP*-Schaper, *SR*-Selchow & Righter, *ST*-Standard Toykraft, *T*-Topper, *TR*-Transogram, *UG*-United Game, *US*-United States Soldier Company, *UT*-Utopia Enterprises, *W*-Whitman.

For further reading see *American Board Games and Their Makers*, Bruce Whitehill, Wallace-Homestead, Radnor, PA, 1992; *Warman's Antique American Games*, Lee Dennis, Warman Publishing Co., Elkins Park, PA, 1986; *Spin Again*, Rick Polizzi and Fred Schaefer, Chronicle Books, San Francisco, 1991; *Toys of the Sixties*, Bill Bruegman, Cap'n Penny Productions, Akron, OH, 1992. The American Game Collector's Association is an active group that can be contacted at AGCA, 49 Brooks Ave., Lewiston, MA, 04240.

Left to right: Tell it to The Judge (Eddie Cantor), 1936, $60-$90; Hand of Fate, 1930s, $70-$90.

	COMPANY	DATE	LOW	HIGH
Across the Continent	PB	1922	$ 180	$ 220
Addams Family	ID	1965	120	160
Addams Family Target	ID	1965	200	300
Agent Zero-M Spy Detector	M	1964	70	90
Air Mail	MB	1927	120	180
Alley Oop	MB	1937	35	45
Amusing Game of Corner Grocer	GP	1887	70	90
Annie Oakley	MB	1950	90	130
Archie Bunker Card	MB	1972	12	18
Archie's	W	1969	20	30
Atom Ant Saves the Day	TR	1966	80	120
Auction Letters	PB	1900	50	70
Auto Fahrt Fur Alles	(German)	1950	60	80
Babe Ruth's Baseball Game	MB	1926	550	800
Barbie's Little Sister Skipper	M	1964	60	80
Barney Google	MB	1923	100	150
Bash!	ID	1967	18	24
Batman	MB	1966	70	95
Batman Target	HB	1966	100	150
Bats in the Belfrey	M	1964	40	60
Battleship	MB	1965	18	22
Beatles Flip Your Wig	MB	1964	150	200
Bewitched Samantha and Endora	G	1965	60	80
Bing Crosby's Call Me Lucky	PB	1954	60	90
Blackout	MB	1939	50	80
Booby Trap	PB	1965	20	30
Bop the Beetle	ID	1963	45	65
Boris Karloff's Monster Game	G	1965	150	200
Branded	MB	1966	40	50
Bulls and Bears	Mc	1896	12,000	18,000
Bulls and Bears	PB	1936	80	120
Bullwinkle Hide 'N' Seek	MB	1961	60	90
Camelot	PB	1930	25	35
Camp Granada	MB	1968	30	50
Candid Camera	L	1963	55	85
Captain America	MB	1966	90	120
Captain Gallant	TR	1956	50	70
Cimarron Strip	ID	1967	90	110
Cities Card Game	AL	1932	30	40
Clue, Sherlock Holmes ed.	PB	1949	50	70
Combat	ID	1963	50	70
Cootie	SP	1949	25	40
Crazy Clock	ID	1964	65	85
Creature of the Black Lagoon Mystery Game	HB	1963	200	300
Dark Shadows	W	1968	90	130
Dark Shadows Barnabas Collins	MB	1969	180	220
Davy Crockett Frontierland	PB	1955	90	130
Dial-a-Quiz	TR	1961	20	30
Dick Tracy Master Detective	SR	1961	55	75
Dick Van Dyke	ST	1965	85	105
Dim Those Lights	PB	1932	200	300

Clockwise from above left: Peter Coodle, 1900, $30-$40; Stop, Look and Listen, 1926, $75-$95; New Pretty Village Church, 1898, $120-$160.

Untouchables, 1961, $80-$100.

	COMPANY	DATE	LOW	HIGH
Dino the Dinosaur	TR	1961	$ 60	$ 90
Disney Fantasyland	PB	1956	70	90
Dr. Kildare	ID	1962	35	45
Dracula Mystery	HB	1963	140	180
Dragnet	TR	1955	80	100
Dynamite Shack	MB	1968	40	50
Electric Questioner	KN	1920	40	55
F-Troop	ID	1965	70	90
Fascination	RM	1962	25	35
Felix the Cat	MB	1960	45	55
Fess Parker/Daniel Boone Trail Blazers	MB	1964	75	95
Finance and Fortune	PB	1936	30	40
Fireball XL-5	MB	1963	120	160
Flintstones Hoppy the Hopparoo	TR	1965	90	130
Flintstones Stone Age	TR	1961	60	90
Flipper Flips	M	1965	60	90
Formula 1 Car Racing	PB	1968	45	65
Frankenstein Mystery	HB	1963	150	200
Game of Man in the Moon	Mc	1901	3000	4000
Game of Venetian Fortune Teller	PB	1898	100	150
Garrison's Gorillas	ID	1967	75	95
Geography Up to Date	PB	1898	45	55
George of the Jungle	PB	1968	80	100
Get Smart, Exploding Time Bomb	ID	1965	90	130
Gidget Fortune Telling	MB	1965	30	40
Gilligan's Island	G	1965	250	350
Godzilla	ID	1963	180	220
Gomer Pyle	TR	1965	50	75
Green Acres	ST	1965	70	90
Green Ghost	TR	1965	70	90
Green Hornet Quick Switch	MB	1966	300	400
Gunsmoke	L	1958	90	140
Hashimoto-San	TR	1963	40	65
Haunted House	ID	1963	150	200
Hector Heathcote, Minute & A Half Man	TR	1963	90	120
Hickety Pickety	PB	1924	30	40
Hogan's Heroes Bluff Out	TR	1966	90	130
Hold the Fort	PB	1895	150	200
Honey West	ID	1965	100	150
Hopalong Cassidy	MB	1950	150	200
Howdy Doody's Own Game	PB	1950	120	160
Huckleberry Hound, Western	MB	1959	60	90
I Dream of Jeannie	MB	1965	90	130
I Spy	ID	1966	80	100
It's About Time	ID	1967	120	180
Jackie Gleason and Away We Go	TR	1956	150	200
Jackie Gleason Story Stage	UT	1955	200	300
James Bond 007 Goldfinger	MB	1966	120	160
James Bond Message for M	ID	1966	300	400
Jetsons Fun Pad	MB	1963	120	160
Jetsons Out of This World	TR	1963	180	220

Top to bottom: Rat Patrol Desert Combat, 1967, $80-$100; Pirate and Traveler, 1936, $50-$70; Twilight Zone, 1964, $150-$200.

	COMPANY	DATE	LOW	HIGH
Jonny Quest	TR	1964	$ 120	$ 180
Ka-Bala	TR	1965	70	90
Kentucky Derby	W	1938	18	22
La Mare aux Grenouilles	(French)	1900	70	90
Land of the Giants	ID	1968	120	180
Land of the Giants Target Game	HB	1968	250	300
Leave It to Beaver, Money Maker	HB	1959	70	90
Leave it to Beaver, Rocket to the Moon	HB	1959	90	140
Let 'Em Have it	AG	1942	40	50
Lie Detector	M	1961	45	65
Little Orphan Annie	MB	1927	200	250
Lost in Space	MB	1965	120	180
Magilla Gorilla	ID	1964	80	100
Man From U.N.C.L.E.	ID	1965	90	130
Mary Poppins	PB	1964	20	30
Melvin The Moon Man	RM	1962	70	90
Mission Impossible	ID	1968	80	110
Mod Squad	RM	1968	65	85
Monkees	TR	1967	80	120
Mouse Trap	ID	1963	45	65
Munsters Card Game	MB	1964	50	60
Munsters Drag Race	HB	1964	200	300
Mystery Date	MB	1966	70	90
Mystic Skull Voodoo	ID	1964	50	75
New Pretty Village Church	Mc	1898	120	160
New Pretty Village Boat House	Mc	1898	120	160
Operation	MB	1965	12	18
Outer Limits	MB	1964	200	300
Palmistry and Psycholgy of the Hand	BB	1919	80	120
Perry Mason	TR	1959	60	90
Peter Coddles Trip (old man, cars)	MB	1925	25	35
Peter Coddles Visit to NY	MB	1888	40	50
Peter Coddles Visit to NY	UG	1910	20	30
Phil Silvers, Sgt. Bilko	GR	1955	70	90
Pigs in the Clover	MB	1930	35	45
Pike's Peak or Bust	PB	1895	100	140
Pirate and Traveler	MB	1936	50	70
Pooch	HB	1956	60	80
Prisoners Base	PB	1896	300	350
Raiders of the Lost Ark	KR	1981	8	12
Rat Patrol Desert Combat	TR	1967	80	100
Rin Tin Tin	TR	1955	80	100
Ring My Nose (clown)	MB	1925	35	45
Risk	PB	1959	40	60
Sea Hunt	L	1960	80	100
Secret Agent Man	MB	1966	50	80
Silly Safari Jungle Game	T	1966	80	100
Six Million Dollar Man	PB	1975	8	12
Skunk	SP	1955	20	30
Snap (swan on cover)	MB	1920	18	25
Space, 1999	MB	1975	15	20

	COMPANY	DATE	LOW	HIGH
Span-It	SB	1948	$ 18	$ 25
Spin 'Em	PB	1938	30	45
Spot a Car Bingo	HB	1950	25	35
Star Trek	ID	1967	80	120
Star Wars	KR	1977	30	40
Stop, Look and Listen	MB	1926	75	95
Stratego	MB	1961	35	45
Teddy Bear Panda ABC	PB	1950	30	40
Tell it to The Judge (Eddie Cantor)	PB	1936	60	90
Tennessee Tuxedo	TR	1963	150	200
The Game of Life	MB	1960	15	20
The Game of India	NG	1950	18	22
Kennedys	TR	1962	100	150
The Merry Milkman	HB	1954	70	90
The Muppet Show	PB	1977	10	15
The Rifleman	MB	1959	90	130
This Is Your Life (R. Edwards)	L	1954	45	65
Through the Locks to the Golden Gate	MB	1918	180	220
Time Bomb	MB	1965	45	65
Time Tunnel	ID	1966	180	220
Time Tunnel Spin to Win	PR	1967	120	180
Tiny Tim	PB	1970	60	80
Tiny Town Post Office (English)	JS	1910	150	200
Touche Turtle	ID	1964	120	180
Touring Card Game	PB	1926	18	22
Twenty-One	L	1956	90	140
Twiggy	MB	1967	60	90
Twilight Zone	ID	1964	150	200
Twister	MB	1966	30	50
Underdog	MB	1964	170	200
Untouchables	TR	1961	80	100
Voodoo Doll	SP	1967	40	60
Wally Gator	TR	1962	90	140
What's the Time?	PB	1898	60	80
When My Ship Comes In, card	GP	1888	45	65
Wipe-out Hot Wheels Race	M	1968	80	100
Wolfman Mystery	HB	1963	200	300
Wonderful Game of Oz (metal pieces)	MC	1921	1500	2500
World War Game	US	1914	500	700
You Bet Your Life, Groucho	L	1955	80	120
Zorro	PB	1966	70	90

Cootie, 1949, $25-$40.

Character Toys

Character toys and memorabilia charm children and adults alike. They are based on familiar faces seen in the comics, heard on the radio or seen on a movie screen or TV. The following items range from the Yellow Kid (turn-of-the century) to Pee-Wee Herman (1980s). Since there is such a diversity of materials, collecting criteria varies a bit. Most of the keywind tinplate character toys have a lithographed or printed finish while cast iron toys are usually painted. Overall the condition reported below is for excellent and better. Prices are given for the item and in many cases a separate range is listed for the item in its original box or package. We do not give a range for toys that are unlikely to be found with their original box nor do we give a price for items that have little value without their packaging such as records. For further information about character and other toys we suggest *Toys of the Sixties*, Bill Bruegman, Cap'n Penny Productions, Akron, OH, 1992; *Toys and Prices,* edited by Roger Case and Tom Hammel, Krause Publications, Iola, WI; *The Official Identification and Price Guide To Antique Toys,* Richard Friz, House of Collectibles, Random House, NY; *Tomart's Price Guide to Action Figure Collectibles*, Carol Markowski, Bill Sikoria, and T.N. Tumbusch, and *A Celebration of Comic Art and Memorabilia*, Robert Lesser, Hawthorn Books, New York, 1975. There are also character items in the following sections of this book, *Little Golden Book, Comic Character Watches, Dolls, Whitman Books, Radios, Premiums, Advertising, Robots and Space Toys Space.*

Three Marx keywind walkers: Amos, Andy, and Harold Lloyd. — Photo courtesy of Phillips Auctioneers.

	UNBOXED	BOXED
A Team, Amy A. Allen, Figure, plastic, Galoob, c. 1984, ht. 6.5"	$ 12-14	$ 20-30
A Team, B. A. Barcus Figure, plastic, Galoob, c. 1984, ht. 6.5"	8-10	18-22
A Team, Hannibal Figure, plastic, Galoob, c. 1984, ht. 6 .5"	5-7	15-20
Addams Family, Gomez Hand Puppet (box), Ideal, c. 1965, ht. 11" .	90-120	200-300
All in The Family, Mug, 1970s	8-10	—
Alvin the Chipmunk, Soakie, c. 1960s	25-32	—
Amos 'N' Andy Fresh Air Taxi Cab, keywind tinplate, Marx, len. 8"	600-900	1000-1500
Amos 'N' Andy Taxicab, cast iron, len. 6"	800-1000	1200-1800

	UNBOXED	BOXED
Amos Walker, keywind tinplate, Marx, c. 1930, ht. 12"	$ 700-1000	—
Andy Gump Car, cast iron, Arcade, c. 1924, len. 5.75"	1200-1800	—
Andy Walker, keywind tinplate, Marx, c. 1930, ht. 12"	700-1000	—
Aquaman, Figure, plastic, Comic Action Heroes, Mego, c. 1975, ht. 3.75"	20-25	$50-70
Archies, Archie Doll, Marx, c. 1975, ht. 10"	12-18	35-55
Archies, Betty, Doll, Marx, c. 1975, ht. 10"	12-18	35-55
Archies, Jalopy, Marx, c. 1975, ht. 10"	25-30	45-65
Archies, Jughead Doll, Marx, c. 1975, ht. 10"	12-18	35-55
Archies, Sabrina Paper Doll	9-12	18-22
Archies, Veronica, Doll, Marx, c. 1975, ht. 10"	12-18	35-55
Babar, Babar, Arthur Figure, Bikin, c. 1989	2-3	8-10
Babar, King Babar Figure, plastic, Bikin, c. 1989.................	2-3	8-10
Babar, Queen Celeste, Bikin, 1989......................................	3-4	10-12
Bambi Soakie, c. 1960s	20-30	—
Banana Splits, Bingo the Bear Doll, Sutton, c. 1970	40-60	90-120
Banana Splits, Drooper the Lion Doll, Sutton, c. 1970	40-60	90-120
Banana Splits, Fleagle Beagle the Dog Doll, Sutton, c. 1970	40-60	90-120
Banana Splits, Snorky the Elephant Doll, Sutton, c. 1970	40-60	90-120
Barnacle Bill The Sailor & Punching Bag, keywind tinplate, Chein, ht. 7.5"	500-800	—
Barney Google Wooden Jointed Figure, Schoenhut, c. 1922, ht. 8.5" ..	400-600	—
Bat Masterson Holster Set, w/ cane & vest, Carnell, c. 1960s	100-150	250-350
Batbike, Corgi, len. 4.25"	40-60	80-100
Batman & Robin Book: *From Alfred to Zowie!,* Golden Press, 1966 ..	15-20	—
Batman & Robin Bookends, 1966, 4" x 7"	70-90	100-140
Batman & Robin Ceramic Figural Bank, 1966	60-80	90-130
Batman & Robin Society Member Button, full color, 1960s	30-40	—
Batman, 45 record, die-cut sleeve in the form of Batman's head c. 1966	—	50-70
Batman, Batcave, Toy Biz, c. 1989	8-12	20-30
Batman, Batcycle, Toy Biz, c. 1989	4-6	10-15
Batman, Batman, Magnetic w/ fly-away action, Mego, c. 1979, ht. 12.5" .	60-90	120-180
Batman, Batmobile w/ remote control, Toy Biz, c. 1989	15-20	30-40
Batman, Batphone, Marx, c. 1966, len. 8"	90-110	140-180
Batman, Batwing, Toy Biz, c. 1989	9-14	20-30
Batman, Ceramic Figural Bank, c. 1966, ht. 7"...................	60-70	80-100
Batman, Charm Bracelet, w/ five on original store card, 1966	30-40	80-100
Batman, Coloring Book, Western Publishing Co.	8-10	20-30
Batman, Figural Ceramic Music Box, Price/National, c. 1970s, ht. 7"	50-70	100-150
Batman, Flashlight, 1976	10-12	20-30
Batman, Flying Copter, Remco, c. 1966	50-70	90-130
Batman, Fork, metal, Imperial, 1966, len. 6"	8-10	15-20
Batman, Hair Brush, plastic figural handle, Avon, 1976 len., 8.5"	8-12	20-25
Batman, Halloween Costume, w/ mask, Ben Cooper, 1960s	20-25	40-60
Batman, Joker van, Toy Biz, c. 1989	7-9	18-22
Batman, Joker, Figural Ceramic Music Box, ht. 7, Price/National c. 1970s	50-70	100-150
Batman, License Plate, 1966, 4" x 7 .5"	10-15	20-30
Batman, Meets Blockbuster Coloring Book, Whitman, 1966	8-10	20-30
Batman, Mug, white plastic w/ illustrations of Batman & Robin	70-90	—

	UNBOXED	BOXED
Batman, Paint By Numbers set, Hasbro, c. 1966	$ 60-80	$ 100-160
Batman, Penguin Figural Ceramic Music Box, Price/National, c. 1970s ht. 7"	50-70	100-150
Batman, Riddler, Figural Ceramic Music Box, Price/National, c. 1970s, ht. 7"	50-70	100-150
Batman, Robin, Flashlight, 1976	8-10	20-25
Batman, Soundtrack LP Record, 20th Century Fox, 1966	—	120-160
Batman, Utility Belt, Ideal, c. 1966	500-700	800-1000
Batman, Wallet, 1966	20-30	—
Batmobile, Bubble Bath, plastic, Avon	10-15	20-30
Batmobile, gold hubs, Corgi, 1966, len. 5"	200-250	350-500
Beatles Paul, Doll, Remco, c. 1964, ht. 5"	70-90	100-150
Beatles, George Doll, Remco, c. 1964, ht. 5"	70-90	100-150
Beatles, John Doll, Remco, c. 1964, ht. 5"	70-90	100-150
Beatles, Ringo Doll, Remco, c. 1964, ht. 5"	70-90	100-150
Betty Boop Composition Figure, c. 1940, ht. 14".	500-700	—
Betty Boop Composition Head Doll, Cameo, ht. 12"	400-600	—
Betty Boop The Acrobat, keywind celluloid & tinplate, ht. 8.5"	500-700	—
Beverly Hillbillies Car, plastic, Ideal, 1963, len. 22"	200-250	400-500
Bewitched, Broom, Amsco, c. 1965, len. 36"	30-50	70-90
Bewitched, Samantha Doll, Ideal, c. 1965, ht. 12"	180-220	300-500
Big Bad Wolf Stuffed Doll, c. 1930s, ht. 21"	700-900	—
Bionic Woman, Bionic Beauty Salon, Kenner, c. 1976	15-20	30-40
Bionic Woman, Jamie Sommers Figure, Kenner, c. 1976	18-22	40-60
Bionic Woman, Sports Car, Kenner, c. 1976	20-30	50-70
Blondie's Jalopy, keywind tinplate, Marx , len. 15"	1500-2000	2200-2800
Bluto Dippy Dumper Truck, tinplate & celluloid, Marx, len. 8.75"	400-600	700-900
Bonanza Holster Set, c. 1960, Halpern Nichols	80-120	150-200
Bonanza, 4 in 1 wagon, plastic, American Character, c. 1966	90-120	200-300
Bonanza, Album, *Party Time*	—	25-35
Bonanza, Ben & Palomino, plastic, American Character, c. 1966	65-85	170-190
Bonanza, Hoss & Stallion, plastic, American Character, c. 1966	75-95	180-220
Bonanza, Jigsaw Puzzle, Ponderosa Ranch	—	25-35
Bonanza, Little Joe & Pinto, plastic, American Character, c. 1966	75-95	180-220
Bonanza, movie viewer, National Broadcasting Co.	10-15	20-30
Bonanza, *One Man with Courage*, paperback, Media Books, 1966	7-9	—
Bonanza, *The Living Legend Of Bonanza*, paperback	8-10	—
Bonzo Scooter, tinplate, Chein, ht. 7"	500-700	—
Boob McNutt, Wooden Jointed Figure, Schoenhut, ht. 9"	1000-1500	—
Bozo the Clown Soakie, c. 1960s	20-30	—
Brady Bunch, Coloring Book, Whitman , c. 1970s	8-10	25-35
Brutus Soakie, c. 1960s	25-30	—
Buck Rogers Police Patrol Spaceship, keywind tinplate, Marx, c. 1939 , len. 12"	800-1200	1800-2200
Buck Rogers, Ardella figure, plastic, Mego, c. 1979, ht. 3.75"	4-6	10-15
Buck Rogers, Atomic Pistol, chrome plating, Daisy, c. 1930s	100-150	200-250
Buck Rogers, Battlecruiser, Tootsie Toy, c. 1937	100-150	200-300
Buck Rogers, Buck Figure plastic, Mego, c. 1979, ht. 3.75"	4-6	10-15
Buck Rogers, Buck figure, plastic, Mego, c. 1979, ht. 12"	15-20	30-50
Buck Rogers, Combat Holster Set, Daisy, c. 1934	180-220	300-400
Buck Rogers, Copper Disintegrator Cap gun, cast iron, c. 1930s	100-150	250-350

	UNBOXED	BOXED
Buck Rogers, Draco figure, plastic, Mego, c. 1979, ht. 3.75"	$ 10-12	$ 20-30
Buck Rogers, Laserscope Fighter, plastic, Mego, c. 1979	12-15	25-40
Buck Rogers, Pencil Case, cardboard, top pictures Buck, c. 1938	30-50	—
Buck Rogers, Pocket Pistol, Daisy, c. 1930s	120-180	250-350
Buck Rogers, Printing Set	60-80	150-200
Buck Rogers, Rubber Band Gun, large litho. cardboard punch-out, c. 1930s, Onward.	30-40	60-80
Buck Rogers, Sonic Ray Gun, plastic, battery powered, Norton Engineering, 1950s	60-90	100-150
Buck Rogers, Star Fighter Command Center, Mego, 1979, c. 1979, 3.75" figs.	25-35	50-70
Buck Rogers, Strato-Kite, Aero Kite, c. 1946	45-65	—
Buck Rogers, Tiger Man figure, plastic, Mego, c. 1979, ht. 12"	15-20	30-50
Buck Rogers, Walking Twiki, plastic, Mego, c. 1979, ht. 12"	20-30	45-65
Buffalo Bill Jr., Western Outfit, c. 1950s	70-90	100-150
Bugs Bunny, Pull String Talking Doll, Mattel, c. 1970s	30-40	80-120
Bullwinkle Soakie, c. 1960s	25-35	—
Buster Brown Dog Cart, cast iron, len. 7.5"	400-600	—
Buttercup & Spare Ribs, Pull Toy, tinplate, Nifty, c. 1925, ht. 7.5" ..	900-1300	—
Captain America, Figure, plastic, Comic Action Heroes, Mego, c. 1975, ht. 3.75"	15-20	40-50
Casper, Talking Ghost Doll, Mattel, c. 1960s, ht. 15"	50-80	150-200
Charlie Chaplin Jointed Doll, Boucher, ht. 7.5"	1800-2200	—
Charlie Chaplin Walker, keywind, Boucher, ht. 8"	1000-2000	—
Charlie McCarthy Benzine Buggy, keywind tinplate, Marx, len. 8"	600-900	1000-1500
Charlie McCarthy Composition Ventriloquist Doll, Effanbee, ht. 20"	500-800	1000-1500
Charlie McCarthy Drummer, keywind tinplate, Marx, ht. 8"	500-700	800-1200
Charlie McCarthy Walker, keywind tinplate Marx , ht. 8"	250-350	400-600
Charlie's Angels, Gift Set, Sabrina, Kelly, & Kris Dolls, Hasbro, c. 1977, ht. 8.5"	30-40	60-90
Charlie's Angels, Jill (Farah Fawcett) Doll, Hasbro, c. 1977, ht. 8.5 ...	25-35	50-70
Charlie's Angels, Kelly (Jacyln Smith) Doll, Hasbro, c. 1977, ht. 8.5" .	20-30	35-45
Charlie's Angels, Kris (Cheryl Ladd) Doll, Hasbro, c. 1977, ht. 8.5" ..	20-30	35-45
Charlie's Angels, Sabrina (Kate Jackson) Doll, Hasbro, c. 1977, ht. 8.5"	20-30	35-45
Cinderella, Drinking Glass, #8, fitted for shoe, c. 1950, ht. 4.63"	9-12	—
Clarabelle Cow, Drinking Glass, red, seated w/ mirror, c. 1936, ht. 4.75"	20-30	—
Cowpuncher Porky, keywind tinplate, Marx, ht. 8"	200-300	400-600
Creature From the Black Lagoon Soakie, Colgate Palmolive, c. 1963, ht. 10"	80-120	—
Dagwood The Driver Car, keywind tinplate, Marx, c. 1935, len. 8" ..	400-600	900-1400
Dagwood's Solo Flight Airplane, keywind tinplate, Marx, len. 9" ..	500-700	900-1200
Daniel Boone Flintlock Pistol, Marx, 1960s	60-80	150-200
Dick Tracy Police Station, w/ car, keywind tinplate, Marx, len. 7.5" ..	250-350	400-600
Dick Tracy Siren Squad Car, tinplate, friction & battery, Marx, len. 11"	250-350	400-600
Dick Tracy Squad Car #1, keywind tinplate, Marx, c. 1939, len. 11" ...	300-400	500-700
Dick Tracy Tinplate Police Squad Car, friction, Marx, len. 6.75" ...	100-150	200-250
Donald Duck Composition & Cloth Doll, in Russian costume,		

	UNBOXED	BOXED
ht. 9" .... $ 1000-1500		—
Donald Duck Duet, keywind Donald & Goofy dancing, c. 1946,		
ht. 10.5" 800-1200		$ 1500-2000
Donald Duck On A Tricycle, tinplate, Linemar, ht. 4" 300-400		600-800
Donald Duck Rowboat, wood & paper, Chad Valley 700-900		—
Donald Duck & Pluto car, hard rubber, Sun Rubber, c. 1950, len.		
6.5" 90-130		—
Donald Duck, Ceramic Figural Cowboy Bank, c. 1940, ht. 6.5" 80-120		—
Donald Duck, Ceramic Figural Milk Pitcher, c. 1940, ht. 6.5" 80-100		—
Donald Duck, Figural Toothbrush Holder, bisque double Donald,		
c. 1940, ht. 4.5" 200-250		—
Donald Duck, Paint Box, litho. tinplate c. 1930s 80-120		—
Donald Duck, Sunshine Straws, c. 1950s ....—		20-30
Donald Duck, The Bubble Duck, plastic, Morris Plastics, c. 1955 90-130		—
Donald Duck, Watering Can, tin, Ohio Art, c. 1930s, ht. 6" 120-180		—
Dopey Soakie, c. 1960s 20-30		—
Dopey, Figurine, plaster, c. 1930s, ht. 14" 70-100		—
Dr. Doolittle, Doll, Mattel, c. 1967, ht. 6" 25-40		80-120
Dr. Seuss, Cat in the Hat Jack in the box, c. 1960s 50-60		90-130
Dumbo, Composition Figure, swiveling trunk, googlie eyes, Cameo		
Doll, c. 1941, ht. 9" 300-500		—
Dumbo, Timothy Mouse Cloth Doll, ht. 14" 300-400		—
Ed Sullivan, Topo Gigio Nodding Head Doll, c. 1960 20-30		40-60
Family Affair, Buffy & Mrs. Beasley Doll Set, Mattel, c. 1967 30-40		80-120
Farfel, Hand Puppet, vinyl & flannel, Juro, c. 1950s 60-80		90-140
Felix The Cat Cloth Doll, ht. 14.5" 500-700		—
Felix The Cat Doll, Schuco, ht. 10.5" 200-300		—
Felix The Cat Standing Figure, composition, ht. 13" 500-700		—
Felix The Cat, Speedy Felix Car, wooden, Nifty, c. 1935, len. 12" . 700-900		—
Flash Gordon Rocketfighter Spaceship, keywind tinplate, Marx,		
c. 1939, len. 12" 500-700		800-1200
Flash Gordon, Arresting Ray Gun, Marx, 1930s 180-230		300-400
Flash Gordon, Easter Egg Decals, features The Phantom & others		
c. 1940 20-30		80-100
Flash Gordon, Figure, standing at attention, wood, ht. 5" 250-350		—
Flash Gordon, Flash Dueling Ming Button, 1970s 6-9		—
Flash Gordon, Radio Repeater Gun, litho. tinplate, Marx, 1930s 200-250		300-500
Flash Gordon, Rocket Fighter, litho. tinplate, Marx, c. 1930s, len.		
13" 500-700		800-1200
Flash Gordon, Solar Commando Figures, litho. card w/ three 3"		
plastic figures, Premier, 1952 50-70		120-160
Flash Gordon, Space Compass, flexible plastic band, 1950s 30-40		60-80
Flintstones, Bamm-Bamm Doll, Ideal, c. 1963, ht. 16" 60-80		160-190
Foghorn Leghorn, Figure, Dakin, c. 1970, ht. 6" 20-30		50-75
Foxy Grandpa Bell Ringer Toy, cast iron, ht. 6.75" 800-1200		—
Foxy Grandpa Doll, composition ht. 17" 900-1400		—
Frankenstein Soakie, c. 1960s 90-120		—
Gabby Hayes fold out book, Bonnie book, c. 1954 80-100		—
Gene Autry Cowboy Spurs, c. 1950 40-60		70-90
Get Smart Agent 86 Pen/Radio, c. 1966 20-30		40-60
Goofy & Wilbur, Drinking Glass, Disney All Star Parade, c. 1939,		

	UNBOXED	BOXED
ht. 4.88"	$ 20-30	—
Green Goblin, Figure, plastic, Comic Action Heroes, Mego, c. 1975, ht. 3.75"	20-25	$ 45-52
Green Hornet, Billfold, c. 1966	20-30	40-60
Green Hornet, Black Beauty Car, Corgi, c. 1966, len. 5"	150-240	350-500
Grumpy, Christmas Light Bulb, c. 1940	25-35	—
Gumby, Electronic Drawing Set, Lakeside, c. 1966	20-25	50-70
Gunsmoke Handcuffs, c. 1950s	15-20	30-40
Happy Hooligan & Rabbit Candy Container, ht. 7.5"	1200-1800	—
Happy Hooligan Donkey Cart, tinplate, Ingap, 7.5"	1200-1800	—
Happy Hooligan Goat Cart, cast iron, 7.5"	1800-2200	—
Happy Hooligan Nodder Donkey Cart, cast iron, len. 6.5"	500-700	—
Happy Hooligan Nodder Horse Cart, cast iron, Kenton, 10.5"	1000-1500	—
Happy Hooligan Walker, keywind tinplate, Chein, ht. 6"	300-500	—
Harold Lloyd Donkey Cart, litho. tinplate c. 1929, Spain, len. 9"	3000-5000	—
Harold Lloyd Walker, keywind tinplate, Marx, ht. 10.75".	600-900	—
Henry On Elephant, keywind celluloid toy, c. 1934, Ck, ht. 8"	1200-1800	2000-3000
Henry On Trapeze, keywind celluloid, Ck, ht. 7.75"	300-500	700-900
Hogan's Heroes, Peri-peeper periscope, ID card, badge	30-40	60-80
Honey West , Doll, plastic, Gilbert, c. 1965, ht. 12"	90-130	200-250
Hopalong Cassidy Holster Light, Aladdin, c. 1950s	250-350	—
Hopalong Cassidy Record Album	60-80	—
Hopalong Cassidy, Belt, leather	20-30	40-60
Hopalong Cassidy, Milk Container, c. 1955, pt.	80-100	—
Hopalong Cassidy, Pocket Knife, black w/ image of Hoppy & Topper	25-35	—
Hopalong Cassidy, Wallet	20-30	30-40
Horace Horsecollar, Drinking Glass, full figure in red, c. 1936 ht. 4.75"	20-30	—
Howdy Doody Piano Band, keywind tinplate, Unique Art, c. 1940, ht. 8.5"	700-900	1200-1500
Howdy Doody Wooden Jointed Figure, c. 1950, ht. 12.5"	400-700	—
Howdy Doody, Figural Ear Muffs	20-30	70-90
Howdy Doody, Jack-in-the-box, plastic, c. 1970s, ht. 5"	18-22	30-50
Howdy Dowdy, Figural Howdy Piggy Bank, porcelain, c. 1950s	150-200	—
Huckleberry Hound Figural Bank, hard plastic, similar to a Soakie, c. 1960s, ht. 10"	25-35	—
Huckleberry Hound Soakie, c. 1960s	25-35	—
Humphrey Mobile, keywind tinplate, Wyandotte, len. 9"	300-500	800-1000
I Dream of Jeannie, Jeanie Doll, Ideal, c. 1966, ht. 18"	200-300	400-600
Ignatz Mouse Car, tinplate litho., Ingap, c. 1930, len. 6"	2500-3500	—
Indiana Jones, Adv. of, Cairo Swordsman Figure, Kenner, c. 1982, ht. 3.75"	8-12	20-30
Indiana Jones, Adv. of, Indy Figure in German Uniform, Kenner, c. 1982, ht. 3.75"	28-32	12-16
Indiana Jones, Adv. of, Marion Ravenwood Figure on card, Kenner, c. 1982, ht. 3.75"	30-40	180-220
Indiana Jones, Adventures of, Desert Convoy Truck, Kenner, c. 1982	35-45	18-22
Indiana Jones, Adventures of, Indy Figure, plastic, Kenner, c. 1982, ht. 3.75"	15-20	60-90
It Takes A Thief, Book #1, paperback	12-18	—
Jackie Coogan Walker, keywind tinplate, German, c. 1920, ht. 7"	600-900	—

	UNBOXED	BOXED

James Bond Doll, w/ suit, plastic (original issue), Gilbert, c. 1964,
ht. 12" .... $ 120-180 $ 300-400

James Bond, Aston Martin Car, battery operated, Gilbert, c. 1965,
len. 12" 200-250   400-500

James Bond, Attaché Case, MPC, c. 1965, 18" x 12" 200-250   400-600

Jeff Felt Stuffed Doll, c. 1930, ht. 12" 100-150

Jetsons, Rosy the Robot, keywind tinplate, Marx, c. 1965 180-220   350-450

Jiggs Cloth Doll, c. 1925, ht. 18" 1200-1800   —

Jiggs Composition & Cloth Doll, ht. 7.5" 200-300   —

Jiggs In His Jazzcar, keywind tinplate, Nifty, c. 1924 , 6.5" 2000-3000

Jiminy Cricket, Christmas light bulb, c. 1950 25-35   —

Jiminy Cricket, Drinking Glass, w/ poem on reverse side, ht. 4.75",
c. 1940 10-15   —

Jiminy Cricket, Hand Puppet, vinyl & cloth, Gund, c. 1960 25-35   50-80

Joe Penner & Goo Goo Walker, keywind, Marx, c. 1939, ht. 8" 500-700   800-1000

Katzenjammer Spanking Toy, cast iron donkey wagon, Kenton,
c. 1906, len. 11.75" 2500-3500   —

Komical Kat Walker, Keywind Tinplate, Gama, c. 1929, ht. 7" 400-600

Krazy Kat Chasing Mice, on a tinplate wheeled platform, Nifty,
c. 1932, 7.5" 600-900   —

Krazy Kat Cloth Doll, c. 1916, len. 3" 600-800   —

Krazy Kat Three Wheel Scooter, keywind, c. 1925, 7.75" 500-700   —

Land of the Giants, Signal Ray Space Gun, Remco, c. 1968 50-70   100-150

Land of the Giants, Target Rifle, Remco, c. 1968, len. 28" 90-140   200-300

Lassie, Stuffed Lassie Doll, c. 1950s 70-120   —

Little Lulu Cloth Doll, Georgene Novelties, c. 1944, ht. 13.5" 400-600   —

Little Nemo, Dr. Pimm Roly Poly, Schoenhut, ht. 11.5" 3000-4000   —

Li'l Abner Dog Patch Band, keywind tinplate, Unique Art, c. 1950,
ht. 9" 500-700   800-1200

Lone Ranger and Silver, keywind tinplate base, Marx 200-250   300-400

Lone Ranger Composition & Cloth Doll, Dollcraft, ht. 20" 600-900   1000-1200

Lone Ranger, Holsters, fiberboard, set of 2, c. 1945, len. 11" 20-30   40-65

Lost in Space, Robot, plastic, AHI, c. 1977, ht. 12" 50-75   100-150

Lost in Space, Robot, plastic, Remco, c. 1966, ht. 12" 250-350   500-700

Lost in Space, Roto Jet Gun, Mattel, c. 1966 700-900   1500-2000

Maggie & Jiggs tinplate squeeze toy, c. 1925, len. 8" 1000-1500   —

Maggie Cloth Doll, c. 1925, ht. 18" 1200-1800   —

Mama Katzenjammer Ball Jointed Figure, Boucher, ht. 7" 400-600   —

Mama Katzenjammer Cloth Doll Tea Cozy, Steiff, c. 1908, ht. 15" . 2000-3000   —

Mama Katzenjammer, celluloid figure, ht. 5" 300-400   —

Man From U.N.C.L.E. Illya Kuryakin Doll, plastic, Gilbert, c. 1965,
ht. 12" 120-180   300-350

Man From U.N.C.L.E. Illya Kuryakin Gun Set, Ideal, c. 1965, len.
8" 180-250   400-600

Man From U.N.C.L.E. Napoleon Solo Doll, plastic, Gilbert, c. 1965,
ht. 12" 60-80   180-230

Man From U.N.C.L.E. Napoleon Solo Gun Set, Ideal, c. 1965 250-300   600-800

Man From U.N.C.L.E. Passport Set, Ideal, c. 1965 45-60   90-130

Man From U.N.C.L.E. Thrush Rifle, Ideal, c. 1966, len. 36" 800-1300   1500-2000

Man From U.N.C.L.E, *ABC's of Espionage*, paperback 8-12   —

Man From U.N.C.L.E, car, blue, fires missiles, Corgi, 1966 50-80   120-160

	UNBOXED	BOXED
Man From U.N.C.L.E, LP Album, RCA, 1966	$ 30-40	—
Man From U.N.C.L.E., MGM Promotional Still	20-30	—
Merrymakers Mouse Band, keywind tinplate, Marx, 1930s ht. 9"	700-900	$ 1200-1500
Mickey & Donald Sand Pail, w/ Daisy & Nephews, Chein, 1930s, ht. 4.5"	80-120	—
Mickey & Minnie Car, wooden, Gong Bell, c. 1933, 10.75"	1200-1900	—
Mickey & Minnie Mouse Playland, keywind, Japan, ht. 10.5"	2500-3500	—
Mickey & Minnie Mouse, Bisque Toothbrush Holder, c. 1930, ht. 4.5"	250-350	—
Mickey Mouse & Cat Wooden Pull Toy, len. 13.5"	500-700	—
Mickey Mouse & Donald Duck Fire Truck, hard rubber, Sun Rubber, c. 1950	90-140	—
Mickey Mouse & Minnie Mouse, Drinking Glass, black on pink, c. 1950, ht. 5.88"	15-20	—
Mickey Mouse Cloth Doll, c. 1930, Knickerbocker, ht. 15"	900-1200	—
Mickey Mouse Cowboy Cloth Doll, Knickerbocker, c. 1935, ht. 19.5"	2500-3500	—
Mickey Mouse Drummer, battery operated, Linemar, c. 1955, ht. 11"	600-800	1000-1500
Mickey Mouse In Rowboat, wooden, Fun-E-Flex, len. 10.75"	2000-3000	—
Mickey Mouse Large Cloth Doll, Knickerbocker, c. 1930s, 15.5"	800-1200	—
Mickey Mouse Piano, litho. wood, c. 1935, Marks Brothers, ht. 10"	1500-2000	—
Mickey Mouse the Magician, tinplate, battery operated, Linemar, ht. 10"	900-1400	1800-2400
Mickey Mouse Tumbling Toy, keywind, Schuco, ht. 4"	200-250	300-400
Mickey Mouse, Donald Duck & Pluto Cup, tug of war, Patriot China, c. 1930s	20-30	—
Mickey Mouse, Recipe Scrap Book, Peter Pan Bread, premium, c. 1930	50-60	—
Mickey Mouse, Seed Packets, Colorforms, c. 1977	—	5-7
Mickey Mouse, Spoon, Mickey on handle, Bransford, c. 1935, len. 5.5"	30-40	—
Milton Berle, Crazy Car, keywind tinplate, Marx, c. 1950s	180-220	300-350
Minnie Mouse Cloth Doll, c. 1930, Knickerbocker, ht. 15"	900-1200	—
Minnie Mouse Knitting, keywind tinplate, Linemar, c. 1950, ht. 6.5"	500-700	900-1200
Monkee Mobile Battery Operated Car, ASC, c. 1967, len. 12"	200-300	500-600
Moon Mullins & Kayo Handcar, Marx, c. 1940, ht. 6"	500-700	800-1000
Mortimer Snerd Walker, keywind tinplate, Marx, len. 8.5"	200-300	400-600
Mr. Ed, Pull String Talking Hand Puppet, Mattel, c. 1962, ht. 12"	20-30	60-90
Mr. Magoo Soakie, c. 1960s	28-36	—
Mr. Magoo, Automobile, tinplate & plastic, battery operated	90-150	250-350
Mummy Soakie, Colgate Palmolive, c. 1963, ht. 10"	80-120	—
Munsters, Herman Doll, Remco, c. 1964, ht. 6"	160-190	300-500
Munsters, Herman Pull String Talking Hand Puppet, Mattel, c. 1964, ht. 12"	150-200	300-400
Munsters, Hypodermic Needle Squirt gun, Hasbro, c. 1964, len. 8"	60-80	150-200
Munsters, Koach Toy, AMT, c. 1964, len. 12"	200-300	500-700
Mutt & Jeff, Jeff Jointed Metal Figure, Boucher, c. 1922, ht. 6.5"	300-400	—
Mutt & Jeff, Mutt Jointed Metal Figure, Boucher, c. 1922, 6.5"	300-400	—

	UNBOXED	BOXED
Mutt Felt Stuffed Doll, c. 1930, ht. 14" .... $ 100-150		—
My Favorite Martian, Beanie w/ antenna, c. 1960s, dia. 7" 50-80		—
Olive Oyl Ballet Dancer Top Toy, tinplate, Linemar, c. 1950 200-250		$ 400-500
Oliver Hardy Cloth Doll, Lenci, ht. 10" 700-1000		—
Orphan Annie Skipping Rope, keywind tinplate, Marx, c. 1937, ht. 5" . 300-400		700-900
Orphan Annie's Sandy w/ Suitcase, keywind tinplate, Marx, c. 1937, ht. 4.5" 250-350		600-800
Orphan Annie, Sandy the Dog playing w/ a ball, Marx, len. 8" 350-450		500-600
Osmonds, Pictorial Activity Book, c. 1970s 7-9		12-18
Peanuts, Snoopy Figural Soap Dish, soft plastic 10-14		18-22
Peanuts, Snoopy, See & Say, Mattel, c. 1960s 20-30		50-80
Pee-Wee's Playhouse, Playset, Matchbox, 1988 18-22		30-50
Pee-Wee's Playhouse, Talking Pee-Wee Doll, c. 1988, ht. 18" 20-30		60-80
Pinocchio The Acrobat, keywind tinplate, Marx, c. 1939, 14.75" ... 300-400		700-900
Planet of the Apes, Cornelius Doll, box, Mego, c. 1973, ht. 8" 35-45		100-150
Planet of the Apes, Zira Doll, box, Mego, c. 1973, ht. 8" 35-45		100-150
Popeye & Olive Oyl Ball Toss, keywind tinplate, Linemar, c. 1950, len. 19" 700-900		1200-1800
Popeye & Olive Oyl Handcar, tinplate, Linemar, len. 9.5" 700-900		1000-1200
Popeye & Olive Oyl Roof Band, Marx, c. 1935, ht. 9.5" 700-900		1200-1800
Popeye & Upright Punching Bag, keywind tinplate, Chein, c. 1935, ht. 8" 1000-1500		—
Popeye Dippy Dumper Truck, tinplate & celluloid, Marx, len. 8.75" 500-700		800-1200
Popeye Express, baggage, wheelbarrow & parrot, Marx, ht. 8" 250-450		800-1200
Popeye Handcar, tinplate & rubber, Marx, c. 1935, ht. 6.5" 700-900		1200-1500
Popeye Heavy Hitter Hammer & Bell Toy, keywind, Chein, c. 1932, ht. 11.5" 1800-2800		3500-5000
Popeye Lamp, cast iron ,w/ litho. paper shade, c. 1935, ht. 17" 700-900		—
Popeye On A Motorcycle, cast iron, Hubley, c. 1938, len. 9" 2000-3000		—
Popeye Overhead Punching Bag, keywind tinplate, Chein, c. 1932, 9.75" 2000-3000		3500-5000
Popeye Rooftop Jigger, keywind tinplate, Marx, c. 1936, ht. 9.75" .. 700-900		1000-1200
Popeye Rowing A Rowboat, keywind tinplate, Hoge, c. 1935, 15.5" 6000-8000		—
Popeye Soakie, c. 1960s 25-35		—
Popeye Somersaulter, keywind tinplate, Linemar, ht. 5" 700-900		—
Popeye Spinach Delivery Motorcycle, cast iron, Hubley 600-800		—
Popeye The Champ Boxing Toy, keywind tinplate & celluloid, Marx, c. 1936, 7" X 7" 2000-2500		3000-5000
Popeye Tinplate Sparkler, Chein, c. 1959, ht. 5", 120-180 200-300		400-600
Popeye Tricycle, keywind tinplate, Linemar, ht. 4" 300-500		600-800
Popeye Wooden Jointed Figure, c. 1932, ht. 10" 300-400		—
Popeye Wooden Jointed Figure, c. 1935, ht. 11" 450-650		—
Popeye Wooden Jointed Figure, w/ cap & pipe, c. 1935, ht. 14" 400-600		—
Popeye, Bubble Blowing, battery tinplate, Linemar, c. 1950s, ht. 8.5" 900-1100		1800-2200
Popeye, Eugene the Jeep, painted wood jointed figure, ht. 7" 700-1000		—
Popeye, Smoking, tinplate, Linemar, ht. 8.5" 800-1000		1500-2000
Popeye, Thimble Theatre Mystery Playhouse, w/ 3 Walkers c. 1939, 9.5 x 12" 1800-2500		—

	UNBOXED	BOXED
Porky Pig Soakie, c. 1960s	$ 20-30	—
Porky Pig with Umbrella, keywind tinplate, c. 1939, Marx, ht. 8.5"	300-400	$ 500-600
Powerful Katrinka Lifting Jimmy, keywind tinplate, c. 1925, ht. 6.75"	3000-4000	—
Rin Tin Tin Stuffed Doll, Smile Novelty, c. 1959	80-120	—
Roy Rogers Bed Spread, c. 1950s	125-175	—
Roy Rogers Guitar, litho. cardboard, c. 1950s	80-100	120-160
Roy Rogers, Fix-It Stage Coach plastic, Ideal, c. 1956	90-130	200-250
Roy Rogers, Lantern, battery operated tinplate, c. 1956	70-90	100-150
Seven Dwarf Doll, Grumpy, Ideal, ht. 7"	200-300	400-600
Seven Dwarf Dolls, Sneezy, Ideal, ht. 7"	200-300	400-600
Seven Dwarfs Doll, Bashful, Ideal, ht. 7"	200-300	400-600
Seven Dwarfs Doll, Doc, Ideal, ht. 7"	200-300	400-600
Seven Dwarfs Doll, Dopey, Ideal, ht. 7"	200-300	400-600
Seven Dwarfs Doll, Happy, Ideal, ht. 7"	200-300	400-600
Seven Dwarfs Doll, Sleepy, Ideal, ht. 7"	200-300	400-600
Shazam, Figure, plastic, Comic Action Heroes, Mego, c. 1975, ht. 3.75"	15-20	40-50
Sightseeing Auto, cast iron, w/ comic character passengers, Kenton, c. 1910, len. 10.5"	5000-7000	—
Six Million Dollar Man, Steve Austin Doll, bionic grip, Kenner, c. 1976	12-18	30-40
Snow White Doll, Ideal, ht. 15.5"	300-400	500-700
Snowflakes & Swipes Pull Toy, litho. tinplate, c. 1929, len. 7.5"	900-1200	—
Sparkplug Wooden Jointed Figure, ht. 9",	400-600	—
Sparkplug, Racing Platform Toy, litho. keywind tinplate, c. 1924, ht. 9"	5000-7000	—
Stan Laurel Cloth Doll, Lenci, ht. 10"	700-1000	—
Superman Figural Ceramic Music Box, Price/National c. 1970s, ht. 7"	50-70	100-150
Superman Rollover Airplane, keywind tinplate, Marx, c. 1940, len. 6"	800-1000	—
Superman Turnover Tank, keywind tinplate, c. 1940, Marx, len. 4"	400-600	700-1000
Superman, Badge, movie promotional, emblem shape (for Superman I)	18-22	—
Superman, Belt Buckle, tin, blue & red, chains portrait, 1940s	120-160	—
Superman, Button, Kellogg's Pep Cereal premium, multicolor litho. tin, 1950s	25-35	—
Superman, Candy Coated Peanuts, box only, illustrated lid, 1966, len. 5"	30-40	—
Superman, Dime Register Bank, litho. tinplate, 1940s	—	260-320
Superman, Doll, composition & wood, painted, jointed w/ cape, Ideal, ht. 13"	1200-1800	—
Superman, Doll, stuffed fabric, full length w/ cape, Toy Works, 1970s, ht. 25"	10-15	22-28
Superman, Pencil Case, Mattel, 1960s	18-22	—
Superman, Standing Figure, Syrocco, 1940s, ht. 5"	3000-4000	—
Superman, *The Magic Ring*, two 78 records, & booklet, Musette, c. 1947	100-150	—
Superman, toothbrush, battery operated	20-30	50-70
Sylvester & Tweety, Sylvester Soakie, c. 1960s	25-35	—
Sylvester & Tweety, Tweety Bird Figure, Dakin, c. 1960s, ht. 6"	8-12	18-22

	UNBOXED	BOXED
Tarzan, Thingmaker Mold, Mattel, c. 1966	$ 20-25	$ 40-50
Three Little Pigs Figure, keywind, Schuco, ht. 4.75"	100-150	200-250
Thumper the Rabbit Soakie, c. 1960s	20-30	—
Tom & Jerry, Jerry Mouse stuffed Toy, Merry Thought, c. 1950s, ht. 6"	45-60	—
Tonto Composition & Cloth & Doll, Dollcraft, ht. 20"	500-700	900-1200
Toonerville Trolley, tinplate, c. 1925, ht. 7"	400-600	700-900
Uncle Wiggily Crazy Car, len. 7"	300-500	600-800
W.C. Fields Doll, Effanbee, ht. 19"	400-600	1000-1500
Wagon Train, 45 Rpm Record, w/ picture sleeve, Mitch Miller & Orchestra, 1957	—	20-30
Wagon Train, Tray Puzzle, Whitman, c. 1960, 14" x 11"	10-15	20-30
Waltons, paper doll	6-8	15-20
Wild, Wild West, Writing Tablet	12-15	—
Winky Dink & You, Magic TV Kit, Standard Toy, 1960s	50-70	—
Wolfman Soakie, Colgate Palmolive, c. 1960s, ht. 10"	80-120	—
Woody Woodpecker Soakie, c. 1960s	25-35	—
Woody Woodpecker, Tray Puzzle	18-22	—
Yellow Kid Figure, cast iron in burlap dress, ht. 6.5"	700-1000	—
Yellow Kid Goat Cart, cast iron, len. 7.5"	400-600	—
Yogi Bear, Magic Slate, c. 1960s	20-30	—

Children's Dishes

This chapter includes both toy dishes and children's tableware. Produced extensively throughout America, Europe and the Orient from the 1880s through the 1950s, they are found in every material common to full size dishes and tablewares. As miniatures of "Mother's" dishes, many are accurate down to the smallest detail. Reproductions and new items made in the style of an earlier period are not worth as much as period pieces.

For further information on children's dishes refer to *The Official Price Guide to Depression Glass* published by The House of Collectibles, Random House, NY, and *Collector's Encyclopedia of Children's Dishes*, Margret & Kenn Whitmyer, collector books, Paducah, KY, 1993.

Left to right: Pitcher, Shirley Temple, blue glass, dia. 6.5", $35-$50; Hopalong Cassidy mug , white milk glass, ht. 3", $25-$35. — Item courtesy of Jim Glaab's Collector's Showcase.

	LOW	HIGH
Bowl, Blue Marble, England, oval, 4.5"	$ 28	$ 33
Bowl, Blue Willow, Made in Japan, 3.5"	28	34
Bowl, Hopalong Cassidy, white milk glass, 5"	25	40
Bowl, Shirley Temple, blue glass, 6.5"	50	60
Butter Dish, pattern glass, Bead & Scroll, clear, w/ dome lid, 4"	135	155
Casserole, Blue Willow, Made in Japan, 4.75"	32	36
Casserole, Blue Willow, Made in Japan, 5"	35	40
Casserole, Blue Willow, Occupied Japan	38	42
Casserole, graniteware, blue & white, w/ lid, 2.88"	75	95
Casserole, Noritake, Bluebird, 6"	30	40
Casserole, Pagodas, England, w/ lid, 5.5"	40	50
Coffee Pot, aluminum., tapered w/ wooden handle lid embossed "Drink Thomson Malted Milk," 1930s, 5"	28	32
Creamer, Blue Willow, Made in Japan, 1.5" -	7	9
Creamer, Blue Willow, Made in Japan, 2"	8	10
Creamer, Blue Willow, Occupied Japan	12	18
Creamer, depression glass, Cherry Blossom, pink, 2.75"	25	30
Creamer, depression glass, Doric & Pansy, pink, 2.75"	25	30
Creamer, glass, Akro Agate, Chiquita, green opaque, 1.5"	3	5
Creamer, Noritake, Bluebird, 1.88"	12	15
Creamer, pattern glass, Acorn, clear, 3.38"	80	100
Creamer, Sunset, Made in Japan, 1.88"	3	5
Creamer, Water Hen, England, 3.13"	20	25

	LOW	HIGH
Crock, lid, brown & gray, 1920s, 4"	$ 9	$ 15
Cup & Saucer, Blue Willow, Made in Japan, cup 1.13"	7	9
Cup & Saucer, Blue Willow, Made in Japan, cup 3.5"	7	9
Cup & Saucer, Blue Willow, Occupied Japan	10	12
Cup & Saucer, depression glass, Cherry Blossom, pink, cup 1.5"	25	30
Cup & Saucer, depression glass, Doric & Pansy, cup 1.5"	25	30
Cup & Saucer, Noritake, Bluebird	7	12
Cup & Saucer, Noritake, Silhouette, pale lavender w/ girl pushing doll buggy, cup 1.25"	9	12
Cup & Saucer, Silhouette, Made in Japan, man & woman, cup 1.5"	6	8
Cup & Saucer, Sunset, Made in Japan, cup 1.25"	6	8
Cup & Saucer, Water Hen, England, cup 2"	15	18
Dishpan, aluminum, flat sides, rolled edge, loop handles, 4"	6	8
Frying Pan, graniteware, blue & white, 4.5"	50	60
Grater, graniteware, blue & white, 4"	70	85
Gravy Boat, Blue Marble, England, 1.5"	30	40
Gravy Boat, Blue Willow, Made in Japan	24	28
Grill Plate, Blue Willow, Made in Japan, 5"	30	40
Mold, graniteware, blue & white, fluted, 2.75"	35	32
Mug, glass, Hopalong Cassidy, white milk glass, 3"	25	35
Pitcher & Wash Bowl, ironstone, white w/ green shading, 24 kt gold bands, roses, scalloped edges, scroll handle, 4"	30	50
Pitcher, graniteware, blue & white, 2.5"	60	80
Plate, Blue Marble, England, 4"	10	12
Plate, Blue Willow, Made in Japan, 3.75"	6	8
Plate, Blue Willow, Made in Japan, 5"	13	15
Plate, Blue Willow, Occupied Japan	8	10
Plate, depression glass, Cherry Blossom, pink, 5.88"	7	9
Plate, depression glass, Doric & Pansy, pink, 5.88"	6	8
Plate, glass, Akro Agate, Concentric Rib, green opaque, 3.25"	2	3
Plate, Hopalong Cassidy, white milk glass, 7"	30	40
Plate, Noritake, Bluebird, 4.25"	5	7
Plate, Pagodas, England, 4.5"	10	12
Plate, Sunset, Made in Japan, 4.25"	3	5
Platter, Blue Marble, England, 4.5"	30	40
Platter, Blue Willow, Made in Japan, 4.63"	20	30
Platter, Blue Willow, Made in Japan, 6"	30	35
Platter, Blue Willow, Occupied Japan	30	35
Platter, Noritake, Bluebird, 7.13"	18	22
Platter, Pagodas, England, 7.13"	25	32
Presentation Cup, porcelain, "To My Sister," pink roses, 24 kt scrolling, closed loop handle, 1890, 2.38"	20	35
Sugar Bowl, Blue Willow, Made in Japan, w/ lid, 2"	10	15
Sugar Bowl, Blue Willow, Made in Japan, w/ lid, 2.75"	10	14
Sugar Bowl, Blue Willow, Occupied Japan, w/ lid	14	18
Sugar Bowl, depression glass, Cherry Blossom, pink, 2.63"	22	26
Sugar Bowl, depression glass, Doric & Pansy, pink, 2.5"	20	30
Sugar Bowl, Noritake, Bluebird, w/ lid, 2.75"	14	20
Sugar Bowl, pattern glass, Block, blue, w/ lid, 4.5"	90	110
Sugar Bowl, Sunset, Made in Japan, w/ lid, 3.13"	8	12
Sugar Bowl, Water Hen, England, w/ lid, 4.5"	25	30

	LOW	HIGH
Table Utensils, tin, five knives w/ 2 piece-riveted bone handles, five forks, 1910, 3.5"	$ 25	$ 35
Teapot, Blue Willow, Made in Japan, w/ lid, 2.63"	35	45
Teapot, Blue Willow, Made in Japan, w/ lid, 3.75"	40	55
Teapot, Blue Willow, Occupied Japan, w/ lid	20	25
Teapot, glass, Akro agate, J.P., transparent green, w/ lid, 1.5"	30	40
Teapot, Noritake, Bluebird, w/ lid, 3.5"	40	50
Teapot, Noritake, Silhouette, pale lavender w/ black silhouette of little girl pushing a doll buggy, 3.5"	40	50
Teapot, Silhouette, Made in Japan, man & woman, w/ lid, 4"	12	18
Teapot, Sunset, Made in Japan, w/ lid, 3.75"	18	22
Teapot, Water Hen, England. w/ lid, 5.25"	40	50
Tea set, china, 9, covered teapot, creamer, covered sugar, two cups, two saucers, white w/ blue shading, 24 kt gold decoration, scalloped edges, German, 1910, tallest 5.5"	90	140
Tea Set, depress. glass, Homespun, pink, 14 pcs, orig box	190	230
Tea Set, glass, Akro Agate, Chiquita, green opaque, 22 pcs, original box	60	80
Tea Set, glass, Akro Agate, Concentric Ring, 21 pcs, marbleized blue, original box	400	475
Tea Set, glass, Akro Agate, Interior Panel, transparent topaz, 8 pcs, original box	40	50
Tea Set, Palissy china, 23 pcs., covered teapot, creamer, covered sugar, 6 cups & saucers, 6 plates, white w/ brown flower, berry & leaf decoration, gold trim, elaborate shape, Palissy blue mark, early 1800s, teapot 4.5" .	200	300
Tea Set, porcelain, 16 pieces, covered teapot, creamer sugar, 6 cups & saucers, teddy bear decoration	300	500
Tea Set, porcelain, 7 pcs., covered teapot, sugar, creamer, 2 cups & saucers, Dolly Dingle decoration	60	80
Tea Set, porcelain, 7 pcs., covered teapot, sugar, creamer, two cups, two saucers, Peter Rabbit decoration	120	180
Toleware, tin, pitcher, cup, saucer, painted blue, and cream w/ still life scenes, 1920, pitcher 2"	30	50
Tumbler, Hopalong Cassidy, white milk glass, 10 oz., 3"	35	45
Tureen, Blue Willow, Made in Japan, w/ lid, 4"	35	45
Tureen, Blue Willow, Occupied Japan, w/ lid	40	50
Tureen, ironstone, lid, moss rose decoration, rococo styling, 24 kt trim on handles, 1890	40	50
Tureen, semi-porcelain, Johnson Brothers, lid, white w/ gold trim & sprays of tiny roses, 1800s, 7" x 4.5"	60	70
Turkey Roasting Pan, aluminum, oval, lid, riveted iron handles on ends of pan & top of lid, 1920s, 5.5" x 3.5"	18	22

Comic Character Watches

Mention "comic character watches" and you will invariably hear the reply, "You mean like a Mickey Mouse watch?" It was Mickey who ushered in the first comic watch in 1933 and the market has been thriving ever since. Prices for watches in their original, colorful boxes have skyrocketed due to scarcity and increasing demand. Promotional watches requiring boxtops or proof of purchase and acquired by mail have gained in popularity.

The prices listed in the MNP column are for mint condition working watches, without their packaging or original boxes; the second price range (MIP) is for working, mint in the package examples. MIP for promo watches means that they come with their original mailing material. We have abbreviated some titles, removed 19 from the date, and substituted PW for pocket watch and WW for wristwatch.

The following are our codes for manufacturers: *BR* -Bradley, *BY* -Bayard, *CT* -Columbia Time, *EX* -Exacta Time, *FW* -Fawcett, *GC* -Glen Clock, *GT* -Gilbert, *HD* -Haddon, *HL* -Helbros, *IG* -Ingraham, *IN* -Ingersol, *L* -Lorus, *PWC* -Patent Watch Company., *RT* -Ralston, *SF* -Starkist Foods, *Sk* -Seiko, *SM* -Smith, *SW* -Swiss (maker unknown), *UK* -Unknown, *UST* -U.S. Time, *W* -Wilane, *WB* -Warner Brothers,

Our consultant for this section is Howard S. Brenner, collector and author of *Comic Character Clocks and Watches,* Books Americana, 1987 (he is listed in the back of this book).

Right: Captain Marvel Wristwatch (larger than deluxe), in original box, $700-$750. Below: Alice in Wonderland Wristwatch , plastic teacup package, $400-$450. — Photos courtesy of Howard S. Brenner

	COMPANY	CIRCA	MNP	MIP
Alice in Wonderland WW, plastic teacup pack. ...	UST	1950	$ 90-130	$ 400-450
Babe Ruth WW, plastic baseball package	EX	1949	250-350	1400-1600
Bambi Alarm Clock	BY	1964	150-200	200-250
Batman WW	TX	1978	60-80	140-160
Betty Boop PW	IG	1934	900-1100	2200-2500
Buck Rogers PW, light. bolt hands, monster bk.	IG	1935	800-900	1400-1600
Bugs Bunny Alarm Clock	IG	1951	400-450	700-800
Bugs Bunny WW	WB	1951	450-500	700-800
Captain Marvel WW (deluxe), 1 jewel	FW	1948	300-350	550-600
Captain Marvel WW (larger than deluxe)	FW	1948	400-450	700-750
Charlie McCarthy Alarm Clock, animated	GT	1938	1500-2000	3000-3500
Charlie the Tuna WW promo	SF	1971	60-80	90-120
Cinderella WW, slipper box	UST	1950	140-160	450-500
Cinderella WW, porcelain statue pack.	TX	1958	120-160	400-450
Dale Evans WW, pop-up display box	IG	1951	200-250	400-500
Dan Dare PW, double animation	IN	1953	700-750	900-1000
Davy Crockett Clock, electric, animated	HD	1954	400-450	500-550
Davy Crockett Clock	UK	1955	200-250	380-420
Davy Crockett WW, powder horn box	UST	1954	140-180	400-450
Davy Crockett WW, 3-D pop-up display box	BR	1956	140-180	400-500
Dick Tracy WW	NH	1948	180-220	450-550
Donald Duck Clock, animated	GC	1950	380-420	600-700
Donald Duck Clock, animated	BY	1964	180-220	280-320
Gene Autry WW	W	1948	250-300	500-600
Gene Autry WW, Six Shooter, animated	NH	1951	500-550	750-850
Goofy WW, runs backwards	H	1972	650-750	1000-1300
Hopalong Cassidy WW, in saddle stand box	UST	1950	140-180	400-450
Hopalong Cassidy Alarm Clock	UST	1950	350-450	600-700
Hopalong Cassidy PW	UST	1950	500-600	900-1100
Howdy Doody WW, moving eye, window box ...	PWC	1954	250-300	500-600
Lone Ranger PW, w/ pistol & holster	NH	1939	400-450	750-850
Lone Ranger WW	NH	1939	320-380	650-750
Little Pig (Disney Fiddler pig)WW	UST	1947	350-400	650-750
Mickey Mouse Alarm Clock, animated wind-up	IN	1933	850-950	1900-2100
Mickey Mouse Alarm Clock, anim., round case	IN	1934	850-950	1900-2100
Mickey Mouse Alarm Clock, elec., revolving MM .	IN	1933	1000-1200	2200-2600
Mickey Mouse Alarm Clock, pocket watch form ..	BR	1979	60-80	100-150
Mickey Mouse Alarm Clock, moving feet	BR	1983	60-80	100-150
Mickey Mouse Clock, Magic Castle, animated	BR	1979	300-350	450-550
Mickey Mouse Clock, square case	IN	1933	850-950	1900-2100
Mickey Mouse Deluxe WW, Mickey on second hand .	IN	1938	500-600	1000-1300
Mickey Mouse PW, shield fob	IN	1933	600-650	1000-1200
MM PW, debossed back, round fob	IN	1933	600-650	1000-1200
Mickey Mouse PW, Bicentennial	BR	1976	100-125	200-300
Mickey WW, "Ambassador to the World"	SK	1986	350-400	450-500
Mickey WW Digital	BR	1973	180-200	250-300
Mickey/Donald WW (1st time tog.)	L	1986	175-200	220-260
Mickey WW, Electric	TX	1968	475-525	650-750
Mickey WW, 50th Birthday	BR	1978	250-300	350-400
Mickey, WW, Pluto Wag. Head (200 made)	BR	1978	750-850	900-1100
MM WW, "Mickey #1," leather band	IN	1933	600-650	800-900

Superman Wristwatch, large pre-war, in original box, $1600-$1800. — Photo courtesy of Howard S. Brenner.

Bugs Bunny Wristwatch, in original box, $700-$800. — Photo courtesy of Howard S. Brenner.

Cinderella Wristwatch, slipper box, $450-$500. — Photo courtesy of Howard S. Brenner.

	COMPANY	CIRCA	MNP	MIP
Mickey Mouse WW, "Mickey #1" steel band	IN	1933	$ 500-600	$ 750-850
Mickey Mouse WW, 1973, 1st issue	BR	1973	160-180	200-230
Mickey Mouse WW Wagging Head, anim.	BR	1978	200-250	320-380
Mickey and Minnie WW, PROMO	SW	1976	60-80	90-110
Minne Mouse WW Anim. Wagging Head	BR	1978	375-425	500-600
Minnie Mouse WW, 1973 1st issue	BR	1973	170-200	220-260
Mister Peanut WW, promo	SW	1975	60-80	90-110
Orphan Annie WW	NH	1948	250-300	450-500
Popeye Alarm Clock, animated	SM	1968	275-325	450-550
Popeye PW, anim., Thimble Theatre char. face	NH	1934	650-700	850-950
Popeye PW	NH	1935	450-500	700-800
Popeye WW	NH	1935	400-450	850-950
Porky Pig WW, round case	IG	1949	350-400	550-650
Raid WW, PROMO	SW	1975	60-80	90-110
Roy Rogers Alarm Clock, animated	IG	1951	350-400	550-650
Roy Rogers PW w/ charm	BR	1959	350-400	700-800
Roy Rogers WW, Roy & Trigger posing on face	IG	1951	350-400	500-550
Roy Rogers WW, posing, round case, pop-up box	IG	1951	300-350	500-550
Snow White WW, large size, pre-war	IN	1939	350-400	550-600
Snow White WW, magic mirror box	UST	1959	160-180	500-550
Star Trek,WW, Spock	BR	1979	25-35	40-50
Star Wars WW, Darth Vader	BR	1977	35-45	50-85
Star Wars WW, R2D2 & C3PO	BR	1977	35-45	50-75
Superman PW	BR	1959	500-550	1000-1200
Superman WW, large pre-war	NH	1939	500-550	1600-1800
Superman WW	NH	1948	350-400	1400-1600
Superman WW, large	TX	1976	90-110	160-180
Superman WW, small	TX	1976	60-80	140-160
Three Little Pigs Alarm Clock, animated Wolf	I	1934	400-450	2200-2600
Three Little Pigs PW, animated, debossed back	IN	1934	800-900	2200-2600
Three Little Pigs WW, figural steel band	IN	1934	1000-1200	2800-3200
Tom Mix, promo WW	RT	1983	300-350	450-550
Woody Woodpecker Alarm Clock , animated	CT	1950	400-450	750-850
Zorro WW, sombrero package	UST	1957	90-130	450-500

Babe Ruth WW, plastic baseball package, $1400-$1600.
— Photo courtesy of Howard S. Brenner.

Cracker Jack

F.W. Ruckenheim and his brother developed this famous mixture of popcorn, peanuts, and molasses. In 1893 they sold it at the Columbian Exposition in Chicago where it was an overnight sensation. In 1896 it was named Cracker Jack and soon after prizes were introduced. At first coupons were used which the customer could trade for various prizes. The company began putting the actual prize in each box by 1912. Cracker Jack prizes have been made of lead, paper, porcelain, plastic, tin, and wood. The little sailor, Jack, is based on the founder's grandson Robert (for trivia fans, the dog's name is Bingo).

The following prices are for items in excellent to mint condition; dates are approximate. For more information see *Cracker Jack Prizes*, Alex Jarmillo, Abbeville Press, NY, 1989.

	LOW	HIGH
Air Corps Wings, metal, emb.	$ 50	$ 75
Badge, junior detective, metal, emb., ht. 1.25"	50	60
Charm for Bracelet, blue celluloid, comical head of man	20	25
Clicker, metal, black & silver, instructions on front, ht. 2.13"	20	30
Clicker, Whistle, metal, emb. CJ, w. 2"	20	30
Coconut Corn Crisp, full-color round tin, ht. 3.5"	70	90
Corkscrew, Angelus, metal, w. 3.75"	50	70
Flip Book, Charlie Chaplin, pre-1922	80	120
Game #1, red, white, & blue, w. 2.5"	40	50
Horse & Wagon, die-cast metal, len. 2"	200	300
Hummer Band, metal, emb, dia. 1"	30	40
Iron-Ons, paper, 4 attached on a sheet, 1945	5	10
Jumper, tin, frog, green & silver, 1935 , len. 1.88"	25	35
Magazine Adv., *Sat. Even. Post*, June, 1919, red, white & blue	15	25
Magic Puzzle, donkey, paper & plastic, w. 1.5"	12	18
Magic Puzzle, fish	12	18
Magic Puzzle, man w/ cigar, marked CJ Co. on reverse	12	18
Paper Booklet, #12, Bess & Bill, ht. 2.5"	70	90
Paper Frog, outside is green, black, & white, opens to red & tan inside	25	35
Paper Golf Top, red, white & blue, rules back, intact	40	55
Paper, Jack at blackboard, turn dial, he writes & erases name, sq. 2"	125	175
Pin, Lady	30	40
Pin, Lady, celluloid, paper insert in back for "CJ 5 Cents"	30	40
Pocket Watch, tin, gold, black, & white, dia. 1.5"	50	70
Postcard, bears, #13	30	40
Postcard, bears, #15	30	40
Puzzle Book, #1, copyright 1917, ht. 4"	30	40
Puzzles, #1-15, complete set	200	350
Rainbow Spinner, cardboard,1920s, len. 2.5"	15	25
Sign, cardboard, red, white & blue box on blue background, 11" x 15"	400	700
Spinner, tin, red, white, & blue illust. of CJ package, w. 1.5"	25	35
Tin Top	25	35
Tin Top, fortune teller	40	60
Tin, standup Harold Teen	70	90
Tin, standup Orphan Annie	90	130
Tin, standup, Perry	70	90
Truck, plastic, emb. on 4 sides, gold, 1940s, len. 1.63"	30	40
Truck, tin, red, white & black, "Cracker Jack," other "Angelus," len. 1.63"	60	80
Whistle, metal, emb. CJ	40	60
Whistle, paper, red & white, rvrs. mkd. CJ Whistle, ht. 2"	25	35
Whistle, tin, silver & blue, 1940s, 2.5"	15	25

Dolls

Doll collecting has grown remarkably in the last twenty-five years to become one of the top hobbies in the United States. It rivals stamps and coins. Individual appeal seems to be the magic ingredient which drives the marketplace. The prices of dolls cover such a wide range that any collector can find a category to fit his budget. Interesting and varied collections can be assembled by specializing in dolls of a certain era, a specific material, or all the various dolls produced by a single manufacturer. Condition is all important. Prices given here are for dolls in excellent condition. Dolls with original or true period clothes will carry an incrementally higher value depending on quality. Deductions must be made for any missing or replaced parts; worn-out or faded clothes and wigs, and most importantly broken, chipped or cracked heads. For further reading see *The Collector's Encyclopedia of Dolls*, Dorothy S., Elizabeth A., and Evelyn J. Coleman, Crown, New York, NY, 1968. *The Collector's Encyclopedia of Dolls Volume II*, Coleman, Dorothy S., Elizabeth A., and Evelyn J., Crown, NY, 1986, *The Official Identification and Price Guide to Antique and Modern Dolls*, Julie Collier, House of Collectibles, Random House, NY, 1989. *Patricia Smith's Doll Values, Antique to Modern*, Collector Books, Paducah, KY, 1992. Our consultant for the bisque doll portion of this section is Matrix Quality Antique Dolls.

Left: SFBJ Paris, early version of the SFBJ 301, no mold number, bisque head, sleep eyes, French jointed body, ht. 24", $1700-$1900. Middle: China head of glazed porcelain, with painted features, molded hair, cloth body and period clothes, ht. 16", $250-$300. Right: Bebe Jumeau'Déposé, bisque head, paperweight eyes, and closed mouth, on Jumeau jointed composition body, ht. 20", $5000-$6000. This doll is earlier than and commands a higher price than a Tete Jumeau. — Photos courtesy of Matrix Quality Antique Dolls.

*Left: Schoenhut Dolly, mint and all original, ht. 17", $650-$700.
Middle: Bye-lo Baby, bisque head, sleep eyes, cloth body, and period
clothes, ht. 12", $475-$525. Brown eyes command a bit more. Right:
Kämmer and Reinhardt Child, bisque socket head, glass sleep eyes,
jointed composition body, period clothes and wig, ht. 24", $900-
$1100. — Photos courtesy of Matrix Quality Antique Dolls.*

	LOW	HIGH
Armand Marseille, '370,' German bisque shoulder head child with wig, glass sleep eyes, open mouth with four teeth, kid leather body with bisque arms. ht. 12"	$ 140	$ 160
Armand Marseille, '370,' ht. 15"	180	220
Armand Marseille, '370,' ht. 20"	360	380
Armand Marseille, '1894,' German bisque shoulder head child with wig, glass sleep eyes, open mouth with four teeth, kid leather body with bisque arms. ht. 12"	180	220
Armand Marseille, '1894,' ht. 15"	240	260
Armand Marseille, '1894,' ht. 20"	380	420
Armand Marseille, '390,' German bisque socket head child with wig, glass sleep eyes, open mouth with four teeth, ball jointed composition body, ht. 12"	180	220
Armand Marseille, '390,' ht. 20"	380	420
Armand Marseille, '390,' ht. 24"	480	520
Armand Marseille, '390,' ht. 30"	750	850
Armand Marseille, 'Florodora,' German bisque shoulder head child with wig, glass sleep eyes, open mouth with four teeth, kid leather body with bisque arms, ht. 12"	140	160
Armand Marseille, 'Florodora,' ht. 15"	180	220
Armand Marseille, 'Florodora,' ht. 20"	360	380
Armand Marseille, '990,' German bisque socket head baby with wig, glass sleep eyes, open mouth with two teeth, five piece composition baby body, ht. 10"	280	320
Armand Marseille, '990,' ht. 20"	460	480
Armand Marseille, '990,' ht. 24"	675	725
Armand Marseille, '971,' German bisque socket head baby with wig, glass sleep eyes, open mouth with two teeth, five piece composition baby body, ht. 10"	300	340

	LOW	HIGH

Armand Marseille, '971,' ht. 20" .... $ 475 — $ 525

Armand Marseille, '971,' ht. 24" .... 700 — 800

Armand Marseille, '326,' German bisque socket head baby with solid
  crown, glass sleep eyes, open mouth with two teeth, five piece composition baby body, ht. 10" .... 340 — 360

Armand Marseille, '326,' ht. 15" .... 525 — 575

Armand Marseille, '326,' ht. 20" .... 675 — 725

Armand Marseille, '341,' known as Dream Baby, German bisque head
  with flange neck, solid crown, glass sleep eyes, closed mouth, cloth
  body with celluloid hands, ht. 9" .... 180 — 220

Armand Marseille, '341,' ht. 13" .... 360 — 380

Armand Marseille, '341,' ht. 20" .... 625 — 675

Armand Marseille, '351,' known as Dream Baby, German bisque head
  with flange neck, solid crown, glass sleep eyes, open mouth with two
teeth, cloth body with celluloid hands, ht. 9" .... 180 — 220

Armand Marseille, '351,' ht. 13" .... 360 — 380

Armand Marseille, '351,' ht. 20" .... 625 — 675

Bye-Lo Baby, 'Grace S. Putnam,' German bisque head with flange neck,
  solid crown, glass sleep eyes, closed mouth, cloth body with celluloid
  hands, ht. 12" .... 475 — 525

Bye-Lo Baby, ht. 15" .... 600 — 700

Bye-Lo Baby, ht. 20" .... 1100 — 1300

Bye-Lo Baby, 'Grace S. Putnam,' German bisque socket head, solid
  crown, glass sleep eyes, closed mouth, five piece composition baby
  body, ht. 13" .... 1100 — 1300

Bye-Lo Baby, ht. 15" .... 1300 — 1400

Bye-Lo Baby, 'Grace S. Putnam,' composition head with flange neck,
  solid crown, painted eyes, closed mouth, cloth body with composition
  hands, ht. 13" .... 340 — 360

Bye-Lo Baby, 'Grace S. Putnam,' German bisque socket head, solid
  crown with wig, glass sleep eyes, closed mouth, all bisque baby
  body with jointed limbs, ht. 4" .... 675 — 725

Bye-Lo Baby, ht. 8" .... 1100 — 1300

China Head, molded hairdo with curly waves, sometimes showing ears,
  black or blonde hair, painted blue eyes, closed lips, cloth or leather
  body, with cloth, leather, china or bisque arms, ht. 8" .... 90 — 125

China Head, ht. 12" .... 200 — 250

China Head, ht. 16" .... 250 — 300

China Head, ht. 24" .... 400 — 450

Heinrich Handwerck, '99,' German bisque socket head child with wig,
  glass sleep eyes, open mouth with four teeth, pierced ears, ball jointed
  composition body, ht. 16" .... 600 — 650

Heinrich Handwerck, '99,' ht. 24" .... 750 — 850

Heinrich Handwerck, '99,' ht. 30" .... 1100 — 1300

Heinrich Handwerck, '109,' German bisque socket head child with wig,
  glass sleep eyes, open mouth with four teeth, pierced ears, ball jointed
  composition body, ht. 16" .... 600 — 650

Heinrich Handwerck, '109,' ht. 24" .... 750 — 850

Heinrich Handwerck, '109,' ht. 30" .... 1100 — 1300

Heinrich Handwerck, '69,' German bisque socket head child with wig,
  glass sleep eyes, open mouth with four teeth, pierced ears, ball jointed

	LOW	HIGH
composition body, ht. 16"	$ 625	$ 675
Heinrich Handwerck, '69,' ht. 24"	750	850
Heinrich Handwerck, '69,' ht. 30"	1200	1400
Heinrich Handwerck, '79,' German bisque socket head child with wig, glass sleep eyes, open mouth with four teeth, pierced ears, ball jointed composition body, ht. 16"	625	675
Heinrich Handwerck, '79,' ht. 24"	750	850
Heinrich Handwerck, '79,' ht. 30"	1200	1400
Heinrich Handwerck, '119,' German bisque socket head child with wig, glass sleep eyes, open mouth with four teeth, pierced ears, ball jointed composition body, ht. 16"	625	675
Heinrich Handwerck, '119,' ht. 24"	750	850
Heinrich Handwerck, '119,' ht. 30"	1200	1400
Heinrich Handwerck, '89,' German bisque socket head child with wig, glass sleep eyes, open mouth with four teeth, pierced ears, ball jointed composition body, ht. 16"	725	775
Heinrich Handwerck, '89,' ht. 24"	850	950
Heinrich Handwerck, '89,' ht. 30"	1400	1600
Heinrich Handwerck, '420,' German bisque socket head character doll with wig, glass sleep eyes, open mouth with two teeth, ball jointed, toddler or baby body, ht. 20"	750	850
Bebe Jumeau 'Déposé, Tete Jumeau, Bte SGDG' in red ink, French bisque socket head child with cork pate and wig, glass paperweight eyes, open mouth with six teeth, pierced ears, ball jointed composition body, ht. 16"	1800	2200
Bebe Jumeau 'Déposé, Tete Jumeau, Bte SGDG,' ht. 20"	2400	2600
Bebe Jumeau 'Déposé, Tete Jumeau, Bte SGDG,' ht. 24"	2800	3200
Bebe Jumeau 'Déposé, Tete Jumeau, Bte SGDG' in red ink, French bisque socket head child with cork pate and wig, glass paperweight eyes, closed mouth, pierced ears, ball jointed composition body, ht. 16"	3500	3800
Bebe Jumeau 'Déposé, Tete Jumeau, Bte SGDG,' ht. 20"	3800	4200
Bebe Jumeau 'Déposé, Tete Jumeau, Bte SGDG,' ht. 24"	4000	4500
Kämmer and Reinhardt '403,' German bisque socket head child with wig, glass sleep eyes, open mouth with four teeth, pierced ears, ball jointed composition body, ht.12"	725	775
Kämmer and Reinhardt, '403,' ht. 16"	725	775
Kämmer and Reinhardt, '403,' ht. 24"	900	1100
Kämmer and Reinhardt, '403,' ht. 30"	1300	1500
Kämmer and Reinhardt, '100,' known as Kaiser baby, German bisque socket baby head with solid crown, painted eyes, open/closed mouth, five piece composition baby body, ht. 12"	550	600
Kämmer and Reinhardt, '100,' ht. 15"	675	725
Kämmer and Reinhardt, '100,' ht. 20"	900	1100
Kämmer and Reinhardt, '126,' German bisque socket head baby with wig, glass sleep eyes, open mouth with two teeth, five piece composition baby body, ht. 12"	475	525
Kämmer and Reinhardt, '126,' ht. 15"	625	675
Kämmer and Reinhardt, '126,' ht. 20"	800	900
Kämmer and Reinhardt, '121,' German bisque socket head baby with wig, glass sleep eyes, open mouth with two teeth, five piece composition baby body, ht. 12"	600	650
Kämmer and Reinhardt, '121,' ht. 15"	750	800

	LOW	HIGH
Kämmer and Reinhardt, '121,' ht. 20"	$ 900	$ 1100
Kämmer and Reinhardt, '122,' German bisque socket head baby with wig, glass sleep eyes, open mouth with two teeth, five piece composition baby body, ht. 12"	600	650
Kämmer and Reinhardt, '122,' ht. 15"	750	800
Kämmer and Reinhardt, '122,' ht. 20"	900	1100
J.D. Kestner, '154,' German bisque shoulder head child with plaster pate and wig, glass sleep eyes, open mouth with four teeth, kid body with bisque arms, ht. 12"	375	425
J.D. Kestner, '154,' ht. 16"	450	500
J.D. Kestner, '154,' ht. 20"	575	625
J.D. Kestner, '148,' German bisque shoulder head child with plaster pate and wig, glass sleep eyes, open mouth with four teeth, kid body with bisque arms, ht. 12"	425	475
J.D. Kestner, '148,' ht. 16"	500	550
J.D. Kestner, '148,' ht. 20"	650	750
J.D. Kestner, '195,' German bisque shoulder head child with plaster pate and wig, glass sleep eyes, inset fur eyebrows, open mouth with four teeth, kid body with bisque arms, ht. 15"	425	475
J.D. Kestner, '195,' ht. 20"	525	575
J.D. Kestner, '171,' German bisque socket head child with plaster pate and wig, glass sleep eyes, open mouth with four teeth, composition all jointed body, ht. 16"	675	725
J.D. Kestner, '171,' ht. 24"	850	900
J.D. Kestner, '171,' ht. 30"	1100	1300
J.D. Kestner, '161,' German bisque socket head child with plaster pate and wig, glass sleep eyes, open mouth with four teeth, composition ball jointed body, ht. 16"	750	850
J.D. Kestner, '161,' ht. 24"	900	1100
J.D. Kestner, '161,' ht. 30"	1300	1500
J.D. Kestner, '167,' German bisque socket head child with plaster pate and wig, glass sleep eyes, open mouth with four teeth, composition ball jointed body, ht. 16"	700	800
J.D. Kestner, '167,' ht. 24"	900	1000
J.D. Kestner, '167,' ht. 30"	1100	1300
J.D. Kestner, '214,' German bisque socket head child with plaster pate and wig, glass sleep eyes, open mouth with four teeth, composition ball jointed body, ht. 16"	725	775
J.D. Kestner, '214,' ht. 24"	900	1000
J.D. Kestner, '214,' ht. 30"	1100	1300
J.D. Kestner, '129,' German bisque socket head child with plaster pate and wig, glass sleep eyes, open mouth with four teeth, composition ball jointed body, ht. 16"	750	850
J.D. Kestner, '129,' ht. 24"	900	1100
J.D. Kestner, 129, ht. 30"	1300	1500
J.D. Kestner, '152,' German bisque socket head child with plaster pate and wig, glass sleep eyes, open mouth with four teeth, composition ball jointed body, ht. 16"	750	850
J.D. Kestner, '152,' ht. 24"	900	1100
J.D. Kestner, '152,' ht. 30"	1300	1400
J.D. Kestner, '174,' German bisque socket head child with plaster pate		

	LOW	HIGH
and wig, glass sleep eyes, open mouth with four teeth, composition ball jointed body, ht. 16"	$ 800	$ 900
J.D. Kestner, '174,' ht. 24"	1000	1200
J.D. Kestner, '174,' ht. 30"	1400	1600
J.D. Kestner, '211,' German bisque socket head baby with plaster pate and wig, glass sleep eyes, open mouth with two teeth, five piece composition baby body, ht.12"	650	750
J.D. Kestner, '211,' ht. 16"	800	900
J.D. Kestner, '211,' ht. 20"	1000	1200
J.D. Kestner, '226,' German bisque socket head baby with plaster pate and wig, glass sleep eyes, open mouth with two teeth, five piece composition baby body, ht.12"	650	750
J.D. Kestner, '226,' ht. 16"	850	950
J.D. Kestner, '226,' ht. 20"	1100	1300
J.D. Kestner, 'JDK,' German bisque socket head baby with solid crown, glass sleep eyes, open mouth with two teeth, five piece composition baby body, ht.12"	550	650
J.D. Kestner, 'JDK,' ht. 16"	700	800
J.D. Kestner, 'JDK,' ht. 24"	1300	1500
J.D. Kestner, 'Hilda,' German bisque socket head baby with solid crown or plaster pate with wig, glass sleep eyes, open mouth with two teeth, five piece composition baby body, ht. 15"	3400	3600
J.D. Kestner, 'Hilda,' ht. 20"	4200	4800
J.D. Kestner, 'Hilda,' ht. 24"	5500	6500
Kewpie, Rose O'Neil, all bisque standing figure, with side glancing eyes, stiff neck with little blue wings, feet joined in standing position, jointed arms with starfish hands, ht. 2"	60	80
Kewpie, Rose O'Neil, all bisque standing figure, ht. 4"	90	110
Kewpie, Rose O'Neil, all bisque standing figure, ht. 6"	150	200
Kewpie, Rose O'Neil, all bisque standing figure, ht. 8"	400	500
Kewpie, Rose O'Neil, all bisque standing figure, ht. 10"	900	1000
Kewpie, Rose O'Neil, all bisque standing figure, ht. 12"	1100	1300
Kewpie, Rose O'Neil, Composition standing figure, with side glancing eyes, stiff neck with little blue wings, feet joined in standing position, jointed arms with starfish hands, ht. 12"	250	350
Schoenhut Baby, wooden socket head with or without wig, painted eyes, open or closed mouth, five piece body, original paint, normal wear, ht. 12"	500	600
Schoenhut Baby, ht. 15"	650	800
Schoenhut Walker, wooden socket baby head with or without wig, painted eyes, open or closed mouth, bent arms and straight hinged legs, original paint, normal wear, ht. 12"	700	850
Schoenhut Walker, ht. 16"	800	950
Schoenhut Dolly, wooden socket head child with wig, decal eyes, open mouth showing teeth, spring jointed body, original paint, normal wear, ht. 14"	400	550
Schoenhut Dolly, ht. 17"	500	700
Schoenhut Dolly, ht. 21"	800	900
Schoenhut Carved Hair, wooden socket head child with hair carved in various hairdos, sometimes with carved ribbon, carved eyes, closed mouth, spring jointed body, original paint, normal wear, ht. 14"	1200	1600

	LOW	HIGH
Schoenhut Carved Hair, ht. 17"	$ 1500	$ 1800
Schoenhut Carved Hair, ht. 21"	1800	2500
Schoenhut Character, wooden socket head child with wig, carved eyes, closed mouth, or showing teeth, spring jointed wooden body, original paint, normal wear, ht. 14"	700	900
Schoenhut Character, ht. 17"	900	1200
Schoenhut Character, ht. 21"	1200	1500
SFBJ '301,' French bisque socket head child with wig, glass sleep eyes, open mouth with four teeth, pierced ears, ball jointed composition body, ht.15	750	850
SFBJ '301,' ht. 20	900	1000
SFBJ '301,' ht. 24"	1100	1300
Shirley Temple, made by Ideal, all composition head and body (in good condition) marked 'Shirley Temple' with size number, socket head, sleep eyes, jointed body, original wig, original dress with label, ht. 11"	550	650
Shirley Temple, ht. 13"	525	575
Shirley Temple, ht. 15"	550	650
Shirley Temple, ht. 18"	650	750
Shirley Temple, ht. 20"	800	900
Shirley Temple, ht. 25"	900	1100
Shirley Temple, ht. 27"	1100	1300
Shirley Temple, made by Ideal, all composition head and body (in good condition) marked 'Shirley Temple' with size number, socket head, sleep eyes, jointed body, original wig, original Captain January blue sailor suit with label and white cap, ht. 11"	550	650
Shirley Temple, ht. 13"	850	950
Shirley Temple, ht. 15"	800	900
Shirley Temple, ht. 18"	900	1100
Shirley Temple, ht. 20"	1000	1200
Shirley Temple, ht. 25"	1200	1400
Shirley Temple, ht. 27"	1400	1600
Shirley Temple, made by Ideal, all composition head and body (in good condition) marked 'Shirley Temple' with size number, socket head, sleep eyes, jointed body, original wig, original Texas Ranger cowgirl outfit with label, gun, holster and hat, ht. 11"	900	1100
Shirley Temple, ht. 13"	900	1000
Shirley Temple, ht. 15"	1000	1200
Shirley Temple, ht. 18"	1100	1300
Shirley Temple, ht. 20"	1200	1400
Shirley Temple, ht. 25"	1400	1600
Shirley Temple, ht. 27"	1600	1800
Shirley Temple, made by Ideal, all composition head and body (in good condition) marked 'Shirley Temple' with size number, socket head, sleep eyes, jointed body, original wig, original Little Colonel southern belle outfit with label and large bonnet, ht. 11"	900	1100
Shirley Temple, ht. 13"	900	1000
Shirley Temple, ht. 15"	1000	1200
Shirley Temple, ht. 18"	1100	1300
Shirley Temple, ht. 20"	1200	1400
Shirley Temple, ht. 25"	1400	1600
Shirley Temple, ht. 27"	1600	1800

	LOW	HIGH

Shirley Temple, made by Ideal, all composition head and body (in good
    condition) marked 'Shirley Temple,' brown color tone, black wig,
    original Hawaiian grass skirt and lei, ht. 18" .... $ 900 $ 1100

Baby Shirley, made by Ideal, composition head with flirty eyes, open
    mouth, socket head on shoulder plate with cloth torso and composition
    limbs, original wig and baby dress with label, ht.12" 900   1100

Baby Shirley, ht. 18" 1400   1600

Simon & Halbig, '1079,' German bisque socket head child with wig, glass
    sleep eyes, open mouth with four teeth, ball jointed composition body,
    ht. 16" 525   575

Simon & Halbig, '1079,' ht. 24" 725   775

Simon & Halbig, '1079,' ht. 30" 1000   1200

Simon & Halbig, '1078,' German bisque socket head child with wig, glass
    sleep eyes, open mouth with four teeth, ball jointed composition body,
    ht. 16" 525   575

Simon & Halbig, '1078,' ht. 24" 725   775

Simon & Halbig, '1078,' ht. 30" 1000   1200

Simon & Halbig, '550,' German bisque socket head child with wig, glass
    sleep eyes, open mouth with four teeth, ball jointed composition body,
    ht. 16" 475   525

Simon & Halbig, '550,' ht. 24" 650   750

Simon & Halbig, '550,' ht. 30" 1400   1600

Simon & Halbig, 'Santa,' German bisque socket head child with wig,
    glass sleep eyes, open mouth with four teeth, red 'V' mark on lower
    lip, ball jointed composition body, ht. 16" 800   900

Simon & Halbig, 'Santa,' ht. 24" 1100   1300

Simon & Halbig, 'Santa,' ht. 30" 1600   1800

Left: Kämmer and Reinhardt '100', Kaiser Baby, solid crown head, painted eyes, composition body, ht. 15", $675-$725. Middle: A Trio of Rose O'Neil Kewpies, The Thinker, ht. 5", $375-$425, flanked by two Standers ht. 3", each $80-$100. Right: Kestner Child, Bisque Head, open mouth, glass sleep eyes, jointed Kestner body with original clothes, ht.23", $1100-$1300. — Photos courtesy of Matrix Quality Antique Dolls.

Dollhouses

Dollhouses and dollhouse furniture are difficult areas to evaluate because of their diversity. Quality craftsmanship and attention to detail are important considerations for wooden items. Because most earlier dollhouses are hand-crafted, price is often determined by collector's individual taste. Collector's of paper on wood examples rely on manufacturer, style and condition. Later, tinplate dollhouses made by Marx and other firms are worth more money if unassembled in the original box with all accessories intact. Dollhouse furniture and accessories have similar criteria, elaborate well crafted early items in excellent condition command the highest prices. Many items have been reproduced or created the style of earlier periods, these items are not worth as much as similar period pieces. Color variations can occasionally affect the prices of plastic dollhouse accessories, prices listed are for more common colors.

	LOW	HIGH
Bliss, lithographed paper on wood, four rooms, marked bliss on front door, 23 x 19 x 11"	$ 1500	$ 2000
Cohn, lithographed tinplate Ranch with pool, 1950s, unassembled in original box	80	100
Cohn, lithographed tinplate Ranch with pool, 1950s, assembled	40	50
Dollhouse, fireplaces in all rooms, simulated carved shingles, stucco exterior, late 1920s	400	600
Dollhouse, wood faced with paper, painted, brick styled chimney, c. 1910, len. 17.5"	600	800
Dutch colonial, wood, c. 1925	500	700
English, wooden, four rooms with staircase, two fireplaces, late 1920s, 23" x 37" x 17"	1200	1800
French chateau style, wooden, windows on three sides, working door, c. 1890	1500	2000
German, wooden, curtained windows, attic, 23" x 27" x 17", c. 1920s	2500	3500
Jayline, lithographed tinplate, 5 rooms, assembled	70	90
Jayline, lithographed tinplate, 5 rooms, unassembled in original box	80	100
Marx, lithographed tinplate Suburban Colonial, 1950s, assembled	45	55
Marx, lithographed tinplate Suburban Colonial with 32 pieces, 1950s, unassembled in original box	150	200
Marx, lithographed tinplate two story Colonial with Disney nursery, 41 pieces of furniture, 1950s, unassembled in original box	180	220
Marx, lithographed tinplate two story Colonial with Disney, nursery, 1950s, assembled, 25" x 10" x 15"	60	80
Mystery Doll House, small, wooden, paneled doors, parquet floors, c.1890s, 11" x 22" x 27"	3500	5500
Nineteenth century style, wooden, shingled roof, clapboard sides, four rooms with hallways and staircase, 2 fireplaces, Victorian furnishings, c.1900	2000	3000
Schoenhut Dollhouse, wooden, faux brick and stone facade, c.1910, 23" x 12" x 16"	600	900
Swiss chalet style, oak base on wheels, stenciled design on exterior, five rooms, Victorian furnishings, c.1895	2600	3600.

Dollhouse Furniture

	LOW	HIGH
Bathtub, tin, paint worn, ht. 2.5", late 19th c.	$ 25	$ 35
Bedroom suite, wood, four pieces, c. 1920s	40	50

	LOW	HIGH
Bowfront chest, Tynietoy scale	$ 55	$ 65
Broom holder, tin, with brooms and dust pan	50	60
Clock, Mantle, Renwal, plastic, c. 1950s	5	7
Dining table, golden oak, scale 1" to 1'	70	90
Drum table, rosewood, top tilts, edge lines in velvet, c. 1900, dia. 3"	70	90
Fireplace, open hearth, pine mantle	25	45
Hepplewhite sofa, Tynietoy, scale	70	80
Ice cream parlor set, 2 chairs with wire mesh seats, table, c.1930s, ht. 3.5"	100	150
Radio, Table, Renwal, plastic, c. 1950s, len. 1"	20	30
Refrigerator, Deluxe, Renwal, plastic, in original box, c. 1950s, ht. 7"	45	65
Refrigerator, Deluxe, Renwal, plastic, no box, c. 1950s, ht. 7"	25	35
Rope bed, ticking mattress and pillow, c. 1920s, 15.5" x 10.5"	80	100
Rug, needlepoint, c. 1920s, dia. 3.5"	25	45
Shaving mirror, mahogany frame and stand, mirror beveled glass, c.1900, H. 4"	80	100
Sink, Deluxe, Renwal, plastic, c. 1950s, len. 6"		
Stove, tin kitchen, with utensils, c.1915, ht. 11"	100	125
Table, Card, folding, Renwal, plastic, c. 1950s, ht.1.75"	8	12
Table, Chair, folding, Renwal, plastic, c. 1950s, ht. 2"	8	12
Table, Kitchen, Renwal, plastic, c. 1950s,	4	6
Teakettle, brass with trivet, c. 1920s	55	75
Telephone, Renwal, plastic, c. 1950s	18	22
Vanity with mirror, Renwal, plastic, c. 1950s, ht. 4"	8	12
Victrola, four-legs, painted wood, c. 1920s, ht. 4.5"	55	75

Fine Miniature Furniture

Chest of drawers, George III. mahogany, late 18th c., ht. 14"	$ 1200	$ 1500
Chest of drawers, George III style, mahogany, 1920s, ht. 10"	100	150
Tea caddy, George III, 18th c., ht. 4.5"	200	300
Victorian dining room set, walnut table and sideboard with marble tops, upholstered chairs	250	300
Wing chair, Federal, upholstered in brocade, ht. 8"	800	1200

G.I. Joe

Joe recently turned thirty and is still going strong. Hasbro introduced him in 1964. The Irwin Company produced some of Hasbro's early vehicles for Joe. Plastic and 11.5" tall, Joe was marketed as a fighting or action figure and not as a doll. Thus the action figure toy was created. A huge success with boys, girls often substituted him for Ken, to act as Barbie's date. Joe has changed with the times. In 1977 Hasbro reduced his height to 8.5". Following the enormous success of the *Star Wars* action-figure line, Joe was reintroduced in the 3.75" size in 1982 and is still being produced. Collectors are beginning to seek these figures. The following list, however, focuses on the earlier 11.5" figures.

The prices below are based on items in excellent or mint condition. Since the same item can be bought at a variety of locations at different prices we devised a range system. The low range covers complete, near mint to mint items without the original box or package (*MNP*). The higher range reflects the prices of complete, near mint to mint items in near mint to mint boxes (*MIP*). Prices below are for complete "like new" items. Completeness is an important factor for G.I Joes.

The Encyclopedia of G.I. Joe, by Vincent Santelmo, Krause Publications, Iola, WI, 1993, describes in great detail what each set contained.

The year listed is the year of introduction, unless it's a reissue or update. Following the date is the series: Action Marine-(*AM*), Action Girl-(*AG*), Action Sailor-(*ALS*), Action Soldiers of the World-(*ASW*), Action Soldier-(*ASD*), Action Pilot-(*AP*), Adventure Team-(*ADT*), and Adventure Pack-(*ADP*)-a designation not a series. Words are abbreviated to conserve space. Following the series is the product number. We have put in *Fig.* (figure), *Unf.* (uniform), or *Equip.* (equipment) to avoid confusion between similarly named sets. Each term encompasses everything that originally came with the set.

	YEAR	SERIES	NO.	MNP	MIP
Action Black Soldier Fig.	1965	ASD	7900	$ 700-900	$ 1200-1500
Action Marine Fig.	1964	AM	7700	180-220	$ 320-380
Action Nurse Fig.	1967	AG	8060	1300-1600	2000-3000
Action Sailor Fig.	1964	ASL	7600	180-220	300-400
Action Soldier Fig.	1964	ASD	7500	150-200	250-300
Air Acad. Cadet Unf. Set	1967	AP	7822	400-600	800-1000
Air Sea Rescue Unf. Set	1967	AP	7825	900-1200	1500-2000
Annapolis Cadet Unf. Set	1967	ASL	7624	500-600	800-1000
Astronaut Unf. Set	1967	AP	7824	550-650	900-1100
Austr. Jungle Ftr.Stnd. Set, w/ fig.	1966	ASW	8205	700-900	1200-1400
Austr. Jungle Ftr. Equip.	1966	ASW	8305	200-250	300-400
Austr. Jungle Ftr. Dlx. Set, fig. & equip.	1966	ASW	8105	1800-2000	2400-3400
Basic Foot Locker	1965	AS	8000	40-50	70-90
Beachhead Flamethrower Set	1964	AM	7718	50-60	80-100
Bivouac Sleeping Bag	1964	ASD	7515	25-35	50-70
British Commando Stnd. Set, w/ fig.	1966	ASW	8204	600-800	900-1200
British Commando Equip.	1966	ASW	8304	190-220	300-350
British Com. Dlx. Set, fig. & equip.	1966	ASW	8104	1600-1800	2200-3200
Combat Fatigue Pants	1964	ASD	7504	40-50	80-100
Combat Fatigue Shirt	1964	ASD	7503	45-55	90-120
Combat Field Jacket	1964	ASD	7505	100-130	180-220
Comma. Post Field Radio Tel. Set	1964	ASD	7520	40-50	80-100
Comma. Post Poncho	1964	ASD	7519	40-50	60-80
Commu. Flag Set	1964	AM	7704	200-250	400-500
Crash Crew Fire Truck Set	1967	AP	8040	1800-2200	3000-3500

	YEAR	SERIES	NO.	MNP	MIP
Deep Freeze Unf. Set	1967	ASL	7623	$ 300-400	$ 500-700
Deep Sea Diver Unf. Set, reissue	1968	ASL	7620	300-450	600-750
Desert Patrol Jeep Set, w/ fig.	1967	ASD	8030	1500-2000	2500-3000
Dress Unf.	1964	AP	7803	800-1000	1400-1800
Fighter Pilot Unf. Set	1967	AP	7823	900-1200	1500-2000
Forward Base Set w/ fig. (Sears)	1966	ASD	5969	300-400	500-700
French Res. Fighter Stnd. Set, w/ fig. .	1966	ASW	8203	650-850	1000-1300
Fr. Res. Fighter Equip.	1966	ASW	8303	160-200	250-300
Fr. Res. Ftr. Dlx. Set, fig. & equip.	1966	ASW	8103	1600-1800	2200-3200
German Soldier Stnd. Set, w/ fig.	1966	ASW	8200	650-850	1200-1400
German Soldier Equip.	1966	ASW	8300	190-220	300-350
Gr. Sold. Dlx. Set, fig. & equip.	1966	ASW	8100	1600-1800	2200-3200
Green Beret Equip.	1966	ASD	7533	70-90	180-220
Green Beret fig.	1966	ASD	7536	900-1200	1800-2200
Grn Brt Mach. Gun Opst , 2 Figs.	1966	ASD	5978	600-800	1100-1300
Japanese Imp. Sold. Stnd. Set, w/ fig. .	1966	ASW	8201	800-900	1300-1600
Jp Imp. Sold. Dlx. Set, fig. & equip. ...	1966	ASW	8101	2000-2200	2500-3600
Japanese Imp. Sold. Equip.	1966	ASW	8301	200-250	300-400
Jet Fighter Airplane	1967	ASD	5396	400-500	800-1000
Jungle Fighter Unf. Set	1967	AM	7732	700-900	1400-1800
M.P. Duffel Bag	1964	ASD	7523	30-40	50-70
M.P. "Ike" Jacket	1964	ASD	7524	50-70	90-120
Mach. Gun Set, w/ fig. (Sears)	1965	ASD	7531	400-450	650-750
Marine Demo. Set (Reissue)	1968	AM	7730	200-250	350-450
Marine Weapons Rack	1967	AM	7727	180-220	340-420
Military Staff Car	1967	ASD	5652	300-350	500-700
Official Jeep Set, w/ eng. sound	1965	ASD	7000	200-300	500-700
Russian Soldier Equip.	1966	ASW	8302	190-220	300-350
Russian Soldier Stnd. Set, w/ fig.	1966	ASW	8202	700-800	1200-1400
Rus. Sold. Dlx. Set, fig. & equip.	1966	ASW	8102	1800-2000	2400-3400
Sea Sled & Frogman Fig. Set	1966	ASL	8050	180-220	350-450
Ski Patrol Equip. Set	1965	ASD	7531	300-400	500-700
Space Capsule Set (Sears)	1966	AP	5979	300-350	600-800
Special Forces Unf. Set, w/ bazooka ...	1966	ASD	7532	400-500	700-900
Talking Action Marine Fig.	1967	AM	7790	400-450	600-700
Talking Action Pilot Fig.	1967	AP	7890	550-650	900-1300
Talking Action Sailor Fig.	1967	ASL	7690	300-400	600-900
Talking Action Soldier Fig.	1967	ASD	7590	190-230	350-450
Talk. Adv. Tm. Black Com. Fig.	1974	ADT	7291	250-350	450-550
Talking Fig. w/ command post items ..	1968	ADP	90517	800-1000	1200-1600
Talking Fig. w/ LSO equip.	1968	ADP	90621	1200-1500	2000-2500
Talk. Fig. w/ Sp. Forces items	1968	ADP	90532	1200-1400	1600-2000
Talk. Mar. Fig., w/ field pack equip. ...	1968	ADP	90712	600-900	1200-1600
Tank Com. Unf. Set	1967	AM	7731	300-400	600-700
West Point Cadet Fig.	1967	ASD	7537	500-600	800-1000

Hot Wheels

Hot Wheels burst onto the toy scene in 1968 as Mattel's answer to Matchbox Toys. Their popularity soared because the product lived up to its name:
- The design of the axles and wheels produced a smooth fast ride
- They emulated the souped up drag racing cars popular at the time
- The metallic paint was attractive

The amazing aspect of collecting Hot Wheels is the number of variations possible for what seems to be the same model. Most differences in value are due to the different paint jobs or details such as wheels, applied logos, and decoration. Many times a model is introduced in a more desirable paint color. Early vehicles finished in metallic pink seem to command higher prices, as the color was discontinued after a short production run. Conversely, common colors produced in huge quantities or for several years often deflate the price of a vehicle. The same model (with slight changes such as color) was introduced over the years but age doesn't necessarily constitute value. Nineteen seventy-three was a disastrous year for Mattel. Trying to cut costs, they removed the button from the package and changed the paint from the metallic Spectra Flame finish to less costly enamels. Sales plummeted. Although terrible for the company, it was a boon for collectors. The 1973 line is more difficult to find than other years, thus prices are consistently higher. Collectors can be fickle-what is thought rare and sought after one year may be displaced by something else the next.

Since the same item can be bought at a variety of locations and because condition and color variations further complicates pricing, we have devised a range system. The low range includes items that are excellent to mint without packing (MNP). The higher-end price reflects the prices of excellent to mint items in excellent to mint boxes (MIP). Therefore prices below are for the best items available; scratched, chipped or altered are not included. We have seen poor-condition Hot Wheels ranging from $1 to the prices listed below and beyond. In our opinion, bad-condition models are worth little unless extremely rare. On the other hand, some special colors (frequently metallic pink) are rare and worth considerably more than the general prices listed here. Because of the many variations, exact identification can be tricky. We have also used the following abbreviations within the descriptions: *rl* .- redline tires, *bwl* .-blackwall tires, *var.*-various paint finishes, *met.*-stands for metallic paint (other colors may also be abbreviated). For each entry, date of manufacture and model number are also listed.

We suggest *Tomart's Price Guide to Hot Wheels* by Michael Strauss, Tomart Publications, Dayton, OH, 1993. This guide has an excellent wheel dating chart and many photos. You may also want to consult *Hot Wheels Newsletter*, 26 Maderas Ave., San Carlos, CA 94070, and *Crusin' Connection,* 2648 E. Workman Ave., West Covina, CA 91791.

	DATE	#	MNP	MIP
Alive '55, var.	1973	6968	$ 80-120	$ 300-400
Alive '55, blue	1974	6968	70-90	300-400
Alive '55, chrome rl. or bwl.	1977	9210	12-18	20-30
Alive '55, dk. grn., op. hood	1983	6968	50-70	90-110
Ambulance, var.	1970	6451	40-60	45-75
Ambulance, white	1970	6451	80-100	100-150
American Tipper, red	1976	9089	16-19	20-25
American Victory, lt. blue	1975	7662	12-18	20-30
AMX/2, var.	1971	6460	35-45	60-80
AMX/2, met. pink	1971	6460	60-70	80-100
Backwoods Bomb, lt. blue	1975	7670	30-40	50-60
Backwoods Bomb, grn. rl. or bwl.	1977	7670	22-38	30-40
Beatnik Bandit, var.	1968	6217	15-25	30-50

	DATE	#	MNP	MIP
Boss Hoss, var.	1971	6406	$ 50-70	$ 100-150
Bragham Repco F1, var.	1969	6264	10-15	25-35
Bugeye, var.	1971	6178	35-45	70-90
Buzz Off, var.	1973	6976	90-120	200-300
Buzz Off, blue	1974	6976	35-45	70-90
Bye-Focal, var.	1971	6187	60-80	175-225
Carabo, var.	1970	6420	25-35	45-55
Carabo, pink	1970	6420	60-70	90-110
Carabo, lt. grn.	1974	7617	30-40	45-55
Carabo, yellow	1974	7617	250-350	400-600
Cement Mixer, var.	1970	6452	25-35	35-45
Chapparal 2G, var.	1969	6256	15-20	30-40
Chapparal 2G, pink	1969	6256	50-70	90-140
Chevy Monza 2+2, green	1975	7671	180-220	250-300
Chevy Monza 2+2, orange	1975	7671	40-50	70-80
Chief's Special, red	1975	7665	30-40	40-60
Classic '31 Ford Woody, var.	1969	6251	12-18	40-60
Classic '36 Ford Coupe, var.	1969	6253	12-18	30-50
Classic '32 Ford Vicky, var.	1969	6250	18-22	45-55
Classic '36 Ford Coupe, lt. blue	1969	6253	35-45	50-70
Classic '36 Ford Coupe, pink	1969	6253	70-90	100-150
Classic '57 T-Bird, var.	1969	6252	20-30	50-70
Classic '57 T-Bird, pink	1969	6252	70-90	100-150
Classic Cord, var.	1971	6472	125-175	300-400
Classic Nomad, var.	1970	6404	40-60	50-80
Cockney Cab, var.	1971	6466	40-50	60-80
Corvette Stingray, red	1976	9241	30-40	45-55
Custom AMX, var.	1969	6267	40-60	80-100
Custom Barracuda, var.	1968	6211	50-60	200-300
Custom Camaro, var.	1968	6208	40-70	200-250
Custom Charger, var.	1969	6268	50-80	100-150
Cust. Con. Mk III, var.	1969	6266	20-30	40-60
Custom Corvette, var.	1968	6215	50-80	180-240
Custom Cougar, var.	1968	6205	60-80	300-400
Custom Eldorado, var.	1968	6218	30-50	100-150
Custom Firebird, var.	1968	6212	40-60	200-250
Custom Fleetside, var.	1968	6213	40-60	100-150
Custom Mustang, var.	1968	6206	60-80	300-400
Custom Police Cruiser, wht.	1969	6269	50-60	80-120
Custom T-Bird, var.	1968	6207	60-80	200-300
Custom VW Bug, var.	1968	6220	12-20	40-60
Demon, var.	1970	6401	15-20	30-40
Deora, var.	1968	6210	40-60	300-350
Double Header, var.	1973	5880	80-100	200-300
Double Vision, var.	1973	6975	80-100	200-300
Drag Race Act. Set (add val. 2 cars in set)	1968	6202	20-30	40-60
Dump Truck, var.	1970	6453	18-22	30-40
Dune Daddy, var.	1973	6967	80-100	220-260
El Rey Special, var. grn.	1974	8273	40-60	70-90
Emergency Squad, red	1975	7650	12-16	40-50
Evil Weevil, var.	1971	6471	35-45	60-80

	DATE	#	MNP	MIP
Ferrari 312P, var.	1970	6417	$ 15-20	$ 30-40
Ferrari 312P, met. red, wht. int.	1970	6417	100-150	180-220
Ferrari 312P, var.	1973	6973	200-250	500-700
Ferrari 512S, var.	1972	6021	80-100	180-240
Fire Chief Cruiser, red	1970	6469	10-14	18-22
Fire Engine, var.	1970	6454	30-50	50-70
Ford J-Car, var.	1968	6214	10-15	30-50
Ford Mark IV, var.	1969	6257	8-12	25-35
Fuel Tanker, white enamel	1971	6018	50-70	100-150
Full Curve Pak	1968	6225	8-10	18-22
Funny Money, gray	1972	6005	50-60	140-180
Funny Money, magenta	1974	7621	30-40	40-60
Grass Hopper, var.	1971	6461	30-40	50-75
Grass Hopper, eng. on hd., green	1974	7622	35-45	50-70
Gremlin Grinder, green.	1975	7652	25-35	40-50
Gun Slinger Jeep, olive	1975	7664	25-35	40-50
Hairy Hauler, var.	1971	6458	30-40	35-45
Heavy Chevy, var.	1970	6408	35-45	50-70
Heavy Chevy Silv. Sp., chr.	1970	6189	40-50	90-110
Heavy Chevy, var.	1974	7619	45-55	80-90
Hiway Robber, var.	1973	6979	80-100	200-250
Hood, var.	1971	6175	30-40	40-60
Hood, met. pink	1971	6175	60-80	90-100
Hot Heap, var.	1968	6219	12-18	30-50
Ice "T," yellow	1971	6184	40-50	120-180
Ice "T," var.	1973	6980	80-120	200-300
Indy Eagle, var.	1969	6263	10-15	30-40
Indy Eagle, gold chrome	1969	6263	50-70	160-200
Jack Rabbit Jack-in-the-Box promo	1970	6421	100-150	200-250
Jack Rabbit Special, white	1970	6421	10-15	35-45
Jet Threat, var.	1971	6179	50-70	100-150
King 'Kuda, var.	1970	6411	30-40	50-70
King 'Kuda, chrome club kit	1970	6190	50-60	80-120
Light My Firebird, var.	1970	6412	18-22	50-60
Lola GT 70, var.	1969	6254	8-12	20-30
Lotus Turbine, var.	1969	6262	10-15	25-35
McLaren M6A, var.	1969	6255	8-12	30-40
Mercedes 280SL, var.	1969	6275	18-22	35-45
Mercedes 280SL, var.	1973	6275	90-120	280-340
Mercedes C-111, var.	1972	6169	80-100	200-250
Mercedes C-111, var.	1974	6169	180-220	300-400
Mighty Maverick, var.	1970	6414	35-45	60-80
Mod Quad, var.	1970	6456	18-22	30-40
Mongoose Rail Drag. (2 Pk), blue	1971	5952	70-90	500-600
Mongoose Funny Car, red	1970	6410	50-60	120-160
Mongoose II, met. blue	1971	5954	70-90	200-250
Moving Van, var.	1970	6455	35-45	50-70
Mutt Mobile, var.	1971	5185	50-80	90-120
Nitty Gritty Kitty, var.	1970	6405	35-45	50-60
Noodle Head, var.	1971	6000	50-80	90-120
Olds 442, var.	1971	6467	200-250	500-600

	DATE	#	MNP	MIP
Open Fire, var.	1972	5881	$ 80-100	$ 180-220
Paddy Wagon, dk. blue.	1970	6402	9-12	25-35
Peepin Bomb, var.	1970	6419	10-15	25-35
Pit Crew, white	1971	6183	60-80	300-500
Porsche 917, var.	1970	6416	12-18	30-40
Porsche 917, var.	1973	6416	180-220	300-500
Power Pad, var.	1970	6459	30-40	60-90
Python, var.	1968	6216	15-20	35-50
Racer Rig, white or red	1971	6194	70-90	250-350
Rear Eng. Mongoose, blue	1972	5699	140-180	300-400
Rear Engine Snake, yellow	1972	5856	140-180	300-400
Red Baron, red, black interior	1970	6400	20-30	30-40
Rocket Bye Baby, var.	1971	6186	50-70	120-160
Rolls R. Sil. Sh., var.	1969	6276	25-45	50-70
S'Cool Bus, yellow	1971	6468	100-150	600-700
Sand Crab, var.	1970	6403	12-18	30-40
Scooper Dump Truck, var.	1971	6193	80-100	200-250
Seasider, var.	1970	6413	50-70	100-150
Shelby Turbine, var.	1969	6265	12-18	30-50
Short Order, var.	1971	6176	40-50	80-120
Side Kick, var.	1972	6022	80-100	175-225
Silhouette, var.	1968	6209	12-18	35-50
Six Shooter, var.	1971	6003	60-80	125-175
Sky Show Fleetside, var.	1970	6436	350-500	600-700
Snake Funny Car, yellow	1970	6409	50-80	200-250
Snake II, white	1971	5953	50-60	200-250
Snake Rail Dragster, white	1971	5951	70-90	500-600
Snorkel, var. (2 pak)	1971	6020	60-80	120-160
Special Delivery, blue	1971	6006	40-60	150-200
Splittin' Image, var.	1969	6261	10-15	30-40
Staff Car	1976	9521	500-700	—
Street Eater, yellow	1975	7669	30-50	80-100
Street Snorter, var.	1973	6971	90-110	250-350
Strip Teaser, var.	1971	6188	50-80	150-200
Sugar Caddy, var.	1971	6418	40-60	60-80
Super Van, Toys R Us	1975	7649	125-175	200-250
Super Van, black	1975	7649	30-40	40-60
Super Van, King Radio	1975	7649	80-100	120-180
Superfine Turbine, var.	1973	6004	200-250	500-700
Sweet -16, var.	1973	6007	80-100	200-300
Swingin' Wing, var.	1970	6422	20-30	40-50
T-4-2, var.	1971	6177	40-50	90-120
Talking Serv. Center	1969	5159	40-70	80-120
Team Trailer, white or red	1971	6019	60-80	150-200
TNT Bird, var.	1970	6407	30-40	60-80
Torero, var.	1969	6260	12-15	30-50
Torero, pink	1969	6260	60-70	80-100
Torino Stocker, red	1975	7647	30-40	40-60
Tough Customer, olive	1975	7655	14-16	30-40
Tow Truck, var.	1970	6450	25-35	45-55
Tri Baby, var.	1970	6424	20-30	40-50

	DATE	#	MNP	MIP
Turbofire, var.	1969	6259	$ 10-15	$ 40-50
Twin Mill, var.	1969	6258	12-22	40-50
Twin Mill II, orange	1976	8240	18-22	25-30
Vega Bomb, orange	1975	7658	35-45	70-90
VW Beach Bomb, surf bds./rear, var.	1969	6274	2000-3000	—
VW Beach Bomb, surf bds./side, var.	1969	6274	40-50	80-100
Volkswagen Bug, orange, bug on roof	1974	7620	30-40	50-60
Volkswagen Bug, orange w/ stripes	1974	7620	140-180	300-400
Waste Wagon, var.	1971	6192	70-90	200-250
What 4, gold	1971	6001	80-100	150-200
What 4, var.	1971	6001	60-80	100-150
Whip Creamer, var.	1970	6457	20-40	40-60
Winnipeg, yellow	1974	7618	60-90	95-135
Xploder, var.	1973	6977	90-120	300-350

Japanese Automotive Tinplate Toys

Two decades before Japan threatened Detroit for the auto market they dominated the post-war tinplate toy industry. Ford, GM, and American Motors refined the art of the automobile in the 1950s and Japan replicated their efforts in toys. A score of Japanese toy companies produced these toys. Even four decades later, very little is known about these firms.

Collectors of post-war Japanese automotive toys favor those models in the 10"-16" category, followed by the 8" category. Many oversized models are less popular because of the amount of shelf space they require. The *creme de la creme* of this area is the 16" 1962 Chrysler Imperial, a car any collector will find space for.

When collecting these vehicles examine them carefully and make sure there are no missing parts, including mirrors and trim. Make sure there is no restoration; battery boxes should be checked closely. Never leave a battery in a toy; it can leak and cause damage. The prices below are for mint without box (MNB) and mint in the box (MIB) examples. Rust, scratches, and restoration will lower these prices. All dates refer to the year the vehicle most closely resembles; production is usually around the same time. These are toys and not exact models, so there are differences between them and their real life counterparts. In the cases where a model looks the same for several years, we used *c.* Abbreviated company names are unidentified firms, as is *UK* (unknown). Regarding power, *BT* stands for battery operated, *BR* battery operated with remote control, *BL* battery operated with lights, and *F* friction powered.

An excellent source of information on this subject is *Collecting the Tin Toy Car 1950-1970*, Dale Kelly, Schiffer Publishing, Exton, PA, 1984. Our consultant for this area is Jack Herbert, collector and contributing author to *Antique Toy World Magazine*, a must-have publication for toy collectors (see our list of publications). Mr. Herbert's address is listed in the back of this book.

Left: '55 Ford flower delivery wagon, $1000-$1200. — Photo courtesy of Jack Herbert.

Right: Jaguar Flower Power, $300-$500. — Photo courtesy of Jack Herbert.

MODEL	YEAR	CO.	SIZE	POWER	MNB	MIB
BMW 600 Isetta, 4 whls. .. c. '50		Bandai	9"	F	$ 500-700	$ 600-800
Buick	'53	Marusan	7"	F	600-800	700-1000
Buick	'59	Nomura	11"	F	600-700	800-1000
Buick	'60	Ichiko	17.5"	F	700-800	900-1100
Buick	'61	Nomura	16"	F	700-900	900-1200
Buick Emerg.Car	'61	Nomura	14"	F	500-600	800-900
Buick, Future Car Conv.	'51	Yonezawa	7.5"	F	800-900	1000-1200
Buick LeSabre	'66	Asahi	19"	F	700-900	800-1000
Buick Sportswagon	'68	Asakusa	15"	F	700-900	800-1000
Buick Station Wagon	'54	UK	8"	BT	400-600	500-700
Cadillac	'51	Marusan	11"	BT	1200-1500	1800-2000
Cadillac	'60	Yonezawa	18"	F	1500-1800	2000-2500
Cadillac	'62	Yonezawa	22"	F	1000-1200	1400-1600
Cadillac	'67	Ichiko	28"	F	1600-2200	2000-2500
Cadillac Convertible	'52	Alps	11.5"	F	1800-2200	2200-2500
Cadillac Convertible	'52	Nomura	13"	BL	400-600	500-800
Cadillac Convertible	'59	Bandai	11"	F	300-400	500-700
Cadillac Convertible	'60	Bandai	11"	F	400-600	500-700
Cadillac Eldorado Conv.	'67	UK	10.75"	F	300-500	400-600
Cadillac Eldorado	'67	Kosuge	10.5"	F	600-700	900-1100
Cadillac Fleetwood	'61	S.S.S.	17.5"	F	300-400	500-700
Cadillac, 4 Door	'59	Bandai	11"	F	300-400	500-700
Cadillac, 4 door	'65	Ichiko	22"	F	700-900	1200-1400
Champion's Racer	c. '54	Yonezawa	18"	F	1200-1500	1400-1800
Chevrolet	'55	Marusan	11"	BL	500-700	700-900
Chevrolet	'62	Asahi	11"	F	400-500	600-700
Chevrolet Camaro	'71	Taiyo	9.5"	BT	150-200	250-300
Chevrolet Convertible	'59	S.Y.	11.5"	F	600-800	800-900
Chevrolet Corvette	'62	Bandai	8"	BT	500-600	600-800
Chevrolet Corvette	'63	Bandai	8"	F	300-350	400-500
Chevrolet Corvette	'68	Taiyo	9.5"	BT	150-200	250-300
Chevrolet Impala Convert. ...	'61	Bandai	11"	F	700-800	900-1000
Chevrolet Impala Sedan	'61	Bandai	11"	F	600-800	700-900
Chevrolet Wagon	'60	UK	12"	F	400-500	500-600
Chrysler Imperial	'62	Asahi	16"	F	10 -15,000	15 -18,000
Citroen	'55	Bandai	12"	F	400-600	500-700
Dodge	'58	Nomura	11"	F	600-800	700-900
Dodge Pick-Up	'59	M.	18.5"	F	1000-1200	1200-1500
Edsel	'58	Asahi	10.75"	F	700-800	900-1200
Edsel Convertible	'58	Haji	10.25"	F	1200-1500	1500-2000
Edsel Station Wagon	'58	Haji	10.5"	F	800-900	1000-1200
Ferrari 250G Convertible	'57	Asahi	9.5"	F	500-600	600-800
Ford	'56	Yonezawa	12"	F	800-1000	1000-1200
Ford	'57	Ichiko	12"	F	800-1200	1000-1400
Ford Cntry Sedan Station Wag.	'61	Bandai	10.5"	F	400-600	500-700
Ford Convertible	'56	Haji	11.5"	F	4000-5000	5000-7500
Ford Convertible, trunk opens	'55	Bandai	12"	F	800-900	900-1200
Ford Country Sedan Sta. Wag.	'62	Asahi	12"	F	800-900	900-1200
Ford Fairlane Convertible	'57	Ichiko	10"	F	400-600	500-700
Ford Flower Del. Wagon	'55	Bandai	12"	F	1000-1200	1200-1500
Ford Galaxie	'65	Mod. Toys	11"	F	400-600	500-700

MODEL	YEAR	CO.	SIZE	POWER	MNB	MIB
Ford GT	c. '68	Bandai	10"	BT	$ 400-600	$ 500-700
Ford Gyron	'60	Ichida	11"	BT	400-600	500-700
Ford Mustang	'65	Bandai	11"	BT	300-500	400-600
Ford Mustang	'67	Bandai	13"	BT	400-600	500-700
Ford Ranchero	'55	Bandai	12"	F	400-600	500-800
Ford Ranchero	'57	Bandai	12"	F	500-600	600-700
Ford Station Wagon	'55	Bandai	12"	F	400-600	500-800
Ford Station Wagon	'57	Bandai	12"	F	400-600	500-700
Ford T-Bird Conv., retract. roof	'62	Yonezawa	11"	BT	400-500	500-700
Ford Thunderbird	'56	Nomura	11"	BL	600-700	700-800
Ford, 2 door	'56	Marusan	13"	F	1800-2200	2500-2800
Good Humor Truck	'50	K.T.S.	10.75"	F	700-900	1000-1500
International Cement Truck	c. '55	S.S.S.	19"	F	1200-1500	1500-2000
Isetta 3 Wheeler	c. '50	Bandai	6.5"	F	500-700	600-800
Jaguar XK-120	'65	Alps	6.5"	F	300-500	400-600
Jaguar XKE	c. '65	T.T.	10.5"	F	400-600	500-700
Land Rover	'60	Bandai	7.5"	F	500-700	700-800
Lincoln	'55	Yonezawa	12"	F	900-1200	1000-1400
Lincoln	'60	Yonezawa	11"	BT	600-800	800-1000
Lincoln Futura	'56	Alps	11"	BT	800-1200	1200-1500
Lincoln Mark II	'56	Line Mar	12"	F or B	2500-3000	3000-3500
Lincoln Mark III	'58	Bandai	11"	F	500-700	600-800
Lotus Elite	c. '58	Bandai	8.5"	F	150-200	200-250
Mercedes Benz 220S	'62	S.S.S.	12"	BT	600-800	700-1000
Mercedes Benz 250 SE	'65	Ichiko	13"	BT	200-300	300-400
Mercedes Benz 300 SL	c. '58	Cragstan	9"	BT	600-800	700-900
Mercedes Benz Racer	'55	Line Mar	9.5"	F	700-900	800-1000
Mercedes Benz Racer W196	'55	Marusan	10"	BT	400-600	500-700
Mercedes Benz (reissued)	'70	Ichiko	24"	F	80-100	90-120
Mercury	'58	Yonezawa	11.5"	F	900-1000	1000-1200
Mercury Cougar	'67	Taiyo	10"	BT	400-600	500-700
Messerschmitt	'56	Bandai	8.5"	F	500-600	700-1000
MG 1600 Mark II	c. '58	Bandai	8.5"	F	175-225	200-300
MG A	'57	Asahi	10"	F	400-600	500-700
MG TD	'55	S.S.S.	6.5"	F	125-175	150-200
MG TF	'52	UK	8.5"	F	300-500	400-600
MG TF	'55	Bandai	8"	F	300-400	400-600
Olds Toronado	'66	Bandai	11"	BT	400-600	500-700
Oldsmobile	'56	UK	10.5"	F	600-800	700-900
Oldsmobile	'58	Yonezawa	16"	F	1200-1800	1800-2000
Opel	c. '55	Yonezawa	11.5"	BL	500-600	600-700
Packard Convertible	'53	Alps	16"	F	5000-7000	7000-8000
Packard Sedan	'53	Alps	16"	F	4000-6000	5000-7000
Plymouth	'56	Alps	12"	BT	500-700	700-800
Plymouth	'61	Ichiko	12"	F	700-900	800-1000
Plymouth Ambulance	'61	Bandai	12"	F	600-700	700-800
Plymouth Convertible	'59	Asahi	10.5"	F	600-700	700-900
Plymouth Hard Top Conv.	'59	Asahi	10.5"	F	500-700	700-800
Pontiac Firebird	'67	Bandai	9.5"	BT	500-600	600-700
Porsche Rally 911	c. '65	Alps	9.5"	BT	300-500	400-600
Rambler Station Wagon	'59	Bandai	11"		400-500	500-600

MODEL	YEAR	CO.	SIZE	POWER	MNB	MIB
Renault 750 .... '58		Masudaya	7"	F	$ 400-600	$ 500-700
Renault 750 .... '58		Yonezawa	7.5"	F	400-600	500-700
Rolls Royce .... '60		UK	10.5"	F	1000-1200	1200-1500
Rolls Royce .... c. '58		Bandai	12"	BT	400-600	500-700
Rolls Royce Convertible ... c.'55		Bandai	12"	F	400-600	500-700
Studebaker ....'53		UK	9"	F	500-600	600-700
Studebaker Avante .... c. '55		Bandai	8"	F	500-600	600-700
Toyota 2000 GT .... '67		Asahi	15"	F	200-250	250-300
Volkswagon Bug .... c. '60		Bandai	15"	BT	450-500	550-600
Volkswagon Bus .... c. '65		Bandai	9.5"	BT	400-600	500-700
VW Convertible Bug .... c. '60		Masudaya	9.5"	F	500-700	700-800
VW Convertible Bug .... c. '60		Taiyo	10.5"	BT	400-600	500-700
VW Pick-Up Truck .... c. '65		Bandai	8"	BR	250-350	400-500

Lunch Boxes

Steel lunch boxes produced from the 1950s to the 1980s were one of the last holdouts of the lithographed metal process once prevalent in the production of toys. In order to deter sandlot warriors from injuring each other, steel boxes were discontinued in the 1980s. Soon after, they burst onto the collecting scene. Buying back a box from their youth, collectors relived grade school memories and the late summer ritual of shopping for school supplies. Collectors also love the diversity of topics represented. Many of the boxes are based on classic TV shows, and they frame their topics like small screens. The steel boxes are not the only ones sought by collectors; some of the vinyl examples are among the costliest. After a meteoric rise, the market cooled in the early '90s. However, today's growing interest in TV memorabilia is bringing in a new group of collectors.

We devised a range system for pricing. Since bottles often become separated from the box, we have given estimates for boxes and bottles separately. The prices below reflect items that are in excellent to mint condition. Rust and dents decrease the value of boxes and bottles. The "NB" designation in the bottle column means that a bottle was not produced for that particular box.

See *The Fifties and Sixties Lunch Box*, by Scott Bruce, Chronicle Books, San Francisco, CA, 1988, and *The Illustrated Encyclopedia of Metal Lunch Boxes*, by Allen Woodall and Sean Brickell, Schiffer Publishing, West Chester, PA, 1992.

Abbreviations: we removed "The" from titles such as "The Munsters," shortened words so that vinyl, with blue steel glass bottle becomes V, bl stl gl bot. Under Features we have listed distinguishing features such as V for Vinyl, if it isn't Vinyl assume it is steel, D stands for dome, Em for embossed. Company name abbreviations are as follows: King Seeley Thermos (KST), Aladdin (A), Adco Liberty (AL), Universal (Un), Air Flite (AF), Ohio Art (OA), Ardee (AR), Okay Industries (OK), and Standard Plastic Products (Stnd). Dates reflect our best approximation.

Clockwise from left: Johnny Lightning, 1971, $60-$80; Roy Rogers & Dale Evans, showing obvious rim ware, 1953, $30-$40; (when mint $100-$130); Johnny Lightning Bottle, 1971, $20-$30.

	BOX	BOTTLE
Action Jackson, OK, 1973	$ 450-550	$ 160-190
Adam-12, EM, A, 1973	60-80	18-22
Addams Family, KST, 1974	80-120	30-50
All American, map, met. hndl., Un, 1954	300-350	50-70
All Star, V, A, 1960	350-450	50-60
Alvin, V, KST, 1963	220-280	60-80
Annie Oakley, A, 1956	180-220	45-55
Archies, EM, A, 1970	55-75	18-22
Astronaut, D, KST, 1960	120-180	40-50
Atom Ant, KST, 1966	150-200	45-55
Batman, EM, A, 1966	140-180	50-60
Beatles, EM, A, 1966	300-350	90-110
Beatles Air Flite, V, AF, 1965	400-500	NB
Beatles Kaboodle, V, Stnd, 1965	500-700	NB
Beverly Hillbillies, EM, A, 1963	120-160	35-45
Bionic Woman, car/bk., A, 1977	25-30	8-10
Black Hole, EM, A, 1980	35-45	8-12
Bonanza, Blk. rim, A, 1968	110-140	40-50
Bond XX, OA, 1966	130-170	NB
Bozo the Clown, A, 1964	180-220	50-70
Brady Bunch, KST, 1970	120-160	50-60
Brave Eagle, KST, 1955	220-260	30-40
Buccaneer, D, A, 1957	180-220	60-80
Bullwinkle, V, bl stl. gl bot., KST, 1962	400-450	100
Bullwinkle and Rocky, Steel, Un, 1962	500-600	190-230
Captain Kangaroo, V, KST, 1964	200-250	40-50
Carnival, Un, 1959	400-450	180-230
Casey Jones, D, Un, 1960	500-700	80-120
Charlie's Angels, EM, A, 1978	40-50	10-15
Chitty Chitty Bang Bang, KST, 1969	60-80	20-30
Chuck Wagon, D, A, 1958	120-180	45-55
Close Encounters, KST, 1978	60-80	10-12
Daniel Boone, A, 1965	90-130	40-50
Davy Crockett/Kit Carson, AL, 1955	190-210	80-100
Disney Fire Fighters, D, A, 1969	70-90	15-20
Disney School Bus, A, 1961	30-40	12-16
Doctor Doolittle, EM, A, 1968	75-95	30-40
Dr. Seuss, EM, A, 1970	65-85	20-30
Dr. Seuss, V, A, 1970	250-300	12-18
Dudley Do-Right, Steel, Un, 1962	500-600	180-240
E.T., EM, A, 1983	25-35	7-9
Eats 'n Treats, V, KST, 1959	180-220	30-40
Emergency, D, A, 1977	70-90	8-12
Empire Strikes Back, KST, 1980	35-45	8-12
Family Affair, KST, 1969	60-80	25-30
Fat Albert & The Cosby Kids, KST, 1973	25-35	5-7
Fess Parker/Daniel Boone, KST, 1965	120-160	30-40
Fireball XL-5, KST, 1964	120-180	35-45
Flag-O-Rama, UN flags, Un, 1954	320-420	70-90
Flintstones, 2nd dsgn., A, 1964	80-100	30-40
Flintstones and Dino, EM, A, 1962	80-120	35-45

Above left to right: Scooby Doo, 1973, $30-$40; Space Orbiter Enterprise, 1979, $35-$45. — Item courtesy of Jim Glaab's Collector's Showcase. Below left to right: Return of The Jedi, 1983, $30-$40; Orbit Bottle, 1963, $60-$90. — Item courtesy of Jim Glaab's Collector's Showcase

	BOX	BOTTLE
Flipper, KST, 1966	$ 90-120	$ 40-50
Flying Nun, EM, A, 1968	80-100	20-30
Fraggle Rock, KST, 1984	12-15	4-6
Gene Autry, Un, 1954	250-300	90-110
Gentle Ben, A, 1968	60-80	15-20
Get Smart, KST, 1966	140-180	35-45
Girl and Poodle, V, AR, 1960	80-100	8-12
Gomer Pyle, EM, A, 1966	90-140	25-35
Green Hornet, KST, 1967	250-300	60-80
Gremlins, EM, A, 1984	12-15	4-6
Grizzly Adams, D, A, 1978	55-75	8-12
Gunsmoke, Red rim, Em, A, 1962	140-180	45-55
Gunsmoke, Splash /bk., A, 1972	50-70	12-16
Gunsmoke, Stage/bk., A, 1973	90-110	12-16
H.R. Pufnstuf, EM, A, 1970	90-110	18-22
Hair Bear Bunch, KST, 1972	30-40	8-12
Happy Days, KST, 1977	45-55	15-20

	BOX	BOTTLE
Hogan's Heroes, D, A, 1966	$ 180-220	$ 60-80
Hopalong Cassidy, curve decal, A, 1950	90-130	35-45
Hopalong Cassidy, full pict., A, 1954	200-250	60-80
Hot Wheels, KST, 1970	50-70	18-24
Indiana Jones, KST, 1984	15-20	4-6
It's About Time, D, A, 1967	190-210	45-55
James Bond-Agent 007, EM, A, 1966	120-180	30-40
Jet Patrol, A, 1957	250-300	45-55
Jetsons, D, A, 1963	750-950	180-240
Johnny Lightning, EM, A, 1971	60-80	20-30
Kiss, KST, 1979	50-70	7-9
Lance Link, KST, 1971	80-120	35-45
Land of the Giants, EM, A, 1969	120-160	35-45
Laugh-In, A, 1969	90-110	15-20
Little House on the Prairie, KST, 1979	35-45	7-9
Lone Ranger, AL, 1954	380-420	NB
Lost in Space, D, KST, 1967	500-600	40-60
Man From U.N.C.L.E., KST, 1966	120-180	40-50
Masters of the Universe, EM, A, 1983	9-14	2-3
Mickey Mouse/Donald Duck, AL, 1954	200-250	80-100
Monkees, V, KST, 1967	250-300	40-50
Mork & Mindy, KST, 1980	28-34	4-6
Munsters, KST, 1965	140-180	50-70
Partridge Family, KST, 1971	40-50	20-30
Pigs in Space, KST, 1979	18-22	4-6
Planet of the Apes, EM, A, 1975	80-100	12-16
Porky's Lunch Wagon, D, KST, 1959	300-350	50-60
Red Barn, clsd. drs., KST, 1957	50-60	14-18
Red Barn, D, op. drs., KST, 1958	40-50	14-18
Return of The Jedi, KST, 1983	30-40	7-9
Roy Rogers Chow Wagon, D, KST, 1958	180-240	40-50
Roy Rogers & Dale Evans, wood bk., bd., KST, 1953	100-130	30-40
Roy Rogers & Dale Evans, hide/8 scns, KST, 1955	80-100	30-40
Scooby Doo, KST, 1973	30-40	4-6
Sesame Street, EM, A, 1980	8-12	4-5
Space: 1999, KST, 1976	30-40	7-9
Space Explorer, A, 1960	300-350	60-80
Star Trek, D, A, 1968	550-650	140-180
Star Wars, KST, 1978	35-45	5-6
Stewardess, V, A, 1962	320-380	30-40
Supercar, steel, Un, 1962	90-120	200-250
Superman, met. hdl., Un, 1954	600-800	150-200
Tom Corbett Space Cadet, curve decal, A, 1952	190-230	60-70
Tom Corbett Space Cadet, full pic., A, 1954	450-500	70-90
Under Dog, Steel, OK, 1973	700-900	200-250
Waltons, EM, A, 1974	25-35	4-6
Welcome Back Kotter, EM, A, 1977	28-36	4-6
Wild, Wild West, EM, A, 1969	150-200	45-55
Winnie the Pooh, V, A, 1967	400-450	40-50
Yellow Submarine, KST, 1969	350-450	90-130
Zorro, blue sky, A, 1958	120-160	40-50

Matchbox Toys

Leslie Smith and Rod**ney** Smith (no relation) started **Lesney** Toys in England in 1947. They produced their first toys in 1948 and had a huge success with a coach produced in 1952 for the Queen's coronation in 1953. In 1953 they started producing small die-cast vehicles packed in what appeared to be matchboxes. These toys are known as the 1-75 Series. They range from approximately 1.5" to 3". Lesney has produced other series over the years but the list below refers mainly to the 1-75 Series. Exceptions are the early toys which have no product number, and the Yesteryear Series, denoted by Y as the first letter in the product code. Both these series are larger than the 1-75 Series. Matchbox toys are still produced, but the Lesney name was removed in 1982.

Since the same item can be bought at a variety of locations at different prices, we devised a range system. The low range covers complete, near mint items without the package. The higher range reflects the prices of complete, near mint (*MNB*) to mint items in the original near mint to mint boxes (*MIB*). Prices below are for complete like-new items. Prices of scratched, chipped or altered examples are not included.. Beware of high prices for poor quality. We have seen many poor-condition Matchbox vehicles ranging from $1 to the prices listed below. In our opinion these bad condition models are worth very little unless extremely rare.

In the listing *sf* stands for super fast wheels and axles, a system Lesney developed to battle Hot Wheels. For the most part, collectors prefer the regular wheels (*rw.*). The numbering system is not foolproof, sometimes a model produced for this country has a different number than the same vehicle originally sold exclusively in England. The letters that precede a number is a system designed by collectors to distinguish different models with the same number, the earlier the letter the earlier the model. Because there are so many variations, exact identification can be tricky. We suggest *Matchbox Toys 1948-1993*, by Dana Johnson, Collector Books, Paducah, KY, 1994.

	YEAR	#	MNB	MIB
Airport Crash Tender	1964	63-B	$ 18-24	$ 28-34
Army Half-track Mk III Person Carr.	1958	49-A	20-30	30-40
Aston Martin DB2 Saloon	1959	53-A	28-34	38-44
Austin A50 Sedan	1957	36-A	20-30	35-40
Aveling Barford Diesel Road Roller	1948	—	300-380	400-500
Bedford Compressor Truck	1956	28-A	32-38	40-50
Bedford Duplé Long Dist. Coach	1956	21-A	38-46	50-60
Bedford Milk Delivery Van	1956	29-A	25-30	35-40
Bedford Tipper Truck	1957	40-A	25-35	40-50
Bedford Ton Tipper	1961	3-B	18-22	28-32
Berkeley Cavalier Travel Trailer	1956	23-A	28-32	35-45
Boat & Trailer, rw.	1966	9-C	8-12	14-18
Cadillac Ambulance, rw.	1965	54-B	18-24	28-32
Cadillac Ambulance, sf.	1970	54-C	6-8	9-12
Cadillac Sedan	1960	27-C	30-35	40-50
Caterpillar Crawler	1964	18-D	18-22	28-32
Caterpillar D8, w/ red blade	1956	18-A	28-32	40-50
Caterpillar Tractor	1955	8-A	40-50	55-75
Cement Mixer	1953	3-A	32-38	40-50
Chevrolet Impala	1961	57-B	25-30	32-38
Citroen DS19	1959	66-A	30-35	42-48
Claas Combine Harvester	1967	65-C	7-9	12-15
Commer 30 CWT Van "Nestle's"	1959	69-A	30-35	40-50
Commer Milk Truck	1961	21-C	28-32	34-38

	YEAR	#	MNB	MIB
Conestoga Wagon, no barrels	1955	—	$ 80-100	$ 140-180
Conestoga Wagon w/ barrels	1955	—	140-180	200-250
Daimler Ambulance	1956	14-A	30-35	40-50
Dennis Fire Escape engine, metal whls.	1955	9-A	30-40	50-60
Dodge Cattle Truck, sf.	1970	37-E	5-7	9-12
Dodge Charger	1970	52-C	5-7	9-12
Dodge Crane Truck, rw.	1968	63-C	9-12	15-20
Dodge Dump Truck, rw.	1966	48-C	12-15	18-22
Dodge StakeTruck, rw.	1967	4-D	8-10	12-16
Dodge Wreck Truck, "BP," rw.	1965	13-D	14-16	20-25
Dumper	1953	2-A	45-50	55-70
ERF 686 Truck	1959	20-B	35-45	50-60
Euclid Quarry Truck	1957	6-B	25-35	40-50
Ferrari F1 Racing Car	1962	73-B	28-32	38-42
Ford Customline Station Wagon	1957	31-A	28-34	40-50
Ford Fairlane Station Wagon	1960	31-B	25-35	35-40
Ford Galaxie Fire Chief Car, rw.	1966	59-C	8-12	15-20
Ford Galaxie Police Car	1966	55-C	15-20	25-30
Ford Mustang Fastback, rw.	1966	8-E	8-10	12-16
Ford Pickup, rw.	1968	6-D	10-14	15-20
Ford Thunderbird	1960	75-A	32-38	42-48
Ford Zodiac Convertible	1957	39-A	40-50	60-80
GMC Tipper Truck, small sf.	1970	26-D	8-10	12-16
Harley Davidson Motorcycle Sidecar	1962	66-B	40-45	55-65
Honda Motorcycle & Trailer, rw.	1967	38-C	12-15	18-22
Honda Motorcycle & Trailer, sf.	1970	38-D	5-6	8-12
Horse-Drawn Milk Cart	1949	—	120-160	200-300
Horse-Drawn Milk Float, gray metal whls.	1954	7-A	50-60	70-90
Hot Rocker Mercury Capri	1973	67-D	4-6	8-10
Hoveringham Tipper	1963	17-C	12-18	24-32
Jaguar, 3.4 Litre	1959	65-A	18-22	28-34
Jaguar, D-Type	1957	41-A	35-40	45-55
Jeep Gladiator Pickup Truck	1964	71-B	18-25	28-32
Land Rover, w/ driver	1955	12-A	30-40	45-55
Leyland Royal Tiger Coach	1961	40-B	15-18	22-28
Lincoln Continental, rw.	1964	31-C	15-18	22-28
Lincoln Continental, sf.	1969	31-D	5-7	9-12
London Bus	1954	5-A	38-44	50-60
Mack Dump Truck, rw.	1968	28-D	8-12	18-22
Massey Harris Tractor, w/fenders	1954	4-A	35-45	60-70
MG Sports Car	1956	19-A	42-48	55-65
Mobile Canteen Refresh. Bar	1959	74-A	40-45	55-65
Pontiac Convertible	1962	39-B	40-45	55-65
Quarry Truck	1954	6-A	38-42	50-60
Rolls Royce Silver Cloud	1958	44-A	22-28	35-45
Saracen Person. Carr.	1959	54-A	28-32	35-55
Scammell Breakdown Truck	1959	64-A	20-25	32-38
VW 1200 Sedan	1960	25-B	30-35	40-50
1862 Am. General Loco.	1959	Y-13-A	35-45	50-70
1909 Thomas Flyabout	1967	Y-12-B	18-22	25-35
1924 Fowler "Big Lion" Showman's Eng.	1958	Y-9-A	55-65	75-85

Mechanical Banks

The values indicated for mechanical banks in this section reflect prices realized at private sales and recent public auctions. When evaluating a bank, one must consider market trends, subject matter, personal taste, and, most importantly, the subtleties of condition. Prices are given for each bank in three condition categories. We define fair as working, with 60% original paint, minor repairs, and some professional restoration. Average is working with 80% original paint, and perhaps a minor repair. Our highest category is not mint but superb, with 98% original paint, no repairs, and working. Superb condition banks are rare and collectors pay a premium price for them. Many banks have been reproduced and most of these are poor quality and easy to detect. Beware of banks that are badly rusted and look like they have been buried in somone's back yard, since that may have been done in order to simulate age. Banks that bear the mark "The Book of Knowledge" are 1930s reproductions that are handsome but worth only a fraction of the originals. Repairs and some reproductions are harder to detect but, with practice, these skills can be developed. As in all areas of collecting, do your homework.

Our consultant for this area is Sy Schreckinger, collector, dealer, appraiser, and contributing author to *Antique Toy World Magazine*. Mr. Schreckinger is also a member of The Mechanical Bank Collectors of America, The Still Bank Collectors Club of America, and the Toy Collectors of America. He is listed in the back of this book. For further reading we recommend *The Bank Book*, Bill Norman, Accent Studios, San Diego, CA 1984, and *Penny Lane*, Al Davidson, Longs Americana, Mokelumne Hill, CA, 1987.

Top row left to right: Bad Accident; Mammy and Child; 'Spise a Mule-jockey over. Bottom row left to right: 'Spise a Mule-bench; Punch and Judy; Eagle and Eaglets. — Photos courtesy of Phillips Auctioneers.

	FAIR	AVG.	SUPERB
Acrobat	$ 2000	$ 5500	$ 11,000
Artillery	375	1100	4500
Bad Accident	900	2500	7500
Bank Teller	20,000	45,000	75,000
Bear and Tree Stump	200	550	2000
Bird on Roof	750	1600	6500
Boy on Trapeze	1200	2750	9000
Boy Robbing Birds Nest	1650	6000	18,000
Boy Scout Camp	2000	7500	17,000
Boys Stealing Watermelons	1000	2500	7500
Bucking Mule	400	1200	2500
Bull Dog, coin on nose	400	1250	4500
Bull Dog Savings	1800	3500	12,000
Butting Buffalo	1800	5500	15,000
Butting Goat	250	550	1600
Cabin	200	450	1500
Calamity	2500	10,000	28,000
Cat and Mouse, balance	700	3000	8500
Chief Big Moon	550	2500	5500
Chimpanzee	1500	3500	13,000
Circus	5500	16,500	45,000
Circus Ticket Collector	750	2000	6500
Clown on Globe	650	2500	9000
Confectionery	4500	9500	28,000
Creedmoor	200	450	2000
Darktown Battery	750	1750	7500
Dentist	3000	8500	23,000
Dinah	200	750	2500
Dog on Turntable	200	400	1800
Dog Tray Bank	1700	4500	9500
Eagle and Eaglets	275	650	2500
Elephant 3 Clowns	750	2000	6000
Elephant Howdah, man pops out	250	550	3000
Elephant Pull Tail	150	450	1200
Frog on Rock	200	500	1500
Frog on Round Base	200	500	2000
Frogs Two	650	2000	8500
Gem	200	400	1200
Girl in Victorian Chair	2500	6500	17,000
Girl Skipping Rope	5500	18,000	65,000
Goat, Frog, Old Man	2000	3500	12,000
Halls Excelsior	100	250	1800
Halls Liliput, w/ tray	200	500	2500
Hen and Chick, white hen	2500	5500	20,000
Hen and Chick, brown hen	2000	4500	16,000
Hindu	800	2500	10,000
Hold The Fort	2000	5000	11,000
Home Bank	400	850	5000
Horse Race, flanged base	3500	10,000	30,000
Humpty Dumpty	500	900	10,000
Indian Shooting Bear	650	2000	7500

Above left to right: Mason; Initiating Bank-First Degree.
Below top row left to right: Artillery; Uncle Sam; Darktown
Battery. Below bottom row left to right: New Creedmoor; Owl
Turns Head; Novelty Bank. — Photos courtesy of Phillips
Auctioneers.

	FAIR	AVG.	SUPERB
Initiating, First Degree	$ 3000	$ 7500	$ 20,000
Jolly N Bank	100	350	1500
Jonah and the Whale, Johah tosses coin into whale's mouth	1200	2500	8500
Leap Frog	1300	2500	9500
Lion and Two Monkeys	450	2000	5500
Lion Hunter	2500	6500	12,000
Little Joe	100	350	750
Magic Bank	550	1500	3500
Magician	1700	4500	14,000
Mammy and Child	1700	5500	16,000
Mason	1700	6500	15,000
Milking Cow	4000	10,000	30,000
Monkey Bank (Hubley)	200	550	1500
Monkey and Coconut	800	3000	6000
Mosque	500	1550	3500
Mule Entering Barn	400	750	4500
New Creedmoor	200	550	2000
Novelty Bank	350	1200	3500
Organ Bank, Boy and Girl	500	1450	3500
Organ Bank, Cat and Dog	200	750	2500
Organ Bank, medium	300	550	1600
Organ Bank, miniature	350	750	2500
Organ Grinder and Performing Bear	2500	3500	12,000
Owl, Slot in Head	350	750	1500
Owl, Turns Head	200	500	1600
Paddy and The Pig	1500	3800	9500
Panorama	2000	8000	18,000
Patronize the Blind Man and His Dog	1800	5500	12,000
Peg-Leg Beggar	800	2500	5000
Pelican	1000	2000	4500
Picture Gallery	5500	16,000	32,000
Pig in a High Chair	200	550	2200
Presto Bank, trick drawer	100	250	1200
Professor Pug Frogs	2800	8500	19,000
Pump and Bucket	750	1500	3500
Punch and Judy	750	2000	5500
Rabbit in Cabbage	250	400	1600
Reclining Chinaman	2500	6500	15,000
Rooster	200	450	2000
Santa Claus at Chimney	1000	2500	6500
Speaking Dog	550	1800	5000
'Spise A Mule, bench	400	1500	4000
'Spise A Mule, jockey	400	1800	5000
Springing Cat, lead	5000	12,000	22,000
Squirrel on Tree Stump	750	2000	4500
Stump Speaker	1500	3500	8500
Tabby	450	1200	2500
Tammany	200	800	2000
Teddy and The Bear	750	1800	4500
Toad on Stump	350	600	2500
Trick Dog, 6-part base	400	1200	3500

	FAIR	AVG.	SUPERB
Trick Pony	$ 400	$ 1500	$ 3500
Uncle Remus	2000	5000	12,000
Uncle Sam	1500	3500	8500
Uncle Tom	200	650	2500
U.S. and Spain	2000	3500	12,000
Watchdog Safe	200	400	2000
Weedens Plantation, tin	800	2000	5500
William Tell	250	750	2500
Wireless	200	400	1200
World's Fair, Columbus	350	850	3000
Zoo Bank	600	1200	3500

Paper Dolls

Paper dolls date to the 1400s and appeared as children's toys in the late 1700s. Collectors usually specialize either in antique examples or in specific types such as celebrity, advertising, works of favorite artists, or companies. Dolls based on movie and TV stars attract collectors from other areas.

A paper doll's collectibility depends upon artist, subject, age, construction, condition, and size. Prices below are for uncut near mint condition examples. Near mint, cut dolls may command prices 20%-50% of uncut dolls. Abbreviations have been used throughout the listings; for example, lg.-large, astd.-assorted, num.-numerous, bk.-book, cstms.-costumes, and clr.-color.

For further information see _The Official Price Guide to Paper Collectibles_, published by The House of Collectibles, Random House, NY; _A Collector's Guide to Paper Dolls_, Second Series, Mary Young, Collector Books, Paducah, KY, 1984; and _Paper Dolls of Famous Faces_, Jean Woodcock, Hobby House Press, Cumberland, MD, 1980.

	LOW	HIGH
Bride & Groom, 1970, Whitman bk. #1989, punch-outs, pink cover	$ 10	$ 12
Bride & Groom, England, 1971, coloring bk. & paper dolls, 2 dolls, astd. outfits	6	8
Candy Stripers, 1973, Saalfield	6	8
Captain Big Bill, 1956, Samuel Lowe	8	12
Career Girls, 1942, Samuel Lowe	25	35
Career Girls, 1950, Samuel Lowe	20	30
Career Girls, by Doris Lane Butler, 1944, Whitman bk. #973, 3 dolls-Ann, Marty, & Dottie, clothlike outfits	35	45
Carmen Miranda, 1942, Whitman #995	90	120
Carmen Miranda, 1952, Saalfield #1558, 2 dolls, astd. outfits	80	100
Carmen Miranda Paper Dolls, by Tom Tierney, 1 doll, astd. cstms.	8	12
Carmen, Rita Hayworth, 1948, 2 dolls, astd. outfits, thin cover	50	70
Dolls Across the Sea, by Queen Holden, 1969, Platt & Munk, Hans, Ingrid, Yvonne, & Juliane, foreign cstms., boxed	8	12
Dolls for All Seasons-Rosy Ruth, by Raphael Tuck, 1 doll w/ 3 dresses & 1 hat	100	150
Dolls of All Nations-Russia, _Boston Sunday Globe_	12	18
Dolls of Other Lands, 1968, Watkins, 6 dolls, 42 cstms.	8	12
Dolly Dingle's World Flight in Italy, December 1932, boy doll, 3 cstms.	20	30
Dolly Dingle's World Flight in Russia, March 1933, 1 doll, pets	20	30
Dolly Dingle's World Flight in Sweden, February 1933, boy, cstms.	20	30
Dolly Dingle's World Flight in Switzerland, September 1931	20	30
Dolly Dingle's World Flight, June 1932, 4 dresses	20	30
Donna Reed, 1959, Saalfield #4412, 2 dolls, astd. clothes, folder	50	70
Doris Day, 1952, Whitman bk. #210325, statuette dolls, astd. outfits, folder	50	70
Doris Day, 1954, Whitman bk. #1179:15, 2 dolls, 8 pages of outfits	60	80
Doris Day, 1955, Whitman bk. #1952, statuette dolls, astd. clothes, folder	60	80
Doris Day, 1956, Whitman bk. #1952, astd. outfits	50	70
Dorothy Provine, 1962, Whitman bk. #1964, 1 doll, astd. outfits, folder w/ handle	35	45
Dr. Kildare & Nurse Susan, #2740, punch-outs, 3 dolls, astd. outfits	25	35
Dr. Kildare Play Book, Samuel Lowe	25	35
Dress-up Doll Book, by Sally de Frehn Ogg, 1953, Treasure bk. # T- 167, 5 dolls, astd. outfits to be colored	20	25
Hansel & Gretel Push-Out Book, 1954, Whitman	12	18
Happiest Millionaire, 1967, Saalfield	10	12
Happy Birthday, 1939, Merrill	30	40
Happy Bride, 1967, Whitman bk. #1958, 4 dolls, 1960s style clothes	18	22

Happy Days Playset Characters, various scenes, characters, incl. Arnold's Drive-
in, & Fonzie's motorcycle .... $ 15 $ 20

Happy Family, 1973, Samuel Lowe 6   8

Happy Holiday, reprint of Carmen Miranda, Saalfield bk. #2722, 2 dolls, astd.
outfits 20   30

Hayley Mills in *Summer Magic*, 1963, Whitman bk. #1966, 1 doll, astd.
cstms., folder 50   70

Hayley Mills in *The Moon Spinners,* 1964, Whitman bk. #1960, 1 doll, astd. clothes .. 50   70

Hedy Lamarr, 1942, Merrill #3482, 2 dolls, 22 outfits, 29 access. 50   60

Hedy Lamarr, 1951, Saalfield 50   60

Hee-Haw, punch-out, by George & Nan Pollard, 1971, C.B.S. Artcraft bk.
#5139, Gunilla, Lulu, Kathy, & Jeannie 15   20

In Old New York, 1957, Saalfield bk. #4411, clr. & paper dolls, bk., 2 dolls, astd.
cstms. 25   35

In Old New York, Saalfield bk. #1772, 2 dolls, 2 pages of cstms., thin cover 25   35

In Our Background, 1941, Samuel Lowe 25   35

Jack & Jill, bk. #1561, 4 dolls, animals, astd. storyland cstms. 15   20

Jack with Magic Eyes, Queen Holden, 1963, James & Jonathan #9301-P,
lg. doll, discs eyes 50   70

Jackie & Caroline, #107 60   80

Journey Friends, toy from Germany, by Ann Eshner, Jack & Jill set, Dec. 1952 10   12

Judy, 1951, Merrill 10   15

Judy & Jim, by Hilda Miloche & Wilma Kane, Simon & Shuster, astd. outfits 40   50

Judy Garland, Queen Holden, 1940, Whitman #996 .... 100 150

Judy Garland, Queen Holden, 1945, Whitman #999, 2 dolls, large assortment
of outfits 100 150

Judy Holiday, 1954, Saalfield bk. #159110, 3 dolls, 4 pages of clothes, thin cover ... 45   55

Julia, 1968, Saalfield 35   45

Julie Andrews, 1958, Saalfield 35   45

June Allyson, 1950, Whitman bk. #970, 2 dolls, astd. outfits 50   70

June Allyson, 1950/1952, Whitman bk. #119015, 8 pages of clothes 50   70

June Allyson, 1953, Whitman bk. #1173:15, 2 dolls, 8 pages of dresses & cstms.. 50   70

June Allyson, 1957, Whitman bk. #2089, 2 dolls, 6 pages of clothes 50   70

June Allyson, 1960s, Watkins/Strathemore bk. #1820, 2 statuette dolls, 1 green,
1 pink & gray, astd. clothes 50   70

June Bride, by Art Tanchon, 1946, Stephens Company bk. #136 25   35

June & Stu Erwin w/ Jackie & Joyce (Trouble with Father), 1954, #159210 ... 50   70

Jungletown Jamboree, Samuel Lowe 6   8

Junior Miss, 1942 , Saalfield bk. #250, large dolls 35   45

Junior Prom, 1942, Saalfield 35   45

Karen Goes to College, 1955, Merrill 35   45

Keepsake Folio-Mini Doll, 1964, Samuel Lowe 15   20

Keepsake Folio-Trudy Doll, 1964, Samuel Lowe 20   30

Kewpie Kin, by Joseph Kallus, 1967, Saalfield bk. #4413, punch-out, wrap-
around dresses, blue cover 20   30

Kewpies, 1963, large Skootles on cover, 2 smaller Kewpies on back, astd. clothes . 25   35

Kewpies in Kewpieville, 1966, Saalfield, Rose O'Neill's dolls 20   30

Kiddie Circus, Saalfield 10   12

Little Ballerina, 1969, Whitman bk. #1963, 4 dolls, astd. outfits, folder 10   15

Little Brothers & Sisters, 1953, Whitman, 4 dolls, astd. outfits 15   20

Little Cousins, 1940, Samuel Lowe 15   20

Little Dolls, 1972, Samuel Lowe 6   8

LOW HIGH

Little Fairy, 1951, Merrill bk. #154715, 4 children w/ astd. cstms. .... $ 30 $ 40

Little Folks Dolls Set, 1900s, Milton Bradley #4727, 3 True-Life dolls, 3 sheets
    of colored clothing, 25 sheets of clothes to color 70   100

Little Girls, 1969, Samuel Lowe 6   8

Little Joy San, McCalls, October 1919, 1 doll, Japanese girl, dress, toy, lantern .. 12   18

Little Kitten to Dress, 1942, Samuel Lowe 20   30

Party Time, 1952, Whitman 10   15

Pat Boone, 1959, Whitman #1985 50   60

Pat Boone, 1959, Whitman bk. #1968, 2 statuette dolls in folder, astd. clothes 50   60

Pat Crowley, 1955, Whitman bk. #2050, 2 dolls, 8 pages of clothes 50   70

Pat The Stand-Up Doll, front & back dresses, 1946, Lowe bk. #1042, astd. clothes ... 35   45

Patches & Petunia, by Betty Bell Rea, 1937, Saalfield bk. #2160, lg. doll, astd.
    clothes 35   45

Patchwork, 1971, Saalfield 8   12

Patchy Annie, 1962, Saalfield 7   10

Patience & Prudence, 1959, Abbott bk. #1807, 2 dolls, astd. outfits, thin cover ... 35   45

Patti Page, 1958, Abbott bk. #1804, 2 dolls, astd. outfits, thin cover 40   60

Patty Duke, 1965, Whitman bk. #1991:59, 2 dolls, 6 pages of punch-out clothes ... 50   70

Polly Pal, 1976, Samuel Lowe 4   6

Preschool, 1958, Saalfield 10   15

Pretty As a Rose, 1963, Saalfield 15   20

Prince & Princess, Saalfield bk. #4464, coloring bk. & paper dolls, punch-outs,
    horse & rider, medieval cstms. 40   50

Princess Diana Paper Doll Bk of Fashion, by Clarissa Harlow & Mary Anna
    Bedford, num. outfits, 40-page bk. 6   8

Prom Home Permanent, 1952, Samuel Lowe 20   30

Puppy & Kitty Cut-outs, 1938, Florence Salter, 21 pieces of clothing 20   30

Quiz Kids, 1942, Saalfield 35   45

Raggedy Ann, 1970, Whitman 6   9

Raggedy Ann, by Ethel Hays Simms, Saalfield bk. #369, thin cover 40   50

Raggedy Ann & Raggedy Andy, 1961, bk. #1728 2 dolls, yellow cover 20   30

Raggedy Ann & Andy, by Ethel H. Simms, coloring & paper doll bk., 1944,
    Saalfield bk. #4409, Marcella & the Raggedies 40   50

Raggedy Ann & Raggedy Andy, by Ethel Hays Simms, 1961, Saalfield bk.
    #2715, Raggedies on front, Marcella on back 30   40

Raggedy Ann & Raggedy Andy Sticker Kit Circus, 1941, #546, sticker pictures ... 25   35

Ranch Family, 1957, Merrill 25   35

Rave Doll Dressing Bk, England, possibly based on The Avengers 50   60

Ricky Nelson, 1959, Whitman bk. #2081, 2 dolls, 6 pages of clothes 60   80

Ride a Pony-Judy & Jill, 1944, Merrill 12   18

Rita Hayworth, 1942, Merrill bk. #3478, 2 dolls, astd. outfits 60   80

Robin Hood, 1973, Walt Disney, press-out finger puppets, scenery & castle 10   15

Robin Hood & Maid Marian, Saalfield bk. #2784, astd. cstms., die-cut covers ... 50   60

School Friends, 1955, Merrill bk. #1556, Linda, Bobbie, & Diane, dresses &
    cowgirl suits 20   30

School Girl, 1942, Saalfield bk. #2400, large dolls, astd. clothes 35   45

Schoolmates, 1947, Saalfield 12   18

Sesame Street Characters, 1976, Whitman, Big Bird, Oscar, Cookie Monster, etc. 6   8

Seven & Seventeen, 1954, Merrill bk. #3441, 4 dolls, astd. clothes 35   45

Seven Children, by Queen Holden, large assortment of clothes 50   70

Shari Lewis, 1958, Saalfield 35   45

LOW HIGH

Shari Lewis & Her Puppets, 1960, Saalfield .... $ 35 $ 45

Sheree North, 1957, Saalfield bk. #1728, front & back dolls, 4 pages of dresses,
    thin cover 40   60

Sherlock Bones, 1955, Samuel Lowe, ... 8   12

Sherry & Terry, Lowe bk. #1847, Kewpie-style dolls 12   18

Shirley Temple, 1930s, adv., front & back doll, blue plaid dress, white collar,
    black tie 45   65

Shirley Temple, 1934, Saalfield bk. #2112, 4 dolls, astd. clothes, num. access. . 100   150

Shirley Temple, 1937, Saalfield bk. #1761, 2 toddler dolls, 2 dresses 70   90

Shirley Temple, 1942, die-cut teenage set, 2 dolls, yellow formal, astd. outfits,
    thin cover 150   200

Shirley Temple, 1950s, Gabriel #300, statuette doll, snap-on clothes, real picture
    faces, num. outfits 40   60

Shirley Temple, 1958, Saalfield bk. #5110, statuette doll, astd. dresses, folder 80   100

Shirley Temple, 1976, Whitman bk. #1986, 1 doll, astd. clothes, pink tote bag 8   12

Shirley Temple-Her Movie Wardrobe, 1938, 1 doll in pink slip, astd. outfits 80   120

Sparkle Plenty, baby from the Dick Tracy comic strip, 1948 30   40

Sports Time, 1952, Whitman bk. #2090, blonde doll in white slip 18   24

Square Dance, 1950, Saalfield #2717, 5 dolls, 6 pages of cstms. 20   30

Stand-Up Dolls, 1960s, Artcraft, 6 dolls 8   10

Star Babies, 1945, Merrill 20   25

Star Trek, 1975, Saalfield bk. #C2272, activity bk., punch-out, stand-up dolls,
    Kirk, Spock, McCoy, Uhura, & Sulu 50   70

Pez Dispensers

Pez is so American, a part of growing up from the 1950s to present day. Like most of us, Pez has its roots in a different country. Eduard Haas introduced it in 1927 in Austria. It takes its name from the German word for peppermint, *pfefferminz*. Originally sold as a breath mint/candy, it came with a handy dispenser with grip (called regulars). Pez redesigned its product for the American market in 1952. They added character heads and introduced fruit flavors. Pez became a kids' candy.

In recent years, Pez collecting has been a very active area, Christie's auction house even included a section of Pez in one of its sales. Collectors tend to concentrate on the head of a Pez dispenser; most do not collect based on stem or container differences. That is because heads can be switched from stem to stem. There is a feet vs. no-feet controversy. Most containers have a rounded base. Some people call them shoes but they are more often are refereed to as no feet (nf). Feet (f) are the bases that appeared on figures beginning around 1987. They are thin, flat, and have a stylized "V" indentation. Many collectors go back to the "only the head matters" theorem, while others place a higher value on no-feet examples. Packaging is also an area of some controversy. Collectors contend that packaging for the most part does not matter since early Pez containers came in unattractive bags or boxes. The matter is harder to determine when evaluating Pez sold on blisterpacks or blistercards. We feel that original packaging will increase the value of an item, especially the more elaborate and interesting packaging. Most notably is the Stand By Me Pez, which must have the orginal packaging, including the movie poster, or it is just a Pez Pal Boy.

The prices below are for mint nonpackaged examples except where noted differently. Pez dispensers are hard to date, so the decades we suggest are our best guess. For further reading we reccommend *Pez Collectibles*, by Richard Geary, Schiffer, Atglen, PA, 1994.

A selection of Pez dispensers. - photo courtesy of Christie's East.

	LOW	HIGH
Eerie Spectres, Air Spirit, fish head, nf, 1980s	$ 30	$ 50
Alpine Man, mustache, Olympics, nf, 1972	300	500
Angel A, sm. light blue eyes, nf, 1980s	15	20
Annie, nf, 1980s	30	40
Arithmetic, nf, 1960s	200	300
Arlene, f, 1980s	2	3
Astronaut A, sm. helmet, nf, 1955	150	250
Astronaut B, pointed helmet, nf, 1970s	70	90
Baloo, blue head, f, 1980s	15	20
Bambi, f, 1980s	5	7
Barney Bear, f, 1980s	10	15
Baseball Glove, ball, nf, 1960s	180	220
Baseball Glove, ball, bat, plate base, 1960s	200	300
Batgirl, soft head, nf, 1970s	70	100
Batman, w/cape, nf, 1960s	100	150
Batman, soft head, nf, 1970s	80	100
Betsy Ross, nf, 1970s	55	75
Big Top Elephant, w/pointed hat, nf, 1960s	50	60
Big Top Elephant, flat hat, nf, 1960s	40	55
Big Top Elephant, hair, nf, 1960s	200	300
Bouncer Beagle, f, 1990s	100	5
Bozo, cutout side, nf, 1960s	90	140
Bride, nf, 1960s	400	500
Brutus, nf, 1950s	100	150
Bullwinkle, nf, 1960s	150	200
Candy Shooter gun, Pez on grip, 1970s	90	140
Captain, nf, 1970s	50	70
Captain America, nf, 1980s	45	65
Captain Hook, nf, 1970s	25	35
Casper, nf, 1960s	60	80
Casper, w/ "Casper" on side, nf, 1960s	80	100
Clown, collar, nf, 1960s	25	35
Cockatoo, nf, 1970s	30	50
Cocoa Marsh Astronaut, nf, 1950s	90	140
Cowboy, nf, 1960s	250	350
Creature from the Black Lagoon, grn head, nf, 1960s	200	250
Crocodile, nf, 1960s	65	85
Daffy Duck, f, 1980s	2	3
Dalmatian Pup, f, 1980s	20	30
Daniel Boone, nf, 1970s	100	150
Dino, f, 1990s	2	3
Doctor, nf, 1960s	45	65
Donald Duck, die-cut face, nf, 1960s	90	120
Donkey Kong Jr., prem. w/card, nf, 1980s	250	350
Dopey, nf, 1960s	100	1500
Droopy Dog, attached ears, f, 1980s	8	10
Easter Bunny, w/rabbit & eggs, cut-out sides, nf, 1950s	300	500
Eerie Spectres Diabolic, nf, 1980s	30	50
Eerie Spectres Scarewolf, nf, 1980s	30	50
Eerie Spectres Spook, nf, 1980s	30	50
Eerie Spectres Vamp, nf, 1980s	30	50

	LOW	HIGH
Eerie Spectres Zombie, nf, 1980s	$ 30	$ 50
Engineer, nf, 1960s	25	35
Fireman, nf, 1960s	10	15
Fishman, looks like Black Lagoon Creature, nf, 1970s	100	150
Foghorn Leghorn, nf, 1980s	30	40
Fozzie Bear, f, 1980s	2	3
Frankenstein, nf, 1960s	200	250
Garfield, w /smile, hat, f, 1980s	3	4
Giraffe, nf, 1960s	35	45
Girl, f, 1980s	1	2
Girl, Pez Pal, nf, 1960s	15	20
Green Hornet, nf, 1960s	200	300
Groom, nf, 1960s	200	250
Henry Hawk, f, 1980s	25	35
Hippo, nf, 1970s	400	500
Hulk, f, 1990s	2	3
Hulk, nf, 1970s	20	30
Indian Brave, nf, 1970s	150	180
Indian Chief, nf, 1970s	55	75
Indian Maiden, nf, 1970s	60	80
Jerry, nf, 1990s	2	3
Jerry, inside of ears pink, nf, 1990s	10	15
Jerry (Tom & Jerry), nf, 1980s	12	18
Jiminy Cricket, nf, 1970s	30	40
Joker, soft head, nf, 1970s	70	90
Make-a-Face, nf, 1970s	1200	1500
Mary Poppins, nf, 1960s	300	500
Mickey Mouse, f, 1980s	2	3
Mickey Mouse D, removable nose, nf, 1970s	10	15
Muselix, nf, 1970s	900	1300
Olympic Snowman, 1976, 1976	200	350
One-Eye Monster, nf, 1960s	50	75
Orange, nf, 1970s	70	90
Pear, nf, 1970s	550	750
Penguin, soft head (Batman), nf, 1970s	70	90
Petunia Pig, nf, 1980s	10	15
Pilgrim, nf, 1970s	70	90
Pineapple, nf, 1970s	600	800
Psychedelic Eye, hand holding eye, nf, 1960s	300	400
Regular, w/ advertising, 1950s	250	350
Santa, full body, 1950s	180	220
Santa, w/ small head, painted face, nf, 1950s	100	150
Snoopy, f, 1980s	1	3
Snowman, nf, 1990s	1	2
Space Trooper, full body., 1950s	300	400
Spaceman, nf, 1950s	90	130
Stand By Me, must be mint in the package, 1980s	200	250
Tinkerbell, nf, 1980s	90	140
Tom, C (Tom & Jerry), f, 1990s	1	2
Uncle Scrooge McDuck, nf, 1980s	8	12
Vucko Wolf, Olympics, 3 variations, ea., f, 1980s	300	500

	LOW	HIGH
Wile E. Coyote, nf, 1980s	$ 18	$ 22
Witch, 1-piece head, embossed stem, nf, 1950s	120	160
Wolfman, nf, 1960s	200	300
Wounded Soldier, nf, 1970s	100	150
Zorro, nf, 1960s	30	40
Zorro, w/ Zorro logo on side, nf, 1960s	80	100

Premiums

The excitement of getting a prize or an extra gift is a temptation for consumers. Combining this with a child's favorite radio, comic book, or television hero creates a powerful inducement to purchase. Premiums gained momentum in the radio days of the Great Depression. Cereal, soap and other companies hosted programs; in turn Radio Orphan Annie, Captain Midnight, The Lone Ranger, and others promoted the host's product. When television replaced radio many programs made the switch as well. These personalities induced young viewers with mail-in offers for membership packages, decoder rings, books, badges and toys. Other premiums were included with the package and occasionally offered at the store.

Collectors actively seek these items. They collect a range of items basing their collection on characters or types of items like decoders or rings. In recent years astounding prices have been paid for rare premium rings. Collectors are also seeking newer premiums from the 1960s and '70s. Quisp and Quake items are currently very popular. Packaging and instructional materials increase the prices of premiums, so don't touch that dial and don't throw that material away. Premiums are still used as sales inducements, mainly by the cereal industry. Prices below are for items in excellent to near mint condition. Each entry contains the character who promoted the product, a brief description of the premium, the date, and the company who made the product.

For further reading see *Radio Premium and Cereal Box Collectibles*, Tom Tumbusch, Wallace Homestead Book Company, Radnor, PA 1991 and *Overstreet Premium Ring Price Guide*, Robert M. Overstreet, Gemstone Publishing, Inc. Timonium, MD, 1994.

	LOW	HIGH
Amos 'N Andy, Amos Driving Cab, cardboard, 1931, Pepsodent	$ 150	$ 200
Bobby Benson, Code Rule, cardboard, 1935, Hecker-H-O	100	150
Buck Rogers, Birthstone Initial Ring, 1939, Popsicle Pete	300	400
Buck Rogers, Repeller Ray Ring, 1930s, Cream of Wheat	2500	3000
Buck Rogers, Ring of Saturn Ring, 1930s, Post	500	800
Buck Rogers, Wilma Pendant, 1930s, Cream of Wheat	80	120
Cap'N Crunch, Button, 1965, Quaker	15	20
Cap'N Crunch, Figural Bank, 1966, Quaker	80	100
Cap'N Crunch, Figural Ring, 1963, Quaker	200	300
Cap'N Crunch, Jean Lefoot Figural Bank, 1966, Quaker	60	80
Cap'N Crunch, Oath of Allegiance, 1964, Quaker	30	40
Cap'N Crunch, Sea Cycle, 1965, Quaker	25	35
Cap'N Crunch, Ship Shake, 1968, Quaker	25	35
Captain Marvel, Pinback, 1940s, Comic	45	65
Captain Marvel, Rocket Raider Compass Ring, 1946, Comics	2000	3000
Captain Midnight, Decoder, 1957	300	350
Captain Midnight, Membership Card, 1939	60	80
Captain Midnight, Mirro-Flash Code-O-Graph, 1946, Ovaltine	180	220
Captain Midnight, Mug, 1940s, Ovaltine	50	70
Captain Midnight, Mystic Sun God Ring, 1947, Ovaltine	2000	3000
Captain Midnight, Secret Squadron Decoder Badge, 1955	180	240
Captain Midnight, Secret Squadron Mem. Manual, 1941, Ovaltine	100	150
Captain Midnight, Shake-Up Mug, 1947, Ovaltine	100	150
Captain Tim, Ivory Stamp Club Album, 72-pg., 1934, Ivory Soap	30	50
Captain Video, Flying Saucer Ring, w/ 2 saucers, 1950s, Powerhouse	800	1200
Captain Video, Mystocoder Instruction Folder, 1950s, TV	100	150
Captain Video, Photo Ring, 1950s, Powerhouse	200	300

	LOW	HIGH
Charlie McCarthy, Diecut-Cardboard Figure, 1938, Chase & Sanborn	$ 80	$ 120
Charlie McCarthy, Spoon, 1938, Chase & Sanborn	30	40
Crackle, Rubber Head Ring, 1950s, Rice Crispies	300	400
Death Valley Days, Story of Death Valley 24 pg.-bk., 1931, Borax	35	45
Dick Tracy, Pocket Flashlight, 1939, Quaker Oats	100	150
Dizzy Dean, Winners Club Member Pin, 1930s, Post Cereal	60	90
Don Winslow, Squadron of Peace Ring, 1939, Kellogs	3000	4000
Droopy Dog, Popping Head Figure, 1960, General Mills	30	40
Eddie Cantor, Trick Cards & Instructions, 1935, Pobeco Toothpaste	30	40
Fibber McGee & Molly, Cast Photo, 1940s, Johnson Wax	25	35
Flash, Flash Pinback Button, 1940s, Comic	100	150
Flash Gordon, Movie Serial Button, 1930s, Theater	80	120
Frank Buck, Black Leopard Ring, Rare Jungleland vers., 1939	4000	6000
Frank Buck, Ivory Initial Ring, 1939, Ivory Soap	300	400
Funny Face, Chug-a-Lug Mug, 1960s, Funny Face	15	20
Funny Face, Walkers, 1960s, Funny Face	80	100
Green Hornet, Seal Ring, 1947, General Mills	900	1200
Green Hornet, Secret Compart. Glow-in-Dark Ring, 1947, General Mills ..	2000	3500
Hopalong Cassidy, Savings Club Folder, 1950s, Savings & Loan	35	55
Howdy Doody, Jack-in-the Box Ring, 1950s, Poll Parrot	3000	5000
Howdy Doody, Pinback, 1950s, TV	40	50
Junior Detective, Junior Det. Corps Captain Badge, 1933, Post Toasties	40	60
Linus The Lionhearted, Stuffed Doll, 1965, Post	40	60
Lone Ranger, Blackout Kit, 1943	150	200
Lone Ranger, Membership Badge, 1935, Silver-Cup Bread	60	90
Lone Ranger, Movie Film Ring, w/ film, 1948, Cheerios	150	200
Lone Ranger, Secret Comp. Ring, 2 Photos, 1945, Kix	600	800
Lone Ranger, Secret Compartment Ring, 1 Photo, 1945, Kix	350	450
Lone Ranger, Silver Bullet/Compass, 1947, Cheerios	40	50
Lone Ranger, Six Shooter Gun Ring, 1947, Kix	100	150
Lone Wolf, Manual 32 pg., 1932, Wrigley Gum	100	150
Mandrake the Magician, Figural Membership Button, 1934, Taystee Bread ..	50	75
Mary Poppins, Chimney Toy, 1964, Kellogs	80	100
Melvin Purvis, Badge, 1936, Post Toasties	60	90
Melvin Purvis, Sacred Scarab Ring, 1937, Post	1000	1500
Orphan Annie, 6 Die-cut Cardboard Shadowettes, 1938	90	140
Orphan Annie, Altascope, 1940s, sold at auction in 1994	*12,650*	
Orphan Annie, Pin, 1934, Ovaltine	50	70
Orphan Annie, Pin, 1935, Ovaltine	50	70
Orphan Annie, Puzzle, 1933, Ovaltine	60	80
Orphan Annie, Secret Guard Magnifying Ring, 1940s	2000	3000
Orphan Annie, Secret Society Manual, 1940, Ovaltine	200	300
Orphan Annie, Shake-Up Mug, 1, full fig., 1931	50	70
Orphan Annie, Shake-Up Mug, 2, bust fig., 1935, Ovaltine	50	70
Orphan Annie, Shake-Up Mug, 3, Annie dancing, 1938, Ovaltine	80	120
Orphan Annie, Shake-Up Mug, 4, jumping rope, 1939, Ovaltine	80	120
Orphan Annie, Sunburst Decoder Pin, 1937, Ovaltine	80	100
Pop, Rubber Head Ring, 1950s, Rice Crispies	300	400
Quake, Earth Digger Car, 1965, Quaker	100	150
Quake, Figural Ring, 1966, Quaker	300	400
Quisp, Friendship Ring, 1966, Quaker	700	900

	LOW	HIGH
Quisp, Meteorite Ring, 1960s, Quaker	$ 300	$ 400
Quisp, Unicycler, 1969, Quaker	80	100
Rootie Kazootie, Club Button, 1950s	30	40
Rootie Kazootie, Lucky Spot Seal Ring, 1950s	350	450
Roy Rogers, Badge/Whistle, 1950, Quaker	80	100
Roy Rogers, Branding Iron Ring, Black Cap, 1948, Quaker	150	200
Roy Rogers, Figural Mug, Plastic, 1950, Quaker	35	55
Roy Rogers, Postcard, 1949, Quaker	20	30
Roy Rogers, Two 45-Record Set, 1950s	80	100
Sekatary Hawkins, Membership Card Oath on Back, 1932, Ralston	30	50
Sgt. Preston, Celluloid Membership Button, 1950s, Quaker	60	80
Sgt. Preston, Totem Pole Set, 1950s, Quaker	70	90
Shadow, Black Stone Crocodile Ring, 1947, Carey Salt	700	1000
Shadow, Blue Coal Glow-in-the Dark Ring, 1941, Blue Coal	400	600
Shadow, Matchbook, 1930s, Blue Coal	80	100
Sky King, Detectowriter, 1950, Peter Pan	90	130
Sky King, Microscope, 1947, Peter Pan	100	150
Sky King, Navaho Treasure Ring, 1950, Peter Pan	180	220
Sky King, Secret Signal Scope, 1947, Peter Pan	100	150
Sky King, Teleblinker Ring, 1950s, TV	150	200
Snap, Rubber Head Ring, 1950s, Rice Crispies	200	250
Superman, Secret Compartment Ring, 1940 Superman Gum sold at auction in 1994	*16,100*	
Superman Tim, Membership Button, 1950	45	65
Ted Williams, Figural Ring w/ Ball on Wire, 1948, Nabisco	800	1000
Tom Mix, Badge, 1945, Ralston	70	90
Tom Mix, Bandanna, 1933, Ralston	75	95
Tom Mix, Book, " Trail of the Terrible Six," 1935, Ralston	25	35
Tom Mix, Brass Compass Magnifier, 1940, Ralston	90	130
Tom Mix, ID Bracelet, 1947, Ralston	90	110
Tom Mix, Illust. Manual, 24 Pg., 1933, Ralston	50	70
Tom Mix, Illustr. Booklet 8 Pg., 1934, Nat. Chicle Gum	40	60
Tom Mix, Paper Face Mask of Tom, 1930s	100	150
Tom Mix, Six Gun Decoder, 1941, Ralston	90	110
Tom Mix, Straight Shooter Bangle Bracelet, 1930s, Ralston	80	100
Tom Mix, Telephone Set, 1938, Ralston	100	150
Trix, Rabbit Mug & Bowl, 1963, Mills	30	40
Valric the Viking, Ring, 1940s, All Rye Flakes	3000	5000
Winnie The Pooh, Plastic Spoon Hanger, 1965, Nabisco	15	20
Wizard Of Oz, *Ozma, The Little Wizard* Book, 1933, Jell-O	60	80
Wonder Woman , Litho. Pinback Button, 1940s, Comic	60	80
Wyatt Earp, Marshall's Badge Ring, 1958, Cheerios	45	65

Robots and Space Toys

The word Robot is derived from Robata for forced labor. Robot first appeared in the 1921 play *R.U.R.* by Czechoslovakian playwright Karl Capek. It was not until the futuristic 1950s that Robots really hit their stride, when toy robots and space craft started to appear. Although some were made in the United States (by firms such as Marx, Remco and Ideal) and Germany, the majority were produced in Japan. Friction drives and keywind mechanisms were employed but battery power increased the complexity of the toy. With batteries, metal monsters and space ships could twirl, spin, light up, roll backwards, change directions, and perform a multitude of other tricks. Collectors call this "action" and it attracts them to these toys.

Most of the toys listed below are Japanese lithographed tinplate with battery power produced in the 1950s and '60s We have noted when the predominate material is something other than tinplate and when a toy is friction or keywind, otherwise assume that it is battery operated. The term *rc* refers to remote control, *UK* stands for manufacturer unknown.

When collecting these toys beware of condition; make sure there are no missing parts, including remote controls, battery boxes, or antennas. Make sure there is no restoration; battery boxes should be checked closely. Never leave a battery in a toy; it can leak and cause damage. The prices below are for mint without box (MNB) and mint in the box (MIB) examples. Rust, scratches, and restoration will lower these prices. In recent years astronomical prices of rare items (over $25,000 at auction for a Robby Space Patrol car) has encouraged people to create new robots such as the Robby Space Patrol, Mr. Atomic and the Rosko Astronauts. Some of these toys are incredible reproductions of the original toy, right down to the box. Other robots are old style new products. Be sure of what you are buying. Robots are listed either by the name that appears on the original box or to the name coined by collectors. Different robots often have the same or similar names. To clarify things, we have listed reference numbers after the name. The B# refers *to Robot-Robots et autres Fusees d'vant la lune*, Pierre Boogaerts, Futuropolis, Paris, 1978. The K# refers to *Robots, Tin Toy Dreams*, Teruhisa Kitahara, Chronicle Books, CA, 1985.

	MNB	MIB
Acrobat (K #119), blue, yellow & red plastic, ht. 10"	$ 100-150	$ 250-350
Action Planet Robot (B #292), keywind Robby style, black & red, w/ sparking mech., Yoshiya, ht. 9"	180-220	300-400
Answer Game Machine (K #105), multicolor w/ buttons for calculations, Ichida, ht. 14"	600-800	900-1500
Apollo 11 Moon Rocket, friction powered, Ashai, ht. 14"	40-60	80-120
Apollo 11 Eagle Lunar Module (B #68), w/ seven automatic actions, Daishin, for Mego, ht. 8"	80-120	200-300
Astro Captain (B #210), keywind, Mego, ht. 6"	70-90	150-220
Astronaut W/ Child's Head (K #65), blue, similar to the Red Cragstan Astronaut, Daiya, ht. 12"	700-900	1000-1500
Atom Boat (B #124), friction drive, Chinese, len. 10"	80-120	200-250
Atomic Robot Man (K #81), keywind, boiler plate style, litho. w/ diecast hands, UK, ht.	400-600	700-1200
Atomic Rocket (B #92), push lever action, w/ side fins displaying Saturn & star motif, Masudaya, len. 6"	150-200	300-400
Attacking Martian (B #191), rotomatic, w/ guns in hinged door chest, ht. 12"	150-200	300-350
Battery Operated Tractor (similar to K #112), red & black w/ 1200 plaque on battery case, Nomura, len. 7"	400-600	700-900
Big Loo Moon Robot, Marx, ht. 38"	600-800	1000-1500
Blink-A-Gear Robot (B #7) black w/ transparent chest panel housing		

	MNB	MIB

rotating gears, Taiyo, ht. 14" .... $ 500-700 | $ 900-1300

Blue Rosko Astronaut (B #230), Rosko toys, ht. 13" .... 900-1300 | 1500-2200

Bulldozer Which A Robot Operates (similar to B #144), silver
robot on blue, & red dozer, UK, len. 9" .... 200-300 | 500-700

Busy Cart Robot (B #269), black & yellow w/ hardhat & wheel-
barrow, Horikawa, ht. 12" .... 700-900 | 1000-1500

Capsule 7 (B #188), w/ rotating astronaut, Masudaya, len. 10" .... 60-90 | 120-180

Chime Trooper (K #137), keywind, boy astronaut plays music,
Aoshin, ht. 9.5" .... 1200-1500 | 2000-3000

Circus 8 Car (B #154), friction, clown robot driving a Circus 8
Mercedes, Ashai, len. 8" .... 500-600 | 700-900

Colonel Hap Hazard (B #61), astronaut in white NASA space suit
w/ whirling copter blade, Marx, ht. 11" .... 800-1000 | 1200-1800

Cragstan X-07 Space Surveillant (B #108), the oval shaped flying
sauce w/ astronaut pilot under bubble dome, Masudaya, len. 9" .... 70-90 | 150-200

Cragstan's Mr. Robot (K #25), red body, litho. chest panel,
swiveling domed-head, Yonezawa, ht. 11" .... 450-650 | 800-900

Cragstan's Talking Robot (K #134), red, similar to the Mercury
robot, Yonezawa, ht. 10" .... 400-700 | 800-1000

Dino Robot (K #97), robot head folds down to reveal a roaring
dinosaur, Horikawa, ht. 11" .... 500-700 | 900-1200

Driving Robot (K #74), keywind, robot driven auto swing, ht. 6" ... 300-500 | 600-900

Dux Astroman, Western Germany, green plastic astroman w/ radar
antenna over clear dome, white head w/ red features, rock
crushing action, rc, ht. 14" .... 1200-1500 | 2000-3000

Earth Man (K #144), tan astronaut, silver helmet w/ sounding &
blinking gun, rc, Nomura, ht. 9" .... 700-900 | 1200-1800

Engine Robot (B #2), keywind, w/ sparks & gears in chest window
panel, ht. 9" .... 180-220 | 300-400

Engine Robot (B #213), gray w/ whirling gears in see-through
chest panel, Horikawa, ht. 9" .... 100-150 | 200-300

Fighting Space Man (B #159), chest panel w/ swiveling gun &
litho. circuitry, Horikawa, ht. 12" .... 100-150 | 200-300

Fighting Space Man (B #159), yellow w/ domed astronaut's head,
Horikawa, ht. 12" .... 200-250 | 300-400

Firebird Space Patrol (K #57), similar to Sonicon Rocket, finished
in green & red, Masudaya, len. 14" .... 300-400 | 500-700

Flying Jeep, circular vehicle on wheels, KKS, ht. 3" .... 70-90 | 120-180

Forbidden Planet Robby The Robot Talking Figure, hard plastic,
Masudaya, c. 1980s, ht. 15" .... 90-140 | 180-230

Forklift Robot (B #270), yellow & w/ red cap, plastic forklift, &
crate, Horikawa, ht. 11.5" .... 1000-1500 | 1800-2400

Friendship 7-Space Capsule (B #95), friction drive w/ interior
floating astronaut, Horikawa, len. 9" .... 50-70 | 100-140

Gear Robot (K #50), chest window gear display & speed control
switch on head, ht. 11" .... 120-180 | 250-350

Great Garloo, green plastic, Marx, c. 1961, ht. 18" .... 250-350 | 500-700

Great Garloo, Son of, keywind, green plastic, Marx, c. 1962, ht. 6" ... 120-160 | 250-350

Hi-Bouncer Moon Scout (K #63), silver astronaut w/ copter blade,
shoots balls from chest, rc, Marx Toys, ht. 12" .... 1000-1500 | 2000-3000

High Wheel Robot (K #32), blue w/ red feet see-through chest

	MNB	MIB
panel, moving gears, rc, Yoshiya, ht. 9"	$ 400-500	$ 600-900
Hysterical Robot (K #128), plastic, laughs & grins, UK, ht. 13"	100-150	200-300
Interplanetary Space Fighter, tinplate vehicle w/ retractable side fins, Nomura, len. 12"	200-300	400-500
Jumping Rocket (B #251), keywind, robot rocket w/ feet, len. 6"	100-150	250-350
King Jet 8 Futuristic Racer (B #119), light blue, friction drive, bubble dome w/ driver, len. 12"	100-150	250-350
Krome Dome (K #131), multicolor plastic w/ clam shaped head & accordion torso, Yonezawa, ht. 10"	60-80	120-180
Laughing Robot, plastic, clown head, ht. 14"	150-180	200-300
Lavender Robot (K #28), a.k.a. Nonstop Robot, lavender w/ litho-graphed machinery panels & gauges, Masudaya, ht. 14"	3000-4500	5000-7000
Lighted Space Vehicle (B #226), blue car w/ domed cockpit, astronaut, & floating ball action, Masudaya, len. 9"	90-140	200-300
Man In Space, tinplate celluloid astronaut, w/ remote control, Alps	70-100	400-600
Man Made Satellite (B #109), litho. base w/ signal missile, Mars, & Earth w/ satellite, Hoku, len. 7"	200-250	400-600
Mars King or Tank Robot (K #133), w/ side-mounted tracks & TV screen in chest, Horikawa, ht. 9"	150-200	300-400
Martian Supersensitive Radar Patrol, friction drive Jeep, UK len. 9"	400-600	700-900
Marvelous Mike Tractor, yellow w/ silver robot operator, Saunders, len. 12.5"	120-160	200-300
Mechanical Sparking Robot (K #77), keywind, red plastic spark panel centered on chest, Yonezawa	70-90	120-170
Mechanical Walking Space Man (K #90), keywind, gray w/ red feet, Sy Toys, ht. 9"	200-250	300-500
Mighty Robot (K #129), keywind, red body w/ gray plastic head & jointed arms, Yonezawa, ht. 9.5"	300-500	600-800
Mirror Man (K #198), gray & red w/ vinyl arms & head, yellow eyes, Bull Mark, ht. 16"	400-600	800-1200
Missile Man (B #260), gray & red, w/ disc antenna & five missiles in hinged chest panel, ht. 16.5"	900-1200	1500-2000
Moon Capsule (B #21), friction, two pilots, Horikawa, len. 6"	50-70	80-120
Moon Detector (B #66), cylindrical shape space vehicle w/ bubble dome front-end & astronaut, Yonezawa, len. 10"	400-600	700-900
Moon Explorer (K #116), dark gray, featuring clock & seesaw mechanical display window, Bandai, ht. 17"	1400-1800	2500-3500
Moon Explorer (K #136), keywind Robby style body w/ domed astronaut head, Yoshiya, ht. 7"	300-400	500-800
Moon Patrol Space Division #3 (B #202), similar to the Robby Space Patrol blue w/ star & satellite motif, astronaut driver & bubble covered astro globe, Nomura, len. 12"	2000-3000	4000-6000
Moon Rocket vehicle (K #169), astronaut in bubble front cockpit & astronaut on roof, Masudaya, len. 10"	80-120	200-250
Moon Space Ship (B #201), light blue, similar to the Robby Space Patrol, but w/ bubble encased radar mechanism, Nomura, len. 13"	1200-1800	2500-3500
Mr. Hustler (B #128), astronaut headed robot w/ flexing shoulders, ht. 11"	180-220	350-450
Mr. Machine, keywind, plastic, later version, mkd. 1977, Ideal, ht. 16"	60-80	100-150

	MNB	MIB

Mr. Machine, plastic, keywind, whistling, c. 1960s, ht. 16" .... $ 180-240 $ 400-600

Mr. Mercury (K #120), gold w/ gray arms & red dome, green pilot-
form eyes, rc, Yonezawa, ht. 13" 600-800   900-1400

Mr. Robot The Mechanical Brain (K #9), keywind & battery, boiler
plate style, (rc), Alps, ht. 8.5" 900-1300   1800-2200

Mr. Xerox (K #35), having guns in open chest, ht. 9" 100-150   200-300

New Fighting Robot (K #42), light up dome on head & guns in
chest, Horikawa, ht. 12" 100-130   200-300

New Space Station (K #157), circular, tinplate w/ plastic bottom,
stop & go action, Horikawa, dia. 10 .5" 500-700   900-1100

Outer Space Patrol (B #253), friction drive w/ astronaut camera-
man, len. 8" 150-200   300-500

Planet Explorer (B #122), tinplate vehicle w/ bubble front &
astronaut, Masudaya, len. 9.5" 80-120   200-250

Planet Y Space Station (B #91), Nomura, dia. 8" 100-150   200-300

R-35 Robot (K #15), bucket-shaped head, remote control box litho.
w/ robots, Masudaya, ht. 7" 700-900   1000-1400

R-7 Flashy Jim (B #51) silver boilerplate style robot, red head-
phones, rc, Ace/S. N. K., ht. 6.5 " 900-1300   1800-2200

R-8 Sparking Robot (B #49), small keywind sparky style robot
blue w/ "R" & "8" on shoulders, ht. 7" 300-500   600-800

Radar Scope Space Scout Robot (B #36), TV image on chest
ht. 9.5" 90-145   200-250

Radicon (K #29), gray textured finish, gauge & light inset in
chest, rc, Masudaya 3500-4500   6000-8000

Ranger Robot (K #113), ribbed clear plastic, smoking action,
Daiya, ht. 13" 600-900   1000-1500

Red Cragstan Astronaut (B #98) w/ gun, Daiya, ht. 14" 1200-1600   2000-3000

Red Rosko Astronaut (B #230), conical shaped dome, walkie-
talkie & dual oxygen tanks, ht. 13" 900-1300   1500-2200

Remote Control Piston Action Robot (K #2), Robby Style, gold
w/ deep blue legs, Nomura, ht. 9" 1200-1800   2500-3500

Robby The Robot (Mechanized Robot) (K. #1) tinplate, black
w/ red accents, 6-battery box, Nomura, ht. 13.5" 900-1600   2000-4000

Robert The Robot (K #99), crankwind, gray plastic, red arms, w/
voicebox, & rc, Ideal, ht. 100-150   200-300

Robot Commando, plastic w ball throwing action, Ideal, ht. 22" 200-300   400-600

Robot in Mercedes, friction drive, w/ sparking gun on hood, len. 8"... 200-300   400-600

Robot Space Auto (B #70), Robby style Robot driving a light
blue roadster, len. 8" 900-1300   1600-2000

Robot St-1, by Strenco, Germany, boilerplate style, w/ coil &
diamond-shaped antennas, ht. 6.5" 500-700   800-1200

Rocket Express, keywind, race to the moon toy, Technofix, ht. 14" ... 150-200   300-400

Rocket Man In Space Armor (B #136), plastic, robot head opens
to reveal an astronaut head, w/ 2 rockets on back, Alps, Rosko,
ht. 12" 1200-1800   2000-3000

Rocket No. 3 (K #156), early, green, red & yellow w/ friction
power, Masudaya, len. 7" 90-140   200-300

Roto Robot (K #132), w/ shooting guns in chest, hinged head
battery compartment, Horikawa, ht. 9" 80-120   180-220

Rt-Z Robotank Z (K #70), gray w/ red & white rockets embossed

	MNB	MIB
on the sides, Nomura, ht. 8"	$ 400-500	$ 600-800
Satellite X-107 (B #162), flying saucer w/ floating astronaut, dia. 8"	50-70	90-140
Sky Patrol (B #239), space boat w/ pilot & swivel gun turret, len. 13.5"	100-150	250-350
Sonicon Rocket (K #54), vehicle which responds to sound, w/ robot driver, Masudaya, len. 13.5"	400-600	900-1200
Space Car (B #40), w/ Robot driver & floating ball, Yonezawa, len. 8"	1000-1500	2000-3000
Space Chick (B #271), keywind, Yone, ht. 3"	40-60	70-90
Space Dog (K #106), keywind, silver w/ spark window, Yoshiya, len. 6.5"	500-600	800-1000
Space Dog (K #106), red w/ friction drive & spark window, Yoshiya, len. 6.5"	500-600	800-1000
Space Explorer (K #104), gray, initially square, raises to reveal head, arms & 3-D TV screen, Yonezawa, ht. open 12"	500-700	800-1200
Space Fighter Rocket Car (B #183), friction, blue, red & yellow w/ two pilots & sparking mechanism, len. 18.5"	400-600	700-900
Space Giant (B #13), Saucer, gray & red w/ domed cockpit (largest flying saucer toy), dia. 12"	700-900	1200-1500
Space Giant Robot (K #l 18), charcoal, w/ red accents, pop-out guns, Horikawa, ht. 16"	100-150	200-300
Space Guard MS-61 (B #257), space tank w/ dual spring-loaded rockets, rc, Masudaya, len. 9.5"	180-220	300-400
Space Patrol (B #239), helmeted driver w/ firing gun, ht. 9"	100-150	200-350
Space Patrol Car (B #82), astronaut driver w/ lighting gun, Nomura, ht. 9.5"	200-300	400-600
Space Patrol X-11 (B #206), green w/ hinged door cockpit, Yonezawa, len. 8.5"	40-60	70-90
Space Ship X-11 (B #161), saucer w/ 2 tinplate pilots & a floating spaceman, Masudaya, dia. 8"	50-65	80-120
Space Sight Seeing Bus (B #285), V shaped astro bus, domed cockpit w/ litho. pilots & passengers, len. 13.5"	100-150	300-400
Space Tank (B #227), bubble dome w/ radar shield & astronaut pilot, Masudaya, len. 8"	70-90	180-220
Space Trip (B #121), a racing game similar to Terre a la Lune, Masudaya, len. 19"	200-250	400-600
Space Whale (K, Yesterday of Toys, #85), keywind, space blue w/ Saturn motif, Yoshiya, len. 8"	500-700	900-1400
Spaceman (B #175), astronaut in silver suit w/ red leggings, white helmet w/ head lamp, flashlight & gun rc, ht. 8.5"	700-900	1000-1500
Sparky Robot (K #84), keywind, silver & red, ht. 6"	180-240	350-500
Star Strider Robot, red & gray, guns in hinged chest, Horikawa, ht. 11"	100-150	200-250
Strolling Space Station, keywind, Yone, dia. 3.5"	50-80	120-180
Swinging Baby Robot (K #72), mechanical tot in keywind swing, Yonezawa, ht. 6"	200-300	400-600
Television Robot (K #52), robot head, double loop antenna & TV in chest, Horikawa, ht. 12"	100-150	200-250
Television Spaceman (B #196), keywind, TV screen chest, Alps, ht. 6"	$ 80-100	$ 150-200

	MNB	MIB
Television Spaceman (B #217), gray, plastic legs, TV screen chest, Alps, ht. 10"	300-500	600-900
Terra Lune (B #120), keywind race to the moon toy, Technofix, German, circa 1947, len. 18"	500-700	800-1200
Tetsujin 28-GO (K #218), keywind, in purple Armor, moveable arms, Nomura, ht. 10"	400-600	700-900
Thor Delta 54 (B #141), friction w/ connected capsule, Daiya, ht. 12"	80-100	150-200
Train Robot (K Yesterday of Toys #28), a.k.a. Sonic Robot, large red & black w/ siren, Masudaya, ht. 14"	2500-4000	5000-8000
Traveling Sam the Peace Corps Man, keywind, stars & stripes litho. body w/ global wheels & flapping jaw, Sy Toy, ht. 7"	120-160	250-400
Tremendous Mike (K #36), keywind, gray w/ red arms & bolt-headed shoulders, Aoshin, ht. 10"	700-900	1200-1800
Twirly Whirly Rocket Ride (K #165), 2 rockets orbiting a tripod base, Alps, ht. 12"	200-300	500-800
Two Stage Earth Satellite (B #54), tinplate rocket w/ crankwind base, Linemar, len. 9"	180-220	300-500
Two Stage Rocket Launching Pad (B #102), technician at control panel screen, w/ silo & 2 rockets, Nomura, ht. 7.5"	300-400	500-800
U.N. Planet Cruiser 751 (B #106), w/ light-up rotary engine, len. 10"	180-220	300-400
UFO X-5 flying saucer, Masudaya, dia. 7"	50-70	80-120
Ultra Man (K #197), gray & green, removable mask, Bullmark, ht. 13"	300-400	500-750
Ultra Man Leo (K #200), keywind, red body & green vinyl head, Bull Mark, ht. 9"	400-600	700-900
Unit 5 Area Radiation Tester Vehicle (B #107), manufacturer unknown (Sears Exclusive), len. 19.5"	200-300	400-600
Universe Car (B #189), blue w/ plastic fins & light-up bubble dome, Chinese, len. 10"	80-120	150-200
Uran (K #188), keywind, tinplate body w/ vinyl head (Uran is the younger sister of Tetsuwan Atom), Nomura/Bandai, ht. 8.5"	500-700	800-1100
V-2 Space Tank (B #-28), w/ Robby style robot driver, Yoshiya, len. 6.5"	60-80	100-150
Voyage a la Lune, friction drive, w/ rocket ship on perforated steel band, Gunthermann, len. 7"	180-220	300-400
Wheel-A-Gear Robot (K #31), similar to Blink-a-Gear Robot, gears are belt driven, retractable antenna on back, Taiyo, ht. 14"	1000-1500	1800-2200
Wind Up Moon Astronaut (B #179), red w/ blue helmet, gun in right hand, Daiya, ht. 9"	700-900	1200-1800
Winkie, keywind, gray tinplate w/ red feet, 3-D winking eyes, meter on chest, Yonezawa, ht. 9"	450-550	700-900
Winner-23 (B #185), jet style vehicle, domed cockpit, len. 6"	80-120	200-300
Wizard Of Oz Tin Man Robot, silver & blue plastic, Remco, ht. 21"	80-140	180-220
X-25 Robot, keywind, round human head & oversized glasses, Daiya, ht. 7"	80-120	180-220
X-70 Space Robot (K #121), petals open to TV camera & screen, UK, ht. 12"	800-1200	1500-2300
X-80 Planet Explorer (B #96), saucer w/ light up central dome,		

	MNB	MIB
dia. 8"	$ 40-60	$ 70-90
X-9 Space Robot Car (K #58), robot-driven green car w/ bubble dome w/ pop-up balls, Masudaya, len. 7"	1200-1800	2000-3000
Z Man Missile (B #250) wheeled, friction powered rocket w/ robot pilot, len. 7"	180-220	300-400

Robert the Robot, by Ideal, 1950s.

Schoenhut Animals

Albert Schoenhut began production of the Humpty Dumpty Circus at his Philadelphia toy company in 1903. Advertised as "The World's Most Popular Toy," the animals and personnel are valued today for their lively representations and charm.

For further information we reccommend *Schoenhut's Humpty Dumpty Circus from A to Z*, by Evelyn Ackerman and Fredrick E. Keller, Era Industries, Inc., Los Angeles, California, 1975. Our consultant for this area is Judith Lile (she is listed at the back of this book).

The following chart gives three prices: good, fair, and excellent for Painted Eye, Glass Eye, and Reduced Size figures. The designation *NA* means that the animal was not produced in that style. Collectors look for pieces that are as close to the original as possible; some paint or fabric wear, and missing ears or tails are considered minor flaws, but repaints, touch ups or replaced clothing affect the prices more significantly

Above left to right: Glass Eye Tiger; early style (two-part head) Clown; Glass Eye Leopard. Below left to right: Glass Eye Donkey; Painted Eye Kangaroo. — Photos courtesy of Judith Lile.

Animals

	Painted Eye			GlassEye			Reduced Size		
	Fair	Good	Exc.	Fair	Good	Exc.	Fair	Good	Exc.
Alligator	$ 200	$ 300	$ 375	$ 350	$ 450	$ 550	—	NA	—
Brown Bear	275	375	450	425	550	650	$ 300	$ 375	$ 450
Buffalo, cloth mane	—	NA	—	450	575	650	—	NA	—
Buffalo, carved mane	200	300	375	600	800	1000	250	325	400
Bulldog	600	750	900	900	1250	1600	—	NA	—
Burro	200	300	350	300	375	450	—	NA	—
Camel, 1 hump	275	325	400	350	475	600	—	NA	—
Camel, 2 humps	200	300	375	900	1300	1600	225	325	400
Cat	800	1100	1500	2000	3000	4000	—	NA	—
Cow	300	400	500	400	650	850	—	NA	—
Deer	300	500	700	500	750	950	—	NA	—
Donkey	75	100	125	100	150	200	60	80	100
Elephant	95	150	175	125	200	275	75	100	125
Gazelle	600	750	1000	1200	1700	2200	—	NA	—
Giraffe	275	350	425	400	500	600	275	350	425
Goose	275	375	450	—	NA	—	—	NA	—
Gorilla	1600	2000	2400	—	NA	—	—	NA	—
Hippopotamus	275	350	400	350	500	600	300	375	450
Horse, brown	125	200	250	225	325	400	75	125	150
Horse, white	150	200	275	225	325	400	75	125	150
Hyena	1100	1500	1800	1800	2800	3800	—	NA	—
Kangaroo	600	750	900	800	1100	1300	—	NA	—
Leopard	275	375	450	400	550	700	250	300	350
Lion, cloth mane	—	NA	—	400	550	650	—	NA	—
Lion, carved mane	225	300	350	600	950	1200	250	300	350
Monkey	300	400	500	—	NA	—	—	NA	—
Ostrich	275	375	500	400	550	700	300	450	600
Pig	250	325	375	325	425	500	300	450	600
Polar Bear	550	700	900	1000	1500	1800	—	NA	—
Poodle, cloth mane	—	NA	—	200	275	350	—	NA	—
Poodle, carved mane	150	200	250	600	850	1000	300	400	500
Rabbit	500	650	800	2000	3000	4000	—	NA	—
Rhinocerous	250	350	450	325	500	650	250	350	425
Sea Lion	400	550	675	500	750	950	—	NA	—
Sheep	300	400	500	450	600	750	—	NA	—
Tiger	275	375	450	400	550	700	200	275	325
Wolf	800	1150	1400	1800	2500	3500	—	NA	—
Zebra	225	300	400	400	550	700	225	325	425
Zebu	1000	1350	1600	2000	2500	3500	—	NA	—

Personnel

	Fair	Good	Exc.	Fair	Good	Exc.	Fair	Good	Exc.
Clown	$ 75	$ 100	$ 150	—	NA	—	$ 75	$ 110	$ 135
Gent Acrobat	600	800	1000	$ 300	$ 450	$ 550	—	NA	—
Hobo	200	300	400	—	NA	—	325	425	500
Lady Acrobat	300	400	450	300	450	550	—	NA	—
Lady Circus Rider	225	300	350	275	375	450	175	225	275
Lion Tamer	300	450	600	300	450	600	—	NA	—
Negro Dude	325	400	450	—	NA	—	375	475	550
Ring Master	300	375	450	350	425	525	—	NA	—

Above: two bisque head Gent Acrobats and a Lady Rider. — Photo courtesy of Judith Lile.

Right: Glass Eye White Horse. Below: rare Zebu. — Photos courtesy of Judith Lile.

Scouting Memorabilia

The Englishman Sir Robert S.S. Baden-Powell founded the Boy Scouts and Girl Scouts in England. Daniel Carter Beard, William Boyce and James E. West developed scouting in America with the Boy Scouts of America, and Juliette Gordon Low for the Girl Scouts of America. The groups are separate and distinct.

Scouting memorabilia includes items from not only the Boy Scouts, but also Cub Scouts, Camp Fire Girls, Brownies and Girl Scouts. Collectibles run from cloth badges to metal neckerchief rings and tools, backpacks, uniforms and manuals. There are more collectors of Boy Scout treasures than of Girl Scout memorabilia. Prices are reasonable and fairly stable.

	LOW	AVG.	HIGH
Ashtray, Kit Carson House, Philmont, 1950	$ 14	$ 17	$ 20
Bank, tin lithographed scout, 1912	40	55	70
Belt and Buckle, gun medal, 1930s	14	18	22
Binoculars, tan leather, 1920s	160	180	200
Blotter, BSA/Coca-Cola, "Be Prepared, Be Refreshed"	12	15	17
Bookends, bronze metal, Girl Scout feeding rabbit	45	50	55
Bookends, metal, first class Emblem, 6" x 6"	47	58	70
Bookmark, green and gold, first class emblem, BSA National Council	8	10	12
Books, Holy Bible, early BSA seal on cover	90	110	130
Cachet Cover, Boy Scout stamp club, 1932	19	22	24
Calendar Holder, cast metal, BSA perpetual, first class emblem	35	45	55
Camera, official 7-piece flash camera kit	27	34	42
Canteen, Wearever seamless, felt cover, 1930s	30	40	50
Cards, 65 BSA job description cards, 1949-1962	11	13	15
Collar Monogram, BSA, brass collar monograms, 1920s	80	110	140
Comb, Official BSA comb and clippers in a case	9	12	15
Compass, Sylva pathfinder, BSA	4	7	11
Cut Outs, Camping with the Scouts, gummed paper in book form, 1930s	40	50	60
Drum, "Boy Scout Drum" tin, dia. 6", ht. 3", 1908	80	120	160
Figurine, Head Scout, signaler, arms move, 2"	40	50	60
Figurine, Kenner doll, Craig Cub Scout	30	37	45
Figurine, Lead Scout kneeling, frying eggs	24	27	30
Figurine, Scout plastic figure, tree and flagpole, 3"	18	21	24
Figurine, Scout with pack and rifle, cardboard, ht. 6"	8	10	12
First Aid Kit, Bauer and Black, gray, oval belt loop kit, rare, 1932	40	50	60
First Aid Kit, Johnson and Johnson, swing clasp, 1942	30	40	50

Star Trek Memorabilia

Star Trek first appeared on N.B.C. on September 8, 1966 but lasted only three seasons. When N.B.C. canceled it, enraged fans bombarded the network with over one million letters of protest. Ironically, the show became even more popular in syndication. Reruns spurred the production of books, pins, fanzines, and toys. "Trekkie" fan clubs and conventions evolved. Speculation regarding the series' return was surpassed only by rumors of a Beatles reunion.

Star Trek-the Motion Picture spawned a lot of material, but the 1979 film was a disappointment. Less material was produced for *Star Trek II- The Wrath of Khan*. That film reestablished *Star Trek* and has been followed by five movies and several new TV shows. The films and programs have created a new generation of fans and collectors.

The prices below are based on items in excellent or mint condition. Since the same item can be bought at a variety of locations at different prices, we devised a range system. The low range covers complete, near mint to mint items without the package. The higher range reflects the prices of complete, near mint to mint items in near mint to mint boxes. Prices below are for complete like-new items. Prices of scratched, chipped, or altered examples are not included.

Abbreviations: Regarding manufacturers, *M*-Mego, *G*-Galoob, *E*-Ertl, *R*-Remco, *Ry*-Rayline, *ID*-Ideal, and *B*-Bradley. To conserve space we have shortened some words. After the manufactutrer we also list the production the item was based on: *TVS*-the original TV series, *NGTV-The Next Generation* TV show, *STMP-Star Trek The Motion Picture* (Star Trek I), *ST III*-Star Trek III, The Movie: *The Search for Spock*, and *FF-The Final Frontier Movie*. Most items in this section are action figures and toys followed by a small group of books. Years listed are approximate.

For more information see *The Official Price Guide to Star Wars And Star Trek*, Sue Cornwell and Mike Kott; *Tomart's Price Guide to Action Figure Collectibles*, Carol Markowski, Bill Sikoria, and T.N. Tumbusch; *Greenberg's Guide To Star Trek Collectibles*, Chris Gentry and Sally Gibson-Downs, and *Toy Shop* listed in the front of this book.

Above: Star Trek The Motion Picture Board Game, $10-$15. Right: Star Trek The Next Generation Phaser, mint in package, $18-$22.

Action Figures and Toys

	MAKER	PROD.	YEAR	MNP	MIP
Andorian, 8"	M	TVS	1974	$ 200-250	$ 400-500
Antican, 3.75"	G	NGTV	1988	20-30	40-50
Arcturian, 3.75"	M	STMP	1979	70-90	120-180
Arcturian, 12"	M	STMP	1979	40-50	70-90
Astro Wlke Tlkes	R	TVS	1968	70-90	110-140
Betelgeusian, 3.75"	M	STMP	1979	80-100	180-220
Cheron, 8"	M	TVS	1974	60-90	120-180
Com. Bridge, 3.75"	M	STMP	1979	50-80	100-150
Data, Dark Face, 3.75"	G	NGTV	1988	22-28	45-55
Data, Flesh Face, 3.75"	G	NGTV	1988	10-12	20-30
Data, blue/green face, 3.75"	G	NGTV	1988	50-70	90-140
Data, spot face, 3.75"	G	NGTV	1988	12-14	20-30
Decker, 3.75"	M	STMP	1979	8-12	18-22
Decker, 12"	M	STMP	1979	50-70	90-140
Dr. McCoy, 8"	M	TVS	1974	30-40	55-75
Dr. McCoy, 3.75"	M	STMP	1979	12-14	20-30
Enterprise Bridge, (8" fig.)	M	TVS	1974	80-120	200-250
Ferengi, 3.75"	G	NGTV	1988	20-30	50-60
Ferengi Ftr Veh, 3.75"	G	NGTV	1988	18-25	35-50
Gorn, 8"	M	TVS	1974	80-100	180-220
Ilia, 3.75"	M	STMP	1979	5-8	14-18
Ilia, 12"	M	STMP	1979	25-35	50-75
Kirk, 8"	M	TVS	1974	15-20	30-40
Kirk, 3.75"	M	STMP	1979	8-12	20-30
Kirk, 12"	M	STMP	1979	40-50	80-100
Kirk, 3.75"	E	ST III	1984	6-9	18-22
Kirk, 7"	G	FF	1989	15-18	30-40
Klaa, 7"	G	FF	1989	15-20	30-40
Klingon, 8"	M	TVS	1974	20-25	40-50
Klingon, 12"	M	STMP	1979	50-60	120-160
Klingon, 3.75"	M	STMP	1979	150-200	70-90

U.S.S. Enterprise Playset, Mint in box, $200-$250; Captain Kirk, ht. 8", by Mego mint no package $15-$20; Lt. Uhura, ht. 8", by Mego mint no package $30-$40. — Items courtesy Jim Glaab's Collector's Showcase

	MAKER	PROD.	YEAR	MNP	MIP
Kruge and dog, 3.75"	E	ST III	1984	$ 8-10	$ 22-28
La Forge, 3.75"	G	NGTV	1988	3-5	9-12
Lt. Uhura, 8"	M	TVS	1974	30-40	60-80
McCoy, 7"	G	FF	1989	15-20	35-40
Megarite, 3.75"	M	STMP	1979	90-120	150-200
Mis. Gam. VI, (8" fig.)	M	TVS	1976	250-350	500-700
Mugato, 8"	M	TVS	1974	125-175	250-350
Neptunian, 8"	M	TVS	1974	80-100	140-220
Phaser	R	TVS	1975	35-45	50-80
Phaser Battle Game	M	TVS	—	200-250	350-450
Picard, 3.75"	G	NGTV	1988	5-7	12-15
Q, 3.75"	G	NGTV	1988	25-35	60-80
Rigellian, 3.75"	M	STMP	1979	70-190	140-180
Riker, 3.75"	G	NGTV	1988	3-4	10-12
Romulan, 8"	M	TVS	1974	250-350	500-700
Scotty, 8"	M	TVS	1974	30-40	60-80
Scotty, 3.75"	M	STMP	1979	9-12	18-24
Scotty, 3.75"	E	ST III	1984	7-9	18-22
Selay, 3.75"	G	NGTV	1988	20-30	40-65
Galileo Craft, 3.75"	G	NGTV	1988	18-22	35-45
Spock, 8"	M	TVS	1974	20-25	45-60
Spock, 3.75"	M	STMP	1979	10-15	25-30
Spock, 12"	M	STMP	1979	30-40	60-90
Spock, 3.75"	E	ST III	1984	9-12	20-30
Spock, 7"	G	FF	1989	10-15	25-35
S.T. Bd. Game,	ID	TVS	1966	—	80-120
Sybok, 7"	G	FF	1989	10-15	25-35
Talosian, 8"	M	TVS	1974	120-160	300-350
The Keeper, 8"	M	TVS	1974	80-100	180-220
Tracer Pistol	RY	TVS	1966	50-70	90-110
Tricorder	M	TVS	1976	70-90	120-160
Worf, 3.75"	G	NGTV	1988	3-5	8-12
Watch, Spock	B	STMP	1979	25-35	40-50
Yar, 3.75"	G	NGTV	1988	8-12	15-20
Zaranite, 3.75"	M	STMP	1979	80-100	180-220

*Super Phaser II Target
Game, mint in box, $45-$65.*

Star Trek Books

Abode of Life, Corey, 1982, pbk.	$ 4-6
Best of Trek, 1974 -1991, based on mag., 16 dif., #1-16 pbks., ea.	3-5
Chekov's Enterprise, W. Koenig, 1980, pbk.	15-20
Come and Be With Me, L. Nimoy, 1978, pbk.	18-22
Covenant of the Crown, Weinstein, 1981, hrdcov, ...	8-12
Death's Angel, K. Sky, 1981, pbk.	12-18
Making of Star Trek II, Asherman, 1982, pbk.	14-18
Star Trek Maps, an intro. to navigation, Jeff Maynard, 1980	70-90
Starfleet Medical Manual, Palestine, Ballentine, 1977, ...	15-20
Coloring book, 1968	20-30

Left to right: Trek Times, $6-$8; Ilia Action Figure, by Mego, Star Trek: The Motion Picture, 3.75", if mint on mint card $14-$18, small damage to this card reduces it to $10-$12.

Star Wars Memorabilia

Star Wars burst on to movie screens in 1977. Stunning special effects made it an instant success. Two equally successful sequels followed, *The Empire Strikes Bac*, (ESB), in 1980 and *Return of the Jedi* (ROTJ) in 1983. Star Wars not only revolutionized special effects, it also introduced a smaller sized action figure. Although sizes vary it is generally known as 3.75" or small figures. Most of the following toys are the 3.75" figures and the vehicles made for them. Kenner made the figures and most of the toys listed below.

Dating carded Star Wars figures is relatively easy. The back of each card pictures each figure in the product line; as the line grows so do the number of illustrations. The original 12 figures are refereed to as 12 backs. Packaging is more important in Star Wars items than any other area. The same figure on a Star Wars card is worth more than on an ESB or ROTJ card and an ESB carded figure is worth more than an ROTJ card. Power of The Force (POTF) produced in 1985, is a series of figures that usually include a collector coin. These figures are generally more valuable than ROTJ or ESB. The other factor affecting price is condition. The first prices quoted are for mint items on mint cards. The other range are for mint complete figures. Many times figures came with weapons or clothing. Loose figures are devalued if they are lacking this original equipment. Because Kenner marketed Star Wars toys worldwide, there is an incredible range of packaging variation. The demand for toys and Star War products continues. With anticipation of a new Star War movie in the late 1990s prices have soared. The sharpest increases are for early small figures, produced for the first movie, in mint condition on mint card. Another area that has seen significant increases are the large figures. For more information see *The Official Price Guide To Star Wars And Star Trek*, Sue Cornwell and Mike Kot; *Tomart's Price Guide to Action Figure Collectibles*, Carol Markowski, Bill Skier, and T.N. Tumbusch, and *1995 Toys and Prices, Krause Publications, 1995*

Left: Speeder Bike in original box, Return of the Jedi, $20-$30.

Right: B-Wing Pilot, Power of the Force, mint on card, $16-$20.

	SERIES	FIGURE	IN PACK.
A Wing Pilot	POTF	$ 8-12	$ 50-70
Admiral Ackbar	ROTJ	4-6	18-22
Amanaman	POTF	20-25	90-120
Anakin Skywalker	POTF	20-30	80-100
AT-AT	—	50-70	150-200
AT-AT Commander	ESB	5-7	35-45
AT-AT Driver	ESB	6-8	35-45
AT-ST Driver	ROTJ	4-5	15-20
B-Wing Fighter	ROTJ	25-35	70-90
B-Wing Pilot	ROTJ	4-6	15-20
Barada	POTF	8-12	50-70
Ben Kenobi, large figure	—	90-110	200-250
Ben (Obi-Wan) Kenobi	SW 20/21 back	8-10	90-110
Ben (Obi-Wan) Kenobi	SW 12 back	8-10	100-130
Ben (Obi-Wan) Kenobi	ESB	8-10	50-60
Ben (Obi-Wan) Kenobi	ROTJ	8-10	25-35
Ben (Obi-Wan) Kenobi	POTF	8-10	70-80
Bespin Security Guard, black	ESB	5-7	35-45
Bespin Security Guard, white	ESB	6-8	40-50
Bib Fortuna	ROTJ	5-7	18-24
Biker Scout	ROTJ	4-6	18-22
Blue Snaggletooth, Sears	SW 20/21 back	90-120	—
Boba Fett, large figure	—	100-150	300-400
Boba Fett	SW 20/21 back	20-30	200-250
Boba Fett, working Rocket Launcher	SW (mail in)	25-35	350-450
Bossk (Bounty Hunter)	ESB	8-10	50-65
C-3PO, large figure	Star Wars	50-75	120-160
C-3PO	SW 12 back	8-10	100-125
C-3PO	SW 20/21 back	8-10	70-90
C-3PO	ESB	8-10	40-50
C-3PO, removable limbs	ESB	8-10	45-65
C-3PO	ROTJ	8-10	25-30
C-3PO	POTF	8-10	50-60
C-3PO bust case, gold chrome	—	18-22	45-55
Cantina Adventure Set, Sears	Star Wars	90-130	350-450
Chewbacca, large figure	—	50-65	120-150
Chewbacca	SW 12 back	8-10	90-110
Chewbacca	SW 20/21 back	8-10	60-90
Chewbacca	ESB	8-10	50-70
Chewbacca	ROTJ	8-10	25-35
Chewbacca	POTF	8-10	40-60
Chewbacca bandoiler strap	ROTJ	3-4	12-18
Chief Chirpa	ROTJ	4-6	18-24
Cloud Car Pilot	ESB	5-7	35-45
Creature Cantina	Star Wars	90-110	30-50
Darth Vader, large figure	—	60-80	150-200
Darth Vader	SW 12 back	8-10	100-125
Darth Vader	SW 20/21 back	8-10	70-90
Darth Vader	ESB	8-10	50-70
Darth Vader	ROTJ	8-10	30-40
Darth Vader	POTF	8-10	70-90

Above left to right: R2-D2 with Sensorscope, Return of the Jedi, mint on card, $40-$50; The Emperor, Power of the Force, mint on card, $30-$50.

Above left to right: Darth Vader Two-Piece Mask, $60-$70; C-3PO Collector's Case, Return of the Jedi, sealed, $45-$55.

	SERIES	FIGURE	IN PACK.
Darth Vader 2 part mask .... —		$ 50-60	$ 60-70
Darth Vader bust case (plastic) .... —		18-22	40-50
Darth Vader TIE Fighter .... Star Wars		25-35	80-110
Death Squad Commander .... SW 12 back		8-10	120-180
Death Squad Commander .... SW 20/21 back		8-10	90-110
Death Squad Commander .... ESB		8-10	70-80
Death Squad Commander .... ROTJ		8-10	50-60
Death Star Droid .... SW 20/21 back		8-10	100-130
Death Star Playset .... Star Wars		60-70	150-190
Dengar .... ESB		6-8	40-50
Desert Sail Skiff .... ESB		5-7	18-22
Droid Factory .... Star Wars		25-35	80-120
Early Bird, 4 figures in mailing box .... Star Wars		80-100	400-500
Early Bird kit .... Star Wars		80-100	400-450
8D8 .... ROTJ		4-5	18-24
Emperor's Royal Guard .... ROTJ		4-5	22-26
Endor Forest Ranger vehicle .... ESB		7-9	20-30
EV-9D9 .... POTF		12-18	90-110
Ewok Assault Catapult .... ROTJ		7-9	20-30
Ewok Combat Glider 8 .... ESB		7-9	20-30
Ewok Village .... ROTJ		30-40	70-90
4-Lom .... ESB		6-8	35-55
FX-7 Medical Droid .... ESB		6-8	50-60
Gamorrean Guard .... ROTJ		4-6	15-20
General Madine .... ROTJ		4-6	15-20
Greedo .... SW 20/21 back		8-10	90-110
Hammerhead .... SW 20/21 back		8-10	90-120
Han Solo, large figure .... —		120-180	350-450
Han Solo .... SW 12 back		10-14	300-350
Han Solo .... SW 20/21 back		10-14	200-300
Han Solo .... ESB		10-14	150-200
Han Solo (Bespin outfit) .... ESB		8-10	60-70
Han Solo (Hoth outfit) .... ESB		10-12	45-65
Han Solo .... ROTJ		10-14	20-30
Han Solo, trench coat .... ROTJ		8-10	25-30
Han Solo .... POTF		10-14	90-120
Han Solo in Carbonite Chamber .... POTF		30-40	180-220
Ice Planet Hoth playset .... ESB		35-45	80-120
IG-88, large figure .... —		200-250	400-500
IG-88 (Bounty Hunter) .... ESB		6-8	45-55
Imperial Commander .... ESB		5-7	30-40
Imperial Dignitary .... POTF		8-12	40-60
Imperial Gunner .... POTF		8-12	60-80
Imperial Shuttle .... ROTJ		30-50	150-200
Imperial Stormtrooper (Hoth battle gear) .... ESB		10-15	70-90
Imperial TIE Fighter vehicle .... Star Wars		25-35	80-110
Imperial Tie Fighter Pilot .... ESB		5-7	55-75
Imperial Troop Transporter .... Star Wars		25-30	90-120
Jabba the Hutt Throne .... ROTJ		10-12	35-45
Jawa, large figure .... —		60-80	175-225
Jawa, cloth cape .... SW 12 back		10-12	100-150

Above: Millennium Falcon, unboxed, $60-$80.

Below left to right: Yoda handpuppet, unboxed, $18-$22; Sy Snootles and the Rebo Band, Return of the Jedi, mint on card, $50-$70.

	SERIES	FIGURE	IN PACK.
Jawa, plastic cape .... SW 12 back		$ 70-90	$ 300-500
Jawa, cloth cape .... SW 20/21 back		10-12	80-90
Jawa, cloth cape .... ESB		10-12	70-90
Jawa, cloth cape .... ROTJ		10-12	30-40
Jawa, cloth cape .... POTF		10-12	50-60
Klaatu .... ROTJ		4-6	15-20
Klaatu, Skiff Guard outfit .... ROTJ		4-6	18-22
Lando Calrissian .... ESB		8-10	35-45
Lando Calrissian, Skiff guard disguise .... ROTJ		6-8	18-24
Lando Calrissian, General Pilot .... POTF		9-14	40-50
Landspeeder .... Star Wars		20-30	50-70
Laser rifle case .... ROTJ		15-20	35-45
Lobot .... ESB		6-8	35-45
Logray .... ROTJ		3-5	15-20
Luke Skywalker .... ROTJ		10-14	25-35
Luke Skywalker .... ESB		10-14	40-60
Luke Skywalker .... SW 20/21 back		10-14	70-90
Luke Skywalker .... SW 12 back		10-14	200-300
Luke Skywalker, battle poncho .... POTF		18-22	70-90
Luke Skywalker (Bespin fatigues) .... ESB		8-10	90-110
Luke Skywalker (Hoth battle gear) .... ESB		8-10	60-80
Luke Skywalker (Jedi knight outfit) .... ROTJ		10-15	60-80
Luke Skywalker, large figure .... —		90-120	200-300
Luke Skywalker, Stormtrooper outfit .... POTF		20-30	120-180
Luke Skywalker X-Wing Pilot .... SW 20/21 back		10-14	100-130
Lumat .... POTF		8-12	30-40
Millennium Falcon Spaceship .... Star Wars		60-80	150-220
Nien Nunb .... ROTJ		4-6	18-24
Nikto .... ROTJ		4-6	15-20
Paploo .... POTF		8-12	30-40
Patrol Dewback Playset .... SW		15-20	40-50
Power Droid .... SW 20/21 back		8-10	90-110
Princess Leia, large figure .... —		90-120	200-300
Princess Leia .... SW 12 back		10-14	200-300
Princess Leia .... SW 20/21 back		8-10	220-260
Princess Leia (Bespin gown) .... ESB		15-20	60-80
Princess Leia, Hoth outfit .... ESB		8-10	45-60
Princess Leia, combat poncho .... ROTJ		10-12	30-40
Princess Leia .... ESB		10-14	180-220
Princess Leia (Boushh disguise) .... ROTJ		10-15	40-50
Prune Face .... ROTJ		5-7	15-20
R2-D2, large figure .... —		50-60	120-150
R2-D2 .... SW 12 back		8-10	90-120
R2-D2 .... SW 20/21 back		10-14	70-90
R2-D2 .... ESB		8-10	40-60
R2-D2, sensorscope .... ESB		8-10	40-50
R2-D2 .... ROTJ		8-10	25-30
R2-D2, pop-up lightsaber .... POTF		25-35	80-100
R5-D4 .... SW 20/21 back		8-10	80-100
Rancor Keeper .... ROTJ		4-5	15-20
Rancor Monster .... ROTJ		10-15	35-45

	SERIES	FIGURE	IN PACK.
Rebel Armored Snowspeeder, vehicle	ESB	$ 30-40	$ 80-100
Rebel Commander	ESB	5-7	30-40
Rebel Commando	ROTJ	4-6	18-22
Rebel Soldier (Hoth battle gear)	ESB	6-8	40-50
Rebel Transport	ESB	25-35	80-100
Ree-Yees	ROTJ	4-6	14-18
Romba	POTF	8-12	30-40
Sand People (Tusken Raider)	SW 12 back	9-12	120-180
Sand People (Tusken Raider)	SW 20/21 back	9-12	90-130
Sand People (Tusken Raider)	ESB	9-12	70-80
Sand People (Tusken Raider)	ROTJ	9-12	45-60
Scout Walker	ESB	20-25	60-90
Slave 1	ESB	30-40	80-120
Snaggletooth	SW 20/21 back	8-10	90-110
Speeder Bike	ROTJ	7-9	20-30
Squid Head	ROTJ	18-22	5-7
Stormtrooper, large figure	—	60-80	200-250
Stormtrooper	SW 12 back	7-9	100-125
Stormtrooper	SW 20-21 back	7-9	60-80
Stormtrooper	ESB	7-9	50-60
Stormtrooper	ROTJ	7-9	100-125
Stormtrooper	POTF	7-9	50-60
Sy Snootles and the Rebo Band, boxed	ROTJ	20-30	50-70
Tauntaun, solid belly	ESB	10-15	25-35
Tauntaun with split belly	ESB	12-18	40-50
Teebo	ROTJ	4-6	18-22
The Emperor	ROTJ	8-10	25-30
Twin-Pod Cloud Car	ESB	20-25	60-90
2-1B	ESB	6-8	50-70
Ugnaught	ESB	6-8	50-60
Walrus Man	SW 20/21 back	8-10	90-110
Warok	POTF	8-12	30-40
Weequay	ROTJ	4-6	18-22
Wicket W. Warrick	ROTJ	5-7	18-22
X-Wing Fighter, battle damage	SW	25-35	90-110
X-Wing Fighter Vehicle	SW	25-35	90-110
Y-Wing Fighter	ROTJ	30-40	80-100
Yak Face	ROTJ	70-90	150-200
Yoda	ESB	6-8	45-55
Yoda handpuppet	—	18-22	30-40
Zuckuss	ESB	6-8	40-55

Still Banks

Still banks are aptly named since there are no mechanical actions required to make the deposit. When collecting still banks, beware of rust, reproductions, and repaints.

The M numbers in the following listing refer to *The Penny Bank Book*, Andy and Susan Moore, Schiffer Publishing, Exton, PA, 1984. The book includes photographs and names of manufacturers of most of the banks listed below. Unless specified, the following banks are made of cast iron. When bronze or copper is noted this refers to the type of finish, just as gold and silver refer to paint colors. Banks featuring several colors are described as "multi." In some cases we have listed paint variations under the description as *var.* (They may have another Moore number that we have not listed.) All measurements are approximate.

Prices are for examples in excellent condition (at least 90% paint intact). These pieces should have no major paint loss, no cracks, repairs, or repaints. Such faults decrease the value of a bank. Mint or near mint condition examples will command a premium price, 20%-50% more than the prices listed below.

Our consultants for this area are Leon and Steven Weiss, owners of Gemini Antiques in New York City, who specialize in antique toys, and still and mechanical banks (they are listed in the back of this book).

Still banks provided a child with a toy that encouraged thrift and saving. Buildings were a popular theme.

	LOW	HIGH
Air Mail on Stand, red, blue, & white accents, ht. 6.38", M848	$ 200	$ 300
Bank of Columbia, nickel, ht. 4.88", M906	100	200
Baseball Player, gold, red, & flesh-tone /var., ht. 5.75", M18	300	400
Basket, woven, bronze finish, ht. 2.88", M917	75	125
Basset Hound, gold, ht. 3.13", M380	800	1000
Bean Pot Nickel Register, red, nickel-finish top, dia. 3.5", M951	150	200
Billiken, gold, ht. 4.13", M74	50	100
Billiken, on throne, gold, red & black, accents, ht. 6.38", M73	100	200
Blackpool Tower, unpainted, ht. 7.38", M984	200	250
Bucket Penny Register, nickel, ht. 2.75", M912	100	150
Buffalo Amherst Stoves, black, ht. 4.38", M556	150	200
Buffalo, small, gold, len. 4.38", M560	100	150
Bungalow, ht. 3.75", M999	200	300
Buster Brown & Tige, gold, red, & multi /var., ht. 5.5", M241	150	200
Captain Kidd, multi, ht. 5.75", M38	300	350
Castle, bronze, ht. 4", M1088	500	700
Cat on Tub, gold, ht. 4.13ʰ, M358	150	200
Cat, w/ ball, gray, ht. 2.5", M352	200	250
Church Towers, ht. 6.75", M956	1200	1500
Clown, gold, red accents, ht. 6.25", M211	75	100

	LOW	HIGH
Colonial House, w/ porch, gold, ht. 3", M993	$ 150	$ 200
Cupola Bank, red, len. 5.5", M1145	300	500
Dog on Tub, gold, ht. 4", M359	150	200
Dog seated, "Cutie," black, red accents, ht. 3.88", M414	100	150
Double-Door Bank Build., dark, gold accents, ht. 5.5", M1125	150	225
Eiffel Tower Bank, ht. 10.38", M1075	700	900
1884 Bank, Small Rabbit, oval base, green & white, ht. 2.25", M569	1200	1500
Elephant on Tub, gold, ht. 5.5", M483	75	100
Elephant on Wheels, ht. 4", M446	250	300
Elephant w/ chariot, gray, red & yellow, len. 7.25", M467	300	400
Elephant w/ howdah, gray, silver & gold, ht. 3.5", M477	75	100
Elephant w/ howdah, large, gold, ht. 4.88", M474	125	175
Empire State Building, lead, ht. 5.63", M1046	100	150
Fidelity Safe, large, black or green, gold trim, ht. 3.5", M863	200	300
Fido, black & gold, red, white trim, ht. 5", M417	50	75
Flat Iron Building, silver, gold trim, small trap, ht. 5.75", M1160	300	450
Frowning Face, ht. 5.75", M12	1000	1200
General Butler, multi, ht. 6.5", M54	2000	2500
Give Billy a Penny, silver, or red, black & flesh-tone, ht. 4.75", M15	300	400
Globe Savings Fund 1888, multi, ht. 7", M1199	1200	1500
Golliwog, multi, ht. 6.25", M85	400	600
High Rise, silver, gold accents, ht. 5.5", M1217	300	400
Home Bank, bronze w/ green wash, ht. 4", M1019	400	500
Horse on Tub, silver paint, ht. 5.5", M510	200	250
Independence Hall, len. 9.38", M1242	1000	1200
Independence Hall, gold, len. 15.5", M1243	2000	3000
Independence Hall, bronze, ht. 9.38", M1244	700	900
Independence Hall Tower, ht. 9.5", M1202	400	600
Indian, w/ tomahawk, multi, ht. 6", M228	200	250
Labrador, black, gold collar, ht. 4.63", M412	300	400
Liberty Bell, Harper, bronze, ht. 3.75", M780	500	700
Lighthouse, ht. 10", M1115	1500	2200
Lion, gold, red accents, ht. 5", M754	50	75
Lion, gold, red accents, ht. 4", M755	50	75
Lion on Tub, decorated, gold, red, & blue, ht. 5.5", M746	100	150
Lion on Tub, small, gold, ht. 4.13", M747	100	150
Lion on Wheels, gold, ht. 4.63", M760	250	300
Litchfield Cathedral, ht. 6.5", M968	200	250
Main Street Trolley, no passengers, gold paint, len. 6.75", M1469	250	350
Middy Bank, metallic finish, ht. 5.13", M36	100	200
Mosque Bank, w/ combination door, gold, ht. 5.13", M1176	300	400
Old Doc Yak, multi, ht. 4.5", M30	600	800
Old Doc Yak, silver, ht. 4.5", M30	500	600
Old South Church, ht. 5.63", M990	2000	2500
Old South Church, ht. 13", M991	4000	5000
One-Car Garage, gold paint, ht. 2.5", M1009	200	300
Palace, black, gold accents, ht. 7.5", M1116	1500	2200
Pershing, copper, ht. 7.75", M150	100	150
Policeman, ht. 5.5", M182	300	400
Polish Rooster, ht. 5.5", M541	1200	1800
Prancing Horse, large, gold, ht. 7.25", M520	100	150

	LOW	HIGH
Prancing Horse, oval base, black, ht. 5.13", M513	$ 100	$ 150
Presto Trick Bank, black & red, ht. 4.5", M1171	400	500
Pupo on Pillow, black & white, ht. 5.5", M442	150	200
Rabbit, Begging, gold, red accents, ht. 5.13", M566	150	200
Roof Bank, dark, gold accents, ht. 5.25", M1122	150	225
Rooster, ht. 4.75", M548	100	150
Safe, Arabian, desert scenes, ht. 4.5", M882	100	150
Safe, Time, nickel, ht. 7.13", M895	350	450
Save & Smile Money Bank, black w/ red lips, ht. 4.25", M24	350	450
Scottie (white metal), red, white or black, ht. 4.75", M433	50	75
Security Safe, Black, gold accents, ht. 6", M889	150	200
Six-Sided Building, ht. 2.5", M1007	150	200
Skyscraper Bank, silver, gold accents, ht. 5.5", M1240	75	100
Soldier, gold, ht. 6", M44	300	400
Spitz, gold, ht. 4.25", M409	300	400
St. Bernard, w/ pack, dark, gold & silver, ht. 5.38", M437	100	150
State Bank, brown, gold accents, ht. 5.75", M1080	75	100
Statue of Liberty, silver, ht. 6.38", M1165	100	150
Tally-Ho, brown, gold & silver, ht. 4.5", M535	125	175
Teddy Roosevelt, gold, silver, & red, ht. 5", M120	200	250
Three "No Evils" Monkeys, gold, len. 3.5", M743	200	250
Tower Bank, comb. lock, red & black, gilt, ht. 7", M1198	1000	1200
Turkey, large, bronze w/ red, ht. 4.25", M585	300	350
Two-Car Garage, silver & blue, ht. 2.5", M1010	200	300
Two Kids, black, green & silver, ht. 4.38", M594	600	800
Two-Faced black boy, large, black & gold, ht. 4.13", M83	150	225
Two-Faced black boy, small, gold & black, ht. 3", M84	75	125
Two-Faced Devil, red, black, & white, ht. 4.25", M31	600	800
U.S. Mail, silver, red trim, comb. trap, ht. 4.75", M835	100	150

Tonka Toys

Tonka began as Mound Metal works in 1946. The firm later moved to Minnetonka, MN. Tonka toys became the post-war symbol of well crafted American toy. In an industry that was turning increasingly to plastic and smaller sizes Tonka's large light pressed steel vehicles ruled sandbox construction sites. Since children used them for heavy duty projects and often left them outside (mom's often banished the heavy toys from the house) condition of Tonka toys is often poor.

In the following listing we give two price ranges, the first, excellent is for a toy that has some light wear but no significant rust or major paint loss, the second is for near mint examples in excellent original boxes. Keep in mind that collectors often pay a hefty premium for mint in mint box examples. Such toys may bring more than prices quoted below. Rusty, damaged pieces will bring significantly less than those in excellent or better condition. For further information see *Collector's Guide to Tonka Trucks*, 1947-1963, Don and Barb DeSalle, L-W Book Sales, Gas City, IN, and *Collecting Toys*, #7, Richard O'Brien, Books Americana, Florence, Alabama, 1995.

	GOOD	MINT
Allied Van Lines #400, 1953	$ 90-110	$ 190-240
Big Mike State Hi-Way Dept. Dump Truck #45, orange w/ V-shape plow, 1958	250-350	500-700
Big Mike State Hi-Way Dept. Dump Truck #45, orange, 1957	200-300	400-600
Car Carrier #840, yellow w/ 3 cars, 1963	200-300	400-500
Carnation Milk Delivery Van #750, 1955	150-200	300-350
Carry-All Tractor Trailer w/ Crane & Clam #170 & #150, yellow & green, 1949	200-250	300-400
Carry-All Tractor Trailer #120, red cab blue trailer, 1949	100-120	180-220
Carry-All Tractor Trailer #120, blue cab, blue trailer w/ #50 Steam Shovel, 1949	200-250	300-400
Cement Truck #120, red & white, 1960	200-250	300-400
Clipper Boat & Trailer # AC360, 1960	80-120	200-250
Crane & Clam #150, yellow & black, 1947	90-140	200-300
Crane & Clam w/ tracks #150, yellow & black, 1949	80-120	200-250
Dump Truck #180, red & green, 1949	100-150	200-250
Dump Truck, red cab, green box, 1955	70-90	160-210
Fire Truck, Hydraulic Aerial Ladder, red w/ # 5 & TFD decals, 1957	200-230	300-400
Gasoline Truck #33, red, 1958	250-400	500-700
Grain Hauler #550, semi, red cab w/ aluminum box, 1952	90-150	200-250
Green Giant Tractor Trailer Transport #650, white w/ green giant decals, 1953	120-180	250-300
Green Giant Utility Truck #175, white w/ Green Giant decals & solid rubber tires, 1953	120-160	280-320
Hydraulic Dump Truck, brown, 1957	70-90	160-210
Jeep Wrecker #375, white, w/ winch & plow, 1964	200-300	400-600
Livestock Semi #500, red, 1952	80-140	190-240
Log Hauler #575, red cab, 1953	90-130	200-250
Minute Maid Box Van #750 w/ dual rear wheels, 1955	250-350	400-600
Pickup Truck #02, bronze, 1960	60-90	120-180
Pickup Truck #02, dark blue, 1956	100-150	200-300
Pickup Truck #02, dark blue, 1958	60-90	120-180
Pickup Truck w/ camper #530, 1963	100-150	200-250
Pickup Truck, Sportsman #05, dark blue w/ cap, 1958	90-130	180-220

	GOOD	MINT
Power lift Truck & Trailer #200, 1948	$ 120-160	$ 200-250
Rescue Van #105, 1960-61	100-150	200-300
Road Grader #600, 1953	50-70	90-110
Sanitary System Truck, #140, rounded back, 1960	250-300	400-500
Sanitary System Truck, #B203, square back, w/ bins & scoop, 1959	300-400	500-700
Ser-vi-Car, # 201, 3 wheel cart, white	60-80	100-130
Star-Kist Tuna Box Van #725, 1954	250-350	400-600
State Hi-Way Dept. Dump Truck, orange, 1956	90-1120	200-250
State Hi-Way Dept. Dump Truck orange w/ side dump, 1957	90-130	200-300
Steam Shovel #100, red & black w/ tracks, 1949	80-130	200-250
Steam Shovel #100, red & black, wheels, 1947	80-130	200-250
Steam Shovel #50, red & blue, 1949	80-120	180-220
Steel Carrier Tractor Trailer #145, cab orange or yellow w/ green box, 1950	100-130	200-250
Suburban Pumper #46 Fire Truck, red w/ # 5 decal & fire hydrant, 1956	200-230	300-400
Tonka Air Express Box Van & "piggyback" trailer, 1959	180-220	350-450
Tonka Farms Stock Rack Truck, 1957	200-250	350-400
Tonka Marine Service #41, blue semi w/ 4 boats, 1959	250-350	450-550
Tonka Service Van #103, 1961	80-130	180-230
Tonka Tanker, 1960	150-200	350-450
Tonka Toy Transport Tractor Trailer #140, red, box features opening doors, 1949	200-250	300-400
Utility Truck #175, Green cab w/ yellow body, 1950	80-130	180-220
Wrecker Truck #250, 1953	100-150	220-280

Fire Engine Suburban Pumper #46, 1956, $200-$230 (unboxed with fire hydrant). — Photo courtesy of George Kerrigan Photography.

Toy and Miniature Soldiers

The soldiers in the following section are lead. Of the various producers of toys and miniature soldiers, we chose Britains, Mignot, and Courtenay.

In 1893 William Britain, founder of a London toy firm, and his sons developed hollow-cast lead toy soldiers. They were cheaper to produce and ship than earlier solid figures. They were packaged in distinctive red boxes with elaborate labels. They established 54mm (2 1/8") as a standard size, and by the early 1900s were outproducing their German and French competitors. Britains production reached a peak between the two world wars and in the 1950s. Pre-World War II sets usually command a premium price and are listed as pre-war in the descriptions below. Production of hollow cast lead figures ceased in 1966. The company now produces a new line of metal toy soldiers and plastic figures. Because Britains improved designs and updated uniforms over the years, there can be many variations of the same set. For further information see *The Art of the Toy Soldier,* Henry I. Kurtz and Burtt R. Ehrlich, Abbeville Press, NY, 1987; and *Britains Toy Soldiers 1893-1932,* James Opie, Harper and Row, NY, 1985.

Three French toy makers founded C.B.G. Mignot in the 1820s. The firm is known for fine quality 55mm toy soldiers representing the French army, with special emphasis on the Napoleonic Wars and World War I. Although still in existence, production is limited, and figures are made for collectors rather than children. The sets listed below were made in the 1970s and '80s. Dates following descriptions refer to the period of the unit represented rather than the year of production. For further information see *The Art of the Toy Soldier,* Henry I. Kurtz and Burtt R. Ehrlich, Abbeville Press, NY, 1987.

Although Richard Courtenay began by producing a line of toy figures in the 1920s, he is best known for his line of high quality, miniature medieval knights, produced from 1938 to 1963. These spectacular figures are now highly sought by connoisseur collectors. The figures represent knights of the 100 Years War, specifically, the Battle of Poitiers (1356). Courtenay assigned numerical designations according to the position of the knight, e.g. a knight lunging with battle ax is position 7. We have listed position numbers in the descriptions below. Courtenay signed many of his figures but not all. An unsigned figure will bring approximately 20% less than the prices listed. For further information see *Heraldic Miniature Knights*, Peter Greenhill, Guild of Master Craftsmen, East Sussex, 1991.

We list two price ranges for Britains and Mignot sets: one for excellent unboxed sets, the second for excellent to near mint condition sets in their original boxes. Courtenay figures are listed with one range for excellent to near mint condition, no box. Set numbers and the number of figures are included for Britains. Prices are based primarily on recent auction results.

Our consultant for this section is Henry Kurtz, co-author of *The Art of the Toy Soldier* and president of Henry Kurtz Limited, an auction house specializing in toy and miniature soldiers. He is a member of the Appraisers Association of America and is listed in the back of this book.

Britains

	# OF FIG.	SET #	UNBOXED	BOXED
11th Hussars, pre-war	5	12	$ 200-250	$ 300-400
16th/5th Lancers, pre-war	5	33	125-150	225-275
1st King George V's Own Gurkha Rifles	8	197	100-125	150-200
3rd Hussars	5	13	300-350	500-600
4.5 Inch Anti-Aircraft Gun	—	1522	200-250	300-400
4th/7th Dragoon Guards, pre-war	5	127	300-350	500-600
6th Dragoon Guards, pre-war	15	106	300-350	500-600
7th Bengal Infantry, pre-war	8	1342	250-350	600-700
9th Queen's Royal Lancers, pre-war	5	24	150-175	250-300

Above: Prewar boxed set of Britains.
Right: Courtenay mounted knight.
Below: Three sets of Mignot soldiers.
— Photos courtesy of Phillips
Auctioneers.

	# OF FIG.	SET #	UNBOXED	BOXED
Arabs of the Desert on Foot, Camels, Horses .	11	224	$ 200-250	$ 300-400
Argyll and Sutherland Highlanders, pre-war	8	15	125-150	200-250
Armoured Car	—	1321	200-250	300-400
Band of the Life Guards in State Dress	12	101	300-400	400-500
Band of the Royal Air Force	12	2116	400-500	700-900
Band of the Royal Berkshire Regiment	25	2093	800-1000	1000-1500
Band of the Royal Marines	12	1291	200-300	400-500
Bikanir Camel Corps, pre-war	3	123	250-350	400-500
Black Watch	6	11	80-100	150-175
Black Watch, pre-war	8	11	125-150	200-250
British Infantry	8	195	80-100	150-175
British Infantry in Tropical Dress	8	1924	200-250	400-500
British Territorial Infantry	8	1537	300-350	400-500
Cameronians	7	1913	700-900	1000-1500
Changing of the Guard	83	1555	600-800	1000-1500
Chinese Infantry	8	241	200-250	350-450
Coldstream Guards	8	2082	90-120	150-200
Coldstream Guards, Three Positions	24	90	450-550	600-800
Colour Party of the Black Watch	6	2111	350-450	500-700
Danish Life Guard	7	2019	200-250	350-450
Drum and Fife Band of the Line	17	321	500-700	1000-1500
Drums and Fifes of the Welch Guards	12	2108	500-700	900-1200
Duke of Connaught's Own Lancers	5	66	100-125	150-200
Egyptian Camel Corps	3	48	125-150	200-250
Egyptian Cavalry	5	115	125-150	175-225
Fire Fighters of the Royal Air Force	8	1758	400-500	700-900
French Foreign Legion in Action	8	2095	200-250	350-450
French Infantry of the Line, pre-war	8	141	200-250	300-400
Gentlemen at Arms	9	2149	500-700	1000-1200
Gordon Highlanders	6	77	80-100	150-175
Gov. General's Horse Guards of Canada	5	1631	125-150	175-225
Greek Evzones	8	196	90-120	150-175
Grenadier Guards	8	312	90-120	150-200
Her Majesty's State Coach	10	1470	200-250	300-400
Indian Army Service Corps	8	1893	120-140	175-225
Italian Cavalry	5	165	400-500	800-1000
Italian Infantry	8	166	250-300	400-500
Japanese Infantry, pre-war	8	134	400-500	700-900
Knight with Mace (mounted, Agincourt)	1	1569	90-120	125-150
Knight with Sword (mounted, Agincourt)	1	1660	90-120	125-150
Knights of Agincourt on Foot	4	1664	100-125	150-200
Life Guards	5	400	100-125	150-200
Mexican Infantry (Rurales), pre-war	8	186	300-350	500-700
Mounted Band of the Life Guards	12	101	300-350	400-500
Mounted Band of the Royal Scots Greys	7	1720	250-350	500-600
Mountain Gun of the Royal Artillery	12	28	200-250	300-400
New Zealand Infantry	8	1542	100-125	175-225
Papal Swiss Guards	9	2022	150-175	250-300
Pipe Band of the Black Watch	20	2109	600-800	1000-1200
Prussian Hussars	5	153	200-300	350-450
Regiment Louw Wepener	8	1900	500-600	900-1200

	# OF FIG.	SET #	UNBOXED	BOXED
Rodeo Set	12	2043	$ 200-300	$ 400-500
Royal Company of Archers	13	2079	200-250	300-400
Royal Engineers Pontoon Sect., Rev. Order	7	203	500-600	800-1000
Royal Horse Artillery at the Gallop	13	39	300-400	400-600
Royal Marine Light Infantry	8	97	500-600	900-1200
Royal Marines	7	2071	90-120	150-200
Royal Marines in Tropical Dress	8	1619	500-700	900-1200
Royal Navy Landing Party	11	79	200-250	300-400
Royal Scots Greys, pre-war	5	32	125-150	200-250
Royal Welch Fusiliers	8	74	80-100	150-200
Russian Infantry	8	133	175-225	300-400
Seaforth Highlanders	17	2062	300-350	500-600
Somersetshire Light Infantry	8	17	125-150	200-250
South Australian Lancers	5	49	300-350	600-800
Standard Bearer, mounted, Agincourt	1	1662	100-125	150-175
State Open Road Landau	10	9402	300-350	400-450
U.S. Cavalry	8	228	90-120	150-175
U.S. Marine Corps	8	228	90-120	150-200
U.S. Marine Corps Band in Summer Dress	25	2112	1000-1500	2000-2500
U.S. Marine Corps Color Guard	4	2101	150-200	200-300
U.S. Military Band "The Snowdrops"	12	1301	300-400	500-700
U.S. Navy Blue Jackets, pre-war	8	230	125-150	200-250
U.S. Navy White Jackets	8	1253	100-125	150-200
Uruguayan Cavalry	4	220	100-125	200-250
Venezuelan Infantry	15	2105	175-225	300-350
Waterloo Period Line Infantry, 1815	9	1518	150-200	200-300
West India Regiment	9	19	200-300	400-500
West Point Cadets	8	299	90-120	150-175
Yeomen of the Guard	9	1257	125-150	200-250
Zulu Warriors of Africa	8	147	100-125	150-200

Mignot

	# OF FIG.	UNBOXED	BOXED
Departmental Guard of Paris (1810)	12	$ 125-175	$ 200-250
English First Life Guards (1815)	6	125-150	200-250
Fr. Napoleonic Marines of the Guard	12	150-175	250-300
Israeli Infantry in Action	12	200-250	250-350
Legion of the North (1806)	12	150-175	250-300
Monaco Royal Guards	12	150-175	200-300
Mounted Band of the Polish Lancers (1810)	11	400-500	700-900
Vistula Legion (1808)	12	150-175	250-300

Courtenay

	SINGLE FIGURE
Boy Prince Philip "Le Hardi," position 21	$ 300-350
Erle of Armagnac, position Z-5	350-450
Erle of Rochechouaret, position 12	300-350
Fallen Knight, Sieur de la Rosay, position 13	350-450
French Knight Matthew de Rouvray, position 7	300-350
King John of France, position 3	350-450
Lord de Chargny, position 6	600-800

SINGLE FIGURE

Lord de la Warr, position 15 .... $ 300-350
Pierre, Sieur de Loigny, position 15 600-800
Sieur de Basentian, position 14 300-400
Sieur John de Landis, position Z-2 300-400
Sir Bartholomew Burghursh, position H-1 500-700
Sir John de Clinton, position H-2 600-800
Sir John Treffrey, position X-2 350-450
Sir Nele Loring, K.G., position H-6 600-800
Sir Thomas Warenhale, position H-3 600-800
Sir William Thorne, position 16 300-400

Lionel Trains

Joshua Lionel Cohen founded America's best-known toy train producer, Lionel, in 1901. In the following descriptions we give the numbers and titles of various locomotives and cars. Descriptions of locomotives contain the wheel configuration, such as 4-4-4; four forward wheels, four wheels in the middle and four in the back. Locomotive descriptions contain engine type, steam or electric (elec.). This describes the style of the locomotive, not the power that runs the toy. Unless otherwise noted, electricity is the power source The number of some locomotives is followed by *E*, which refers to an E-Unit reverse system. *Sp* following a number stands for Special. Gauge for cars and locomotives is listed, such as *Std.* (Standard), and *O*. Gauge refers to the track width. Although specific years are not listed, *post* and *pre* indicate if an item was produced before WW II (pre) or after WW II (post).

The following prices are given in a double-range format. The first range for items in good condition, having scrapes and some light corrosion. The second range is for items in excellent or like-new condition.

There are many variations of Lionel trains. Color and stylistic differences can dramatically influence prices. The prices below, unless specified, are for the more common variations.

For further information we recommend *Lionel Trains Standard of the World*, Donald S. Fraley, M.D., Ed., Train Collectors Association, 1976; *Greenberg's Pocket Price Guide to Lionel Trains*, Allen W. Miller, Kalmbach Publishing, Waukesha, WI, 1994; *Greenberg's Guide To Trains*, 1901-42, volumes I-III; and *Greenberg's Guide to Trains 1945-69*, volumes I-VI. The Train Collector's Association can be reached at TCA, P.O. Box 248, 300 Paradise Lane, Strasberg, PA 17579, 717-687-8623.

Our consultant for this area is Stuart Waldman collector and owner of Toy Treasures specializing in Trains and Antique Toys (he is listed in the back of this book).

Original boxes, like the one pictured above, add value to the set. - photo courtesy of Phillips Auctioneers.

	GOOD	EXCELLENT
5, Loco 0-4-0, No Tender, steam, Std., pre	$ 450-550	$ 650-750
6, Loco 4-4-0, steam, Std., pre	450-550	650-750
6, Sp., Loco 0-4-0, steam, Std., pre	1400-1600	2800-3200
7, Loco 4-4-0, steam, Std., pre	1800-2200	2800-3000
9E, Loco 0-4-0, elec., Std., pre	550-650	900-1100
10, Loco 0-4-0, elec., Std., pre	90-110	180-220
16, Ballast, Std., pre	90-110	140-160
17, Caboose, Std., pre	65-80	90-110
31, Combine, Std., pre	60-80	90-100
32, Mail, Std., pre	60-80	90-100
33, Loco 0-4-0, elec., Std., pre	60-80	90-110
33, Loco 0-6-0, elec., Std., pre	400-600	800-1000
34, Loco 0-6-0, elec., Std., pre	400-600	900-1100
38, Loco 0-4-0, elec., Std., pre	90-110	180-200
42, Loco 0-4-4-0, square, elec., Std., pre	450-550	1100-1300
50, Loco 0-4-0, elec., Std., pre	90-110	180-220
53, Loco 0-4-4-0, elec., Std., pre	1800-2200	3500-4000
53, Loco 0-4-0, elec., Std., pre	900-1100	1400-1600
54, Loco 0-4-4-0, elec., Std., pre	2800-3000	3800-4000
61 Sp., Loco 0-4-4-0, Schwartz, elec., Std., pre	900-1100	1800-2200
117, Caboose, Std., pre	45-55	60-80
150, Loco 0-4-0, elec., O, pre	60-80	90-110
152, Loco 0-4-0, elec., O, pre	90-100	110-130
153, Loco 0-4-0, elec., O, pre	90-100	110-130
154, Loco 0-4-0, elec., O, pre	140-160	180-220
156, Loco 0-4-0, elec., O, pre	280-320	450-500
158, Loco 0-4-0, elec., O, pre	90-110	140-160
201, Loco 0-6-0, steam, O, pre	280-320	380-420
203, Loco 0-6-0, steam, O, pre	280-320	380-420
203, Loco 0-4-0, armored, elec., O, pre	650-750	900-1100
204, Loco 2-4-2, steam, O, pre	90-110	140-160
214R, Refrigerator, Std., pre	280-320	575-600
224E, Loco 2-6-2, steam, O, pre	140-160	180-200
225E, Loco 2-6-2, steam, O, pre	160-180	220-260
226E, Loco 2-6-4, steam, O, pre	240-260	340-380
227, Loco 0-6-0, steam, O, pre	450-550	650-760
228, Loco 0-6-0, steam, O, pre	650-750	900-1100
229, Loco 2-4-2, steam, O, pre	60-80	90-110
233, Loco 0-6-0, steam, O, pre	900-1100	1400-1600
238, Loco 4-4-2, steam, O, pre	140-160	180-220
248, Loco 0-4-0, elec., O, pre	40-60	80-100
249, Loco, steam, O, pre	140-160	180-220
250, Loco 0-4-0, elec., O, pre	40-60	90-110
250E, Loco 0-4-0, Hiawatha, steam, O, pre	450-550	700-800
251, Loco 0-4-0, elec., O, pre	180-220	380-420
252, Loco 0-4-0, elec., O, pre	60-80	90-110
253E, Loco 0-4-0, elec., O, pre	90-110	180-220
254, Loco 0-4-0, elec., O, pre	180-220	380-420
255E, Loco 2-4-2, steam, O, pre	180-220	280-320
256, Loco 0-4-4-0, elec., O, pre	450-550	650-750
258, Loco 2-4-2, steam, O, pre	40-60	90-110

	GOOD	EXCELLENT
259, Loco 2-4-2, steam, O, pre	$ 40-60	$ 90-110
260E, Loco 2-4-2, steam, O, pre	180-220	280-320
261, Loco 2-4-2, steam, O, pre	60-80	110-130
262, Loco 2-4-2, steam, O, pre	90-110	130-160
263E, Loco 2-4-2, steam, O, pre	180-220	280-320
263E, Loco 2-4-2, blue, steam, O, pre	450-550	650-750
264E, Loco 2-4-2, steam, O, pre	180-220	380-420
289E, Loco 2-4-2, steam, O, pre	90-110	140-160
309, Pullman, Std., pre	50-70	90-110
310, Baggage, Std., pre	50-70	90-110
318E, Loco 0-4-0, elec., Std., pre	90-110	180-220
322, Observation, Std., pre	50-70	90-110
380E, Loco 0-4-0, elec., Std., pre	180-220	280-320
381E, Loco 4-4-4, elec., Std., pre	1800-2200	2800-3200
384, Loco 2-4-0, steam, Std., pre	180-220	350-400
385E, Loco 2-4-2, steam, Std., pre	450-550	650-750
390, Loco 2-4-2, black, steam, Std., pre	450-550	650-750
390E, Loco 2-4-2, blue, steam, Std., pre	900-1100	1800-2200
392, Loco 4-4-2, steam, Std., pre	450-550	900-1100
400E, Loco 4-4-4, steam, Std., pre	900-1100	1800-2200
400E, Loco 4-4-4, blue, steam, Std., pre	1800-2200	2800-3200
402E, Loco 0-4-4-0, elec., Std., pre	450-550	650-750
408E, Loco 0-4-4-0, elec., Std., pre	900-1100	1800-2000
431, Diner, Std., pre	375-400	575-625
450, Loco 0-4-0, Macy's Sp., elec., O, pre	180-220	380-420
600, Pullman, O, pre	60-75	90-100
601, Observation, O, pre	60-75	90-100
652, Gondola, O, pre	20-25	30-40
653, Hopper, O, pre	35-45	50-60
671, Loco 6-8-6, steam, O, post	140-160	180-220
681, Loco 6-8-6, steam, O, post	90-110	140-160
700, Loco 0-4-0, elec., O, pre	180-220	280-320
700E, Loco 4-6-4, Sc. Hud. 5344, steam, O, pre	900-1100	1400-1600
701, Loco 0-4-0, elec., O, pre	180-220	280-320
703, Loco 0-4-0, elec., O, pre	900-1100	1400-1600
708, Loco 0-6-0, steam, O, pre	900-1100	1400-1600
726, Loco 2-8-4, steam, O, post	180-220	380-420
736, Loco 2-8-4, steam, O, post	140-160	180-220
746, Loco 4-8-4, N & W, steam, O, post	550-650	900-1100
752E, Loco Streamliner, Diesel, O, pre	240-260	380-420
763E, Loco 4-6-4, Scale Hudson, steam, O, pre	650-750	850-950
773, Loco 4-6-4, Hudson, steam, O, post	750-850	1100-1300
804, Tank, Shell, O, pre	30-40	50-60
805, Box Car, O, pre	30-40	50-60
806, Cattle, O, pre	35-45	50-60
807, Caboose, O, pre	25-35	40-50
820, Floodlight, O, pre	90-110	140-160
831, Lumber, O, pre	18-22	28-32
831, Flat, O, pre	18-22	28-32
1100, Handcar Mickey & Minnie, pre	300-400	600-900
1103, Handcar Bunny & Basket, pre	500-600	700-900

	GOOD	EXCELLENT
1105, Handcar Santa, pre	$ 500-600	$ 700-900
1107, Handcar Donald Duck, pre	300-400	600-800
1651E, Loco 0-4-0, elec., O, pre	40-60	65-80
1661E, Loco 2-4-0, steam, O, pre	40-60	65-80
1662, Loco 0-4-0, steam, O, pre	60-80	90-110
1663, Loco 0-4-0, steam, O, pre	90-110	140-160
1664, Loco 2-4-2, steam, O, pre	60-80	90-110
1666, Loco 2-6-2, steam, O, post	40-60	70-90
1674, Pullman, steam, O, pre	60-80	90-110
1689E, Loco 2-4-2, steam, O, pre	90-110	140-160
1835E, Loco 2-4-2, steam, Std., pre	450-550	650-750
1910, Pullman Car, Std., pre	1800-2200	900-1100
1911, Loco 0-4-0 early, elec., Std., pre	900-1000	1800-2200
1911 Sp., Loco 0-4-4-0, elec., Std., pre	2400-2600	3800-4200
1912, Loco 0-4-4-0, elec., Std., pre	1800-2200	3800-4200
1912 Sp., Loco 0-4-4-0, elec., Std., pre	3800-4200	5500-6000
2037, Loco 2-6-4, steam, O, post	90-110	140-160
2055, Loco 4-6-4, steam, O, post	90-130	160-180
2056, Loco 4-6-4, steam, O, post	90-130	160-180
2810, Derrick, O, pre	140-160	180-220
2816, Hopper, O, pre	140-160	180-220
3357, Hydraulic Maint. Car, O, post	90-110	180-220
3409, Helicopter Car, O, post	90-110	180-220
3413, Mercury Capsule Car, O, post	140-160	240-260
3470, Target Launcher, O, post	65-80	140-160
3472, Automatic Milk Car, O, post	65-80	140-160
3510, Satellite Car, O, post	90-110	180-220
3859, Dump, O, pre	60-75	90-100

Trolls

Do you have trolls? You may have them or remember them from the mid-1960s to the early 1970s. Although trolls have existed in folklore for hundreds of years, the trolls we are addressing trace their roots to the late 1950s in Denmark, when Thomas Dam made a troll for his daughter. By the mid-1960s Dam produced and exported the dolls with crazy hair and scrunched up faces. They were a sensation which in turn, created a troll-collecting frenzy and competition for Dam from Scandia House (they later joined forces) and Uneeda Doll Company who called their trolls "Wishniks." There were also lower-quality imitators. The following listing focuses on Dam and Wishniks. In the 1990s another wave of troll mania hit, introducing trolls to a younger generation. After their burst of success, the Dam toys were not available in the United States for many years. They are now marketed here as Norfins. Wishniks never really left the scene, with its company repackaging and releasing trolls over the years. Dam Trolls were the standard of the troll world, just as their successors, Norfins, are today. The troll market also boasts Russ Trolls, Magic Trolls, and Treasure Trolls, and again a host of lower-quality imitators.

The following are just a few of the thousands of trolls produced. Since trolls are still manufactured and identification is an art rather than a science, do some research. Compare new and old, high quality and cheap imitators. The Dam Animals, some of the most widely sought trolls, were recast from the original molds by Norfin in 1990. They were limited to a run of 500, sold for $50 and comprise the large horse, the large cow, the large elephant, and the lion. Since the edition was so limited, it probably will have little or no effect on the price of the originals. Dam trolls may bear a variety of "Dam" markings, and Wishniks may bear the double horseshoe mark, or "Uneeda Wishnik" or "Uneeda Dolls."

The prices below are based on items in excellent to mint condition with original clothing, accessories, and tags. Packaging is not as important as in other areas but it always adds value and desirability. Permanent marks and stains on the trolls themselves, as well as damaged hair and clothes, adversely affect value. Clothing and accessories are an important factor in determining value. Some trolls were sold without clothes, therefore clothes aren't really an issue. Many times trolls are redressed or missing part of their original ensemble. Replacement clothes may add some value, but crisp, bright original clothes with original accessories are the trolls most sought after by collectors. The following descriptions list what is currently known as outfits and accessories for the specific troll.

For further information see *Troll Identification & Price Guide* by Debra Clark, Hobby House Inc., Cumberland, MD, 1993, and *Collector's Guide to Trolls*, by Pat Petersen, Collector Books, Paducah, KY, 1994. See also Troll Monthly, *Trolling Along*, 585 Washington St., Whitman, MA 02382

	LOW	HIGH
Astronaut Troll, w/ helmet/space suit, Dam, ht. 7"	$ 60	$ 80
Black Troll, girl, Dam, ht. 12"	300	400
Boy in Raincoat Bank, w/ pants & cap, Dam, ht. 7"	40	60
Cow, limited edition, Dam, ht. 7"	60	80
Cow, small, Dam, ht. 3"	120	180
Cow, with bell, Dam, ht. 6"	120	180
Cowboy, w/ guns & hat, Wishnik, ht. 5.5"	12	18
Cowboy Bank w/ hat, six shooters, kerchief, shirt, & pants, Dam, ht. 7"	45	65
Doctor, in 2 piece uniform, w/ hat & stethoscope, Dam, ht. 3"	15	25
Donkey, Dam, ht. 3"	30	40
Donkey, w/ jointed head, Dam, ht. 9"	120	180
Double-Nik, Two Headed Troll, Wishnik, ht. 4"	50	60
Elephant, blue, w/ cap, bow tie & saddle blanket, Japan, ht. 4"	20	30
Elephant, Dam, ht. 3"	30	40

	LOW	HIGH
Elephant, Dam, ht. 6"	$ 140	$ 220
Giraffe, Dam, ht. 11.5"	90	130
Girl in Raincoat Bank, w/ pants & cap, Dam, ht. 7"	40	60
Here Comes the Judge *Laugh In Troll,* in printed black smock, Wishnik, ht. 6"	40	50
Horse, Dam, ht. 3"	30	50
Hula-Nik, w/ skirt, Wishnik, ht. 5"	25	35
Hunt-Nik, w/ rifle, pants & checked flannel shirt, Wishnik, ht. 3"	25	35
Iggy-Normous, in Cave Man outfit w/ tag, Dam, ht. 12"	100	150
Iggy-Normous, in Sailor Costume, tag, Dam, ht. 12"	120	180
Indian (girl) Bank, w/ headband, feather, belt, & wrap, Dam, ht. 7"	50	70
It's A Dam Dam World, book, by Hal Goodman & Larry Klein	10	15
Lion, Dam, ht. 5"	75	100
Monkey, R. Shekter, ht. 3.5"	25	35
Mouse, Dam, ht. 5"	60	80
Nurse, uniform, hat, and shoes, Scandia House, ht. 3"	15	25
Outa Sight, groovies series, w/ rhinestone eyes & outfits printed w/ various sayings, Wishnik, ht. 3"	18	25
Pirate (boy) Bank, w/ striped shirt, 1 earring, pants, belt, & eye patch, Dam, ht. 7"	50	70
Pirate (girl) Bank, striped shirt, 2 earrings, pants, belt, vest & hat, Dam, ht. 7"	50	70
Playboy Bunny, including tail, tie, ears, & cuffs, Dam, ht. 5.5"	40	50
Playboy Bunny, including tail, tie, ears, & cuffs, Scandia House, ht. 3"	20	30
Rock-Nik, black & red outfit w/ attached Guitar, Hong Kong, ht. 6"	20	30
Santa, Dam, ht. 12"	175	225
Sock-It-to-Me, Troll w/ large white eyes, dressed in smock w/ *Laugh-In* expressions, Wishnik, ht. 6"	50	60
Superman, in man of steel costume w/ cape, Wishnik, ht. 5.5"	50	70
Tartan Girl, Dam, ht. 12"	125	175
Troll Boy Bank, purple & white outfit, Dam, ht. 7"	35	40
Troll Car, log-shaped, Irwin	70	90
Troll Cave Carrying Case, Standard Plastics, ht. 9.5"	20	30
Troll Girl Bank, purple & white outfit, Dam, ht. 7"	35	40
Troll Lamp, featuring a 5.5" troll on wooden base, Wishnik, ht. 18"	80	100
Troll with Tail & jointed head, Dam, ht. 6.5"	150	200
Turtle, molded green shell, Dam, ht. 3"	175	225
Viking, w/ molded plastic hat, one piece outfit w/ belt & red wrist tag, Dam, ht. 6.5"	120	160

Viewmaster

Visitors to the 1939 World's Fair were treated to many spectacular new inventions, including the Viewmaster, which was introduced there by Sawyer. The invention of Harry Gruber, Viewmaster produced reels for the war effort. Pre-1945 single reels were either dark blue with a gold sticker or blue and tan. These early reels command a premium price among collectors. After the war, Sawyer did numerous travel sites and National Parks reels. In 1952 they purchased their competitor, Tru-Vue, thereby acquiring the licensing rights to Disney productions. Some of the most sought after reel packs are those depicting classic TV shows and cartoons from the 1950s and 1960s. There is a lot of cross-over collecting from the television memorabilia field. The firm stopped selling three-packs in 1980 but are still in business. Having been owned by five different companies, including Sawyer and GAF, they are now owned by Tyco. Collectors love the frozen-time aspect of Viewmaster, this century's stereoscope.

The prices below are based on items in near mint to mint condition, which means no damage to the reels or package, including all flaps (4). If the package states that instructions are enclosed they should be there. Blister packs should display virtually no signs of wear. We removed "The" in several titles for ease of use. All those listed are three-packs except those that specify *1R* (one reel), or *BP* (Blister pack). Dates are approximate and the number of each pack is listed after the date.

Above, left to right: Steve Canyon (B582), $40-$60; World's Fair (B760). $18-$25. Right: Captain Kangaroo (B560), $20-$30.
— Items courtesy of Stephen Kiss.

	LOW	HIGH
Addams Family, 1965	$ 70	$ 90
Batman-Catwoman, 1966, B492	35	45
Beverly Hillbillies, 1963, B570	30	40
Bonanza, 1965, B471	25	35
Brave Eagle, 1956, B466	25	35
Bryce Canyon, 1955, A346	8	10
Bugs Bunny & Elmer Fudd, 1R, 1951, 800	7	9
California State Tour, 1950, A170	18	22
Daniel Boone, 1965, B498	25	35
Dark Shadows, 1968, B503	70	90
Death Valley, 1950, A203	12	18
Deputy Dawg, 1962, B519	25	35
Desert Wildflowers, 1956, 985-A	4	6
Dr. Who, BP, 1975, Bd214	60	80
Flipper, 1966, B485	20	25
Flying Nun, 1966, B495	25	35
Gene Autry 1R, 1950, 950	12	15
Goldilocks & the Three Bears, 1R, 1946, FT6	7	9
Grand Canyon, 1950, A361	7	9
Green Hornet, 1966, B	80	100
Jack and the Beanstalk, 1R, 1951, FT3	6	9
Land of the Giants, 1975, B494	40	60
Laugh-In, 1969, B497	25	35
Little Black Sambo, 1R, 1948, FT8	18	24
Lone Ranger, 1956, B465	25	35
Long Island, 1957, 57-A	3	5
Lost in Space, 1965, B482	80	100
Man From U.N.C.L.E., 1966, B484	45	60
Mission Impossible, 1967, B505	20	30
Mod Squad, 1969, B478	20	30
Monkees, 1967, B493	45	55
Munsters, 1964, B481	80	100
New York World's Fair, 1964, A671	25	35
Planet of the Apes, B507	30	40
Popeye, 1962, B516	12	18
Queen Elizabeth Visits Canada/USA, 1957, B925	15	20
Roy Rogers 1R, 1955, 945	10	12
Secret Squirrel & Atom Ant, 1966, B535	25	35
Sequoia National Park, 1954, 117	8	12
Six Million Dollar Man, 1974, B559	9	12
Star Trek TV Series, 1968, B499	40	60
Tarzan Rescues Cheetah, 1R, 1950, 975	5	7
Thunderbirds, 1965, B453	50	70
Time Tunnel, 1966, B491	50	60
Tom and Jerry Cat Trapper, 1R, 1951, 810	6	8
Voyage to the Bottom of the Sea, 1966, B483	40	50
Welcome Back Kotter, 1977, J19	15	20
Wild Bill Hickok, 1959, B473	30	40
Wizard of Oz, 1957, FT45abc	30	40
Woody Woodpecker, 1955, B522	20	25
Yellowstone National Park, 1948, A361	7	9
Zorro, 1958, B469	40	50

Transportation

Automobiles

Although the antique car market is not as hot as it was ten years ago, prices are still strong and favored models are increasingly difficult to secure. The cars listed in this selection are given in six categories: A) salvageable only for parts, B) restorable, C) working order, but deteriorated, D) very good, drivable original or good amateur restoration, E) fine, well restored or well maintained original with minimal wear, F) excellent, professional quality restoration or perfect original. For further information, see *The Standard Guide to Cars and Prices*, edited by James T. Lenzke and Ken Buttolph, published by Krause Publications.

	A	B	C	D	E	F
Auburn						
1915						
All models	$ 1000	$ 3500	$ 6000	$ 11,000	$ 20,000	$ 30,000
1916						
All models	1000	3500	6000	12,000	20,000	30,000
1917						
All models	1000	3500	6000	12,000	20,000	28,000
1918						
Model 6-39	1000	3000	5000	10,000	18,000	25,000
1919						
Model 6-39, sedan	600	2000	3000	6500	11,000	16,000
1920						
Model 6-39, sedan	700	2200	3700	7500	13,000	19,000
1921						
Model 6-39, sedan	700	2100	3600	7500	13,000	18,000
1922						
Model 6-51, sedan	700	2400	4000	7500	13,000	19,000
1923						
Model 6-63, sedan	700	2200	3600	7400	13,000	18,000
1924						
Model 6-43, sedan	700	2200	3700	7500	13,000	19,000
1925						
Model 8-88, sedan	700	2300	4000	8000	14,000	20,000
1926						
Model 8-88, sedan	750	2500	4000	8000	14,000	20,000
1927						
Model 8-88, sedan	750	2400	4000	8000	14,000	20,000
1928						
Model 8-88, sedan	800	2500	4200	8400	15,000	21,000
1930						
Sedan	1000	3000	5000	9000	16,000	23,000
1932						
Sedan	1200	4000	6500	12,000	22,000	30,000
1934						
Sedan	1000	3000	5000	10,000	17,000	23,000
1936						
Sedan	1200	4000	6500	13,000	23,000	33,000

	A	B	C	D	E	F
		Buick				
1918						
Sedan	$ 700	$ 2100	$ 3500	$ 7000	$ 12,000	$ 17,500
1920						
Sedan	400	1300	2200	4400	8000	11,000
1922						
Sedan	400	800	1500	2500	6000	7500
1924						
Sedan	500	1200	2000	4000	7000	9000
1926						
Sedan	500	1200	2200	4000	6000	10,000
1928						
Sedan	500	1300	2500	4000	7500	11,000
1930						
Sedan	500	1500	2500	5000	9000	12,000
1932						
Sedan	750	2000	3000	6000	11,000	16,000
1934						
Sedan	700	1800	3000	4500	9000	12,000
1936						
Limited Series Sedan	700	2200	3600	7200	12,000	18,000
1938						
Limited Series Sedan	800	2500	4000	8000	14,000	20,000
1940						
Limited Sedan	1000	2500	4500	10,000	16,000	24,000
1942						
Century	500	1500	2600	5000	9000	13,000
1946						
Roadmaster Convertible	1000	3500	6000	12,000	20,000	30,000
1950						
Roadmaster Convertible	1000	3000	5000	10,000	18,000	25,000
1953						
Roadmaster Convertible	1000	3000	5000	10,000	18,000	25,000
1955						
Roadmaster Sedan	400	1200	2000	4000	7000	10,000
1957						
Convertible	1000	3000	5000	10,000	18,000	25,000
1959						
Sedan	400	700	1200	2500	4000	6500
1961						
Sedan	200	600	1000	2000	4000	6000
1963						
Sedan	200	600	1000	2200	4000	6000
1965						
Sedan	200	500	900	2000	3500	5000
1967						
Sedan	150	350	750	1500	3000	4000
1969						
Sedan	150	300	700	1200	2500	3800
1971						
Skylark	125	250	700	1200	2300	3300

	A	B	C	D	E	F
1973						
Electra	$ 150	$ 400	$ 750	$ 1400	$ 3000	$ 4500
1974						
Electra	150	400	750	1500	3000	4200
1975						
Regal	125	200	650	1100	2400	3400
1976						
Skylark	125	250	700	1200	2500	3500
1977						
Century	125	250	700	1200	2500	3600
1978						
Riviera	200	600	1000	2000	4000	6000
1979						
LeSabre	150	300	750	1400	3000	4000
1980						
Riviera	250	700	1100	2300	4500	6500
1983						
Skylark	150	350	750	1500	3000	4200
1985						
LeSabre	200	600	1000	2200	4000	5500
1986						
Somerset	200	500	800	1900	3400	5000

Cadillac

	A	B	C	D	E	F
1903						
Model "A"	$ 1300	$ 4000	$ 7000	$ 14,000	$ 24,000	$ 34,000
1907						
Model "G"	1200	3600	6000	12,000	20,000	30,000
1912						
Model 30	1400	4200	7800	15,000	25,000	37,000
1918						
Type 57	1300	4200	7500	13,000	23,000	34,000
1927						
Fleetwood	1700	5500	9000	18,000	32,000	44,000
1930						
Series 353, sedan	1700	5500	9000	18,000	32,000	46,000
1931						
Series 370, sedan	6000	18,000	30,000	60,000	100,000	140,000
1935						
Fisher body	2000	6000	10,000	18,000	32,000	47,000
1940						
Series 62, convertible	2000	7000	11,000	22,000	38,000	54,000
1948						
Sedan	850	2600	4200	8500	15,000	21,000
1954						
Series 75	1000	3500	5500	11,000	20,000	28,000
1960						
DeVille, sedan	600	1800	3000	6000	10,000	15,000
1963						
El Dorado	1000	3000	5000	10,000	17,000	24,000
1968						
Calais	400	1000	1500	3000	6000	9000

	A	B	C	D	E	F
1973						
DeVille .... $ 300	$ 700	$ 1100	$ 2300	$ 4400	$ 6300
1977						
Fleetwood 350	700	1200	2300	4700	6700
1980						
Seville 350	700	1100	2400	4700	6500
1985						
DeVille 200	700	1000	2300	4500	6500

Chevrolet

	A	B	C	D	E	F
1913						
Classic .... $ 1200	$ 3500	$ 6000	$ 12,000	$ 20,000	$ 30,000
1918						
Series "D" 850	2600	4300	8500	15,000	22,000
1923						
Sedan 350	750	1200	2400	5000	7000
1927						
Model "AA," sedan 350	750	1200	2400	5000	7000
1931						
Model "AE," sedan 500	1500	2500	5000	9000	13,000
1934						
Master Coupe 400	1200	2000	4000	7000	10,000
1937						
Master Sedan 450	1000	1600	3300	6300	9000
1939						
Master 85, station wagon 900	2700	4500	9000	16,000	23,000
1942						
Fleetwood 500	1000	1700	3600	6500	9500
1946						
Stylemaster 350	800	1500	3000	5700	8000
1951						
Styleline Special 350	800	1300	2600	5300	7500
1955						
Bel Air, sedan 400	1300	2300	4500	8000	11,000
1958						
Biscayne 200	600	1000	2200	4000	6000
1961						
Impala, sedan 200	650	1100	2300	4300	6000
1966						
Chevelle 150	400	750	1600	3200	4500
1969						
Impala, station wagon 150	350	750	1500	3000	4000
1970						
Camaro 500	1500	3000	5000	9000	13,000
1974						
Nova 150	300	750	1400	2800	4000
1977						
Monza 125	250	700	1200	2500	3500
1981						
Citation 125	250	700	1200	2500	3500
1985						
Celebrity 150	400	750	1500	3000	4000

	A	B	C	D	E	F

Corvette

	A	B	C	D	E	F
1955						
Convertible .... $ 1500	$ 5000	$ 8000	$ 16,000	$ 28,000	$ 40,000
1963						
Sport Coupe 1000	3000	5000	10,000	20,000	27,000
1972						
Convertible 700	2000	3000	7500	13,000	19,000
1986						
Corvette 500	1600	2600	5500	9000	14,000

Chrysler

	A	B	C	D	E	F
1925						
Town Car .... $ 500	$ 1600	$ 2700	$ 5000	$ 9000	$ 13,000
1928						
Series 62, sedan 350	800	1400	2700	5500	8000
1931						
Series 77, coupe 550	1700	2800	5700	10,000	15,000
1933						
Royal Sedan 500	1600	2700	5500	9500	14,000
1939						
New Yorker 550	1700	3000	5800	10,000	14,000
1942						
Saratoga, coupe 400	1300	2200	4500	8000	12,000
1949						
Crown Imperial 500	1600	2700	5500	10,000	14,000
1953						
New Yorker 400	1000	1700	3000	6000	10,000
1957						
LeBaron 500	1600	2700	5500	10,000	14,000
1960						
Saratoga, sedan 200	600	1000	2500	4000	6000
1964						
Newport, sedan 125	250	700	1200	2500	3500
1968						
New Yorker 250	600	1000	2000	4000	5500
1972						
Imperial 200	600	1000	2200	4000	6000
1977						
LeBaron 150	300	700	1300	2800	4000
1981						
Newport 150	400	750	1600	3000	4500
1985						
Laser 150	400	750	1600	3000	4400

Desoto

	A	B	C	D	E	F
1930						
Model "CK" Coupe .... $ 450	$ 1000	$ 1700	$ 3500	$ 6500	$ 9500
1934						
Airflow 400	1200	1800	4000	7000	10,000
1940						
S7 Deluxe 350	800	1250	2500	5000	7000

	A	B	C	D	E	F
1946						
S11, sedan .... $ 200	$ 700	$ 1200	$ 2400	$ 4500	$ 6500
1953						
Powermaster 6 300	700	1200	2400	4700	7000
1958						
Firesweep, sedan 200	600	1000	2300	4000	5700
1960						
Adventurer, sedan 200	600	1000	2000	3700	5500

Dodge

	A	B	C	D	E	F
1917						
Coupe .... $ 350	$ 900	$ 1600	$ 3000	$ 6000	$ 9000
1923						
Sedan 200	500	900	2000	3500	5000
1930						
Series "DD," sedan 350	800	1500	3000	6000	8000
1934						
Convertible 1200	3500	6000	12,000	21,000	30,000
1939						
Coupe 450	1000	1600	3500	6500	9000
1946						
Coupe 350	800	1300	2500	5500	8000
1953						
Coronet 350	750	1200	2500	5000	7000
1957						
Royal Sedan 200	600	1000	2500	4000	5500
1960						
Seneca 200	500	900	2000	3500	5000
1963						
Polara Sedan 200	500	900	2000	3500	5000
1966						
Monoco 250	600	1000	2200	4000	5500
1969						
Monoco 150	400	800	1800	3500	4600
1973						
Colt 100	200	600	1000	2200	3000
1976						
Crestwood 125	250	700	1200	2500	3500
1980						
Diplomat 150	300	700	1200	2600	3800
1984						
Aries 150	350	750	1500	3000	4000
1986						
Lancer 200	500	1000	2000	3500	5000

Ford

	A	B	C	D	E	F
1909						
Model "T" .... $ 750	$ 2200	$ 4000	$ 7800	$ 13,000	$ 20,000
1914						
Model "T" 500	1500	2700	5000	9000	15,000
1926						
Model "T," coupe 400	800	1400	2500	5500	7500

	A	B	C	D	E	F
1930						
Model "A," station wagon .	$ 600	$ 1800	$ 3000	$ 6000	$ 10,000	$ 14,000
1935						
Model 48, sedan	500	1100	1700	3500	6500	9500
1939						
Model 922, coupe	400	1300	2300	4500	8000	11,000
1942						
Model 21A, sedan	400	800	1200	2500	5000	7000
1952						
Sedan	200	500	850	2000	4000	5500
1956						
Mainline	200	600	1000	2200	4000	6000
1958						
Thunderbird, convertible	1000	3000	5500	12,000	20,000	30,000
1962						
Galaxy 500, sedan	200	500	900	2000	3500	5000
1964						
Sprint	400	1300	2300	4600	8000	11,000
1967						
Futura	200	500	800	2000	3500	5000
1970						
Cobra	700	2400	4000	8000	14,000	20,000
1972						
Maverick	150	300	700	1200	2500	4000
1974						
LTD	150	350	750	1300	2700	4000
1978						
Thunderbird	250	650	1000	2000	4000	6000
1982						
Escort	150	300	700	1200	2600	3800
1985						
Tempo	125	250	700	1200	2500	3500

Hudson

	A	B	C	D	E	F
1911						
Model 33	$ 1000	$ 3000	$ 5000	$ 10,000	$ 18,000	$ 26,000
1915						
Sedan	700	2000	3500	7000	12,000	18,000
1920						
Coupe	450	1100	1700	3700	7000	10,000
1924						
Sedan	350	800	1500	2800	6000	8000
1928						
Coupe	450	1500	2500	5000	9000	12,000
1931						
Sedan	500	1000	1700	3500	6500	10,000
1934						
Challenger, coupe	350	750	1300	2500	5500	8000
1937						
Custom 6, sedan	350	750	1200	2400	5000	7000
1939						
Big Boy	600	1700	3000	6000	10,000	15,000

	A	B	C	D	E	F
1942						
Traveller	$ 400	$ 1000	$ 1700	$ 3500	$ 6500	$ 9000
1950						
Pacemaker, sedan	500	1200	2000	4000	7000	10,000
1953						
Hornet, sedan	400	1200	2000	4000	7000	10,000
1957						
Sedan	450	1200	2000	4000	7000	10,000

Lincoln

	A	B	C	D	E	F
1920						
Sedan	$ 1200	$ 4000	$ 7000	$ 14,000	$ 23,000	$ 33,000
1923						
Towncar	2000	5000	9000	17,000	30,000	45,000
1926						
Convertible	2000	7000	11,000	22,000	39,000	55,000
1929						
Town, sedan	1200	4000	6000	12,000	22,000	33,000
1932						
Model "KB," sedan	1500	4700	7500	15,000	26,000	38,000
1936						
Zephyr	900	3000	5000	10,000	18,000	25,000
1939						
Series "K," sedan	1500	5000	8000	15,000	27,000	40,000
1942						
Zephyr, sedan	500	1600	2700	5500	9500	14,000
1950						
Cosmopolitan, sedan	400	1300	2200	4500	8000	11,000
1956						
Capri, sedan	500	1500	2500	5000	9000	13,000
1960						
Premier, sedan	500	1000	1700	3500	6500	10,000
1965						
Lincoln Continental, sedan	400	800	1500	3000	6000	8500
1967						
Lincoln Continental, sedan	400	800	1500	3000	6000	8500
1970						
Continental Mark III	500	1500	2500	5000	8500	12,000
1975						
Mark IV	500	1000	1700	3500	6500	9000
1980						
Versailles	200	600	900	2000	4000	6000
1983						
Towncar	350	700	1200	2400	5000	7000

Mercury

	A	B	C	D	E	F
1940						
Sedan	$ 500	$ 1000	$ 1700	$ 3500	$ 6500	$ 9500
1942						
Coupe	400	1300	2200	4500	8000	11,000
1946						
Sedan	350	800	1500	3000	6000	8500

	A	B	C	D	E	F
1951						
Mercury, convertible .... $ 750	$ 2500	$ 4000	$ 8000	$ 14,000	$ 20,000
1955						
Montclaire, sedan 350	900	1500	3000	6000	8500
1957						
Monterey, sedan 300	700	1200	2400	4500	6500
1959						
Parklane, convertible 900	2700	4500	9000	15,000	23,000
1961						
Meteor 600 200	500	900	2000	3700	5500
1962						
Comet 200	600	1000	2200	4000	5500
1964						
Comet, sedan 200	500	900	2000	3500	5000
1967						
Capri 200	600	1000	2200	4000	5500
1970						
Marquis 150	400	750	1500	3000	4500
1974						
Cougar 200	600	1000	2300	4000	5700
1975						
Bobcat 125	250	700	1200	2600	3700
1977						
Marquis 150	300	750	1400	3000	4200
1979						
Zephyr 150	300	700	1200	2500	3700
1981						
Grand Marquis 200	500	900	2000	3400	5000

Nash

	A	B	C	D	E	F
1918						
Sedan .... $ 500	$ 1000	$ 1700	$ 3500	$ 6500	$ 9500
1920						
Coupe 400	900	1700	3000	6000	9000
1922						
Sedan 350	750	1200	2500	5000	7000
1925						
Light 6, sedan 200	500	900	2000	4000	5500
1928						
Standard, sedan 350	750	1200	2400	5000	7000
1930						
Single, coupe 350	700	1300	2700	5000	8000
1933						
Ambassador, coupe 500	1500	2500	5000	9000	12,000
1935						
Lafayette 350	750	1300	2500	5000	7000
1937						
Ambassador, sedan 350	750	1200	2300	5000	6500
1940						
Ambassador, coupe 350	750	1400	2700	5500	8300
1942						
Ambassador 600, sedan 350	700	1200	2400	5000	7000

	A	B	C	D	E	F
1946						
600 .... $ 200	$ 500	$ 900	$ 2000	$ 3500	$ 5000
1949						
600 Custom 200	600	1000	2200	4000	6000
1952						
Statesman, sedan 200	600	1000	2300	4000	6000
1955						
Rambler 200	600	1000	2200	4000	6000
1957						
Rambler 200	600	1000	2000	3700	6000

American Motors Corporation

	A	B	C	D	E	F
1958						
American Super .... $ 200	$ 600	$ 900	$ 2200	$ 3900	$ 5500
1962						
Ambassador 150	350	750	1500	3000	4500
1965						
Classic 150	300	750	1400	3000	4000
1967						
Rebel 150	250	700	1200	2500	3700
1969						
Rambler 150	300	700	1200	2700	4000
1972						
Hornet SST 150	400	700	1300	2700	4000
1974						
Matador 150	300	700	1300	2700	4000
1977						
Gremlin 150	300	700	1200	2500	3500
1980						
Concord 150	300	700	1200	2500	3500
1983						
Alliance 150	300	700	1200	2500	3500

Oldsmobile

	A	B	C	D	E	F
1905						
Touring Car .... $ 1200	$ 4000	$ 6500	$ 13,000	$ 23,000	$ 35,000
1909						
Model "Z" 1500	5000	8000	17,000	30,000	40,000
1912						
Defender 1300	4000	7000	14,000	25,000	34,000
1915						
Model 42 1000	3000	5000	10,000	18,000	26,000
1917						
Model 45 1000	3000	5000	10,000	20,000	27,000
1920						
Model 37-B 400	1300	2300	4500	8000	12,000
1923						
Model 43-A, sedan 500	1200	1800	4000	7000	10,000
1926						
Coupe 350	900	1500	3000	6000	9000
1929						
Sedan 400	800	1500	3000	6000	8500

	A	B	C	D	E	F
1931						
Model F-31 .... $ 500	$ 1500	$ 2500	$ 5000	$ 8000	$ 12,000
1934						
Model F-34 400	1000	1700	3500	6500	9500
1938						
F-38 450	1000	1600	3400	6000	9000
1940						
Series 70 400	1000	1600	3500	6500	9000
1942						
Station wagon 1000	3000	5500	12,000	20,000	30,000
1946						
Special Series, convertible ... 800	2500	4000	8500	15,000	21,000
1949						
Futuramic 76, sedan 200	600	1000	2000	4000	6000
1953						
Classic, convertible 1000	3500	6000	12,000	20,000	30,000
1956						
Series 98, sedan 400	1300	2200	4500	7500	10,000
1959						
Series 88, sedan 400	750	1300	2500	5000	8000
1961						
Dynamic 88 300	700	1000	2200	4200	6000
1963						
Jetfire 350	1000	1600	3300	6000	9000
1965						
Cutlass 350	800	1200	2500	5000	8000
1967						
Vista Cruiser 200	600	1000	2000	3700	5500
1969						
Delta 88 350	750	1200	2500	5000	7000
1971						
98 200	500	900	1800	3600	5000
1973						
Cutlass 150	300	700	1200	2700	4000
1976						
Omega 125	200	650	1200	2400	3500
1979						
Delta 88 150	300	750	1300	2700	4000
1981						
98 200	500	900	2000	3500	5000
1983						
Cutlass 150	450	750	1700	3300	5000

Packard

	A	B	C	D	E	F
1904						
Model "L" .... $ 2300	$ 7500	$ 13,000	$ 25,000	$ 45,000	$ 65,000
1912						
Model "NE" 1500	4500	7000	15,000	25,000	37,000
1915						
Model 5-48 2000	6000	10,000	18,000	30,000	45,000
1921						
Single 6 1200	4000	7000	12,000	21,000	35,000

	A	B	C	D	E	F
924						
ingle 8, sedan	$ 1000	$ 3300	$ 6000	$ 11,000	$ 20,000	$ 30,000
928						
tandard, coupe	1000	3000	5000	10,000	17,000	25,000
931						
Model 833, coupe	2000	7000	11,000	23,000	40,000	60,000
932						
Model 900, sedan	1000	3500	6000	11,000	20,000	30,000
933						
Model 10005, sedan	2000	6000	10,000	20,000	40,000	55,000
935						
eries 1204, coupe	2000	7000	11,000	23,000	40,000	60,000
937						
Model 120-C, sedan	1000	3500	6000	12,000	20,000	30,000
939						
Model 1801, convertible	2000	5000	10,000	18,000	31,000	45,000
942						
eries 2001	700	2200	3600	7500	13,000	20,000
946						
lipper	500	1500	2500	5000	9000	14,000
949						
uper Eight, sedan	1000	2000	4000	7000	13,000	20,000
953						
atrician	700	2000	3500	7000	12,000	18,000
956						
aribbean	1200	4000	6000	12,000	20,000	30,000

Pierce-Arrow

	A	B	C	D	E	F
903						
One cylinder	$ 1200	$ 4000	$ 6500	$ 12,000	$ 24,000	$ 35,000
906						
Great Arrow	3000	8000	13,000	30,000	50,000	70,000
909						
Model 40	2000	6000	10,000	20,000	34,000	50,000
913						
Model 66A	3000	10,000	16,000	30,000	50,000	80,000
915						
Model 66A	3000	10,000	17,000	35,000	60,000	85,000
919						
Model 48-B-5	2500	8000	13,000	27,000	45,000	63,000
923						
Model 38, sedan	1200	4000	6500	13,000	24,000	35,000
926						
Model 33, touring car	2000	7000	12,000	23,000	40,000	55,000
929						
Model 126	3000	9000	15,000	30,000	48,000	68,000
933						
Model 1236	1700	5000	9000	18,000	30,000	45,000
936						
alon 12	2000	5000	9000	18,000	30,000	42,000
938						
ierce-Arrow 8	1500	4000	7000	15,000	25,000	40,000

	A	B	C	D	E	F

Plymouth

	A	B	C	D	E	F
1928						
Model "Q," sedan	$ 350	$ 800	$ 1500	$ 3000	$ 6000	$ 8500
1933						
PC, coupe	400	1000	1600	3300	6000	9000
1937						
Roadking	300	700	1200	2500	4500	6500
1940						
P9 Roadking	300	700	1200	2300	4500	7000
1946						
P15 Deluxe, sedan	200	600	1000	2200	4000	5700
1949						
Deluxe	300	800	1200	2500	5000	8000
1952						
Cambridge	300	700	1300	2500	5000	7500
1955						
Plaza	200	700	1200	2500	4500	6200
1959						
Suburban	200	500	900	2000	3700	5500
1962						
Belvedere	200	500	900	2000	3500	5000
1966						
Valiant	200	400	800	1500	3000	4500
1969						
GTX	700	2300	3500	7300	12,000	19,000
1971						
Regent Wagon	150	300	700	1300	2700	4000
1974						
Fury	150	250	700	1200	3000	4000
1976						
Volare	150	300	750	1500	3000	4000
1978						
Arrow	150	300	700	1200	2500	3750
1981						
Reliant	150	300	700	1300	2600	3800
1984						
Tourismo	150	400	750	1700	3000	4500

Pontiac

	A	B	C	D	E	F
1926						
Model 6-27	$ 400	$ 1000	$ 1500	$ 3000	$ 6000	$ 9000
1929						
Model 6-29A, sedan	400	800	1200	2400	5000	7500
1932						
Model 302, sedan	400	1300	2200	4300	7500	11,000
1936						
Silver Streak, sedan	400	750	1250	2500	5000	7000
1939						
Special Series, coupe	400	1000	1600	3200	6000	9000
1941						
Torpedo	350	800	1400	2600	5500	8000

	A	B	C	D	E	F
1946						
Torpedo, coupe	$ 300	$ 700	$ 1200	$ 2400	$ 5000	$ 7000
1949						
Chieftain	300	700	1200	2400	4800	7000
1953						
Chieftain	400	900	1500	2500	5000	8000
1957						
Chieftain	300	700	1200	2500	5000	7000
1960						
Safari	200	700	1100	2300	4500	6500
1963						
Catalina	300	700	1000	2300	4000	6500
1966						
GTO	500	1500	3000	5000	10,000	15,000
1968						
Tempest	300	700	1000	2000	3700	6000
1970						
GTO	800	2300	4000	8000	14,000	20,000
1972						
Bonneville	200	500	800	1700	3200	4800
1975						
LeMans	100	200	700	1200	2400	3500
1978						
Sunbird	100	200	600	1100	2200	3000
1980						
Phoenix	150	300	700	1200	2700	4000
1984						
Parisienne	150	450	800	1800	3300	5000

Studebaker

	A	B	C	D	E	F
1905						
Model 9502	$ 1000	$ 3000	$ 5000	$ 10,000	$ 18,000	$ 27,000
1909						
Model "B"	1200	4000	7000	14,000	24,000	34,000
1914						
Model 1 SC	900	2700	4500	9000	16,000	23,000
1918						
Series 19, sedan	350	900	1500	3000	6000	8500
1923						
Model EK, coupe	500	1200	2000	4000	7000	10,000
1927						
Commander, coupe	500	1100	1800	3500	7000	10,000
1930						
Dictator, sedan	500	1000	1700	3500	6500	10,000
1933						
Commander, coupe	600	2000	3000	6000	11,000	16,000
1936						
President 8, sedan	400	1300	2200	4300	7500	12,000
1939						
Model "G," sedan	350	750	1200	2400	5000	7200
1942						
Commander Skyway	500	1500	2500	5000	9000	13,000

	A	B	C	D	E	F
1947						
Champion, sedan	$ 200	$ 600	$ 1000	$ 2000	$ 4000	$ 6000
1951						
Champion Deluxe	300	650	1200	2400	4200	6000
1956						
Champion	150	400	750	1700	3300	4700
1959						
Lark Regal	200	600	900	2000	3500	5500
1965						
Daytona	200	500	900	2000	3700	5500

Aviation

Aviation memorabilia includes any item dealing with airplanes. From commercial airlines to the air force, hobbyists are collecting any type of aviation memorabilia available. These include: stewardess wings, pilot goggles, pins, buttons, helmets, entire airplanes or just parts of airplanes

	LOW	AVG.	HIGH
Activity Book for Children, cut-outs of 7 classic planes, 10" x 15", 1930 .	$ 70	$ 90	$ 110
Bombardier's Panel, WWII	180	240	300
Book, *The Romance of Air Fighting* by R.W. Anderson, 1917	60	75	90
Book, Signal Corps Pilot's Book, used by a cadet in 1917, hardcover, 5.5" x 6"	100	120	140
Booklet, Souvenir of the Harvard/Boston Aviation Meet, 1911	190	225	260
Button, brass, pictures world globe and reads "U.S. Air Mail," c. 1930 ..	20	25	30
Cap, canvas with built-in earphones, Bakelite phones, c. 1930-1934	100	115	130
Coffee Mug, porcelain, Tactical Air Command General White, 3"	30	40	50
Drinking Cup, leather, Pan American Airways System, 4", c. 1930	30	35	40
Game, Flying For Fun, card game based on stunt pilot maneuvers, 1928 ..	70	85	100
Magazine, *The Alexander Aircrafter*, September, 1927, full color cover, 22 pages, 5.5" x 8"	60	65	70
Military Pass to MacGill Air Field, Florida, dated August 14, 1942	10	20	30
Notebook, personal notes from Officer's Training Course, 1918, diagrams .	130	180	230
Pamphlet, *National Air Races*, Int. Aeronautical Exposition, 8" x 11", 1928	90	110	130
Pilot Goggles, Bakelite, screw off lenses, made by Wilson, c. 1930	60	75	90
Pilot Goggles, fur lined, yellow tinted lenses, elastic band, c. 1925	60	70	80
Pinback Button, Earhart's Friendship, full color celluloid premium of Bond's Bread	10	15	20
Pinback Button, Lincoln Beachey, aviator and stunt pilot, 1.5", 1915	110	125	140
Pocket Watch, Graf Zeppelin, *Trail Blazers Around The World: Magellan 1522*, c. 1930	480	575	670
Postcard, biplane over Paris, black and white, unused, c. 1910-1912	30	35	40
Postcard, Hanriot Monoplane in flight, black and white, unused	30	40	50
Slides, set of 100 slides of planes in silhouette, in original box, WWII	120	145	170
Trade Catalogue, Bird Aircraft Corporation, 17 pages, 1931	60	80	100
Watch Fob, aluminum shell, pictures dirigible, *U.S. Navy, Duralumin*, c. 1935	50	55	60
Wreck Fragment, piece of a Douglas SBD-3 dive bomber, 5', WWII	40	45	50

Bicycles

A steerable wooden horse on wheels, built in 1818, the Draisienne is considered the first modern bicycle. The first pedal driven bicycle appeared in Scotland in 1839. Later versions include the Velocipede, the High-Wheeler and the safety bike.

Bicycles built before 1900 are the most collectible. Of particular note are the 1861 Velocipede with front wheel pedals and the 1885 Rover. Tricycles and quadricycles are especially rare and collectible. The Wright Brothers of Dayton, Ohio, and Columbia were top manufacturers of the early bicycle.

Penny farthing high wheel bicycle, $5500 at auction — Photo courtesy of Northeast Auctions.

	LOW	AVERAGE	HIGH
Adult tricycle, 1885	$ 7000	$ 8500	$ 10,000
Boneshaker, 1850	2750	3750	4750
Boneshaker, 1870	1770	2465	3160
Buggy, spoked triangle pedal high wheeler, 1886	800	1000	1200
Chainless, 1853	260	330	400
Chainless safety, 1900	340	435	530
Columbia chainless, 1856	330	400	470
Columbia high wheeler, 1901	2000	2750	3500
Columbia, 3 wheeler tandem tricycle, 1888	5000	6000	7000
Eagle, 50 inch high wheeler, 1872	3500	4250	5000
Eagle, high wheeler with brake, 1865	5000	6000	7000
Fifty inch high wheeler, 1878	2000	2500	3000
Fifty-six inch high wheeler, 1898	1000	1300	1600
High wheeler bicycle, 1885	2000	2500	3000
Scooter, 1927	350	400	450
Solid tire safety, 1890	1350	2000	2750
Spring fork 1862	1050	1210	1370
Tandem, 1914	450	500	550
Tandem, adult tricycle, 1885	10,000	11,000	12,000
Tandem, bicycle, 1895	550	710	870
Two wheeler, 1896	550	690	830
Two wheeler, 1914	210	270	330

Railroad Memorabilia

Before airplanes and the interstate highway system, railroads crisscrossed the United States with mile after mile of track. Railroad memorabilia enthusiasts love tracking down mementos of the rail era. Many collectors concentrate on defunct lines in their area, therefore there are regional differences of what people collect and how much they pay for items. Other collectors concentrate on a topic regardless of region. The following prices are for items in excellent condition. Beware of items with no identifying marks or provenance. Railroads did not mark all their items, but many pieces are touted as being from a particular railroad that are not.

Left to right: lantern, with colored bullseye lenses, B & M ht. 16", $100-$150; ticket case, Erie c.1920, ht. 30", $600-$800.

	LOW	AVG.	HIGH
Ashtray, Erie RR, glass, diamond in center	$ 10	$ 11	$ 12
Ashtray, New York Central RR, crystal, blue, pictures, diesel	18	20	22
Beer Mug, Chessie System, glass, side logo w/ cat	30	35	40
Booklet, NH & H, "Arranged Freight Train Service," c. 1920	10	13	16
Brochure, Erie RR, "The Erie Limited," w/ timetables and maps, 8" x 11", 1929	20	25	30
Candle Holders, Penn. RR, silverplate, pr., ht. 3.5"	250	300	350
Cordial Glass, 20th Century Limited, embossed glass	20	25	30
Cordial Glass, New York Central System, tall, side logo	10	13	15
Cordial Glass, Santa Fe, etched glass	15	18	21
Dessert Fork, New York Central RR, "New Pattern," Hall and Elton ...	15	18	21
Formal Dinner Fork, New York Central RR, "King's Pattern"	15	18	21
Horseradish Pot Holder, Pennsylvania RR, glass & silver plate, (2 pieces) 1926	120	150	180
Juice Glass, C & O, emb. "For Progress"	8	10	12
Juice Glass, New York Central RR, emb., side marked, 6 oz.	8	9	10
Lantern, Signal, Erie RR, ht. 12"	50	62	75
Lantern, w/ colored bullseye lenses, Erie RR, ht. 16"	100	125	150
Map, New York Central System, color, 1924	20	25	30
Menu, Burlington Northern, 4-sided folder, "form 2813"	12	14	16

	LOW	AVG.	HIGH
Menu, Burlington Northern, Breakfast, folder, April 1970, 5" x 7" ...... $ 3		$ 4	$ 5
Napkin, Rock Island Line, linen w/ logo 10		11	12
Pass, Lake Shore and Western, 1882 25		30	35
Pass, Maine Central RR, 1898 20		25	30
Pass, Memphis and Little Rock RR Co., 1883 25		30	35
Pass., Milwaukee and Northern, 1888 25		30	35
Poster, New York Central, "Low Fare Excursions to Watkins Glen, 1931," 6" x 15" 20		25	30
Poster, New York Central, "State Fair, Syracuse, September 7 to 12, 1931," 7" x 14" 25		30	35
Serving Spoon, New York Central RR, "King's Pattern" 15		18	20
Station Master's Brass Candlestick Phone, w/ head set, Erie RR, c. 1925 300		350	400
Stock Certificate, Market Street Railway Co., San Francisco, green and black w/ eagle vignette, c. 1925 15		18	20
Sugar Bowl, Pennsylvania RR, silver plate, w/ keystone emblem, 1929 ht. 4" 90		110	130
Ticket Case, Erie Lackawana, c.1920, hinged slant door, ht. 30" 600		700	800
Timetable, Angelina and Naches River System, July 1938 10		13	15
Timetable, Ashley Drew and Northern System, 12/38 12		14	16
Timetable, Atlanta Birmingham and Coast Line System, Nov. 1936..... 12		14	16
Timetable, Baltimore & Ohio, Baltimore Division, October 1965 4		5	6
Timetable, Baltimore & Ohio, Chicago Terminal, April 1969 5		6	7
Timetable, Boston and Albany RR, poster style w/ large woodcut c. 1880, 18" x 24" 200		250	300
Timetable, Ft. Worth and Denver, Wichita Falls and Amarillo Division, October 1936 10		13	16
Water Glass, 20th Century Limited, embossed glass, 8 oz. 20		25	30
Water Glass, Baltimore & Ohio, embossed glass, pictures Capitol Dome 15		18	20
Water Glass, New York Central RR, embossed G, side marked, 10 oz. 12		15	18
Water Glass, Santa Fe, embossed glass, 8 oz. 8		10	12
Water Glass, Union Pacific, crest at side, 8 oz. 7		8	9
Wine Glass, New York Central RR, embossed, side marked, 4 oz. 8		9	10

Phototography and other Contributions

Bill Bertoia Auctions
2413 Madison Avenue
Vineland, NJ 08360
609 692 1881

Christie's East
219 East 67th Street
New York, NY 10021
212 606 0430

Eclectic Antiques
PO Box #475
Lynnwood, WA 98046

Douglas-Chew Ho

James D. Julia Inc.
PO Box 830
Fairfield, ME 04937
207 453 7125

George Kerrigan Photography
56 West 22nd Street
New York, NY 10010
212 645 7979

Kessie & Co. Antiques and Gifts
163 East 87th Street
New York, NY 10128
212 987 1732

Stephen Kiss

Northeast Auctions
PO Box 363
Hampton, NH 03842

Phillips Fine Art Auctioneers
406 East 79th Street
New York, NY 10021
212 570 4830

Sotheby's
1334 York Avenue
New York, NY 10021
212 606 7000

Thelma Shaffer

Dorothy Shelton

ABOUT THE AUTHORS

ERIC ALBERTA has headed the Collectibles Department at both Christie's and Phillips auction houses. With over twenty-five years' experience, he now runs an appraisal and consulting firm.

ART MAIER teaches appraising at New York University. He is a consultant for international auction houses and their clients.